International Privacy, Publicity and Personality Laws

Other books by Michael Henry include:

Media Industry Transactions – Butterworths 1998

Media Industry Documentation – Butterworths 1998

Current Copyright Law – Butterworths 1998

Entertainment Law Volume 15 Encyclopaedia of Forms and Precedents
Fifth Edition Reissue – Butterworths 1998

Publishing and Media Law – Butterworths 1994

Practical Lending and Security Precedents (Security Over Intellectual
Property Section)
FT Law & Tax 1992

International Agency and Distribution Agreements (UK Section)
Butterworths 1989

Entertainment Law Volume 15 Encyclopaedia of Forms and Precedents
Butterworths 1998

The Film Industry – A Legal and Commercial Analysis
Longman 1986

Jaques the Fatalist (Translation)
Denis Diderot – Penguin Classics 1986

10% net receipts from the proceeds of the sale of this book shall be donated
to the Diana, Princess of Wales Memorial Fund, registered charity no.
1064238.

International Privacy, Publicity and Personality Laws

General Editor

Michael Henry
Partner, Buchanan Ingersoll

United Kingdom	Butterworths, a Division of Reed Elsevier (UK) Ltd, Halsbury House, 35 Chancery Lane, LONDON WC2A 1EL and 4 Hill Street, EDINBURGH EH2 3JZ
Australia	Butterworths, a Division of Reed International Books Australia Pty Ltd, CHATSWOOD, New South Wales
Canada	Butterworths Canada Ltd, MARKHAM, Ontario
Hong Kong	Butterworths Hong Kong, a division of Reed Elsevier (Greater China) Ltd, HONG KONG
India	Butterworths India, NEW DELHI
Ireland	Butterworth (Ireland) Ltd, DUBLIN
Malaysia	Malayan Law Journal Sdn Bhd, KUALA LUMPUR
New Zealand	Butterworths of New Zealand Ltd, WELLINGTON
Singapore	Butterworths Asia, SINGAPORE
South Africa	Butterworths Publishers (Pty) Ltd, DURBAN
USA	Lexis Law Publishing, CHARLOTTESVILLE, Virginia

© Reed Elsevier (UK) Ltd 2001

A CIP Catalogue record for this book is available from the British Library.

ISBN 0 406 90805 2

ISBN 0-406-90805-2

9 780406 908056

Printed and bound by Bookcraft (Bath) Ltd, Midsommer Norton, Avon

Visit Butterworths LEXIS *direct* **at: http://www.butterworths.com**

Contributors

Introduction
Michael Henry
Buchanan Ingersoll, London

Argentina
Ernesto Aracama Zorraquin of Marval, O'Farrell & Mairal, Buenos Aires

Australia
Robert Todd of Blake Dawson Waldron, Sydney
Ian Smith

Austria
Dr Meinhard Ciresa, Vienna

Belgium
Alexandre Cruquenaire of the University of Namur, Namur
Benoit Van Asbroek of Van Asbroek & Coltenie, Louvain-La-Neuve

Brazil
Peter Dirk Siemsen of Dannemann Siemsen Bigler & Ipanema Moreira, Rio de Janeiro

Canada
Louise Potvin of the Canadian Department of Justice, Quebec
Robert Howell of the University of Victoria, British Columbia
Tom McMahon of the Canadian Department of Justice, Ottawa

Denmark
Peter Blume of the Faculty of Law, University of Copenhagen, Copenhagen

Eire
Don McAleese of Matheson Ormsby Prentice, Dublin

Finland
Rainer Hilli of Roschier-Holmberg & Waselius, Helsinki
Tanja Liljeström

France
Charles de Haas of Gilbey de Haas, Paris

Germany
Dr Thomas R Klötzel of Thümmel Schütze & Partner, Stuttgart

Greece
Dr Leonidas Kanellos of Kokkas-Kanellos & Associates, Athens

Hong Kong
Simon Deane of Deacons Graham & James, Hong Kong

Iceland
S B Einarsdóttir of Faktor Patentbureau, Reykjavik

India
Pravin Anand of Anand and Anand Advocates, New Delhi
Gitanjli Duggal of Anand and Anand Advocates, New Delhi

Italy
Patrizio Menchetti of Studio Legale Menchetti, Lucca

Japan
Yoshimi Ohara of the Intellectual Property Center, Osaka

Luxembourg
Anne Baudoin of Le Gouëff Advocates, Luxembourg
Stéphan Le Gouëff of Le Gouëff Advocates, Luxembourg

Netherlands
JCS Pinckaers of Trenité Van Doorne, Amsterdam

New Zealand
Ken Moon of AJ Park & Son, Auckland
Bona Lee of Allen & Overy, Hong Kong

Norway
Lee A Bygrave of the Norwegian Research Centre for Computers and Law, Oslo
Ann Helen Aarø of Wiersholm, Mellbye & Bech, Oslo

Portugal
César Bessa Monteiro of Abreu, Cardigos & Associates, Lisbon
Rita Paínho of Abreu, Cardigos & Associates, Lisbon

Singapore
Michael Hwang of Allen & Gledhill, Singapore
Andrew Chan of Allen & Gledhill, Singapore

South Africa
Owen Dean of Spoor & Fisher, Pretoria

Spain
Professor Isabel Hernando of the Facultad de Derecho San Sebastian, San Sebastian

Sweden
Thomas Lindqvist of Advokatfirman Hammarskiöld, Stockholm
Claes Langenius of Advokatfirman Hammarskiöld, Stockholm

Switzerland
François Dessemontet, Professor for the Law of Obligations and Intellectual Property Law, Universities of Lausanne and Fribourg

United Kingdom
Robyn Durie of Linklaters & Paines, London

United States of America
Bruce P Keller of Debevoise & Plimpton, New York
Jeremy Feigelson of Debevoise & Plimpton, New York
Craig Bloom of Debevoise & Plimpton, New York
Lisa Green of the National Broadcasting Co

Preface

From our vantage point on the cusp of the 20th and 21st centuries, it is, perhaps, difficult for us to imagine living in a world without international conventions, a world where international trade would be impossible without detailed knowledge of the laws of every country.

Thanks to the huge efforts of our forebears who pioneered international conventions on copyright, trade marks and patents, and thus created a minimum universally-applicable set of standards (at least among conventional countries), we modern intellectual property lawyers inhabit a world of certainty where trade with foreign countries is almost as straightforward as national transactions.

Few practising lawyers are qualified to advise on the laws of more than one jurisdiction, yet most of us routinely advise on complex international transactions, frequently with no more than a passing thought for issues of foreign law. In a world without international conventions, this state of affairs would be impossible.

Yet it is precisely this situation which exists in the areas of privacy, publicity and personality rights. The range and diversity of legislation relating to privacy, publicity and personality throughout the world is both striking and stimulating. It is one of the last remaining important tracts of international law remaining to be codified.

There are no applicable international conventions which deal with these issues. The European Convention on Human Rights, (which the UK has recently implemented in the Human Rights Act 1998), documents a number of basic human rights, and deals with privacy issues. It has yet, however, to achieve truly international status, since its adherents (with the exception principally of certain Commonwealth countries) are primarily confined within the European land mass. It does not deal comprehensively with publicity or personality issues.

Privacy, publicity and personality rights are of crucial importance, in relation to the place of the individual in society. The human rights issues raised by our rapidly developing technology are becoming increasingly complex; the contrast between the developed countries and the developing world is becoming increasingly stark; meanwhile the role of the communications media, not only in reflecting but also shaping our society, grows ever more important.

It seems inevitable that the first quarter of the 21st century will lead to the increasing globalisation of our culture, and both the pace and direction of this change are likely to be determined by the communications media. The challenge we face will be to ensure that as commercial practices and laws become harmonised, we chose the best models to guide us.

This book presents a snap-shot of relevant privacy, publicity and personality laws in 29 different jurisdictions at the end of the 20th century. The task of selecting and co-ordinating the contributions from such a distinguished range of international contributors has been lengthy, and at times (for some of those involved) frustrating. Like wartime convoys, collective works of joint authorship tend to progress at the speed of the slowest vessel, and the publication of the work is a testament to the perseverance and skill of the editorial staff at Butterworths.

I would particularly like to express my thanks and gratitude to those eminent practitioners from all over the world who have so freely given of their time and energy to document the richness and diversity of the laws relating to privacy, publicity and personality.

It is not an exaggeration to state that this work breaks completely new ground. It is to be hoped that it will stimulate thought and debate on the future development of the laws of privacy, publicity and personality.

Michael Henry
15 November 2000

Contents

1 INTRODUCTION

A   Scope of this work

1.01   The rapid development of the communications media during the 20th century has raised a number of fundamental issues in the human rights area and specifically:

(1) the conflict between freedom of expression and the individual right of privacy;

(2) the right of the individual to authorise the use or prevent the use of their name/likeness for publicity purposes; and

(3) the difficulties arising in a global society dependent on mass media as a result of the absence of any right protecting an individual's personality.

This work consists of a detailed analysis of the laws relating to privacy, publicity and personality in 29 different jurisdictions, including the US, (where there is substantial case law on these matters).

B   Privacy

1   European Convention on Human Rights and the Human Rights Act

1.02   The Human Rights Act 1998 was incorporated into UK law on 1 October 2000 and with it not only the legislative provisions that reflect the European Convention on Human Rights ('ECHR') but the entire body of jurisprudence that makes up the case law of the European Court.

The Human Rights Act has a significant impact on the already fast-developing areas concerning the media, freedom of expression and the nascent right to privacy.

Freedom of expression, encompassing the rights to publicity and personality, is enshrined in Articles 8 and 10 of the ECHR. (The full text of the ECHR may be found in the Appendix.)

2   Article 10 – European Convention on Human Rights

1.03   Article 10 specifies that everyone has the right to freedom of expression which can only be restricted if the restriction is prescribed by law, the claimant pursues a legitimate aim and the right is necessary in a democratic society.

These exceptions are to be construed narrowly in accordance with the European Court's ruling in *Sunday Times v UK.*[1]

Article 10 of the ECHR (Freedom of Expression) states as follows:

> 'Everyone has the right to freedom of expression. This right shall include freedom to hold opinions and to receive and impart information and ideas without interference by public authority and regardless of frontiers. This article shall not prevent States from requiring the licensing of broadcasting, television or cinema enterprises.
>
> The exercise of these freedoms, since it carries with it duties and responsibilities, may be subject to such formalities, conditions, restrictions or penalties as are prescribed by law and are necessary in a democratic society, in the interests of national security, territorial integrity or public safety, for the prevention of disorder or crime, for the protection of health or morals, for the protection of the reputation or rights of others, for preventing the disclosure of information received in confidence, or for maintaining the authority and impartiality of the judiciary.'

The right covers all types of expression whether political, commercial or artistic. The freedom relates to the giving and receiving of information so that content is largely irrelevant and there is no public interest requirement. The European Court has consistently held that press freedom is of particular importance *Jersalid v Denmark*[2] and outlawed gagging by prior restraint or by forcing disclosure of confidential sources.

1.04   There are a number of cases where the domestic courts have attempted to prohibit publication of government 'secrets' pursuant to specific legislation. In the *Spycatcher* case[3] the Observer and Guardian newspapers were successful in Strasbourg and the more recent case of ex-MI5 agent David Shayler is unlikely to get that far. In these cases the allegedly confidential status of information cannot be sustained.

In *Goodwin v UK*[4] a journalist had been fined for failing to disclose the source of his information about a company's financial report. The European Court stated:

> 'Protection of journalistic sources is one of the basic conditions for press freedom… without such protection the vital public watchdog role of the press may be undermined'. It went on to say: …'the potentially chilling effect of an order of source disclosure is incompatible with Article 10 unless justified by an overriding requirement in the public interest…limitations on confidentiality of journalistic sources call for most careful scrutiny by the court.'

In *Elton John v Express Newspapers*[5] the court had to consider section 10 of the Contempt of Court Act 1981 which protects the confidentiality of sources 'unless necessary in the interests of justice or national security or for the prevention of disorder or crime'. One of the paper's journalists had obtained a draft of Counsel's advice in litigation concerning John and his accountants,

1   (1991) 14 EHRR 229, E Ct HR.
2   (1994) 19 EHRR 1, E Ct HR.
3   (1996) 22 EHRR 123, 3 Ct HR.
4   *A-G v Guardian Newspapers Ltd (No 2)* [1988] 3 All ER 545.
5   [2000] 3, All ER 257, [2000] 1 WLR 1931, [2000] EMLR 606, [2000] NLJR 615, 144 Sol Jo LB 217, CA.

Price Waterhouse Coopers. Morland J ordered the journalist and his editor to provide an affidavit specifying whether the source of the information was known and if so identifying such source.

On appeal the court considered that legal professional privilege was not to be equated with an overriding public interest. '… it is important that when orders are made requiring journalists to depart from their normal professional standards, the merits of their doing so in the public interest are clearly reinforced.'

3   Article 8 – European Convention on Human Rights

1.05   Article 8 of the ECHR (Right to respect for private and family life) states as follows:

> 'Everyone has the right to respect for his private and family life, his home and his correspondence.
>
> There shall be no interference by a public authority with the exercise of this right except such as is in accordance with the law and is necessary in a democratic society in the interests of national security, public safety or the economic well-being of the country, for the prevention of disorder or crime, for the protection of health or morals, or for the protection of rights and freedoms of others.'

The right to privacy has been implied in the UK domestic law of confidence but is necessarily broader. It extends protection to the person rather than just the information. The UK courts have been slow to grant injunctive relief or prior restraint orders in cases alleging breach of confidence where there is an obvious public interest in disclosure.

In *Service Corpn International plc v Channel Four Television*[6] the court refused a funeral home's application for an injunction to prevent the broadcast of a documentary exposing allegedly abusive treatment where the information had been obtained as a result of covert filming.

If the claim had been brought in privacy by the families who had used the home against the appropriate regulatory body, the court would have had to balance the competing rights to freedom of expression and privacy. It could not have ruled as it did that the claimant's application was in truth an attempt to protect reputation brought under guise of breach of confidence, because prior restraint is not available in defamation proceedings.

1.06   The most recent domestic decision in which the concept of privacy was explored is the Court of Appeal's judgment on the Broadcasting Standards Commission's appeal in a case involving secret filming by the BBC in a public place. At first instance the court ruled that DSG Retail Ltd (Dixons) as a body corporate did not have a right of privacy and that filming in a shop to which the public necessarily has access cannot amount to infringement unless what is filmed itself has a private element.

Liberty joined in the appeal and made submissions arising out of both the ECHR jurisprudence and case law from the Canada Charter of Rights and Freedom which were reflected in the BBC's own submissions to the court.

---

6   [1999] EMLR 83.

Dixon's arguments also explored international jurisprudence and research on the assimilation of the human rights in a country's legal infrastructure.

In allowing the appeal all three judges referred to the concept of privacy in the ECHR and concluded that there was nothing to prevent its application to a company. Clandestine filming was held to be objectionable because it was done without justification and was therefore an unwarranted infringement of Dixons' privacy under the Broadcasting Act 1996 that governs the BSC's regulatory role.

4   Data protection

1.07   The Data Protection Act 1998 was implemented in March 2000 and it affects privacy law not only in the UK but throughout the world. The Act was passed in compliance with the EU Directive on the Protection of Personal Data and applies to all computerised data on EU nationals.

This means that data cannot be transferred to countries without adequate protection and any foreign jurisdiction dealing with such data must comply with the eight principles which ensure the fair collection, transmission and storage of this information.

1.08   Traditionally the US has not legislated to protect private information - some argue that this is because of its emphasis on the First Amendment, the more cynical point to the lucrative data-mining industry that has sprung up.

After a two-year dialogue and with a real threat to continuing economic activity between Europe and the US, the US Department of Commerce has now reached an accord with the European Commission.

US companies are able, with effect from 1 November 2000, to self-certify their compliance with the 'safe harbour principles' by annual registration with the Department of Commerce.

The US government has already passed statutory regulations dealing with online privacy in the financial and banking industry and it is thought that there will soon be federal legislation to protect online privacy generally.

5   International privacy rights

1.09   The extent to which individuals in the UK are protected against intrusion into their privacy is markedly less than in many other jurisdictions.

Covert filming and video surveillance is outlawed in many countries (including Belgium, Brazil, Denmark, Finland, France, etc), and there are numerous other examples where laws of other jurisdictions confer rights which do not exist in the UK.

1.10   A right to oblivion, or a right to be forgotten exists in a number of countries including Belgium, France, and Switzerland. This right permits an individual whose life it not dedicated to public activities to enjoy the peace and quiet necessary for the free development of their personality.

Some jurisdictions, such as France, permit individuals to ensure that their addresses and pseudonyms remain secret, and it is noticeable that many foreign jurisdictions provide significantly more protection against intrusion into privacy than is provided under UK law.

The law of Switzerland, for example, prevents the filming of tearful or joyful behaviour, such as weeping at funerals or mild or wild sexual endearment, and German law provides extension protection for a persons 'individual sphere' which the law recognises may exist in locations such as restaurants, hotels, sporting arenas, telephone booths or even the countryside.

1.11 By comparison with these foreign legislative provisions, the laws of the UK appear comparatively under-developed.

C   Publicity and personality

1   *Publicity rights and personality rights*

1.12   Although some jurisdictions – notably the US – provide a right of publicity which gives significant protection for individuals against the misappropriation of their identity or performance, the laws of the UK make no such provision.

Equally absent from the scope of legal protection in the UK and other countries is the personality right, or the exclusive right of an individual to exploit their name, likeness and other attributes in a commercial manner. Although it is possible to obtain limited trade mark protection for the signatures of individuals, the absence of any protection for wider personality rights appears incongruous in a society where merchandising, product endorsement, and the cult of the celebrity are so prominent.

1.13   As the process of globalisation of our culture continues, there will be increasing pressure towards harmonisation of international laws relating to personality and publicity rights. It may be that those jurisdictions which provide strong protection for personality and publicity rights may expect to stimulate commercial growth in areas such as merchandising, fashion, and other activities associated with popular culture.

If jurisdictions which fail to provide protection for personality and publicity rights perceive themselves to be commercially disadvantaged, then it is likely that we will witness significant change over the coming years, as international laws become harmonised.

1.14   From experience derived from the harmonisation of European laws on copyright and related rights, the probability is that harmonisation will tend to select high degrees of protection rather than low ones. Two factors determine this outcome.

First, European union law respects vested rights of individuals: any harmonisation which results in individuals in any European Union State receiving a lesser degree of protection than they enjoyed before harmonisation is therefore out of the question.

Secondly, on purely pragmatic grounds, equality of protection between contracting States can be effected as soon as legislation is implemented, without any need for a transitional period, if the maximum term of protection is selected. If, however, the minimum level of protection is selected, a significant transition period would be required before equalisation was achieved in all contracting States.

D Conclusion

1.15 The negotiation of the great international conventions on copyright, trade marks and patents was instigated by commercial interests, which required certainty and guaranteed minimum standards of protection between participating States.

Commercial entities who are active in the areas associated with the communications media and popular culture all have a direct interest in ensuring that laws and commercial practices which respect rights of publicity and personality are developed and enacted in those jurisdictions which currently do not provide these basic protections.

There is also a pressing need to eliminate the incongruity where the private life (or individual sphere) of a British footballer is protected if he is in France or Germany, but not if he is in the UK. British laws protecting individual privacy are weak when compared to the well-developed laws in other jurisdictions. In the UK itself, the contrast between the draconian regime regulating news reporting by broadcasters in the UK and the lax regulation of the press by the Press Complaints Commission, which appears utterly powerless to curb the worst excesses of the tabloids, is dramatic. The case for maintaining this unjustifiable distinction in a post-convergence era is completely unconvincing, and there is an urgent and compelling need for law reform in the area.

2 ARGENTINA

Ernesto Aracama Zorraquin

A Privacy

1 Relevant laws

2.01 The following are the sources of legislation in Argentina relating to the right of privacy.

2 Rules arising from the Constitution

2.02 The National Constitution was enacted on 1 May 1853 and subsequently amended in 1860, 1866, 1898, 1951 and 1994. Sections 18 and 19 of the National Constitution, read in part, as follows:

> 'Section 18: a person's domicile may not be violated nor may their correspondence, letters or private papers or documents; a law shall determine in which cases and on which grounds they may be seized and opened.
> Section 19: the private acts and affairs of individuals which do not adversely affect the public order or morals, or injure any third party, are reserved to God alone and exempt from judges' authority.'

3 Treaties having constitutional hierarchy

2.03 The National Constitution, section 75(22) states that:

> 'no treaties, therein mentioned ... overrule any section of the first Part of this constitution and must be construed as supplementary to the rights and guarantees therein acknowledged.'

According treaties a constitutional hierarchy does not mean that they are incorporated into the Constitution but that they are added to the internal Argentine law, with the same hierarchy as that of the Supreme Law but without forming a part of it.

2.04 The main relevant treaties are.

(1) *The American Declaration of an Individual's Rights,* approved at the IX American International Conference, in Santa Fe de Bogotá, Colombia,

in 1948. Section V of this Declaration provides that 'Any person has the right to be protected by law from abusive attacks affecting his/her honour, good name and private and family life.'

(2) *The Universal Declaration of Human Rights*, adapted and enacted by resolution 217 A (III) passed by the General Meeting of the United Nations on 10 December 1948, section 122 of which states that: 'Nobody shall be subject to arbitrary defamation of his/her private life, family, domicile, letters and correspondence, or honour or good name. Any person is entitled to be protected by law from insults or defamation.'

(3) *The International Pact on Political and Civil Rights*, adopted by resolution 2200 (XXI) of the General Meeting of the United Nations, signed in New York City on 19 December 1966.[1] Section 17 states as follows:

'1   Nobody shall be subject to arbitrary or illegal interference in their private life, family, domicile, correspondence or letters, or unlawful attacks against their honour or reputation (good name).

2   All persons are entitled to be protected by law from insults or defamation.'

(4) *The American Convention on Human Rights* (San José de Costa Rica Pact), subscribed in San José, Costa Rica, on 22 November 1969.[2] Section 11 states:

'1   Every person is entitled to have their honour be respected and their dignity acknowledged.

2   Nobody shall be subject to arbitrary or abusive insult or defamation on their private life, family life, domicile, letters or correspondence, or illegal attacks to their honour or reputation.

3   All persons are entitled to be protected by law from insults or defamation.'

4   Laws

Civil Code

2.05   Section 1071 *bis*, incorporated to the Civil Code by Law 21.713[3] states as follows:

'Any person who arbitrarily interferes with another's life, by publishing pictures, disclosing correspondence, adversely affecting another with their usage and customs or feelings, or disturbing their privacy in any other way, shal lif such acts are not considered criminal offences, be compelled to cease performing them, if they have not previously ceased, and to pay compensation to be equitably fixed by the judge, according to the circumstances of the case; in addition, the judge, at the request of the injured party, may also order the publication of the judgment in a local newspaper, if such measure is considered appropriate remedy.'

---

1   Approved by the Argentine Republic under Law 22.313 (sanctioned on 17 April 1986; enacted on 5 June 1986, published with the Official Bulletin on 13 May 1986).
2   Approved by the Argentine Republic, by Law 23.054 (enacted on 1 March 1984, enacted on 19 March 1984, published with the Official Bulletin on 27 March 1984, ratified on 14 August 1984).
3   Sanctioned on 30 September 1975, enacted on 15 October 1975 and published on 22 October 1975.

The Criminal Code and in particular its provisions are referred to in paras **2.06**, **2.07** and **2.10**.

5   Crimes against one's honour

2.06   Slander, defamation or false accusation of any crime which results in the filing of a public action may be punishable with imprisonment for a term of one to three years.[4]

Any person who dishonours or injures the reputation of another person, shall be punished with a fine from 1,500 to 90,000 pesos or with imprisonment from one month to one year.[5]

6   Violation of secrets

Unauthorised opening

2.07   Any person who opens a letter, envelope or telegram, or intercepts a telephonic message or any other kind of communication or letter which is not addressed to them, or a message or notice or other private paper, or suppresses or diverts from its final destination any letter or correspondence not addressed to them, shall be punished with imprisonment from 15 days to six months.[6] If the person guilty of such crime publishes or discloses the content of a letter or other communication, he or she shall be punished with imprisonment from one month to one year.

Unauthorised publication

2.08   Any person who is in possession of a letter or other communication not intended to be published, and who unduly publishes it, even though it was addressed to them, shall be punished with a fine from 1,500 to 90,000 pesos, if such act causes injury to third parties.[7]

Unauthorised disclosure

2.09   Any person who, due to their status, occupation, employment, profession or art, knows any secret, the disclosure of which may cause any injury, and discloses it without any reasonable cause, shall be punished with a fine from 1,500 to 90,000 pesos and shall be disqualified from their profession.[8]

2.10   The provisions of the Criminal Code described here arise from the text arranged by the Executive Order 3.992 and passed on 21 December 1984. These provisions are applied both to Argentine citizens and to citizens of foreign countries. The basic rule for protecting the right to privacy is in section 19 of the National Constitution, which reads as follows:

> 'The private acts and affairs of individuals which do not adversely affect the public order or morals or injure any third party are reserved to God alone and exempt from the judges' authority.'

---

4   National Constitution, s 109.
5   National Constitution, s 110.
6   National Constitution, s 153.
7   National Constitution, s 155.
8   National Constitution, s 156.

This constitution thus acknowledges the existence of a '*derecho personalísimo*' (a personal right which is inalienable and truly personal) which protects a person from publicity and other interference with private life in order to preserve social needs and the public interest.[9]

2.11 Pursuant to the constitution, only those actions of men which do not adversely affect the public order or morals or are injurious to third parties are protected.

7 *Civil Code, section 1071 bis*

2.12 Consequently, the provision of section 1071 *bis* of the Civil Code states as follows:

> 'Any person who arbitrarily interferes with another person's life by publishing pictures, disclosing their correspondence and letters, injuring another third party's habitual acts and doings or feelings, or adversely affecting in any other way their privacy, shall if such acts are not criminal offences, be compelled to cease performing the same, if they have not been previously brought to an end, and to pay compensation to be fixed equitably by the judge, according to the circumstances of the case; in addition, the judge, at the request of the injured party, may also order the publication of the judgment in a local newspaper, if such measure is considered appropriate remedy.'

8 *Subjects*

Living persons

2.13 Any living individual is protected by law because each of us has an activity, an individual autonomy that must not be invaded by third parties, provided we do not affect public order or morality, or injure third parties.

2.14 The Supreme Court of Justice in the judgment rendered in the case *Ponzetti de Balbín, Indalia E et al v Editorial Atlántida SA et al* made a distinction between public and private persons. As regards the former it also distinguished between civil servants and others who are not civil servants such as sportsmen, cinema and television actors, famous persons, scientists or persons being socially known and the like. Even though it acknowledged that all of them are entitled to the protection of their privacy, it pointed out that public persons, whether civil servants or not, are less entitled to it by reason of the right of society to know all aspects of the private life of a person, to the extent they may in some way, affect the community.

2.15 Of course, not everything that may be of interest to the public at large, or to those who are simply curious, may be considered in the public interest. The latter must be actual and not refer to past acts of the person whose privacy has been injured and must be assessed under a strict criterion.[10]

---

9   Cifuentes.
10 *Menen, Carlos v Editorial Perfil SA.*

Dead persons

2.16   So far as concerns dead persons, it is considered they lack privacy because they are no longer subjects capable of acquiring rights and contracting duties.

Legal persons

2.17   The interpretation of section 1071 *bis* of the Civil Code and the circumstances which the courts have heed to, constitute a privacy violation, 'the act of publishing pictures', 'injuring another person's habitual actions or feelings', and the like have led legal authors to conclude that legal persons are excluded from section 1071 of the Civil Code.

9   *Requirements for action for invasion of privacy*

2.18   In order for invasion of privacy to be considered to have occurred for the purposes of section 1071, it is necessary that some or all of the following requirements be met:

(1)   some disturbance or interference with a person's private life where, for example, someone intervenes or does something which interferes with another's private life without being requested to do so;[11]

(2)   such interference or disturbance was arbitrary, and carried out by a person 'without [them] being entitled to do so'[12] or contrary to justice, reason, or capriciously performed. An action for invasion of privacy will not occur for the purposes of section 1071 *bis* if:

  (a)   it is not arbitrary;[13]

  (b)   it deals with the exercise of a person's own right or the fulfilment of a legal duty, as, for example, when it derives from an extension of parental authority;

  (c)   it was necessary for the administration of justice, as, for example, the publication of pictures or identikits drawn by the police in order to facilitate the arrest of persons accused of having committed crimes;

  (d)   it is based on the maintenance of the public order;

  (e)   the injured party consents to it; or

  (f)   a third party's privacy would be adversely affected in any way.

2.19   Section 1071 sets forth some cases, including publication of pictures or photographs, divulging correspondence and letters, disturbance or humiliation of any third party in their habitual acts and doings or feelings, and adversely affecting another's privacy in any way.
These cases are only listed as examples and there are other factors particular to the circumstances of each case which need to be considered in order to determine whether is an invasion of privacy.

---

11 Rivera, Julio C.
12 Rivera.
13 Belluscio, Zannoni.

2.20 Taking pictures of a person's property, for the purposes of advertising and without the owner's authorisation, constitutes an invasion of privacy.[14] A similar invasion occurred when, as a joke, an announcement of a person's death was published while the person was still alive.[15]

Freedom of the press

2.21 The National Constitution, section 19, provides for freedom of the press. The courts have held that the freedom of press consists of publishing ideas in the press without prior censorship, but it does not afford protection to persons who use the press as a means doing unlawful acts. The courts have also stated that the right to private life protects all persons, including those having a public life.[16]

2.22 Cases that have not yet been adjudged by Argentine courts include:

(1) covert filming;
(2) filming over private property (from the air);
(3) public order aspects (obstructing the highway, riotous assembly, and the like);
(4) recording conversations whether open or covert;
(5) sifting of rubbish;
(6) staking out/following use of assumed identity to obtain information;
(7) use of security camera footage for reporting events; and
(8) use of telephoto lenses.

10 *Remedies for invasion of privacy*

Criminal offences

2.23 Where appropriate, the specific laws relating to the punishment of crimes and the general provisions of the Civil Code as regards the payment of appropriate compensations will be relevant. In all the other cases, the remedies provided by section 1071 *bis* of the Civil Code will be appropriate.

Civil offences

2.24 The remedies are:
(1) that the interference with another's private life be brought to an end;
(2) that compensation be paid to the injured person; and
(3) publication of the judgment.

2.25 The action set forth in section 1017 *bis* clearly is an action to bring the act complained of to an end. In addition, the injured person is entitled to demand payment of compensation, which shall be fixed 'equitably by the judge according to the circumstances'.

---

14 Compare *Mieres, Roberto C v Safrar SA*, National Civil Court of Appeals, Division C, 9 February 1978, published in La Ley, 1978-C-369; *Weil, Andrés D v Sevel Argentina SA et al*, National Civil Court of Appeals, Division, in La Ley, 1986-E-614.
15 *Aldama, Ángel v Souvenir Publicidad*, Civil Court of Appeals, Division C, 22 April 1991, in El Derecho Vol 97, p 327.
16 As in the already quoted case: *Ponzetti de Balbín*, see para **2.14** above.

2.26   A person whose private life has been interfered with, may request publication of the judgment in a local newspaper, 'if such measure is considered appropriate remedy'. Publication of the judgment is not automatically carried out – the judge must consider whether it is appropriate or not as a suitable remedy.

B   Publicity

1   *Relevant laws*

2.27   The specific laws of the Argentine Law System protecting the names of individuals are Law 18.248 on the individual's name[17] and Law 22.362 on trade marks and trade names, which in section 3(h) forbids the registration of a person's name and nickname as a trade mark without their consent, or their heirs' consent up to the fourth generation inclusively.

2   *Name and personality*

2.28   Since name and personality are considered to be indivisible, as stated by Pliner, the legal defence of a person's name may involve the protection of other assets of their personality such as their honour, their professional name, artistic name, commercial name, success or fame, family status, identity and also sometimes their property and goods.[18]
In the Argentine legal system, an individual's name is protected through civil actions and criminal sanctions and by the intervention of the administrative authority.[19]

3   *Protection of name*

2.29   From the civil point of view, the protection of an individual's name is provided for by sections 20 and 21 of Law 18.248.

Acknowledgment or claim

2.30   Section 20 of Law 18.248 provides for an action requesting the acknowledgement or claim, and states as follows:

> 'The person, whose name is being used, may demand its acknowledgement and request the prohibition of any future use by the defendant; and they shall also be entitled to request the publication of the judgment at the defendant's expense.'

Acción de contestación

2.31   Section 21, para 1 of Law 18.248, creates the right of *acción de contestación* or an action requesting the usurpation of the name. It states that:

---

17   Sanctioned on 26/12/86, enacted on 19 June 1969, and published with the Official Bulletin on 24 June 1969, as amended by Laws 23.162, 23.264 and 23.515.
18   Rivera.
19   Pliner.

'If the name belonging to a person is used by any other, the former may bring an action in court requesting the latter to stop unduly using their name, without prejudice to the recovery of appropriate compensation, if appropriate.'

Unlawful use of name

2.32   Section 21, para 2 of Law 18.248 creates a right of action requesting suppression of unlawful (improper) use of the name. It states that:

'When a person's name is maliciously used to name things or characters in a play, movie or television programme, and such use morally injures or adversely affects the property or assets or said person, the latter may request that such use be brought to an end and such person is paid a compensation for damages. In both cases, the Judge may fix the penalties or sanctions authorised by section 666 *bis* of the Civil Code.'

The purpose of this action is to make a person stop using the name of the plaintiff whenever such use is malicious.

2.33   In order for an action to be viable, it is necessary for the following requirements to be met:

(1)   ownership of the name by the plaintiff;

(2)   malicious use by the defendant of the name of the plaintiff for the purpose of naming a thing or character in a play, movie or television programme. The existence of fraud or deceit is not necessary;

(3)   damage to the property or assets of the plaintiff or injury affecting their reputation, honour, feelings or emotions *(daño moral)*.

4   *The* Little Dragon Chipy *case*

2.34   National case law applied this legal provision in the case of *Chipy, Aída C et al v Productos García Ferré SA*.[20] In this case, the well-known cartoonist García Ferré created a character called '*Drangocito Chipy*' (Little Dragon Chipy).
Mrs Aída C Chipy and her sisters sued Producciones García Ferré SA and requested that the use of the character should be brought to an end and sought compensation for the injury suffered by the plaintiffs affecting their reputation, honour, feelings or emotions. The plaintiffs also sought compensation for the damage to their assets and property caused by the use of their surname as the name of a character in a television cartoon, which invaded their privacy and encouraged as a result of its publicity, mistaken and humiliating comparisons.

2.35   The Court of Appeal sustained the complaint brought by Mrs Chipy, and held that:

'It is reasonable that the plaintiffs should be entitled to request that the defendant stops using their surname as the name of the character in the cartoon represented by a dragon called "Dragoncito Chipy" ("Little Dragon Chipy"), and their interest in doing so lies both from the material and moral point of view. Even though there is no confusion because

20 Finally adjudged by the National Court of Appeals in Civil Matters, Division B, on 27 October 1980 (JA Volume 1981-II-p 611).

logically there is no identity at all, it is considered as an invasion which constitutes an undue (improper) use of a name, and it is also legitimate to secure for the owners of the name the right to have their name respected for elementary social reasons and as prescribed by law.'

The court ordered the defendant to stop using the surname Chipy and to pay the plaintiffs the sum of $2,000,000 as a compensation for the *daño moral* as well as the costs of the case at the original and appellate courts.

5   Right to prevent registration of a personal name as a trade mark

2.36   No application may be made to protect an individual's name, nickname or picture without their consent or that of their heirs. This right continues until the fourth generation, and is set out in section 3(h) of Trade Marks Law 22.362, enacted on 28 December 1980. Therefore an individual's name may not be registered as a trade mark without that individual's consent or their heirs' consent.

2.37   Argentine courts, by applying this rule, have rejected applications to register the trade marks 'CHURCHILL'[1] and 'RHOOSEVEL' because it may be confused with the name of the president Theodore Roosevelt;[2] and have also declared null and void the registration of the trade mark 'PICASO'.[3]

2.38   Law 22.362, section 3(h), also protects an individual's nickname. By reason of the application of its provisions, the registration of the trade mark 'PELÉ', the nickname of the famous footballer Nelso Arantes Do Nascimiento, was denied.[4]

2.39   Section 3(h) of the Trade Marks Law 22.362 forbids the registration as a trade mark of a person's picture without their consent or their heirs' consent until the fourth generation. If the appropriate authority has awarded registration to an aggrieved person or to their heirs, they may request its nullity. It was thus resolved by the Supreme Court of Justice in *Guerrier, Bouvard's widower v Garese, Antonia*.[5] This provision must be supplemented by the one set forth by section 1071 *bis* of the Civil Code, which protects the persons' privacy.

C   Personality

1   Right to reproduce one's image

2.40   The general legal textbooks and opinions (Cifuentes, Rivera) state that the right to reproduce one's image is a *derecho personalísimo* (a personal right

1   *Enrigue Hughes ex party*, 4 August 1987, Patents and Trade marks 1947-545.
2   *Re Ricardo Fernández, ex party*, Patents and Trade marks 1931-331.
3   Federal Court of Appeals of the Federal Capital City, Division I, case 2248 of 14 April 1987.
4   Federal Court of Appeals of the City of La Plata, Division I, judgment rendered on 30 March 1979, La Ley 14 November 1979.
5   Judgment rendered on 30 April 1941, Fallos 189:315.

which is inalienable and truly personal) that entitles its holder to object to any third parties' seizure, reproduction, publication or divulging of that image without his/her consent or the agreement of the law.

2.41 Initially, the right to reproduce one's image was restricted to photographs. Nowadays, it is understood that this protection is extended also to the reproduction of the human being's voice.

2.42 It is debateable whether the right to one's image is an independent right or if otherwise, it is merely an aspect of the right to privacy. At present the prevailing view is that it is an independent right. Therefore, the seizure, reproduction or publication of an image constitutes an infringement of the individual's right independently of whether it affects that individual's right to privacy.

Of course, it does not imply that through the use of the image the right to private life, privacy or the right to one's honour may be adversely affected. As we have seen in the paragraphs dealing with privacy, section 1071 *bis* of the Civil Code considers that the publication of pictures may interfere with a person's private life.

In this sense, the judgment rendered on 2 November 1988 by the National Civil Court of Appeals, Division C[6] upheld that the right to one's image may be infringed even though it does not affect a person's honour or privacy.

2 Copyright law restrictions relating to photographs and pictures of individuals

2.43 Section 3 of Law 11.723 on copyright[7] states as follows:

'A person's photograph may not be sold without the express consent of said person and, after his/her death, without the express consent of his/her spouse and children or their direct descendants, or in default thereof by his/her father or mother.

Should there be no spouse, children, father or mother, or no direct descendants of the children, the photograph may be freely published. Any person who has given his/her consent may revoke the same by paying a compensation for damages.

A photograph may be freely published where it relates to scientific, educational and cultural matters in general, or to facts or events of public interest or to those facts that had been publicly performed.'

2.44 Before commenting on these rules, it should be borne in mind:

(1) that the provision of Law 11.723 does not refer to the photographer but to the person who is featured in the photograph. It establishes his/her rights and restricts the rights of the photographer;

(2) that the expression 'picture or photograph', as stated by Rivera, must be considered in a wide sense, because it includes drawings, portraits, paintings, sculptures, television, cartoons, and any other way of capturing

---

6   JA, IV-20-88.
7   Sanctioned on 26 September 1933, enacted on 28 September 1933 and published on 30 September 1933.

and/or reproducing the human image (Cifuentes);

(3) from the independent nature of the right to reproduce one's image, it arises that the taking and/or distribution of another person's image without his/her consent, or whenever it is not authorised by the law,[8] is unlawful.

3 Requirements for consent

2.45 Section 31 of Law 11.723 is very precise when it refers to the requirements for consent:

> 'A person's photograph may not be sold, traded or marketed without his/her express consent and, after his/her death, without the express consent of his/her spouse and children or their direct descendants, or in default thereof by his/her father or mother.'

2.46 The legal textbooks and doctrine (Rivera) understand that the consent is strictly restricted to the purpose for, or the circumstances under which, it has been given. Thus, a person who authorised the publication of their image for a certain magazine or newspaper may object to its being used again.[9] The judgment rendered by Division A of the National Commercial Court of Appeals on 02/24/66[10] resolved that:

> 'The consent of the party who is interested in the publication of his/her photograph must be express. If there are many interested persons and they disagree among themselves, the final decision is taken by the judicial authority. If a sum of money is received as a consideration for a picture, it is presumed that the person has consented thereto. After thirty years have elapsed from the death of the person who has been photographed, the publication of the photograph is free.'

Any person who has given his/her consent may revoke it by paying compensation for damages.

4 Circumstances where publication of a picture/photograph is permitted

2.47 Law 11.723, section 31, para 4 states that free publication of a picture is permitted in the following cases:

(1) whenever the publication of the picture is related to scientific, educational and cultural purposes in general; and

(2) whenever it is related to facts or events of public interest or those that have been publicly performed.

2.48 The first case must always constitute a non-injurious publication and, pursuant to Rivera, all necessary measures must be adopted to avoid the

---

8   Law 11.723, s 31, para 4.
9   Judgment rendered by a court of original jurisdiction in civil matters on 20 September 1978) (El Derecho, Vol 81, p 459; judgment rendered by the National Civil Court of Appeals, Division G, on 4 May 1988). JA VII/13/88.
10 La Ley 122-159.

identification of the person photographed or filmed. As regards the second case, the judgment rendered by the National Court of Appeals in Civil Matters, Division F, on 26 August 1980[11] held as follows:

'When the reproduction of a person's image is related to facts, events or ceremonies of a public nature or publicly performed, the restriction of the subjective right to the image is wholly justified, because the photographed person's image is merely an element of the fact, event or ceremony of public interest or publicly performed (riot, military magazine, funeral procession, fire).'

The fact that the photograph or the video is taken at a public place does not authorise the focus to be placed on a person directly in such a way as to allow his/her identification (Rivera).

Finally, Argentine courts have held that the reproduction of a photograph taken at a sports match in a magazine containing erotic material is unlawful.[12]

2.49   In those circumstances where a picture is taken for commercial purposes (as in advertising activities) the person photographed, who may, according to Goldstein, resemble an actor will retain his/her moral rights and will be able to object to any use of the photograph that injures his/her image or personal good name.

---

11 JA, 1981-II-288.
12 National Civil Court of Appeals, Division A, judgment rendered on 27 October 1987. La Ley, 19 April 1988).

3   AUSTRALIA

Robert Todd
Ian Smith

A   Introduction

3.01   This chapter outlines the protection afforded by Australian law to privacy, personality and publicity. Presently, this protection is provided not through any discrete or coherent regime but through an eclectic amalgam of statute and common law.
Nevertheless, the next decade may see some consolidation in this area of the law, driven by legislative responses[1] to the rapid penetration of new information technologies.

3.02   This chapter examines the ways in which the law, and the attitudes of law and policy makers have changed to accommodate growing public concerns regarading intrusions into individual privacy. It also outlines the ways in which privacy and related laws in Australia extend beyond the protection of individual rights to protect valuable commercial interests, for example in maintaining corporate identity or confidentiality.

3.03   In outlining the Australian law, this chapter separates the areas of discussion into two parts. The first deals with the protection afforded to an individual's privacy and the second deals with the protection of personality and publicity which applies to both individuals and commercial entities.

B   Privacy

1   Introduction

3.04   In Australia, there is no absolute right to or protection of privacy under either the common law or statute.[2]
Despite this, the law has developed sanctions against intrusion in certain circumstances. These sanctions reflect the growing community concern over

---

1   The Commonwealth government has announced its intention to legislate to 'support and strengthen self regulatory privacy protection in the private sector'.
2   See *Australian Consolidated Press v Ettingshausen* (13 October 1993, unreported), NSW CA; *South Australian Police v Carbone* (1997) 68 SASR 200.

invasions of privacy, in particular the use by government agencies of personal information such as credit records,[3] and incursions by the media into the private lives of individuals.

3.05 Further, it has not only been the law makers who have recognised the growing public concern with privacy. Many industry bodies have instituted guidelines or codes of practice[4] which, while in themselves lacking the force of law, are still widely recognised as the basis for appropriate privacy safeguards. For example, the Australian Journalists' Code of Ethics provides that journalists: 'shall respect private grief and personal privacy and shall have the right to resist the compulsion to intrude on them'.[5] This code has no legislative force and therefore no legal sanction attaches to a breach.[6] Failure to observe such provisions in the Australian Broadcasting Codes may, however, be a relevant matter in the Australian Broadcasting Authority's periodic review of broadcasting licences.[7]

3.06 Though there is no all-encompassing law of privacy in Australia, the law does afford some protection. The remainder of this section concentrates on the types of protection available and examines in more detail the public perception of the need for such protection.

2   Legislation governing privacy in Australia

Protection of stored information

3.07 The High Court of Australia in the 1993 decision *Johns v Australian Securities Commission*[8] recognised an important principle in relation to information privacy. It stated that information collected under statutory compulsion for one purpose may not be used for other purposes in the absence of the consent of the data subject (although the implications of the decision could be restricted to the specific legislation which was then under consideration).

3.08 This principle is reflected in the Privacy Commissioner's National Principles for the Fair Handling of Personal Information (discussed at para

---

3   Privacy Act 1988 (Cth).
4   The codes of practice covering the mainstream media in Australia are:
   — Australian Broadcasting Corporation Code of Practice;
   — Australian Subscription Television and Radio Association Codes of Practice;
   — Commercial Television Code of Practice;
   — Commercial Radio Codes of Practice;
   — Herald and Weekly Times Professional Policy;
   — Country Press Association of New South Wales Code of Ethics;
   — Special Broadcasting Service Code of Practice.
5   Clause 9; see also the television and radio codes of the Federation of Australian Commercial Television Stations and the Federation of Australian Radio Broadcasters.
6   The Press Council of Australia, an independent body, regularly adjudicates on complaints about publications and by agreement newspapers publish its findings, although it does not impose any other sanctions.
7   Section 44 of the Broadcasting Services Act 1992 (Cth) details that the Australian Broadcasting Authority 'may impose a condition on a commercial television broadcasting licensee or commercial radio broadcasting licensee:
   (a) requiring the licensee to comply with a code of practice that is applicable to the licensee...'
8   CLS 1993 HC 91.

3.67) and is also reflected in the recent State initiatives in enacting of privacy legislation.

The Privacy Act 1988 (Commonwealth)

3.09   The Privacy Act 1988 (Cth) safeguards personal information obtained and held by Commonwealth and Australian Capital Territory ('ACT') government departments and agencies, and by private sector case managers.

3.10   The Privacy Act limits access to certain types of recorded information, by prescribing the methods by which the information is to be collated and stored, and the persons to whom access is to be granted. For example, the Privacy Act limits the collection, use and disclosure of the tax file numbers of Australian citizens to purposes related to taxation and the payment of Commonwealth assistance.[9] In the same way, it controls the content and circulation of consumer credit files held by credit reporting agencies and consumer credit information passing between credit providers. It also provides individuals with the right to complain to the Privacy Commissioner if they believe that there has been an interference with their right to privacy in relation to this information.[10]

3.11   The Privacy Act establishes information privacy principles which the Commonwealth Government departments and agencies are obliged to follow when handling personal information. They are as follows:

(1)   information collected must be used for the stated purpose;

(2)   individuals are entitled to know the purpose for which the information is being sought about them;

(3)   the government should ensure that collected information is accurate and up-to-date;

(4)   collected information should be kept secure and free of unauthorised access;

(5)   accurate records must be kept of stored information;

(6)   people should be entitled to access information concerning themselves;

(7)   inaccurate information should be corrected;

(8)   information should be checked for accuracy before being used by the government;

(9)   personal information will not be used except for the purpose to which it is relevant; and

(10) individuals may object to personal information being used for purposes other than that for which it was collected.

3.12   Despite these provisions, the scope of the Privacy Act is quite limited: it does not regulate common intrusive practices such as video or optical surveillance, intrusions into household privacy, or limit the effect of direct marketing operations. Further, the Privacy Act does not regulate State or local government information-gathering or the similar activities of private firms or individuals, although the Australian Federal Government has recently announced the extension of certain privacy provisions to the private sector.[11]

---

9   Privacy Act 1988 (Cth), s 14; Sch 2 Interim guidelines concerning the collection, storage, use and security of Tax File Number information.
10 Privacy Act 1988 (Cth), Part IIIA, Credit Reporting.
11 See para **3.68** below.

3.13 In relation to the collection of personal information by government agencies, the New South Wales Court of Appeal, in a similar vein to the High Court in the *Johns* case mentioned above, has acknowledged that:

> '"record keepers" [have an obligation to] handle personal information in accordance with Information Privacy Principles based on OECD Guidelines, regulating matters such as the manner and purpose of collection of personal information, storage and security, and limits on use'.[12]

However, the extent and nature of this obligation has not been judicially considered.

3.14 In 1991, further legislation was introduced in the form of the Data-Matching Programme (Assistance & Tax) Act (Cth) which regulates data-matching between certain Commonwealth Government departments.

3.15 A limited form of privacy protection was introduced by the Telecommunications Act 1997 (Cth). Part 13 of that Act prohibits the disclosure by carriers, service providers and others, of certain information acquired as a result of their normal business activities. The Privacy Commissioner will monitor compliance in this regard.

Remedies under the Privacy Act

3.16 Certain penalties are detailed in the Privacy Act where information has been used, contrary to the provisions of the Privacy Act. For example, a person found to have gained unauthorised access to credit information files or credit reports can be subject to a fine not exceeding $30,000.[13]
Individuals who have been wronged may make a complaint to the Federal Privacy Consumer who may award compensation in certain circumstances.[14]

3.17 Furthermore, the voluntary codes of conduct employed by certain industries, such as the Banking Code of Conduct detail remedies available where there has been a breach. The Banking Industry Ombudsman, for example, has the capacity to make binding determinations on banks who have breached the Code and may award a settlement or compensation up to $150,000.

State privacy initiatives

3.18 With the exception of the Australian Capital Territory, which is subject to the provisions of the Privacy Act, there was, until recently, no specific State privacy legislation in Australia.

3.19 There was some ad hoc legislation in some States with some relevance to privacy. These included the Privacy Committee Act 1975 (NSW), the Invasion of Privacy Act 1971 (Qld) (discussed at para **3.28**), the Fair Trading Act 1987 (SA) and the Health Records (Privacy Access) Act 1997 (ACT). In South Australia a form of privacy regulation exists by virtue of a Cabinet

---

12 *Civil Aviation Authority v Australian Broadcasting Corpn* (1995) 39 NSWLR 540 at 554 per Kirby P. See also *Attorney-General (New South Wales) v Time Inc Magazine Co Pty Ltd* (15 September 1994, unreported), NSW CA at 10-11 per Gleeson CJ. Both cases involved mass media publications which were alleged to be contempts of court.
13 Privacy Act 1988, s 18s.
14 Privacy Act 1988, s 27.

Administrative Instruction of 1989 which regulates the handling of personal information in the public sector.

3.20   Recently, there have been some State initiatives which both improve and extend the State privacy regimes in Australia.

New South Wales

3.21   New South Wales became the first Australian State to introduce privacy legislation with the enactment of the Privacy & Personnel Information Protection Act 1998. This Act repeals the Privacy Committee Act 1975 and imposes information protection principles upon State public sector agencies.

3.22   The new Act permits privacy codes to be formulated by individual public sector agencies in substitution for the information protection principles contained in the Act, subject to endorsement by the State Privacy Commissioner.

3.23   The key features of the Act include:

(1)   the Act is not intended to override the operation of the Freedom of Information Act 1989 (NSW);

(2)   the Act essentially targets the collection of personal information by public sector agencies;

(3)   public sector agencies must, when collecting personal information, adhere to a variety of requirements including ensuring that the information is collected direct from the specific individual, ensuring the individual knows why the information is being collected, ensuring the information remains up-to-date and relevant to the stated purpose, ensuring the information is not kept longer than necessary, ensuring the individuals know what information is held about them, altering information which is demonstrated to be inaccurate and ensuring the information is only used and disclosed for the specific purpose;

(4)   the information protection principles contained in the Act may be modified by public sector agencies by them adopting an approved privacy code of practice, approval being provided by the State Privacy Commissioner;

(5)   public sector agencies are specifically prohibited from doing anything which contravenes any information protection principle;

(6)   specific exemptions from compliance with the information protection principles include legitimate activities by law enforcement agencies and investigative agencies, circumstances in which compliance may prejudice the interest of the individual, and activities by such bodies as the Police Service, the Police Integrity Commission and the New South Wales Crime Commission;

(7)   public sector agencies are required to prepare privacy management plans;

(8)   the Act creates the position of State Privacy Commissioner with the powers to receive complaints about any alleged violation of, or interferences with, the privacy of an individual. The Privacy Commissioner must endeavour to resolve these complaints by conciliation;

(9)   a person not satisfied with an internal review can apply to the Administrative Decisions Tribunal which can, in addition to other remedies, compensate them up to the value of $40,000;

(10) public sector agencies responsible for keeping public registers are prohibited from disclosing any personal information kept in a register unless the agency is satisfied that it is to be used for a purpose relating to the purpose of the register or the Act under which the register is kept.

3.24 Both Victoria and Queensland have moved in the last twelve months towards recognising the right to privacy through legislation. However these moves have since been overshadowed by the Commonwealth Governments initiatives in the area.

Access to stored information

3.25 The Commonwealth, States and Territories have all enacted legislation dealing with freedom of information. This legislation does not so much protect an individual's privacy, as allow an individual to ascertain what type of personal information relating to them is being held by governments and government authorities.[15] It does this by providing minimum standards for access to documents in the possession of ministers, departments and public authorities.

3.26 The legislation is as follows:

(1) Freedom of Information Act 1982 (Commonwealth);

(2) Freedom of Information Act 1989 (ACT);

(3) Freedom of Information Act 1989 (New South Wales);

(4) Freedom of Information Act 1989 (South Australia);

(5) Freedom of Information Act 1982 (Victoria).

3.27 The Freedom of Information Act 1982 (Commonwealth) gives members of the public rights of access to official documents of the Commonwealth Government and its agencies.[16] The State Acts provide similar access within their particular jurisdictions.

Interception and recording of private communications

Listening devices legislation

3.28 The Commonwealth, State and Territory Listening Devices Acts regulate the use of phone taps and 'bugs' to record private conversations. The legislation is as follows:

(1) Telecommunications (Interception) Act 1979 (Cth);

(2) Listening Devices Act 1992 (ACT);

(3) Listening Devices Act 1984 (NSW);

(4) Listening Devices Act 1990 (NT);

(5) Invasion of Privacy Act 1971 (Qld);

(6) Listening Devices Act 1972 (SA);

(7) Listening Devices Act 1991 (Tas);

(8) Listening Devices Act 1969 (Vic);

---

15 *Commonwealth v John Fairfax & Sons Ltd* (1980) 147 CLR 39; *Breen v Williams* (1994) 35 NSWLR 522.
16 Freedom of Information Act 1982 (Cth), s 11.

(9) Listening Devices Act 1978 (WA).

These Acts, though differing slightly in their provisions, generally prohibit any person from intercepting, authorising the interception, or enabling the interception of communications.

3.29 'Interception' in the Telecommunications (Interception) Act 1979 (Cth) is defined as 'listening to or recording, by any means, such a communication in its passage over [a] telecommunications system, without the knowledge of the person making the communication'.[17]
This covers 'wire tap' situations, the interception by radio frequency scanner of mobile telephone communications and the recording of conversations by means of a device attached to a telephone receiver.[18] There has been some debate as to whether the Commonwealth Act also extends to recordings made by a device placed adjacent to a telephone, for example, a tape recorder. The current view seems to be that the passage of communication over a telecommunications system is complete once the communication has been emitted from the telephone receiver.[19]

3.30 The various State and Territory regimes take over from the operation of the Commonwealth Act in dealing with the post-transmission recording of telephone communications.[20]

3.31 The State and Territory legislation essentially prohibits the recording of a private conversation where the consent of all of the parties to the conversation has not been obtained. This prohibition applies uniformly to someone who is not a party to the conversation. Where the recording is made by a party to the conversation, it is unlawful only in New South Wales,[1] South Australia,[2] Tasmania,[3] the Australian Capital Territory[4] and the Northern Territory.[5] The Acts do provide exceptions to the general prohibition, for example where the recording or interception is made pursuant to a warrant or authorisation.[6]

3.32 Further, in some jurisdictions the prohibition does not apply in circumstances where one of the parties to the conversation makes or consents to the recording and the recording was reasonably necessary for the protection of that party's lawful interests.[7] It has been held that the consent of a party to a recording must be obtained prior to, not after, the relevant communication and the onus of establishing that the exception applies lies with the party seeking to invoke it.[8]

---

17 Section 6(1).
18 *R v Migliorini* (1981) 38 ALR 356.
19 *R v Oliver* (1984) 57 ALR 543; *In the Marriage of Parker & Williams* (1993) 117 FLR 1; cf *R v Curran* (1983) 50 ALR 7545.
20 *In the Marriage of Parker* & *Williams* (1993) 117 FLR 1.
1 Listening Devices Act 1984 (NSW), s 5(1).
2 Listening Devices Act 1972 (SA), s 4.
3 Listening Devices Act 1991 (Tas), s 5.
4 Listening Devices Act 1992 (ACT), s 4.
5 Listening Devices Act 1990 (NT), s 8.
6 Listening Devices Act 1992 (ACT), s 4(2); Listening Devices Act 1984 (NSW), s 5; Listening Devices Act 1991 (Tas), s 5; Listening Devices Act 1990 (NT), s 8(2); Listening Devices Act 1972 (SA), s 6.
7 Listening Devices Act 1992 (ACT), s 4(3); Listening Devices Act 1984 (NSW), s 5(3); Listening Devices Act 1972 (SA), s 4(2); Listening Devices Act 1991 (Tas), s 5(3).
8 *Miller v TCN Channel 9* (1988) 36 A Crim R 92.

3.33 The Telecommunications (Interception) Act 1979 (Commonwealth) provides ancillary liability, prohibiting any person from authorising or doing anything to enable the interception of communications over a telecommunications system.[9]

3.34 The Commonwealth Act also prohibits any person making use or further communicating an intercepted communication, restraining its further publication.[10] It was held in *John Fairfax Publications Pty Ltd v Doe*[11] that the prohibition against publication in the Commonwealth Act may be enforced by a person whose communication has been intercepted. Further relief may be sought by 'an aggrieved person' under the Commonwealth Act, which enables a court to make 'such orders against the defendant as the court considers appropriate'.[12]

Trespass legislation

3.35 The Commonwealth and certain State parliaments have enacted what might be termed trespass legislation which reinforces the common law in relation to specific sites such as diplomatic missions, hospitals and other 'enclosed lands'.[13]
These Acts prescribe that trespass on these defined lands will constitute a criminal offence punishable by either fine, or imprisonment, or both.[14]

3   *The common law*

3.36 Australia is a federation whose political and legal system reflects its English heritage. A part of this heritage is the common law – that is, law based originally on the unwritten common customs of England. The common law has developed over time and operates, in Australia, in conjunction with the law set down by the Parliaments of the Commonwealth, States and Territories.

3.37 The common law in Australia is still influenced by the decisions made in other common law countries such as England and Canada, and in recent years the High Court of Australia and the State appellate courts have also looked towards American and European civil law jurisdictions for persuasive authority.

3.38 An important element of the common law is the law of torts (that is, the law governing civil wrongs other than breaches of contract, which can be redressed, in general, by an award of damages).[15] The law of torts has, over time, developed restraints on intrusions into the privacy of others, specifically through the development of the torts of trespass, nuisance and the development of protections against the misuse of confidential information.

9 Section 7.
10 Section 63.
11 (1995) 130 ALR 488.
12 Section 107A.
13 Public Order (Protection of Persons and Property) Act 1971 (Cth);
    Enclosed Lands Protection Act 1901 (NSW);
    Trespass Act 1987 (NT);
    Invasion of Privacy Act 1971 (Qld);
    Summary Offences Act 1953 (SA);
    Police Offences Act 1935 (Tas);
    Summary Offices Act 1966 (Vic).
14 See below at paras **3.39** ff.
15 Fleming, JG *The Law of Torts* (7th edn, 1986).

Trespass to property

3.39   It is a fundamental common law right for a person in possession of premises to exclude others from those premises.

3.40   In a recent decision the High Court of Australia stated that:

'Every unauthorised entry upon private property is a trespass, the right of a person in possession or entitled to possession of premises to exclude others from those premises being a fundamental common law right.'[16]

3.41   This fundamental right is embodied in the tort of trespass. Trespass is committed where a person:

(1)   enters onto land without the consent, express or implied, of the occupier; or

(2)   enters onto land with the consent of the occupier, but does not leave within a reasonable time of being asked by the occupier to do so; or

(3)   places an object on land without the consent of the occupier.

However, such conduct is actionable only if the occupier was entitled to the exclusive possession of the land at the time of the relevant entry and if the entry was intentional. In the tort of trespass, 'land' includes the buildings on the land and the air space above the land to a height necessary for the ordinary use and enjoyment of the land.

3.42   With respect to privacy, the tort of trespass serves only to protect an individual in so far as their land is trespassed upon for an unauthorised or unlawful purpose. For example, a news journalist who enters land solely in order to seek an interview does not necessarily commit a trespass. Entry to seek an interview does not of itself interfere with the occupier's possession or injure the occupier or the occupier's property. Such entry may offend, distress or embarrass the occupier, or lead the occupier to claim that their privacy has been invaded, but those matters do not in themselves constitute a trespass.

3.43   There is no remedy in Australian law for conduct which, without more, causes offence, distress, embarrassment or invades privacy.[17] However, refusal to leave a property after a request to do so may constitute trespass.[18] The High Court of Australia has held that the consent to entry of an occupier of land may be expressed or implied. In *Halliday v Nevill* it stated that:

'if the path or driveway leading to the entrance of such a dwelling is left unobstructed and with entrance gate unlocked and there is no notice or other indication that entry by visits generally or particularly designated visitors is forbidden or unauthorised, the law will imply a licence in favour of any member of the public to go upon the path or driveway to the entrance of the dwelling for the purpose of lawful communication with, or delivery to, any person in the house. Such implied or tacit licence can be precluded or at any time revoked by expressed or implied refusal or withdrawal of it.'[19]

---

16 *Coco v The Queen* (1994) 120 ALR 415 at 417.
17 Acts beyond this may amount, in certain circumstances, to an assault.
18 *Baker v The Queen* (1983) 153 CLR 338; *Lincoln Hunt Australia Pty Ltd v Willesee* (1986) 4 NSWLR 457.
19 (1984) 57 ALR 331 at 333.

3.44   In Australia there has been some debate as to when entry onto land to film, photograph or interview can be said to be pursuant to an implied licence. In *Lincoln Hunt Pty Ltd v Willesse*, Young J held that the implied consent of persons visiting business premises was limited to those seeking to do business with the owner of the premises and did not extend to any other class of persons:

> '...whose motives were to go onto the premises with video cameras and associated equipment or report or to harass the inhabitants by asking them questions which will be televised.'[20]

3.45   It has been suggested that any implied licence to enter property, to take photographs or videotape can be expressly negatived, for example by the use of signs forbidding entry by a particular class of persons.[1] It should also be noted that in Australia there is no prohibition on photographing or filming premises or persons from outside the land on which they are present. This was discussed in *Bathurst City Council v Saban* where the court stated that:

> 'Such authorities as there are have been consistent that, at least in the ordinary case, there is no tortious conduct involved in taking a photograph of someone else or of someone else's property without their consent.'[2]

Trespass to person

3.46   This includes assault and battery and unlawful imprisonment, all of which can be used, though in limited circumstances, to protect an individual's privacy.[3] For example, an individual may bring an action for unlawful imprisonment if they are effectively unable to exit their residence as a result of media presence.

Nuisance

3.47   The tort of nuisance is committed if a person unreasonably interferes with an occupier's use or enjoyment of land. Such interference may include noise, smell, light, vibrations or obstructions. It is important to note that the use or enjoyment of the land includes not simply its physical use but also the pleasure and amenities which the occupier usually derives from their occupancy. However, to constitute a nuisance the interference must be substantial and unreasonable, as opposed to merely trivial interference or interference flowing from the reasonable exercise of another person's rights to use of their own or public land.[4]

3.48   Nuisance does not protect an individual's privacy to the extent of preventing filming or the taking of photographs.
It has been held that it is not an unreasonable interference simply to observe, film or photograph premises or persons on land, as the rights of the occupier do not include a freedom from view.[5] This contrasts with the situation where photography is accompanied by the noise of an aircraft or a group of journalists

---

20   (1986) 4 NSWLR 457.
1   *Church of Scientology v Transmedia Productions Pty Ltd* (1987) ATR 80-101.
2   [1985] 2 NSWLR 704 at 706–707.
3   *Boughey v The Queen* (1996) 161 CLR 10.
4   *Victoria Park Racing and Recreation Grounds Co Ltd v Taylor* (1937) 58 CLR 479.
5   *Baron Berntstein of Leigh v Skyviews and General Ltd* [1978] QB 479.

for example. The tort of nuisance may extend to cover the situation of a stake out, as the act of 'watching and besetting' premises is an actionable nuisance. Therefore, whilst the mere action of filming and photographing land is generally not a nuisance, if it is accompanied by a constant surveillance of the land it may be unlawful.[6] In *Langridge v Fox* Pigeon J observed that a cameraman:

> 'coming up very close with the camera could amount to a wrongful act...Pedestrians on the streets must not be obstructed. This would amount to an offence and possibly a nuisance...if a pedestrian felt intimidated or a pedestrian felt that he or she could not move in a way that the pedestrian wished.'[7]

Confidentiality

3.49   It is important to distinguish between an obligation of confidentiality and a privacy obligation.

3.50   A confidentiality obligation attaches to information which is inherently secret, and which has been conveyed by one person to another on the understanding that secrecy will be preserved. There is an obligation to maintain that secrecy.

3.51   A privacy obligation, such as those obligations provided in the Privacy Act, on the other hand, can attach to the handling of information which is not necessarily secret. The information may be available from diverse sources, including public registers. There is, however, an obligation to use that information for a limited purpose only.

3.52   Australian law provides some protection to information which can be classified as confidential. A situation of confidence may arise as a result of a particular relationship, for example a formal relationship of employer and employee, or from particular contractual duties or more generally where a person confides in another in circumstances that make it clear that they do not wish the information to be disclosed.[8]

3.53   Essentially, the courts look to the following issues in resolving an action for breach of confidence:

(1)   whether the information was imparted in circumstances of confidence; and

(2)   whether the obligation of confidence was made plain; and

(3)   whether there was an unauthorised use of the information.

The usual remedy for a breach of confidence is a court ordered injunction to prevent the continued misuse of the information or an award of monetary damages.

3.54   Generally, the court will not grant final or interlocutory injunctions where damages will provide adequate compensation for the continuing

---

6   *Hubbard v Pitt* [1976] QB 142; *Re Van Der Lubbe* (1949) 49 SR (NSW) 309; *Re DG Whelan Rentals Pty Ltd* (1983) 67 FLR 472; *Boral Bricks New South Wales Pty Ltd v Frost* (1987) ATR 80-097.
7   (5 August 1997, unreported), West Australian Supreme Court.
8   *Smith Kline & French Laboratories (Australia) Ltd v Secretary, Department of Community Services and Health* (1991) 20 IPR 643.

breach.[9] A party seeking an interlocutory injunction must also establish a prima facie case with sufficient probability of success and satisfy the court that the balance of convenience favours the granting of injunctive relief.[10]

Limits of the common law

3.55 The common law has developed restraints in certain areas, but it by no means represents a unified body of law protecting an individual's right to privacy.

3.56 Examples of areas where the law provides no remedy are:

(1) the taking of photographs of a person without their permission, even where the person is on his or her own premises;

(2) a journalist approaching a person on their premises for an interview;

(3) conduct which causes offence, distress or embarrassment but which is not an assault, defamatory or a trespass;

(4) revealing private information unless defamatory or in breach of an obligation of confidence, or copyright (this is dealt with in the next section on personality).

4   Public policy: the changing attitude

3.57 Privacy is recognised in public international law as a basic human right, and a recent survey by the Australian Privacy Commissioner highlights its importance as a social issue, ranking it higher than concern over the economy or the environment.[11]
Of principal concern are the limited current controls over industry and business with regard to the use, or misuse, of personal information.

3.58 The growth of modern technology is also perceived by the public as a significant threat to privacy. Public concerns have been raised over the safeguarding of personal information, such as tax records or credit history and in particular over threats to privacy in the home. The Commissioner's survey reveals that eight out of ten Australians are more concerned with this latter aspect of privacy than with the desire to keep their personal information private.

3.59 In many ways it is far easier for governments to legislate to safeguard information, as there are relatively few bodies entitled to collect this information and they can be easily targeted for legislative and regulatory guidelines. In contrast, the protection of home privacy and the integrity of private property is a far more difficult task both conceptually, as it may infringe other conflicting rights of access to information, and in terms of enforcement.

3.60 It has been seen in this chapter that there have been recent State legislative initiatives in this area, in particular, the New South Wales Privacy and Personnel Information Protection Act 1998. Other States have also moved towards the enactment of legislation.

---

9   *American Cyanamid Co v Ethicon Ltd* [1975] AC 396 at 406.
10   *Beecham Group Ltd v Bristol Laboratories Pty Ltd* (1968) 118 CLR 618.
11   'Community Attitudes to Privacy' Information Paper Number Three.

3.61 In Victoria, the Data Protection Bill 1998 was introduced with the intention of providing privacy protection, in a similar way to the Privacy Act, but with respect to personal information handled by Victorian-based organisations and personal information handled in Victoria by business, State and local government and other organisations. The Bill proposes the adaptation of the Federal Privacy Commissioner's national principles to both the public and private sectors on a default basis, leaving organisations with the ability to develop and have endorsed their own tailored codes of practice.

3.62 In Queensland, the Queensland Legal Constitutional and Administrative Review Committee published a report in May 1998 entitled Privacy in Queensland. This report recommended the introduction of privacy controls on the State public sector though the development of legislation. Some of the key recommendations were:

(1) measures should be taken to ensure greater protection of personal information held by Queensland government departments and agencies;

(2) information privacy principles should be introduced in Queensland;

(3) a Queensland privacy commissioner should be appointed;

(4) the information privacy principles should be implemented by legislation, and not by lesser statutory instruments;

3.63 Importantly, the legislation should apply to local governments as well as private service providers contracted by Queensland government departments and agencies performing services otherwise performed by those departments or agencies.

These moves, however, may have been superseded by the recent Commonwealth Government initiative on the extension of privacy protection.

3.64 On 16 December 1998, the Australian Federal Government announced its intention to legislate to protect the privacy of personal data handled by the private sector. In part this was designed to pre-empt rival State legislation, such as the proposed Victorian data protection legislation and the recommendations by the Queensland Legal Constitutional and Administrative Review Committee. It was also prompted by fears that Australian companies would be excluded from lucrative European markets because of the absence of national privacy standards. Under this latest plan the Federal Government will provide legislative backing for industry-based privacy codes developed under its privacy framework, rather than detailed government regulation. In response, some consumer groups have questioned whether the Commonwealth Privacy Commissioner's Office has adequate resources to act as the de facto enforcement mechanism for industry codes.[12]

3.65 It was foreshadowed that this scheme would apply a 'bench-mark' legislative framework to both the public and private sectors in Australia while allowing the development, review and registration of tailored industry codes where required to meet specific sector or concerns.

3.66 Advantages in this approach would include:

(1) the Australian private sector would become subject to privacy regulation which most would see to be in the community interest;

(2) by regulating the private sector as well as the Commonwealth public

---

12 *Australian Financial Review* (1998) 17 December 4.

sector, the Federal Government would be moving in a manner consistent with many overseas jurisdictions;

(3) compliance with the EU Directive would be assured (assuming business act in accordance with the legislation); and

(4) the effects of inconsistent State legislation in relation to the private sector would be avoided.

The government has determined that this 'light touch' legislative regime will best achieve consistency and certainty by following the Privacy Commissioner's National Principles for the Fair Handling of Personal Information.

3.67 These National Principles outline appropriate conduct for organisations dealing with personal information. They include that:

(1) an organisation should only collect information that is necessary for one or more of its legitimate functions;

(2) information should only be collected by lawful means;

(3) that the organisation should take reasonable steps to ensure that the subject of the information is aware of the identity of the organisation, knows that they are able to gain access to the information, the purposes for which the information is collected, and to whom it is to be disclosed;

(4) the organisation should take all reasonable steps to ensure the accuracy of the information at the time of collection or use;

(5) the information should be kept secure;

(6) the information should be readily accessible by the subject and be corrected when shown to be wrong.

Effectively the scheme will be based on industry codes with legislative intervention only where industry codes are not adopted.

3.68 There are some notable exceptions from the scheme, in particular employee records, so that businesses which hold no personal data, other than employee data, will not be affected. Also, personal information collected and used by the media for journalistic purposes will be exempted.

C Publicity and personality

3.69 If the essence of privacy is the ability to keep information out of the public domain, its corollary is an individual's ability to control and therefore exploit the public release of personal information. This is what is meant by the rights of publicity and personality.

3.70 Like that afforded to privacy, the protection afforded to individuals and commercial entities in Australian law with respect to the use or misuse of their personality, or against unwanted publicity is limited.

1 Legislation dealing with publicity and personality

3.71 The principal legislative regime in this area is the network of Acts regulating the use of intellectual property in Australia, and aspects of the

Trade Practices Act 1974.[13] The most significant application of these provisions is in the protection of business reputation.

Intellectual property statutes

Copyright Act 1968 (Commonwealth)

3.72   In Australia, the Copyright Act 1968 (Cth) in conjunction with relevant international treaties and conventions is the principal form of protection to prevent the 'pirating' or misuse of material which is categorised as the intellectual property of another. In this respect, aspects of personality which fall within copyright are protected under Australian law.

3.73   In essence an author under Australian law has the capacity to exploit their work or material without others being able to copy that 'creative output'.[14] The Copyright Act sets up a regime whereby copyright owners are entitled to monetary remuneration upon the use by others of their particular work. It also specifies the remedies available to an author in the event of the unauthorised exploitation of the subject matter of the copyright. These provisions allow the owner of a copyright to bring an action for infringement and to seek relief in the form of an injunction, award of damages (including punitive damages for flagrant breach) or account of profits.[15] Further, criminal penalties apply to the most deliberate forms of copyright infringement.[16]

Designs Act 1906 (Commonwealth)

3.74   As part of the development of a business reputation, a business often develops logos or designs which are indicative of a product or services. The ability of an organisation to register an industrial design affords a further protection to its business reputation.

3.75   Designs are governed by the Designs Act 1906 (Commonwealth) which establishes a system whereby new or original designs for the visual presentation of a commercial product may be registered. The Act details the procedure for registration[17] and specifies remedies for infringement, including the grant of an injunction, an awry of damages, or an account of profits.[18]

Trade Marks Act 1995 (Commonwealth)

3.76   In Australian law, trade marks are governed by the Trade Marks Act 1995 (Clh). Trade marks may include devices, labels and names which indicate that goods or services originate from a particular organisation.[19] In a similar way to the Designs Act the Trade Marks Act details the procedure for registration and the penalties for infringement of a trade mark.[20]

Trade Practices Act – passing off

3.77   Part V of the Trade Practices Act 1974 (Clh) and its equivalent State

13   Trade Practices Act 1974 (Commonwealth), ss 52, 53C and 53D.
14   McKeogh and Stewart, *Intellectual Property in Australia*, Butterworths, Sydney 1991.
15   Copyright Act 1968 (Cth), s 115.
16   Copyright Act 1968 (Cth), ss 132,133,135,203A–203H.
17   Designs Act 1906 (Cth), Pt IV.
18   Designs Act 1906 (Cth), s 32B.
19   Trade Marks Act 1995 (Cth), s 6, 17.
20   Trade Marks Act 1995 (Cth), s 126.

and Territory legislation[1] now provide strong legislative tools to protect businesses in trade or commerce against abuse of their professional or commercial reputation. Section 52 of the Trade Practices Act provides that:

> 'A corporation shall not, in trade or commerce, engage in conduct that is misleading or deceptive or is likely to mislead or deceive'.

Section 53 of the Trade Practices Act provides that:

> 'A corporation shall not, in trade or commerce, in connection with the supply or possible supply of goods or services or in connection with the promotion by any means of the supply or use of goods or services:
>
> (a) represent that goods or services have sponsorship, approval, performance characteristics, accessories, uses or benefits they do not have;
>
> (b) represent that the corporation has a sponsorship, approval or affiliation it does not have.'

3.78 Whilst not strictly concerned with the protection of business reputation or personality, these provisions have the effect of enabling commercial competitors to bring actions for misrepresentation of association with, or endorsement of, a particular product. This is due to the fact that while Part V of the Trade Practices Act was primarily intended to protect Australian consumers, the Act also allows civil proceedings by 'any other person'[2] and it has been routinely used by traders to prevent trade libel and damage to business reputation. On the face of it, the provisions do not require a trader to show that they actually possesses a well-known name, image or reputation, providing that the false representation of an association with the plaintiff's product by the defendant can be established. However, the terms 'sponsorship', 'approval' and 'affiliation' have been treated by the courts as amounting to formal or authoritative condemnation,[3] and it is unlikely that an applicant who can show only an inappropriate suggestion of association with their product or service without also proving its reputation among consumers will be able to satisfy a court that the conduct complained of amounts to misrepresentation of 'sponsorship, approval or affiliation'.

3.79 Therefore, the policy behind the Trade Practices Act hinges on the premise that the Act is designed to protect consumers from buying goods or services that have been falsely associated with another product or personality. In so doing, the Act, albeit tacitly, serves to protect against the unauthorised exploitation of reputation or personality.

2   Common law

3.80 As already observed, in Australia there is no common law right of privacy. Equally the common law does not recognise any discrete rights protecting a person's commercial interests in the integrity or commercial

---

1   Fair Trading Act 1985 (Vic), s 11; Fair Trading Act 1987 (NSW), s 42; Fair Trading Act 1987 (SA), s 56; Fair Trading Act 1987 (WA), s 10; Fair Trading Act (QLD), s 38; Fair Trading Act 1990 (TAS), s 14; Consumer Affairs and Fair Trading Act 1990 (NT), s 42; Fair Trading Act 1992 (ACT), s 12.
2   Trade Practices Act 1974 (Cth), s 80(1).
3   *10th Cantanae Pty Ltd v Shoshana Pty Ltd* (1987) 10 IPR 289.

exploitation of their personality, image or name.[4] However, several existing causes of action in tort may provide some protection to commercial interests in identity and name.

Passing off

3.81   The protection that the common law in Australia provides to personality and publicity has emerged primarily from the adaptation of the tort action of passing off, rather than the recognition of distinct proprietary rights of personality and publicity, as have evolved in US law.

3.82   In relation to individuals, primarily this development has been in response to the lucrative modern business of 'character merchandising' and 'celebrity endorsement', where the passing off action protects an individual's 'commercially valuable reputation'[5] and indirectly restricts the unauthorised use of their persona, by prohibiting the misrepresentation of their endorsement of products or services. In this respect the tort of passing off complements section 52 of the Trade Practices Act as the primary means of protecting individual and business reputation.

3.83   The common law action of passing off requires the plaintiff to establish that a misrepresentation has been made in the course of trade or business to customers or prospective customers and that it is reasonably foreseeable that this misrepresentation will injure the plaintiff's own business or goodwill. Therefore, in order for the tort of passing off to be made out, three key elements must be satisfied:

(1)   the subsistence of some reputation or goodwill on the part of the plaintiff or owner of the reputation;

(2)   deceptive conduct on the part of the person or corporation alleged to have acted in breach of the owners' rights; and

(3)   the existence or threat of damage to the plaintiff as a result of that conduct.

3.84   It was an Australian Court, in *Henderson v Radio Corpn Pty Ltd* that first applied the action of passing off to the practice of character merchandising, nearly 40 years ago. It did so by relaxing the 'common field of activity' requirement, previously imposed by the English courts in relation to passing off actions.[6]

3.85   In the *Henderson* case this allowed the plaintiff ballroom dancers to be characterised as 'competitive in a broad sense' with the defendant record producers who had used the dancers' image on a dance record. The court held that the plaintiffs had been presented as endorsing the defendant's record in the course of their professional activities. Subsequently, Australian courts seem to have accepted the broad proposition that an action for passing off lies where there is a misrepresentation by the defendant that the plaintiff has endorsed or approved a particular product, service or business.[7]

---

4   *Ettingshausen v Australian Consolidation Press* (13 October 1993, unreported), NSW CA.

5   *Henderson v Radio Corpn Pty Ltd* (1960) 60 SR NSW 576 at 604.

6   *McCulloch v Lewis A May (Produce Distributors) Ltd* (1947) 65 RPC 58.

7   *10th Cantanae Pty Ltd v Shoshana Pty Ltd* (1987) 10 IPR 289; *Hogan v Koala Dundee Pty Ltd* (1988) 12 IPR 508; *Hutchence v Southseas Bubble Co Pty Ltd* (1986) 64 ALR 330; *Honey v Australian Airlines Ltd* (1989) 14 IPR 264; and *Talmax Pty Ltd v Telstra Corp* (1996) 36 IPR 46.

3.86 The Australian courts have also been relatively astute to the nuances of modern advertising, in accepting a flexible and expansive approach to the kind of misrepresentation that will suffice for the purposes of liability. In this respect, they seem to have flirted with the recognition of a tort of 'misappropriation of personality'.

3.87 In *Hogan v Koala Dundee Pty*,[8] Pincus J suggested that there was 'a degree of artificiality in deciding image-filching cases on the basis that the vice attacked is misleading the public about licensing arrangements'. Subsequently, in *Pacific Dunlop Ltd v Hogan*[9] the plaintiff complained of the use of a short sequence from the movie *Crocodile Dundee* in a television advertisement for a brand of shoes. In the course of his judgment in the Full Federal Court, Burchett J observed that:

> 'To ask whether the consumer reasons that Mr Hogan authorised the advertisement is therefore to ask a question which is a mere side issue, and far from the full impact of the advertisement. The consumer is moved by a desire to wear something belonging in some sense to Crocodile Dundee (who is perceived as a persona, at most an avatar, of Mr Hogan). The arousal of that feeling by Mr Hogan himself could not be regarded as misleading, for then the value he promises the product will have is not in its leather, but in its association with himself. When, however, an advertisement he did not authorise makes the same suggestion, it is misleading; for the product sold by that advertisement really lacks the one feature the advertisement attributed to it.'[10]

This begs the question of whether the defendant's conduct was a misleading representation of Hogan's endorsement or an appropriation of Hogan's personality and image per se, founded on a latent right of publicity. However, despite his observations, Burchett J framed his decision squarely in the traditional terms of passing off, even if signalling that the court did not require an unequivocal representation of endorsement in order to make out the action.

3.88 This more conservative approach was highlighted by the decision of the Federal Court in *Honey v Australian Airlines Ltd*[11] where the athlete Gary Honey sought unsuccessfully to restrain the use of his photograph on advertising posters. Northrop J concluded that he was not satisfied that a reasonable number of persons, on seeing the poster would have concluded that the plaintiff had given his endorsement to Australian Airlines. Similarly, in *Newton-John v Scholl-Plough (Australia) Ltd*,[12] the defendant used a celebrity lookalike in a television commercial, but the court held that this did not go 'to the extent of suggesting an association'.

Other common law causes of action

Injurious falsehood

3.89 Injurious falsehood was a tort that originally protected against unwarranted attacks on title to land but has been extended over time to misleading and deceptive statements about goods. Now, to the extent that

---

8   (1988) 12 IPR 504.
9   (1989) 14 IPR 398.
10 (1989) 14 IPR 398 at 429–430.
11 (1989) 14 IPR 264.
12 (1986) 11 FCR 233.

injurious falsehood applies to disparaging comments with respect to goods and services, this cause of action has been superseded by section 52 of the Trade Practices Act. Further, injurious falsehoods with respect to a person have now been subsumed by that person's right to sue in defamation.

Defamation

3.90   At common law, a person's reputation is protected largely by the tort of defamation and to some extent this also protects aspects of privacy.

For example, while the defence of public interest has been applied to publications that comment on the public conduct of people holding political office,[13] this generally does not provide a defence for publication of their private details. For the defence of public interest to succeed publication of any details must be relevant to the public and it must relate to matters that the public are legitimately interested in or concerned about. What is determined to be legitimately in the public interest is largely governed by the morés of the time and the nature of the publication. The public interest defence is a mechanism that goes part way to ensure private information that is not in the public interest is not published. Likewise the defence of qualified privilege affords publishers the right to publish information that is prima facie defamatory, if they can show that a 'public interest' will be served.

3.91   The law of defamation within Australia varies between each State and Territory. Some States apply the common law, others apply a mix of both the common law and statute, and finally, some States are governed solely by statutory provisions. This makes a journalist's job extremely difficult.

3.92   A defamatory statement is a statement which holds a person up to 'hatred, ridicule or contempt' or 'tends to lower the person in the estimation of a right thinking ordinary decent Australian'.

3.93   To be defamatory an imputation need have no actual effect on a person's reputation. The law only looks to its tendency. Public opinion has to be measured from time to time, and the place of broadcast is also considered in measuring how defamatory an imputation is. A defamatory statement may be conveyed by words or visual images either singularly or in conjunction. An imputation may be conveyed even though it is not apparent on the face of the words alone, however there may be a certain class of person who is aware of some additional fact which makes the statement defamatory. Accordingly defamation does not need to be direct and can be conveyed in inference.

It is also important to note that the intention of the reader is irrelevant in determining whether a statement is defamatory.

3.94   A person will establish a cause of action in defamation if there are three elements present:

(1)   that the words carry a defamatory imputation – 'meaning';

(2)   the matter is capable of identifying the person – 'identification';

(3)   the matter has been communicated to at least one other person – 'publication'.

So whilst the law of defamation will allow a person to protect his reputation and therefore give a person some control over the use or misuse of aspects of his or her personality, it does not extend to words which merely injure the

---

13   *Renouf v Federal Capital Press of Australia Pty Ltd* (1977) 17 ACTR 35.

feeling or cause annoyance but which otherwise do not reflect on character or reputation. However it has been held that the use of a person's name without his authority may be restrained by an injunction, regardless of whether there is a defamatory imputation conveyed or not, if the use is calculated to cause him pecuniary loss.[14]

3.95 Again, although the law goes some way to protecting an individual's reputation, it does not provide an absolute right amounting to the prevention of the use or misuse of a person's likeness or character.

D Conclusion

3.96 This chapter has sought to outline the ways in which privacy, personality and publicity are protected in Australian law. In so doing it has demonstrated that this protection is achieved almost parenthetically through a collection of different statutes and common law actions. This is a product both of history and expediency, allowing law and policy makers to shirk the fundamental questions that would be raised in any attempt to reconstitute these laws into a coherent regime. The challenge for the next decades will be whether the law as it now stands can cope with the increased scope for infringement of privacy, personality and publicity brought by technological developments. Eventually it seems inevitable that the nettle will have to be grasped and these laws will have to be reformulated by legislation into something approaching a coherent regime of individual and commercial rights in Australia. The recent moves by the Commonwealth Government to strengthen privacy protection may be seen to be a first step in this direction.

---

14 *Tolley v Fry* [1930] KB 467. See the judgment of Greer LJ at 478.

4 AUSTRIA

Dr Meinhard Ciresa

A Introduction

4.01   The concept of general protection of the private sphere ('privacy') is unknown in the Austrian legal system. Apart from the right to protection of one's private and family life (European Convention on Human Rights, Article 8), which is guaranteed by the Constitution but is (only) a defensive right against governmental intervention or intrusion, the Austrian legal system contains only a few specifically-worded rights for the protection of the individual which, in a broader sense, also serve the purpose of protecting the individual's privacy against third parties. However, there is no general statutory prohibition, or prohibition established by case law, according to which the life of an individual or individual facets of it may not be publicly known by third parties in general.

B Privacy

1   Films and photographs

4.02   There is no separate right or statutory provision from which it would be possible to infer that there is a prohibition to take photographs of, or film a person. Only the utilisation of the finished film or individual photographs may, subject to particular conditions (see below at para **4.19**), constitute an infringement of, or intrusion into, the right of personality of the person shown.

4.03   As regards filming on private property, the only approach is the right of 'inviolability of property',[1] which would make it possible to prohibit filming on private property.[2] The title to property also covers the airspace above the private land.[3] However, the title does not provide for any protection against

---

JBl = Juristische Blätter (general law journal), year, page.
MR = Medien und Recht (special law journal on media and law), year, page.
ÖBl = Österreichische Blätter für Gewerblichen Rechtsschutz und Urheberrecht (special law journal on intellectual property & copyright law), year, page.

1   ABGB [Austrian General Civil Code], s 364.
2   OGH [Austrian Supreme Court] 25 October 1988 MR 1989, 22.
3   OGH 27 August 1969 JBl 1971, 90.

the taking of photographs of, eg, a building on public property and subsequent selling of the photographs, because this does not infringe the title.[4] Indirectly this also results from an exemption of the Austrian *Urheberrechtsgesetz* [Copyright Statute] of 1936, which provides for a 'freedom of the streetscape'.[5] This provision mainly stipulates that outside views of buildings taken by means of photographs may be copied without limit unless private property has to be entered.

4.04   The title to property applies to everyone and not only to Austrian citizens. A person whose title to property is infringed may, within 30 days of the day of the infringing act, file an action for *Besitzstoerung* [action to ascertain an act of violation of undisturbed possession] or, alternatively, a prohibitory action.

2   Tape recordings

4.05   With respect to tape recordings of discussions, one has to distinguish whether the statement recorded was intended solely for the person recording the same or not. If the former is the case, the recording as such is not an illegal act. However, the distribution of this recording to third parties – without the consent of the speaker – is prohibited by the Austrian Criminal Code.[6]

4.06   The misdemeanour is punishable by imprisonment of up to one year or a fine of up to 360 times the daily rate. The multiplier of the daily rate depends on the gravity of the offence, whereas the amount of the daily rate depends on the income of the person convicted. With respect to this provision one has to take into account the fact that the offender is not prosecuted ex-officio, ie by the public prosecutor, but by the injured party. The injured party has a limitation period of six weeks from learning of the illegal act in order to be able to exercise their right to file an action.[7] If this period expires, the party who has suffered from such infringement of their rights will lose their right of prosecuting the offender.

3   Personal data

4.07   Pursuant to the constitutional provision of the Data Protection Act 2000, section 1 (BGBl [Federal Law Gazette] 165/99), everybody is entitled to secrecy with respect to personal data relating to them to the extent they have an interest that is worth protecting, in particular with respect to the safeguarding of their private and family life. This protection applies irrespective of whether the data was processed electronically or not.

4.08   Both Austrians and foreign citizens are entitled to the right of protection of data; it has to be asserted by means of filing an action in the ordinary civil courts. The right guarantees the right to information, correction and deletion of data which was obtained or processed electronically in an inadmissible way.

---

4   OGH 25 October 1988, MR 1989, 23.
5   Copyright Statute 1936, s 54, para 5.
6   Criminal Code, s 120.
7   Code of Criminal Procedure, s 46.

C Publicity

1 Rights in one's name, life and voice

4.09   The protection of a person's name is regulated by section 43 of the Austrian General Civil Code, which has been in force since 1811. The right to a name which is embodied in the Civil Code is a personal right, which applies to both foreign citizens and Austrians. The story of the life of a certain person[8] or their voice is, however, not protected.

4.10   The name as an identification mark of a certain person is protected. It is not the name as such that is protected but the personality identified by it. Section 43 of the Austrian General Civil Code not only protects the family name but also the fictitious name (pseudonym, pen-name, stage name), the name of legal entities, the trade name (company name) and the names of political parties.

4.11   Section 43 of the Austrian General Civil Code grants the holder of the name the right to use his or her name and exclude every other person from doing so.

4.12   If the use of a name is based upon one's personal right, this will not be considered unauthorised use as anybody is entitled to use his or her own name in business.[9] However, this entitlement is limited in so far as the name may only be used in such a way as to avoid confusion with names used by another person in an authorised manner. Unfair use of names is therefore inadmissible without exception and excludes any claiming of the right to use one's own name.

2 Right to prevent use of one's name

4.13   Section 43 of the Austrian General Civil Code grants the holder of the name the right to use his or her name and to exclude any other person from using the same. The right is conditional on the fact that interests of the holder of the name which are worth protecting are impeded or impaired by unauthorised use of the name by a third party. In this connection it is sufficient that the holder of the name be unjustifiedly associated with certain actions of the other person, or if the impression is given that idealistic or economic/business relations exist between the holder of the infringed name, and the third party.[10]

4.14   The person whose rights have been infringed is entitled to a claim – irrespective of fault – in respect of unauthorised use of the name. This claim must be brought before the civil courts of justice. The prohibitory action may also be combined with a petition for the granting of an interim injunction.

---

8   OGH 7 February 1992, ÖBl 1992, 75.
9   OGH 11 February 1997, ÖBl 1998, 43; OGH 13 July 1999, JBl 2000, 35 regarding domain names.
10 OGH 24 February 1998, ÖBl 1998, 298; 11 February 1997, ÖBl 1998, 43.

3   Trade mark protection of names

4.15   There is, in principle, the possibility of obtaining trade mark protection for the name of a person in the Austrian Patent Office[11]. The right to obtain trade mark registration applies to everyone party to the Madrid Agreement and its protocol, not only to Austrian citizens.

4.16   Case law provides that a claim may be brought pursuant to section 51 of the Trade Mark Act against non-authorised use of a name protected by trade mark.[12] This claim must be brought before the ordinary civil courts. The law does, in principle, provide for a claim to damages;[13] however, such claims are almost never asserted in practice due to a lack of concrete evidence of damage.

D   Personality

1   Rights in photographs and pictures

4.17   The protection of pictures of persons (photographs, portraits) is embodied in section 78 of the Copyright Statute, which entered into force on 1 July 1936.[14] Although this is a personal right of the person shown in the picture, and has nothing to do with the copyright in the photograph, it has – contrary to the system – been regulated by the Copyright Statute.

4.18   It is not only Austrian citizens who are protected. Everyone whose picture is used in Austria against the provisions of section 78 of the Copyright Statute will also be protected.

2   Respect of justified interests of pictured persons

4.19   Section 78 of the Copyright Statute provides that pictures of persons may not be exhibited publicly nor distributed or disseminated in any other way by which they would be made accessible to the public, if this violates justified interests of the persons depicted. If the person depicted is already deceased and did not approve of or give instructions to publish the same, the admissibility of the publication of the picture depends on the justified interests of their close relatives. The exclusive purpose of section 78 of the Copyright Statute is the protection of the personality of the person depicted, while their economic interests are protected by a claim under enrichment rules pursuant to general civil law.[15]

11 Eg 'Anton Bruckner' for class 30 [Pastries and Chocolate], ÖBl 1998, 219.
12 OGH 17 September 1996, ÖBl 1997, 83 regarding British Football Association; 29 October 1996, ÖBl 1997, 72.
13 Trade Mark Act, s 53.
14 BGBl 1936 No 111.
15 Austrian General Civil Code, s 1041 (OGH 6 December 1994, ÖBl 1995, 284).

3   Protection against public exhibition

4.20   Section 78 of the Copyright Statute exclusively protects the person concerned against public exhibition of their picture, but not against the taking of photographs of them.

4.21   The picture does not have to be a portrait. Even if not all features of the person depicted are clearly shown, as, for example, in the case of a photograph of a larger group of people, this can still be a picture of a person within the meaning of section 78 of the Copyright Statute. The relevant point is whether the person (as depicted) can be recognised or not.[16] For the purpose of assessing the above, not only the picture alone but also the way of distributing the same and the circumstances under which it is published are to be considered, such as, eg a listing of names and functions of the persons shown within the scope of a picture story.[17] Even if the eyes are covered, this does not exclude applicability of section 78 of the Copyright Statute if the personal appearance of the person depicted can be clearly identified, eg because of figure, haircut and other features.[18] This may, for example, be the case in connection with a picture story about happenings in a rural area where one would recognise a person depicted because of only very few characteristics because they are known to you personally.

4   Infringement of 'justified interests'

4.22   A prerequisite for protection pursuant to section 78 of the Copyright Statute is the infringement of the 'justified interests' of the person depicted.

4.23   The legislators, intentionally, did not define the term 'justified interests' in detail in order to leave a broad scope for interpretation in individual cases. According to decisions of the Austrian Supreme Court justified interests of the person depicted are in any case infringed if the person is exposed, debased or disparaged by the picture, if their private life is disclosed, or if the picture is used in any other way which might cause misinterpretation.[19] The infringed interests of the person depicted are 'justified' if they are worth protecting. When assessing whether this is the case or not this has to be done objectively.[20]

4.24   If detrimental statements are made about the person depicted in connection with the publication of a picture, according to court decisions not only the picture itself but also the connection to the published text is of relevance.[1] This applies both to the publication of a picture in print media and on TV. In this context, both the text immediately accompanying the picture, and other texts which the viewer still recalls when the picture appears, must be taken into consideration.[2]

4.25   If the person depicted agrees to publication of the picture, they are no longer protected.[3] When judging whether the person depicted consented to

16   OGH 27 February 1996, MR 1996, 149.
17   OGH 20 October 1964, ÖBl 1965, 49.
18   OGH 14 March 1989, MR 1989, 54; 20 September 1994, MR 1995, 63.
19   OGH 29 September 1987, ÖBl 1988, 139.
20   OGH 21 November 1989, ÖBl 1990, 187.
1   OGH 13 May 1997, MR 1997, 254.
2   OGH 10 November 1992, MR 1995, 55.
3   OGH 13 May 1997, MR 1997, 149; 15 April 1997, MR 1997, 150.

publication of the picture, the purpose and scope of the consenting statement has to be taken into account. Consent to publication of a picture in a certain case, therefore, does not justify publication in a different context and in different media.[4] The consent need not be express but may also be implicit.[5] If a person attends a public event and notes that people are being filmed and photographs are being taken there, they normally cannot object to the mere reporting of this event or the use of their picture in that connection.

5 Nude and/or embarrassing photographs

4.26 The most intimate sphere of one's personality is also protected in the case of persons who are publicly known.[6] Publication of a nude photograph infringes the justified interest of the person depicted because it is an intrusion into their privacy. The only thing which is relevant is that the picture can clearly be discerned as a nude photograph. Even if a nude photograph is a realistic photomontage, this does not change anything about the fact that distribution of the same infringes the justified interests of the person depicted.[7] To show persons in embarrassing or disadvantageous positions is likewise inadmissible.[8]

6 Photomontage

4.27 Distribution of disfiguring pictures (eg photomontage) is inadmissible in any case. However, not every photomontage is a disparaging disfigurement. For example, the Austrian Supreme Court (OGH) decided that the joining together of the faces of two politicians, which joining can be discerned as such, in the form of a photomontage was admissible as a political statement.[9]

7 Use of pictures for advertising purposes

4.28 Utilisation of a picture for advertising purposes usually infringes the justified interests of the person depicted because it suggests that the person made available their picture for advertising purposes in return for compensation.[10]

8 Publication of pictures and the 'pillory effect'

4.29 When publishing pictures in conjunction with detrimental reports, one has to distinguish between persons who are publicly known and other persons.

4   OGH 11 July 1995, MR 1996, 67; 15 April 1997, MR 1997, 150.
5   OGH 17 July 1996, MR 1997, 88.
6   OGH 17 September 1996, MR 1997, 28.
7   OGH 17 September 1996, MR 1997, 28.
8   OGH 28 January 1997, MR 1997, 145.
9   OGH 28 January 1997, MR 1997, 145.
10 OGH 3 April 1990, MR 1990, 141.

4.30   If the identity of the person depicted is only made known visually to a broad public by publication of the picture, this leads, according to court decisions, to an unwanted 'pillory effect'. Therefore, pursuant to case law,[11] publication of pictures in the case of persons who are not publicly known is only admissible, when weighing the pros and cons of the interests leads to the result that the interest in publishing the picture prevails over the justified interests of the person depicted, eg if the published picture itself is of additional informative value.

4.31   A person is not generally known if their appearance is only known to a limited group of the public.[12] Thus, public figures of the recent past are also protected if their appearance is not publicly known.[13] Case law provides that publication of a picture of persons who are regularly exposed to the public is of informative value if the photograph is connected with the public activity of the person depicted. When reporting on up-to-date events, publication of a picture of a person's private life may be appropriate in the individual case, however, this cannot be assumed without reasons. In no case, however, may the publication serve the purpose of satisfying curiosity and desire for sensation.[14]

4.32   If publication of the picture is of no important information value, the question of whether the accompanying allegations are true or not is irrelevant.[15] If the publication is of an informative value, the accompanying text has to be checked. If this is incorrect[16] or dishonourable[17] the balance of interests will, in any case, be in favour of the person depicted.

4.33   If the depicted person is publicly known because of their appearance, publication of a picture as such does not usually constitute an infringement of their justified interests. However, in the case of politicians or other persons who are known by the public, publication of pictures in connection with disparaging reports should not be admissible, without limits. In any case, publication of a picture will be inadmissible if the person depicted (because of the accompanying reports) is associated with events which they have nothing to do with.[18]

9   Remedies for infringements of rights

4.34   A person whose rights are infringed by making their picture accessible to the public in violation of section 78 of the Copyright Statute is entitled to forbearance,[19] removal,[20] damages[1] and publication of the judgment.[2]

4.35   According to court decisions the person whose rights have been infringed is only entitled to an adequate compensation for the publication of

---

11 OGH 15 October 1996, MR 1997, 148.
12 OGH 19 September 1995, MR 1996, 33; 15 October 1996, MR 1997, 148.
13 OGH 10 October 1995, MR 1996, 35.
14 OGH 10 November 1992, MR 1993, 59.
15 OGH 10 November 1992, MR 1993, 59; 17 January 1995, MR 1995, 143.
16 OGH 10 November 1992, MR 1995, 55; 4 May 1993, MR 1993, 146.
17 OGH 8 November 1994, Mr 1994, 237.
18 OGH 27 May 1997, MR 1997, 209.
19 Copyright Statute 1936, s 81.
20 Copyright Statute 1936, s 82.
1   Copyright Statute 1936, s 87, paras 1 and 2.
2   Copyright Statute 1936, s 85, para 1.

the picture in the form of an enrichment claim, which is based upon the exploitation of a level of awareness about the person, which can be measured in terms of money.[3] Section 81 of the Copyright Statute entitles the person whose rights have been infringed to a right to forbearance that is independent of fault, which right is subject to either the danger of recurrence or the danger of commission of an act. In order to secure the right to forbearance, interim injunctions may be petitioned for, which may be granted without evidence of imminent danger.[4]

4.36   A person whose rights have been infringed pursuant to section 87, para 1 of the Copyright Statute is entitled to damages with respect to the property loss, and in the case of ordinary negligence lost profit also has to be reimbursed. Pursuant to section 87, para 2 of the Copyright Statute a person injured is entitled to an adequate compensation for disadvantages which do not constitute loss of property. However, in order to be entitled to compensation for immaterial damage, the impairment must exceed the annoyance (which is normally associated with any kind of infringement of the protection of pictures) and must constitute a quite serious insult.[5]

3   OGH 6 September 1983, ÖBl 1984, 141.
4   Copyright Statute 1936, s 81, para 2.
5   OGH 29 May 1996, MR 1996, 185; 21 November 1989, MR 1990, 58.

5   BELGIUM*

Alexandre Cruquenaire
Benoit Van Asbroek*

A Privacy

1 *The right to privacy*

5.01   The right to privacy can be defined as the freedom to develop personal relations without any outside interference.[1] Privacy can also be defined in a negative way as 'anything that does not regard the public life of a person'. It implies the control of what a person wants to reveal about themselves.[2]

5.02   This chapter will develop the rules governing the right to privacy and then tackle some related practical issues. In Belgian law, the right to privacy of each individual is acknowledged by three fundamental texts (see para **5.04**). Two specific Acts protect privacy against particular forms of interferences (see para **5.08**).

5.03   Specific topics in connection with the right to privacy and personality will also be tackled: videosurveillance (see para **5.32**); photographs of a person's assets (see para **5.38**); biographical narratives (see para **5.46**); use of name (see para **5.54**); and finally, the right to image (see para **5.58**).

2 *Arrangements regarding the right to privacy*

5.04   The right to privacy is founded upon two major international texts incorporated within the Belgian legislation:

(1)   Article 8 of the European Convention on Human Rights[3] which states that:

---

*   This chapter reflects the law in Belgium as at October 1998.

**   The authors express their warmest acknowledgments to Professor Yves Poullet (University of Namur) for the submitted documentation with respect to the Personal Data Act and for his accurate suggestions concerning the privacy section of this chapter.

1   F Rigaux, *La vie privée, une liberté parmi les autres?*, Travaux de la Faculté de Droit de Namur, Brussels, (Larcier, 1992) at p 18.

2   F Rigaux, *La protection de la vie privée et des autres biens de la personnalité*, Brussels, Bruylant (1990) nr 684.

3   Incorporated in the Belgian law: cf Belgian State Gazette (*Moniteur Belge*), 19 August 1955.

'1. Everyone has the right to respect for his private and family life, his home and his correspondence.

2. There shall be no interference by a public authority with the exercise of this right except such as is in accordance with the law and is necessary in a democratic society in the interests of national security, public safety or the economic well-being of the country, for the prevention of disorder or crime, for the protection of health or morals, or for the protection of the rights and freedoms of others.

(2) Article 17 of the International Covenant on Civil and Political Rights (ICCPR)[4] which states that:

'1. No one shall be subjected to arbitrary or unlawful interference with his privacy, family, home or correspondence, nor to unlawful attacks on his honour and reputation.

2. Everyone has the right to the protection of the law against such interference or attacks.'

5.05 The Belgian Supreme Court has ruled that any international Act ratified by the Kingdom of Belgium supersedes any related internal texts.[5] The above-mentioned texts can therefore be pleaded directly in any proceeding.

5.06 Furthermore the Belgian Constitution, amended on 17 February 1994 states in its Article 22[6] that:

'Everyone has the right to respect for his private and family life, except in the circumstances and with respect to the conditions determined by law. The law or the decree warrants the protection of this right'.

Up to now, two specific Acts have been enacted on the basis of this constitutional principle (see para **5.09**).

5.07 In the event of any breach of a term of these general provisions, the injured party can initiate in the Belgian civil courts either a procedure on the merits of the case, or an interim relief procedure.

3   Specific Belgian laws relating to privacy

5.08 There are two relevant laws relating to privacy: first, the Act relating to privacy protection with regard to the processing of personal data[7] (see paras **5.09–5.25**); and second, the Act relating to the privacy protection against the monitoring of private communications and telecommunications[8] (see para **5.26**).

---

4   *Moniteur Belge*, 6 July 1983.
5   Cass, 27.05.1971, *Pas*, 1971, I, p886.
6   '*Chacun a droit au respect de sa vie privée et familiale, sauf dans les cas et conditions fixés par la loi. La loi, le décret ou la règle visée à l'article 134 garantissent la protection de ce droit*' (*Moniteur Belge*, 17 February 1994).
7   Loi du 8 décembre 1992 relative à la protection de la vie privée à l'égard des traitements de données à caractère personnel, *Moniteur Belge*,18 March 1993, p 5801.
8   Loi du 30 juin 1994 relative à la protection de la vie privée contre les écoutes, la prise de connaissance et l'enregistrement de communications et télécommunications privées, *Moniteur Belge*, 24 January 1995.

4 *The Privacy Commission*

5.09 Before examining the material scope of the Personal Data Act (hereafter, 'PDA') it is necessary to specify the role of the Belgian 'Commission for the protection of privacy'[9] ('the Privacy Commission').

5.10 The Privacy Commission is part of the Ministerial Department of Justice. Its composition reflects the socio-economic trends of Belgian society (PDA, Article 24). The Privacy Commission plays a triple role:

(1) it receives the notifications from the data controller (PDA, Article 18);

(2) it has an important consultative power regarding the PDA application and its improvement (PDA, Articles 29 and 30);

(3) it can be notified by individuals in case of breach of the PDA. It acts as a mediator (PDA, Article 31) and denounces the PDA infringements[10] to the Public Prosecutor (PDA, Article 32). The intervention of the Privacy Commission in litigation does not prevent recourse to the courts (PDA, Article 31, section 1).[11]

5 *Scope of the Personal Data Act*

5.11 The material scope of the PDA is determined by two concepts:[12] that of 'personal data' and that of the 'processing' of such data.

Personal data

5.12 'Personal data' is any data related to an identified or identifiable individual.[13] The EU Personal Data Directive,[14] which was transposed into Belgian legislation by a Bill of 11 December 1998,[15] adds that: 'to determine whether a person is identifiable, account should be taken of all the means likely reasonable to be used either by the controller or by any other person to identify the said person'.[16]

5.13 The PDA does not define the concept of 'data'. According to the preamble of this Act, any sort of information could be regarded as data (eg, the

---

9   The so called 'Commission de la protection de la vie privée' or 'Commissie voor de bescherming van de persoonlijke levenssfeer'.

10 The infringements to the main PDA provisions are criminal offences (PDA, arts 37–43).

11 Cf para **5.22** below.

12 Cf G Baeteman and MJ Van Vlasselaer, *De bescherming van het privé-leven ten aanzien van de gegevensverwerking*, Antwerp (Kluwer, 1993).

13 PDA, art 1, s 5. See also art 2a of the EU Directive 95/46/EC.

14 'Loi du 11 décembre 1998 transposant la directive 95/46/EC du 24 octobre 1995 du Parlement européen et du Conseil relative à la protection des personnes physiques à l'égard du traitement de données à caractère personnel et à la libre circulation de ces données', Belgian State Gazette (*Moniteur Belge*), 3 February 1999, pp 3049–3065). About the application of the self-executive provisions of a Directive, see J Verhoeven, *Droit de la Communauté européenne*, Précis de la Faculté de Droit de l'Université Catholique de Louvain, Brussels (Larcier, 1996) at pp 261 ff.

15 Directive 95/46/EC of the European Parliament and of the Council of 24 October 1995 on the protection of individuals with regard to the processing of personal data and on the free movement of such data.

16 26th Recitals of the EU Directive 95/46/EC, *JOCE*, 23 November 1995, L 281/31.

information contained in a picture or in a fingerprint).[17] The PDA extends to personal data in both private and public sectors.[18]

Processing of data

5.14 Both manual files and automated processing of personal data are within the scope of the PDA.[19]

5.15 The maintenance of a manual file is defined as the compilation and the storing of personal data in a logically structured manner enabling systematic consultation (PDA, Article 1, section 4).[20] A difference has to be made between a file ('fichier' or 'bestand') and a record ('dossier'), the first one being more structured than the second.[1] The distinction between these two concepts is rather unclear since it depends on the degree of structure permitting (or not) a systematic consultation of the data, although every record is, in principle, intended to be consulted.[2]

5.16 According to the Privacy Commission, one has to determine whether the data can be accessed and handled *rapidly*.[3] The alternative criterion proposed by the Privacy Commission will be of little practical help since, like the legal criterion, it is subjective.

5.17 The automated processing of personal data covers any set of operations carried out wholly or partially by automatic means relating to the registration and storage of personal data, as well as to the modification, erasing, consultation or dissemination of such data (PDA, Article 1, section 3).[4] The linking factor of the different operations mentioned by the definition must be found in the purposes of processing: all operations contributing to a common purpose constitute a 'set of operations'.[5]

5.18 Directive 95/46/EC adopts a broader approach to the concept of processing. Any operation, such as collection, recording or consultation, which is performed on personal data can be considered processing.[6] Moreover, this approach could raise problems in the context of the Internet: any consultation of personal data, made available on the web, could be considered to be the

---

17 MH Boulanger, C De Terwangne et T Leonard, 'La protection de la vie privée à l'égard des traitements de données à caractère personnel', *JT*, 1993, p 371. For the picture, cf paras **5.32** ff on videosurveillance.

18 C Van den Eynden, 'Data protection in Belgium', in *Business Guide to Privacy and Data Protection Legislation*, (1996) p 39.

19 PDA, art 1, s 1.

20 S Louveaux, 'Comments on the EU Data Protection Directive: the Belgian perspective', http://ltc.law.warwick.ac.uk/jilt/dp/2louveau/default.htm. See also: Cass, 16.05.1997, *JT*, 1997, p 779.

1 Cf Commission de protection de la vie privée, avis n° 7/92 du 12 mai 1992, *Doc Parl*, Chambre, sess Extr, 1991–1992, nr 413/12, pp 79–97.

2 M-H Boulanger, C De Terwangne et T Leonard, 'La protection de la vie privée à l'égard des traitements de données à caractère personnel', *JT*, 1993, p 371. *Adde* Commission de protection de la vie privée, avis n°2/92 du 25 février 1992 concernant un projet d'arrêté royal relatif au traitement de données à caractère personnel en matière de crédit à la consommation, in *Rapport d'activités 1992–1993*, p 74.

3 Commission de protection de la vie privée, *note sur la distinction fichier-dossier*, 10/IP/96/189/048, nr 5.

4 Simple registration without storage does not constitute an 'automated processing'.

5 MH Boulanger, C De Terwangne et T Leonard, 'La protection de la vie privée à l'égard des traitements de données à caractère personnel', *JT*, 1993, p 371.

6 Cf art 2b.

processing of such data. Such a view is in contradiction with the aim of the Directive which seems to apply to making personal data available for consultation, rather than the act of consultation itself.[7]

6 *Data protection principles*

5.19 The personal data protection instituted by the PDA is based on the purpose-limitation principle[8] which, according to Article 5,[9] covers two aspects: (1) the legitimacy of the processing; and (2) the conformity of the processing with the legitimate declared purposes.[10]

Legitimacy of processing

5.20 The principle of legitimacy implies that the purpose of the processing must be determined, declared and legitimate. The legitimacy of processing depends on its transparency (determination and prior information with regard to the processing purposes)[11] and the proportionality between the legitimate purpose of the processing and the need to attempt privacy.[12] The controller of the file ('maître du fichier' or 'houder van het bestand')[13] has then to notify the Privacy Commission of the considered processing and its purposes.[14] The subject of the data must be informed about the identity of the file controller, the purposes of this processing and their right to access and rectify the data related to them.[15]

---

7 MH Boulanger and C De Terwangne, 'Internet et le respect de la vie privée', in *Internet face au droit*, Cahiers du CRID, nr 12, pp 198–199. *Contra, cf* Projet de loi transposant la Directive 95/49/EC du 24 octobre 1995 du Parlement européen et du Conseil relative à la protection des personnes physiques à l'égard du traitement des données à caractère personnel et à la libre circulation de ces données, *Doc Parl*, Chambre des Représentants, sess ord 1997–1998, nr 1566/1, Commentaire des articles, p 13.
8 This principle must be viewed as the cornerstone of each personal data protection law (cf CNIL, *Dix ans d'informatique et libertés*, Paris, Economica, 1988, p 81 ff).
9 *'Les données à caractère personnel ne peuvent faire l'objet d'un traitement que pour des finalités déterminées et légitimes et ne peuvent pas être utilisées de manière incompatible avec ces finalités; elles doivent être adéquates, pertinentes et non excessives par rapport à ces finalités'* (personal data can only be processed for determined and legitimate purposes and cannot be processed in a way incompatible with those purposes).
10 JP Buyle, L Lanoye, Y Poullet et V Willems, 'Chronique de jurisprudence: l'informatique (1987–1994)', *JT*, 1996, p 233.
11 Cf T Leonard et Y Poullet, 'Les libertés comme fondement de la protection des données nominatives', in F Rigaux, *La vie privée, une liberté parmi les autres?*, Travaux de la Faculté de Droit de Namur, Brussels, Larcier, 1992, p 232 ff. See particularly the PDA, arts 4 and 9 regarding the obligation of information of the data subject.
12 S Gutwirth, 'De toepassing van het finaliteitsbeginsel van de privacywet van 8 december 1992', *TPR*, 1994, p 1432. *Adde* MH Boulanger, C De Terwangne et T Leonard, 'La protection de la vie privée à l'égard des traitements de données à caractère personnel', *JT*, 1993, p 377.
13 See the PDA, art 1, s 6 which defines the 'maître du fichier' as the individual or legal entity who or which can decides on the purposes of the processing and the types of data to be processed.
14 PDA, art 17.
15 PDA, arts 4 and 9 (right to information).

Conformity of processing

5.21　The principle of conformity implies that the content of the processing must respect the legitimate declared purposes which were assigned to it.[16] It also implies that the personal data has to be adequate, relevant and not excessive in relation to the said purposes (ie the proportionality relationship between the data collected and processed, and the purposes of such processing).[17]

7　Interim rules

5.22　The PDA[18] grants to every individual the right to specific recourse to 'interim relief' from the President of the civil courts.[19] The ability to order payment of damages has been discussed.[20] In any event, this recourse does not affect the possibility of initiating an examination of the merits of the case, which permits the awarding of damages.

Up to now, case law on this area has been very limited since the vast majority of individuals either have no knowledge of their rights in these matters, or do not realise the practical implications of the unlawful use of data related to them.

8　Directive 95/46/EC and amendments to the Personal Data Act

5.23　The transposition of the Directive 95/46/EC implies an amendment of the present Belgian PDA. A new bill adapting the PDA is now under discussion at the Belgian Parliament.[1] The first version of the draft bill has been criticised by the Privacy Commission[2] since it did not fully make use of the manoeuvrability margin allocated to the Member States by the Directive.[3]

---

16 J-P Buyle, L Lanoye, Y Poullet et V Willems, 'Chronique de jurisprudence: l'informatique (1987–1994)', *JT*, 1996, p 236.
17 Y Poullet, 'Droits et devoirs du ficheur', in *Quelle Commission pour quelle vie privée?*, actes juridiques de la journée d'information du 3 mai 1993, Brussels, Presses du Moniteur belge, p 55.
18 PDA, art 14.
19 However, this procedure is for use in an emergency. The court President decides on the merits of the case.
20 Up to now, two decisions have awarded damages in case of PDA infringement: Civ Brussels (prés), 22.03.1994, *JT*, 1994, p 841; Civ Nivelles (prés), 15.11.1994, *J*, 1995, p 289. *Contra*: Civ Brussels, 12.04.1995, unpublished, RG nr 95/53/A.
1 Projet de loi transposant la Directive 95/49/EC du 24 octobre 1995 du Parlement européen et du Conseil relative à la protection des personnes physiques à l'égard du traitement des données à caractère personnel et à la libre circulation de ces données, *Doc Parl*, Chambre des Représentants, sess ord 1997–1998, nr 1566/1.
2 Avis n° 30/96 du 13 novembre 1996 relatif à l'avant-projet de loi adaptant la loi du 8 décembre 1992 relative à la protection de la vie privée à l'égard des traitements de données à caractère personnel à la Directive 95/46/EC du 24 octobre 1995 du Parlement européen et du Conseil relative à la protection des personnes physiques à l'égard du traitement des données à caractère personnel et à la libre circulation de ces données.
3 On the extent of that margin, cf Y Poullet, 'The European Directive relating to the protection of physical persons with regard to the processing of personal data and its free circulation – a state of relative harmony', in *EC Data protection Directive: interpretation – application – transposition*, Darmstadt, STMV, 1997, pp 24 ff.

5.24   A sensitive question is the necessary reconciliation of the right to privacy with the freedom of expression. The Directive invites Member States to provide partial exemptions for journalistic purposes.[4] The Privacy Commission considers that the PDA applies to the files maintained by journalists and thus recommends partial exemptions in order to preserve the freedom of expression and the principle of the secrecy of journalistic sources. The latter could have to be revealed in the absence of exemptions.[5]

5.25   The first version of the draft bill, which gave to the courts the task of finding a balance between the two fundamental rights, was severely criticised by the State Council ('Conseil d'Etat' or 'Raad Van State').[6] So, the new version of the draft bill[7] stipulates effectively exemptions relating to the processing of sensitive personal data[8] provided relatively severe conditions are respected, particularly with regard to the public[9] character of the processed data and the means reasonably used for the necessary prior verification of the data accuracy[10] (Article 3, section 3(a) – new). Partial exemptions to the obligation of information of the data subject, to the right of access and rectification of said subject and to the duty of prior registration in order to protect the journalistic sources secret have also been provided (Article 3, section 3(b), (c) and (d) – new).

9   Monitoring of communications

Private communications

5.26   Wire tapping is regulated by the Act of 30 June 1994 relating to privacy protection against the monitoring of private communications and telecommunications.[11] All (tele)communications which are not intended to be heard by everybody have to be considered as 'private' (tele)communications, whatever means are used for the transmission, the place where the words are raised, or the type of content that is sent (images, digitalised data, etc).[12]

---

4   'Member States shall provide for exemptions or derogations from the provisions of this Chapter, Chapter IV and Chapter VI for the processing of personal data carried out solely for journalistic purposes or the purpose of artistic or literary expression only if they are necessary to reconcile the right to privacy with the rules governing freedom of expression' (art 9).

5   Avis n° 09/95 du 5 avril 1995 concernant *l'application de la loi du 8 décembre 1992 relative à la protection de la vie privée à l'égard des traitements de données à caractère personnel par les médias*, in Commission de protection de la vie privée, Rapport d'activité 1994–1995, pp 19–20, *Adde* Avis n° 30/96, op cit, p 6.

6   Projet de loi transposant la Directive 95/49/EC..., Avis du Conseil d'Etat, *Doc Parl*, Chambre des Représentants, sess ord 1997–1998, nr 1566/1, pp 96 ff.

7   Projet de loi transposant la Directive 95/49/EC..., Texte de la loi du 8 décembre 1992 dans l'hypothèse où cette loi serait modifiée suivant le projet de loi transposant la Directive 95/46/EC du 24 octobre 1995 du Parlement européen et du Conseil, *Doc Parl*, Chambre des Représentants, sess ord 1997–1998, nr 1566/2, pp 33–34.

8   Personal data with regard to race, ethnic origins, sexual behaviour, beliefs, political opinions, ... (art 6) and medical data (art 7).

9   Data made public by the referred person or in relation with his public character or the public character of the event he is involved in.

10 It implicitly refers to an ethical obligation on the part of journalists.

11 HD Bosly and D Vandermeersh, 'La loi belge du 30 juin 1994 relative à la protection de la vie privée contre les écoutes, la prise de connaissance et l'enregistrement de communications et télécommunications privées', *Rev dr pén* (1995) p 340. See also T Henrion, 'Les écoutes téléphoniques', *JT*, 1995, pp 205 ff.

12 Exposé des motifs, *Doc Parl*, Sénat, sess Ord 1992–1993, nr 843/1.

5.27 The Act protects private information and data only during their transmission (Articles 90 *ter* to 90 *decies* inserted in the Belgian Criminal Procedure Code by the above-mentioned law).[13]

5.28 The tapping of private communications can only be carried out in particular conditions[14] listed by the law and under the control of an investigation judge. The PDA should apply to the tapping of private communication as such an activity implies the processing of the personal data collected.[15] The Privacy Commission considers the provisions of the PDA could offer a more flexible and appropriate solution in these matters than the specific law on wire tapping.[16] Besides, the systematic recourse to an investigation judge imposed by the law is criticised by the investigation judges who are inundated with multiple requests.

5.29 The recording by individuals of private conversations without the consent of all the persons concerned infringes their right to privacy and makes the use of the tapes as judicial evidence unacceptable. This matter has been discussed by F Rigaux.[17]

Tracing of communications

5.30 A recent draft bill is aimed at relaxing the legal requirements regarding phone number tracing.[18] It allows phone number tracing by the Public Prosecutor and, in emergency cases by police officers.[19] Under this draft bill, three types of measures are distinguished according to the importance of the attempt to privacy, namely the identification of phone numbers, communication tracing and communication tapping.

5.31 The Privacy Commission criticises the new powers given to police officers in emergency circumstances.[20] It has also criticised the delegation to the government of the task of setting the technical means imposed to the telecommunication operators for permitting the tapping of private

---

13 T Henrion, 'Les écoutes téléphoniques', *JT*, 1995, p 209. About some questions relating to the application of the provisions of the law to the new technologies (e-mail, etc), see D Vandermeersh, 'Le droit pénal et la procédure pénale confrontés à Internet', in *Internet sous le regard du droit*, Brussels, Éditions du Jeune Barreau de Bruxelles (1997) p 253.

14 Notably with regard to specific incriminations.

15 Commission de protection de la vie privée, avis n° 23/93 du 14 décembre 1993, *Doc Parl*, Sénat, sess ord, 1992–1993, nr 843/1. *Adde* Commission de protection de la vie privée, *Avis relatif au projet de loi concernant l'identification et le repérage des numéros de postes de communication ou de télécommunication et portant modification des arts 90ter, 90quater, 90sexies et 90septies du Code d'instruction criminelle*, p 2.

16 Ibid.

17 *La protection de la vie privée et des autres biens de la personnalité, op cit*, nr 139. *Adde* Corr Gent, 10-06-1988, *TGR*, (1989) p 27. *Contra*: J-P Masson et N Massage, op cit, p 729

18 C Du Brulle, 'Repérages téléphoniques: la Justice tend l'oreille', *Le Soir*, 5 October 1998, p 12.

19 Ministère de la Justice, *Projet de loi concernant l'identification et le repérage des numéros de postes de communication ou de télécommunication et portant modification des articles 90 ter, 90 quater, 90 sexies et 90 septies du Code d'instruction criminelle*, art 2.

20 Commission de protection de la vie privée, *Avis relatif au projet de loi concernant l'identification et le repérage des numéros de postes de communication ou de télécommunication et portant modification des articles 90ter, 90quater, 90sexies et 90septies du Code d'instruction criminelle*, p 3.

communications.[1] In particular, concerning e-mails, the Privacy Commission fears the limitation of the encryption key size and/or the imposition of the recourse to key escrows. The Privacy Commission believes that this would constitute an excessive measure infringing Article 8 of the European Convention on Human Rights and in addition to this Article 22 of the Belgian Constitution requires the intervention of the Parliament to state any new limitation to the right to privacy.[2]

10 *Videosurveillance*

Possible applicability of the Personal Data Act

5.32 The first question to be addressed is whether this activity falls within the scope of the Personal Data Act. Images can constitute personal data in so far as they are related to an identifiable individual.[3] The Privacy Commission refers to the definition of the 'processing' (PDA, Article 1, section 3) to exclude any system which does not store picked up images.[4] The Privacy Commission also tries to limit the concept of personal data to the sole images systematically used to identify individuals.[5] Strictly speaking, the purpose of most videosurveillance systems is not the identification of persons but the protection of given places against intrusion. Those systems should then be excluded from the field of the PDA provisions.[6]

5.33 The teleological criteria used by the Privacy Commission reduce the extent of the concept of 'identifiable' by replacing the criteria of the use of reasonable means with the criteria of the initial intention of the data controller.[7] The implementation of the Directive 95/46/EC will supersede the restrictive vision expressed by the Privacy Commission.[8]

Possible implications of applicability of the Personal Data Act

5.34 The possible application of the PDA to the use of videosurveillance would have had dramatic implications, which it is believed will now be avoided for the reasons stated at the end of para **5.33** above. The principle of fair collection (legitimacy) requires, in particular, the prior information of the

---

1 Ibid, p 4. See also *Projet de loi concernant l'identification et le repérage des numéros de postes de communication ou de télécommunication...*, op cit, art 10.

2 Commission de protection de la vie privée, *Avis relatif au projet de loi concernant l'identification et le repérage des numéros de postes de communication ou de télécommunication...*, p 5.

3 Cf Projet de loi relatif à la protection de la vie privée à l'égard des traitements de données à caractère personnel, *Rapport fait au nom de la Commission de la Justice par Monsieur Vandenberghe*, Doc Parl, Sénat, sess extr, 1991–1992, nr 445/2, p 57. *Adde* Sénat, Questions et Réponses, nr 136, December 6, 1994, p 7133.

4 Avis n° 14/95 du 7 juin 1995 relatif à *l'applicabilité de la loi du 8 décembre 1992 relative à la protection de la vis privée à l'égard du traitement de données à caractère personnel à l'enregistrement d'images et ses conséquences, in Commission de protection de la vie privée, Rapport d'activité* 1994–1995, p 31 (compare with art 2b of the Directive).

5 Ibid.

6 P De Hert, O De Schutter and S Gutwirth, 'Pour une réglementation de la vidéosurveillance', *JT*, 1996, p 573.

7 P De Hert, O De Schutter and S Gutwirth, 'Pour une réglementation de la vidéosurveillance', *JT*, 1996, p 575.

8 Cf O De Schutter, 'Vidéosurveillance et droit au respect de la vie privée', *Journ Proc*, 1996, nr 298, p 10. Cf also above with regard to the provisions of the Directive.

data subject.[9] As a result, the processing of data collected by means of secret video systems should be regarded as illegal.[10] The role of videosurveillance systems would then be merely dissuasive.

5.35 Collected images could also be considered as 'sensitive' data should the ethnic origins (PDA, Article 6) or the state of health (PDA, Article 7) of a person be inferred from such data. The processing of sensitive data, ie in practice virtually any image featuring a human being, is only permitted:

(1) for the sole purposes laid down by or in implementation of the law (PDA, Article 6);
   [The Privacy Commission curiously suggests the stipulation of a general authorisation for the processing of visual data.[11] This suggestion was criticised by the legal commentators since the role of the Commission is obviously not to reduce privacy protection.[12]]

(2) with the prior written consent of the data subject or under the control and the liability of a practitioner of a medical profession (PDA, Article 7).

The images from an illegal video system cannot be used as evidence and must be rejected by the courts.[13]

5.36 The Privacy Commission has recently issued a positive opinion with regard to a monitoring system of the Saint-Gilles prison (Brussels) visitors, for security purposes.[14]

B Publicity and personality

1 *Photographs of a person's assets*

5.37 The question of the use of an individual's physical appearance will be examined in paras **5.58** ff.[15]

5.38 The owner of an asset can forbid anybody from taking or using a photograph of his asset if such an action would infringe his right to privacy (see para **5.39**). The rightholder of a work of art, and in certain circumstances the owner of a work of art, can also forbid the taking and use of a photograph of the said work of art (see para **5.40**). Aerial pictures require in any event a special government licence.[16]

---

9   The Privacy Commission (avis n° 14/95, op cit, p 32) suggests the hanging of a clearly visible written notice near the video system.
10 P De Hert, O De Schutter and S Gutwirth, 'Pour une réglementation de la vidéosurveillance', *JT*, 1996, p 573.
11 Avis n° 14/95, op cit, pp 32–33.
12 P De Hert, O De Schutter and S Gutwirth, 'Pour une réglementation de la vidéosurveillance', *JT*, 1996, p 573.
13 HD Bosly, 'La régularité de la preuve en matière pénale', *JT*, 1992, p 122.
14 In *Journal de droit des jeunes*, nr 178, October 1998, pp 21–22.
15 Cf infra, s 7.
16 Cf Arrêté royal du 21 février 1939 réglementant la prise de vues aériennes au dessus du territoire national et le transport d'appareils photographiques à bord d'aéronefs, *Moniteur Belge*, 16 March, 1939.

2   *Fixing and reproduction of private assets*

5.39   The fixing and reproduction of an image of a private asset is forbidden where it results in privacy infringement.[17] The possible occurrence of a privacy infringement depends on the viewable character of the assets involved: if the assets are not viewable without the consent of their owner, they relate to their owner's privacy and cannot then be photographed without his/her consent.[18] Such authorisation is required, for example, if it is necessary to enter a private property to view the assets.[19] Failing that, the owner could also use their right to respect for their home to sue the photographer.[20]

3   *Reproduction of works of art*

5.40   The author has an exclusive right to authorise the reproduction of his or her works (in whatever form, or on whatever medium).[1] He/she also has a moral right to the respect of the integrity of his or her work.[2] There are some exceptions to the patrimonial rights of the author, like the quotation right, which has a narrower scope than the fair use concept prevailing in the US. The new author's right law[3] permits, without prior consent of the author, the reproduction of short quotations of any artwork for critical, scientific, controversial or teaching purposes.[4]

5.41   The issue of quoting from an artistic work remains controversial. The majority of the authors pursuant to French case law consider that a full reproduction of an artistic work, even at a reduced size, cannot be regarded as a short quotation.[5] According to the French Supreme Court, a reproduction of an excerpt of an artistic work, which fits the concept of a short quotation, breaches the moral right to respect the integrity of the artistic work and is thus unlawful.[6]

5.42   In view of the fact that the new Belgian author's right law is not limited to short quotations from literary works but refers explicitly to artistic works, it should be considered, in order to enable short quotations from artistic works, that the Belgian legislative power admits in this case a limited attempt to respect the integrity of the primary artistic work.

This interpretation of the Belgian author's law has not yet been discussed by any published relevant case law. According to the authors of the present chapter the social necessity of quoting from any artistic work associated with the

---

17   T Gr Inst Paris, 11-07-1996, *Jurisdata*, 050277.
18   P Kayser, 'L'image des biens', *Dalloz*, 1995, Chron, p 292.
19   T Gr Inst Paris, 27-09-1976, *RIDA*, July 1977, p 158.
20   ECHR, art 8 and art 15 Belgian Constitution.
1   Article 1, s 1 de la loi du 30 juin 1994 relative au droit d'auteur et aux droits voisins (cf infra).
2   On the moral right to integrity, cf art 1, s 2 AL.
3   Loi du 30 juin 1994 sur le droit d'auteur et les droits voisins, *MB*, 27 July 1994.
4   Article 21 AL.
5   A Berenboom, *Le droit d'auteur et les droits voisins*, Brusses, (Larcier, 1997) pp 129 ff. A et B Strowel, 'La nouvelle législation belge sur le droit d'auteur', *JT*, 1995, p124 and with certain nuances B Van Asbroek, 'l'œuvre BD Multimédia, Essai comparatif en droit belge et droit français', in *Droit d'auteur et Bande dessinée*, Brussels, Paris, Bruylant, LGDJ, 1997, pp 177 ff.
6   Cass, fr, 05/11/93, JCP, 1994, II, 22201, comments Françon. This case law is severely criticised by the major french commentators. Read in PY Gautier, *Propriété littéraire et artistique*, Paris, PUF, 1996, nr 143 and quoted references.

general principle of freedom of expression, balanced with the necessary so-called disinterest status of the author of the secondary work[7] should lead to an extensive interpretation of the concept of 'short quotations' which would consider the concept of shortness not only with respect to the work quoted but also with respect to the entire works of the relevant artist. In this case a limited amount of full reproduction of artistic works in a secondary artistic work would be possible without prior authorisation of the primary author. Such interpretation would tend to reconcile the concepts of short quotations and fair use.

Article 10 of the Berne Convention for the protection of literary and artistic works[8] which allows quotations of artworks of any kind without making any more reference to the necessary shortness of the quotations should promote this suggested broad interpretation.

5.43   An analysis of the guidelines with respect to the amount and the length of acceptable quotations would exceed the scope of the present article. These questions have been thoroughly examined by Lionel Bochurberg.[9] The reproduction of an artistic work is also permitted without the author's consent when the artwork is located in public spaces, in so far as the artistic work does not constitute the image's main subject (AL, Article 22, sections (1),(2°)).[10]

5.44   Finally, the reproduction of an entire artistic work is permitted for information purposes and in the limits of news events review (AL, Article 22, sections (1), (1°)).[11]

5.45   The owner of an artistic work can forbid the taking of, or the use of photographs of 'his' artistic work if it is not located in a public space. This power is based on property[12] and/or on contractual rights issues. For example, art museums can contractually regulate the photography of artistic works which are in the public domain.

4   Biographical narratives

5.46   Can the facts belonging to the privacy of an individual be freely stated? The answer to that question lies in the balance to be struck between the right to freedom of expression and the right to privacy.[13] The courts weigh the interests at stake and, according to the circumstances, decide which of those fundamental rights will prevail.[14]

---

7   PY Gautier, *Propriété littéraire et artistique*, Paris, PUF, 1996, nr 143.
8   Revised in Paris, 24 July 1971 (due to be incorporated into Belgian law – see GATT Agreement on TRIPs).
9   L Bochurberg, *Le droit de citation*, Paris, Masson, 1994, p 153.
10 B Edelman, 'La rue et le droit d'auteur', *Dalloz*, 1992, chron, XVIII, p 95, nr 20. *Adde* Paris, 23 octobre 1990, *Dalloz*, 1990, IR, 298 (the 'Géode' case).
11 B Vincotte, 'Droit d'auteur et comptes-rendus d'actualité', note sous Brussels, 21 septembre 1994, *RGDC*, 1996, pp 38–47.
12 See s 4.1 on the viewable character of the involved artwork.
13 Civ Brussels (réf), 06-04-1995, *Journ Proc*, nr 286, p 23.
14 J Milquet, 'La responsabilité aquilienne de la presse', *Ann Dr Louvain*, 1989, p 43.

5.47   The statement of information relating to a person's privacy requires, in principle, the consent of the person involved. But account must be taken of the behaviour of that person.[15] The privacy accorded to public figures should reflect the fact that certain facts of their private lives which are normally reported become newsworthy and then 'available' even without their consent.[16] The general public has a legitimate interest in information about all the facts reporting to a public figure's privacy which are related to his or her public activities and/or with what he or she publicly expresses.[17] Some events of the privacy of public figures become 'news events' and can then be freely stated.[18] These limitations to the privacy scope only affect public figures. Persons coming into the public sphere because of their implication in news events are to be put in the same category as public figures.

5   Right to oblivion

5.48   In this context, a problem which occurs frequently is that of the statement of facts related to a judicial condemnation. The freedom of expression allows the facts at stake to be stated solely during the trial. Indeed, case law has held that the right to privacy includes a 'right to oblivion' which could be defined as a right permitting the individual whose life is not dedicated to public activities to demand the peace and quiet necessary for the free development of his personality.[19] A person involved in a trial enters the news through that trial and leaves the public sphere as soon as the trial is over.[20]

5.49   The French Supreme Court,[1] whose case law has inspired Belgian decisions, admits exceptions to the right to oblivion in so far as the related facts were lawfully stated at the trial's time and as long as a subsequent statement can have a real interest, which is obvious, for instance, if the facts have an 'historical' importance.[2]

6   Personality distortion and right to honour

5.50   Another relevant question is that of the accuracy of biographical information. The tort rules permit any fault committed in the exercise of the freedom of expression which causes damage to the mentioned person to be actionable. Damage could either consist in a personality distortion or in an offence against the subject's right to honour. Personality distortion exists every

---

15 F Rigaux, *La protection de la vie privée et des autres biens de la personnalité*, Brussels, Bruylant, 1990, nr 684.
16 Ibid, nr 201.
17 H De Page, *Traité élémentaire de droit civil belge*, Tome II, *Les Personnes*, volume I, par J-P Masson, Brussels, Bruylant, 1990, p 57. *Adde*: A Strowel, 'Démêlés judiciaires autour d'*Une Paix royale* de Pierre Mertens', *JT*, 1996, p 199; J Ravanas, *La protection des personnes contre la réalisation et la publication de leur image*, Paris, Bibliothèque de droit privé, 1978, p 141; P Kayser, *La protection de la vie privée par le droit*, Presses Universitaires d'Aix-Marseille, 1995, nr 153 ff.
18 C Bigot, 'Protection des droits de la personnalité et liberté de l'information', *Dalloz*, 1998, Chronique, p 238.
19 Civ Namur, 17-11-1997, *JT*, 1998, p 187.
20 Civ Brussels, 30-06-1997, *JT*, 1997, p 715. *Adde:* F Rigaux, 'Justice et presse: réflexions comparatives', *JT*, 1996, p 44.
1   Cass fr, 20-11-1990, *JCP*, 1990, nr 21908.
2   Cf A Strowel, 'Liberté de rappeler des faits contre droit au silence: les contretemps de la presse', *JLMB*, 1998, pp 785 ff.

time a personality which is different from the subject's real personality is suggested to the public.[3]

5.51 So far as concerns the right to honour, there is no need to specifically identify the person concerned.[4] The right to honour[5] protects against defamatory accusations[6] and/or insults, without making any distinction between the private and the public life of the individual.[7]

5.52 The tort is relatively easy to prove when a false or incorrect fact is attributed to the relevant person. Evidence is more difficult to bring in the case of critical observations about the subject's personality.[8] Even the author of a biographical narrative is bound by a duty of fairness and is not allowed to distort the subject's personality, although the right to freedom of expression requires freedom to criticise to be maintained.[9] Prohibition against censorship prevents legal proceedings being commenced before publication of a narrative which is possibly prejudicial to honour.[10]

5.53 In the case of personality distortion by a periodical, the injured party can refer to their right of reply[11] and force the publisher to publish a reply written by them. Publication of the judgment is another form of compensation frequently sought.[12]

7 Use of name

5.54 A person's name is considered to be one of their attributes. Every person holds a right to their name.[13] That right enables the holder to forbid each use of their name, even without demonstrating any particular patrimonial

---

3 J Mestre, 'La protection, indépendante du droit de réponse, des personnes physiques et des personnes morales contre l'altération de leur personnalité aux yeux du public', *JCP*, 1974, nr 2623, para 7–18.
4 Cf Civ Brussels, 23-03-1993, *JT*, 1993, p 579 (about the case of a publication questioning the honesty of a municipality management without specifically identifying the persons responsible).
5 Cf ICCPR, art 17 (above).
6 About the libel incrimination, cf Penal Code, arts 443–452.
7 A Strowel, 'Démêlés judiciaires autour d'*Une Paix royale* de Pierre Mertens', *JT*, 996, p 197.
8 Personality distortion can also result from the publishing of a photograph (P Kaiser, *La protection de la vie privée par le droit*, Presses Universitaires d'Aix-Marseille, 199, p 189).
9 Civ Brussels, 26.04.1991, *JT*, 1992, p 315. About the application of the civil responsibility rules in case of satirical or fictional works, cf E Montero, 'La responsabilité civile des médias', in *Prévention et réparation des préjudices causés par les médias*, Brussels, (Larcier, 1998) pp 121–124.
10 Civ Brussels (réf), 22-08-1991, *Pas*, 1992, III, 1. *Adde* JP Masson and N Massage, 'Chronique de jurisprudence: les personnes (1991–1993)', *JT*, 1994, p 729. See also: Civ Brussels (réf), 05-02-1997, *A & M*, 1997, p 200; Brussels (réf), 08-05-1998, *JLMB*, 1998, p 1046.
11 Cf Loi du 23 juin 1961 relative au droit de réponse, *Moniteur Belge*, 8 July 1961. About the possible extension of the right to reply to the Internet sphere, cf F Jongen, 'Droit de réponse dans la presse et l'audiovisuel', in *Prévention et réparation des préjudices causés par les médias*, Brussels (Larcier, 1998) pp 55–56.
12 For example: Civ Namur, 17-11-1997, op cit.
13 About the right to the name, cf AC Van Gysel, 'Examen de jurisprudence (1991–1996) les personnes', *RCJB*, 1998, pp 452–453. *Adde* Civ Liège, 12-12-1997, *JLMB*, 1998, p 819.

damage.[14] Indeed, each person has a moral right to control the use of their name.[15] However, a person is not able to forbid the use of their name in a fictional work if there is no risk of confusion existing between the fictional figure and that person.[16]

5.55 The Benelux Uniform Trade marks Law (BUTL) expressly permits the registration of a person's name as a trade mark (Article 2).[17] Three main conditions are required for the trade mark validity: (1) the distinctive character of the registered sign; (2) its lawfulness; and (3) its availability.

5.56 A sign is considered as 'distinctive' when it permits the identification of the product referred to in such manner as to distinguish its origin from that of other products.[18] A sign is considered unlawful if it is likely to mislead the public about the product properties or its origin. Availability of any sign depends on the third parties' rights (marks, personal name, trade name).

5.57 The name holder's consent is obviously required for registration of a person's name. This consent must be obtained in good faith. If this is not done, the registration of a name which is homonymous with the name of a person will be invalid. A person whose name is homonymous with a registered trade mark may continue to use his or her name but not in the same territory as a trade mark.[19]

8 Right to image

5.58 Each individual has an exclusive right to the use of their 'image'. The 'right to image' enables any individual to prevent any unauthorised use of a reproduction of his visual features.[20] An 'image' could be defined as any lasting reproduction of the visual features of a specific and recognisable person.[1] The 'right to image' is based on the privacy general arrangements (ECHR, Article 8; ICCPR, Article 10; Belgian Constitution, Article 22)[2] and on the provisions of Article 10 of the new author's right law.[3] The 'right to image' exceeds the limits of privacy and applies to every use of an individual's likeness.

---

14 Civ Brussels (réf), 11-02-1991, *JT*, 1991, p 567.
15 H De Page, op cit, nr 138 ff.
16 Brussels (réf), 12-01-1994, *RW*, 1994–1995, p 229.
17 Loi du 30 juin 1969 portant approbation de la Convention Benelux en matière de marques de produits et annexe signée à Bruxelles le 19 mars 1962, *Moniteur Belge*, 14 October 1969.
18 Cf A Braun, *Précis des marques*, Brussels, (Larcier, 1995) pp 97 ff.
19 A Braun, *Précis des marques*, Brussels, (Larcier, 1995) pp 50 ff.
20 R Lindon, note sous Paris, 25-10-1982, *Dalloz*, 1983, p 343. *Adde:* Paris, 10-09-1996, *RDPI*, 1996, nr 68, p 63 ; Civ Brussels (réf), 04-10-1995, unpublished, RG nr 95/1469/C, p 4. M Isgour and B Vincotte, *Le droit à l'image*, Brussels (Larcier, 1998) p 68.
1 Cf above.
2 This article states that neither the author, neither the owner of a portrait, nor any other possessor of a portrait has the right to reproduce or to publicize it without the consent of the represented person or of his or her entitled beneficiary during the 20-year period commencing on his or her death ('*Ni l'auteur, ni le propriétaire d'un portrait, ni tout autre possesseur ou détenteur d'un portrait n'a le droit de le reproduire ou de le communiquer au public sans l'assentiment de la personne représentée ou celui de ses ayants droit pendant 20 ans à partir de son décès*').
3 B Michaux, 'La bande dessinée et les droits des tiers', in *Droit d'auteur et bande dessinée*, Brussels-Paris, Bruylant-LGDJ (1997) p 200.

5.59 The 'right to image' implies therefore a visual representation of a specific and recognisable person. Only the textual description of an individual does not come under the 'right to image'.

5.60 However, a visual representation in whatever form could lead to a breach of someone's 'right to image': strip,[4] painting,[5] and so on. The represented person must be recognisable.[6]

5.61 There is no need for an absolutely identical representation, so long as the person is recognisable (by his attitudes, features or by a caption[7]) by any third person. Therefore, the Paris Court (Tribunal de Grande Instance) ruled that the actress Catherine Deneuve could refer to her 'right to image' with regard to a representation of her bust because her nearest and dearest could recognise her.[8] Account has to be taken of the person's attitude. The rights of a person with regard to their image end with their death.

5.62 The prerogatives transmitted to the rightholder relate only to images made during that person's life.[9] It is therefore impossible to refer to the 'right to image' about the representation of mortal remains. The forbidding of such representation could only be based on the prejudice to the late person's memory and/or to the family's honour.[10]

9 Public figures and persons involved in news events

5.63 Unless formally refused, a person's consent will be presumed in certain circumstances: public figures, persons involved in a news event, and (sometimes) persons in a public place.

5.64 The consent of a public figure can be presumed with regard to any reproduction of their visual characteristics relating to their public activities or opinions.[11]

5.65 Public persons are also able to refer to their right to privacy.[12] Their presumed consent can only be assumed for information purposes, to the exclusion of any commercial use.[13] The consent of persons involved in a news event can also be presumed, but only for immediate information purposes.[14]

---

4   Cass fr, 14.03.1900, *Dalloz*, 1900, I, 497.
5   Trib Gr Inst Lyon, 18.02.1976, *JCP*, 1978, II, 18900.
6   J Corbet, note sous Civ Brussels, 19.06.1981, *RW*, 1981–1982, col 2616.
7   Trib Gr Inst Paris, 29.03.1978, quoted by P Fremond, *Le droit de la photographie. Le droit sur l'image*, Paris, Publicness, 1985, p 352.
8   For a 20-year time period.
9   M Isgour and B Vincotte, *Le droit à l'image*, Brussels (Larcier, 1998), p 85. About the commercial use of President Pompidou's image, cf Trib Gr Inst Paris (réf), 04.04.1970, *JCP*, 1970, II, 16328.
10 M Isgour and B Vincotte, *Le droit à l'image*, Brussels (Larcier, 1998), p 96.
11 This issue is treated in M Isgour and B Vincotte, *Le droit à l'image*, Brussels (Larcier, 1998), p 109 and following. *Adde* Trib Gr Inst Paris, 25.04.1994, *Jurisdata*, 043178.
12 About the limits of said right, cf above.
13 J Milquet, 'La responsabilité aquilienne de la presse', *Ann Dr Louvain*, 1989, p 64.
14 M Isgour and B Vincotte, *Le droit à l'image*, Brussels (Larcier, 1998), p 96.

10 Consent to use of image

5.66 Can a person's consent in relation to the use of his or her image be deduced from the sole fact that he or she walks on the street? Great care is required: in fact, privacy can partially exist in public places.[15] Some authors recommend a distinction depending on the main subject of the photograph.[16] The consent of the represented person could be presumed if they are not the main subject of the photograph.[17] Otherwise, the represented person's consent is necessary.

5.67 The authors are divided upon the necessity (or not) of consent for the mere taking of a photograph in a public place independently of the use of the photographs concerned. There are different opinions in this matter. Some authors consider that the right to control the use of photographs has necessarily to be completed by the right to control the photograph being taken.[18] Others believe that nothing forbids the taking of a photograph of a person in a public space.[19] F Rigaux considers that the person who enters the public sphere implicitly waives his right to forbid his image being taken and used for some purposes (see above).[20]

5.68 This opinion cannot be shared: the sole fact of leaving a private area cannot a priori be interpreted as a will to publicise. Indeed, it is not always possible to avoid public places, even when a person wants some elements of their privacy to be kept secret.[1] So far as the act of taking a photograph results in an image which is of a durable character, which is perhaps legitimately objected to by the person represented, the person represented should retain their right to forbid its taking and/or use.

5.69 Consent for the use of a person's image is interpreted in a restrictive way: consent for a specific use does not imply the consent for another use.[2] In a recent case involving the reproduction of images of parents of missing children in a neo-fascist political leaflet, the Brussels Civil Court ('Tribunal de Première Instance' or 'Rechtbank van Eerste Aanleg') went further and affirmed that the express consent of the person represented is required for any use or reproduction of their physical appearance.[3]

5.70 In addition, the person represented has the right to withdraw and can always cancel any consent given for a specific use of their physical appearance.[4]

15 Y Marecellin, *Photographie et loi*, Paris, CEDAT, 1997, p 124.
16 X Dijon, *Le sujet de droit en son corps: une mise à l'épreuve du droit subjectif*, Brussels (Larcier, 1982) p 159.
17 M Isgour and B Vincotte, *Le droit à l'image*, Brussels (Larcier, 1998), p 66. *Adde* D Acquarone, 'L'ambiguïté du droit à l'image', *Dalloz*, 1985, Chron, nr 2.
18 P Kaiser, *La protection de la vie privée par le droit*, Presses Universitaires d'Aix-Marseille, 199, p 184.
19 Cf the case relating to the use of Jacques Brel photographs representing him as a sick man going downstairs in an airport (quoted by M Isgour and B Vincotte, *Le droit à l'image*, Brussels (Larcier, 1998), p 108).
20 F Rigaux, *La protection de la vie privée et des autres biens de la personnalité*, Brussels, Bruylant, 1990, p 760.
1 Civ Bruxelles (réf), 23.10.1998, unpublished, RG nr 98/1553/C. It seems quite excessive and may be prejudicial to the right to the freedom of expression.
2 Civ Brussels (réf), 04.10.1995, op cit.
3 For a 20-year time period.
4 Com Brussels, 24.02.1995, *Ing-Cons*, 1995, p 333.

6   BRAZIL

Peter Dirk Siemsen[1]

A   Introduction

6.01 The subject matter of personality rights is an area which finds ample protection in Brazil through constitutional provisions,[2] several laws[3] and extensive jurisprudence (mostly related to image and name protection).

6.02 Among the many authors, who have analysed and commented on the various features concerned with the protection of personality rights, the conclusions of Professor Rubens Limongi França are of particular interest,[4] ie that the area needed better arrangement in view of three fundamental aspects – the physical; the intellectual; and the moral one – which basically characterise the personality rights.

1   Personality rights – França classification

6.03 Starting from these three aspects, Professor França established the following classification of personality rights:

1   Rights to physical integrity:
    (a)   right to life and to food;
    (b)   right over one's own living body;
    (c)   right over one's own dead body;
    (d)   right over the living bodies of others;
    (e)   right over the dead bodies of others;

---

1   Lawyer and industrial property agent, Senior partner of Dannemann, Siemsen, Bigler & Ipanema Moreira, Rio de Janeiro and São Paulo, Brazil, former President of AIPPI, ASIPI, ABPI and LES-Brazil.
2   1988 Constitution, of 5 October 1998, art 5, items V, X, XII, XXVII, XVIII, XXIX.
3   Industrial Property Law no 9279/96 of 15 May 1996; Law no 5772/71 of 21 December 1971; Decree-Law no 1005 of 21 October, 1969; Decree-Law no 254 of 28 February 1967; Decree-Law no 7903 of 27 August 1945; Copyright Law (Law no 9610/98 of 19 February 1998; Law no 5998/73 of 14 December 1973; Consumer Protection Law no 8078/90 of 11 September 1990 and amendments; Law no 9296/96 of 24 July 1996; Civil Code (Law no 3071/16 of 1 January 1916) and amendments; Criminal Code (Decree-Law no 2848/40, of 7 December 1940) and amendments; Code of Civil Procedures (Law no 5869/73 of 11 January 1973); Code of Criminal Procedures (Decree-Law no 3689 of 3 October 1941).
4   Rubens Limongi França, 'Manual de Direito Civil', vol I, 3rd edn, São Paulo, 1975, Editora RT, p 403.

    (f)   right over separate parts of the living body;

    (g)   right over separate parts of the dead body.

2   Right to intellectual integrity:

    (a)   right to the freedom of thought;

    (b)   personal right of a scientific author;

    (c)   personal right of an artistic author;

    (d)   personal right of an inventor.

3   Right to moral integrity:

    (a)   right to the civil, political and religious freedom;

    (b)   right to honour;

    (c)   right to distinction;

    (d)   right to modesty;

    (e)   right to personal, domestic and professional secrecy;

    (f)   right to the image;

    (g)   right to the personal, family and social identity.

2 *Personality rights – Miranda classification*

6.04   On the other hand, one of the most prominent Brazilian jurists, Pontes de Miranda, classified the personality rights as being the:

(1) right to life;

(2) right to physical integrity;

(3) right to psychic integrity;

(4) right to freedom;

(5) right to truth;

(6) right to honour;

(7) right to one's own image;

(8) right to equality;

(9) right to one's name;

(10) right to one's pseudonym;

(11) right to one's trade name;

(12) right to intimacy.

6.05   Considering that the matter of protecting personality rights is treated unequally in the different countries and by different authors, and consequently classifications of personality rights have been subject to extensive controversy, the above classifications seem broad and flexible enough so as to embody the ample spectrum of personality rights which will continue to emerge through case law and new means of communication.

3 *Constitutional personality right*

6.06   In Brazil, although the first important decision relating to the protection of names dates back to 1936, it was with the adoption of the 1988 Constitution that personality rights in their broadest sense became a constitutional right.

6.07   Article 5 of the Constitution provides that all are equal before the law, without distinction of any nature, guaranteeing to Brazilians and foreign citizens living in Brazil the inviolable rights to life, freedom, equality, safety and property, and proceeds to specify these rights.

6.08   Item V of Article 9 of the Constitution confers the right to compensation in the case of material or moral damages, or damages to the image of a person.

6.09   Under item IX of Article 5, the Constitution guarantees the freedom of intellectual and artistic expression, scientific activity and communication, regardless of censorship or licence.

6.10   The inviolability of the intimacy, private life, honour and image of persons is guaranteed under item X, which also guarantees, in the case of violation, compensation for resulting material or moral damages.

6.11   Also, the secrecy of the postal service and communication of data by telephone or other telegraphic means is guaranteed, except in the case of a duly justified judicial order (item XII).

6.12   Authors of copyright works, inventions and other industrial creations such as designs and utility models and owners of trade marks, service marks and other distinctive signs, as well as trade names have their rights recognised by the Constitution (items XXVII and XXIX).

6.13   The reproduction of the human image and voice, even at sporting activities, and the participation of individuals in collective works are duly protected in accordance with item XXVIII(a).

B   Privacy

1   *Aspects of privacy*

6.14   As mentioned above, the right to privacy is guaranteed by Article 5, items X and XII of the Federal Constitution.[5]

6.15   There is no doubt that: covert filming; filming on private property; filming over private property (from the air); recording of conversations (whether open or covert); sifting of rubbish; use of security camera footage for reporting events and use of a telephoto lens for invading privacy, infringe the provisions protecting intimacy and privacy, so long as not authorised by express judicial order.

6.16   However, there is one decision by the Civil Court of Appeal of the State of São Paulo which did not consider the recording of a telephone conversation with the purpose of obtaining proof for a business negotiation, to be an invasion of privacy and found this to be licit and morally legitimate.[6]

---

5   Some details can be found implemented in the Law of the Press (Law 5250/67), presently under review at the Brazilian Congress and in Law no 9296 of 24 July 1996, which regulates item XII of art 5 of the Federal Constitution.
6   Interlocutory appeal 488.433 – 5th Chamber of the 2nd Civil Appeal Court of the State of São Paulo – June 1997.

6.17   The Civil Court of Appeals of the State of Rio de Janeiro ordered the search and seizure of a film which recorded facts which caused the death of a young girl and was being exhibited in cinemas. The search and seizure had been requested by the girl's parents.[7]

C   Publicity

1   *Right to intimacy*

6.18   The right to intimacy, which covers the private life of a person, embodying personal and family aspects, which include the image and the honour, biographies, diaries, memories, etc is covered by Article 5, item X, of the Federal Constitution. Whenever publications refer to public figures or famous personalities, the difficulty is always to evaluate the fine line which exists between the interests of the public and the privacy to which such personalities should be entitled. In Brazil the law guarantees such privacy as long as the publications do not cover public events or occurrences.

2   *Trade mark protection in respect to a person's name*

6.19   Since the time of the first trade mark law, Brazilian legislation on trade marks contained provisions regulating the conditions under which a person's name could be registered as a trade mark. The present law has been the broadest in protecting not only personal names or signatures but also family or patronymic names, images of third parties, well-known pseudonyms or nick-names and single or collective artistic names without the consent of the owner, his heirs or successors (Article 124, XV and XVI, of the Industrial Property Law).

6.20   Jurisprudence interpreting the application of the various trade mark laws is available since 1936, when the Court of Justice of the State of São Paulo, in the case of *Lápis Johann Faber Ltda v L Faber & Cia Ltda*, rendered the following decision:

> 'The right to one's name is absolute, deriving from the human personality itself; an individual makes use of his personal name in accordance with his free will, proceeding with the activity he chooses. This rule however is limited by another, which does not allow someone to take undue advantage at another's expense by means of unfair competition. If the similarity between two conflicting names entails confusion of the consumer, the use of this name as a trade mark by someone who commences the activity by availing himself of the reputation gained by his homonym is forbidden. The use of the surname to commit unfair competition does not constitute the exercise of a right but a fraud, an abuse, which the courts do not hesitate to repress.'[8]

---

7   *Hilton Calasans Rodrigues and his wife v Artenova Filmes Ltda*–Civil Appeal no 51200 – 1st Chamber of the Civil Court of Appeals of the State of Rio de Janeiro – 16 June 1980.
8   Civil Appeal no 20.904 (Campinas) – *Lápis Johann Faber Ltda v L Faber & Cia Ltda*, in Revista dos Tribunais no 101, May 1936.

6.21   In the case of *John Woodbury Inc v Esther Woodbury*, the Superior Court established that there are limitations to the use of a surname whenever such use results in unfair competition, undue enrichment at another's expense, or the counterfeiting of a trade mark.[9]

6.22   The most important decision regarding the requirement that a well-known pseudonym cannot be registered without express authorisation, was rendered by the Federal Court of Appeals in the case of 'Paco Rabanne', the famous pseudonym of the Spanish couturier Francisco Rabaneda.[10]

6.23   However, in the case of 'Robert Lewis', having established that it was a fanciful name not identifying any existing person, the Federal Court of Appeal decided that a consent which had been requested by the National Institute of Industrial Property was not due.[11]

6.24   The protection given to personal names against attempts of registration by third parties was confirmed by decisions rendered in the cases of 'Mary McFadden', 'Claude Montana', 'Gianni Versace', 'Rayond Weil', 'Pierre Cardin' and 'Howard Johnson'.[12]

6.25   In the case of *Thomas Othon Leonardos v Leonardos Decorações Ltda*, the court decided that the surname is entitled to a special protection and that the right to the civil name is personal, absolute and non-transferable.[13]

6.26   The problem resulting from the coexistence of identical personal names has been solved by the courts by allowing the first registrant for such personal name to register the same without any special condition, but requiring that a second party carrying an identical personal name can only register it in a fanciful form.

D   Personality

1   *Misuse of person's image*

6.27   In relation to the misuse of a person's image for the purpose of advertising for publicity, the rules of the National Council of Publicity Agencies establish that:

'Section 9 – Protection to intimacy

Article 34 – This Code condemns the publicity that:

(a)   makes use of images or citations of living persons, unless their previous and express authorisation has been given;

---

9   Extraordinary Appeal no 23.893-STF – *John Woodbury, Inc v Esther Woodbury*, in the Judicial Gazette no 63, 18 March 1957.
10   Appeal in Writ of Mandamus no 98.865 – *Concorde Ind de Roupas Ltda v INPI (National Institute of Industrial Property)*, in the Judicial Gazette of 3 March 1983.
11   Civil Appeal no 64.845-TFR – *Robert Lewis do Brasil Modas Ltda v INPI (National Institute of Industrial Property)*, in the Judicial Gazette of 16 December 1982.
12   Published in Trademark Gazettes of 19 June 1984, 5 June 1984, 11 March 1986, 4 October 1983, 25 June 1985 and 5 May 1987.
13   Civil Appeal no 12.004 – *Thomas Othon Leonardos v Leonardos Decorações Ltda*, in Revista Forense no 279/237-39, July/September 1982.

(b) offends religious beliefs and other susceptibilities of descendants or of whoever is related to dead people whose image or reference appears in the advertising;

(c) reveals disrespect to the dignity of the human being and to the family institution;

(d) disrespects private property and its limits.

Article 35–The above rules do not apply to:

(a) pictures of large groups or crowds in which individuals can be recognised but do not involve a defamatory, offensive or humiliating context;

(b) advertising of books, films, radio and TV programmes and related activities in which the persons appearing are authors or participants.'

2   Unauthorised use of images

6.28 A number of decisions referring to unauthorised use of images or photographs have been issued, among which the following are of interest:

(1) *Maison Brunet Ind e Com Ltda and Luisa Brunet v Editora Abril:*[14] Luisa Brunet is a well-known model in Brazil, who granted the rights to use her name and image to the plaintiff. The defendant had used the name of Luisa Brunet in an article published in a magazine together with the image of a counterpart. The court preliminarily decided that Maison Brunet was not entitled to proceed with the action, but then, on the merit, decided, under Article 5, item X, of the Federal Constitution, in favour of Luisa Brunet's claim, limiting the same to moral damages, as there had been no material damage.

(2) The right to an image is also the subject of a decision rendered by the Court of Justice of the State of Rio de Janeiro in relation to the unauthorised use of the images of the World Champion National Soccer Team by the Confederação Brasileira de Futebol and Editora Abril SA in a sticker album. The claim was deemed valid pursuant to Article 5, items X and XXVIII, of the Federal Constitution.[15]

(3) There have been several decisions on the unauthorised use of photographs for commercial purposes consolidating the application of the provisions of Article 5, item X, of the Federal Constitution.[16]

14 Civil Appeal no 4209/90 – *Maison Brunet Ind e Com Ltda v Editora Abril SA*, in Diário Oficial do Rio de Janeiro III, 26 September 1991, p 156.

15 Civil Appeal no 4.452/90 – *Carlos Alberto Torres v Confederação Brasileira de Futebol and Editora Abril SA* in Diário Oficial do Rio de Janeiro III, 16 May 1991, p 139.

16 Writ of Mandamus no 391-87 – *Luma de Oliveira v Benicio e Brandão Ind e Com de Roupas Ltda* in Diário Oficial do Rio de Janeiro III, 5 May 1988; Civil Appeal no 91.688-1 – *Paulo Tadeu Ostapenko and wife v Três Livros e Fascículos Ltda* in Revista dos Tribunais 629/106-107, March 1988; Appeal no 81483-1 – *Carlos Rogério Salomão v Grow Jogos e Brinquedos SA e Klaus Mitteldorf Arquivo de Imagens S/C Ltda* in Revista dos Tribunais 624/65-68, October 1987; Civil Appeal no 3559/88–*Paulo Greven v Distribuidora Record de Serviços de Imprensa SA*, in Diário Oficial do Rio de Janeiro III, 15 December 1988; Civil Appeal no 35.436, in Revista dos Tribunais 628/92-96, February 1988; Civil Apeal no 129.556-1 – *Helio Barbini and son v Editora C Ltda*, in Revista dos Tribunais 668/78-80, June 1991; Civil Appeal no 4215/89 – *Alexandre Silva de Abreu v Página Dois Promoções e Publicidade Ltda e Discovery Bolsas e Artigos Esportivos*, in Diário Oficial do Rio de Janeiro III, 24 September 1992; Extraordinary Appeal no 115.838-7-SP – *Sandra Rico Panzoldo v Paramount Lansul SA e Abril SA Cultural e Indústria* in Diário da Justiça, 3 June 1988.

(4) In accordance with a decision rendered by the Court of Justice of the State of Rio de Janeiro, a person renounces his right to privacy when a photograph containing his image is taken in the course of a public event, such as the Rio Carnival.[17]

17 Civil Appeal no 31.525 – Published in Revista Forense no 292/257-8, October/ December 1985.

7   CANADA

Louise Potvin*
Robert Howell**
Tom McMahon

A   Introduction

7.01   Canada is a federation. *The Constitution Act 1867* divides legislative jurisdictions between the federal and provincial governments.[1] Of the ten provinces, nine have a common law foundation for private law, 'received' from English law.[2] Québec is a civil law province originating in the earlier French colonisation of North America. Civil law for private law in Québec has been retained.[3] There are three common law territories, administered more directly by the Federal Crown, but with certain measures of autonomy.

7.02   The consequences of these constitutional and political divisions in presentation of a concept as broad as 'privacy' is the need to consider federal and provincial legislative jurisdictions as well as common law and civil law initiatives. These sources necessarily are interwoven. A broad demarcation may, however, be made. Federal constitutional and legislative provisions that relate to privacy issues, may be characterised as public law, especially in a context of criminal law sanctions, an exclusively federal jurisdiction.[4] On the other hand, common law and (in Québec) civil law is an exclusively provincial constitutional jurisdiction concerning private law relationships. In between these perspectives, provincial legislation, in subject areas that are constitutionally of provincial competence, may concern either public or private law relationships. For example, the *Charter of Human Rights and Freedoms* in

---

*   In 1999, I adopted a baby girl from Vietnam, Lilian Mai (Nguyet Tuyet Mai), and would like to dedicate my work in this article to her.
**   The authors would like to thank Philip Kennedy (U Vic 1999) for his checking of footnote citations.

1   *The Constitution Act 1867*, ss 91 and 92. See Schedule to the Constitution Act 1982 (UK), this Act itself being Schedule A (French) and B (English) to the Canada Act 1982, c 11 (UK). (*The Constitution Act 1867*, was enacted originally as the British North America Act 1867, 30 & 31 Vict, c 3 (UK).)
2   The expression 'English law' refers to the common law and equity of England (ie decisions of the English courts of common law and chancery) as well as statutes of the English Parliament (to 1707) and the Parliament of the 'United Kingdom of Great Britain' from 1707. There is a 'reception date' for the receipt of this law in each former colony or territory. The law had to be suited to local circumstances. See Howell 'Important Aspects of Canadian Law and Legal Systems' in *Law Libraries in Canada* (ed JN Fraser, 1988) Carswell, Agincourt, Ont at pp 63–66.
3   See The Québec Act 1774, 14 Geo III, c 83 (UK). Prior to 1866 the civil law was uncodified. From 1 August, 1866 the Civil Code of Lower Canada was in effect and from 1994, the Civil Code of Québec, SQ 1980, c 39.
4   *The Constitution Act 1867*, s 92(27).

Québec,[5] unique in the sense of being the only provincially created 'Charter' of judicially enforceable human rights and freedoms,[6] encompasses both public and private relationships. Yet, in four common law provinces, legislation has created 'statutory torts of privacy', limited essentially to private relationships.[7]

7.03   A further factor that must be considered is the perceived distinction between 'privacy' and 'publicity' or property interests in personality rights. Within the constitutional framework of Canada, publicity interests are essentially within provincial jurisdiction, except to the extent that they may be encompassed within the federal powers of criminal law or specific categories of intellectual property law, such as copyright, registered trade marks or industrial design.[8] However, the concept of 'privacy' and 'publicity' are, in fact, significantly interwoven.

Since the present article is the first attempt to deal with some privacy issues in Canada in a global fashion encompassing criminal law, civil law (covering both common law and Québec law) as well as constitutional law, bringing these various aspects of privacy law together in a unique and coherent article is particularly challenging.

B   Privacy

1   *The Canadian Charter of Rights and Freedoms*

7.04   The starting point is the *Canadian Charter of Rights and Freedoms*.[9] Any law that conflicts with the *Charter* can be declared unconstitutional and of no force or effect. The *Charter* was not adopted until 1982. There is no express hierarchy of rights.[10] However, in cases where both privacy and freedom of expression issues are present, the Supreme Court of Canada has generally protected privacy – even though freedom of expression is an expressly protected right in the *Charter* and 'privacy' is not.[11] The Supreme Court has also held that freedom of the press and other media of communication does not give

---

5   Charter of Human Rights and Freedoms, RSQ c 12 (1977), as am SQ 1982, c 61 (replacing the original statute SQ 1975, c 6).
6   The Québec *Charter* is not an entrenched constitutional document. It was enacted by legislation. However, s 52 stipulates that that the *Charter* shall prevail over other statutes unless those other statutes are expressed to apply despite the *Charter*. See text accompanying para **7.41**, n 16 below.
7   See Privacy Act, RSBC 1996, c 373; Privacy Act, RSM 1987, c P-125; Privacy Act, Nfld RS, 1990 c P-22; and Privacy Act, RSS, 1978 c P-24.
8   See *The Constitution Act 1867* s 91(27) (criminal law), s 91(23) (copyright) and s 91(2) trade and commerce for registered trade mark and industrial design).
9   *Canadian Charter of Rights and Freedoms*, Part I, ss 1–34, Constitution Act 1982, c 11 (UK) (hereinafter referred to as 'the *Canadian Charter of Rights and Freedoms*' or simply 'the *Charter*').
10 *Dagenais v Canadian Broadcasting Corp* [1994] 3 SCR 835 at 877.

journalists any greater right to freedom of expression than is enjoyed by the general public.[12]

7.05 The *Charter* limits only *government* actions. The privacy interests directly protected by the *Charter* are only those that arise in a confrontation between the state and the citizen or those that arise from the wording of a statute. Where the news media investigate and publish embarrassing details of a person's life, the *Charter* does not directly limit the media. However, it is accepted that the common law and interpretation of the Civil Code in Québec should be developed to conform with 'Charter values'.[13] This affects, in particular, proceedings in nuisance, trespass and defamation.

7.06 The principal section of the *Charter* that relates to privacy is section 8: 'Everyone has the right to be secure from unreasonable search or seizure'. The protection afforded by this provision does not apply unless there is an invasion of a reasonable expectation of privacy. This will depend on the overall facts of a case. To be reasonable, a search or seizure must be validly authorised and the manner in which it is carried out must be reasonable. The purpose of section 8 is to protect against invasions of privacy *before* they occur, not after. Therefore, whether a search is reasonable does not depend on what was found.[14]

7.07 A number of other provisions of the *Charter* are important to protect privacy interests. Section 7 provides that 'everyone has the right to life, liberty and security of the person and the right not to be deprived thereof except in accordance with the principles of fundamental justice'. The phrase 'principles of fundamental justice' means that section 7 has both a procedural 'due process' aspect to it *and* a substantive justice aspect. While the Supreme Court of Canada has commented in a number of cases that section 7 will protect privacy interests, the court has not yet faced a case where a plaintiff has alleged a violation of section 7 rights because of an invasion of privacy or undue publicity. The main context in which privacy interests have arisen under section 7 is that of a criminal trial where accused persons have a right to full disclosure of all relevant information to enable them to properly defend themselves. In

11 In *Hill v Church of Scientology* [1995] 2 SCR 1130, the court upheld a large defamation award against the Church of Scientology; in *R v Lucas* [1998] 1 SCR 439, the Supreme Court of Canada upheld the offence of criminal defamation; and in *Aubry v Les Éditions Vice-Versa* [1998] 1 SCR 591, the Supreme Court of Canada found a violation of the Québec *Charter of Human Rights and Freedoms* (an ordinary statute that is not part of the Constitution) when a magazine published a photograph of a woman without her knowledge or consent, even though freedom of expression is a constitutionally protected freedom in both the *Québec Charter* and the *Canadian Charter of Human Rights and Freedoms*.
12 *CBC v New Brunswick (AG)* [1991] 3 SCR 459; *CBC v Lessard* [1991]3 SCR 421.
13 *RWDSU v Dolphin Delivery* [1986] 2 SCR 573 at 603; *R v Salituro* [1991] 3 SCR 654 at 675; *Dagenais v CBC* [1994] 3 SCR 835 at 875–78; *Hill v Church of Scientology of Toronto* [1995] 2 SCR 1130 at 1169.
14 *CBC v NB* [1991] 3 SCR 459; *CBC v Lessard*, [1991] 3 SCR 421; *R v Lloyd* [1994] BCJ No 3169 (BCSC).While the basic rules were laid down in cases such as *Hunter v Southam Inc* [1984] 2 SCR 145; *R v Dyment* [1988] 2 SCR 417 and *R v Duarte* [1990] 1 SCR 30, there are a number of cases which suggest that the place makes a difference as to whether a search will be reasonable. There are lower expectations of privacy, and therefore lower requirements on a search, when the search is in the context of entering the country (*R v Simmons* [1988] 2 SCR 495), in the context of a friend's apartment (*R v Edwards* [1996] 1 SCR 128), or in the context of a friend's car (*R v Belnavis* [1997] 3 SCR 341).

sexual assault cases, victims have resisted disclosing therapeutic records to the accused, but while expressing sympathy for these privacy interests, the Supreme Court has allowed for the possibility of disclosure of even these records where a court is satisfied they are relevant.[15]

7.08　Section 2 of the *Charter* protects freedom of thought, belief, religion, expression and association. While there are few cases that are concerned specifically with 'privacy', it seems safe to presume that in most cases a court would protect individuals from government actions that would force them to disclose their beliefs and associations.[16]

2　Criminal law and privacy

Covert filming and photography

7.09　There is no *general* crime or offence of covert filming, videotaping or photographing another, including the use of telephoto lens or security camera surveillance. Specific prohibitions include:

(1)　covert videotaping in private circumstances by police or state authorities without a warrant;[17]

(2)　in British Columbia, making a visual depiction that will identify doctors, service providers and patients within a specified area around an abortion service facility.[18]

Generally, police authorities may photograph an accused person without his

---

15　See Jody van Dieen 'O'Connor and Bill C-46: Differences in Approach,' (1997) 23 Queen's LJ 1. Bill C-46, SC 1997, c 30, establishing strict procedures and a rigorous test between an accused's right to a full defence and the privacy of a witness has been held to be constitutional. See *R v Mills* (1999), 139 CCC (3d) 321 (SCC).

16　Section 319 of the Criminal Code makes it a criminal offence to communicate statements in any public place (but not in private) that incite hatred against identifiable groups where such incitement is likely to lead to a breach of the peace, or to communicate statements 'other than in private conversation' with an intent to wilfully promote hatred against any identifiable group, unless the accused can show the statements to be true (among other defences). These provisions have been upheld by the Supreme Court of Canada in *R v Keegstra* [1996] 1 SCR 458. Interestingly, the offence of publishing a statement that the accused 'knows to be false and that causes or is likely to cause injury or mischief to a public interest' was held to be unconstitutional: *R v Zundel* [1992] 2 SCR 731. The Supreme Court of Canada upheld the removal of a school teacher from the classroom even though the teacher did not express his anti-Semitic views in the classroom: *Taylor v Canada Human Rights Commission* [1990] 3 SCR 892. These cases raise the issue of the liberty of private thought, and the relationship between expression in one's private life and how that expression may be used against a person in their employment. Note also that s 319 makes a distinction between public statements and private statements.

17　*R v Wong* [1990] 3 SCR 36. Note that the Supreme Court of Canada found that there is a reasonable expectation of privacy in what happens in a hotel room, even though the suspects had issued invitations to strangers to attend at the hotel room, for the purpose of illegal gambling. LaForest J for the majority of the Supreme Court (at 43) stated: 'the broad and general right to be secure from unreasonable search and seizure guaranteed by s 8 is meant to keep pace with technological development, and accordingly, to ensure that we are ever protected against unauthorised intrusions upon our privacy by the agents of the state, whatever technical form the means of invasion may take'. See also *R v Mercer* (1992) 7 OR (3d) 9 (Ont CA).

18　See Access to Abortion Services Act, RSBC 1996, c 1, s 3.

or her consent,[19] and Canadian criminal law has no specific 'peeping tom' offence.[20] Videotapes made by news media may be obtained by police authorities and used as evidence in a prosecution.[1]

Stalking, staking out and harassment

7.10 The Criminal Code contains several provisions that seek to ensure that persons have a reasonable expectation of privacy in their movements in public. These provisions are as follows.

Criminal harassment

7.11 Subsection 264(1) creates the offence of criminal harassment to the effect that:

> 'no person shall, without lawful authority and knowing that another person is harassed or recklessly as to whether the other person is harassed, engage in conduct referred to in subsection (2) that causes that other person reasonably, in all the circumstances, to fear for their safety or the safety of anyone known to them'.

Subsection (2) provides that the conduct in subsection (1) consists of:

> '(a)   repeatedly following from place to place the other person or anyone known to them;
>
> (b)   repeatedly communicating with, either directly or indirectly, the other person or anyone known to them;
>
> (c)   besetting or watching the dwelling-house, or place where the other person, or anyone known to them, resides, works, carries on business or happens to be; or
>
> (d)   engaging in threatening conduct directed at the other person or any member of their family.'

Mischief

7.12 Section 430 covers conduct that would obstruct, interrupt or interfere with any person in the lawful use, enjoyment or operation of property. However, 'no person commits mischief within the meaning of this section by reason only that he attends at or near or approaches a dwelling-house or place for the purpose only of obtaining or communicating information'. This section has

---

19 *R v Dilling* (1993)84 CCC (3d) 325 (BCCA); *R v Shortreed* (1990), 54 CCC (3d) 292 (Ont CA).

20 *Frey v Fedoruk* [1950] SCR 517; *R v Davidson* [1990] OJ No 2793 (Ont HC) (QuickLaw). However, see s 177, *Criminal Code*, RSC, c C-34 and *Lipiec v Borsa* [1996] OJ No 3819 (Ont Gen Div), where the judge held the plaintiffs liable for deliberate invasion of privacy for erecting a commercial style surveillance camera near the roof of their house aimed directly at the defendant's yard, for no purpose other than to keep the defendants under constant surveillance. The judge noted: 'Intentional invasion of privacy has also been recognized as actionable in Ontario in several cases. See *Roth v Roth* (1991) 4 OR (3d) 740 (Gen Div); *Saccone v Orr* (1981) 34 OR (2d) 317 (Co Ct); *S & A Nagy Farm Ltd v Repsys* [1987] OJ No 1987 (Dist Ct).'

1 *CBC v NB* (AG) [1991] 3 SCR 459; *CBC v Lessard* [1991] 3 SCR 421; *R v Lloyd* [1994] BCJ No 3169 (BCSC).

not, however, been interpreted in a manner that would afford meaningful privacy protection to occupiers.[2]

Intimidation

7.13   Section 423 sanctions conduct where a person:

> 'wrongfully and without lawful authority, for the purpose of compelling another person to abstain from doing anything that he has a lawful right to do, or to do anything that he has a lawful right to abstain from doing ... (c) persistently follows that person about from place to place, ...

> (e) with one or more other persons, follows that person, in a disorderly manner on a highway,

> (f) besets or watches the dwelling-house or place where that person resides, works, carries on business or happens to be, or

> (g) blocks or obstructs a highway. ...'

Subsection (2) provides that a 'person who attends at or near or approaches a dwelling-house or place, for the purpose only of obtaining or communicating information, does not watch or beset within the meaning of this subsection'.

Private communications

7.14   The principal provision in the Criminal Code concerning interception of 'a private communication' is section 184(1). The interception must be 'wilful' and be 'by means of any electro-magnetic, acoustic, mechanical or other device'. The section encompasses oral communications as well as electronic transmission of images, sounds or intelligence.[3]

7.15   No offence is committed under this section if the interceptor has the consent of *either* the originator *or* the intended recipient of the communication. Of course, while not an offence under this provision, an interception with the consent of merely one participant in the communication may be a tortious breach of privacy.[4] The requirement that the interception be 'wilful' removes from the provision any mere overhearing of a communication.[5]

7.16   Section 184(1) will apply in circumstances where an originator of a communication reasonably believes that the communication will not be intercepted. Primarily, this will involve telephone communications, but may

---

2   See *R v Maddeaux* (1997) 33 OR (3d) 378 (CA) finding that loud noises can interfere with enjoyment of property. Contrast *R v Drapeau* (1995) 96 CCC (3d) 554 (Que CA) (no conviction for watching or staring at a neighbour and making objectionable noises).

3   The definition in s 183 of 'private communication' is limited to 'any oral communication, or any telecommunication...'. The expression 'telecommunication' is defined in the Interpretation Act (Canada), RSC 1985, c I-21, s 35 as 'any transmission, emission or reception of signs, signals, writing, images, sounds or intelligence of any nature by wire, radio, visual or other electromagnetic system'.

4   Where an interception is by police or state authorities, the interception with the consent of only one party is an unconstitutional search. See *R v Duart* [1990] 1 SCR 30.

5   *R v Kennedy* [1996] J No 4401 (CA) (QuickLaw).

also include e-mail[6] and radio communication (eg cellular telephones), although the latter is specifically covered by section 184.5 and, in that context, the interception can be either 'malicious', 'or for gain even if not malicious'. Accordingly, a news media interception, while not being malicious, may well be 'for gain'. The precise scope of this provision awaits interpretation.

Personal data

7.17 There are federal (and provincial) enactments that protect personal information and data under the control of governments. An analysis of these enactments is beyond the scope of the current context.

7.18 A federal data protection law, that would apply to the handling of personal information by private parties, was enacted in 1998 and currently applies to federally-regulated private sectors parties.[7] The legislative intention of this Act is to apply also to all private sector parties, unless a province has a reasonably equivalent law. At the present time, only the province of Québec would be found to have an equivalent law.[8]

3   *The common law provinces*

Common law

7.19 Consistently with other Commonwealth jurisdictions, there is little direct protection of privacy at common law in Canada. This, of course, is a sharp contrast to the vigorous common law privacy protections that developed in the US from the seminal article by Warren and Brandeis in 1890,[9] and which were categorised by Prosser[10] into four situations involving:

(1) intrusions;

(2) public disclosure of private facts;

(3) placing another in false light in the public eye; and

(4) appropriation of name or likeness.

This jurisprudence does provide a guide or source for common law development, but to date this approach has not been accepted and, indeed, was expressly rejected in one province.[11]

---

6   See the meaning of 'a private communication', at n 3 above. It is unclear whether e-mail can be 'intercepted' after it has been received in a computer. The Criminal Code, s 183 defines 'intercept' as including 'listen to, record or acquire a communication...'. Is it still a 'communication' after it has been received? See also Criminal Code, s 430(1.1) (obstructing, interrupting or interfering with data) and s 342.1 (accessing, intercepting computer services). See also *R v Weir* [1998] AJ No 155 (Alta QB) (QL) for an indication of reasonable exportation of e-mail privacy.

7   *Personal Information Protection and Electronic Documents Act*, SC 2000 c 5.

8   In Québec see *An Act respecting personal information in the private sector*, SQ 1993, c 17. Section 1 excludes journalists from application of the Act. The federal Act also contains significant exclusions for journalists.

9   See Warren and Brandeis 'The Right to Privacy' (1890) 4 Harv L Rev 193.

10 See Prosser 'Privacy' (1960), 48 Cal L Rev 383, 389–401.

11 See *Parasiuk v Canadian Newspapers Co* [1988] 2 WWR 737 (Man QB). See also *Turton v Buttler* (1987) 42 CCLT 74 (Alta Master). See generally, LD Rainaldi, *Remedies in Tort* (Toronto, Carswell, 1988), vol 3 at 24-9 to 24-12.

7.20 Canadian common law recognition of privacy interests may be noted as:

(1) a few instances of a direct recognition of privacy interests;[12]
(2) a consistent trend in Ontario of a refusal to dismiss summarily claims of privacy violation;[13]
(3) the encompassment of privacy injury within established torts, such as, for example, trespass to land or private nuisance;[14] and
(4) the inclusion of privacy injury within the fledgling tort of appropriation of personality.[15]

7.21 Despite this historical absence of any common law general right of privacy, such an approach may still be recognised in Canada,[16] to enhance the many ways in which the common law provides an indirect protection of privacy.

Statutory privacy torts

7.22 Four provinces (British Columbia, Manitoba, Newfoundland and Saskatchewan) have enacted privacy acts that create statutory torts related to the invasion of privacy.[17] The purpose of the Acts has been described as 'to introduce into the law a broad and generous protection of an individual's interest in privacy'.[18]

7.23 Proceedings may be heard only by superior courts.[19] In Saskatchewan and Newfoundland, there is a limitation period of two years.[20] The death of the person whose privacy is alleged to have been violated extinguishes the right of action in three provinces.[1]

7.24 None of the Privacy Acts attempt to define 'privacy'. They simply state that the violation of another's privacy is wrongful and tortious if wilful and without a claim of right[2] or substantial, unreasonable and without claim of right.[3]

---

12 See eg *Saccone v Orr* (1981) 34 OR (2d) 317 (Co Ct) and *Roth v Roth* (1991) 4 OR (3d) 740 (GD). See also para **7.09**, n 20 above.
13 See LD Rainaldi, *Remedies in Tort* (Toronto, Carswell, 1988), vol 3, at 24-9 to 24-12.
14 See eg *Motherwell v Motherwell*, [1976] 6 WWR 550 (Alta CA) where the defendant made numerous harassing telephone calls.
15 See eg *Dowell v Mengen Institute* (1983) 72 CPR (2d) 238 (Ont HC). The tort of appropriation of personality in Canada is essentially proprietary, but in this instance would have applied in a privacy context had not the plaintiff been found to have consented to the procedure and disclosure—the publication of the results of an 'encounter group' on the difficulties of being unemployed at which the plaintiff had become very emotional.
16 See n 12 above and LD Rainaldi, *Remedies in Tort* (Toronto, Carswell, 1988) vol 3 at 24–12.2 noting that the issue of a general right to privacy 'has never been addressed at the highest appellate levels'. See also AM Linden *Canadian Tort Law* (6th ed) (Toronto, Butterworths, 1997) at 55–59.
17 See para **7.02**, n 7 above.
18 Osborne 'Case Comment on *Milton v Savinkoff*' (1993) 18 CCLT 292.
19 BC, s 4; Nfld, s 8; Man, s 1(a); Sask, s 5.
20 Nfld, s 10 (with possible extension to seven years); Sask, s 9.
1 BC, s 5; Nfld, s 11; Sask, s 10.
2 BC, s 1(1); Nfld, s 3(1); Sask, s 2.
3 Man, s 2(1).

Statutory guidelines

7.25 Some statutory guidelines are provided for in the interpretation of the concept of privacy. For instance, section 1(2) of the British Columbia Act states that everyone is entitled to a degree of privacy which is reasonable in the circumstances, due regard being given to the interests of others.[4]

7.26 In deciding whether a violation of privacy has occurred, the following factors should also be considered:

(1) the nature, incidence and occasion of the act or conduct;[5]

(2) the effect of the act, conduct or publication on the health, welfare or social, business or financial position of the affected person;[6]

(3) the distress, annoyance or embarrassment suffered by the affected person;[7]

(4) the conduct of the person affected, and of the defendant, before and after the publication (including any apology or offer of amends by the defendant).[8]

Proof of damage

7.27 Proof of damage is not required in each province.[9]

Remedies

7.28 In Manitoba, Saskatchewan and Newfoundland,[10] the courts can award damages, grant an injunction, order the defendant to account to the plaintiff for any profits that have accrued or may subsequently accrue to the defendant by reason of the violation of privacy, order the defendant to deliver up to the plaintiff articles or documents that come into his or her possession by reason or in consequence of the violation, or give any other necessary relief.[11] The British Columbia Act makes no special provision for the kind of relief that is available.

Use of another person's likeness for commercial purposes

7.29 In Manitoba, Saskatchewan and Newfoundland,[12] the unauthorised use of someone's likeness to advertise or promote the sale of, or other trading in, property or services, or for other purposes of gain to the user, is a violation of privacy if the person in question is identifiable or identified and the user intended to exploit that person's likeness. In British Columbia, an entirely separate tort is created specifically in this context.[13] There can be no liability unless the plaintiff is sufficiently identified. In a group context, the plaintiff's presence must be emphasised by the composition of the picture or otherwise, or the plaintiff must be recognisable and the defendant intended in using the picture to exploit the name or reputation of the person represented.

---

4   See also Sask, s 6(1) and Nfld, s 3(2).
5   BC, s 1(3); Nfld, s 3(2); Man, s 4(2)(a); Sask, s 6(2)(a).
6   Sask, s 6(2)(b); Man, s 4(2)(b).
7   Man, s 4(2)(d).
8   Sask, s 6(2)(d); Man, s 4(2)(e).
9   BC, s 1(1); Man, s 2(2); Sask, s 2; Nfld, s 3(1). Contrast the position in Québec. See para **7.49** below.
10 Man, s 4(1); Sask, 7; Nfld, s 6.
11 Manitoba has no residual clause granting 'any other relief'.
12 Man, s 3(c); Sask, s 3(c); Nfld, s 4(c).
13 Section 3(3).

Defences

7.30   Various defences may be raised. They vary depending on the province in which the action is brought. They include consent; that the act was done by a peace officer acting in the course of his or her duty for the prevention of crime or the discovery or investigation of perpetrators of a crime, or by a peace officer engaged in an investigation in the course of his or her lawful duty; that the act was in lawful defence of persons or property; and that with respect to any published matter, the publication was in the public interest.[14]

Case law

7.31   The courts have not attempted to define the nature and scope of privacy and have avoided directly adopting American privacy law.[15] The approach has been simply on a case-by-case basis. Most have been in British Columbia. For convenience, they may be presented in the following contexts:

(1)   the taking of photographs, videotapes or other means of surveillance;[16]

(2)   the use of a 'tracking' device affixed to the plaintiff's property;[17]

(3)   the publication of photographs or videotapes;[18] and

(4)   the use of the plaintiff's name or likeness.[19]

Most of these proceedings failed.[20]

7.32   Two cases require particular attention. First, in *Milton v Savinkoff*,[1] the plaintiff inadvertently left her vacation pictures in the defendant's jacket pocket, including one photograph in which she appeared topless. The defendant subsequently gave the photograph to another of the plaintiff's acquaintances, who passed it on to another friend. The plaintiff sued the defendant for breach of her privacy. The British Columbia Supreme Court found no breach of privacy for the following reasons: the plaintiff had not sought the return of her photographs until she found that they had been shown to her friend; she 'had little concern about the development of her photograph in a semi-nude condition by an unknown film developer in Hawaii';[2] she had been careless in leaving the photographs in the defendant's jacket pocket and the defendant had not acted out of malevolence. The decision has been criticised as the

---

14   BC, s 1(3); Nfld, s 5; Man, s 5; Sask, s 4.

15   See Warren and Brandeis 'The Right to Privacy' (1890) 4 Harv L Rev 193.

16   *Belzberg v BCTV Ltd* [1981] 3 WWR 85 (BCSC 1980) (and broadcast of tape); *Insurance Corporation of BC v Somosh* (1983), 51 BCLR 344 (BCSC); *Silber v BCTV Ltd* (1985), 25 DLR (4th) 345, 69 BCLR 34 (BCSC) (and broadcast of tape); *Penny v Manitoba Public Insurance Corp* (1991), 72 Man R (2d) 10, 12 (QB) and *Richardson v Davis Wire Industries Ltd* (1997), 33 BCLR (3d) 224, 237 (BCSC).

17   *Davis v McArthur* (1969), 10 DLR (3d) 250 (BCSC) *rev* (1970), 17 DLR (3d) 760 (BCCA).

18   *Wooding v Little* (1982), 24 CCLT 37 (BCSC).

19   *Joseph v Daniels* (1986), 4 BCLR (2d) 239, 11 CPR (3d) 544 (SC).

20   One success was *Insurance Corporation of BC v Somosh* (1983), 51 BCLR 344 at 354 (BCSC) (Counterclaim). See also *Unger v Lutz* (1996), 24 BCLR (3d) 124, 130 (BCSC) (obiter dictum) and *Ferguson v McBee Technographics Inc* (1989), 58 Man R (2d) 119 (QB) (motion to strike out portion of affidavit concerning recording by eavesdropping after obtaining the consent by only one party to a telephone conversation).

1   (1993) 18 CCLT (2d) 288 (BCSC).

2   *Milton v Savinkoff* (1993) 18 CCLT (2d) 288 (BCSC) at 291.

'unauthorised circulation of a personal and embarrassing photograph would appear to be a paradigm breach of privacy'.[3] Osborne's view is that any waiver by the plaintiff of her right to privacy would be valid only in relation to the film developer, to whom the plaintiff would be unknown. Additionally, the context did not involve a 'delicate balance of the interests of privacy and the public's right to know';[4] rather, the photograph was shown to others to 'satisfy idle curiosity'.[5]

7.33 Secondly, *Joseph v Daniels* presents the situation of a commercial utilisation of the persona of a person who may be characterised as a non-celebrity.[6] The absence of effective identification of the plaintiff from the photograph precluded both appropriation of personality at common law as well as under the statute.[7] Nevertheless, the case does present a potential merging of the perspective of privacy and publicity.[8]

4 Civil law in Québec

7.34 The right to privacy and to one's likeness has been protected in Québec as follows:

(1) by judicial recognition of invasion of privacy being within Article 1053 of the (former) *Civil Code of Lower Canada*: '[e]very person capable of discerning right from wrong is responsible for the damage caused by his fault to another, whether by positive act, imprudence, neglect or want of skill';

(2) from 1975, by express inclusion in the Québec *Charter of Human Rights and Freedoms*; and

(3) from 1994, by express inclusion in the *Civil Code of Québec*.[9]

Recognition by the courts of the right to one's likeness

7.35 Under Québec law, a person's right to his or her likeness is infringed when the person's picture is circulated without his or her consent. This specific right was first recognised in a 1973 case[10] in which a company used a photograph of a teacher who was employed as a manual labourer during the school vacation period. The picture was used on an advertising poster that showed him bare-armed in work clothes. The teacher was humiliated and

---

3 See Osborne 'Case Comment on *Milton v Savinkoff*' (1993) 18 CCLT 292 at 295.
4 Osborne 'Case Comment on *Milton v Savinkoff*' (1993) 18 CCLT 292 at 288.
5 Osborne 'Case Comment on *Milton v Savinkoff*' (1993) 18 CCLT 292. Osborne acknowledges that the context may have been different if the photograph had been taken in a public place or if the plaintiff had been making a political statement exposing her breasts (see p 296).
6 *Joseph v Daniels* (1986), 4 BCLR (2d) 239, 11 CPR (3d) 544 (SC) involved a body builder who may have been known to the local bodybuilding community but who would not have been likely to have been known in the general community.
7 *Joseph v Daniels* (1986), 4 BCLR (2d) 239, 244–245.
8 See para **7.20**, n 15 above and para **7.60** below.
9 See generally, Potvin 'Protection Against the Use of One's Likeness in Québec Civil Law, Canadian Common Law and Constitutional Law' (1997) 11 [Can] IPJ 203 (Part I), 295 (Part II) and L Potvin, La personne et la protection de son image: Étude comparée des droits québécois, français et de la common law anglaise (Cowansville: Yvon Blais, 1991).
10 *Rebeiro v Shawinigan Chemicals (1969) Ltd* [1973] CS 389.

embarrassed by the mockery of his students. The Superior Court ruled that some persons may not enjoy having their photographs on advertising posters and that this is a matter for each person to decide. The court said: [Translation] 'A person whose photograph is published without authorisation can sue for damages'.[11]

7.36　According to this rule, the simple fact that a person's likeness has been published without that person's consent is a sufficient basis for an action in damages. However, if the context is such as to involve a legitimate interest in the public knowing of a situation, the person will probably not be able either to prevent his or her likeness from being published or to obtain financial compensation. In 1971, in the leading case of *Field v United Amusement Corporation Ltd et al*,[12] a Montreal hairdresser participating in the Woodstock rock music festival was filmed without his knowledge while undressing with his girlfriend in a place they believed to be out of view. The sequence stopped at the point when they disappeared into the high grass. The Superior Court refused to allow the hairdresser's application to stop the film from being shown in a Montreal cinema, or even to cut the sequence in which he appeared. Among its findings, the court stated that the film was a documentary of public interest that showed the behaviour of a crowd estimated at 500,000 people.

7.37　However, Glenn has commented that consent to observation by those in the vicinity cannot be extended to subsequent publication to the world at large.[13] Should a distinction therefore be made between consent to observation and consent to publication? Osborne suggests that there may be an implied consent to publication if the plaintiff is knowingly involved in an activity likely to attract attention or if the media are known to be present.[14]

Protection under the *Québec Charter*

7.38　Publishing a person's photograph without his or her consent may infringe fundamental rights enshrined in the *Québec Charter of Human Rights and Freedoms*,[15] which came into force in 1975. The principal privacy-related Articles of the *Charter* read as follows:

> 'Section 4:　Every person has a right to the safeguard of his dignity, honour and reputation.
>
> Section 5:　Every person has a right to respect for his private life.'

The right to protect one's private life comes into conflict with another right protected by the *Charter*, namely the right to freedom of expression:

> 'Section 3:　Every person is the possessor of the fundamental freedoms, including freedom of conscience, freedom of religion, freedom of opinion, freedom of expression, freedom of peaceful assembly and freedom of association.'

7.39　The *Charter* also contains a provision as to how rights and freedoms are to be exercised.

11　*Rebeiro v Shawinigan Chemicals (1969) Ltd* [1973] CS 389 at 391.
12　*Field v United Amusement Corporation Ltd* [1971] CS 283.
13　See 'Civil Responsibility – Right to Privacy in Québec – Recent Cases' (1974), 52 Can Bar Rev 302.
14　See Osborne 'Case Comment on *Milton v Savinkoff*' (1993) 18 CCLT 292 at 91 ff.
15　RSQ, 1977 c C-12, as amended by the *Act to Amend the Charter of Human Rights and Freedoms*, SQ 1982, c 61 (replacing the original statute SQ 1975, c 6).

'Section 9.1:   In exercising his fundamental freedoms and rights, a person shall maintain a proper regard for democratic values, public order and the general well-being of the citizens of Québec.'

In this respect, the scope of the freedoms and rights, and limits to their exercise, may be fixed by law.'

7.40   Moreover, the *Charter* provides for the following remedies:

'Section 49:   Any unlawful interference with any right or freedom recognised by this Charter entitles the victim to obtain the cessation of such interference and compensation for the moral or material prejudice resulting therefrom.'

In case of unlawful and intentional interference, the tribunal may, in addition, condemn the person guilty of it to exemplary damages.

7.41   Finally, in enacting section 52 of the *Charter*, the Québec legislature placed the *Charter* [Translation] 'at a higher level than other statutes'.[16] It states the following:

'No provision of any Act, even subsequent to the Charter, may derogate from sections 1 to 38, except so far as provided by those sections, unless such Act expressly states that it applies despite the Charter.'

Protection under the new *Civil Code of Québec*

7.42   The new *Civil Code of Québec*,[17] in force since 1 January 1994, expressly prohibits the unauthorised use of a person's likeness on the basis of invasion of privacy. The Legislature has thus codified the right to one's likeness recognised by previous judgments. The relevant Articles of the *Civil Code of Québec* read as follows:

'Article 35:   Every person has a right to the respect of his reputation and privacy.
No one may invade the privacy of a person without the consent of the person or his heirs unless authorised by law.

Article 36:   The following acts, in particular, may be considered as invasions of the privacy of a person:

(1)   entering or taking anything in his dwelling;

(2)   intentionally intercepting or using his private communications;

(3)   appropriating or using his image or voice while he is in private premises;

(4)   keeping his private life under observation by any means;

(5)   using his name, image, likeness or voice for a purpose other than the legitimate information of the public;

(6)   using his correspondence, manuscripts, or other personal documents.'

Article 3 of the *Civil Code of Québec* also recognises the right to privacy as a personality right:

---

16   Morel, 'La coexistence des chartes canadienne et québécoise: problèmes d'interaction' (1987), 17 RDUS 62.
17   SQ 1991, c 64.

'Every person is the holder of personality rights, such as the right to life, the right to the inviolability and integrity of his person, and the right to the respect of his name, reputation and privacy.'

These rights are inalienable.

Case law

7.43 In addition to the cases of *Rebiero* and *Field* discussed earlier,[18] the proceedings brought under the sources noted above have involved the following contexts:

(1) the use of the plaintiff's name or likeness to sell a product;[19]

(2) the publication of photographs or broadcasting of videotape that casts the plaintiff in a 'false light';[20] and

(3) the publication of a photograph that presented a factual situation that was embarrassing and in respect of which the public interest did not require publication;[1]

(4) the publication of an article in a newspaper revealing highly personal information that was true, but in respect of which the public interest did not require publication;[2] and

(5) an intrusive situation of encouraging harassing communications.[3]

The *Aubry* case

7.44 The case of *Aubry v Les Éditions Vice Versa Inc*[4] is a landmark decision. For the first time, the Supreme Court of Canada has considered the consequence of publication of a photograph taken without permission. This case arose before the 1994 *Civil Code of Québec* and it was governed by civil

---

18 See para **7.35**, nn 10–12 above and accompanying text.

19 See *Bogajewicz v Sony of Canada Ltd* (1995), 128 DLR (4th) 530 (Que SC); *Bélasky v 3164055 Canada Inc* [1986] RRA 851 (Sup Ct); and *Cohen v Queenswear International Ltd* [1989] RRA 570 (Sup Ct).

20 See *Hudson v CHLT-TV Inc* [1986] RJQ 2651 (SupCt) (the plaintiff being videotaped leaving a police van along with five other suspects of serious crimes. These other suspects were charged, but the plaintiff was not – yet the television station repeatedly broadcast the videotape); and *D'Alexis v Société de publication Merlin Ltée* (Sup Ct (Montreal), No 500-05-007199-878, Jan 10, 1995, LPJ 95-5042 (Forget J)) (privacy not violated by the publication of one photograph of the plaintiff in the company of a victim of a murder in Haiti.)

1 See *Thomas v Les Publications Photo-Police Inc* (Ct of Quebec, Longueuil, No 505-02-001116-957 July 8, 1997) (Chicoine J). The plaintiff was the wife of a man accused of sex crimes and described in the defendant newspaper as a 'sexual weirdo'. The plaintiff was photographed leaving the court with her husband. The plaintiff was identified as the accused's wife and their address was given. Substantial damages were awarded.

2 See *Valiquette v The Gazette* [1991] RJQ 1075, 8 CCLT (2d) 302 (SC), varied [1997] RJQ 30 (CA). The plaintiff was HIV positive and suffering from AIDS. He was a school teacher. The publication revealed these facts. The plaintiff's sexual orientation became public. The purpose in publishing was to reveal the fact of the illness. The Superior Court expressed the situation as 'the interests of commerce have taken precedence over the public interest and the right to privacy', ibid at 1078.

3 See *Robbins v CBC* (1957), 12 DLR (2d) 35 (Sup Ct) concerning the broadcasting by a radio station of the plaintiff's name and address and encouraging contact with him after he had complained about a program.

4 [1998] 1 SCR 591 (L'Heureux-Dubé, Gonthier, Cory, Iacobucci and Bastarache JJ, Lamer CJ and Major J dissenting, affd [1996] RJQ 2137 (Lebel and Biron JJA, Baudouin JA dissenting), aff [1991] RRA 421.

liability law and the *Québec Charter*.

7.45 A photographer shot a picture of a 17-year-old student without permission and sold it to a magazine dedicated to the arts. The young woman was depicted sitting on the steps of a building in Montreal, a public place. It was published without consent. The trial judge found the photographer and the publishing house jointly at fault. The defendants were ordered to pay $2,000 in damages to compensate her for moral prejudice (embarrassment and humiliation) since classmates had laughed at her. The trial judge based its ruling notably on the *Québec Charter*'s provisions enshrining the right to privacy. The Court of Appeal affirmed the trial judge's decision.
The Supreme Court split 5–2 to uphold the award made by the trial judge. The majority held that although the infringement of a right guaranteed by the *Québec Charter* gives rise to an action for moral and material prejudice, such an action is subject to the civil law principles of recovery. As a result the traditional elements of liability must be established, namely fault, damage and causal relation.

7.46 The Supreme Court ruled that the right to one's image is an element of the right to privacy under section 5 of the *Charter*. If the purpose of the right to privacy is to protect a sphere of individual autonomy, it must include the ability to control the use made of one's image. Therefore a publication of one's image without consent is remedial.

7.47 The Supreme Court noted exceptions to this rule based on a public right to information and more particularly the freedom of artistic expression encompassed within the right to freedom of expression protected by the *Québec Charter*.

7.48 The Supreme Court found the following factors in considering the balance of protection of privacy with freedom of expression:

(1) a public interest can be established if a person 'is engaged in a public activity or has acquired a certain notoriety';

(2) this includes artists and politicians and especially 'those whose professional success depends on public opinion';

(3) a person may be cast into the public interest by a public activity, such as 'an important trial, a major economic activity having an impact on the use of public funds, or … public safety'; and

(4) a person participating as part of a crowd (eg a sporting event or demonstration) or as a merely incidental element of scenery is deemed in public and is not protected.[5]

7.49 The Supreme Court also stipulated that damage must be sustained. Mere infringement of a right guaranteed by the *Québec Charter* is not actionable per se.[6] The majority found evidence of damage.[7] The dissenting judges did not.[8]

7.50 A significant aspect of *Aubry*, for not only the law in Québec, but, perhaps, for the whole of Canada, was the rejection by the Supreme Court of

5   Ibid at 616 and 617.
6   Ibid at 620.
7   Ibid.
8   Ibid at 608 (Lamar CJC), Major J concurring at 625.

the American principle of so-called 'sales vs subject' for balancing issues of privacy and free expression as seen below. However, the court's reference to American law was to a 'Right of Publicity' proceeding, focused not on privacy protection but on interference with a property interest.[9] This may invite some reconciliation, but nevertheless, the position is clear that a much greater weight was given by the Supreme Court to the interest in privacy or autonomy than would have been the position in the US.

7.51 Before pursuing this matter further, the Canadian developments in the context of 'publicity' rights must be considered.

C Publicity

1 Publicity rights

7.52 Publicity rights at common law in Canada, the Commonwealth and the US have been conceptualised as *proprietary* rights. In the US, the proceeding known as 'Right of Publicity' developed from the perceived inadequacy of privacy as a concept to provide for commercial or proprietary losses for usurpation of the name, image, likeness or persona of a celebrity.[10] Subsequently, the US Supreme Court, interpreting Ohio common law, affirmed the proprietary nature of Right of Publicity by categorising it as a 'discrete kind of "appropriation"' presenting objectives 'analogous to the goals of patent and copyright law' protecting 'the right of an individual to reap the reward of his endeavours'.[11] In effect, this can be seen as a discrete category of the general tort of unfair competition by misappropriation of business values.[12] Some other Commonwealth jurisdictions have, to date, focused on the development of the tort of passing off in attempting to achieve a remedy for celebrities in this context.[13] This may also have been recognised in Canada.[14] There are, however, considerable conceptual difficulties in such restructuring of the tort of passing off.

---

9 Ibid at 617– 618 with reference to *Estate of Presley v Russen*, 513 F Supp 1339 (DNJ 1981), and *Current Audio Inc v RCA Corpn* (1972) 337 NYS 2d 949 (Sup Ct 1972) (including 'literary property'), see para **7.33**, n 7 above and para **7.62** below.
10 The seminal authority is *Haelan Laboratories Inc v Topps Chewing Gum Inc* 202 F 2d 866 (2d Cir, 1953). See Howell 'The Common Law Appropriation of Personality Tort' (1986), [Can] IPJ 149, 160.
11 See *Zacchini v Scripps-Howard Broadcasting Co* 433 US 562, 572–573 and 576–577 (1977).
12 See Shipley 'Publicity Never Dies: It Just Fades Away: The Right of Publicity and Federal Preemption' (1981), 66 Cornell L Rev 673, 675. The tort of misappropriation of business values flows from *International News Service v Associated Press*, 248 US 215 (1918). See generally, J Thomas McCarthy on *Trademarks and Unfair Competition* S 10.47 et seq (4th edn, 1997).
13 See eg *Hogan v Koala Dundee Pty Ltd* (1988) 83 ALR 187 (Aust FC); *Pacific Dunlop Ltd v Hogan* (1989) 87 ALR 14 (Aust FC); and *Mirage Studios v Counter-Feat Clothing Co Ltd* (1990) 18 FSR 145 Ch. See also Howell 'Publicity Rights in the Common Law Provinces of Canada' (1998) 18 Loy of LA Ent LR 487, 499–501. However, see *Tot Toys v Mitchell* [1993] 1 NZLR 325, 363 (NZHC) noting that New Zealand law might contemplate a separate tort of appropriation of personality.
14 See *Paramount Pictures Corp v Howley* [1991] 5 OR (3d) 573, 582 (Ont GD).

7.53 The unique contribution of Canadian common law has been the recognition of a tort of Appropriation of Personality as a distinct tort not requiring the establishment of a likelihood of public deception or confusion, as is required for passing off. The new proceeding is predicated on simply a substantial 'taking' or 'misappropriation' of the value attaching to the persona of another for the purpose of marketing the usurper's goods or services. This development in 1973 in *Krouse v Chrysler Canada Ltd*[15] followed upon the tort of passing off being found inapplicable as the parties (the plaintiff football player and the defendant automobile producer) were hardly in a relationship that would cause public confusion as to an 'association' between them, particularly as the test of association prevailing at that time was the 'common field of activity' rule.[16] The case of *Krouse* might, indeed, be seen as a hybrid between passing off and misappropriation by the emphasis in one part of establishing an element of 'endorsement' by the plaintiff of the defendant's product.[17] However, as has been noted elsewhere, no requirement of public deception or confusion was sought and that therefore the 'endorsement' element might be seen as a factor in the establishing of a sufficient level of 'taking' or 'misappropriation'.[18]

7.54 Furthermore, the Ontario Court of Appeal in developing the tort of appropriation of personality expressly recognised:

(1) a tort of this nature was contemplated within Commonwealth common law, being derived from the source of all new torts, the seminal proceeding of 'the action on the case';[19]

(2) a specific comparison of the tort with 'an action for trover or conversion in its modern form';[20] and

(3) a favourable comparison of the tort with the American principle of 'Right of Publicity', although with the acknowledgement that such a proceeding had not in itself yet been recognised in Canada or England.[1]

7.55 Subsequent cases have all proceeded on a misappropriation theory.[2] Two recent cases have reinforced the proprietary nature of the interest protected by finding the publicity rights protected under the tort of appropriation of personality to be descendible and exercisable by the estate of a deceased celebrity.[3] The issues that descendibility presents have been analysed

---

15 *Krouse v Chrysler Canada Ltd* (1973), 1 OR (2d) 255, 40 DLR (3d) 15 (Ont CA).
16 *Krouse v Chrysler Canada Ltd* [1972] 2 OR 133, 25 DLR (3d) 49, 68 (at trial).
17 *Krouse* (Ct App) at 40 DLR (3d) pp 18, 19, 27 and 29, see para **7.53**, n 15.
18 This interpretation is discussed fully in Howell 'The Common Law Appropriation of Personality Tort' (1986) 2 [Can] IPJ 149, 170–172.
19 Ibid at 40 DLR (3d) 27.
20 Ibid at 40 DLR (3d) 27.
1 Ibid at 23–24, 27 and 31.
2 See *Athans v Canadian Adventure Camps Ltd* (1977), OR (2d) 425, 80 DLR (3d) 583 (Ont HC); *Racine v CJRC Radio Capitale Ltee*, (1977), 17 OR (2d) 370 (Co Ct); *Heath v Weist-Barron Sch of Television*, (1981), 34 OR (2d) 126 (HC); *Dowell v Mengen Institute* (1983) 72 CPR (2d) 238 (Ont HC) *Joseph v Daniels* (1986), 4 BCLR (2d) 239, 11 CPR (3d) 544 (SC);*Gould Estate v Stoddart Publishing Co* (1996) 30 OR (3d) 520 (GD) affd on other grounds (1998), 39 OR (3d) 545 (CA); *Shaw v Berman*, [1997] 72 CPR (3d) 9 (Ont GD); and *Horton v Tim Donut Ltd* (1997) 75 CPR (3d) 451, affd (1997), 75 CPR (3d) 467 (Ont CA).
3 See *Gould Estate v Stoddart Publishing Co* [1996] 30 OR (3d) 520 (GD) revd on other grounds and *Horton v Tim Donut Ltd* (1997) 75 CPR (3d) 451, 459–460.

elsewhere,[4] together with some now established basic elements of the proceeding.[5]

7.56 Beyond issues of descendibility, two significant situations remain problematic. The first is the potential to include non-celebrities. The second is the balance to be drawn between private autonomy and public free expression. These situations require an analysis of the relationship of privacy and publicity interests and, in Canada, the relationship of common law and civil law initiatives.

7.57 Before engaging in this, mention should be made of options to protect publicity interests through other areas of law including: the moral right of integrity in copyright,[6] registered trade mark[7] or possibly under provisions of the *Trade-marks Act* preventing persons from adopting any mark 'consisting of, or so nearly resembling as to be likely to be mistaken for … any matter that may falsely suggest a connection with any living individual',[8] or by expanded version of the tort of passing off.[9]

2   *The relationship of privacy and publicity*

7.58 The seminal theory by Warren and Brandeis in 1890[10] to utilise the concept of 'privacy' as a compendious vehicle for the miscellany of non-physical interferences with an individual's autonomy, ultimately yielded in the US to a division between privacy and publicity.[11] A similar distinction has evolved under French civil law between infringement of a purely private interest and 'droit à l'image' preventing the use of a person's likeness for commercial purposes.[12]

7.59 Such a distinction is natural and inevitable. Privacy and publicity protect different interests and values. Their interwoven relationship cannot, however, be ignored. Publicity loss is usually suffered by celebrities, but this is merely

---

4   See Howell 'Publicity Rights in the Common Law Provinces of Canada' (1998) 18 Loy of LA Ent LR 487, at 504–508.
5   See Howell 'Publicity Rights in the Common Law Provinces of Canada' (1998) 18 Loy of LA Ent LR 487, at 494–495.
6   Copyright Act, RSC 1985, c C-42, s 28.2(1)(b) when an author's work is 'used in association with a product, service, cause or institution'. See Howell, 'Character Merchandising: The Marketing Potential Attaching to a Name, Image, Persona or Copyright Work' (1991), 6 [Can] IPJ 197, at 200–203.
7   See Howell, 'Character Merchandising: The Marketing Potential Attaching to a Name, Image, Persona or Copyright Work' (1991), 6 [Can] IPJ 197, at 213–217, esp at n 46.
8   Trade-marks Act, RSC 1985, c T-13, s 9(1)(k). See *Baron Phillipe de Rothchild SA v Casa de Habana Inc* (1987), 19 CPR (3d) 114, 17 CIPR 185, 186 (Ont HC) and Carson v Reynolds (1980), 49 CPR (2d) 57 (FCTD). However, see Howell, 'Character Merchandising: The Marketing Potential Attaching to a Name, Image, Person or Copyright Work' (1991) 6 [Can] IPJ 197 at 215–216 noting the potential unconstitutionality of using this federal statutory provision as a 'statutory tort'.
9   See Howell, 'Character Merchandising: The Marketing Potential Attaching to a Name, Image, Persona or Copyright Work' (1991), 6 [Can] IPJ 197, at 206 and para **7.52**, n 13 above.
10 See Warren and Brandeis 'The Right to Privacy' (1890) 4 Harv L Rev 193.
11 See para **7.52** above.
12 See L Potvin, 'La personne et la protection de son image: Étude comparée des droits québécois, français et de la common law anglaise', para **7.34**, n 69, and J Ravanas, 'La protection des personnes contre la réalisation et la publication de leur image, thèse de l'université d'Aix-Marseille III, preface by Pierre Kayser, Paris, LGDG 1978.

a reflection of greater commercial or marketing value. Celebrities can also suffer privacy loss in the nature of anguish and humiliation. Likewise, non-celebrities can suffer publicity loss when their image is used for commercial purposes. Some measure of value or worth is implicit in the very desire of a person to 'take' or exploit the persona of another.

If, therefore, the primary distinctions between privacy and publicity concern:

(1) the nature or type of injury that is sustained; and

(2) how the interest may be utilised, including the conceptual ability to licence, assign or provide for inheritance;

all that needs to be decided is whether to encapsulate both interests within one proceeding (howsoever it may be described), or to retain two separate proceedings.

7.60 In Canadian common law the tort of appropriation of personality has been concerned mainly with celebrities in publicity contexts, but it has also been utilised with respect to non-celebrities in a privacy context. The conceptual threshold, a substantial 'taking' without consent can encompass both.[13] Care must, however, be taken to ensure that the tort is not equated with the tort of passing off for which evidence of business goodwill or reputation as well as public confusion as to source, are essential elements. In Québec, proceedings have concerned principally non-celebrities and privacy injury, but have included commercial usage[14] and at least one instance of a celebrity plaintiff.[15] The Québec *Charter of Human Rights and Freedoms*, section 4 ('Every person has a right to the safeguard of his dignity, honour and reputation') and the *Civil Code of Québec*, section 4 ('Every person has a right to the safeguard of his dignity, honour or reputation') are, it is suggested, sufficiently encompassing of both privacy and publicity interests. This may also be the position with the statutory privacy torts in the four common law provinces with these provisions, particularly British Columbia with the separate statutory tort, actionable without proof of damage, for the unauthorised use of a person's name or portrait for commercial purposes.[16]

7.61 However, even if one proceeding is sufficiently wide to include both privacy and publicity interests, each will still require to be a separate head or category within the proceeding. For example, issues of assignment, licence or inheritance may be determined differently according to whether the interest is one of privacy or one of publicity.

7.62 The public interest in free expression may present a further difference between interests in privacy and publicity, although in Canada any difference in application may be minimal. In the US the 'well-known' qualified privilege to report matters concerning 'public officials' and 'public figures' has extended

---

13 See paras **7.20**, n 15 and **7.33** above and Howell, 'Publicity Rights in the Common Law Provinces of Canada' (1998), 18 Loy of LA Ent LR 487, 496–497. See also Vaver, 'What's Mine Is Not Yours: Commercial Appropriation of Personality Under the Privacy Acts of British Columbia, Manitoba and Sasketchewan' (1981), 15 UBCLR 241, 256–261 providing a theory of a 'right to control' use by another of one's personality.

14 See *Rebeiro v Shawinigan Chemicals (1969) Ltd* [1973] CS 389 and *Bogajewicz v Sony of Canada Ltd* (1995) 128 DLR (4th) 530 (Que SC).

15 *Bogajewicz v Sony of Canada Ltd* (1995) 128 DLR (4th) 530 (Que SC).

16 *Privacy Act* RSBC 1996 c 373, s 3.

to privacy contexts,[17] but was rejected with respect to publicity.[18] The public interest in publication was, therefore, seen to be of greater weight in a privacy context. In publicity proceedings a distinction between promoting sales and reporting news is applied.[19] This so-called 'sales vs subject' principle has been applied in Canada in *publicity* contexts,[20] but was rejected by the Supreme Court of Canada in *Aubry*, a case involving strictly *privacy*.[1] The use in Canada of any defence of qualified privilege will not necessarily follow the position in the US.[2] Accordingly, in Canada, a much higher level of autonomy has been applied in a privacy context. In a publicity context, given that the level of autonomy is already high in the US, this is also likely to be so in Canada. However, it is problematic whether a 'sales vs subject' approach will continue to apply in common law publicity after *Aubry*.

D Conclusion

7.63 Privacy is a broad concept. At a federal level, in Canada privacy themes can be identified in the interpretation of key provisions in the *Canadian Charter of Rights and Freedoms* and in provisions of the Criminal Code. Québec is the only province with a (non-entrenched) *Charter of Human Rights and Freedoms* that expressly protects privacy. The civil law in Québec similarly protects privacy. Four common law provinces have enacted statutory privacy torts. Canadian common law includes a distinct tort of appropriation of personality. It has to date been invoked primarily in a publicity context, but can also encompass privacy interests. It presents a unique initiative in Commonwealth common law development and one that has been urged in the UK.[3] Hopefully, the attempt to cover in this chapter various aspects of privacy law in a systematic fashion will offer useful insight to readers and particularly those who are not familiar with the Canadian legal system. Moreover, the Supreme Court of Canada in *Aubry* has taken the opportunity to articulate policy criteria to better interpret the concept of privacy in Québec civil law. This interpretation and the policy choices may well be influential in interpreting statutory and common law provisions throughout the rest of Canada. This could provide the potential of a unified policy with respect to balancing private interests in individual autonomy with public interests in disclosure of elements of private life.

17 See eg *Time Inc v Hill* 385 US 374 (1967). The rule is derived from *New York Times Co v Sullivan* 376 US 254 (1964).
18 See *Zacchini v Scripps-Howard Broadcasting Co* 433 US 562, 571–578 (1977).
19 See eg *Groucho Marx Productions, Inc v Day & Night Co* 523 F Supp 485, 492 and *Estate of Presley v Russen* 513 F Supp 1339, 1356 (DNJ 1981).
20 See *Gould Estate v Stoddart Pub Co* (1996), 30 OR (3d) 520, 526–527 (GD) affd on other grounds (1998), 39 OR (3d) 545 (CA); *Shaw v Berman* [1997] 72 CPR (3d) 9, 18 (Ont GD) and *Horton v Tim Donut Ltd* (1997) 75 CPR (3d) 451 affd (1997), 75 CPR (3d) 467 (Ont CA).
1 *Aubry v Les Éditions Vice Versa Inc*,discussed in para **7.50** above.
2 See *Hill v Church of Scientology* [1995] 2 SCR 1130 at 1180–1188 where the Supreme Court of Canada rejected application of the principle in a defamation proceeding. See R Martin, *Media Law*, Irwin Law, 1997 at pp 154–158.
3 See Frazer 'Appropriation of Personality – A New Tort' (1983) 99 LQR 281 (recommending a statutory tort) and Hilton and Goldson 'The New Tort of Appropriation of Personality: Protecting Bob Marley's Face' [1996] 55 CLJ 56; see also Nest, 'From "ABBA" to Gould: A Closer Look at the Development of Personality Rights in Canada' (1999) 5 Appeal 12–17 and JG Fleming, *The Law of Torts*, (9th ed) (Sydney, Aust LBC Inf Serv 1998) at 787. However, contrast Flagg, 'Star Crazy: Keeping the Right of Publicity Out of Canadian Law' (1999) 13 [Can] IPJ 179.

8   DENMARK

Peter Blume

A Privacy

1 *Constitutional right*

8.01   In the Danish Constitution of 5 June 1953 there is no general rule on the protection of privacy corresponding to Article 8 of the European Convention on Human Rights. In section 72 some form of protection is stated. According to this rule:

> 'The dwelling shall be inviolable. House searching, seizure, and examination of letters and other papers as well as any breach of the secrecy which is to be observed in postal, telegraph, and telephone matters shall take place only under a judicial order unless particular exception is warranted by Statute.'

The rule concerns only the relationship between State and citizen. Regardless of its impressive beginning it is mainly a procedural rule which has little bearing on the actual level of protection in Danish law.

2 *Other legislative provisions*

8.02   The basic statutory regulation is found primarily in chapter 27 of the Penal Code.[1] The code originally[2] came into force on 1 January 1933. Other important statutes are the Private Registers Act,[3] which was amended in 1991, and to some extent the Public Authorities Registers Act.[4] Both of these Acts originally came into force on 1 January 1979.

As is also the case with other rules mentioned below, these statutory rules apply to all persons as long that they are within Danish jurisdiction. Foreign citizens are accordingly covered. By way of introduction it should be observed that the Penal Code applies to all situations and in particular is relevant with respect to surveillance issues while the specific aim of the Registers Acts is to protect personal information, mainly but not exclusively in computerised form. There is a fairly long tradition for such data protection

---

1   Consolidated no 648 of 12.8.1997.
2   Act no 126 of 15.4.1930.
3   Consolidated no 622 of 2.10.1987.
4   Consolidated no 654 of 20.9.1991.

but although informational privacy is extremely important today the main emphasis is placed on more traditional forms of privacy in the following paragraphs.

3   Films and photographs

8.03   Different forms of filming can be an infringement of privacy. According to section 264a of the Penal Code,[5] it is an offence to film on private property. The rule is applicable when the area is not freely accessible, implying that it is in some way secluded. A car, for example, is private property. The rule applies to all kinds of filming and the location where the filming takes place is of no importance. This can be on or outside or over the property. The equipment used – telephoto lenses etc – is also of no importance. Whether filming takes place covertly or openly is likewise of no consequence. The rule furthermore includes use of binoculars to survey private property.

8.04   As is the case with other provisions in the Penal Code below, the main rule is that the private victim must bring the charge against the offender. Charges can be brought by the public prosecution on request. Violations can result in fines or imprisonment up to six months.

8.05   Filming outside private property can also invade privacy and be punishable according to section 264d of the Penal Code. This rule applies to filming in areas which are freely accessible in situations where the pictures disclose information etc that is private or clearly has no public interest. As above the methods applied have no relevance for the assessment. The nature of the pictures taken is decisive. Examples can be photographs of traffic victims or children who are forcibly removed from their home. Another example is prostitutes at work.[6] It should be mentioned that there are no special rules with respect to public figures and in principle they have the same sphere of privacy as other citizens. In practice this rule is used with caution as it must be balanced against considerations of freedom of information. Violations can result in fines or imprisonment for up to six months.

8.06   Act 278 of 9 June 1982 forbids private persons from surveying public places using television or video. Such surveillance of pedestrian streets etc cannot take place, although this is permissible on private property, including shops. There are no concrete cases with respect to this Act, but there is an increased tendency for public authorities to use surveillance not least in relation to traffic control.

8.07   According to the Private Registers Act, sections 3(2) and 4(1) it is not permissible to store or disclose photographs of shoplifters in order to prevent such crime. However, the individual shop may keep such a photograph as long as criminal proceedings have not ended. This is a firm rule stated in the decisions of the Data Protection Agency.

---

5   Inserted in the code by Act no 89 of 29 March 1972.
6   As stated by the High Court in (1969) Ugeskrift for Retsvæsen, p 233 (the Danish law report).

4   Postal and telephone secrecy

8.08   Postal secrecy is protected under section 263 of the Penal Code. All forms of traditional post are protected against interception and intrusion. This covers all methods used to acquire knowledge of the contents. In this respect the rule applies to both closed and open mail. If a letter is thrown out with the rubbish it is still protected as it will be if it has been torn to pieces by the owner. To read it after sifting through rubbish is an offence. It must be assumed that the rule also applies to e-mail and subsection 2 specifically applies to information (or programs) in data transmissions. Violation of section 263 is punishable by fines or imprisonment for up to six months.

8.09   Section 263 also applies to telephone calls and furthermore to recording of conversations in situations where the person has no lawful access, eg closed meetings. The rule applies regardless of whether the recording takes place openly or covertly. In a recent case,[7] a person who had placed a radio transmitter and a microphone in the apartment of his former girlfriend was sentenced to 14 days' suspended imprisonment and a fine of 2,000 D kr.

8.10   According to section 7f of the Private Registers Act, corporations are not allowed to register automatically the telephone numbers dialled from the corporation. The purpose of this rule is to protect the privacy of employees.

5   Stalking

8.11   Stalking or pursuing a person can also be a criminal offence according to section 265. This, however, presupposes that the stalker has been previously warned by the police. The duration of such a warning is five years. Violation of this rule is punishable by fines or imprisonment for up to six months. In one decision,[8] a warned person was fined 1,000 D kr because he, through the Danish State radio, had sent greetings to his former girlfriend.

8.12   Besides the decisions mentioned above there have not recently been published cases concerning these forms of invasions into privacy. This also includes civil cases but in general it should be emphasised that the level of damages in such cases is fairly low and this, among other things, is the reason for the low number of lawsuits.

---

7   (1997) Ugeskrift for Retsvæsen, p 198.
8   Printed in (1996) Ugeskrift for Retsvæsen, p 1087.

B Publicity

1 Use of name and biography

8.13 The legal regulation of the use of names and biography is minimal in Danish law. Act no 193 of 29 April 1981 on names contains the rules on how a person acquires a name and according to section 7 there are certain surnames that are protected indicating that other people cannot freely use these names which are placed on a list maintained by the Ministry of Justice. This rule and the Act in general applies to all persons within Danish jurisdiction. This is the only general protection of names.

8.14 Use of another person's name can be a violation of the law, but this depends on the actual situation. If the name is used to commit fraud it will be *this* act and not the name misuse in itself which is punishable.

8.15 The question of whether trade mark protection can be obtained is regulated by Act no 162,[9] which originally came into force on 1 January 1992. According to section 2 (1, no 1) this is possible but it is only commercial use of the name which is protected (section 4). Another person who has the same name can still use the name commercially provided that this is done fairly (section 5).

8.16 There are no rules that protect biographies. Once again it will depend on the actual situation whether a violation of some rule has included such misuse. There have been no calls for a regulation in Danish law on publicity and it is not likely that such rules will be introduced.

C Personality

1 Personality rights

8.17 In general there is no specific statutory protection of a person's personality in Danish law. With respect to public figures, where the problem is relevant the only rules are found in the Ethical Code of the press. The Code, based on section 34 of Act no 348[10] on media responsibility, is binding for the mass media. According to the Code, the personality must not be used in such a way that the person is identified with an idea, cause etc, which is against his beliefs. It is a vague rule and there is no advisory practice with respect to its use. In general freedom of information is given predominance and there is in particular a long tradition of using the resemblance of people in cartoons etc.

8.18 With respect to advertising there are special rules on radio/television in Statutory Instrument no 491.[11] Usage of personality can take place but the integrity of the person must be respected. There are no advisory cases as to the interpretation of these rules.

---

9 Of 21 February 1997 (consolidated).
10 Of 6 June 1991.
11 Of 11 June 1997.

8.19   Usage of public figures in advertising is, however, an increasing problem. In recent years there have been several incidents where such usage has occurred without the consent of the person in question. These cases have been settled out of court and the level of damages is unknown. However, compared to other countries it is probably fairly low.

9 EIRE (REPUBLIC OF IRELAND)

Don McAleese

A Privacy

9.01 There is no specific legal code in Irish law which governs the protection of privacy per se. Instead what protection does exist, exists as a result of a number of legal safeguards which have evolved from three different sources, namely, the Constitution, legislation and the common law. The level of protection afforded by each will be examined individually.

9.02 The most extensive review to date of the extent to which privacy is protected under Irish law has been by the Irish Law Reform Commission in the Consultation Paper they published on 'Privacy: Surveillance and the Interception of Communications'.[1] Although the Consultation Paper examines privacy in the context of surveillance and communications, it also examines the extent to which privacy is protected generally under Irish law. As a follow up to the Consultation Paper the Law Reform Commission recently published its Report on 'Privacy: Surveillance and Interception of Communications',[2] the recommendations of which are dealt with below.

1 The Constitution

9.03 The 1937 Constitution of Ireland does not explicitly recognise a right to privacy, however the Irish Supreme Court has held[3] that the right to privacy is an 'unenumerated right' and is protected under Article 40.3.1 of the Constitution. This is the Article that states:

> '...the State guarantees in its laws to respect, and, as far as practicable, by its laws to defend and vindicate the personal rights of the citizen.'

9.04 Aside from the protection afforded under Article 40.3.1 of the Constitution, the courts have recognised that there are other specific elements of privacy which are protected by the Constitution:

> '...there is a guarantee of privacy in voting under Article 16, s 1, sub-s 4, the secret ballot; a limited right of privacy given to certain litigants

---

1 Published 1996.
2 LRC 57-1998, 30 July 1998.
3 *McGee v Ireland* [1974] IR 284.

under laws made under Article 34; the limited freedom from arrest and detention under Article 40, s 4; the inviolability of the dwelling of every citizen under Article 40, s 5; the rights of citizens to express freely their convictions and opinions, to assemble peaceably and without arms, and to form associations and unions – all conferred by Article 40, s 6, sub-s 1; the rights of the family under Article 41; the rights of the family with regard to education under Article 42; the right of private property under Article 43; freedom of conscience and the freedom of expression and practice of religion under Article 44. All these matters may properly be described as different facets of the right to privacy ...'[4]

9.05 Notwithstanding the fact that privacy has been explicitly recognised as an unenumerated constitutional right since 1974, subsequent case law has shown that it is only in rare cases that the Irish courts will recognise a specific breach of this constitutional right. Possibly the best known case where a breach has been recognised is *Kennedy & Arnold v Ireland*.[5] The first two plaintiffs were political journalists and their telephones were tapped pursuant to a warrant issued by the Minister for Justice under section 56 of the Post Office Act, 1908. While the Minister did have legislative authority to make such an order in a given case, it was accepted by him that he had made the order without justification. Hamilton P in the High Court held that the right to hold private telephone conversations without deliberate and unjustified intrusion by the State was an aspect of the constitutional right to privacy and awarded the plaintiffs damages accordingly.[6]

9.06 Another noted case was the decision by the Irish Supreme Court in *Norris v The Attorney General*.[7] The applicant was a well known public figure, a noted Joycean scholar and a prominent gay rights campaigner. He challenged the constitutionality of sections 61 and 62 of the Offences Against the Person Act 1861 which had the effect of criminalising homosexual acts by men. He claimed, inter alia, that these sections infringed his constitutional right to privacy in that they were an unwarranted intrusion into his private life. The Supreme Court held that, having regard to the Christian nature of the State, the immorality of the deliberate practice of homosexuality, the damage that such practice causes to the health of citizens and the potential harm to the institution of marriage, there was no inconsistency between the terms of any of the impugned sections and the provisions of the Constitution and that, therefore, the right to privacy claimed by the plaintiff could not prevail against the sanctions imposed by those sections.[8]

9.07 The *Norris* case is an example of the general approach adopted by the Irish Courts when dealing with allegations of a breach of privacy – they balance the right to privacy against any other relevant constitutional right in making a determination on whether there has been a breach of the right or not.

4   *Per* McCarthy J in *Norris v The Attorney General* [1984] IR 36.
5   [1987] IR 587.
6   The two journalists each received £20,000 whilst the wife of one of the journalists, who was also a plaintiff, was awarded £10,000.
7   Op cit fn 3.
8   This controversial decision was appealed to the European Court of Human Rights, [1989] 13 EHRR 186, who ruled that the provisions of the 1861 Act was contrary to the European Declaration on Human Rights and as a result homosexual acts were decriminalised by s 2 of the Criminal Law (Sexual Offences) Act 1993.

9.08 The recent decision of the High Court in *Maguire v Drury*[9] is further evidence of the reluctance of the Irish judiciary to expand the constitutional right to privacy. In this case a mother sought to prevent a number of Irish national newspapers from reporting the events surrounding her marriage break-up, alleging that publication of the story would amount to a breach of her constitutional right to privacy. The newspapers were ready to publish accusations by her husband that she was having an affair with a priest. O'Hanlon J refused to grant an injunction preventing publication on the grounds that to do so would be an infringement of the right of the freedom of expression. He acknowledged that publication of the article would cause distress both to her and her children but still felt unable to grant the relief sought.

9.09 Finally, since the decision in *State (Nicolaou) v An Bord Uchtála*[10] it has been possible for a non-citizen to invoke a constitutional guarantee before the Irish courts. It is unclear whether non-citizens are afforded the same degree of constitutional protection as citizens, however Hamilton P in the *Kennedy & Arnold* case indicated that the right to privacy was also available to non-citizens.

2 *Legislation*

9.10 The Law Reform Commission in its Consultation Paper[11] identified a diverse range of statutes addressing a wide variety of issues which either create offences or lay down provisions, the breach of which may have the effect of directly or indirectly creating a privacy type protection. These include the following:

(1) Section 8(1) of the Railways (Conveyance of Mails) Act 1838 as amended by the Postal and Telecommunications Services Act 1983 empowers An Post (the Irish national postal service) to make reasonable regulations for the security of mails conveyed by mail, the breach of which is an offence. No such regulations have been made.

(2) Section 37 of the Malicious Damage Act 1861 as amended by the Criminal Damage Act 1991 makes it an offence to damage or interfere with the sending of communications by way of telegraphy. This offence covers telephone tapping.

(3) Section 45 of the Telegraphy Act 1863 as amended by the Postal and Telecommunications Services Act 1983 makes it an offence for an employee of the Irish national telecommunication company (Bord Telecom Eireann) to wilfully or negligently omit to transmit or deliver a message.

(4) Section 7(2) of the Conspiracy and Protection of Property Act 1875 makes it an offence to persistently follow a person about from place to place. Section 7(4) of the Act makes it an offence to watch and beset the house or other place where a person resides, works or carries on business. An offence is only committed if the accused acts wrongfully

---

9 [1995] 1 ILRM 108.
10 [1966] IR 567.
11 The Law Reform Commission Consultation Paper on 'Privacy: Surveillance and the Interception of Communications'.

and without lawful authority with a view to compelling the other person from abstaining or doing any act which that person has a legal right to do or abstain from doing.

(5) Section 11 of the Post Office (Protection) Act 1884 as amended by the Postal and Telecommunications Services Act 1983 makes it an offence for an employee of a telegraph company to divulge the purport of a telegram.

(6) Section 51 of the Post Office Act 1908 as amended by the Postal and Telecommunications Services Act 1983 makes it an offence for a person to unlawfully open a mailbag or postal package.

(7) The Wireless Telegraphy Acts 1957 – 1988 contain various offences relating to the improper divulging of communications sent by way of wireless telegraphy.

(8) The Postal and Telecommunications Services Act 1983 creates a number of offences involving interference with mail and postal packages and interception of telecommunication messages. Section 98 of the 1983 Act as amended by section 13 of the Interception of Postal Packets and Telecommunications Messages (Regulation) Act 1993 makes it an offence for a third party to record any telephone conversation or to disclose the existence, substance or purport of any such recorded message. It is not however an offence to record a telephone conversation if either the person making the telephone call *or* the person receiving the call consent to its recording.

(9) Section 5 of the Criminal Damage Act 1991 makes it an offence to gain access to data through the means of a computer without authorisation. A person operating a computer in the State may be convicted for accessing data kept both inside and outside the State, whereas a person who operates the computer outside the State can only be convicted for accessing data kept inside the State.

(j) Section 10 of the Non-Fatal Offences Against the Person Act 1997 makes it an offence for any person, without lawful authority or reasonable excuse, by any means including by use of the telephone to harass another by persistently following, watching, pestering, besetting or communicating with him or her.

9.11 The Law Reform Commission also identified legislation in the broadcasting area which imposes privacy obligations.[12] Specifically, section 18(1B) of the Broadcasting Authority Act 1960 as substituted by section 3 of the Broadcasting Authority (Amendment) Act 1976 provides that the Irish national broadcaster (RTE) shall not, in its programmes and in the means employed to make such programmes, unreasonably encroach on the privacy of the individual. Similarly, with respect to independent broadcasting, sections 9(1)(E) and 18(1) of the Radio and Television Act 1988 require every sound broadcasting contractor and television programme service contractor to ensure that in programmes broadcast by them, and in the means employed to make such programmes, the privacy of any individual is not unreasonably encroached upon.

---

12 Op cit, p 173.

9.12   The Law Reform Commission also points out that in contrast to broadcasting, the print media are not subject to specific statutory regulation, but rather are governed by the general law of the State.[13] The National Union of Journalists produces a Code of Conduct for its members, and the Code has been accepted by many of the Irish national newspapers as part of a House Agreement with the Union. The Code lays down certain rules relating to the means by which information, photographs and illustrations may be obtained, and the obligations of journalists with regard to intrusion into private grief and distress.

3   The Data Protection Act 1988

9.13   This Act regulates the collection, processing, keeping, use and disclosure of personal data that is processed automatically. The Act ratifies the 1986 Council of Europe 'Convention for the Protection of Individuals with regard to the Automatic Processing of Personal Data'. The Act establishes a number of 'data protection principles' which a 'data controller' is obliged to adhere to. The Act also imposes a duty of care on both data controllers and 'data processors' in regard to the collection or use of 'personal data' or information owed by them to 'data subjects'. The Act establishes the Office of the Data Protection Commissioner who is responsible for the registration and control of data controllers and data processors.

9.14   The way the Act protects the privacy of individuals is by imposing restrictions on data controllers and data processors as regards their dealings with information relating to individuals. The Data Protection Commissioner is empowered by the Act to take action against data controllers and/or data processors who are in contravention of the Act. It should however be noted that the Act does not apply to information which is held or processed manually whether by card indexes, ledger files or otherwise, though the EU Directive on Data Protection, which member states of the EU are obliged to bring into force by the 24 October 1998, does deal with non-automatic processing.

4   The Freedom of Information Act 1997

9.15   The main purpose of this Act is to allow members of the public to have a right of access to records held by public bodies. Balanced against this aspiration of transparency is a correlative protection of privacy. The preamble to the Act makes it clear that the right of access to records is subject to the right to privacy:

> 'An Act to enable members of the public to obtain access to the greatest possible extent consistent with the public interest and the right to privacy'.

9.16   Section 7 of the Act entitles people to apply to a public body for access to records kept by that public body. This general entitlement to access records is, however, subject to the exemptions contained in Part III

---

13 Op cit, p 175.

of the Act. The public body shall refuse to grant access to records on the grounds that, inter alia, the information is confidential (section 26) or is personal information (section 28). 'Personal information' is defined as:

'....information about an identifiable individual that—

(1) would in the ordinary course of events, be known only to the individual or members of the family, or friends, of the individual, or

(2) is held by a public body on the understanding that it would be treated as confidential,

and without prejudice to the generality of the foregoing includes—

(1) information relating to the educational, medical, psychiatric or psychological history of the individual,

(2) information relating to the financial affairs of the individual,

(3) information relating to the employment or employment history of the individual,

(4) information relating to the individual in a record falling within *section 6(6)(a)* [types of personnel records held by public bodies],

(5) information relating to the criminal history of the individual,

(6) information relating to the religion, age, sexual orientation or marital status of the individual,

(7) a number, letter, symbol, word, mark or other thing assigned to the individual by a public body for the purposes of the identification or any mark or other thing used for that purpose,

(8) information relating to the entitlements of the individual under the Social Welfare Acts as a beneficiary .... or required for the purpose of establishing whether the individual, being a claimant .... is such a beneficiary,

(9) information required for the purpose of assessing the liability of the individual in respect of a tax or duty or other payment owed or payable to the State or a health board or other public body or for the purpose of collecting an amount due to the individual in respect of such a tax or duty or other payment,

(10) the name of the person where it appears with other personal information relating to the individual or where the disclosure of the name would, or would be likely to, establish that any personal information held by the public body relates to that individual,

(11) information relating to the property of the individual (including the nature of the individual's title to the property), and

(12) the views or opinions of another person about the individual but does not include —

I in a case where the individual holds or held office as a director or occupies or occupied a position as a member of staff, of a public body, the name of the individual or information relating to the office or position or its functions or the terms upon and subject to which the individual holds or held that office or occupies or occupied that position or anything written or recorded in any form by the individual in the course of and for the purpose of performance of the functions aforesaid,

II in a case where the individual is or was providing a service for a public body under a contract for services with the body, the name of the individual or information relating to the service or the terms of the contract or anything written or recorded in any form by the individual in the ordinary course of and for the purposes of the provision of services, or

III the views or opinions of the individual in relation to a public body, the staff of a public body or the business or the performance of the functions of a public body.'

9.17   This very detailed definition of personal information operates so as to protect the information privacy[14] of an individual in light of the new entitlement to access publicly-held records. So while the Freedom of Information Act's principal aim is to allow for more access to publicly-held information it also provides a minimum level of privacy protection.

5   Common law

9.18   There is uncertainty as to whether there exists a general right to privacy at common law in Ireland. There is no express cause of action for breach of privacy, per se, though the courts have not ruled out the possibility that one may exist.[15] Also, it should be noted, that decisions of courts from other common law jurisdictions such as England, Australia or Canada, whilst not binding on an Irish Court can be cited with persuasion in litigation before Irish courts. This would not preclude the citing in an Irish court of decisions of other common law jurisdictions on privacy-related issues.

9.19   Despite the fact that there appears to be no general right to privacy under Irish law, one can look to other branches of the law such as tort and equity which can have the effect of protecting the privacy of individuals in given circumstances.

Trespass to land

9.20   The common law tort of trespass to land[16] operates so as to provide people who suffer a physical intrusion upon their land a cause of action. This may be of relevance in situations where a photographer enters upon another's land to take photographs. There is no requirement to show damage or loss as a result of the intrusion; the mere entering upon another's land without permission is sufficient to give rise to a cause of action. The interest protected by trespass is not privacy, but rather a person's possession in land,

---

14 'Information Privacy' was one of the three aspects of privacy identified by the Canadian Department of Justice in their 1972 study 'Privacy and Computers'. The other two aspects are territorial privacy and privacy of the person.
15 *Desmond and Dedeir v Glackin* (25 February 1992, unreported), HC.
16 See generally Chapter 23, McMahon and Binchy, *Irish Law of Torts* (2nd Edn).

so the tort will not be effective in combating surveillance conducted off the person's land.

9.21 It can be argued that the use of a highway outside a person's land (that part of the highway being the property of the landowner) for taking photographs of that land does amount to trespass.[17] The issue of whether aerial photography may amount to trespass has not yet been addressed by the Irish courts, though the English case of *Bernstein of Leigh (Baron) v Skyviews & General Ltd*[18] which held that, in general, aerial photography did not amount to trespass, would be of persuasive authority if argued before an Irish court.

Private nuisance

9.22 In order to sue in private nuisance one must establish that there has been an unreasonable and substantial interference with the enjoyment of land. In order to succeed in this tort one must have an interest in the land which is subject to the alleged nuisance. Unlike trespass to land, however, the tort is not actionable per se and damage must generally be established.

9.23 There is potential to use this tort so as to combat the situation where premises are besieged by photographers and reporters and indeed the English case of *Hubbard v Pitt*[19] held that the watching and besetting of a premises could amount to a private nuisance. As the Irish and English law of nuisance are substantially similar, the case could be of persuasive authority in this jurisdiction.

Trespass to the person

9.24 The tort of trespass to the person, which principally involves assault and battery, may operate so as to protect persons from breaches of privacy. If an act of surveillance results in a direct injury to the person that person may have a cause of action.

9.25 Of particular relevance to protection of privacy is the extension of the concept of trespass to the person to include a right of recovery where a person has suffered emotional suffering owing to intentional or negligent acts of another. This aspect of the tort is as yet undeveloped in Ireland, though there have been developments in the US. It is, in theory at least, open to an Irish court to hold that where a person has been followed or been subject to over-exuberant surveillance which results in them suffering emotional stress, that such behaviour amounts to a trespass to the person.

Trespass to goods

9.26 Again the tort of trespass to goods may provide an incidental protection for the privacy of an individual. The tort involves the wrongful interference with another person's chattels. One can see it being of potential use in cases of phone tapping if the tapping involves physical interference with a phone line. However, the tort will only be of use where the plaintiff owns the phone line, and in most cases the phone company rather than the individual owns the phone line. The tort may be of similar use in cases

---

17 *Hickman v Maisey* [1900] 1 QB 752.
18 [1978] 1 QB 479.
19 [1976] 1 QB 142.

where a bugging device has been placed in a person's telephone receiver without that person's consent.

Defamation

9.27   The fact that a statement is true is invariably a good defence to a claim of defamation and so it is hard to see how an action for defamation could be extended to encompass a breach of privacy. If, however, personal information or photographs, which are acquired by surveillance or without the consent of an individual, are doctored in such away as to damage the reputation of the individual, an action in defamation may succeed.

9.28   The Irish courts are presently of the view that a breach of privacy per se does not amount to libel as the countervailing right of freedom of expression cannot be overridden on grounds of privacy alone. The fact that the breach of privacy may give rise to considerable stress, even when children are involved, will not in itself be sufficient to prevent the publication of the offending piece.[20]

Malicious falsehood

9.29   The tort of malicious falsehood may also be used to prevent the publication of personal information; the requirements necessary to establish the tort are that the defendant maliciously published false words about the plaintiff and that special damage followed the publication which was the direct and natural result of the publication.[1] Again this doctrine falls well short of a general privacy protection.

The doctrine of confidentiality

9.30   An action for breach of confidence is a civil remedy which protects against the disclosure or use of information which is not publicly known and which is entrusted to a person in circumstances which imposes an obligation on that person not to disclose the information without the authority of the person who entrusted them with the information. The main distinction between the concepts of confidence and privacy is that a right of action for breach of confidence arises primarily due to the nature of the relationship between the parties involved whereas a right of action for a breach of privacy arises due to the nature of the information concerned.[2]

9.31   While there have been a number of decisions in Ireland on the doctrine of confidentiality[3] there has been little in-depth analysis of the doctrine as it applies in the context of privacy.

Copyright

9.32   Under Irish law, copyright subsists in original literary, dramatic, musical and artistic works as well as in sound recordings, cinematographic

---

20 *Maguire v Drury* [1995] 1 ILRM 108, where O'Hanlon J approved of the corresponding English decision in *R v Central Independent Television plc* (9 February 1994, unreported), CA.

1   *Kaye v Robertson* [1991] FSR 62.

2   The Law Commission for England and Wales' Report on Breach of Confidence.

3   *Attorney General for England and Wales v Brandon Book Publishers* [1987] ILRM 135 and *House of Spring Gardens Ltd v Point Blank Ltd* [1984] IR611.

films and broadcasts.[4] To the extent that any of these contain personal information, it is possible that copyright law may afford protection of privacy. There is, however, one considerable limitation to copyright being used to protect privacy. A copyright infringement is only actionable at the suit of the copyright owner. Therefore, where there has been a recording of a telephone conversation, or an unwanted photograph taken, the copyright in such works will belong to the person who makes the recording or takes the photograph and not the individual who is subject of the recording or the photograph.

9.34 This situation however may change. A working draft of the Copyright and Related Rights Bill 1998 includes a provision, section 111, in Chapter (16) which deals with moral rights. The section entitled 'Right to Privacy in Photograph and Films' provides:

'... a person who, for private and domestic purposes, commissions the taking of a photograph or the making of a film has, where copyright subsists in the resulting work, the right not to have the work or copies of the work made available to the public.'

9.35 Subsection (2) of this section goes on to provide:

'... the act of making available to the public, or authorising the making available to the public, of the work or copies of the work without the authority of the commissioner of the work infringes the right conferred by Subsection (1).'

9.36 Subsection (3) provides that this new privacy right will not be infringed by acts which under other sections of the Bill would not infringe the copyright in the work. These include acts done in reliance on registration of design (section 73); advertisement of sale of artistic work (section 89); making of subsequent works by same artist (section 90); photographs of television broadcasts or cable programmes (section 96) and exceptions to the integrity right (section 107).

6   Conclusions

9.37 There is no comprehensive protection of privacy under Irish law. Apart from these rare cases where the courts will recognise a constitutional right to privacy, a plaintiff must look to other areas of the law for assistance in the protection of their privacy interests. From a plaintiff's point of view these piecemeal provisions are an inadequate means of protecting privacy. Notwithstanding, it still remains open for the Irish Supreme Court to impose a broader right to privacy founded both on the Constitution and common law.

9.38 The Law Reform Commission has put forward a number of proposals for reform of privacy laws in Ireland.[5] They can be summarised in the following paragraphs.

---

4   See the Copyright Act 1963.
5   Chapters 7 – 10, The Law Reform Commission Report on 'Privacy: Surveillance and the Interception of Communications', LRC 57-1998.

The creation of a civil liability for privacy-invasive surveillance and harassment

9.39 As regards civil liability, the Law Reform Commission has proposed the creation of the tort of privacy-invasive surveillance and a tort of harassment. Because of its limited remit, the Commission does not recommend the creation of a general privacy tort, but rather restricts it to the protection of the right of privacy against the threat proposed by surveillance. It recommends that the new tort should protect a 'reasonable expectation' of privacy. The court in a given case will have to weigh up the various factors in deciding whether the tort has been committed. The Commission states that the ordinary and natural incidences of everyday life, such as being photographed by a tourist must be tolerated. The Commission wants to keep the definition of surveillance open-ended so as to cover new technological developments as they evolve, though it recommends that it include aural and visual surveillance irrespective of the means employed and that it includes the interception of communications.

9.40 The 'subsidiary recommendation' of the Commission is the creation of a tort of harassment. Harassment occurs 'where any person, without lawful authority or reasonable excuse, by any means, including by use of any communicating device, harasses another by persistently following, watching, pestering, besetting or communicating with him or her'.[6] The Commission does however advise against the creation of a group offence of collective besetting.

9.41 The Commission proposes the exercise of a legal duty, power or right of the defendant as a defence to these new torts. As regards remedies, the Commission advises that the new torts should be actionable without proof of damage and that damages be available to plaintiffs. In addition, a plaintiff should have the option of seeking injunctive relief so as to prevent the commission of the tort.

The creation of civil liability for the disclosure, dissemination or publication of information or material obtained as a result of privacy-invasive surveillance or harassment

9.42 The creation of civil liability for the unjustified disclosure, dissemination or publication of information material is ancillary to the two new torts of invasive surveillance and harassment. In simple terms, the imposition of this civil liability will prevent people from bearing fruit from the commission of the new torts. The Commission recommends that liability extends to information, etc, obtained overseas by methods which if used in Ireland would have constituted privacy-invasive surveillance. The Commission advises that consent should constitute a defence to this civil offence and that preventive orders and damages be available as remedies.

Proposed criminal, regulatory and supplementary provisions

9.43 In total, the Commission proposes the creation of four new criminal offences aimed at protecting the right to privacy – an offence of installing a

6   Chapter 10, p 121.

surveillance device in a dwelling with a view to surveillance or to using such a device from outside the dwelling with a view to spying on the dwelling; an offence of trespass done for the purpose of surveillance, namely, trespass on private property (either by unlawfully entering thereon, or by unlawfully remaining therein) effectuated for the purpose of obtaining information thereon concerning any (natural) person; an offence of using devices to spy on private conversations, such as, by using oral or optical devices to spy on people's conversations in circumstances where a 'reasonable expectation of privacy' arises and where the consent of no party to the conversation has been obtained and; ancillary offences aimed at the disclosure of information obtained as a result of the new criminal offences. The Commission recommends a broad range of defences to the proposed new offences, including consent and the necessary protection of one's own rights. In addition to these criminal provisions the Commission recommends the establishment of regulatory provisions directed at surveillance by State authorities, including the police.

9.44 The above recommendations have been presented to the Taoiseach in accordance with the Law Reform Commission Act 1975 for consideration by the Government. It is unlikely that there will be a legislative response to these proposals in the immediate future and as such, the piecemeal legal safeguards as described above will continue to apply.

B Publicity

9.45 The concept of an exclusive right to control the use of one's own name has attracted little legislative or judicial attention in Ireland thus far. There is no equivalent in Irish law to the right of publicity which exists under US law. The only means whereby a person can attempt to protect the unlicensed exploitation of his/her name or biography is by resorting to more conventional common law causes of action ie passing off, trade mark infringement, copyright infringement and defamation. The measure of protection afforded by these respective causes of action will in most cases fall well short of the desired level of protection.

Passing off

9.46 Passing off is a common law action which can be used to protect a person's proprietary interest in their goodwill. The principles which underline an action in passing off were outlined by Budd J in *Polycell Products Ltd v O'Carroll, T/A Dillon, O'Carroll*:

> 'To establish merchandise in such a manner as to mislead the public into believing that it is the merchandise or product of another is actionable. It injures the complaining party's right of property in his business and injures the goodwill of his business. A person who passes off the goods of another acquires to some extent the benefit of the business reputation of the rival trader and gets the advantage of his advertising'.[7]

---

7   [1959] Ir Jur Rep 34.

9.47   The three main requirements are that a person must have acquired a particular reputation in the eyes of the public; that persons wishing to buy his goods are likely to be misled into buying the goods of the defendant; and that he is likely to suffer damage thereby.[8]

9.48   The requirement that there be some underlying commercial activity to which the goodwill is attached means that many public figures will find themselves unable to avail themselves of the action in the event that their name is used to endorse a product without their consent. In fact, it is only really in the situation where a person actively trades in certain goods or services, and the offending person decides to trade in the same goods or services using that person's name, that a claim in passing off will be successful. The aim of the tort of passing off is to prevent the unjustified expropriation of goodwill associated with a product and not the unwarranted use of a person's name.

Trade mark law

9.49   Section 8(1)(b) of the Trade Marks Act 1996 provides that if a word is devoid of distinctive character it cannot be registered as a trade mark. It is possible therefore that a common surname could be considered devoid of distinctive character. Notwithstanding this reservation, it is nevertheless possible for a name or surname to be registered as a trade mark, so long as it is deemed to have the requisite amount of distinctiveness.[9]

9.50   So trade mark legislation does offer the potential for protection of a person's name. The efficacy of this protection is however questionable as it is subject to the normal restrictions that apply to trade marks. For instance, in order to avoid having a registration revoked a person must be able to show that the mark has been put to genuine use in that State in relation to the goods or services for which it was registered within five years from the date the trade mark was actually registered.[10] One further restriction is that section 15(2) of the 1996 Act provides that an honest use by a person of their own name and address cannot amount to an infringement of another person's registration.

Copyright law

9.51   It is generally accepted that a single word cannot constitute a 'work' and therefore is ineligible for copyright protection.[11]

Character merchandising

9.52   Character merchandising, which is an extension to the tort of passing off, is being developed as a means of protecting a person's name in other jurisdictions,[12] but has yet to be developed in this jurisdiction. Indeed the

---

8   *Per* Lord Jauncey in *Warnick v Townsends & Sons (Hull)* [1979] AC 731 and Budd J in the Irish case of *Polycell Products Ltd v O'Carroll* [1959] Ir Jur Rep 34.
9   Section 6(2) of the Trade Marks Act 1996 specifically lists 'personal names' as being an example of a trade mark.
10   Section 51(1)(a).
11   *Exxon Corpn v Exxon Insurance Consultants Int* [1982] RPC 69.
12   Most notably in Australia with the cases *Henderson v Radio Corpn* [1969] RPC 218 and *Hogan v Pacific Dunlop* [1989] 12 IPR 225.

tort has only recently gained credence in the UK with the decision in *Mirage Studios v Counter Feat Clothing Co*.[13] The aim of the tort is to prevent the unlicensed use of a 'character' in relation to the promotion of goods. The experience with this tort in Australia has shown that it is virtually impossible for a claim to succeed on the basis of the unlicensed use of a person's name and that a plaintiff will only be likely to succeed where there is an unlicensed use of a fictional character's name.[14]

9.53   The experience of these common law jurisdictions will be of obvious influence in the event that character merchandising rights are asserted before the Irish courts. *Clark and Smyth* have put forward the argument that the constitutional protections in relation to property and a good name may assist an Irish litigant in a character merchandising case.[15]

Defamation

9.54   Defamation has only a limited potential use as a means of protecting a person's name from unwarranted exploitation. It is only where the use of a person's name would be likely to lower their reputation in the eyes of the public that an action will be successful. A good example of a case where this occurred is the English House of Lord's decision in *Tolley v JS Fry and Sons Ltd*,[16] where an amateur golfer successfully argued that a visual caricature which also used his name to promote the defendant's brand of chocolate constituted defamation as it brought into question his amateur status.

1   Conclusions

9.55   Currently there is no 'right of publicity' under Irish law, indeed there have been very few cases before the Irish courts where individuals have raised the question of there being an unwarranted use of their name or biography. There are no immediate proposals to legislate in this area either and the Law Reform Commission in its Consultation Paper declined to put forward any recommendations on the topic as it felt that the issue was primarily a commercial rather than a privacy matter.[17]

C   Personality

9.56   There is no tort of misappropriation of personality or similar such protective measure in Irish law. The general common law rule as enunciated in *Sports & General Press Agency v Old Dogs Publishing Co*[18] still holds true, ie

---

13 [1991] FSR 145.
14 Contrast the decisions in *Sony Music Australia Ltd & Michael Jackson v Tansing* [1993] 27 IPR 649 (the *Michael Jackson* case) and *Twentieth Century Fox v South Australia Brewing* [1996] 34 IPR 225 (the *Simpson's Duff beer* case).
15 Clark and Smyth, *Intellectual Property Law in Ireland*, 1997, Butterworths (Ireland), p 475.
16 [1931] AC 333.
17 Op cit, para 9.70.
18 [1916] 2 KB 880.

there is a right to photograph anyone in a public or in a private place (where no trespass is involved) without their consent and to publish that photograph. The reality is that there is very little that a person can do to prevent the unwarranted use of their image. The following are a few possible grounds upon which an applicant could attempt to base his claim against an unauthorised use of his personality.

Copyright law

9.57 By virtue of section 10(3) of the Copyright Act 1963 the copyright in a photograph either lies with the person who took the photograph or the person who commissioned it. Therefore an individual has little recourse under copyright law to protect his/her personality in the case where a photographic journalist is taking a picture. A person can, however, prevent the publication of a photograph which they themselves commissioned or took. This gives a certain measure of protection to 'private' photographs.[19]

Character merchandising

9.58 As mentioned in the previous section, this doctrine is as yet unrecognised in Ireland. Most likely the Irish courts will be influenced by the developments and case law in other common law jurisdictions in the event that character merchandising rights are asserted before them. The experience of other common law jurisdictions has however shown that the doctrine, at its present stage of development, provides little if any protection against the commercial exploitation of the image of a real as opposed to a fictional character.

Privacy

9.59 Again the tort of invasion of privacy has yet to be recognised under Irish law, though there is potential for Irish courts to do so. A recent Irish case which threatened to bring this to the fore involved the Irish model Laura Birmingham and the Sunday Mirror. The newspaper obtained topless pictures of the model, taken while she was in her changing rooms and then published them. She sued the newspaper, alleging, inter alia, that the newspaper by obtaining and publishing the photographs had breached her right to privacy. The case, however, never went to trial but the model did receive a substantial monetary settlement from the newspaper.

1   Conclusions

9.60 There is no direct or specific measure whereby an individual can protect their personality under Irish law. The few indirect means that do exist fail to provide an adequate means of redress for an individual who has suffered from an unauthorised exploitation of their personality. There are two principal types of situation where a person might seek to prevent an unauthorised use of their image. First, when their image is being exploited

---

19 See also earlier comments on the possibility of a right to privacy in photographs and films being created when the Copyright and Related Rights Bill 1998 is enacted.

for commercial gain eg by associating their image with a certain product, and secondly where the use of their image in some way invades their privacy. Irish law has not yet formulated a means of redress for individuals in such situations.

10 FINLAND

Rainer Hilli
Tanja Liljeström

A Privacy

1 General provisions relating to privacy

10.01 In Finland, both natural and, to the extent applicable, legal persons enjoy constitutional protection against incursions into the privacy of their home, confidential communications, and personal lives. These rights are applied and enforced through criminal law and data protection legislation.

10.02 In principle, Finnish law also recognises that an individual has a right to prohibit and control others' use of his identity for commercial purposes. However, the statutory protection afforded to an individual's property rights in his name, likeness, and other aspects of identity is still fairly uncodified. Provisions applicable to the right of publicity are primarily found in intellectual property and unfair competition law.

10.03 An individual's right to his personal information has traditionally been protected through criminal law. Judicial relief has been granted against actions whereby an individual has been caused harm, such as unlawful entry, eavesdropping and illicit observation, as well as statutes concerning invasion of privacy through mass media. The entry into force of the Personal Data File Act in 1988, replaced in 1999 by the Personal Data Act, provided a significant change to the situation, since the data protection legislation aims towards the prevention of incursions into the privacy of individuals through use of personal information.

2 Applicable legislation

10.04 The inviolability of the privacy of one's personal life, home, and postal, telephone, and other confidential communications is guaranteed in Finland as a constitutional right. Freedom of speech is also guaranteed as a constitutional right and this includes the right to express and receive information, opinions, and messages unhindered in advance by anyone. These rights were first set forth in 1919 in the Constitution Act,[1] one of four documents that comprise Finland's constitutional laws. In 1995 these fundamental rights were amended into their present form to reflect the

---

1   17 July 1919/94A.

technology and social developments of the past few decades. At the same time, the scope of application of the Constitution Act was extended to include all persons under Finnish jurisdiction.

10.05 The purpose of a constitutional provision establishing a fundamental right is to safeguard the rights of individuals from encroachment by the State through governmental, administrative or legislative acts in the area covered by the provision. Constitutional protection is primarily seen as protection in relation to the exercise of public power and can therefore, as a rule, not be invoked in disputes between private individuals or entities. Instead, the exercise of constitutional rights is arranged through statutes enacted by the Finnish Parliament. However, courts are allowed to use constitutional provisions in their reasoning within the limits of the wording of the Act in question.

10.06 The Finnish Penal Code was first published on 19 December 1889 and came into force on 14 April 1894. Since then, the Penal Code has undergone several partial reforms, which have extended to virtually every Chapter of the Code. The scope of application of the Penal Code, as set forth in its first Chapter, is fairly wide. In addition to covering unlawful acts done in Finland, the Penal Code may also be applied to offences committed abroad by Finnish residents, and to offences committed by foreign residents against Finland, a Finnish citizen or resident, or a Finnish corporation, institution or foundation.

10.07 The exercise of the constitutional right to freedom of speech is governed by several statutes, the most important one being the Freedom of the Press Act.[2] The Act sets forth the rights and obligations of everyone enjoying the right to freedom of speech under the Constitution Act in relation to publication of printed writings, which are defined in section 2 of the Press Act as every kind of writing which has been reproduced by means of a printing machine or other means of the same nature, as well as pictures, maps, lyrics to musical works, and plays performed in public. The dissemination of information in other forms, such as radio and television broadcasts, is regulated by specific statutes, such as the Radio Broadcasting Responsibility Act[3] and the Radio and Television Act[4] but follows the main rules established in the Press Act.

10.08 The collection, use, and dissemination of personal data in Finland is governed by the Personal Data Act[5] as well as the provisions of the Convention for the Protection of Individuals with regard to Automatic Processing of Personal Data[6] and the Data Protection Directive. The Data Act is a general law providing for the protection of personal information. It is applicable to data files maintained both by government authorities and private enterprises. The Data Act applies to the processing of personal data by entities that have a place of business or operations in Finland, or which are otherwise within Finland's legal jurisdiction. The Data Act also applies when the processing of personal data uses devices located in Finland other than simply for transmitting data via Finland.

---

2   4 January 1919/1, 'Press Act'.
3   12 March 1971/219.
4   9 October 1998/744.
5   22 April 1999/523.
6   1/21/1981, 'Data Protection Convention'.

The Data Act is comlemented by the Act on Privacy and Data Security in Telecommunications (99/565, the 'Telecoms Privacy Act'), which promotes the protection of privacy and data security in the subscription to and use of telecommunications services. Under the Telecoms Privacy Act, all communications (including e-mail and other telecommunications via the Internet) are confidential unless the sender has intended the transmission to be public. Pursuant to this rule, third parties may not store, open, listen to, tap, intercept, or otherwise conduct surveillance on, communications.

3   *Privacy of one's personal life*

10.09   The right to privacy of one's personal life has traditionally been conceived as the right of every person in Finland to legitimately control what, when, and how information concerning his or her personal life is disclosed to the public. The Constitution Act, section 1 provides that protection of this constitutional right is to be set forth in law. Today, enforcement of this protection is provided, inter alia, under the Penal Code and the Data Act.

10.10   Under section 27:3a of the Penal Code, a person who unlawfully, through the use of mass media or in another similar manner, publicly spreads information, an insinuation or an image of the private life of another person, conducive to causing him damage or suffering, shall be sentenced for invasion of privacy to imprisonment for at most two years or fined. Publication that deals with a person's behaviour in public office or in a public duty, in professional life, political activity or in another comparable activity, when this is necessary in dealing with a socially important matter, shall not be considered an invasion of privacy.

10.11   An individual's private life is generally considered to encompass his or her family life, personal relations, leisure activities, state of health, wealth, and political, religious and other opinions. However, the publication of information concerning such conditions is prohibited under the Penal Code, section 27:3a only when such publication is liable to cause damage or suffering, the deciding factor being whether the information in question is of such a nature that its publication would cause harm to an average individual.

10.12   A legal right to publication may be based on the express or implied consent of the individual. Such consent must be obtained voluntarily in order to be valid, and the individual must be able to comprehend the significance and consequences of the consent. The purpose for which the consent is given determines its extent. It must be noted that, under criminal law, the consent may be withdrawn at any time prior to the publication. Under private law, however, a withdrawal of consent may constitute a breach of contract and lead to liability for damages.

10.13   For the purposes of the Penal Code, section 27:3a, mass media is deemed to comprise the press, literature, visual and aural technical media, and the use of outdoor advertisements, posters, flyers and the like distributed in public. An invasion of privacy can thus only be committed with the help of a technical medium. An element of publicity must also be present, ie there must be a possibility that anyone can receive the message.

10.14 The scope of protection offered under the Penal Code, section 27:3a to the private lives of persons exercising social power, such as politicians or high-powered officials or businessmen, is very limited compared to private individuals. As stated above, damaging or embarrassing details of the lives of private individuals may never be published without proper consent, however, information of a corresponding nature concerning public persons can be published if the information concerns the exercise of power and has social importance.

10.15 Although not directly comparable with public figures, so-called celebrities and entertainers are also considered to enjoy a more limited degree of protection with regard to their private lives. Celebrities are considered, through their choice of profession, to have tacitly consented to a certain extent to having information concerning their private lives published in the mass media. On the other hand, such tacit consent has not been considered to extend to the publication of private information liable to cause damage or suffering, and may naturally also be withdrawn with respect to private information in general.

10.16 As stated earlier, the exercise of the right to freedom of speech through publication of printed writings is governed under the Press Act, and the rules set out therein regarding content regulation are to a material extent repeated in the Radio Broadcasting Responsibility Act. The provision concerning freedom of speech in section 10 of the Constitution Act prevents the authorities from exercising prior censorship of any form of speech, however, the publication of printed writings covered by the Press Act may in certain circumstances be suspended or banned. Under section 37 of the Press Act, a printed work that is criminal in content may be adjudged forfeit, as defined in the Penal Code. The Penal Code, section 2:17 provides that, if the contents of a publication, writing or pictorial presentation are declared to be offensive, the copies in the possession of the author, publisher, editor, producer, distributor or seller, as well as the plates and patterns which are solely intended for the production of said product, shall be declared forfeit and rendered unusable. Deliberate distribution or re-publication of a forfeited work is punishable by a fine or imprisonment for up to six months. Under section 42 of the Press Act, a publication that is perceived to be criminal in content may be seized at the request of the party involved while charges concerning said contents are dealt with by a court of law.

10.17 Invasion of privacy is a complainant offence meaning that the public prosecutor cannot bring charges unless the complainant has reported the offence for the purpose of bringing charges. The period of limitation for the bringing of charges or requesting that charges be brought for a complainant offence is one year from the day the complainant gained knowledge of the offence and the offender.

10.18 Compensation for damages resulting from the publication of information in violation of the Penal Code, section 27:3a, the Press Act, the Radio Broadcasting Responsibility Act can be claimed according to the Act on Compensation for Damages.[7] Under section 5:6 of the Damages Act, personal injury such as suffering can be compensated if it is caused by, inter alia, prejudice to a person's honour or privacy. Damage that is not directly connected to personal injury is defined as economic loss. Under

---

7   31 May 1974/412, 'Damages Act'.

section 5:1 of the Damages Act, an economic loss can only be compensated if it results:

(1) from a punishable act;

(2) from the use of public authority; or

(3) where other particularly pressing grounds exist for compensation.

10.19 Naturally, criminal charges need not be brought. However an award of damages on the basis of violation of privacy requires that proof be presented of the punishable nature of the act.

4 Privacy of the home

10.20 The right to privacy of the home is interpreted in a conceptual as well as a tangible sense. Traditionally, the right to privacy of the home has been conceived as the right to control physical access to the tangible premises owned, rented, or otherwise lawfully occupied by a person. In a conceptual sense, the right to privacy of the home is considered to include the right to restrict activity conducted on, or in close proximity to, one's tangible premises which effects an impermissible intrusion on one's right to privacy.

10.21 The principal statute protecting the constitutional right to privacy of the home in its tangible sense is found in the Penal Code, section 24:1.1. Accordingly, any person who, without lawful reason or permission, intrudes on the premises of another or who refuses to comply with an order to leave the premises, could be fined or imprisoned for up to six months for trespassing. Premises protected under this provision include houses, rooms or apartments used as residences or business premises, as well as associated courtyards, gardens and staircases.

10.22 Privacy of the home in its conceptual sense is protected under the Penal Code, section 24:3b, which prohibits the use of technical devices to listen to or record what occurs in the premises of another, or to watch or monitor a person staying in such premises, without permission. Such eavesdropping or illicit observation is punishable by a fine or imprisonment for up to one year. Preparation for eavesdropping or illicit observation is punishable by a fine or imprisonment for up to six months. The wording of the provisions covers any unauthorised listening in on or recording of conversations, as well as observing, photographing or filming occurring in an area protected under the right to privacy of the home set forth in the Penal Code, section 24:1.1. Thus, recording conversations or filming in public places are not restricted activities as such. However, the publication of information thus obtained may be punishable under the Penal Code, section 27:3a if such publication constitutes an invasion of privacy. Naturally, this also applies to the publication of information obtained through eavesdropping or illicit observation, provided such information is deemed to be of a private nature. Information which is not deemed to be private can be published even though it was obtained through a criminal act.

5 Privacy of confidential communications

10.23 The Constitution Act, section 8.2 provides that the privacy of postal, telephone and other confidential communications is inviolable. The Telecoms Privacy Act, section 4 further provides that telecommunications are confidential unless intended by the sender to be public. A person who has received or otherwise gained knowledge of a confidential telecommunication not addressed to him may not unlawfully disclose or use information on the contents or existence of the message. A breach of this confidentiality obligation is punishable as a violation of telecommunications confidentiality under the Penal Code, section 38:2 by a fine. The unlawful retrieval of information, whether in voice, telex, text, picture or data form, transmitted through a telecommunications network is punishable as a violation of communications privacy under the Penal Code, section 38:3 by a fine or imprisonment for up to one year.

10.24 The Penal Code establishes a subjective guideline for determining when voice communications are private. Accordingly, individuals are entitled to legal protection for their voice communications when they had no reason on a case-by-case basis to expect that such voice communications would be heard by anyone else other than the intended party. The unlawful eavesdropping through the aid of special technical devices or the unlawful and surreptitious recording of such private voice communications is criminalised under the Penal Code, section 38:3. Arguably, the determination of whether or not a voice communication is private cannot depend solely on subjective expectations. The measure of expectation of privacy also depends on what expectations a reasonable person in similar circumstances would be entitled to.

6   Public order aspects

10.25 The Penal Code criminalises, *inter* alia, breaching the peace in a public place or causing a disturbance (section 17:13), resisting an official (section 16:1), riotous assembly (section 17:2) and the use of identification belonging to another in order to mislead a public official (section 16:5). Interference with road or tramway traffic is punishable under the Road Traffic Act.

7   Data protection

10.26 The Data Act, section 3(1) defines personal data as a description of an individual or an individual's characteristics or living circumstances which can be recognised as depicting a certain individual or his family or those living with him or her in the same household.

10.27 The scope of application of the Data Act depends to a great extent on whether the data collected and used fulfils the definition of personal data. The operative words in the definition include *description* and *individual*. These operative words have been interpreted to exclude from the scope of the Data Act undertakings, funds and associations. However, unlike the previous Personal Data File Act, the Data Act also applies to personal data related to individuals in their capacity as professionals, entrepreneurs, and public persons as well as key employees of undertakings with regard to data relevant to their private circumstances. The Data Act also does not apply to the collection and use of such singular data as a name that does not in any way describe a natural person his or her characteristics or living style. The Data Act also does not apply to the collection, recording and use of personal data for normal private use, nor does it affect the right to publish printed matter.

10.28　The provisions of the Act regulate personal data files maintained with the aid of automatic data processing as well as personal data stored on cards or in lists. The collection and entry of personal data in registers is permitted only under the provisions of the Act. In brief, a personal data file may only be maintained for predetermined purposes. An enterprise that collects, registers, and maintains personal data in a personal data file ('File Controller') may only register information that concerns individuals with whom the File Controller has a customer, service or other comparable relationship. Compliance with the Act is supervised by the Data Protection Ombudsman and the Data Protection Board.

10.29　The personal data file may contain only information that is necessary for the purposes of the File Controller. Sensitive information may be registered in certain circumstances specifically described by law. Sensitive information is described in the Act as personal data that describes an individual's race or ethnic origin; political, social, and religious convictions; physical health or handicaps or sexual behaviour.

10.30　In general, personal data maintained in a personal data file may be used only for the purpose for which it was collected. Personal data maintained in a personal data file may be disclosed, disseminated, or conveyed and personal data files may be combined only in those circumstances stipulated in the Act.

10.31　Dissemination of personal data is a form of processing, and is therefore subject to the general processing rules under the Data Act. Personal data may be processed only if at least one of the following applies:

(1)　the data subject has unambiguously consented to the processing;

(2)　the data subject has given an assignment for the processing, or processing is necessary in order to perform a contract to which the data subject is a party, or in order to take steps at the request of the data subject before entering into a contract;

(3)　the processing is necessary to protect the vital interests of the data subject;

(4)　the processing is based on legislation, or is necessary for compliance with a task or obligation to which the file controller is bound by virtue of legislation or an order issued on the basis of legislation;

(5)　the data subject has a customer or service relationship with, or membership in, or other similar relevant connection with, the operations of the file controller;

(6)　the personal data relates to the clients or employees of a group of companies or other comparable economic group, and this is processed within that group;

(7)　the processing is necessary for purposes of payment services, data processing or other comparable tasks undertaken by a third party on the assignment of the file controller, or

(8)　the matter concerns generally available personal data on the status, duties, or performance of a person in a public corporation or business, and the personal data is processed to safeguard the rights and interests of the file controller or of a third person receiving the data.

The Data Protection Board may grant a file controller permission to process personal data on other grounds than those authorised above, provided that such processing is necessary (i) to safeguard data subjects' vital interests, (ii) to perform a task of public benefit, or (iii) for the exercise of the public authority of the file controller or of a third person receiving the personal data. Permission to process personal data may also be granted to pursue the legitimate interests of the file controller, or of a third person receiving the personal data, provided that such processing does not jeopardise the protection of data subjects' privacy or rights.

File controllers have a general duty to ensure that the data subject can obtain information regarding the file controller, the purpose of the processing, the destination of regular disclosures of personal data contained in the file, and the information necessary for the exercise of the data subject's rights with respect to the processing in question. This information must be provided when collecting and registering personal data or, if the data is not obtained directly from the data subject and is intended to be disclosed, when the data is disclosed for the first time. Data subjects are also entitled to prohibit the file controller from using or disseminating their personal data for the purposes of direct marketing, telemarketing, directory assistance, and market and opinion research.

10.32   Violations of the obligations and conditions placed on file controllers or the use or dissemination of inaccurate personal data triggers strict liability for financial damages and for more than minor suffering under the Data Act, section 47 and criminal liability under the Penal Code, section 38:9.

8   Finnish jurisprudence concerning privacy

10.33   The most recent decision of the Finnish Supreme Court concerning the protection of privacy under the Penal Code, section 27:3a was rendered on 11 June 1997. A daily newspaper had published an article concerning certain arson attacks, which identified the wife of the head of the local fire department as the culprit. The Supreme Court stated that, since it had not even been suggested that the fire chief himself had been involved in the events, there were no acceptable grounds for making public the fact that he was married to the suspect. The publisher and editor of the paper and the author of the article were obligated to pay the fire chief FIM 50.000 in compensation for suffering caused by invasion of privacy.

B   Publicity

10.34   As a general rule, an individual is entitled to prohibit the use of his name in cases where the name is used to invoke his identity without permission. However, aside from privacy statutes, the remedies available to private individuals with regard to such unauthorised use are few.

1   Applicable legislation

10.35   The Names Act[8] governs the determination and changing of the surname and forename of persons habitually resident in Finland. The Names

---

8   9 August 1985/694.

Act offers a limited degree of protection for names and symbols through the provisions concerning the adoption of a new surname. However, the Names Act does not contain other restrictions pertaining to the actual use of personal names.

10.36 The legislation on trade marks is laid down in the Finnish Trade Marks Act.[9] The provisions of the Trade Marks Act apply equally to goods and services. The Trade Marks Act allows trade marks to be held by Finnish as well as foreign entities and persons. Trade name protection, as regulated by the Trade Names Act,[10] follows for many parts rules similar to those of trade mark protection.

10.37 The Unfair Business Practices Act[11] contains provisions providing for protection against, inter alia, misleading advertising and unfair utilisation of goodwill. The Act applies to entrepreneurs conducting business in Finland.

2   Use of a person's name and biography

10.38 Under section 12 of the Names Act, a surname that has been entered into the Finnish Population Register or a name that is commonly known to have been established as the name of a given Finnish or foreign family cannot be approved as a new surname, unless there is a special reason for the approval. In the absence of a special reason a name cannot be approved as a new surname if it may be misapprehended in connection with, or confused with, the name of a foundation, association or other organisation, a registered trade name or trade mark or other protected symbol used in trade, or a generally known pseudonym. Under section 19.1 of the Names Act, a person who considers that the approval of an application for a new surname would infringe his rights has the right to submit an objection to the County Government. The holder of a name or symbol protected under section 12 may also bring an action for an order of forfeiture of a surname already acquired upon application, provided such action is brought within five years of the entry of the surname into the Population Register. An action for the forfeiture of a surname can be taken up for consideration in a Finnish court if the defendant is habitually resident in Finland.

10.39 A person's biography may in some cases fulfil the definition of personal data under the Data Act. However, while biographical information would in situations involving private natural persons be subsumed in the definition of personal data protected under the Data Act, section 3(1), (ie a description of a person or a person's characteristics or living circumstances which can be recognised as depicting a certain individual or his family or those living with him or her in the same household), the same will not always hold true for situations involving legal persons and professionals, entrepreneurs, and public figures. Under section 17 of the Data Act, specific data concerning data subjects connected through a certain profession, education, status or accomplishment in the area of culture, sports, business

9   7/1964, as amended.
10   2 February 1979/128.
11   22 December 1978/1061.

and the like, may be published in a register without the permission of the data subjects, provided that the protection of the data subject's privacy is not thereby endangered. Naturally, a person's biography may not be published if such publication would constitute an invasion of privacy under the Penal Code, section 27:3a.

3   Trade mark protection

10.40   Under section 1 of the Trade Marks Act, a trade mark may consist of any symbol that can be represented graphically and that serves to distinguish its proprietor's goods or services. Hence, a personal name may be registered as a trade mark, provided it fulfils the requirement of distinctiveness. However, a trade mark may not be registered if it is composed of or contains anything that is likely to give the impression of being, eg the name or likeness of another person (unless such a name or likeness clearly refers to someone who died a long time ago), unless the person whose right is concerned agrees.

10.41   A sole right to a trade mark may be acquired even without registration after the mark has become established. The Trade Marks Act, section 2 provides that a trade symbol shall be regarded as established if it has become generally known in the appropriate business or consumer circles in Finland as a symbol specific to goods or services purveyed in business by the proprietor of the trade mark.

10.42   As a general rule, a name or trade name of another may not be used as a trade mark or part of a trade mark. However, this prohibition does not concern cases where the name included in the trade mark is the applicant's personal name. Under section 3 of the Trade Marks Act, any person may use his surname in his business as a symbol for his goods or services unless its use is liable to cause confusion with the protected trade mark of another, or with a name, or trade name that another is already lawfully using in his business. If the use of the name is likely to cause confusion with an earlier trade mark, a court of law may decide, where reasonable, that one or both of the trade marks may only be used in a specific manner, eg with the addition of a place name or some other explanatory feature.

10.43   Administrative action to object to the registration of a trade mark can be taken by any party with a qualified interest within two months after public announcement of the registration. A person or entity may oppose registration of a trade mark by filing a written submission with the National Board of Patents and Registration within two months of the date of the public notice regarding the application. If a trade mark has been registered in violation of the Trade Marks Act, the registration shall be invalidated. Furthermore, the exclusive right to a trade mark is forfeited if the trade mark has, after its registration or establishment, evidently lost its distinctive power or has become misleading or contrary to law, public order or morality. A court of law can decide on the declaration of invalidity of a registration and forfeiture of a trade mark when a suit to that effect is brought against the proprietor of the mark by anyone who suffers inconvenience as a result of the trade mark.

10.44   The use of a trade mark may be prohibited by a court of law, irrespective of any time limits, to the extent deemed necessary if the trade mark is misleading to the public. Action for prohibition may be brought by a public prosecutor, by anyone suffering inconvenience due to the use of the mark, or an interest group of relevant merchants or professionals. When prohibiting the use of a trade mark, the court may also, as deemed necessary, order that a mark placed on goods, packaging, brochures, business documents, or the like in violation of the prohibition, be removed or altered so as not to be misleading, or that the property be destroyed or altered in a specified manner. The property may also be confiscated pending the said order.

10.45 Infringement of a trade mark is not specifically defined in the Trade Marks Act, but it does set forth the content of the exclusive right and the punishment prescribed for the violation of such an exclusive right. Under section 4.1 of the Trade Marks Act, an exclusive right to a trade mark, whether acquired by registration or through establishment, means that no-one other than the holder of the trade mark may, without proper consent, use in trade for his goods a symbol likely to be confused with the said trade mark, whether on goods or their packaging, in advertising or business documents, or otherwise, including oral use.

10.46 Hence, if a symbol is likely to be confused with a trade mark already protected under the Trade Marks Act, the provisions of the Act concerning infringement apply. In general, protection against unauthorised use is provided only with regard to goods of the same or similar kind as those to which the trade mark refers. Irrespective of this, the likelihood of confusion of trade marks may be invoked if a symbol is widely known in Finland and the use of another similar symbol would result in an unjustified exploitation of the distinctive power or goodwill of the earlier mark or would be likely to diminish it.

10.47 Action against trade mark infringement can be taken through civil or criminal proceedings. Deliberate infringement of a trade mark right is punishable under section 39.1 of the Trade Marks Act by a fine as a trade mark misdemeanour or, if the infringement is severe enough, under the Penal Code, section 49:2 as an industrial property right crime, for which the penalty is a fine or imprisonment for up to two years.

10.48 Both civil action and criminal charges for trade mark infringement have to be brought by the holder of the trade mark. Also an exclusive licensee whose licence is entered in the Trade Mark Register is considered an injured party in infringement matters. Criminal charges may be brought by the public prosecutor only if the injured party has reported the offence for prosecution.

10.49 An injunction against present and any future infringements can be requested either in civil or criminal proceedings taken against the infringer. Precautionary measures can also be requested under Chapter 7 of the Code of Procedure, which contains general provisions regarding, eg seizure and interlocutory injunctions.

10.50 Action for compensation for damages must be brought within three years from the date when the injured party learned about the infringement and the party guilty thereof, in any event no later than ten years after the infringement took place.

10.51 The District Court of Helsinki is the competent court of first instance in matters concerning title to and forfeiture of a trade mark, invalidation of registration and prohibition of use of a trade mark, infringement of trade mark right and actions for declaring whether a right to a trade mark exists and whether a certain act infringes such a right. The decisions of the District Court of Helsinki can be appealed to the Court of Appeals and, subject to a leave of appeal, further to the Supreme Court.

4 Trade name protection

10.52 Under section 4 of the Trade Names Act, a trader may use his surname as a trade name, unless such use is liable to cause confusion with the protected trade name or trade mark of another. Another trader may not use a similar trade name in the area where the trader uses his surname as a trade name.

10.53 The use of another person's name as a trade name is restricted under section 10 of the Trade Names Act, according to which a trade name may not without proper consent contain anything which may be perceived as the surname, pseudonym, or other such name of another person (unless it clearly refers to someone who died a long time ago) or anything which may be confused with the protected trade name or trade mark of another.

10.54 The Trade Names Act, section 18 provides that the use of a trade name may be prohibited by a court of law if the trade name or its use is contrary to good business practice or public order or misleading to the public, or if it infringes another's right to a trade name. Furthermore, if a trade name has been registered in violation of the Trade Names Act, the registration can be invalidated by a court of law. An action for prohibition or for invalidation of a trade name registration can be brought by anyone suffering inconvenience due to the trade name.

10.55 Deliberate infringement of a trade name right is punishable under section 22 of the Trade Names Act by a fine. Criminal charges may be brought by the public prosecutor only if the injured party has reported the offence for prosecution. Action for compensation for damages must be brought within five years from the date when the infringement took place.

10.56 In an infringement case, the court may order that a mark placed on goods, packaging, brochures, business documents, or the like in violation of the prohibition is to be removed or altered so as not to be misleading, or that the property is to be destroyed or altered in a specified manner. The property may also be confiscated pending the said order.

10.57 The District Court of Helsinki is the competent court of first instance in matters concerning title to a trade name, invalidation of registration and prohibition of use of a trade name, infringement and a trade mark right and actions for declaring whether a right to a trade mark exists and whether a certain act infringes such right. The decisions of the District Court of Helsinki can be appealed to the Court of Appeals and, subject to a leave of appeal, further to the Supreme Court.

5 Copyright protection

10.58 The Copyright Act,[12] section 51 prohibits the publication of a literary or artistic work under such a pseudonym or signature that the author of the work may be confused with the author of a previously disseminated work. The protection granted to an author's pseudonym or signature is thus similar to that of trade symbols. The provision serves to prevent the unauthorised exploitation of the goodwill associated with the author's name. The provisions of section 51 are applicable regardless of who created the work or where the work was published.

10.59 Under section 56a of the Copyright Act, anyone who deliberately or out of gross negligence violates the said provision shall be punished by a fine for a copyright offence. If the infringement is severe enough, it is punishable under the Penal Code, section 49:1 as a copyright crime, for which the penalty is a fine or imprisonment for up to two years. A violation of section 51 is subject to public prosecution. The author is entitled to compensation for damages for any loss, mental suffering or other injury caused by a copyright crime. The court may also prescribe that the infringing property be destroyed or altered in specific ways, or conveyed to the injured party against a compensation corresponding to their cost of manufacture, or rendered such that their unauthorised use is prevented.

6 Unfair competition

10.60 According to section 1 of the Unfair Business Practices Act, good business practice may not be violated, nor may practices that are otherwise unfair to other entrepreneurs be used in business. This general clause has been regarded as a complement in certain situations where commercial identifiers are not subject to statutory protection under intellectual property legislation. The general clause could, therefore, be applicable for the protection of a personal name that is not subject to trade mark or trade name protection but nevertheless is distinctive and valuable for the person using the name in his business.

10.61 The Unfair Business Practices Act applies to entrepreneurs conducting business in Finland. Thus, a person's right to bring an action on the basis of the Unfair Business Practices Act hinges on his or her status as an entrepreneur. In the preparatory words of the Act, an entrepreneur is defined as a person or entity carrying out operations aimed towards achieving an economic result. In court practice, this has been interpreted as including the professional activities of a performing artist, irrespective of whether the activities are conducted through a company or by the artist as a sole entrepreneur. A private person who is not an entrepreneur can therefore not refer to the Unfair Business Practices Act to prohibit the commercial use of his name. Even an entrepreneur is required to establish that the practice is likely to harm his business.

10.62 An entrepreneur may be prohibited, under section 6 of the Unfair Business Practices Act, from continuing or repeating practices that violate good business practice. The prohibition may be enforced with the threat of

---

12 8 July 1961/404.

a fine. Action for a prohibition may be brought before the Market Court by an entrepreneur against whom the practice in question is directed or whose activity said practice may endanger, or by a registered organisation supervising the interests of entrepreneurs. The Market Court is a special court which hears and decides cases relating to, inter alia, the regulation of marketing which falls under its competence pursuant to the Consumer Protection Act and the Unfair Business Practices Act. A judgment of the Market Court is not subject to ordinary appeal, however, anyone who has been ordered to pay a fine imposed conditionally as reinforcement of an injunction or corrective action may appeal the decision to the Supreme Court in respect of the amount of the fine.

7 Finnish jurisprudence concerning publicity

10.63 In the Market Court decision 1981:18, rendered on 1 October 1981, the applicability of the general clause to the protection of names was affirmed. In its decision, the Market Court held that the unauthorised use of a pop artist's stage name and likeness in marketing was contrary to good business practice. The Market Court considered the artist to qualify as an entrepreneur under the Unfair Business Practices Act due to the professional nature of his activities. Since the stage name was deemed to be established in marketing and generally associated with the artist in Finland, it was considered to have a certain economic importance and commercial value.

C Personality

1 Personality rights generally

10.64 In Finland, there is no special legislation concerning the use of a person's image. As a rule, a person is not entitled to prohibit the use of his image in cases involving normal use in, eg news reporting or other activities covered by the right to freedom of speech. Thus, a person is not entitled to receive economic compensation for the publication of his image in reporting public events. However, a person's right to privacy may not even in these cases be violated. An image may therefore not be used in a manner which is liable to infringe the subject's right to privacy without proper consent. On the other hand, as a rule, the unauthorised use of a person's image for commercial purposes is not permitted.

2 Applicable legislation

10.65 The protection of an individual's right to privacy afforded by the provisions of the Penal Code and the Data Act also extends to the use of images relating to his private life. In addition, the unauthorised commercial use of a person's image may be contrary to statutes concerning unfair marketing practices.

10.66   The Unfair Business Practices Act[13] contains provisions providing for protection against, inter alia, misleading advertising and unfair utilisation of goodwill. The Finnish Market Court may enjoin business entities to refrain from using such practices and issue conditional fines to ensure compliance.

10.67   The Consumer Protection Act[14] applies to the marketing and sales of goods, interests, and services to consumers and contains mandatory legislation regarding the use of marketing methods which are considered contrary to good practice or otherwise unfair to consumers. Compliance with the Consumer Protection Act is supervised by the Office of the Consumer Ombudsman.

3   Use of a person's likeness for reporting public events

10.68   As a rule, the publication of an image taken in a public place only violates a person's right to privacy if the purpose of the image is to specifically present such behaviour on the part of the individual that the publication of the image would be likely to cause him harm. If the main purpose of such an image is to present, eg a view of a street, a building, a public event or a public figure, the publication of the image does not constitute an invasion of the privacy of a private individual thereby coincidentally depicted, even if the individual is clearly identifiable.

4   Use of a person's likeness for reporting their private life

10.69   The primary rule concerning the use of a person's image is the Penal Code, section 27:3a, which penalises the publication of an image pertaining to a person's private life. Conviction is conditional upon the unauthorised nature of the publication, whether the publication of the image is liable to cause damage or suffering, and criminal intent. Damages for personal injury and economic loss resulting from an invasion of privacy may be claimed under the Damages Act.

5   Use of a person's likeness in advertising

10.70   The use of a person's image for a commercial purpose such as advertising has in court practice been deemed to constitute a violation of good business practice under section 1 of the Unfair Business Practices Act. The use of a person's image in advertising may also be prohibited as misleading advertising under section 2 of the Act if such use is liable to give the impression that the person in question endorses the advertised product or service. Under section 2, no-one may use a false or misleading expression concerning one's own business or the business of another, if the said expression is likely to affect the demand for or supply of a product or harm the business of another.

13 22 December 1978/1061.
14 20 January 1978/38.

10.71 In determining whether a particular marketing act is contrary to good business practice under section 1 of the Act, the Market Court has applied the ICC International Code of Advertising Practice, which prohibits the unauthorised portrayal or imitation of persons both in a private or public capacity in advertising. Thus, the use of a person's image in marketing without proper permission thereto can generally be said to be contrary to good business practice under Finnish law.

10.72 However, as stated before, the Unfair Business Practices Act only applies to entrepreneurs, and the protection afforded only covers business activities. Consequently, since judicial relief under the Act is not available to non-entrepreneurs, a private person cannot have the commercial use of his image prohibited by referring to section 1 or section 2 of the Unfair Business Practices Act. However, since the use of misleading expressions in marketing is also prohibited under section 2:2 of the Consumer Protection Act, private persons have the option of alerting the Consumer Ombudsman, who may issue an injunction prohibiting the marketing operation, or bring the matter before the Market Court.

10.73 Injunctions against activities contrary to the Act on Unfair Business Practices or the Consumer Protection Act can be ruled by the Market Court and significant wilful conduct contrary to the said statutes is also criminalised. Under section 6 of the Unfair Business Practices Act and section 7 of the Consumer Protection Act, an entrepreneur may be prohibited by the Market Court from continuing or repeating practices that constitute a violation of good business practice or are liable to mislead the public. The prohibition may be enforced with the threat of a fine.

10.74 A deliberate violation of section 2 of the Unfair Business Practices Act and of the provisions concerning misleading marketing in the Consumer Protection Act is punishable by a fine or imprisonment for up to six months. Violation through gross negligence is punishable by a fine. Charges for such an offence or violation shall be brought before a general District Court. The public prosecutor may not bring charges unless the injured party has reported the matter for prosecution.

6   General tort law

10.75 The significance of tort law in Finland is indirect, meaning that it is applicable if no specific rules or regulations are found. As a rule, natural and legal persons in Finland must bear their own losses unless it can be demonstrated that grounds exist under written law or legal practice to attach liability for the damage to another person. The basis for compensation must be the other person's act, omission, negligence, or other description of a chain of events that incurs liability. The party demanding compensation must demonstrate that the damage indeed resulted from the described event.

10.76 The Damages Act provides compensation for injury to person or property. The Act distinguishes between material and immaterial injury: material injury is, as a rule, defined as visible injury to an individual's person or property; immaterial injury concerns pain, inconvenience, and suffering. Under the Act, suffering can be compensated only if it is caused by certain crimes. Immaterial injury to property cannot be compensated under the Act. Compensation is available for purely economic losses only if they result from a punishable act, from the use of public authority, or if other particularly pressing grounds exist for compensation. Courts have interpreted the last expression fairly strictly. Thus, a claim for compensation for immaterial injury or economic loss resulting from use of one's image that is not punishable under specific legislation is not likely to succeed.

7 Unjust enrichment

10.77 An action for refund of benefit by unjust enrichment can be brought against someone who has gained (eg financial benefit) at the expense of the complainant. The party demanding restitution is required to demonstrate a causal connection between his own loss and the other party's gain.

A person whose image has been used in marketing without proper authorisation could thus claim that the party using the image has gained benefit by unjust enrichment, the benefit being the fee the person depicted would have charged for consenting to the use of his image.

8 Finnish jurisprudence concerning personality

10.78 In the Supreme Court decision 1986 II 131, rendered on 15 October 1986, the unauthorised use of the image of a famous racing driver in a television commercial for a print magazine was not deemed to be unlawful. The racing driver had sued the publisher of the magazine for damages, stating that the use of the image had caused him significant economic loss by damaging his chances of negotiating advertising contracts with other publishing companies. Furthermore, in using the image, the publisher had made use of a valuable advertising commodity without paying the compensation usually charged for that commodity. The Supreme Court found that since the image was, save a few non-essential differences, the same as the one published in the magazine and the magazine also had other content relating to the racing driver, the image was deemed to have been used to describe the contents of the magazine in a manner that was not tortious.

10.79 In the Supreme Court decision 1982 II 36, compensation for damages was awarded for the unauthorised commercial use of a private individual's image although the said use was not deemed to constitute an invasion of privacy. A had been photographed with his permission in a public place. The photographs were conveyed to B, who used an image from which A could be clearly identified, in a travel brochure and advertising poster. B had not established that A had consented to the said use of his image. Although the Supreme Court found that the publication of the image had not constituted an invasion of A's privacy because the image had not conveyed information about A's personal life, B was ordered to pay FIM 2.000 in damages to A for using his image in the said promotional activities without proper permission. Since A had not presented any evidence of any damage actually suffered by him as a result of the use of his image, the Supreme Court apparently based its decision to award damages on the assumption that the commercial use of a person's image is in itself liable to cause that person suffering. This interpretation was affirmed in the Supreme Court decision 1989:62, rendered on 26 May 1989, where the parents of a child whose image had been used in advertising without permission were awarded FIM 2.000 in damages for the suffering caused by the unwanted attention the parents were subjected to as a result of such use, again despite the fact that the occurrence of damage had not been established by the plaintiffs.

11 FRANCE

Charles de Haas

A Introduction

1 Searching for a balance

11.01 The protection of privacy, personality rights and the rights to one's likeness are the object of strict regulation in France, in ways that are both complex and subtle.

11.02 Such protection is complex because it frequently results from the evolving application of very general principles case-by-case through jurisprudence.

11.03 Furthermore, it is subtle because such protection necessitates the search for a balance between several fundamental freedoms and general principles of law, particularly the right of free enterprise and the freedom of expression on the one hand and the protection of personality rights on the other.

11.04 The balance is far from fixed, as it changes with society's sensibilities and customs. Drawing conclusions from illustrated cases may therefore lead to errors of interpretation.

B Privacy

1 Principal texts

11.05 Initially the general principle of civil liability set out in Article 1382 of the Civil Code was invoked by victims and used by courts in order to ensure the protection of privacy in France. The French legislature then intervened with the law of 17 July 1971, 'tending to reinforce the guarantee of individual rights of citizens', that established the right of the respect of privacy as an entitlement of individual rights.

11.06 Article 9 of the Civil Code reasserts the terms of Article 8 of the European Convention on Human Rights (ECHR) of 1950, which was already directly applicable in France, by affirming the existence of a right attributed to the individual.

Article 8 of the European Convention on Human Rights

11.07

'RIGHT TO RESPECT FOR PRIVATE AND FAMILY LIFE
1. Everyone has the right to respect for his private and family life, his home and his correspondence.
2. There shall be no interference by a public authority with the exercise of this right except such as is in accordance with the law and is necessary in a democratic society in the interests of national security, public safety or the economic well-being of the country, for the prevention of disorder or crime, for the protection of health or morals, or for the protection of the rights and freedoms of others.'

Article 9 of the Civil Code

11.08

'Each individual has the right to the respect of his privacy.'
'The judges can, without prejudice to compensation for damages suffered, prescribe all measures, such as sequestration, seizure and others, suitable for preventing or causing to cease an invasion of privacy; these measures may, in case of urgent matters, be ordered through a summary proceeding.'

11.09   Numerous specific laws then follow from these general principles in order to prevent invasion of privacy under particular circumstances and will be cited when describing the more specific contents of this system of protection.

2   *Status of foreign citizens and international privacy rights*

11.10   The right to have one's privacy respected was established as a human right by the ECHR (Articles 8 and 14), which was ratified by France, consequently all foreign citizens enjoy the full protection of this right without any condition of reciprocity being required by the system of their State of origin.[1]

11.11   As far as International Privacy Rights are concerned, jurisprudence of the Cour de Cassation (supreme court for civil and criminal matters) considers that 'the law of the place where the facts were committed' must be applied.[2]

11.12   Finally, French courts will be competent if the defendant resides in their jurisdiction or if the offence was committed there or if the damage was suffered there.[3] The Brussels Convention, in instances where it is applicable, does not substantially modify the rules of domestic law on this point.

---

1   Cour d'Appel de Paris, 14 June 1995, Juris Data No 02 4843.
2   Cour de Cassation 1st Civile, 13 April 1988, Jurisclasseur 1988 Ed G IV, 212.
3   Articles 42 and 46 of the New Civil Procedure Code.

3   *General content of protection*

11.13   The legislator was careful not to give a definition to the notion of privacy. Definitions have nevertheless been proposed, in particular:

> 'the right to the respect of privacy is a right for a person to be free to lead his own existence as he sees fit, with a minimum of external interference' (M Hebarre).

11.14   The ECHR itself is more specific:

> 'privacy is violated when the autonomy, peace or tranquility of personal or family activities is undermined, also noise nuisances and more generally pollutions that affect physical well-being or that undermine the enjoyment of the pleasure of domicile constitute violations of the right of Article 8 of the ECHR.'

11.15   In general, it must be noted that this protection of privacy rather logically yields before a number of circumstances, in particular:

(1)   when the reported fact stems from the public life of the subject (artist, politician, etc) and is therefore neither intimate nor private;

(2)   when the subject dies, as protection then ceases in principle – '...the right to bar any form of disclosure of one's private life ... belongs only to the living' – and heirs can only complain about offences to the honour or to the memory of the deceased,[4] unless the invasion of privacy of the deceased affects by extension the privacy of the heirs; [5]

(3)   when the reported fact belongs to history, even recent history;[6] and

(4)   when the subject himself consents, expressly and specifically, to the collecting or to the disclosure of information of a private nature. Authorisation cannot be general and permanent. However, the use of information must be made strictly within the limits of the authorisation.

11.16   Beyond these general principles, we shall consider under what more specific circumstances this complex system of protection applies.

4   *Covert filming (or recording)*

11.17   The general law relating to privacy prohibits the filming or transmitting of images of an individual without his consent, except when the individual appears in public outside the sphere of privacy.[7]

11.18   The criminally punishable offences of spying on someone's privacy[8] and of using the product of this spying[9] are liable to constitute an invasion of one's private life.

---

4   Cour d'Appel de Paris, 1st Chamber A, 23 November 1993, Légipresse 1994, 7 No 114 II, p 32.

5   Such an invasion exists when the book 'the Great Secret' disclosed the state of François Mitterrand's health following his death, Cour de Cessation, 1st Civil Chamber, 14 December 1999, JCP 2000 II 10.241, s 5 or when the photograph of the corpse of the murdered Prefect of Corsica was published during the period of mourning, Cour d'Appel de Paris, 24 February 1998, D.98.225.

6   Concerning Costa Gavras' film Z: Tribunal de Grande Instance de Paris, 6 June 1971, Dalloz 1971 Jur, p 678.

7   Cf paras 11.13 to 11.16.

8   Article 226-1 of the New Penal Code.

9   Article 226-2 of the New Penal Code.

11.19   The offence has been judged to include photographing an individual (even well-known) on his death bed[10] and the use of an intercom to overhear the conversations of employees.[11]

5   The domicile

11.20   There are a number of laws which protect rights in relation to domiciles, including laws against making openings or spy-holes into one's neighbour's domicile,[12] the offence of breach of domicile,[13] the offence of spying from a distance into private places[14] and the presumption of legitimate defence by a resident in the case of entry at night by break-in, violence or ruse into their domicile. In addition, the individual's right to keep their address secret is protected.

11.21   Therefore, according to the Tribunal de Grande Instance of Paris (civil trial court of general jurisdiction): 'the disclosure in the press of the address of domicile or of residence of an individual without the latter's consent constitutes an illicit invasion of privacy'.

11.22   The Paris Court reached a similar conclusion in condemning the disclosure to the public of the personal address of the Prince of Monaco.[15]

> 'The domicile belongs to the domain of privacy ... the reproduction of photographs taken in the private home of an individual without his authorisation ... violates his privacy'.[16]

11.23   This protection does not, however, cover abuses such as the attempt to escape from an obligation, particularly a contractual one,[17] and does not prevent the Post and Telecommunication regulations from requesting additional fees for non-disclosure of the particulars of an individual in the directories.[18]

6   Filming on private property

11.24   The publication of the photograph or film of an individual's residence cannot be punished through the application of Article 9 of the Civil Code, unless it constitutes an invasion of privacy 'by the disclosure of facts of a private nature'.[19]

---

10 Cour de Cassation Criminelle, October 21, 180, Revue Trimestrielle de Droit Civil 1983, p 112d.
11 Tribunal Correctionnel, lower criminal court of Saint-Etiénne, April 19, 1997, Dalloz 1978, J 123, Note Lindon,
12 Civil Code, arts 676 to 680.
13 Articles 226-4 and 432-8 of the New Penal Code.
14 Article 226-1 of the New Penal Code.
15 Cour d'Appel de Paris, 2 June 1976, Dalloz 1977, p 364.
16 Tribunal de Grande Instance de Paris, 1st Chamber, 8 January 1986, Dalloz 1987 Somm, p 138, obs R Lindon.
17 Action of creditors or the legitimate request of an insurer – cf Cour de Cassation Civile, 30 June 1992, Jurisclasseur 1993 II.22.001 Note Daverat.
18 Conseil d'Etat 30 December 1998, JCP 1999, IV, 1759.
19 Cf in particular, Cour de Cassation 2nd Civile, 29 June 1988, Bulletin Civil II No 160.

11.25 The activity of filming from the air will constitute an invasion of privacy if the aerial photography of a building includes the image of its occupants or of its interior lay-out, which would normally be hidden from the view of outsiders. The disclosure of the facts relative to one's private life must be identified.

11.26 Where aerial photography involves low flying over residential zones, the persons carrying out this activity must request from the prefect the exemption provided by Article 5 of the Order of 10 October 1957, relative to flight over urban areas and gatherings of people.[20]

11.27 The publication of an individual's likeness can be considered an invasion of privacy which will be criminally punishable 'if it involved an individual found in a private place'[1] or if it involved publication by dissimulating it within a montage of words or image.

11.28 The rights of individuals to their likeness are considered later in this work.

In addition, according to recent case law, the ownership of the right to enjoy and dispose of things, including private property and real property would comprise a right in the likeness of the things (including photographs) at least with regard to any commercial exploitation thereof.[2]

7   *Interception of mail and telephone calls*

11.29 The inviolability of correspondence is established by the ECHR (Article 8-1), though subject to interference by government authorities pursuant to Article 8, paragraph 2, and is considered in France as a higher principle of constitutional value.[3] French jurisprudence therefore confirms the protection of the secrecy of correspondence and telephone communications.

11.30 If a letter of a confidential nature is presented in court, case law seems to accept it as proof[4] even if the person responsible for the violation of confidentiality incurs general civil liability.[5]

11.31 French criminal law provides that the interception of correspondence or telephone calls, with respect to both individuals and government employees, is an offence.[6] The only exception to this protection concerns interception ordered by judicial authorities.[7]

---

20 See Rép Ministérielles No 28356 and 28386 of 20 July 1987 and Rép Ministérielle No 22133 Journal Officiel de l'Assemblée Nationale, Q 12 February 1990, p 678.
1   Article 368-372 of the Penal Code.
2   Cour de Cassation, 1st Civil Chamber, 10 March 1999, see however several harsh critics in JCP Ed E 1999 PU s 5, p 1482, JCP Ed G 1999 10.07, RIDA No 181, p 243 and Droit & Patrimoines 1999 Bulletin p 300, p 7.
3   P Kayser – La Protection de la Vie Privée par le Droit – 3rd Ed Economica 1945, pp 304 and 528.
4   Cf Mélanges Pierre Voirin – article of, P Kayser, p 445.
5   According to art 1382 of the Civil Code.
6   Articles 186 and 187 of the Penal Code which are applicable even against policemen in charge of the protection of the French President at the Elysée Palace: Cour d'Appel de Paris, 30 September 1996, GP 1997 J1.
7   According to art 186-1 of the Penal Code.

11.32 The New Penal Code prohibits the opening, removal, delay or diversion and fraudulent reading of correspondence[8] or the distribution of an edited dissimulation of recorded words without the consent of the party concerned.[9]

8 Personal information

11.33 Disclosure of the pregnancy of the actress Isabelle Adjani was condemned on the grounds of the protection of privacy.[10] But the pregnancy of Princess Stephanie of Monaco was considered to be a public event capable of disclosure, taking into account the fact that it was not concealed from the public.[11]

11.34 So far as disclosure of financial information is concerned, if it relates to public figures who are known for financial or economic reasons then it can be disclosed.[12] In other cases disclosure is, in principle, prohibited.

9 Personal identification

11.35 A person's name, by its very nature, is not something which may be kept secret since it is intended to allow the public to individualise a given person. An individual's last name or surname is not in itself confidential. However, in certain circumstances, in particular in the field of the arts, if a pseudonym is adopted in order to conceal from the public one's true identity, this is then considered a matter of privacy.

11.36 Therefore, the Cour d'Appel de Paris, in a decision of 15 May 1970, considered that the following 'must in particular be sheltered from violation: the right to one's name, image, voice, privacy, honour and reputation, the right to being forgotten and the right to *one's own biography*'.[13]

11.37 In this case, the periodical concerned was accused of having, for purely commercial purposes, disclosed to the public (which was previously unaware of such matters) the last name or surname of the singer Tenenbaum, the real name of Jean Ferrat, his domicile in Ivry, his telephone number and the place of his second home in the Ardèche.

11.38 Protection against the identity of an individual being abusively exploited to the detriment of their private life is provided by the legislature by a special regulation applicable to nominative data and its automated processing.

8   Articles 226-15 and 432-9 of the New Penal Code.
9   Article 226-7 of the New Penal Code.
10 Cour d'Appel de Paris, 26 February 1981, Dalloz 1981, 457.
11 Tribunal de Grande Instance de Nanterre, 17 June 1998, Légipresse 1998 No 154I, 107.
12 See in particular the publication by *Le Nouvel Observateur* of the 100 wealthiest people in France, Cassation Civile, 4 October 1989, Bulletin Cassation No 307, p 204 and publications by 'Le Canard Enchaîné' of financial information relating to managers of big firms: CEDH, 21 January 1999, D 1999 IR 46.
13 Recueil Dalloz Sirey 1970 JPN, p 466.

10 Protection of nominative data and its automated processing

11.39 'Nominative information' and 'nominative data' are taken to mean all information whose object is a natural person 'with the exclusion of artificial persons', such as corporate bodies and companies, which allows for identification of the person.[14] This information includes a person's last name or surname, their first name and their domicile. It also includes other information of a personal nature.

11.40 The law of 6 January 1978 'relative to information, data files and freedoms' instituted this protection, which applies principally to:
(1) the creation of automated data processing, and
(2) all lists, computer-based or not.

11 Protection of automated processing of nominative data

11.41 Article 5 of the law of 6 January 1978 defines the notion of automated data processing either as 'the totality of operations realised by automated means' whose function is 'the collection, recording, development, modification, consultation and destruction of nominative information', or as 'the exploitation of files or data bases and especially the interconnection or comparison, consultation or communication of nominative information'.

(1) For the public sector, only a law or a regulatory instrument can create such data processing.

(2) Non-public data processing that manifestly does not constitute an invasion of privacy or a violation of freedoms must be declared beforehand to the CNIL (Commision Nationale Informatique et Liberté, National Data Processing and Freedom Commission).

(3) All other private data processing must be the object of a request for the opinion of the Commission (CNIL).

(4) All data processing is made public by the CNIL with the exception of those important for national security, national defence and public safety.

(5) Finally, data processing for research purposes in the field of health is subject to a more complex procedure of prior opinion and authorisation.

12 Protection of nominative data files per se

11.42
(1) Certain information can never be recorded (racial origins, political, philosophical or religious views, trade-union memberships or memberships related to lifestyles), unless by express agreement on the part of the concerned party and it is recorded:
  (a) for churches and religious, philosophical, political or trade-union groups for their members and correspondents;
  (b) for written and audio-visual press organisations; and
  (c) for reasons in the public interest by order of having received approval of the Conseil d'Etat, the highest administrative court, following a proposition or opinion in conformity with the CNIL.

14 Cf art 4 of the law of 6 January 1978.

(2) The collecting of nominative information in order to record it in any data file whatsoever by fraudulent, dishonest or unlawful means is prohibited. Any natural person has the recognised right 'to oppose for legitimate reasons the use of nominative information concerning himself in data processing'.[15]

(3) A person collecting information has the obligation, with respect to each individual concerned, to inform that person as to who is to receive the information and the individual's right to have access to and to rectify the nominative data concerned.

(4) Any person who orders or carries out the processing of information is responsible for ensuring the security of information collected.

11.43 Any breaches of these provisions are criminally punishable from Class 5 misdemeanors to fines of up to 2,000,000 francs and prison sentences of up to 5 years.

13 *Public order aspects (obstructing the road, riotous assembly, etc)*

11.44 In principle, participation in public demonstrations does not fall within the scope of privacy protection (cf supra, concerning the right to one's likeness). However, information relating to political opinions (including participation in demonstrations) cannot be recorded except for public interest reasons after having received the approval of the Conseil d'Etat (the highest administrative court), following the opinion of the Commision Nationale Informatique et Liberté (CNIL, National Data Processing and Freedom Commission).[16]

11.45 That apart, the photographing, filming and publication of public events is lawful even if individuals can be recognised.[17] However, a participant or a demonstrator must not play a particular rôle or be presented in the foreground.[18]

14 *Recording of conversations (whether overt or covert)*

11.46 The recording of a conversation which is essentially of a private nature without the consent of all its participants constitutes an invasion of privacy.

11.47 If the conversation is by telephone, as we have seen, it is protected from interception, recording and broadcast or distribution[19] as well as from broadcast or distribution without the consent of the concerned party.[20]

---

15 Article 26, para 11 of the law.
16 See paras **11.42** and **11.43** above.
17 Cour d'Appel de Paris, 10 January 1985, and Tribunal de Grande Instance Paris, 9 April 1992, Gazette du Palais 1993, 2, 5.320.
18 Cf Tribunal de Grande Instance Paris, summary proceeding, 6 June 1974, J 95 note Lindon, or, for the disclosure of the participation at a demonstration of homosexuals, Cour d'Appel de Paris, 14 June 1985, Dalloz 1986 IR 50.
19 See para **11.29**.
20 Article 226-7 of the New Penal Code.

11.48   Finally, the invasion of privacy by spying and the use of the product of this spying may also be the objects of the application of Articles 226-1 and 226-2 of the New Penal Code.[1]

15 Sifting through rubbish

11.49   In itself, the sifting through and removal of rubbish is not unlawful. However, the disclosure of information relevant to a person's private life, even if lawfully collected beforehand, is unlawful under the common law.

16 State of health

11.50   Even public figures have the right to maintain their state of health secret. A newspaper was taken to court for having published the photograph, taken without the knowledge of his family circle, of the young and seriously ill son of the actor Gérard Philipe.[2] Even when the subject dies, the subsequent disclosure of the state of Francoir Mitterrand's health affects by extension, the privacy of the heirs.[3]

11.51   The disclosure of a politician's psychiatric confinement was also deemed unlawful.[4]

11.52   An unknown individual obtained 100,000 francs in damages and the publication of the judicial decision following the posting of information revealing that the individual had AIDS.[5]

17 Use of an assumed identity in order to obtain information

11.53   Whatever the means (even lawful) employed in order to obtain information, its disclosure to the public is unlawful if it touches on matters of privacy. Surveillance of an individual is possible, provided it does not interfere with their privacy (eg by violating their domicile by violation of Articles 226-4 and 432-8 of the New Penal Code).

11.54   On the other hand, the use of a false identity, if it can lead to a confusion with a regulated professional or public office, is prohibited and punishable under Article 258-1 of the Penal Code. Using a false identity may also lead to evidence being ruled inadmissable if it is not obtained by honest means.

11.55   Recently, a brokerage firm was unable to prove an order by admitting evidence of a recorded telephone conversation with a client who had not been informed that the conversation was being recorded.[6]

---

1   See para **11.17**.
2   Summary Proceeding, Paris, 13 March 1965, JCP 1965 II 14 443, Note Lindon and 2nd Cassation, 12 July 1966, Jurisclasseur 1996 Ed G II 14 223.
3   Cour d'Appel de Paris, 13 March 1996, JCP ed 6 1996 II, 22632 and Cour de Cassation 1st Civil Chamber, 14 December 1999 JCP 2000 II 10.241 s 5.
4   By decision of the Cour d'Appel de Paris of December 1997.
5   Cour d'Appel de Paris, 24 August 1990, non-published but cited by Jean-Pierre Ancel, Gazette de Palais 1994, 2nd sem, p 990.
6   Cour d'Appel de Paris, 15 May 1998, Recueil Dalloz Sirey 1998 No 31 IR, p 196.

18 Use of security camera footage for reporting events

11.56   Security cameras are not generally set up in private places, otherwise an invasion of privacy would obviously be perpetrated and the offence of spying on an individual's private life[7] might be committed using information thus obtained.[8]

11.57   Where security cameras are set up in public places, and the events they monitor take place in public; they cannot, in principle, violate a person's privacy. There are special circumstances, however, where scenes considered as private can take place in public and be protected.[9]

11.58   It should also be borne in mind that the dissemination of an individual's likeness even outside their privacy requires their consent (cf supra, regarding rights to one's likeness).

19 Use of telephoto lens

11.59   Apart from the disclosure of facts concerning a person's private life and restricted by the terms of common law,[10] the use of a telephoto lenses may constitute the offence of spying on an individual's private life[11] as will using information obtained from this.[12]

11.60   Orders have been made restraining the use of photographs of Brigitte Bardot on her private property taken with a telephoto lens[13] as well as against photographs of Grimaldi[14] and of Princess Diana and Mr Fayed on a yacht.[15]

20 Remedies

11.61   In urgent cases involving an invasion of privacy, Article 9 of the Civil Code provides that the summary proceedings judge is competent to deal with matters (paragraph 2). The matter can be brought before such a judge as quickly as desired (from hour to hour if necessary).

11.62   Measures to prevent publication have been ordered, such as prohibition by the levying of a dissuasive penalty, or even seizing of newspapers.[16] Interference in an individual's private life must, however, be serious if not intolerable because the sanction against it is not reversible (cf the publication of the photograph Gérard Philipe's child on his hospital bed despite his fright and his objections, already cited).[17]

7   Article 226-1 of the New Penal Code.
8   Article 226-2 of the New Penal Code.
9   Cf concerning the resident of a burning building who jumps out a window, judgment of the Tribunal de Grande Instance of Nanterre, 18 January 1995, note ch Amard, Petites Affiches 1998, No 34, p 13.
10 On the basis of art 9 of the Civil Code.
11 Article 226-1 of the New Penal Code.
12 Article 226-2 of the New Penal Code.
13 Cour d'Appel of Paris, 1 December 1965, Jurisclasseur 1966.
14 Tribunal de Grande Instance de Nanterre 8 April 1998, Légipresse 1998 No 155, I 122.
15 Tribunal de Grande Instance de Paris, 13 December 1999 Légipresse No 171, p 62, giving rise to a fine of FF 150.000 and damages of FF 100.000 granted to their heirs.
16 See especially Cour de Cassation 1st Civile, 18 May 1972, Jurisclasseur 1972 Ed G II, 17 209.
17 See para **11.50** above.

11.63 Most often, when the violation is not intolerable or sufficiently serious, the freedom of the press regains the upper hand and only future actions are restricted (seizing of negatives, prohibition of further publication under penalty, etc).

11.64 The following have been judged as being intolerable:

(a) publication of a person's features on their deathbed;

(b) disclosure of a surgical operation;

(c) exposing the reasons for a spouse's jealousy; and

(d) publication of an image that shows the private parts of the body.

11.65 The summary proceedings judge does not generally have the power to order the payment of damages but the following are illustrations of the range of orders that may be made:

(1) removal of an excerpt from a publication;[18]

(2) affixing of a mask on the face of an individual in order to make him unrecognisable;[19]

(3) publication of a warning at the beginning of a film;[20]

(4) destruction of photographic negatives[1] or other documents that are evidence of an invasion of privacy;[2]

(5) the awarding of damages, generally of a small amount from 1 symbolic franc to 10,000 francs when the wrongdoing essentially causes emotional distress, except in specific cases. The gravity of the tort can sometimes increase the damages; 115,000 francs were therefore awarded to the Rainier family of Monaco,[3] 350,000 Francs to the same Grimaldi[4] and 100,000 francs to each of the actors that played in a comedy that was then shown, without their knowledge, with erotic sequences;[5]

(6) publication of the decision at the expense of the perpetrator of the invasion of privacy, particularly when the violation was committed via the press;[6]

(7) Finally, criminal prosecution can be sanctioned in respect of violations of any of the laws mentioned above.

---

18 Tribunal de Grande Instance de la Seine, 18 March 1966 Dalloz 1966, 2nd sem, p 568.
19 Cassation Civile, 14 March 1990, Dalloz 1990, I, p 497 and Tribunal de Grande Instance de Paris, 3rd of 2nd section, 16 January 1975.
20 Cour d'Appel de Paris, 5 January 1972, Dalloz 1972, p 445, Note Duterte.
1   Tribunal de Grande Instance to Paris, 25 May 1983, Dalloz. 1984, IR, p 332.
2   Cour d'Appel de Bordeaux, 18 March 1998, Jurisdate No 043197.
3   Tribunal de Grande Instance de Paris, 2 June 1976, Dalloz 1977, p 364.
4   Tribunal de Grande Instance de Nanterre 8 April 1998, Légipresse 1998 No 155, I 122.
5   Tribunal de Grande Instance de Paris, 20 April 1977, Dalloz 1977, p 610.
6   Cour d'Appel de Paris, 28 November 1989, Dalloz 1989, p 410.

C Personality rights

1 Principal laws

11.66 Numerous and disparate laws might be applied for the protection of an individual's name and biography. In addition to the laws relating to the protection of privacy cited above, the relevant laws include:

(1) The law of 29 July 1881, in relation to defamation and the right of response.

(2) Article L 121.1 of the Intellectual Property Code for author's moral rights, ie in particular the right of the author to have published their paternity of a work, or, on the contrary, to have it cancelled (in force since 1957).

(3) Article 9-1 of the Civil Code for the respect of the presumption of innocence (in force since 1993).

(4) Article L 711-4 of the Intellectual Property Code provides that a personality right thwarts the adoption of a trade mark (took effect on 28 December 1991, but codified an old jurisprudence).

(5) Article L 713-6 of the Intellectual Property Code that provides that a homonym maintains concurrent rights notwithstanding registration of the name as a trade mark (took effect on 28 December 1991).

(6) Article 226-8 of the New Penal Code, which prohibits the publication of a dissimulated montage of words or images without the consent of the concerned party.

2 Status of foreign citizens

11.67 The system of personality rights (which includes the right to one's own biography and name) has already been described from the viewpoint of a foreign national.

11.68 However, since the right of trade marks is likely to be superposed, we note that according to Article L 712-11 of the Intellectual Property Code foreign citizens domiciled or established in France benefit from French law as do French citizens and as do foreign nationals (or foreigners assimilated to nationals) from member countries of the European Union by application of Articles 2 and 6-2 of the Paris Convention.

11.69 Foreign citizens from non-union member nations who are neither domiciled nor established in France can still benefit from the French system if, reciprocally, French citizens are protected in their country, again by application of Article L 712-11 of the Intellectual Property Code.

3 Aspects of personality rights generally

11.70 In French law, the concept of personality rights is quite wide and is not limited to the protection of one's name and of one's biography; it involves all the inseparable fundamental rights of the individual, including:

(1)   right to one's honour and reputation;

(2)   right to respect of privacy (already examined);

(3)   individual freedoms, at least in their subjective content; and

(4)   moral rights of authors.

11.71   Established legal authorities are rather unclear on the nature and even the exact contents of these rights.[7] If, for the purposes of this work, we limit ourselves to presenting the specific contents of only those rights relative to one's biography and name, we note a certain number of common characteristics:

(1)   They have a purely moral content as well as a patrimonial content, since the consent that is required of their holder, particularly for comercial use, can be exchanged for money.

(2)   The distinction is particularly evident upon the death of the concerned party since rights having financial value pass on to the heirs, whereas most moral rights end (except the moral right of the author according to Articles L 121-2 and L 121-3 of the Intellectual Property Code and the right to defend the honour and reputation of the deceased, excluding defamation according to Article 34 of the law of 29 July 1881).

(3)   From a subjective point of view, personality rights are negatively analysed, ie they permit the owner to prohibit others from enjoying what is reserved for himself or herself. This includes the ability to prohibit others from using certain elements of one's biography or from deforming them or from using one's name otherwise than from the purposes of identification.

(4)   When the individual concerned consents to use or commercial exploitation that they can otherwise prohibit, their consent must be specific and strictly respected within any limits.

11.72   So far as concerns the right to one's name, the present section will not explore regulations of the *état civil* (legal status according to the official registry), which do not fall at all within the scope of personality rights.[8] Basically, this involves the principle of *the immutability* of one's name, which requires all French citizens to bear the patronymic that is present on their birth certificate, but permits:

(1)   the right to use a pseudonym in the context of literary or artistic activities;

(2)   the right of a married woman to use her husband's name;

(3)   the limited ability to request a name change (in case of legitimate interest if the name is ridiculous, ignominious or foreign-sounding).

4   Rights in a person's 'biography'

11.73   There are two aspects of a person's biography which are protected, namely the publication of the elements of a person's private life and a public disclosure which presents a person in a false light.

---

7   Cf Denis Tallon, Répertoire. Civil Dalloz, October 1996, ss 7 and 11.

8   For the recent reform and simplification of the *état civil* see '*Les Décrets du 16/10/1997 sur l'Etat Civil*' presented in GP 98 No 77/78, Doc, p 2.

Elements of a person's private life

11.74 Any publication of biographical elements belonging to the sphere of privacy without the consent of the person concerned constitutes, in principle, an unlawful invasion of privacy under the general conditions previously examined (cf supra).

11.75 However, several difficulties arise specifically from the public disclosure of biographical elements.

(a) First, when public figures are involved it is not always easy to determine the boundary between public life – which can be disclosed – and private life – which must remain secret. The funeral of the father of the tennis champion Yannick Noah was initially considered by the Tribunal de Grande Instance as an element of his private life, before being excluded from it in appeal.[9] More recently however, the funeral of the actor Yves Montand was considered as an event strictly protected by privacy.[10]

(b) Secondly, the freedom to information can in certain exceptional circumstances justify disclosure of biographical elements, when *the facts also belong to history* provided that the facts are old enough.[11]

(c) Finally, the question of knowing whether allusion to facts that are already known, and may even be publicly notorious, is permitted, has not yet been coherently resolved by case law.

11.76 Therefore, the published details of the romantic liaison of a famous actress, though well known, were unlawful;[12] however the Cour de Cassation refused to grant a right to 'forget' facts arising from the private sphere which had previously been lawfully disclosed to the public as a result of legal proceedings.[13]

Public disclosure which presents a person in a false light

11.77 In this situation the problem is not so much the disclosure of information as its falsification.

In the most serious cases, the criminal offence of defamation is liable to be committed,[14] ie 'the allegation or imputation of a fact that offends the honour or the respect of the person'. Except in the case where the offence may be considered as an invasion of privacy, the defamer can exonerate himself if he proves either the truth of his allegations[15] or his good faith (that is

---

9   Cour d'Appel de Paris, 13 March 1986, Dalloz 1986, IR, 445. Kaiser suggests distinguishing between this kind of borderline event according to the intentions demonstrated by the concerned party himself – 'La Protection de la Vie Privée par le Droit,' Economica, 3rd edition, s 155, p 194.
10 Tribunal de Grande Instance de Nanterre, 15 February 1995, GP 1995 1,282.
11 See, however, the very recent historical facts Simone de Beauvoir disclosed in 'La Cérémonie des Aidieux', describing the final, painful moments of Jean-Paul Sartre's life, cited by Jean-Pierre Ancel, Gazette Palais, 2nd sem 1995, p 988, s 226, and Costa Gavras' film Z – Tribunal de Grande Instance de Paris, 30 June 1971, Dalloz 1971 – Juris, p 678.
12 Tribunal de Grande Instance de Paris, 16 January 1985, unpublished but cited by Jean-Pierre Ancel, article mentioned above.
13 Cour de Cassation, 1st Civil, 30 November 1990, Bulletin Cassation, No 256, p 181.
14 Articles 31 to 34 of the law of 29 July 1881.
15 Article 35, para 3 of the law of 29 July 1881.

established only if there were serious reasons to believe in his allegations). Civil or criminal actions are barred by a statute of limitations that ends three months from the date the offence was committed or from the last investigative or legal action.

11.78 So far as concerns audio-visual material, the publication of a montage of words and images may consitute an offence[16] if it involves the inexact presentation of an individual in public. An election campaign poster which consisted of a montage of a photograph of a couple out for a walk and a political caption has therefore been found unlawful.[17] For an offence to be committed the montage must be published, must not be obvious or expressly mentioned, and must have been made without the consent of the person or persons represented.

11.79 The legislature has also protected individuals being prosecuted but not yet definitely condemned by the presumption of innocence provided by Article 9 of the Declaration of the Rights of Man and of the Citizen of 1789, later established as a constitutional principle.

11.80 Article 9-1 of the Civil Code assures the right of every individual to the respect of the presumption of innocence and upholds this right by allowing the victim to request the judge to order the publication of a statement, and to grant compensation, in the form of damages. Legal action is barred by the statute of limitations after three months from the date of publication of the offence. The individual, once finally cleared of criminal charges, has the right to have the acquittal advertised and the right to resume the period of limitations for legal action, which the individual could not exercise until being cleared. Case law has confirmed the efficiency of said legislation[18] which is going to be strengthened[19] in the near future.

11.81 Where information is disclosed in the course of an interview, case law has considered that an implied contract has been concluded according to which:

(1) the interviewer has the right to use the elements gathered and is considered to be the author of the whole;

(2) the interviewee cannot revoke his consent to the broadcast or publication of the interview; and

(3) the interviewer has an express obligation not to distort the interviewee's presentation of himself or of his opinions. The burden of proving the accuracy of reporting the interviewee's declarations falls on the interviewer, whose hand-written notes will not constitute sufficient proof.[20]

---

16 Articles 370, para 1, of the Penal Code and 226-8 of the New Penal Code.
17 Cour d'Appel de Paris, Chambre d'Accusation, 26 February 1974, Jurisclasseur 1975 II, 17903.
18 Cour de Cassation, 1st Civil Chamber, 12 November 1998, JCP 1999 IV, 3512.
19 A government bill is going to be voted to forbid (in addition) any reproduction of persons linked with manacles...as the Attorney General and the accused who has been put up before public as guilty to publish corrective press releases.
20 Cour d'Appel de Paris, 9 March 1990, Dalloz 1990 IR, 85.

11.82 When an individual's biographical elements are presented without consent (and without any interview having been conducted), case law prevents:

(1) the inclusion of remarks not made;[1]

(2) the use of images in such a way as to give rise to any inference.[2]

11.83 If, however, a biographical element is presented in a work of fiction, the risk of depicting a person in a false light is excluded if a clear warning is given to the public.[3]

5 *Rights in a person's name*

11.84 Use of a patronym (family name or surname) is a necessary means of distinguishing individuals in society. Given its essential role for identification, a person's last name or surname, as a patronym, is no longer the object of a property right, and this has been the position in France for more than 100 years.

11.85 The right to one's name, therefore, is simply one category of personality rights. One's name may also constitute a distinctive sign, in particular a trade mark, a trade name or a company name, and as such it is then protected in an entirely different way, in view of its specific character.

An individual's name taken as an element of personality outside of any use as a distinctive sign

11.86 Taken as an element of personality, an individual's name is protected against interference in one's private life, particularly when it is kept secret through the use of a pseudonym or when it is associated with other information or with computerised date processing.[4]

11.87 Apart from such invasions of privacy, since by general definition an individual's name is not secret, it is rarely in itself the object of protection as an element of personality. However, when the name is well known, it can be the subject of being presented in a false light (cf supra).

11.88 A rather large number of lawsuits have been initiated as a result of works of fiction (novels, films, etc) in which characters are given the names of living individuals. Legal action is possible by the individual bearing the name, though only where a prejudicial confusion can be made between the individual and the character in the novel, film or play. This would be the case if the name is rare and renowned or generally known.[5]

---

1 See from among the numerous decisions of the *Marlene Dietrich* case, Cour d'Appel de Paris, 16 March 1955, Dalloz 1955, J 295.
2 See, for example, the photograph of a person in a night club used to illustrate a magazine about homosexuality, Tribunal de Grande Instance d'Aix, summary proceedings, 18 March 1983, unreported but cited by Kaiser, op cit, p 135, note 76.
3 See the invented love story between Empress Eugénie and Ferdinand de Lesseps, Tribunal Civil de la Seine, 18 January 1939, S 1939, 2.183.
4 Cf Tribunal Civil de la Seine, 1 December 1926, Revue Trimestielle de Droit Civil 1927.411 and Tribunal de Grande Instance de la Seine, 22 October 1963, p 1964.1.86
5 See paras **11.35** ff.

11.89 If the name is more common, other elements (situations, dialogues, scenarios, etc) must necessarily cause the prejudicial confusion,[6] otherwise the request will be rejected.[7] There is prejudicial confusion only if the character is presented in a grotesque, ridiculous, odious or unpleasant manner that would taint the homonym's honour or respectability.

11.90 For other cases, and keeping to the essential, if the name is sufficiently well known and/or rare, it can, as any other element of personality (such as one's likeness), still be the object of exploitation for profit, which is prohibited by French law without the consent of the name bearer. As an example, the use of the first and last names of a character performing a feat in a video game was found to be unlawful.[8]

11.91 We will see that the fame or rarity of a name also leads to decisive consequences as far as the right to distinctive signs is concerned.

An individual's name taken as a distinctive sign, particularly as a trade mark

11.92 There are essentially three difficulties that must be examined when one considers using an individual's name as a distinctive sign:

(1) the name's distinctive character;

(2) the availability of the patronymic name as a distinctive sign; and

(3) the rights of homonyms that remain despite the appropriation of the name as a distinctive sign.

6 *The distinctive character of patronymic names*

11.94 Particularly with respect to trade marks, this distinctive character is denied by certain foreign laws; however, French law recognises it in Article L711-1 of the Intellectual Property Code.

11.95 The possibility of borrowing a person's name to compose a corporate or company name has also been recognised by jurisprudence, with the person's signature on the corporate or company byelaws constituting authorisation.[9]

11.96 By analogy, the same rule has been extended to first names[10] and to pseudonyms, as Article L 711-1 of the Intellectual Property Code formally specifies.

11.97 It would only be otherwise if the name developed and ended up designating the product or service itself.[11] The administration (INPI –

---

6   See in particular Cour d'Appel de Paris, 10 July 1957 Dalloz 1957.622.

7   Cf concerning a character in a television series named Mr Pic, Cour d'Appel de Paris, 7 February 1989 Dalloz 1990.124, note Hassler.

8   Tribunal de Grande Instance de Chalon-sur-Saône, 29 July 1988 Bulletin Information Cour de Cassation 1989 1/2, No 135.

9   Cassation Com, 12 March 1985 and 25 February 1990, Annales de la Propriété Intellectuelle 1985, 3 and 1990, 3.

10 Cour d'Appel de Paris, 1 June 1970 and 7 February 1978, Annales de la Propriété Intellectuelle 1971, 84 and 1979, 352.77.

11 As with 'Brillat Savarin' for a cheese, Cour d'Appel de Paris 18 August 1985 Jurisclasseur Ed G 1987.II.901.

National Institute for Industrial Property), however, appears to want to refuse the registration of famous names as trade marks when the designated products and services are in more or less direct relation to the field of activity in which the well-known name is famous.[12]

7 *The availability of an individual's name as a distinctive sign*

11.97 As with all distinctive signs, the name must be available for use as a trade mark with regards to all possible prior rights. In examining the availability of a trade mark, Article L 711-4 of the Intellectual Property Code sets out a long list of possible prior rights:

(1) prior registered or well-known trade marks;

(2) prior corporate names;

(3) prior trade names and signs;

(4) prior '*appellations d'origine*' (labels denoting place of origin);

(5) prior copyright;

(6) designations of public territorial bodies; and

(7) finally personality rights.

11.98 Personality rights include the right to one's likeness, which has already been successfully opposed to the appropriation of this likeness as a trade mark.[13]

11.99 However, frequent conflicts arise from the desire of one party to appropriate the patronymic name of another party as a trade mark without the consent of its bearer. Consent is necessary only when the name is rare and famous, because in that case it can cause confusion prejudicial to the name holder. There are a number of decisions to this effect in respect of famous names such as Luynes,[14] Noailles[15] and Boissy d'Anglas.[16]

11.100 On the other hand, the names 'Dop' and 'Savignac' were considered by the courts as being too common to create a risk of confusion when they were adopted as trade marks.[17]

11.101 Similar jurisprudence has developed with respect to pseudonyms.[18] The general position (exceptions aside) is that first names were judged as being too common to be able to bar their adoption as trade marks.[19]

---

12 Cf Belioz for records, cassettes and presentations, Propriété Industrielle Bulletin Documentaire 302 III.108 or Glenn Miller for tape recorders and record players, Propriété Industrielle Bulletin Documentaire 307 III.102.

13 Cour d'Appel de Paris, 1 June 1947, Annales de la Propriété Intellectuelle 1940-1948, p 395.

14 Cour d'Appel de Paris, 24 January 1962, Annales de la Propriété Industrielle 1962, p 97.

15 Cour d'Appel de Paris, 21 March 1973 Annales de la Propriété Industielle 1974, p 164.

16 Cassation Civile, 19 June 1961 Annales de la Propriété Intellectuelle 1968, p 188 and 1970, p 236.

17 Cassation Civile, 19 December 1967 and 26 May 1970, Annales de la Propriété Industrielle 1968, p 188 and 1970, p 98.

18 Cour d'Appel de Paris, 30 October 1985, Annales de la Propriété Intellectuelle 1986, p 157.

19 Cassation Commerciale, 26 April 1988, Annales de la Propriété Intellectuelle 1988, p 163.

11.102 Where the owner of a rare and famous patronymic name has given his consent to another party allowing the latter to adopt it as a distinctive sign, the owner's heirs cannot retract his consent after a lengthy period.[20]

11.103 When the name, which is by nature distinctive, is available and appropriated as a distinctive sign, particularly as a trade mark, homonyms nevertheless still retain concurrent rights.

8 Rights concurrently retained by homonyms

11.104 Even if a patronymic name is appropriated as a trade mark, this appropriation in no way prevents homonyms, who are natural persons, from using their own name to designate themselves, even in the context of their commercial activity.

11.105 This right is recognised by Article 2 of the former law on trade marks (of 31 December 1964) and has been consistently recognised by jurisprudence.

11.106 Moreover, according to Article L 713-6 of the Intellectual Property Code:

> 'The registration of a trade mark does not hinder the use of the same sign or of a similar sign as:
> (a) A corporate name, trade name or shop name when this use is … the act of another party in good faith employing his own patronymic name;
> … However, if this use interferes with his rights, the holder of the registration can request that it be limited or prohibited.'

11.107 Only a natural person or natural persons bearing the same name (or a nearly identical name) benefit(s) from this provision, to the exclusion of artificial persons such as corporations[1] and even of holders of identical pseudonyms.[2]

11.108 A married woman who, according to legal documents, retains her maiden name does not benefit from the option provided by Article L 713-6 of the Intellectual Property Code.[3]

11.109 The court has pronounced that the provision may be extended to benefit the relatively uncommon first name Francesco,[4] however the decision was criticised by the most official doctrine.[5]

11.110 The possibility of concurrently using a name that has already been appropriated as a trade mark does not directly benefit a company, which is an artificial person. However, it can benefit the company indirectly through

---

20 Cf concerning the shop sign 'Au Duc de Praslin', Tribunal de Grande Instance de Paris, May 25, 1984 Gazette du Palais 1996 No 215 and 216, p 11.

1 Cour d'Appel de Paris, 21 May 1985, Annales de la Propriété Intellectuelle 1986, p 119.

2 Cour d'Appel de Paris, 17 September 1984, Annales de la Propriété Intellectuelle 1985, p 189.

3 Cour d'Appel de Reims,12 June 1985, Annales de la Propriété Intellectuelle 1986, p 107.

4 Cour d'Appel de Paris, 6 March 1979, Annales de la Propriété Intellectuelle 1983, p 257.

5 Paul Mathely – Le Nouveau Droit des Signes Distinctifs/The New Law of Distinctive Signs – Ed JNA 1994, p 192.

the intermediary of a physical person bearing that name if the latter manages or controls the company, as is implied in the text of Article L 714-6 of the Intellectual Property Code, which provides that a homonym can use his name in the form of a corporate name. Use must be limited to use as a corporate name, a trade name or a shop name and must not be detrimental to the trade mark owner. If use is detrimental to the trade mark owner, concurrent use can be regulated or, more often, prohibited.[6]

9   Remedies

11.111   When interference with personality rights (especially with an individual's biography or name) constitutes an invasion of privacy, it is necessary to refer to decisions already presented on this matter (cf supra). In other cases, the victim will have a cause of action before civil courts, it having already been noted that the Tribunal de Grande Instance has exclusive jurisdiction in trade mark matters by application of Article L 716-3 of the Intellectual Property Code.

11.112   If the damage for which remedy is sought is of a commercial nature, the rules of the common law of civil liability are applicable and the court must evaluate – if necessary by appraisal through experts on a case-by-case basis – the costs and losses suffered. It should be borne in mind that French judges as a general rule are not very generous in such matters.[7]

D   Publicity

11.113   This section will examine only the system of protection of an individual's likeness, other than through an invasion of privacy. Indeed, we have already seen that one's likeness is well protected in the context of the privacy of private life.[8] However, the protection of one's likeness extends far beyond the sphere of privacy in French law.

1   The basis for protection

11.114   This protection is not based on any law, rather on jurisprudence that has been considerably developed since the nineteenth century. The author proposes various theories to base it on, noting in particular:

(1)   development of the protection of privacy;

(2)   a right to private property;

(3)   a form of personality right;

(4)   a specific patrimonial right; and

(5)   even copyright.[9]

---

6   Cf prohibited use of the names Lapidus – Cassation Commerciale, 2 May 1984, Annales de la Propriété Industrielle 1984, p 49 and Leclerc – Cassation Commerciale, 9 November 1987, Annales de la Propriété Industrielle 1988, p 159.
7   For details on evaluation methods, see Jurisclasseur Ed E 1997, supplement No 5, p 30.
8   See para **11.27** above.
9   By likening physical appearance to a work of art : Acquarone, Recueil Dalloz Sirey 1985 Chronique XXIV.

11.115 Whatever the basis may be, this is indeed an exclusive right very close to an intellectual property right since it may be enforced against any third party, except under exceptional circumstances.[10]

2 *Status of foreign citizens and international privacy law*

11.116 The points previously made in relation to the protection of privacy are applicable here.[11]

3 *General aspects of protection*

11.117 Traditionally, extra-patrimonial content is distinguished from patrimonial content, ie a sort of moral law of a discretionary nature from a more material content that can be put on the market. Implementation of the protection requires that the individual can be recognised from the likeness.[12]

11.118 Protection is therefore not merely limited to the face; it can extend to the shape of the body and to any recognisable detail of the body.[13] However, a mere resemblance cannot be considered a violation of an individual's right to his face.[14]

11.119 Generally speaking, the content of this right is considered in a negative manner: it is the right to prohibit the production and distribution of an individual's likeness without the subject's consent. Without the subject's consent, the jurisprudence has nevertheless exposed several exceptions to the exercise of this right:

(1) when the image is incidental and was taken in a public place;

(2) when it concerns a subject of a current event and is published soon after;

(3) when it concerns the reporting of a trial (whose proceedings are public); and

(4) when it concerns the likeness of a public figure in his public life.

4 *Reporting public events*

11.120 In principle, the right to one's likeness cannot impede upon the freedom to report upon public events. Subjects photographed or filmed, therefore, cannot prevent the publication of images made on the occasion of a public event, except under special circumstances.

The publication of a photograph taken in a public place, such as in a department store, is lawful, though the subjects were photographed in a

---

10 See paras **11.117** to **11.119**.
11 See paras **11.10** to **11.12**.
12 Cour d'Appel de Versailles, 27 January 2000 D 2000 IR 56.
13 Tribunal de Grande Instance de la Seine, 26 June 1966, Jurisclasseur 1966 II, 14875 regarding the hand.
14 Concerning the actor Gérard Depardieu, see Tribunal de Grande Instance de Paris, 17 October 1984, Dalloz 1985, IR 324.

normal pose.[15] The same lawfulness holds for the photograph of a person praying in a synagogue.[16]

11.121 However, we have already seen that the subject must not play any particular role in the foreground.[17] The publication of a photograph of slovenly dressed tourists in order to illustrate how poorly the French dress when they travel in a foreign country was judged unlawful.[18]

11.122 Public figures (politicians, artists, athletes, etc) are required to accept that they may be the main subject of a photograph or film illustrating their own public life. To this extent, the publication of their image is lawful even without their express consent, which is assumed.[19] However, such publication must be made for the purposes of providing information and not for publicity purposes or for commercial exploitation.[20]

11.123 Where, however, a public figure acts merely as a private individual, he retains all the rights of a private individual, including those rights available in relation to public places.[1]

5 Reporting one's private life

11.124 The protection of common law is fully applicable whether the person is a public figure or not. We refer to our comments concerning the protection of privacy in general, which apply where an individual's likeness is used in violation of their privacy. The taking of an image with a camera is also criminally punishable by Article 226-1 of the New Penal Code.

6 Advertising for publicity purposes (and commercial exploitation)

11.125 The likeness of any well-known person has a commercial value that may be very significant. Taking this fact into account, jurisprudence has further provided a right to an individual's likeness in the context of such use.[2]

11.126 Therefore, in order to use a celebrity's likeness, the user must have special consent, in general by way of contracts that are increasingly elaborate.[3] This authorisation is strictly interpreted. Thus, the showing of a film sequence that was not expressly authorised has been found unlawful.[4]

---

15 Cour d'Appel de Paris, 19 September 1994, Revue Trimestrielle de Droit Civil 1995 326.
16 Cour d'Appel de Paris, 11 February 1987, Dalloz 1987, Som 385.
17 See paras **11.45** and **11.46**.
18 Cour d'Appel de Paris, 24 March 1965, Jurisclasseur 1965 II 14 305.
19 See among several decisions: Cour d'Appel de Paris, 26 February 1991, D 1991 2.538.
20 Cf for post cards, Cour d'Appel de Paris, 26 February 1991, cited above or, further for 'pin's' (brooches) showing the image of the television presentator Dechavanne : Cassation 1ère Civile 13 January 1998, Jurisclasseur 1998 Ed G , 10.082 and Légipresse 1998 No 52 p 77.
1 Where he cannot be seen as the central or particular subject: Cour d'Appel de Paris, 16 June 1986, Dalloz 1987 Som 136.
2 The Petula Clark case, Cour d'Appel de Paris, 1 December 1965, previously cited.
3 Cf 'Les contrats de transfert de renommée' Richard Gilbey and Charles de Haas, 5 Jurisclasseur Ed E 1989 No 21 p 29.105.
4 Cour d'Appel de Paris, 1st Chamber, 24 January 1994, Légipresse No 111 III, p 72.

11.127   The responsibility of proving authorisation and the conditions of use falls upon the person exploiting the image[5] and the publisher cannot therefore simply accept what the photographer tells him.[6]

11.128   This basic, quasi-commercial right can itself be transferred to the heirs.[7]

7   Remedies

11.129   When protection of the right to one's likeness merges with that of privacy, the judges will use the privacy law procedure (cf supra). We note, however, that the remedies ordered appear more extensive, and that there is a greater likelihood in obtaining the order for the irreversible seizure or removal of publications in which the image appears, even if the violation is not intolerable.[8]

11.130   So far as concerns the amount awarded in damages, decisions vary widely and in the end appear rather arbitrary. Emotional distress would seem to be capable of being unconditionally and symbolically redressed, at least by the awarding of a symbolic franc, but then actual loss must be established.

11.131   If the likeness is published without authorisation, the harm is essentially in terms of emotional distress.[9] This loss has been judged as limited, even almost non-existent:

(1)   when involving the publication of a photo of a baby in a catalogue;[10]

(2)   when the contentious likeness has already been the object of wide distribution;[11]

(c)   when the poor quality of the photograph makes the subject difficult to recognise;[12] and

(d)   when the likeness is transmitted for only several seconds during a television programme.[13]

11.132   When concerned with the publication or distribution of the likeness of public figures, the judge may refer to the 'going rate' (established by expert witness if necessary) in order to award on the basis of lost earnings, *at most* the sum equivalent to what could have been paid contractually, in accordance with the principles of the allocation of damages by virtue of Articles 1382 and 3 of the Civil Code.

---

5   Jurisclasseur Ed E 1989 No 21 p 29.105.
6   Tribunal de Grande Instance de Paris, 18 December 1985, Dalloz 1986, IR 446.
7   Tribunal de Grande Instance d'Aix en Provence, 24 November 1988, Jurisclasseur 1989, II 21 329.
8   Tribunal de Grande Instance de Paris, 4 April 1970, Jurisclasseur 1970, II 16 328, the Pompidou case.
9   Cour d'Appel de Paris, 18 February 1971, Jurisclasseur 1971, II 16 774.
10 Tribunal de Commerce de la Seine, 12 May 1934, Gazette du Palais 1934, 2.238.
11 Tribunal de Grande Instance de Paris, 27 February 1970, Jurisclasseur 1970, II 16 293
12 Cour d'Appel de Versailles, 4 October 1988, Dalloz 1989, Som 359.
13 Tribunal de Grande Instance de Lyon, 18 February 1976, Jurisclasseur 1978, II 18 900.

11.133   If private life is disclosed through publication of photographs of public figures, damages are greater.[14]

---

14 200,000 Francs for Caroline de Monaco and 150,000 Francs only for her lover: Tribunal de Grande Instance de Nanterre, 8 April 1998, Légipresse 1998 No 155 I, 122.

12 GERMANY

Dr Thomas R Klötzel

A Privacy and personality

1 Constitutional basics

12.01 Privacy ('Privatsphäre') is considered as being an integral part of a person's general personality right ('allgemeines Persönlichkeitsrecht'). From a German perspective it is not possible to distinguish privacy on the one hand from personality on the other. Since the constitutional and the civil law rights or criminal liability resulting from an infringement or violation of the general personality right are the same, privacy and personality shall be dealt with in one joint section.

12.02 The general personality right which exists as a matter of principle for legal entities as well as individuals is guaranteed in Article 2(1) read in conjunction with Article 1(1) of the Basic Law ('Grundgesetz'), Germany's constitution which came into force on 24 May 1949. Articles 2(1) and 1(1) of the Basic Law protect everyone's right to the free development of his or her personality in so far as that person does not violate the rights of others and does not breach the constitutional order or the moral standards. The consitution further warrants that the dignity of man is inviolable and that it is the duty of all State authorities to respect and protect such dignity.

12.03 The term 'everyone' clearly includes all foreign citizens.[1] In the civil law it is also settled that legal entities are within the sphere of protection of Article 2 (1) of the Basic Law to the extent of their respective purposes as determined in their objects. In their case, the constitutional guarantee of free development means protection of their freedom to trade and their appearance in public as employer and business enterprise.[2]

12.04 The Federal Constitutional Court has further constantly held that as a consequence of the general personality right, the individual is entitled

---

1 Maunz/Dürig, Basic Law, art 2, para 66.
2 Bundesgerichtshof (Federal Supreme Court) Neue Juristische Wochenschrift 1994, 1281; in this judgment the Federal Supreme Court held that a company's reputation is infringed if a speaker at a seminar distributes copies to the audience of the annual financial statements of the company as published in the Federal State Gazette without blackening the name of the company; the Federal Constitutional Court did not accept a constitutional complaint against this judgment, cf Bundesverfassungsgericht (Federal Constitutional Court) Neue Juristische Wochenschrift 1994, 1784.

to ask the State and the courts for protection and that the Civil Courts have to observe in their decision-making the constitutional guarantees in order to ensure their value-determining character ('wertsetzender Gehalt') in the application of the law.[3]

2 Privacy and personality rights

12.05 Privacy describes a person's life at home, within his or her family and their private life not only within their own four walls but also – depending on the circumstances – outside. In a recent judgment of the Federal Supreme Court in proceedings brought by Princess Caroline of Monaco, it was held that privacy may also exist in public if a person expresses his or her intention to be left alone in an objective manner.[4]

12.06 Other aspects of the general personality right are the individual sphere ('Individualsphäre') which protects the personality and the freedom of self-determination and the intimate sphere ('Intimsphäre') which includes a person's thoughts and emotions, their various forms of expression and all other aspects which require, by virtue of their nature, secrecy such as information about their health or their sex life.[5] The intimate sphere is absolutely protected and cannot be exposed to the public at all.[6]

3 Freedom of expression

12.07 The area of conflict of the rights described above results from Article 5 of the Basic Law which protects freedom of expression. Article 5(1) of the Basic Law in particular guarantees:

(1) everyone's right to freely express and disseminate his or her opinion orally, by writing and pictures and to freely inform himself or herself using generally accessible sources; and

(2) the freedom of the press and the freedom of reporting by means of broadcasting and film.

12.08 Any censorship is excluded. Article 5(2) of the Basic Law limits these rights to communicate by the provisions of the general laws, the statutory provisions for the protection of the young and the right of the inviolability of the honour of a person. The freedom of art and science, research and teaching are separately governed by Article 5(3) of the Basic Law.

---

3 Bundesverfassungsgericht (Federal Constitutional Court) Neue Juristische Wochenschrift 1999, 483 in connection with the right to have published a correction in the print media.
4 Bundesgerichtshof (Federal Supreme Court) Neue Juristische Wochenschrift 1996, 1128; in a landmark decision of the Federal Constitutional Court of 15 December 1999 the judgment of the Federal Supreme Court was upheld in this respect, cp Archiv für Presserecht 2000, 76 et seq.
5 Court of Appeal Hamburg Neue Juristische Wochenschrift 1967, 2314.
6 Bundesgerichtshof (Federal Supreme Court) Neue Juristische Wochenschrift 1988, 1984.

4 Media activity v privacy and personality

12.09 The word 'media' describes the various instruments of communication and transport of information. It includes printed media, film and broadcasting[7] and, in the global world, information technology.

12.10 Historically, the protection of a person's privacy and personality against media publication was achieved by the criminal law only. An individual civil right was created by interpreting certain provisions of the criminal code as laws having a protective effect ('Schutzgesetze') within the meaning of section 823(2) of the Civil Code, the violation of which resulted in a general right to seek damages against a wrongdoer. Section 824 of the Civil Code protected against the allegation and dissemination of incorrect statements of fact which jeopardised the credit of a person or had a detrimental effect on his or her future career. Moreover, sections 22 and 23 of the Act on the Author's Rights in respect of Artistic Works and Photography ('Kunsturhebergesetz')[8] provided protection against the publication or dissemination of a person's image.[9]

12.11 As a consequence of the constitutional recognition of a person's general personality right, German case law[10] accepted such right as 'some other right' ('sonstiges Recht') within the meaning of section 823(1) of the Civil Code[11] and thus as an absolute right, the violation of which entitles the injured party to seek a restraining order, a revocation and/or damages.

12.12 The following sections outline the various activities of the media and the regulatory framework which has to be observed when individual rights are involved.

5 Advertisements

12.13 In a recent judgment, the Federal Supreme Court has recognised that the right to keep the private sphere free from public relations material forms part of the general personality right. In the case, a person had put onto his letterbox a sticker requesting that no advertisements should be inserted. Nevertheless, a company which distributed advertisements in the form of leaflets ignored the plaintiff's request. The firm in whose interests the advertisements were distributed was ordered to refrain from inserting advertising material into the plaintiff's letterbox.[12]

---

7 V Gamm Frhr, *Persönlichkeits- und Ehrverletzungen durch Massenmedien*, 1969, 1.
8 This Act of 9 January 1907, Reichsgesetzblatt (Law Gazette of the former German Reich), 7 was largely abolished with effect from 1 January 1966 when the Copyright Act came into force but remains to date in force with respect to the protection of images.
9 Cf Löffler, *Presserecht*, 4th edition 1997, s 6 of the Landespressegesetz (State Act on the Press), paras 55 ff.
10 Federal Supreme Court Amtliche Entscheidungssammlung des Bundesgerichtshofes in Zivilsachen (Official Case Reports of Bundesgerichtshof (Federal Supreme Court) in civil matters) 13, 334; 24, 72(78); Federal Constitutional Court Amtliche Entscheidungssammlung des Bundesverfassungsgerichts (Official Case Reports of Bundesverfassungsgericht (Federal Constitutional Court)) 30, 173(194).
11 The German Civil Code is of 18 August 1896, Reichsgesetzblatt (Law Gazette of the former German Reich) 195 and has thereafter been amended various times; ss 823 et seq Civil Code deal with the law of tort.
12 Judgment dated 20 December 1988, Amtliche Entscheidungssammlung des Bundesgerichtshofes in Zivilsachen (Official Case Reports of Bundesgerichtshof (Federal Supreme Court) in civil matters) 106, 229.

6   Correction of statements in the media

12.14   The right of a person to request the printing and publication of the correction of statements of fact ('Gegendarstellung') published and/or broadcast in the media is considered as an aspect of the general personality right granted under Articles 2(2), 1(1) of the Basic Law.[13] Such 'right of reply' means an immediately enforceable right of a person concerning whom facts were published in the media to present his or her own version to the same forum.[14]

12.15   The statutory provisions in this rather complex field of law governing the correction and publishing of media statements are permissible limitations of the freedom of the media as constitutionally guaranteed in Article 5 of the Basic Law.[15] The Federal Constitutional Court has recognised that these rights form part of a special field of law protecting the individual against interference of the modern mass media with the general personality right.[16]

12.16   As far as media statements on the Internet are concerned, these are at present not covered by the right to request a correction of a statement.[17] However, in view of the problems in distinguishing media – and telecommunication services and taking into account the existence of certain push-services regularly appearing and edited like printed media, it is suggested to apply these rules to the Internet as well. Section 2 (5) of the Act on Telecommunication Services – TDG – expressly preserves the application of the media laws of the States ('Länder').[18]

7   General principles of media regulation

12.17   In Germany, the regulation of the law of the media falls under the competence of the Länder. The Federal Government has not yet exercised its power pursuant to Article 72(2) of the Basic Law to establish a uniform statutory framework for the media law. Every State therefore has its own law of the press.[19] The right to request the correction of a statement in the print and broadcast media is recognised in all press laws of the German Länder without any material differences.[20] It is considered as a right sui generis which exists in addition to other rights such as the right to request to refrain from doing something, to withdraw a statement or to seek compensation/damages.

---

13   Bundesgerichtshof (Federal Supreme Court) Neue Juristische Wochenschrift 1976, 1198; it is thus clearly available to foreign parties too.
14   Löffler/Golsong/Frank/Martin, The Right of Reply in Europe, 1974, 34.
15   Seitz/Schmidt/Schoener, Der Gegendarstellungsanspruch in Presse, Film, Funk und Fernsehen, 2nd edition 1990, para 7 et seq; Löffler/Ricker, Handbuch des Presserechts, 3rd edition 1994, ch 23, para 3 et seq.
16   Bundesverfassungsgericht (Federal Constitutional Court) Neue Juristische Wochenschrift 1983, 1179.
17   Cf Ory, Archiv für Presserecht 1996, 105(110); Landgericht (Regional Court) Düsseldorf Archiv für Presserecht 1998, 420.
18   Hoeren/Sieber/Helle, Handbuch Multimedia-Recht, 1999, Chap 8.1, para 180.
19   Cf the list giving all relevant particulars of Löffler, op cit Einl zu Bd 1, paras 89 ff.
20   Cf the actual statutory provisions with respect to print media and broadcasting, Löffler/Sedelmeier, op cit s 11 of the Landespressegesetz (State Act on the Press), paras 1 ff.

8 Right to require correction

12.18 Pursuant to section 11(1) of the Landespressegesetz (State Act on the Press)[1] of the Baden-Württemberg Press Act a person or entity ('Stelle') is entitled to request the printing and publishing of reply in respect of a statement of fact that had been published in a periodical. The responsible editor and the publisher are jointly and severally liable for fulfilment of such right. Section 11 of the Landespressegesetz (State Act on the Press) reads as follows:

'(1) The responsible editor and the publisher of a periodical printed publication are under the obligation to print a correction of the person or entity which is affected by a statement of fact made in the printed publication. The obligation extends to all secondary editions of the printed publication in which the statement of facts has been published.

(2) The obligation to print a correction does not exist if the affected person or entity has no legitimate interest in the publication, if the size of the correction is not appropriate or in case of advertisements which exclusively serve business activities. If the correction does not exceed the size of the objected text, it is deemed as appropriate. The correction must be limited to statements of fact and may not have any criminal content. It requires the written form and must be signed by the affected party or its legal representative. The affected party or its representative can request the printing only, if the correction is received by the responsible editor or the publisher without delay, at the latest, however, within three months after the publication.

(3) The correction must be printed without additions or omissions in the next number which follows the receipt of the correction and which has not yet been closed for printing in the same section of the printed periodical and in the same type face of the objected text; it may not be published in the form of a letter to the editor. The printing is free of charge. He who replies to the correction in the same number, must limit himself to statements of fact.

(4) The civil courts have jurisdiction for the enforcement of the right to a correction. Upon request of the affected party, the court may order that the responsible editor and the publisher have to publish the correction in the form as set out in sub-paragraph 3. These proceedings are governed by the regulations of the Civil Proceedings Act on interlocutory relief. An imminent danger that the enforcement of the right is threatened to be frustrated must not be shown to the court. Proceedings on the merits shall not be made.

---

1 The reference to s 11 of the Landespressegesetz (State Act on the Press) of the Baden-Württemberg State Press Act is deemed to refer to all the other relevant state laws including the respective obligations of other media; it should be noted, however, that although the general principles are the same in all Länder, their are some differences in detail; Löffler/Sedelmeier, op cit s 11 of the Landespressegesetz (State Act on the Press) paras 229 ff is specifying the various differences in the law of the Länder.

(5) The sub-paragraphs 1 to 4 do not apply to true and accurate reports on public sessions of the legislative or resolving bodies of the federal state, the Länder and municipalities (associations of local governments) as well as the courts.'

12.19 There is abundant case law dealing with the interpretation and application of the right to request the printing of a correction. In view of the procedural regulation of section 11(4) of the Landespressegesetz (State Act on the Press) which excludes proceedings on the merits, the highest court instances in this type of proceedings are the respective Regional Courts of Appeal. There is no appeal to the Federal Supreme Court which could create a uniform application of the respective statutory provisions. However, despite several efforts to harmonise the law in this field, diversity of the law has been described as being a sad reality.[2]

12.20 As far as broadcasting is concerned, a vast field of regulations varying from *Land* to *Land* applies to public and private broadcasting as well.[3] Although it was for quite some time highly disputed whether the right to correct a media statement in radio or television was permissible, it is nowadays well settled that the principles which have been established for print media apply in relation to incorrect broadcast media statements too, with some peculiarities resulting from the different nature of these media forms.[4]

12.21 So far as concerns filming, there are no statutory provisions dealing with the correction of statements in this form of media. In general, a right to correct incriminating statements of fact in a film is not available. However, several authors argue that the general principles granting a right to correct media statements should be applied by way of analogy to the film as well.[5] Below, some issues of practical importance will be mentioned.

9 Practical aspects of corrections

12.22 A correction can only be requested and made with respect to statements of fact. There is abundant case law distinguishing the expression of an opinion ('Meinungsäußerung') and/or a value judgment ('Werturteil') from a statement of fact. A statement of fact normally exists if it is possible to verify the issues relating to such statement by way of an evidentiary process.[6] It is, however, not required that evidence is effectively taken. Provability is sufficient.[7] Intrinsic circumstances such as motive or the intent for an extrinsic event are considered as well as statements of fact.[8] A lot of

---

2 Wenzel, Das Recht der Wort- und Bildberichterstattung, 4th edition 1994, paras 11.30 and 11.31.
3 Cf with further references Löffler/Sedelmeier, op cit s 11 of the Landespressegesetz (State Act on the Press) paras 243 ff.
4 Wenzel, op cit paras 11.259 ff.
5 Cf Seitz/Schmidt/Schoener, op cit paras 33 ff with further references.
6 Cf Bundesgerichtshof (Federal Supreme Court) Gewerblicher Rechtsschutz und Urheberrecht 1989, 222.
7 Bundesverfassungsgericht (Federal Constitutional Court) Neue Juristische Wochenschrift 1999, 483.
8 Bundesgerichtshof (Federal Supreme Court) Monatsschrift für deutsches Recht 1951, 404.

uncertainty exists.[9] The interpretation of the statement, however, must always be made from the viewpoint of the average reader or viewer.[10]

12.23 So far as concerns statements of fact in advertisements, there is no uniform law. Whereas in several Länder (eg Baden-Württemberg, Berlin etc) advertisements for business purposes are generally exempted from the right to request a correction, other Länder (eg Bayern, Hamburg etc) and almost all legislation dealing with broadcasting also allow the correction of incorrect statements in advertisements.[11]

12.24 A correction may not have a criminal character[12] and is limited to a statement of fact. However, whether the correction is true or not, is not required to be considered. In the case of a correction which is setting out an 'obviously untrue statement', a request may lack a legitimate interest and be unenforceable.[13]

12.25 Where several statements are made in the same article, the correction must cover all statements.[14]

12.26 If the incriminating statement was printed on the front page, the full correction must also be printed there. The Regional Court of Appeal Karlsruhe held that if the front page of the edition intended to contain a correction to a statement printed on the *front* page of a previous edition only contains a reference to a correction being printed *inside* the magazine, the right to have a correction printed is not fulfilled.[15]

12.27 Some uncertainty exists with respect to the form of a correction of a media statement. While it is clear that any correction must be made in writing, there is conflicting case law as to whether a correction submitted by way of facsimile letter is sufficient or whether the editor/publisher responsible must receive the original of the correction.[16] As a matter of principle, in case of statutory form requirements which are not at the disposition of the parties, the transmission of documents via facsimile cannot be considered as sufficient for complying with the written form. Moreover, the signature must be made in the handwriting of the person affected by the statement. Whether representation of a person on the basis of a Power of Attorney is permissible, varies from *Land* to *Land*.[17]

12.28 A distinction is made between the request to print a correction and the correction of the statement itself. In practice, it is common to send a covering letter requesting the printing of the correction which is enclosed with such request and signed in accordance with the above requirements.[18]

---

9 Löffler/Sedelmeier, op cit, s 11 of the Landespressegesetz (State Act on the Press) para 93 is describing the situation as gambling.
10 Seitz/Schmidt/Schoener, op cit, para 306 with further references.
11 Seitz/Schmidt/Schoener, op cit, paras 280 ff.
12 Wenzel, op cit, para 11.114.
13 Löffler/Sedelmeier, op cit s 11 of the Landespressegesetz (State Act on the Press) para 63.
14 Wenzel, op cit, para 11.46.
15 Oberlandesgericht (Regional Court of Appeal) Karlsruhe Neue Juristische Wochenschrift 1993, 1476.
16 Cf Oberlandesgericht (Regional Court of Appeal) Hamburg Neue Juristische Wochenschrift 1990, 1613: original must be received; Oberlandesgericht (Regional Court of Appeal) Müchen Neue Juristische Wochenschrift 1990, 2895: facsimile letter is sufficient.
17 Wenzel, op cit, paras 11.137 ff.
18 Seitz/Schmidt/Schoener, op cit, paras 109 ff.

12.29   A request is deemed to have been made without undue delay if it is received within two weeks after publication of the incriminating statement. A fixed time limit, however, does not exist.[19]

12.30   Although a correction must be printed without additions or omissions, it is generally permissible to add an editorial comment ('Redaktionsschwanz') to the printed correction of a statement, if such comment is limited to factual statements.[20]

10 Data protection

12.31   In the landmark decision of the Federal Constitutional Court dated 15 December 1983 regarding several constitutional complaints against the Census Act 1983, it was decided that the individual's right to be protected against the unlimited collection, recording, use and dissemination of personal data is covered by the general personality right.[1] Following extensive discussions, on 1 June 1991, the Federal Data Protection Act came into force.[2] The German Länder have thereafter on different dates enacted their respective State Data Protection Acts.[3]

12.32   The purpose of the legislation in this field is to create a regulatory framework which applies not only to the public and administrative sector but also to the private sector governing the collection, processing and use of personal data in order to protect an individual against a violation of his or her general personality right.

12.33   In the private sector, this protection is achieved by section 33 et seq of the Data Protection Act pursuant to which a person whose data has been recorded is entitled to be informed and may request information on, correction, deletion and/or blocking of his or her data.

12.34   Section 41 of the Data Protection Act provides for the so-called media privilege. The rights granted pursuant to section 33 et seq of the Data Protection Act do not apply to print, film or broadcasting media organisations that process and/or utilise personal data for their own journalistic-editorial work. However, sections 5 and 9 of the Data Protection Act have to be observed by media enterprises as well. These provisions provide for the secrecy of data and the obligation to implement technical and organisational structures to protect data.

11 Lookalikes

12.35   A company tried to enter into a contract with a well-known German singer for the production of a television advertisement for its products. No agreement could be reached. The company engaged a lookalike. The television advertisement was broadcast several times on different channels

---

19 Seitz/Schmidt/Schoener, op cit, paras 131 ff.
20 Cf Wenzel, op cit, paras 11.187 ff.
1   Amtliche Entscheidungssammlung des Bundesverfassungsgerichts (Official Case Reports of Bundesverfassungsgericht (Federal Constitutional Court)) 65, 1.
2   Bundesgesetzblatt (Federal Law Gazette) 1990, I 2954.
3   Eg Baden-Württemberg on 27 May 1991; Thüringen on 29 October 1991; Bayern on 23 July 1993 etc.

on German television. The Court of Appeal Karlsruhe considered the broadcasting of the advertisement as a violation of the singer's general personality right and allowed a claim for compensation.[4] It was sufficient that several factors (first name, costume, beard etc) were directly referring to the singer and that in the Court's view a considerable part of the viewers (more than 10 per cent) thought that the singer was advertising the products of the company.

12   Rights in images and photographs generally

12.36   According to section 33 of the Kunsturhebergesetz, a person or entity disseminating or publishing an image in contravention of sections 22 and 23 of the Kunsturhebergesetz shall be guilty of an offence and shall be liable on conviction to imprisonment for a term not exceeding one year or to a fine.

12.37   Section 22, Sentences 1 and 2 of the Kunsturhebergesetz reads as follows:

'Images may only be disseminated or publicly be presented with the approval of the person shown. The approval is deemed to have been granted if the person shown received a consideration for the production of the image.'

12.38   Sentences 3 and 4 of section 22 of the Kunsturhebergesetz deal with images of deceased persons. In general, for a period of ten years after the death of the person, approval must be sought from the next of kin. Even after this, the publication of an image may be considered as a violation of the personality right of the deceased.[5]

12.39   Section 22 of the Kunsturhebergesetz applies to all forms of images whether obtained by covert filming, filming on private property,[6] filming from the air,[7] use of security camera footage for reporting events or the use of telephoto lenses.

12.40   Section 22 of the Kunsturhebergesetz does not prohibit the taking of an image but only its dissemination and publication. However, case law has recognised that the shooting of a picture itself can be considered as a violation of the general personality right.[8] The photographer has acquired the ability to dispose of the image of the person shown. But not every

4   Oberlandesgericht (Regional Court of Appeal) Karlsruhe Versicherungsrecht 1996, 600; the Federal Supreme Court did not accept an appeal against the judgment.
5   Schricker/Gerstenberg, Urheberrecht, 1987, ss 22 and 60 of the Kunsturhebergesetz, para 24 with examples.
6   Trespassing on private property may be considered as a criminal offence under section 123 of the Criminal Code if the trespasser has entered into dwellings, business premises or any other protected area ('befriedetes Besitztum').
7   Pursuant to s 27 (2) of the Act on Air Traffic, outside the regular air traffic, pictures or films from the air can only be taken and be disseminated with governmental approval; such approval will be granted by the competent authorities of the Federal States, s 31(2) No 15 of the Act, except for applicants from outside of Germany who have to apply to the Federal Ministry for Traffic.
8   Bundesgerichtshof (Federal Supreme Court) Neue Juristische Wochenschrift 1957, 1315; Löffler, op cit, s 6 of the Landespressegesetz (State Act on the Press), para 119 with further references.

picture taken may be considered as an illegal infringement of such personal right. The nature and the purpose of the act permit the balancing of the interests involved. Determining factors are the importance of the invasion and the purpose of the picture being taken which must be evaluated on a case-by-case basis.[9]

12.41 The protection accorded by section 22 of the Kunsturhebergesetz covers any form of image of one or more persons. It is necessary that the person shown can be recognised.[10] However, it is sufficient if the individual shown can only be identified by a small number of people on the basis of certain elements such as appearance, haircut, jersey etc. There need not be any intention to present a recognisable person.[11]

12.42 Approval does not require any particular form. It may be given expressly or implicitly. An implied approval may arise from the circumstances, in particular if the person shown had accepted the taking of the pictures knowing that they would be published at a later stage.[12] The onus of proof for the existence of approval is upon the media. Evidence must be given in order to prove that the person shown approved the actual form of dissemination or public presentation.[13]

13 Exceptions to protection of images and photographs

12.43 Section 23 of the Kunsturhebergesetz is enumerating several exceptions, allowing dissemination and publication of images without an approval pursuant to section 22.

12.44 Section 23 of the Kunsturhebergesetz reads as follows:

'(1)　　Without the approval required pursuant to section 22 the following may be disseminated or be publicly presented:

1　　Images having a historic context;

2　　Pictures upon which the persons appear as an accessory to a landscape or some other locality only;

3　　Pictures of assemblies, parades or similar events at which the persons shown have participated;

4　　Images, which have not been produced upon order, if their dissemination or public presentation serves a higher interest of the art.

9　Cf Court of Appeal Schleswig Neue Juristische Wochenschrift 1980, 352 – secret video filming of an employee during work, allowed; Court of Appeal Berlin Neue Juristische Wochenschrift 1980, 894 – taking of a picture of a playing child for the purpose of securing evidence, allowed; Bundesgerichtshof (Federal Supreme Court) Neue Juristische Wochenschrift 1995, 1955– private video surveillance of public area on a regular basis and for a longer period, not allowed.

10　Amtliche Entscheidungssammlung des Bundesgerichtshofes in Zivilsachen (Official Case Reports of Bundesgerichtshof (Federal Supreme Court) in civil matters) 26, 349.

11　Bundesgerichtshof (Federal Supreme Court) Neue Juristische Wochenschrift 1979, 2205.

12　Amtliche Entscheidungssammlung des Bundesgerichtshofes in Zivilsachen (Official Case Reports of Bundesgerichtshof (Federal Supreme Court) in civil matters) 49, 288.

13　Amtliche Entscheidungssammlung des Bundesgerichtshofes in Zivilsachen (Official Case Reports of Bundesgerichtshof (Federal Supreme Court) in civil matters) 20, 345; see as well Wenzel, op cit, para 7.41.

(2)   Such right does not apply to a dissemination or public presentation, if by such means a legitimate interest of the person shown or, if the person has died, his or her family is violated.'

12.45   The rationale behind section 23 of the Kunsturhebergesetz is a balancing of the interest between the individual general personality right of the person shown and the public information interest.[14]

12.46   Of utmost practical importance is the scope of section 23(1) No 1 of the Kunsturhebergesetz. There is abundant case law dealing with the scope and interpretation of this exception. The salient aspects are the following:

(1)   Historic context describes any event which for whatever reason has created an interest of the public. In its judgment dated 26 June 1929, the former *Reichsgericht* held that historic context refers to all aspects of present life, which are recognised by the public and receive its attention and are the object of broad circles' 'thirst for knowledge'. Such interest need not necessarily continue to exist in the future.[15]

(2)   Individuals are to be distinguished as 'absolute historical persons' or 'relative historical persons' ('absolute oder relative Personen der Zeitgeschichte'). Absolute historical persons are persons who independently of a single event are in the public eye. Generally speaking, these persons are prominent personalities involved in politics, arts, sports etc.[16] Examples are members of royal families, heads of states, famous artists and actors, top athletes, football stars etc.[17] Relative historical persons are persons who have lost their anonymity in connection with a certain event. The right to publish images of these persons is limited to a presentation made in connection with the reporting on the respective event.[18]

12.47   A determining factor of the exception provided by section 23(1) No 2 of the Kunsturhebergesetz is the question of whether the person shown is merely an 'accessory' who could be removed without destroying the object and character of the picture.[19] If the individual shown is the determining factor of the picture, then his or her approval is clearly required.

12.48   The provisions of section 23(1) No 3 of the Kunsturhebergesetz also refer to a public event/situation and not to persons.[20] The determining factor of the picture is the assembly, parade or similar event. There is some dispute as to whether the images of members of the police force who are involved with a demonstration can be shown. Although police forces are in view of their particular duties not participants in the demonstration, the prevailing opinion considers a restrictive interpretation of section 23(1) No 3 of the Kunsturhebergesetz as not permissible under Article 5(1) of the Basic Law and the right of the press to report on these events.[1]

---

14 Löffler/Steffen, op cit, s 6 of the Landespressegesetz (State Act on the Press) para 129.
15 Entscheidungssammlung des Reichtsgerichts in Zivilsachen (Official Case Reports of the former Reichsgericht in civil matters) 123, 80.
16 Löffler/Steffen, op cit, s 6 of the Landespressegesetz (State Act on the Press) para 131.
17 Cf the list with examples from case law Schricker/Gerstenberg, op cit, ss 23 and 60 of the Kunsturhebergesetz, para 11.
18 Löffler/Steffen, op cit, s 6 of the Landespressegesetz (State Act on the Press) para 132.
19 Schricker/Gerstenberg, op cit, ss 23 and 60 of the Kunsturhebergesetz, para 18
20 Wenzel, op cit, para 8.23.
1   Löffler/Steffen, op cit, s 6 of the Landespressegesetz (State Act on the Press) para 138.

12.49   Section 23(1) No 4 of the Kunsturhebergesetz has little practical importance. It is applied to images which are published for scientific purposes.[2]

14 Balancing of interest

12.50   It follows from section 23(2) of the Kunsturhebergesetz that the exceptions of section 23(1) do not apply without limitation. The purpose of section 23(2) is to ensure that the general personality right of the individual will be observed even though the image falls under an exception of section 23(1). In its decision dated 10 May 1957 the Federal Supreme Court held that historical persons did not have to accept in principle that pictures are taken within their private environment without their knowledge for the purpose of publication. This limitation follows from the general personality right, which protects every individual against violations of his or her private sphere if such violation is not warranted by a higher interest. The simple interest of the public in a historical person is not sufficient to justify the publication of images of the private sphere of an individual which were secretly taken.[3]

12.51   In the above mentioned judgment,[4] the Federal Supreme Court confirmed the necessity of balancing the information interest of the public against the private, legitimate interest of an individual arising under the general personality right and extended the private sphere. By referring to American case law and the 'right to be alone' as an element of the right to privacy, the court did not accept that privacy ends at the front door of the house. Privacy may also exist in public if the person expresses in an objective manner that he or she wants to be alone, or if the person acts in such manner as he or she would not act in general public and the situation is of a private character. This sphere of protection is violated if pictures are published which were taken secretly or by surprise. In addition, the court has clearly said that the above broader approach also applies to absolute historical persons. The most important elements of the judgment are the following:

(1)   Secluded locations may exist in restaurants, hotels, sport arenas, telephone booths or nature, if the person no longer appears as a member of the public.

(2)   The situation must be of private character and the person must act in a personal way which is not meant for the eyes of third parties.

(3)   Keyhole journalism and pictures taken by surprise are unlawful not only in the private sphere of the person's dwelling but also if the person takes his or her private sphere outside.

(4)   In balancing the conflicting interests, the information value of the published images has to be taken into account as well; if pictures are taken merely out of curiosity or the desire for sensation with the simple interest of entertainment, then the interests of the public in information cannot outweigh the legitimate right of a person to have his or her personality right respected.

---

2   Wenzel, op cit, para 8.27.
3   Bundesgerichtshof (Federal Supreme Court) Neue Juristische Wochenschrift 1957, 1315.
4   Bundesgerichtshof (Federal Supreme Court) Neue Juristische Wochenschrift 1996, 1128.

12.52 In its landmark decision of 15 December 1999,[5] the Federal Constitutional Court confirmed the ruling of the Federal Supreme Court that privacy may not only exist at home. It was recognised that privacy outside the own four walls may exist or be created by a person in the event that, depending on the actual circumstances of each individual case, such person may reasonably, and hence perceptibly for third parties, believe that she or he is not in the public eye. Any public place where a person is usually amongst others does never qualify as a private place. It is not the person's behaviour that constitutes privacy, but only the actual condition of the respective locality. However, if a person has allowed media reports on his or her private life such as an exclusive home-story, such person is estopped from seeking judicial protection. The constitutional protection of the personality is not granted for the purpose of commercialisation of the personality.

12.53 Moreover, a new aspect has been decided regarding the parent-child relationship. The Federal Constitutional Court reconfirmed its position that children require special protection in order to warrant a proper development of their personalities. As a consequence, Article 6 of the Basic Law which guarantees special protection by the state of matrimony and family, reinforces the general personality right. Whilst the Federal Supreme Court in its above judgment (para **12.52**) inter alia held that a photograph showing Princess Caroline of Monaco with her daughter Charlotte canoeing on the river Sorgues in the Provence near St Rémy did not violate the personality right of the Princess, the Federal Constitutional Court was of the opinion that the Federal Supreme Court must reconsider its decision by taking into account the constitutional considerations regarding the special protection of the family and therefore vacated and remitted the judgment on this point to the Federal Supreme Court.

Finally, the Federal Constitutional Court summarised the conditions under which it will consider constitutional complaints as follows:

(1) The lower courts must have ignored that constitutional rights must be observed in the interpretation and application of the civil law;

(2) the scope of the relevant constitutional rights was incorrectly or insufficiently determined or their relevance was not correctly weighted, thus resulting in a wrong balancing of the conflicting legal rights;

(3) the decision is based on the above mistake.

On the basis of the foregoing, only recently in March/April 2000 the Federal Constitutional Court in a series of Orders did not accept constitutional complaints for decisions due to lack of general constitutional relevance, the non-existence of a particularly important detriment of the applicant and lack of sufficient prospects of success.[6]

12.54 In a further recent decision, the Federal Supreme Court had to balance the personality right of an absolute historical person under section

---

5 Archiv für Presserecht 2000, 76 et seq.
6 Further details may be sourced from the website of the Federal Constitutional Court under http://www.bundesverfassungsgericht.de regarding Constitutional Complaints No. 1 BvR 2223/96, 1 BvR 1213/97, 1 BvR 1454/97, 1 BvR 2479/97, 1 BvR 150/98, 1 BvR 151/98, 1 BvR 158/98, 1 BvR 768/98, 1 BvR 2080/98, 1 BvR 2109/98, 1 BvR 2116/98, 1 BvR 1353/99, 1 BvR 1505/99.

23(2) of the Kunsturhebergesetz against the right to publish images of such person without approval pursuant to section 23(1). A German company distributed a CD with music of Bob Dylan which was recorded during a live concert. The CD contained an inlay showing several images of Bob Dylan. The Federal Supreme Court reversed a judgment of the Court of Appeal and held that an absolute historical person must not be made an object of the economic interests of some other party. The dissemination of the images was also made for advertising purposes with the intent of enhancing sales of the CD.[7]

12.55   A famous football player was unsuccessful in stopping distribution of, and receiving compensation from, a football calendar, the title picture of which showed the player in a scene of a match between the national teams of Greece and Germany. The Federal Supreme Court accepted the information interest of the public was higher than the right of the player to participate in the earnings made as a result of the sale of the calendar.[8]

12.56   The famous ice skating star Katarina Witt was also not successful before the Regional Court of Appeal Frankfurt in enforcing a claim for compensation for the unauthorised publication of a nude picture in a Sunday Magazine. In 1998, Ms Witt had posed for the Playboy magazine. The Magazine used a photograph from the website of Playboy and published it with a satirical article under the heading 'People you talk about'. Since the size of the picture was only 2.5cm x 3cm and the accompanying text was comparing Ms Witt's role in the former German Democratic Republic with her new life, the Court was of the opinion that the information interest of the public should prevail. The Senate emphasised that the nude picture was not published in a sensational manner and was obviously required to explain the satirical text.[9] A decision on a constitutional complaint which has been filed has not yet been rendered. In view of the recent reluctance of the Federal Constitutional Court to deal with these matters following its landmark decision of 15 December 1999, it is rather unlikely that the complaint will be successful.

12.57   Another field of practical importance is that involving filmed historical documentations or reports on contemporary history involving persons. If material is used showing a person who was previously a relative historical person, the approval of such person is generally required. If after the balancing of the information interest of the public and the general personality right of the individual shown, the interest of the person prevails, approval will be necessary.

12.58   In that context, the Federal Constitutional Court held that the public interest in respect of information on criminals is time-limited and declines, the longer ago the criminal offence has been committed.[10]

12.59   If a report deals with a person who could be regarded in the past as an absolute historical person, then any publication of images is permissible

---

7   Bundesgerichtshof (Federal Supreme Court) Neue Juristische Wochenschrift 1997, 1152.
8   Bundesgerichtshof (Federal Supreme Court) Gewerblicher Rechtsschutz und Urheberrecht 1979, 425.
9   Archiv für Presserecht 2000, 185 et seq.
10 Amtliche Entscheidungssammlung des Bundesverfassungsgerichts (Official Case Reports of Bundesverfassungsgericht (Federal Constitutional Court)) 35, 202; see as well Court of Appeal Hamburg Archiv für Presserecht 1985, 209.

without the approval of such person. However, such person must have played an important role which is required for the understanding of the historical events. This has been recognised for prominent Nazis and notorious doctors at concentration camps.[11] Even though these persons may live in seclusion today, the Federal Supreme Court held that a report can be made dealing with their earlier function and their present position.[12] In general, persons who have gained importance in connection with certain events occurring during the Third Reich are relative historical persons. The Court of Appeal Frankfurt has recognised that a public interest in naming persons who are still alive in connection with former events is permissible, as the public interest takes precedence over the individual interest of such person.[13] However, information on the actual living circumstances of such a relative historical person is only permissible if such person presently holds an exposed position in respect of which the previous actions of such person are relevant.[14]

15 Imitation of voice

12.60   In its judgment of 8 May 1989, the Court of Appeal Hamburg had to decide whether it was permissible in connection with a radio advertisement for the voice of a deceased famous German actor to be imitated by a voice impersonator. The Court considered the use of the voice as a violation of the general personality right and did not allow the use of the voice.[15] By way of analogy the regulation of section 22(2) of the Kunsturhebergesetz[16] was applied as setting out a general principle in the field of the general personality right.

16 Interception of post and telephone calls and recording of conversations

12.61   Article 10 of the Basic Law provides for constitutional protection of the secrecy of mail, postage and telecommunications. Although this constitutional guarantee primarily addresses the relationship between the individual and the State, the Federal Supreme Court in its judgment of 20 February 1990 held that the principle also applies among individuals. The opening of a letter is a violation not only of the general personality right of the sender but also the right of the addressee. Whether the mail is read or not makes no difference.[17]

12.62   So far as concerns recording and publication of telephone conversations, the Federal Supreme Court has recognised that such recording and publication requires the consent of the participants in the conversation. Otherwise a violation of the general personality right will be

11 Löffler/Riecker, Handbuch des Presserechts, 3rd edition 1994, ch 42, para 16.
12 Bundesgerichtshof (Federal Supreme Court) Neue Juristische Wochenschrift 1966, 2353.
13 Archiv für Presserecht 1980, 52.
14 Löffler/Riecker, op cit, ch 42, para 16.
15 Oberlandesgericht (Regional Court of Appeal) Hamburg Neue Juristische Wochenschrift 1990, 1995.
16 See para **12.37** above.
17 Cf Bundesgerichtshof (Federal Supreme Court) Betriebs-Berater 1990, 739.

committed. Whether the conversation is of a private nature only or relates to political matters in which the public has an interest, is irrelevant. Although there is no absolute protection, there must be a balancing of the individual rights and the freedom of the print media. This principle also applies if the respective material has been obtained by way of an unlawful and criminal act and is offered to an organisation of the press which was not involved in such act. The material may only be published and disseminated if the information value for the public outweighs the interest of the individual to keep the matters in question private and secret.[18]

12.63   The Federal Supreme Court accepted an exception, where minutes of a confidential meeting were recorded in writing and disseminated later. Such record was neither considered authentic nor objective. Publication did not therefore violate the personality right of the participants of such meeting.[19]

12.64   Chapter 15 of the Criminal Code sets out the rules in relation to violations of one's personal and intimate sphere. Section 201 of the Criminal Code prohibits the recording of words which are not spoken in public, their interception with technical equipment and the use of any such record or material obtained. The maximum term of imprisonment on conviction is three years or a fine. Pursuant to section 202 of the Criminal Code, a person who opens a closed letter or other document which is not addressed to him or her shall be liable, on conviction, to imprisonment for a term not exceeding one year or to a fine. Unauthorised access to protected data is a criminal offence according to section 202a of the Criminal Code which provides for imprisonment on conviction for a term not exceeding three years or a fine.

17 Remedies

12.65   As a matter of principle, an affected party is free to choose the enforcement of his or her rights under civil or criminal law or a combination of both. Normally these matters are dealt with in civil proceedings. An affected party may seek restraining orders, the correction of statements, compensation for his or her actual damage etc.[20]

18 Jurisdiction

12.66   Where criminal acts are committed by the media, section 7(2) of the Criminal Proceedings Act concentrates criminal jurisdiction on the persons responsible for the acts at the place where a domestic printed publication is published[1] or from where a radio or television broadcast is made.[2] As far as foreign media is concerned, the privilege of concentration does not apply. The 'flying jurisdiction' continues to exist wherever a

18 Amtliche Entscheidungssammlung des Bundesgerichtshofes in Zivilsachen (Official Case Reports of Bundesgerichtshof (Federal Supreme Court) in civil matters) 73, 120.
19 Amtliche Entscheidungssammlung des Bundesgerichtshofes in Zivilsachen (Official Case Reports of Bundesgerichtshof (Federal Supreme Court) in civil matters) 80, 25(41/42).
20 Löffler/Riecker, op cit, ch 41, para 5.
1   Löffler/Riecker, op cit, ch 32, 2.
2   Löffler/Kühl, op cit, Vorbem, s 20 ff of the Landespressegesetz (State Act on the Press) para 17.

criminal act is completed.

12.67 As regards civil jurisdiction, the general provisions of the Civil Proceedings Act and – in a cross border context - the statutory provisions of the Brussels/Lugano Conventions on Jurisdiction and the Enforcement of Judicial Decisions in Civil and Commercial Matters ('the Conventions')[3] apply.

12.68 Pursuant to section 12 et seq of the Civil Proceedings Act and Articles 2 and 53 of the Conventions, jurisdiction and venue lies at the residence or place of business of the respective party. Of particular importance to foreign media is section 32 of the Civil Proceedings Act which creates international jurisdiction for causes of action in tort at the place where the tort was committed. In the absence of any particular provision governing the international jurisdiction of German courts, it is well settled that local jurisdiction implies international jurisdiction.[4] Moreover, Article 5(3) of the Conventions, which applies to any tort or act which is deemed to be a tort or claims arising from such an act, provides for jurisdiction at the place where the tortious act occurred.

12.69 Under section 32 of the Civil Proceedings Act, violations of the general personality right by the media, are committed at any place where printed media was distributed in accordance with the determination of the publisher.[5] The same applies to violations by way of broadcasting and the Internet. In such cases, any court in the district where the broadcasting was received[6] or electronic information could be accessed has jurisdiction.[7] The 'flying jurisdiction' therefore continues to exist in civil matters for domestic and/or foreign media activities. A plaintiff may bring an action at the place where the tortious act was committed or, alternatively, where the protected right was violated.[8]

12.70 The Federal Supreme Court has recognised that under section 32 of the Civil Proceedings Act interim relief in the form of a protective restraining order may be sought as well.[9] The prevailing legal doctrine further allows remedies arising under section 1004 of the Civil Code.[10]

12.71 Some dispute exists as to whether the right to request the correction and printing of a media statement may be pursued under section 32 of the Civil Proceedings Act. The prevailing opinion denies such procedural

---

3 The 4th Agreement on the Accession of Austria, Finland and Sweden to the Brussels Convention (EuGVÜ 1989) of 29 November 1996 has not yet come into force in the Federal Republic of Germany; the Lugano-Convention of 16 September 1988 came into force on 1 March 1995, Bundesgesetzblatt (Federal Law Gazette) 1995 II, 221.

4 Amtliche Entscheidungssammlung des Bundesgerichtshofes in Zivilsachen (Official Case Reports of Bundesgerichtshof (Federal Supreme Court) in civil matters) 44, 46.

5 Confirming its earlier case law cf Amtliche Entscheidungssammlung des Bundesgerichtshofes in Zivilsachen (Official Case Reports of Bundesgerichtshof (Federal Supreme Court) in civil matters) 131, 332 (335).

6 Oberlandesgericht (Regional Court of Appeal) München Entscheidungen der Oberlandesgerichte in Zivilsachen (Report of decisions of the Regional Court of Appeals) 1987, 217.

7 Cf Landgericht (Regional Court) Düsseldorf Neue Juristische Wochenschrift-Rechtsprechungs-Report Zivilrecht 1998, 979.

8 Amtliche Entscheidungssammlung des Bundesgerichtshofes in Zivilsachen (Official Case Reports of Bundesgerichtshof (Federal Supreme Court) in civil matters) 124, 237(245).

9 Bundesgerichtshof (Federal Supreme Court) Betriebs-Berater 1956, 382.

10 Zöller/Vollkommer, ZPO, 21st edition 1999, s 32, para 14 with further references.

possibility in view of the particular character of the right under the various press laws.[11]

12.72 Under Article 5(3) of the Conventions similar principles apply.[12] However, three aspects should be mentioned:

(1) In the decision of the European Court in the matter *Fiona Shevill, Ixora Trading Inc, Chequepoint SARL, Chequepoint International Ltd/ Presse Alliance SA* it was held that in cases involving the violation of a general personality right (the 'honour'), the affected party can bring an action not only in the State where the publisher is resident, but in any other contracting State where the publication has been distributed and where a violation of rights occurred ('flying jurisdiction'). However, only the Courts of the first State may award damages incurred by the affected party, although courts in the second State can only adjudicate those damages which occurred within their jurisdiction.[13]

(2) Doctrine suggests that under Article 5(3) of the Conventions jurisdiction arises in respect of claims to correct media statements, printed or broadcast.[14] This opinion is persuasive. Article 5(3) of the Conventions has a broader scope of application than section 32 of the Civil Proceedings Act. It expressly applies to claims of a tortious nature. The right to request a correction is based on the violation of a general personality right and has thus a tortious character. The provisions of the Conventions have to be interpreted autonomously.

(3) Some uncertainty exists as to whether Article 5(3) of the Conventions should apply as well to applications for protective interim orders. The Federal Supreme Court had submitted a case where this question arose to the European Court for decision.[15] However, the matter was struck off the roll there, so that the issue is not yet decided.[16] Since the form of the relief granted is a question of the *lex fori*, Article 5(3) of the Conventions should apply as well to remedies against tortious acts that are threatening.[17]

12.73 In actions which have a value of an amount not exceeding DM 10,000, the local District Courts will be competent. In the case of a request which is of immaterial nature (eg a request to correct a media statement), the interest of the claimant is decisive. Matters having a value of more than DM 10,000 fall within the competence of the Regional Courts. Chambers specialising in media law have been established within the various Regional Courts which are highly professional in dealing with this type of litigation. In practice, the value of normal media litigation ranges between DM 12,000 and DM 30,000.[18]

---

11 Seitz/Schmidt/Schoener, op cit ,442 with further references.
12 Cf European Court on 30 November 1976 – *Bier/Mines de Potasse d'Alsace* Neue Juristische Wochenschrift 1977, 493.
13 Neue Juristische Wochenschrift 1995, 1881.
14 Geimer/Schütze, Europäisches Zivilverfahrensrecht, 1997, art 5, para 171.
15 Monatsschrift für deutsches Recht 1995, 282.
16 Kropholler, Europäisches Zivilprozeßrecht, 6th edition 1998, art 5, para 59.
17 Geimer/Schütze, op cit, art 5, para 174.
18 Wenzel, op cit, para 11.219.

19 *Applicable law*

12.74 German private international law has no special conflict rules governing violations of the general personality right. As the general personality right is considered an absolute right within the meaning of section 823 of the Civil Code, the Federal Supreme Court has applied the principles developed in connection with the proper law of a tort.[19] *Sedes materiae* of conflict rules applying to a tort are the newly enacted articles 40 to 42 of the Introductory Act to the Civil Code which enact the principle of *lex loci delicti commissi*.[20] Accordingly, the tortious liability is determined by the law of the place where the wrongful act was committed.[1] A distinction is made between the place where the act was committed and the place where the violation of the right occurred. Both places fall under the *lex loci delicti commissi* rule.[2] If these places are located within different jurisdictions, an injured party may choose the law which is more beneficial to his or her interests.[3] However, it must be noted that pursuant to Article 40(3) of the Introductory Act to the Civil Code, the liability of a German wrongdoer which is governed by a foreign law is subject to certain limitations. Claims arising under a foreign law cannot be made in the event that these claims:

(1) go much further than necessary for the adequate compensation of the injured person; or

(2) apparently serve other purposes than adequate compensation of the injured person; or

(3) are in conflict with regulations on liability implemented in any convention which is binding on the Federal Republic of Germany.

The earlier provision of Article 38 of the Introductory Act to the Civil Code which generally limited the liability of the wrongdoer to what was awarded under German law was considered in doctrine as a violation of the non-discrimination rule under Article 6 of the European Union Treaty.[4] Nevertheless, the courts always applied the former Article 38 of the Introductory Act to the Civil Code.[5] Whether the attempt of the German legislator to dilute the intended control of foreign law is still discriminating remains to be seen.

12.75 As regards the right to request a correction of a media statement, the principles above developed in connection with the former Article 38 of the Introductory Act to the Civil Code applied with some modifications. In view of the fact that the right to request a correction is a right *sui generis* taking into account the characteristics of the media, it is suggested to limit the broad approach of the *lex loci delicti commissi* to the place, where a printed publication is officially published or, in case of broadcasting, to the place

---

19 Bundesgerichtshof (Federal Supreme Court) Neue Juristische Wochenschrift 1996, 1128.
20 Cf Bundesgesetzblatt (Federal Law Gazette) 1999 I, 1026 of 31 May 1999.
1   Cf Amtliche Entscheidungssammlung des Bundesgerichtshofes in Zivilsachen (Official Case Reports of Bundesgerichtshof (Federal Supreme Court) in civil matters) 119, 137(139).
2   Cf Oberlandesgericht (Regional Court of Appeal) Hamburg Archiv für Presserecht 1998, 643.
3   Bundesgerichtshof (Federal Supreme Court) Neue Juristische Wochenschrift 1981, 1606.
4   Cf Ehmann/Thorn, Archiv für Presserecht 1996, 20(24).
5   Eg Oberlandesgericht (Regional Court of Appeal) Hamburg Archiv für Presserecht 1996, 69.

from where the radio or television product is officially broadcast.[6] Since the new legislation on the proper law of tort does not address these issues, it is to be expected that the courts continue to apply their earlier case law.

12.76 Pursuant to section 7 of the Criminal Code, German criminal law is applicable in respect of acts committed abroad against a German national, if the act is at the place where it is committed a criminal offence as well. According to section 3 of the Criminal Code, German criminal law applies to any criminal act committed within the territory of the Federal Republic of Germany regardless of the nationality of the wrongdoer.[7] If the same act was committed in several Länder and different provisions of the media laws of these Länder apply to such act, German Courts have held the wrongdoer responsible under the strictest rule.[8]

20 Liability under tort law

12.77 *Sedes materiae* and the main sources of the German tort law are sections 823 to 853 of the Civil Code. In general terms, a tort under section 823(1) of the Civil Code is an unlawful violation of a protected absolute right of a third party. As already mentioned earlier, it is well settled in German case law that the general personality right is considered as 'some other right' the unlawful violation of which gives rise to a claim for damages.[9]

12.78 As opposed to the general principles of tort law pursuant to which any violation of an absolute right is deemed to be unlawful, the courts have held that in the case of a violation of the general personality right, the illegality has to be established on a case-by-case basis by way of balancing the conflicting interests.[10]

12.79 Therefore, a violation of the general personality right by the media does not constitute an unlawful act, if it is justified for specific grounds which can be summarised as follows:

(1) An act is not considered unlawful, if the freedom of the media guaranteed in Article 5 of the Basic Law outweighs the general personality right of a person or entity.[11]

(2) Section 193 of the Criminal Code embodies the general principle of

6   Cf Seitz/Schmidt/Schoener, op cit, paras 53 ff.
7   Löffler/Kühl, op cit, Vorbem, ss 20 ff, para 25 of the Landespressegesetz (State Act on the Press).
8   Cf Löffler/Kühl, op cit, Vorbem, ss 20 ff, para 21 of the Landespressegesetz (State Act on the Press), is criticising that approach and suggests the application of the law which is most closely connected to the violation.
9   It should be noted that with respect to business enterprises, German case law has recognised the absolute right of the established and exercised commercial business ('Recht am eingerichteten und ausgeübten Gewerbebetrieb') as being some other right; in the media law this can be of relevance in case on test reports on products of a business undertaking, cf Löffler/Ricker, op cit, ch 42, paras 52 ff.
10 Löffler/Ricker, op cit, ch 41, para 3.
11 Amtliche Entscheidungssammlung des Bundesverfassungsgerichts (Official Case Reports of Bundesverfassungsgericht (Federal Constitutional Court)) 7, 198 (207/208) where the Federal Constitutional Court considered Article 5 of the Basic Law as an expression of the most prominent human right and cited verbatim Benjamin N Cardozo's dictum that the freedom of expression is 'the matrix, the indispensable condition of nearly every form of freedom'; further Amtliche Entscheidungssammlung des Bundesgerichtshofes in Zivilsachen (Official Case Reports of Bundesgerichtshof (Federal Supreme Court) in civil matters) 45, 296.

the protection of legitimate interest in defamation cases. The information interests of the public and the exercise of the appropriate standard of journalistic care are decisive for determining whether a legitimate interest exists.[12] The obligation to duly investigate reports increases proportionately to the weight of the likely violation of personality rights.[13] The Federal Constitutional Court has held that the freedom of the press implies duties which grow in the same manner as the relevance of the constitutional guarantee of the freedom of the media.[14]

(3) A particular problem exists with respect to incorrect statements of fact. There is never a legitimate interest in disseminating wrong information. Therefore, the right to refrain from maintaining an incorrect statement and to request its withdrawal arises even if the wrong information was sourced with all due journalistic diligence and care. However, in such a case, a claim for damages might be excluded.[15]

12.80 A tort further requires a fault either in the form of a wilful or negligent act. For practical purposes, a fault is deemed to exist if the violation of the general personality right is not justified under the above principles.[16]

12.81 Section 823(2) of the Civil Code gives rise to a claim in tort, if no absolute right was violated but a legal regulation having a protective effect has been breached. In the field of the general personality right some notable regulations are section 185 et seq of the Criminal Code which protects honour (libel and slander, defamation) and the personal and intimate sphere.[17]

12.82 Section 824 of the Civil Code deals with a tort resulting from the allegation and dissemination of incorrect statements of facts which jeopardise the credit of a person or have a detrimental effect to his or her future career.

12.83 Pursuant to section 826 of the Civil Code a tort arises in case of a wilful act committed with the intent to cause damage to another party in breach of the public policy. In media law, this can occur under the strict principles applying to the publication of demands for boycott.[18]

12.84 If a tort has been committed, the wrongdoer has to make good the violation of the respective right. This obligation includes the right to request a restraining order, withdrawal, correction and amendment of a statement,

---

12 Löffler/Ricker, op cit, ch 41, paras 9 and 10.
13 Bundesgerichtshof (Federal Supreme Court) Gewerblicher Rechtsschutz und Urheberrecht 1969, 147(151).
14 Amtliche Entscheidungssammlung des Bundesverfassungsgerichts (Official Case Reports of Bundesverfassungsgericht (Federal Constitutional Court)) 12, 113(130); recently, Kepplinger in Zeitschrift für Rechtspolitik (Journal for Law Politics) 2000, 134 et seq. has critiqued the granting of certain privileges to the media privilege by arguing that the original rationale of identifying the interest of the media with the interest of the public is no longer existing. In contrary, modern media are pursuing their own interests often on the back of individuals the rights of whom are on the books, but in practice due to a number of reasons exercised in a rather limited manner only.
15 Löffler/Ricker, op cit, ch 41, para 10.
16 Löffler/Ricker, op cit, ch 41, para 3.
17 Cf Palandt/Thomas, Bürgerliches Gesetzbuch, 58th edition 1999, s 823, paras 141 and 149
18 Löffler/Ricker, op cit, ch 42, paras 60 ff.

compensation of the actual damage and, pursuant to section 847 of the Civil Code, the moral damage.[19]

12.85 The amount of damage is determined by section 249 et seq of the Civil Code, whose general principle is that the party liable for damage has to re-create the status which would exist had the tort not occurred (status quo ante).

12.86 In a recent decision in a *Princess Caroline of Monaco* case, the Federal Supreme Court expressly confirmed that the right to withdraw and correct an incorrect statement does not generally exclude the additional right to seek compensation. Depending on the circumstances of each case, it must be established whether the violation goes to the root of the personality and also whether the wrongdoer initially declined to withdraw the statement. The court held that wilful violations of personality right were committed for the purpose of increasing sales solely in pursuit of the commercial interests of the defendant. Compensation is given if there is a correlation between the violation of the personality right and the profits made. The amount of compensation must have some prohibitive effect against the commercialisation of violation of the general personality right in order to provide effective protection. DM 30,000 were considered as insufficient.[20] The practical effects of this landmark decision remain to be seen.[1] In the European context for the purpose of balancing the conflicting interests, it is fair and equitable to attempt to create equality of arms ('Waffengleichheit') between the media and individuals.[2]

21 Correction of media statements

12.87 As already set out above in para **12.14**, German media law recognises a special remedy for the correction of media statements. Error on the part of the editor or publisher is not required. The remedy is limited to printing/broadcasting of a correction. Compensation for damages is not granted.

22 Removal of interference

12.88 Section 1004 of the Civil Code which expressly protects property has been developed by case law to provide protection against any interference with the general personality right and other legitimate interests.[3] The most important aspect of this remedy is that there is no requirement of fault on the side of the interferor.[4] Two forms exist:

19 Cf Palandt/Thomas, op cit, s 823, paras 198 ff.
20 Amtliche Entscheidungssammlung des Bundesgerichtshofes in Zivilsachen (Official Case Reports of Bundesgerichtshof (Federal Supreme Court) in civil matters) 128, 1(13,16); the Court of Appeal Hamburg whereto the matter was re-transferred for fixing the amount of liability awarded DEM 180,000.—; see below, para **12.101**.
1 Cf Stürner, Archiv für Presserecht 1998, 1; Gounalakis, Archiv für Presserecht 1998, 10 who is criticising the recent decision of the Federal Supreme Court as 'judication for prominents'.
2 Cf Prinz in Zeitschrift für Rechtspolitik (Journal for Law Politics) 2000, 138 et seq.
3 Palandt/Bassenge, op cit, s 1004, para 2 with further references.
4 Amtliche Entscheidungssammlung des Bundesgerichtshofes in Zivilsachen (Official Case Reports of Bundesgerichtshof (Federal Supreme Court) in civil matters) 34, 99(103) where the Federal Supreme Court expressly held that the remedy under s 1004 of the Civil Code was created in order to release a plaintiff from the difficult proof of a fault.

(1) The affected party may seek an order to rectify an existing act and the consequences of the interference with its rights;

(2) If an interference or violation is threatened, a protective restraining order may be sought. Normally the essential prerequisite of this remedy is the danger of repetition. If such danger does not exist, the remedy will not normally be available.[5] In some circumstances, however, the remedy may be available in case of an interference or violation threatened for the first time.[6]

12.89 Pursuant to section 1004(2) of the Civil Code the remedy is excluded, if the owner of the right is obliged to accept the interference or violation. Such obligation generally exists if the act is justified under the principles set out above under para **12.79** et seq.

23 Unjust enrichment

12.90 The Federal Supreme Court has recognised that in the case of the unlawful publication of an image, the person affected may seek compensation under the statutory regime of unjust enrichment pursuant to section 812 et seq of the Civil Code. For the purpose of calculating compensation the Courts work on the basis of a hypothetical licence agreement between the person whose image is shown and the person who uses it without permission. The amount of compensation is the fee which the person could have sought for having his or her image used.[7] Such compensation must be reasonable[8] and take into account factors such as the extent of circulation, any use by way of advertisement, the public relations effect etc.[9] Claims under the principle of unjust enrichment are of particular importance, because they arise independently of any claim for damages under the law of tort.[11] Some uncertainty exists in cases where the person whose image is used would never have agreed to dissemination of his or her image. Although some case law[10] (and the prevailing legal doctrine[12] suggests that the claim under unjust enrichment arises in any event, there have been reported cases where claims have been rejected.[13]

12.91 Finally it should be noted that none of the above remedies excludes the other. An affected party may plead all possible causes of action cumulatively and in the alternative.

---

5 Amtliche Entscheidungssammlung des Bundesgerichtshofes in Zivilsachen (Official Case Reports of Bundesgerichtshof (Federal Supreme Court) in civil matters) 2, 394.
6 Palandt/Bassenge, op cit, s 1004, para 29 with further references.
7 Amtliche Entscheidungssammlung des Bundesgerichtshofes in Zivilsachen (Official Case Reports of Bundesgerichtshof (Federal Supreme Court) in civil matters) 20, 345(353/354).
8 Bundesgerichtshof (Federal Supreme Court) Neue Juristische Wochenschrift 1981, 2402.
9 Löffler/Steffen, op cit, s 6 of the Landespressegesetz (State Act on the Press), para 320 with examples from case law.
10 Wenzel, op cit, para 9.9
11 Amtliche Entscheidungssammlung des Bundesgerichtshofes in Zivilsachen (Official Case Reports of Bundesgerichtshof (Federal Supreme Court) in civil matters) 81, 75(82)
12 Cf Wenzel, op cit, para 9.7; Löffler/Steffen, op cit s 6 of the Landespressegesetz (State Act on the Press), para 320 with further references.
13 Eg Oberlandesgericht (Regional Court of Appeal) Hamburg 1995, 504.

24 Interlocutory relief

12.92 By its nature, interlocutory relief is not available in relation to all remedies arising as a result of violations of the general personality right. This type of relief is generally aimed at preserving a certain state of affairs pending final resolution of a dispute. In respect of monetary claims for compensation, the granting of interlocutory relief is unlikely. An order requiring the interim withdrawal of a statement pending the final resolution on the merits is also considered impractical.[14]

12.93 However, as mentioned above under para **12.18** et seq, the right to correct printed media statements must usually be enforced by means of interlocutory relief. Section 11(4) of the Baden-Württemberg Press Act expressly states that there is no requirement to demonstrate to the Court the existence of any imminent danger of threatened frustration of the enforcement of such right.[15]

12.94 In practice, interlocutory orders are most commonly encountered in connection with restraining orders,[16] as with, for example, a court order prohibiting further dissemination of an image which has been distributed in the printed media without the approval of the person shown.

12.95 Pursuant to section 935 of the Civil Proceedings Act, a preliminary injunction may be sought if a change in the status quo could frustrate or substantially impede a party's rights. Although there is no general presumption that such change is likely to occur, in view of the constitutional guarantee of the protection of the general personality right German courts are generally willing to grant this form of relief. In particular, if the petitioner has unsuccessfully requested the respondent to give a written undertaking to refrain from committing further unlawful acts, an interlocutory order will be made, if the right has been violated and the petitioner has shown a cause of action.

12.96 Interlocutory relief may be granted on an ex parte basis under section 937(2) of the Civil Proceedings Act. The practice of the courts varies. Normally an oral hearing will take place. If there is a likelihood that an application for an interlocutory order is to be made to a court, the prospective respondent may submit a protective brief ('Schutzschrift') against the prospective petitioner setting out the respondent's version of the story and expressly requesting the court not to decide on an ex parte basis.

12.97 Upon application by the respondent, the court is required to give the petitioner a certain time limit in which to commence regular proceedings, failing which the interim order may be set aside with costs to be borne by the petitioner, in accordance with section 926(2) of the Civil Proceedings Act.

---

14 Cf Löffler/Steffen, op cit, s 6 of the Landespressegesetz (State Act on the Press), para 302.
15 Cf for the different regulations Seitz/Schmidt/Schoener, op cit, paras 478 ff.
16 Löffler/Steffen, op cit, s 6 of the Landespressegesetz (State Act on the Press), para 282.

25 *Examples for compensation adjudicated*

12.98   Some examples of the abundant case law in this field are set out below. As a matter of principle, under German law damages are awarded on the basis of restitution in kind. In lieu of restitution, the creditor may seek pursuant to section 249 of the Civil Code the amount of money which is required to effect restitution. Damages are generally calculated either in a concrete or an abstract manner. The affected party must substantiate and prove its damages in a precise manner. Pursuant to section 287 of the Civil Proceedings Act, a court has only very limited discretion to estimate damages. An expert opinion can be sought on the amount of damages when determining, for example, the reasonableness of a hypothetical licence fee for the publication of an image etc.

12.99   German law does not recognise the concept of punitive damages. However, as a consequence of recent case law, it is suggested that in cases of violation of personality rights by the media, the amount of compensation may have a punitive element.[17]

12.100   Under the existing civil law system, damages for breach of moral rights can only be requested in case of a tort pursuant to section 847 of the Civil Code and will be awarded as compensation for the purpose of allowing the affected party to enjoy what they were not able to enjoy as a result of the tortious act. The courts have accepted that this form of compensation has the function of granting satisfaction to the affected party.[18]

12.101   German courts are rather conservative in awarding damages. Spectacular sums cannot be expected. However, in order to better protect the personality rights of prominent persons against unauthorised media reports, there is a tendency to award higher amounts of compensation by accepting the principle that the compensation awarded should have some preventive effect.[19]

12.102   Gerstenberg[20] has collected cases and materials regarding violations of the right to a person's image showing the amounts of compensation adjudicated by German courts of which some examples will be given below. Some recent case law is also considered:

(1)   DM 500 as compensation for publishing an advertisement showing a famous actor on a motorcycle.[1]

(2)   DM 10,000 as compensation for an advertisement for a product relieving impotence showing a well-known horseman.[2]

(3)   DM 1,000 as the hypothetical licence fee for two advertisements in respect of television sets showing a scene from a TV series.[3]

(4)   DM 10,000 as compensation for defamation of a TV announcer as 'milked goat'.[4]

---

17   Stürner, Archiv für Presserecht 1998, 8.
18   Cf Palandt/Thomas, op cit, s 847, para 4 with further references.
19   Engels/Schulz, Archiv für Presserecht 1998, 574.
20   Cf Schricker, op cit Entsch of the Kunsturhebergesetz.
1   Bundesgerichtshof (Federal Supreme Court) Neue Juristische Wochenschrift 1956, 1554.
2   Bundesgerichtshof (Federal Supreme Court) Neue Juristische Wochenschrift 1957, 1315.
3   Bundesgerichtshof (Federal Supreme Court) Neue Juristische Wochenschrift 1961, 558.
4   Bundesgerichtshof (Federal Supreme Court) Neue Juristische Wochenschrift 1963, 902.

(5) DM 3,050 as the hypothetical licence fee for showing the back of a goalkeeper in an advertisement for TV sets.[5]

(6) DM 25,000 as compensation for the use of a photograph of a suspect in a terrorist murder case with sensational text.[6]

(7) DM 20,000 as compensation for the unauthorised use of a firm's business name for public relations activities.[7]

(8) DM 2,000 as compensation for the unauthorised use of a picture of a person hiking in the mountains in a public relations brochure.[8]

(9) DM 10,000 as compensation for printing a misleading headline suggesting that a politician was willing to pose for nude pictures.[9]

(10) DM 4,000 as compensation for the unauthorised publication of a nude picture taken at a public beach in Spain.[10]

(11) DM 10,000 as compensation for a report on a person swearing an oath of disclosure regarding his financial circumstances.[11]

(12) DM 6,000 for showing a photograph of a person having a criminal background with handcuffs.[12]

(13) DM 5,000 as compensation for publication of a false report which was not verified by contacting the affected person.[13]

(14) DM 6,000 as compensation for a person being described in an article as a 'swindler'.[14]

(15) DM 30,000 as the hypothetical licence fee for the unauthorised publication of a photograph originally taken for a body-painting action advert.[15]

(16) DM 15,000 as compensation for defamation in a report ('biggest wash-out').[16]

(17) DM 180,000 as compensation for the printing and publication of an invented interview with Princess Caroline of Monaco.[17]

5   Bundesgerichtshof (Federal Supreme Court) Archiv für Presserecht 1979, 345.
6   Oberlandesgericht (Regional Court of Appeal) Düsseldorf Archiv für Presserecht 1980, 54.
7   Bundesgerichtshof (Federal Supreme Court) Gewerblicher Rechtsschutz und Urheberrecht 1981, 846.
8   Oberlandesgericht (Regional Court of Appeal) Frankfurt Archiv für Presserecht 1986, 140.
9   Oberlandesgericht (Regional Court of Appeal) Hamburg Archiv für Presserecht 1988, 247.
10 Oberlandesgericht (Regional Court of Appeal) Oldenburg Archiv für Presserecht 1989, 556.
11 Oberlandesgericht (Regional Court of Appeal) Hamburg Archiv für Presserecht 1992, 376.
12 Oberlandesgericht (Regional Court of Appeal) Frankfurt Archiv für Presserecht 1993, 753.
13 Oberlandesgericht (Regional Court of Appeal) Hamburg Archiv für Presserecht 1994, 42.
14 Landgericht (Regional Court) Berlin Archiv für Presserecht 1994, 324.
15 Landgericht (Regional Court) Hamburg Archiv für Presserecht 1994, 526.
16 Landgericht (Regional Court) Oldenburg Archiv für Presserecht 1994, 679.
17 Oberlandesgericht (Regional Court of Appeal) Hamburg Neue Juristische Wochenschrift 1996, 2870.

(18) DM 10,000 as compensation for the use of a photograph in advertisements on bus-stops; although the face of the person shown was made unrecognisable, their identity was nonetheless clear.[18]

(19) DM 10,000 as the hypothetical licence fee for using the first name of the coach of the German national football team ('Berti') in an advertisement.[19]

(20) DM 155,000 as the hypothetical licence fee for violation of a well-known singer's personality right by using a lookalike.[20]

(21) DM 20,000 as compensation for the unauthorised publication of a photograph showing a semi-nude (abdomen) woman with a frivolous caption.[1]

B   Publicity

1   *Publicity rights generally*

12.103   For the purposes of this publication, the term publicity is limited to the legal issues relating to the use of a person's name and/or biography.

Constitutional rights

12.104   The right of a person to his or her name is another aspect of an individual's general personality right. The constitutional aspects outlined above under para **12.1** et seq therefore apply.

Protection of name

12.105   Protection of a person's name is provided by section 12 of the Civil Code, which reads as follows:

'If the entitled party's right to use a name is denied by another or if the interest of the entitled party is violated by another's unauthorised use of the same name, the entitled party has the right to request such other party to remove the interference. If further interference is threatening, he can seek a restraining order.'

12.106   A party's right to his or her name is considered an absolute right within the meaning of section 823(1) of the Civil Code.[2] Following the introduction of the new Trademark Act of 25 October 1994,[3] section 12 of the Civil Code has lost some of its importance, in particular in the field of the protection of names, signs and marks attaching to business enterprises. Section 5 of the Trademark Act has substituted section 16 of the Act against

18 Landgericht (Regional Court) Berlin Archiv für Presserecht 1997, 732.
19 Landgericht (Regional Court) Düsseldorf Archiv für Presserecht 1998, 238.
20 Oberlandesgericht (Regional Court of Appeal) Karlsruhe Archiv für Presserecht 1998, 326.
1   Oberlandesgericht (Regional Court of Appeal) Hamm Archiv für Presserecht 1998, 304.
2   Bundesgerichtshof (Federal Supreme Court) Neue Juristische Wochenschrift 1959, 525.
3   Bundesgesetzblatt (Federal Law Gazette) I 3082.

Unfair Competition,[4] which provided for the protection of certain business activities in the field of competing enterprises.[5]

12.107 Although originally section 12 of the Civil Code was meant to protect an individual's name only, it is well settled in case law that the name of legal entities[6] and the name of a company/firm which is different from the name of its owner[7] are within its scope of protection.

12.108 A distinction is made between the so-called name by operation of law ('Zwangsname') which attaches to a person/entity as a result of statutory provisions such as the family name (section 1616 et seq of the Civil Code) or the firm's name (section 17 et seq of the Commercial Code) and the name by choice ('Wahlname'). The latter form which usually is a pseudonym or fictitious name is also protected under section 12 of the Civil Code. There is some dispute as to whether it is necessary for a pseudonym to have attained a certain degree of recognition in the public in order to be protected.[8]

12.109 There is no particular protection of a person's biography under section 12 of the Civil Code. However, rights and remedies in case of utilisation of another person's biography can be considered as a violation of the general personality right of such person and give rise to the remedies as set out above under para **12.1** et seq.

2   *Trade marks, signs and domain names*

12.110 It is well settled that section 12 of the Civil Code protects signs or marks which are similar to names.[9] There is some uncertainty as regards domain names used on the Internet. Domain names under the Top Level Domain '.de' are now registered in Germany with DENIC EG. However, DENIC does not exercise any control whether the respective domain name violates the right of a third party. Pursuant to DENIC's standard Registration Agreement[10] an applicant has to give a declaration that the proposed domain does not violate any rights. Upon request of a third party threatening to start legal proceedings against the applicant, DENIC will put the domain on a Wait-Status. As a consequence, the applicant will not be able to transfer its domain but has to wait for the outcome of the proceedings. There is no

---

4   Of 7 June 1909 Reichsgesetzblatt (Law Gazette of the former German Reich) 499 with several amendments and modifications, latest change as of 17 December 1999 Bundesgesetzblatt (Federal Law Gazette) I 2448.

5   Cf for the general impact of the introduction of the Trademark Act on the Act on Unfair Competition, Berlit, Neue Juristische Wochenschrift 1995, 365.

6   As well for legal entities under public law Amtliche Entscheidungssammlung des Bundesgerichtshofes in Zivilsachen (Official Case Reports of Bundesgerichtshof (Federal Supreme Court) in civil matters) 124, 173.

7   Amtliche Entscheidungssammlung des Bundesgerichtshofes in Zivilsachen (Official Case Reports of Bundesgerichtshof (Federal Supreme Court) in civil matters) 14, 155.

8   Cf Amtliche Entscheidungssammlung des Bundesgerichtshofes in Zivilsachen (Official Case Reports of Bundesgerichtshof (Federal Supreme Court) in civil matters) 30, 7; Münchener Kommentar/Schwerdtner, Bürgerliches Gesetzbuch, Vol. 1, 3rd edition 1993, s 12, para 25; Palandt/Heinrichs, op cit, s 12, para 8.

9   Palandt/Heinrichs, op cit s 12, para 10 with further refenences.

10 DENIC Registration Agreement is published on http://www.denic.de.

possibility to commence proceedings concerning the Top Level Domain '.de' under the Uniform Domain Name Dispute Resolution Policy of the Internet Corporation for Assigned Names and Numbers ICANN.[11]

12.111 However, there is conflicting case law as regards the scope of application of section 12 of the Civil Code in the field of domain names. The Court of Appeal Hamm accepted that a famous name[12] when used as a domain name is protected under section 12 of the Civil Code.[13] Likewise, the Regional Court of München[14] has held that the Internet address is considered as a name in the meaning of section 12 of the Civil Code. However, the Regional Court of Köln expressed the view that the domain name does not have the function of a name as envisaged by section 12 of the Civil Code but is merely a combination of letters or figures similar to a telephone or bank account number.[15] In a recent decision of the Court of Appeal Hamburg it was held that a domain name falls under section 12 of the Civil Code, if it has distinctive features.[16] The Court of Appeal Stuttgart also accepted that a domain name is protected under section 12 of the Civil Code, if such a name is recognised by the public as a name of a certain enterprise. Further, the mere registration of a name itself is considered to be a violation, not simply its use.[17] These judgments are persuasive, but it should be noted that it is an inherent requirement of section 12 of the Civil Code that a name must have a distinctive character.[18]

12.112 Protection generally commences upon use of the name or its acceptance by the public. Violation accords the affected party the right to seek a restraining order against use of the same name or a similar name if such use is likely to give rise to the risk of confusion. However, in the case of a violation of statutory provisions such as sections 1 and 3 of the Act against Unfair Competition, section 12 of the Civil Code shall not apply. Any legitimate interest in the name will be accepted in order to give a

11   On 24 October 1999, the ICANN Board adopted a set of rules for Uniform Domain Name Dispute Resolution Policy setting out the procedure and other requirements for each stage of the dispute resolution administrative procedure. Such procedure is administered by dispute resolution service providers accredited by ICANN such as the WIPO Arbitration and Mediation Centre. However, these arbitration proceedings apply to Top Level Domain '.com', '.net' and' '.org' only.

12   A famous name normally exists if it is known by more than 80% of the public, cf Amtliche Entscheidungssammlung des Bundesgerichtshofes in Zivilsachen (Official Case Reports of Bundesgerichtshof (Federal Supreme Court) in civil matters) 114, 105 depending on the nature of products or fields of operation; prior to that decision 65% up to 80% were considered as sufficient

13   Cf Oberlandesgericht (Regional Court of Appeal) Hamm Neue Juristische Wochenschrift-Rechtsprechungs-Report Zivilrecht 1998, 909 – krupp de -

14   Landgericht (Regional Court) München Neue Juristische Wochenschrift-Rechtsprechungs-Report Zivilrecht 1998, 973 – juris de -.

15   Landgericht (Regional Court) Köln Neue Juristische Wochenschrift-Rechtsprechungs-Report Zivilrecht 1998, 976 –Pulheim de-. Meanwhile the Oberlandesgericht (Regional Court of Appeal) Köln has decided that domain names have the function of a name, Neue Juristische Wochenschrift-Rechtsprechungsreport Zivilrecht 1999, 622 - herzogenrath.de –.

16   Oberlandesgericht (Regional Court of Appeal) Hamburg, Judgment dated 5 November 1998 Computer und Recht 1999, 184.

17   Oberlandesgericht (Regional Court of Appeal) Stuttgart Archiv für Presserecht 1998, 662; see as well Oberlandesgericht (Regional Court of Appeal) München, Der Betrieb 1999, 2510 - rolls-royce.de -.

18   Cf Palandt/Heinrichs, op cit, s 12, para 12.

cause of action under section 12 of the Civil Code. The courts have applied a broad approach. The risk of confusion which is an inherent requirement of any action under section 12 of the Civil Code[19] is always considered as supporting a legitimate interest.[20] Special considerations apply in the case of famous names. They are not only protected against a risk of confusion but also against any infringement of their exclusive nature and public relation value.[1]

3 Remedies for breach of publicity right

12.113   The general aspects of the remedies arising under section 12 of the Civil Code such as jurisdiction and proper law as set out above under para **12.66** et seq apply in relation to a person's/entity's right to their name. The relevant aspects of section 12 of the Civil Code are discussed below.

Foreign parties

12.114   As a matter of principle, the name of a foreign party is also protected under section 12 of the Civil Code.[2] The right arises as soon as the name is used within the territory of the Federal Republic of Germany.[3] The name must be used in a way which justifies the assumption that a continuing activity within the jurisdiction is contemplated.[4]

Substantive matters

12.115   The rights arising under section 12 of the Civil Code are twofold. First, the denial of the right to use a particular name gives rise to a claim for removal of interference regardless of any negligent act committed by the interfering party.[5] However, this remedy is only of limited practical importance.[6]

12.116   Secondly, the unauthorised use of a name gives rise to the right to seek whatever relief is necessary to remove the unlawful interference.[7] If the risk of repetition ('Wiederholungsgefahr') exists, the party entitled may apply for a restraining order prohibiting the future use of the name.[8]

---

19 Münchener Kommentar/Schwerdtner, op cit, s 12, para 105.
20 Palandt/Heinrichs, op cit, s 12, paras 28 and 30 with further references.
1   Cf Bundesgerichtshof (Federal Supreme Court) Neue Juristische Wochenschrift-Rechtsprechungs-Report Zivilrecht 1992, 940, 942 – Mercedes -.
2   Pursuant to art 10 of the Introductory Act to the Civil Code, the name of a person is governed by the person's nationality; the proper law of companies/firms is determined by the law of the state where the effective management of the company/firm is located, cf Amtliche Entscheidungssammlung des Bundesgerichtshofes in Zivilsachen (Official Case Reports of Bundesgerichtshof (Federal Supreme Court) in civil matters) 97, 269 (271); the effect of the CENTROS-decision of the European Court of Justice, cf. Neue Juristische Wochenschrift 1999, 2027, on this point remains to be seen.
3   Amtliche Entscheidungssammlung des Bundesgerichtshofes in Zivilsachen (Official Case Reports of Bundesgerichtshof (Federal Supreme Court) in civil matters) 34, 91.
4   Amtliche Entscheidungssammlung des Bundesgerichtshofes in Zivilsachen (Official Case Reports of Bundesgerichtshof (Federal Supreme Court) in civil matters) 75, 172.
5   Palandt/Heinrichs, op cit, s 12, para 32.
6   Cf Münchener Kommentar/Schwerdtner, op cit, s 12, para 97.
7   Cf Amtliche Entscheidungssammlung des Bundesgerichtshofes in Zivilsachen (Official Case Reports of Bundesgerichtshof (Federal Supreme Court) in civil matters) 107, 384 regarding the removal of Emil Nolde's name from a forged painting.
8   Palandt/Heinrichs, op cit, s 12, para 34.

12.117   Section 12 of the Civil Code does not contain any provisions for the granting of damages. This is exclusively governed by section 823 et seq of the Civil Code. The principles and examples set out above under para **12.65** et seq apply *mutatis mutandis*.

13 GREECE

Dr Leonidas Kanellos

A Privacy

1 The protection of privacy under Greek law

13.01 The protection of privacy in Greece has traditionally been considered a fundamental human right. Nowadays this right is subject to violations from new technological methods of privacy invasion, such as identity cards, biometrics, surveillance of communications, Internet and e-mail interception, video and workplace surveillance and so on. However, although the term 'privacy' is used in many statutes, there is no legal definition of it. In practice, this concept has mainly been specified by case law and legal literature.

13.02 According to legal writers, privacy may be defined as the person's 'right to be left alone'. The private sphere is the minimum space which is necessary to the individual if he is to exercise his personal, professional and social activities without interference from intrusive third parties.[1]

13.03 Private life includes but is not limited to sensitive personal information about family life, health, sex, religion, friendship, profession, property, political beliefs, ideas and other data characterising a person that the person wishes to keep private and shielded from publicity.

13.04 A right to privacy is recognised by Greek legislation for persons whether they are well-known or not. However, it is accepted that due to their social status, some categories of people such as celebrities or politicians, who are by definition 'in the public eye', should tolerate more intrusion into their private space than ordinary people.[2]

13.05 A major concern of political democracy in Greece has been to enable the press to criticise politicians as part of a wider public debate, and as a means of ensuring proper accountability on the part of public servants. Nevertheless, it is always a delicate matter for courts to evaluate in any particular case whether the publication or communication of facts, value-judgments or opinions amounts to an abuse or violation of privacy.

---

1 Sourlas, *Commentary on articles 57-60 of Civil Code*, see also: Krippas, *Freedom of the press*, volume I, 1970 and Dagtoglou, *Press and Constitution*, 1989.
2 In this direction Athens Court of Appeal 10745/1991, Nomiko Vima, 40, 1992, p 290.

Consequently, the scope of privacy may differ from person to person, from time to time and place to place, in accordance with social habits, morality and the person's position in society.[3]

13.06 Privacy is safeguarded in Greece by international conventions, constitutional provisions, civil and criminal code provisions as well as specific laws covering the written and electronic press.

2 Privacy protection by international conventions

13.07 Greece has signed and ratified the European Convention for the Protection of Human Rights and Fundamental Freedoms of 4 November 1950 and its Protocols.[4] Thus, the Convention and the ratified Protocols became an integral part of domestic law and prevail over any contrary statutory provision. Under Articles 46 and 25 of the ECHR, Greece has also recognised the jurisdiction of the European Court of Human Rights together with the right of an individual to petition the European Commission of Human Rights. Consequently, the Hellenic Courts may apply Articles 8 and 10 of the ECHR in order to strike a balance between freedom of expression and protection of privacy.[5]

3 Privacy protection by the Hellenic Constitution

13.08 The Hellenic Constitution of 1975[6] contains a set of fundamental rules covering privacy and the broader right to personality, such as Article 2, para 1 (respect of human value), Article 5, para 1 (free development of personality), Article 7, para 2 (respect of human dignity), Article 9 (protection of home and family life), and Article 19 (secrecy of correspondence). Those fundamental rights are reflected in several civil and penal law provisions.

13.09 More specifically, Article 9, which recognises the rights of privacy and secrecy of communications, states:

'(1) Each man's home is inviolable. A person's personal and family life is inviolable. No house searches shall be made except when and as the law directs, and always in the presence of representatives of the judicial authorities.

(2) Offenders against the foregoing provision shall be punished for forced entry into a private house and abuse of power, and shall be obliged to indemnify in full the injured party as the law provides.'

13.10 Article 19 states:

'The privacy of correspondence and any other form of communication is absolutely inviolable. The law shall determine the guarantees under

---

3   Michaelides-Nouaros, *The protection of private life and the freedom of the press*, To Syntagma 1983, p 379.
4   The ratification instruments of the European Convention are in chronological order: Law 2329/1953, Legislative Decrees 53/1974 and 215/1974, Law 1705/1987 and Law 1841/1989.
5   In this direction: Athens District Court 11656/1995, Supreme Court (Areios Pagos) 812/1980, Athens Court of Appeal 594/1998.
6   The Hellenic Constitution of 11 June 1975 is available in English translation at http://www.uni-wuerzburg.de/law/gr00t___.html.

which the judicial authority is released from the obligation to observe the above-mentioned right, for reasons of national security or for the investigation of particularly serious crimes.'

13.11 The right to privacy may often be subject to violations by third parties as well as by the press that is also guaranteed the right of freedom of information. This right, laid down in Article 14 of the Constitution, is considered as an invaluable component of the freedom of expression, which is fundamental to the democratic society.

13.12 Article 14 on Freedom of Expression and Press states:

'(1) Any person may express and propagate his opinion orally, in writing, or in print with due adherence to the laws of the State.

(2) The press is free. Censorship and all preventive measures are prohibited.

(3) The seizure of newspapers and other printed matter, either before or after circulation, is prohibited ...'

13.13 By exception, seizure after publication is permitted upon instruction by the Public Prosecutor because of:

(1) insult to the Christian and all other known religions;

(2) insult to the person of the President of the Republic;

(3) a publication which discloses information relating to the composition, armament, and disposition of the armed forces or the fortifications of the country, or aims at violently overthrowing the political system or is directed against the territorial integrity of the State; and

(4) obscene publications which manifestly offend public decency, in the cases specified by law.

13.14 The above constitutional provisions, as interpreted by courts on a case-by-case basis, mark the necessary limits to the democratic freedoms of opinion and press, speech and expression in order to avoid conflicts with rights to personality.

4 *Privacy protection by civil law*

13.15 The above constitutional principles concerning privacy and personality have been transferred to the Hellenic Civil Code. More specifically, Articles 57–60 of the Civil Code define the general rules for protection of personality. This concept also includes a person's name and intellectual works. According to Article 57 a person who has suffered an unlawful offence on his personality has the right to claim the cessation of such offence as well as non-recurrence in the future. If the offence was directed against the personality of a deceased person the right referred to above shall belong to the spouse, the descendants, the ancestors, the brothers, the sisters and the legatees appointed by testament. A further claim for damages based on the provisions governing unlawful acts is not excluded.[7]

7 Greek Civil Code, translated by C Taliadoros, 1992.

13.16   Article 58 safeguards the right to the name, Article 59 provides for the reparation of moral prejudice suffered by the person offended, while Article 60 protects persons suffering unlawful infringements of their intellectual property rights. Privacy violations may arise by any unlawful act performed without the person's consent, irrespective of the means or technical equipment used.

13.17   The publication of false facts or value-judgments about an individual or their activities, recording conversations, filming or photographing on private property, intercepting phone calls or opening letters, are in principle illegal and constitute violations of privacy and personality rights. Article 281 of the Civil Code provides that any right must be exercised in accordance with the requirements of good faith and morality also giving consideration to the social and economic scope of this right.

13.18   On the basis of the above general principles, a person whose privacy is violated may commence legal proceedings in order to prevent the publication of such document or recording, to oblige offenders to provide compensation for the damage by any appropriate means and abstain from any similar offences in the future. A person seeking remedies for a violation of their privacy may also claim damages on the basis of Articles 330, 914, 919, 920 and 932 of the Civil Code in contractual liability, negligence and tort. In such a case, they will have to prove default on the part of the defendant, ie a violation of his privacy, a damage which will often be only moral, and a causal relationship between the default and the damage suffered. The court can order the offenders to provide compensation for the damage by paying financial compensation to the plaintiff. The judge may prevent the publication of documents, recording or articles concerning privacy, and order the restitution, seizure or destruction of the documents or unlawful recordings.

5   Privacy protection by criminal law

13.19   Notwithstanding the civil law protection, making a false statement about someone could give rise to criminal liability. Since the press in a democratic society has the freedom to inform and criticise on matters of public interest, it must be allowed to make public any information that offends, shocks or even insults an individual. Nevertheless, the publication of false statements or facts about a person can result in custodial or pecuniary penalties for journalists or editors. Seizure of journals is permitted by the Hellenic Constitution only in the very exceptional cases stated above.

13.20   In all of these cases, the Public Prosecutor must, within 24 hours of the seizure, submit the case to the judicial council which, within a further 24 hours, must decide whether the seizure shall be maintained or withdrawn, otherwise the seizure shall be lifted automatically ('ipso jure'). The publisher of the seized newspaper or other printed matter and the Public Prosecutor are allowed to appeal to the Court of Appeal and the Supreme Court (Areios Pagos).[8] The law determines the manner in which erroneous publications will be rectified through the press. After at least three convictions within a five-year period for crimes committed through the press, the court shall

---

8   Hellenic Constitution, art 14, paras 3, 4.

order the permanent or temporary suspension of issue of the publication. In serious cases, the court can also prohibit the practice of the profession of journalist by the person convicted, as provided by law. Such suspension or prohibition shall commence from such time as the sentence becomes irrevocable. Press offences shall be deemed 'offences in *flagrante delicto*' and shall be judged by the courts as the law provides. The law also determines conditions and qualifications for the practice of journalism and requires transparency in financing newspapers and periodicals.[9]

13.21   According to the Criminal Code an offence is an act, which is illegal, imputable to the offender and punishable under the law.[10] Articles 361-365 of the Criminal Code on defamation and libel may be invoked in order to establish a criminal offence committed by journalists against a person. Pursuant to Article 367 negative comments on scientific, artistic or professional works do not constitute unlawful acts when expressed in a document issued by a public administration or in order to exercise a recognised right or safeguard 'a justified interest'. The acts of wiretapping, illegal recording, accessing digital data or computer memories and breach of secrecy of communications are punishable under Articles 370A, 370B, 370C and 370D of the Criminal Code.

13.22   The above provisions have been added to Article 370 by Law 1805/ 1988 on incriminating forgery. This law has been criticised as being too far-reaching since it extends the meaning of 'writing', as defined in Article 13 of the Code, to all electronic or magnetic materials in which any information, image, symbol or sound is incorporated, if those means can be proved to have a legal interest, such as computer memories, photographs, cinematographic films, videotapes, sound recordings etc.[11] Any person who by any technical means records private communications, uses such recordings or markets technical equipment facilitating the above acts is subject to severe penalties of fines and imprisonment. The same penalties apply to the illegal accessing of computer memories or data in violation of state or scientific secrets.

6   Privacy protection by specific laws on the press

13.23   The first laws on the civil and penal liability of the press in Greece were adopted in 1931[12] and 1938.[13] Those laws have been amended several times in recent years.[14] In addition to the general liability rules, as described above, there are today in Greece several provisions which define the sanctions to be pronounced by courts against activities of the press infringing individual rights. Law 1178/1981, as amended by Law 2243/1994, obliges the owner of any journal or periodical to compensate victims for any

---

9   Hellenic Constitution, art 14, para 5 and cons.
10   B Lolis, *The Greek Penal Code*, Sweet & Maxwell, London, 1973.
11   L Kanellos, *Copyright Software Protection in the EC*, Kluwer, 1993, p 102.
12   Law 5060/1931, which has been abolished by Law 2243/1994 with the exception of arts 29 and 30.
13   Articles 32, 37 and 38 of Law 1092/1938 introducing general rules remain still valid. Breach of those rules implies administrative sanctions together with the persons right to seek relief.
14   Laws 1178/1981, 1738/1987, 1806/1988, 1868/1989 and 2243/1994 have amended without totally abolishing the legislation on the press.

pecuniary or moral prejudice which occurs as a result of publication, independently from the outcome of any pending penal proceedings. By virtue of the above law, pecuniary compensation for moral prejudice caused by a publication may not be less than 10 million GRD for the daily newspapers in Athens and Thessaloniki and 2 million GRD for other newspapers or periodicals, unless the person demands a smaller sum in compensation.[15]

13.24   Cases are decided pursuant to a simplified procedure described in Articles 663–676 of the Code of Civil Procedure.[16] Some commentators argue that it is necessary to adopt a coherent, actual law on the press by assembling the numerous disparate public and private law provisions into a coherent system of statutes. However, journalists' associations oppose this idea since they believe the adoption of a new law could disturb the institutional equilibrium established by tradition between the State, the government, the press and the citizens.

7   *Privacy protection by media laws*

13.25   Initially focusing on the written press, privacy protective legislation in Greece has progressively been extended to include all mass communication media such as books, pamphlets, periodicals, newspapers, motion pictures, phonograph records, radio, television and means of telecommunication.

13.26   However, by virtue of Article 15 of the Constitution, the increased constitutional protection of Article 24 applies only to the written press. This means that no equivalent freedom of expression right is expressly recognised in the electronic media. In fact, Article 15 on media supervision reads:

> '(1) The provisions on the protection of the press contained in the aforegoing article shall not be applied to motion pictures, phonography, radio, television, and all other similar means of transmitting speech of image.
>
> (2) Radio and television are placed under the immediate supervision of the State and shall aim at the transmission of objective information and news under conditions of equality, as well as works of literature and art, safeguarding in every case such quality in the broadcasts as may become necessary by the social function thereof and the cultural development of the country'.

13.27   Constitutional requirements on State control have been transposed into sector specific broadcasting rules concerning quality, pluralism, impartiality and objectivity of radio and television broadcasts. For instance, Law 1730/1987 on ERT, which is the State radio and television, specifies that emissions should respect individual privacy.[17] Equally, the Broadcasting

---

15   Law 1178/1981 para 2 as amended by Law 2243/1994 which abolished special criminal provisions on the press.

16   This procedure is followed in labour law disputes and aims at the immediate satisfaction of the plaintiff.

17   Law 1730/1987, art 3e.

Act (Law 2238/1995) and the new Act on subscriber radio and television services (Law 2644/1998[18]) specify that radio and television broadcasts (including advertisements) 'must respect personality, private and family life, professional, social, scientific, artistic, political or any other activity of the person, the image or name of whom appear on the screen'[19] in accordance with Article 15, para 2 of the Constitution and EC Directive 89/552/EEC, as implemented in Greece.[20] The above legislation also provides for a right of rectification and a right of reply.

13.28 The National Council for Radio and Television (NCRT), which is the independent regulatory authority in the broadcasting sector, is entitled by the law to recommend to the Minister of Press and Mass Media severe administrative fines and penalties to be pronounced against radio and television broadcasts which violate the above provisions. Recently, the Council of State confirmed the legality of sanctions pronounced by the Minister of Press and Mass Media against a private television broadcaster for breach of broadcasting rules of ethics. According to this decision, taken on recommendation of the NCRT, the way in which journalists last summer dealt on a popular current affairs programme with an incest case which had occurred in a provincial city led to the public vilification of the family. The sanctions against the television station included a 100 million GRD administrative fine together with a 10-minute temporary suspension of its programme for 5 consecutive days. According to the Council of State, sanctions had to be maintained since this broadcast directly violated the Constitution which requires a high quality of television programmes and respect for human dignity.[1]

13.29 Beyond general civil and penal liability rules, specific privacy protective provisions define the civil liability of the editors and journalists in cases of breach of professional codes of conduct, dissemination of untrue defamatory rumours against persons resulting in damages and other personal injuries. Sanctions are meant to apply to the press and journalists in cases of personal libel, heresy, sedition, blasphemy, obscenity, and other positive and negative expressions on freedom of the press which may violate rights to privacy.

8 *Privacy protection by telecommunication laws*

13.30 Traditional press legislation has been supplemented by a new generation of technology-related laws such as telecommunications and data protection acts. Most of the above laws implement relevant European Union Directives adopted to enhance privacy protection in the Information Society. A specific statute (Law 2225/1994) guarantees secrecy of communications. It establishes a special committee made up of representatives of all political parties represented in Parliament which is entitled to perform audits and controls at the premises of all telecommunications operators in order to ensure respect of the above constitutional requirements on secrecy. In the

---

18 See the electronic newsletter LABnews September–October 1998 at http://www2.echo.lu/legal/en/news/9810/chapter6.html#1.
19 Law 2328/1995, art 3b.
20 Presidential Decree 236/1992 has implemented in Greece the Directive 89/552/EC.
1 'LABnews- November 1997' at http://www2.echo.lu/legal/en/news/9711/chapter6.html#61.

same direction Law 2246/1994 (the Telecommunications Act) and its implementing regulations, in conjunction with Codes of Ethics on the provision of telecommunication services, also introduce the telecommunications operators' obligation to guarantee secrecy of communications and data transmitted over their networks.

13.31 The National Telecommunications Commission (NTC), which is the independent regulator in the telecommunications sector in Greece, is entitled to pronounce administrative fines and penalties against infringers. However, in the past, judicial investigations have been conducted in order to find out if the above provisions have been respected. For instance, in June 1994, a parliamentary investigation committee recommended the indictment of former Prime Minister Mitsotakis and 30 persons from his administration on charges of wire-tapping political opponents from 1989 to 1991. In January 1995, the Parliament voted to drop all charges against Mitsotakis, and the Supreme Court ordered the dismissal of other charges in April 1995. The late Greek prime Minister Andreas Papandreou was also investigated for illegally wire-tapping his political opponents.[2]

13.32 In view of the dramatic growth of the Internet as a communications medium the public dialogue has begun in Greece on the necessity of developing a legislative framework which guarantees both secrecy of communications and the need to foster the perspectives of electronic commerce and online transactions. In this respect, the Technical Chamber of Greece has launched a pilot project which aims at the distribution of digital certificates to private firms. Equally, the Ministry of Development has set up a Committee to study the questions of security on the Internet and on-line transactions. The Hellenic Government will announce in the near future a framework for public policy on cryptography, electronic signatures and accreditation of certification authorities. The measures to be adopted should strike a balance between the rights to privacy, security and integrity of communications, the development of the national cryptography industry, and lawful access to data for law enforcement and national security.

9   Privacy protection by data protection law

13.33 The Data Protection Act (Law 2472/1997) passed by Parliament is designed to guarantee a basic level of protection of privacy. The Act is in line with EU Data Protection Directive 95/46/EC and the 1981 Convention of the Council of Europe. It lays down a set of guidelines, principles and rules relating to the use, processing, storage and export of personal data both in electronic and manual files and sets up an independent Personal Data Protection Authority. Its mission is to supervise the implementation of the law and the other rulings pertaining to the protection of individuals against the processing of personal data. It also exercises other powers delegated to it from time to time. The Act also contains provisions relating to the registration and notification of electronic data processing, and defines the licensing requirements which apply to the establishment of databases

---

2   The Reuters European Community Report, 10 June 1997 and the Reuters European Community Report, 23 April 1993.

containing personal data and the transfer of personal data overseas. Transborder data transmission from Greece to EU countries is unrestricted. Transmission of data to other countries requires that a licence be granted by the Data Protection Authority on the criterion of reciprocity. Data subjects are entitled to access and correct the data relating to them, and to claim compensation where loss or damage is suffered as a result of the use or disclosure of such data. Infringement of the legislation entails administrative, civil and penal liability.

B Publicity

1 *Name protection*

13.34 Protection of a person's name against any contest or unauthorised use can be afforded both by civil and commercial law provisions. Protection includes not only national persons but also legal entities, such as professional companies[3] and associations.[4]

13.35 Use of a person's name, either in public or in a biography, without their consent may be restricted, on the basis either of the aforementioned Article 58[5] of the Civil Code or of the general rules of liability. In some provisions, the Civil Code uses the term 'name' either as a synonym for both first and family name[6] or just as only family name.[7] Name protection also includes pseudonyms, professional titles such as 'professor', 'doctor', 'ambassador' or military ranks such as 'General', 'Major' etc. Titles of nobility or distinction can neither be conferred upon, nor recognised in Greek citizens by virtue of Article 4, para 7 of the Constitution. Use of a person's name to name an animal does not entail attack on the person's name but on their honour.[8]

13.36 This protection applies to all persons, irrespective of their citizenship. If the right of a person to bear a given name has been challenged by another person or if anyone made unlawful use of a given name, the person who suffers prejudice may claim the cessation of the offence as a well as the non-recurrence thereof in the future.

13.37 Apart from the civil law provisions, the protection of one's name has been recognised by the Criminal Code. Under Articles 216–217 any person who uses a false name or falsifies an official document (passport, identity card) in order to obtain profit for himself or another person incurs criminal penalties including a custodial sentence and/or fine.

13.38 Facts relating to privacy may not be disclosed in a biography, except with the consent of the person concerned. Nevertheless, no person has the

---

3   Legal entities have additional commercial law protection, however, art 58 of the Civil Code applies by analogy.
4   Stathopoulos, Georgiadis, *Civil Code, Article by Article Commentary*, art 58 and Athens Court of Appeal 1146/197.
5   This Article has similar scope with arts 12 of the German Civil Code, 29 of the Swiss Civil Code or 7–9 of the Italian Civil Code.
6   Civil Code, arts 85, 1369, 1960.
7   Civil Code, arts 1388, 1452, 1493, 1531, 1537, 1582.
8   Stathopoulos, Georgiadis,*Civil Code, Article by Article Commentary*, p 111.

right to prevent the publication of biographies analysing public or historical events in which they have taken part. In such cases, publication should be permitted, even if the consent of the person concerned has not be obtained, as long as the facts are truthfully, objectively and impartially described.

13.39 Publication of public events may be punished as a violation of a person's reputation, in cases where a specific fact has been maliciously and publicly attributed to a person, a fact that may cause an injury to the person's reputation (defamation) if the proof of this specific fact is prohibited and libel if the proof is legally permitted and the fact is not proved. The penalties incurred (custodial sentence and fine) will depend on the circumstances of the defamation, libel or slander, and also depending on the factual circumstances of the insult.

2   Trade mark protection

13.40   A trade name is the name which a merchant uses in his commercial activities. Normally, if the merchant is a natural person, his trade name will coincide with his name as a citizen (first name and family name). Trade names and distinctive titles are protected by virtue of Articles 13 and 14 of the Law 146/1914 on Unfair Competition together with trade mark legislation (Law 2239/1994 as amended by PD 353/1998). Trade mark protection may be granted to a person's name as well as to first name and pseudonyms. Protection is granted provided the name is registered as a trade mark at a special department of the Ministry of Development by following a simplified registration procedure which controls the existence of a former registration of a similar product or service.

13.41   Civil protection of a trade mark gives the proprietor the right to sue for refraining from use of the trade mark and/or for damages. The provisional remedies procedure referred to above may be resorted to here as well, in which case the court may order the preliminary seizure of products bearing the counterfeit or imitation trade mark.[9] By virtue of the legislation the intentional use of such a trade name or distinctive sign belonging to another is punishable by imprisonment and fines.[10]

C   Personality

1   Personality rights

13.42   As explained above, the Greek law, jurisprudence and legal theory[11] traditionally accept that the right to privacy is a derivative of a broader right of personality. According to Greek law, the latter is an absolute, autonomous, non transferable 'composite' or 'framework right' since it also includes several particular dependent rights such as right to respect of honour, reputation, personal integrity and professional image. Any unlawful act of any third natural person, legal entity, public or private authority may

9   Rokas, *Introduction to Greek law*, Longman 1992.
10   K Kerameus, P Kozyris, *Introduction to Greek Law*, Kluwer-Sakkoulas 1993, p 188.
11   Gazis, *General Principles of Civil law*, 1973.

violate the right of personality. The aforementioned provisions on privacy protection equally apply on personality.

13.43   Under the Hellenic Code of Civil Procedure, provisional remedies can be ordered by courts in order to safeguard a personality right. Those measures can be intended to conserve, so as, for example to secure the future satisfaction of a substantive right,[12] or intended to regulate, so as for example to provisionally arrange disputed situations through orders for specific acts, omissions or indulgences, such as in disputes related to possession, unfair competition, family relations labour law etc.[13]

13.44   In this respect, the Greek courts have ruled that personality rights are violated by the pollution of natural environment[14] and pollution of the sea[15] which violates the relevant citizens' right to enjoy a clean environment. In labour law, subjective evaluation of an employee[16] or transfer of a public servant to a remote area[17] by an employer has been found to infringe personality rights. In commercial law, the courts have also ruled that the use of the trade mark 'Jesus' for clothing goods also violates people's religious feelings.[18] Personality rights can also be injured in cases of unauthorised use of a person's image for advertising purposes.[19] Equally, intellectual property rights of a composer may be infringed by a record company having omitted to mention the company's name on a disc's front cover.[20] However, in some cases the courts have found that personality rights of a spouse are not violated where the husband uses in divorce proceedings videotapes recorded without the wife's consent since common marital life justifies such acts[1] or when the employer makes negative comments about an employee which are based on the employee's bad performance.[2] Equally, personality rights are not infringed when persons are filmed during public events, spectacles or ceremonies.

13.45   Consequently, one could conclude that Greek law offers an adequate arsenal of legal remedies for personality and privacy protection. Nevertheless, constant technological evolution creates new threats for those individual rights. Even with the adoption of legal and other protections, violation of privacy still remains a concern. National laws cannot keep up with global technology, whose development continually creates significant gaps in protection. Without continuous and adequate supervision and enforcement, the mere presence of laws will not provide adequate protection. There are widespread violations of laws relating to the surveillance of communications, even in the most democratic of countries.[3] Annual reviews of human rights violations find that many countries engage

---

12   Greek Code of Civil Procedure, arts 704–727, 737–738.
13   Greek Code of Civil Procedure, arts 731–736 .
14   Serres First Instance Court 12/1994.
15   Nafplion First Instance Court 163/1991.
16   Supreme Court (Areios Pagos) 962/1993.
17   Athens First Instance Court 277/1991, Athens Court of Appeal 2723/1994.
18   Athens District Court 2327/1985.
19   Areios Pagos 940/1995.
20   Athens First Instance Court 1293/1987.
1   Areios Pagos 673/1983, Thessaloniki Court of Appeal 735/1993.
2   Areios Pagos 835/1972.
3   See in this respect: Global Internet Liberty Campaign- 'Privacy and Human Rights' An International Survey of Privacy Laws and Practice on the Internet at http://www.gilc.org/privacy/survey/intro.html#threats.

in illegally monitoring the communications of political opponents, human rights workers and journalists. Police services, even in countries with strong privacy laws, still maintain extensive files on citizens not accused or even suspected of any crime. Companies regularly flaunt the laws, collecting, disseminating and using personal information for marketing purposes.

13.46 Extreme vigilance is therefore required from individuals, privacy protection groups, consumer organisations and the legislators. In addition to developing adequate technological means of ensuring privacy protection in order to comply with European and international data protection, encryption and other legislation, it is also important to create international legal remedies in order to protect privacy and personality without compromising our societies' smooth transition to the Information Society.

14 HONG KONG

Simon Deane*

A Introduction

14.01 Over the past few years, there have been significant legislative developments in Hong Kong in relation to the protection of the privacy of individuals. A lot of this activity was no doubt inspired by fears (so far unrealised) about the handover of sovereignty of Hong Kong to the communist People's Republic of China ('PRC'). It is interesting to note, however, that even the mini-constitution drafted for Hong Kong by China tries to protect some aspects of individual privacy as well as various basic individual freedoms.

This survey of the law in Hong Kong will attempt to summarise the recent legislative enactments and the impact they have on issues of privacy, publicity and personality and then briefly consider recent proposals by various Law Reform Commissions. Next, the common law position, the use of a person's name and likeness and the availability of trade mark protection will be considered very briefly. A final section will look at the following areas in the light of the summary of the law in Hong Kong: covert collection of data such as use of telephoto lenses, telephone tapping; sifting rubbish; use of an assumed identity; open collection of data on or over private property; using cameras or by staking out by the police and the press.

B Legislation

1 The Basic Law

14.02 The Basic Law[1] was adopted by the government of the PRC on 4 April 1990 and became law in Hong Kong on 1 July 1997 when the PRC resumed sovereignty. It is effectively the PRC's mini constitution for Hong Kong and, amongst other things, it has a separate Chapter dealing with the Fundamental Rights and Duties of Residents. The two articles of most direct relevance to this survey are Articles 29 and 30, set out below in full:

---

*   This chapter is dedicated to my daughter, Jade.
1   Or to give it its full title, The Basic Law of the Hong Kong Special Administrative Region of the People's Republic of China.

Article 29:

> 'The homes and other premises of Hong Kong residents shall be inviolable. Arbitrary or unlawful search of, or intrusion into, a resident's home or other premises shall be prohibited.'

Article 30:

> 'The freedom and privacy of communication of Hong Kong residents shall be protected by law. No department or individual may, on any grounds, infringe upon the freedom and privacy of communication of residents except that the relevant authorities may inspect communication in accordance with legal procedures to meet the needs of public security or of investigation into criminal offences.'

14.03 It will be noted that these articles only apply to 'Hong Kong residents'. Hong Kong residents are defined in Article 24[2] as persons with right of abode and those without right of abode but who are qualified to obtain Hong Kong identity cards. Persons with right of abode are:

(1) Chinese born in Hong Kong and Chinese born outside Hong Kong but who have lived in Hong Kong for 7 years, and any of their children born outside Hong Kong;

(2) non-Chinese who have lived in Hong Kong for 7 years who have taken Hong Kong as their place of permanent residence, and their children under 21; and

(3) other people who before 1 July 1997 had the right of abode in Hong Kong.

14.04 Those without right of abode but who are entitled to a Hong Kong identity card are, very broadly, those who are permitted to work in Hong Kong and their children and those who are otherwise permitted to remain in Hong Kong for more than 180 days. The rights under the Basic Law are also available to any other individual in accordance with law.

14.05 Article 29, as has been seen, protects the privacy of Hong Kong residents' homes or other premises – only lawful search or intrusion is permitted. Article 30 protects the freedom and privacy of communication. No government department or individual is permitted *on any grounds* to infringe this freedom, although the authorities may do so to meet the needs of public security or in order to investigate criminal offences provided proper legal procedures are followed. This exception (which is, arguably, necessary for the purposes of safeguarding the public interest and crime prevention) is quite limited in that it does not extend to any non-governmental authorities – it remains to be seen how widely the 'needs of public security' will be construed. But Article 30 would seem to prevent any private eavesdropping on Hong Kong residents' communications.

14.06 Mention should also be made of Article 27 of the Basic Law which, among other things, provides for 'freedom of speech, of the press and of publication'. These rights potentially conflict with the privacy rights provided for in Articles 29 and 30. However, it is submitted that there is no real conflict as it is not strictly necessary for the press to eavesdrop or gain

---

2   There have recently been some highly controversisal court decisions c oncerning the interpretation of this and other related sections of the Basic Law which are not relevant for the purposes of this survey.

access to Hong Kong residents' property to enjoy freedom. (Problems might arise, however, where third parties pass on to the press the 'fruits' of their invasion of someone's privacy – these problems are touched upon below in the light of other legislation and the common law).

14.07 Whether Hong Kong residents will seek to rely upon the Basic Law as a means of enforcing rights to privacy is another matter. The Basic Law does not itself lay down any sanctions for breach of its provisions, so enforcement of rights may be problematic. Further, under Article 158, ultimate power to interpret the Basic Law lies with the Standing Committee of the National People's Congress of the PRC. However, Hong Kong's courts are authorised to interpret provisions of the Basic Law which are within the limits of Hong Kong's autonomy, and other provisions (provided guidance is sought from the Standing Committee where relevant provisions concern affairs which are the responsibility of the PRC Government or concern the relationship between Hong Kong and the PRC Government). As matters within the limits of Hong Kong's autonomy are not necessarily clear cut, in practice, the Hong Kong courts regrettably may be reluctant to interpret the Basic Law.

14.08 In any event, the Basic Law is more a statement of general principles in so far as individual rights are concerned. It is submitted therefore that it is unlikely to be relied upon to any great extent as a source of law to protect those rights. Relevant provisions may need to be 'clarified' by further legislation in respect of these principles. However, Article 11 provides that 'no law enacted by the legislature of the Hong Kong Special Administrative Region shall contravene [the Basic] Law,' thus establishing the Basic Law's pre-eminence.

2   Hong Kong Bill of Rights Ordinance

14.09 This Ordinance came into force on 8 June 1991 and provides for the incorporation into Hong Kong law of the International Covenant on Civil and Political Rights ('ICCPR'). It binds only the Government and all public authorities, and persons acting on their behalf. It cannot be relied upon against an invasion of privacy by newspapers and other members of the private sector.

14.10 Article 14 of section 8 of this Ordinance is of relevance to this survey and it is set out below in full.

'Protection of Privacy, family, home, correspondence, honour and reputation

(1)   No one shall be subjected to arbitrary or unlawful interference with his privacy, family, home or correspondence, nor to unlawful attacks on his honour and reputation.

(2)   Everyone has the right to the protection of the law against such interference or attacks.'

This particular right would appear to apply to everyone in Hong Kong whether a 'Hong Kong resident' or not. To some extent, the Bill of Rights Ordinance reflects Articles 29 and 30 of the Basic Law – it prohibits arbitrary or unlawful interference with an individual's home[3] and with his/her

---

3   Article 29, Basic Law.

correspondence[4] by government bodies or agents. In practice, this will not prevent public authorities interfering with an individual's privacy or home provided they do so in accordance with the law and follow prescribed legal procedures. The interference must also not be arbitrary so there must be good grounds for doing so. In addition, Article 14 provides protection against unlawful attacks on honour and reputation. Section 6 of the Ordinance deals with remedies for breach of the Ordinance – courts and tribunals are given power to grant such remedy or relief or make such order in respect of breaches of the Ordinance as they have power to grant or make in relevant proceedings and as they consider appropriate and just in the circumstances.

14.11 Brief mention should be made of Article 39 of the Basic Law and its relationship with the Bill of Rights Ordinance. Article 39 provides for the ICCPR to be implemented in Hong Kong and that rights and freedoms of Hong Kong residents shall not be restricted in such a way as to contravene the ICCPR. Although the Bill of Rights Ordinance attempts to implement the ICCPR, it only binds the Government and public bodies, whereas the ICCPR is intended to bind the private sector as well. Article 39 of the Basic Law, however, would appear to suggest that protection should also be available against infringements of rights by the private sector. The Hong Kong courts have not yet had to address this apparent anomaly.

3 Personal Data (Privacy) Ordinance

14.12 The Personal Data (Privacy) Ordinance ('PDPO') is the primary legislation in Hong Kong concerning the protection of personal privacy. The legislation was enacted in August 1995, but only came substantially into force in December, 1996 and one of the provisions (relating to the transfer of personal data out of Hong Kong) has still not been brought into effect.

14.13 The PDPO protects 'personal data'. This is defined as any data relating to any living individual, from which it is practicable for the identity of the individual to be directly or indirectly ascertained and in a form in which access to or processing of the data is practicable; 'data' is defined as any representation of information (including an expression of an opinion) in any document; and 'document' includes, in addition to a document in writing:(1) a disc, tape or other device in which non-visual images are embodied so as to be capable, with or without the aid of some other equipment, of being reproduced from the disc, tape or other device and (2) a film, tape or other device in which visual images are embodied so as to be capable, with or without the aid of some other equipment, of being reproduced from the film, tape or other device.

The PDPO therefore applies to all living individuals in Hong Kong, not just to Hong Kong residents and covers most forms of data about individuals provided such data is contained in documents and is in a form in which access to or processing of is practicable - 'idle gossip' about someone does not constitute personal data unless it has been taped or transcribed.

14.14 The PDPO regulates 'data users' who are persons who control the collection, holding, processing or use of personal data whether on their

---

4   Article 30, Basic Law.

own or jointly or in common with others, and expressly binds the Government. The PDPO also establishes a Privacy Commission for Personal Data. The principal function of the Commission is to monitor and supervise compliance with the legislation and, where appropriate, to enforce its provisions. The foundation of the legislation is *the six data protection principles* which are set out in the First Schedule of the PDPO. Very briefly, the six principles cover the purpose and manner of collection of personal data, the accuracy and duration of retention of personal data, the use of personal data, security of personal data, general information about use of personal data to be made available by data users and the right of access to personal data and the right to correct them if wrong. The PDPO requires data users to comply with these six principles unless the legislation requires or permits otherwise. There are, as one might expect, some exemptions and relevant ones will be discussed below. Contravention of a principle does not constitute a criminal offence although it may found a civil claim in respect of any loss suffered including injury to feelings. Apart from this, the principal remedy for a breach by a data user of the PDPO is a complaint to the Privacy Commissioner. The Commissioner, as mentioned, has wide powers to inspect data systems and carry out investigations of a data user's practices to ascertain whether there has been a breach. If the Commissioner determines that there has been a breach, he has power to serve an enforcement notice on a data user requiring the relevant breach to be remedied. Breach of an enforcement notice is a criminal offence punishable by a fine of up to HK$50,000 and imprisonment for up to two years. In addition to enforcement via the Privacy Commissioner, there would seem to be no reason why aggrieved data subjects should not also be able to seek redress through the courts, by, for example, applying for injunctive relief to restrain a data user from a particular activity. The injunction is however a discretionary remedy and it is possible a court might hold that the proper way to deal with an alleged breach of the PDPO is to use the complaint procedure laid down by the PDPO.

14.15   In the context of this survey, data protection principles 1 and 3 are of particular relevance and for this reason they are set out below in full.

'Principle 1 – purpose and manner of collection of personal data

(1)   Personal data shall not be collected unless —

    (a)   the data are collected for a lawful purpose directly related to a function or activity of the data user who is to use the data;

    (b)   subject to paragraph (c), the collection of the data is necessary for or directly related to that purpose; and

    (c)   the data are adequate but not excessive in relation to that purpose.

(2)   Personal data shall be collected by means which are —

    (a)   lawful; and

    (b)   fair in the circumstances of the case.

(3)   Where the person from whom personal data are or are to be collected is the data subject, all practicable steps shall be taken to ensure that -

    (a)   he is explicitly or implicitly informed, on or before collecting the data, of —

        (i)   whether it is obligatory or voluntary for him to supply the data; and

        (ii)   where it is obligatory for him to supply the data, the consequences for him if he fails to supply the data; and

   (b)   he is explicitly informed —

        (i)   on or before collecting the data, of —

            (A)   the purpose (in general or specific terms) for which the data are to be used; and

            (B)   the classes of persons to whom the data may be transferred; and

        (ii)   on or before first use of the data for the purpose for which they were collected, of —

            (A)   his rights to request access to and to request the correction of the data; and

            (B)   the name and address of the individual to whom any such request may be made,

unless to comply with the provisions of this subsection would be likely to prejudice the purpose for which the data were collected and that purpose is specified in Part VIII of this Ordinance as a purpose in relation to which personal data are exempt from the provisions of data protection principle 6.'

'Principle 3 – use of personal data

Personal data shall not, without the prescribed consent of the data subject, be used for any purpose other than —

   (a)   the purpose of which the data was to be used at the time of the collection of the data; or

   (b)   a purpose directly related to the purpose referred to in paragraph (a).'

14.16   Key points to note about principles 1 and 3 are that:

(1) personal data must not be collected except for a lawful purpose directly related to a function/activity of the data user;

(2) personal data must be collected by lawful and fair means in the circumstances of the case;

(3) all practicable steps must be taken to tell a data subject whether he/she is obliged to supply the data being collected, what the data will be used for, to whom the data may be transferred and of his/her rights of access; and

(4) personal data cannot be used for a purpose different from the purpose they were collected for without the consent of the data subject.

The third key point mentioned above would appear to place a fairly onerous obligation on a person wishing to collect data, effectively requiring that individuals be given notice of their rights when the data was being collected and an opportunity to refuse to supply the data if it is not obligatory to supply them.

14.17   In practice the protection against the particular invasions of privacy with which this survey is concerned afforded by the obligation to give notice of rights etc (which will be referred to here now as the 'notification duty') may be fairly limited. This is because of the final part of subsection (3) of principle 1 which releases data users from the notification duty, if to comply with this duty would be likely to prejudice the purpose for which the data were being collected and that purpose has the benefit of an exemption from principle six (the right of access to personal data and to correct data if wrong).

14.18 As mentioned, the PDPO provides for a number of exemptions from principles 3, 6 and other provisions in respect of purposes for which personal data may be used. The most significant exemptions in the context of this discussion are for purposes relating to safeguarding Hong Kong's 'security interests' (these include immigration control, defence and international relations), prevention of crime, financial regulation by public and quasi-public authorities such as the Monetary Authority, the Securities and Futures Commission and the Hong Kong Stock Exchange, and news activity. In all of these areas, if the exemption applies, it will not be necessary for the data user to comply with the notification duty in the collection of the data if to do so would be likely to prejudice the purpose for which the data was being collected.

14.19 It will be interesting here to examine the exemption relating to 'news activity'. 'News activity' is very widely defined – it means any journalistic activity, including gathering news, preparation/compilation of articles/programmes about news or observations on news or current affairs for the purpose of dissemination to the public; or the dissemination to the public of such articles, programmes or observations. Rightly or wrongly, there is no requirement that the activity be in the public interest. The PDPO exempts personal data held by a newspaper company (or any other data user whose business includes news activity) solely for the purpose of news activity from:

(1) principle 6,

(2) the obligation established by the Ordinance to give copies of the data to the data subject, and

(3) the Commissioner's power to investigate a complaint, unless and until the data is published or broadcast.

As will have been noted, there is no 'notification duty' where there is an exemption from principle 6. There is an absolute exemption from the Commissioner's power to carry out his own inspection of a newspaper's data system or his own investigation (ie not initiated by a data subject's complaint).

14.20 However, the newspaper company is still obliged to collect the data for a lawful purpose using lawful means which are fair in the circumstances of the case. Although the meaning of 'fair in the circumstances of the case' is not entirely clear, the words would suggest that collection of data using underhand methods or trickery is prohibited by the PDPO.

The *Eastweek* case

14.21 There has been one interesting, although not entirely satisfactory, case on this particular area. A photographer from 'Eastweek', a popular Chinese magazine, took a photograph of a young woman on the street for use in an article in the magazine on women's fashion. The photograph was taken using a long-range lens and the young woman did not know she was being photographed. The photograph was later used in the magazine with an unflattering caption. The lady's consent was not obtained for the publication of her photo. She complained to the Privacy Commissioner and he found that the publisher was in breach of principle 1(2) – personal data had been collected by means which were not fair in the circumstances. The publisher appealed to the Court of First Instance for judicial review of the Privacy Commissioner's decision and Keith JA delivered the judgment of the court on 24 September, 1999.[5] There was an appeal from this decision to the Court of Appeal and the appeal court delivered its verdict on 28 March, 2000.[6]

First Instance

14.22   The three most important points considered by the court at first instance were (i) whether the photograph could constitute personal data for the purposes of the PDPO; (ii) whether the circumstances of the taking of the photograph also constituted a breach of principle 1(3) and the 'notification duty' and (iii) whether the Commissioner was correct to find that the taking of the photograph was an unfair collection of personal data in breach of principle 1(2). It is worth examining the first instance decision in view of the unsatisfactory nature of the decision of the Court of Appeal.

(i)   The judge was very doubtful whether a photograph could constitute 'data' for the purposes of the PDPO but as neither side argued that it did not constitute data, he reluctantly accepted that it did. With respect to the judge, his doubts were rather surprising. The combination of the definitions of 'data', 'documents' and 'personal data' seem to make it fairly clear that photographs can constitute 'personal data'; to reiterate, 'personal data' is any data from which it is practicable to identify an individual directly or indirectly; 'data' is any representation of information in any document; and a 'document' includes a film in which visual images are embodied so as to be capable of being reproduced. A photograph of an individual is a 'document' containing a 'representation of information' (that individual's visual likeness) from which it is practicable to identify the individual.

(ii)   The judge considered why the Commissioner had not decided that there had also been a breach of principle 1(3) (see above). At first sight, the Commissioner's decision here is a little surprising since contravention of this paragraph of principle 1 seems to be even more clear than contravention of principle 1(2). However, perhaps the decision can be explained by the fact that the 'news activity' exemption could not apply in relation to principle 1(2) whereas it might apply in relation to principle 1(3). The Commissioner obviously felt that he would be on safer ground relying on principle 1(2). The judge concluded that the use of the words 'collection' and 'supply' of data in the context of taking a photograph might give rise to difficult questions of semantics so that the Commissioner preferred to base his criticism of Eastweek on the firmer ground of a breach of principle 1(2). It is submitted, however, that photographing a person does amount to the collection of personal data and that allowing a photograph of one's visual likeness to be taken constitutes the supply of personal data. If this is correct, the photographer did owe the 'notification duty' and

5   See *Eastweek Publisher Limited and Eastweek Limited v The Privacy Commissioner for Personal Data*, HCAL 98/98.
6   See CACV 331/1999.

should have given the notice required by principle 1(3) either before or at the time he took the photograph (subject to it being practicable to do so (see also paragraph (iii)(02) below) and there not being a 'news activity' exemption available in respect of the purpose of the photograph).

(iii)   The judge agreed with the Commissioner's finding that the taking of the photograph in these circumstances was in breach of principle 1(2). The following were some of the conclusions which the judge was able to reach with respect to the fairness of collection of personal data.

(1)   It was accepted that collection of data in the course of 'news gathering' was relevant to fairness. The implication of the judgment was that if data were collected in connection with journalistic activity, the collection did not need to be 'fair'. This tends to follow the proviso to principle 1(3) which states that the notice requirement of principle 1(3) does not apply if to give the notice would be likely to prejudice the purpose for which the data were collected and the purpose is an 'exempt purpose' under the PDPO, such as 'news activity' (see above).

> The judge agreed with the Commissioner that the taking of the photograph did not amount to 'news activity' because the article in which it was used was 'only a commentary on dress sense and criticism of individual taste of a few individuals based on the random thoughts of the reporter, rather than a report on fashion trends or street fashion'. This conclusion by the Commissioner and the judge was probably the most important of those made in this case. If the photograph had been used in a more serious article, it is possible that both the Commissioner and the judge would have found that the 'news activity' exemption provided for in the PDPO *did* apply.

(2)   It was accepted that, in some cases, it might be impracticable to obtain the consent of a person to the collection of data about him/her by taking a photograph and that in such a case it might be fair to take the photograph without the subject's consent. However, in this particular case, (a) the photographer had no reasonable grounds to believe he could obtain the subject's consent and (b) Eastweek had no policy of publishing photos in such a way as to avoid identification of the subject where his/her consent to publication had not been obtained. So the taking of the photograph was held to be unfair.

(3)   The fairness of the collection of the data had to be judged by reference to the circumstances of the case. The subjective state of mind of the photographer about this was not relevant.

(4)   Factors relevant to fairness included (a) the equipment used, (b) the circumstances of the collection eg whether on a genuine journalistic assignment in a public place involving no trickery, deception or intrusive or covert operations and (c) whether the data would be used fairly after collection. In this last case, the judge noted that the PDPO did not prohibit the unfair use of data but focused instead (through principle 3) on the purpose of the use of data. This led him to conclude that an intention to use data unfairly was relevant in determining whether their collection was by unfair means.

(5)   It could not be assumed that a data subject would always consent to the taking of his/her photograph or its subsequent publication.

(6)   The existence of a policy as to the publication of photographs with or without the data subject's knowledge or consent (such that, for example, if no consent had been obtained, data would either not be used or only used if the identity of the subject was not revealed) was relevant to fairness of collection.

Court of Appeal

14.23   The magazine appealed and by a two-to-one majority, the appeal court found in favour of the magazine. The following important points can be extracted from the judgments of the majority judges:

(1)   Photographs did constitute personal data for the purposes of the PDPO;

(2)   In the particular circumstances of the case, there was no act of personal data collection. The Court of Appeal found that the lower court had not sufficiently considered the question of 'collection'. It did not expressly disapprove of the other conclusions reached by the lower court.

It is difficult to understand the reasoning of the judge, Ribeiro JA, in his judgment but he seemed to be saying that the anonymity of the lady in question and the 'irrelevance' of her identity to the magazine meant that the magazine was not collecting personal information. For there to be personal data collection for the purposes of the PDPO, there had to be an act of compilation of information about an identified person or about a person whom the data user intended, or sought, to identify. The data collected must constitute personal information which attaches to the identified subject.

As mentioned, it is difficult to understand the reasoning of Ribeiro JA here. First, it is difficult to see how an exact likeness of a person in a photograph is not personal information attaching to a person, whether identified or not - surely a photograph is the best way of identifying a person and is better than a name or an ID card number for doing this. Second, on the one hand, he agreed that a photograph of an individual constituted personal data for the purposes of the PDPO, whilst on the other hand, he argued that taking a photograph of someone without also establishing their identity did not constitute collection of personal data. He seems to be introducing different levels of importance to different types of personal data - a name (or an ID Card number) would appear to be more important than a person's likeness contained in a photograph. Alternatively, the judge seems to be saying that the data user's state of mind is relevant - was the identity of the actual data subject of any importance to the data user?

With respect, these distinctions are untenable. The PDPO's definition of personal data (see above) does not allow for any distinction in type, quality or importance. The attempt to attribute a special meaning to 'collection' is also fanciful. Indeed the judge who agreed with Ribeiro JA's decision (Godfrey VP) admitted that there was nothing in the PDPO which supported their view.

The judge also sought to justify his conclusion by cross-referring to a number of other sections of the PDPO which, he said, showed that the legislation was only intended to relate to the personal data of identified persons; eg principle 3 (see above) – the requirement to obtain a data subject's consent to the use of his personal data assumes knowledge of his identity. The provisions referred to, however, cover entirely different circumstances to those at issue and it is difficult to see their relevance. If anything, the relevant provisions only served to highlight the fact that the magazine may have been in breach of the PDPO. For example, in the principle 3 example above, surely this only emphasizes that the lady's consent should have been obtained before her personal data were used in the article.

(3)   The distinction summarised in the last paragraph was important in order to preserve legitimate journalistic activity and photo-journalism. Examples of taking photographs of crowds jostling in queues for an initial public share offering, teenagers smoking for the purposes of an article on health and racegoers at Happy Valley horse race track were given to illustrate the fact that, even though individuals may be identifiable from the photographs, any newspaper taking these photographs (and then publishing them) would not be seeking to collect personal data but simply to illustrate an article of news.

These situations are, however, in this writer's view, readily distinguishable from the circumstances of the *Eastweek* case. The situations listed constitute newsworthy events of interest to the public in themselves. In those particular circumstances, it would be fair to collect the personal data of the people in question in that manner. In the *Eastweek* case, the lady in question was specifically selected by the journalist from a busy street scene to illustrate an article - the street scene and the lady were not, in themselves, newsworthy, but the journalist sought to make them so by writing his own thoughts about the lady's fashion sense – he even gave the lady a nickname for the purposes of the article.

(4)   There might be circumstances when taking a photograph might constitute collection of personal data, for example, when the photograph is to be included in a dossier about an identified subject.

(5)   The PDPO should not unduly inhibit legitimate journalistic activity, although the legislation clearly would in some circumstances apply to the press.

This conclusion probably explains why the Court of Appeal allowed the magazine's appeal. The majority judges were reluctant to be seen to be clamping down on press freedom. Their concerns are understandable to some extent, particularly given Hong Kong's unique political situation. However, the PDPO does contain protections/exemptions applicable to news activity (see above) and, as noted by the dissenting judge, Wong JA, it is necessary to balance freedom of the press against freedom of the individual – a free press is also a responsible press. In this case, however, the exemptions were simply not applicable.

(6)   The PDPO did not establish general privacy rights against all possible forms of intrusion. It simply sought to protect 'information privacy' as opposed to 'personal privacy'.

This statement is clearly correct. However, given the definition of personal data in the legislation ie the type of information which the legislation was intended to protect, it is difficult to see how the Court of Appeal could conclude that there was no breach of the PDPO.

14.24   The Commissioner cannot begin an investigation based on a complaint about a newspaper company's activities until the relevant data has been published or broadcast. The specific remedies afforded by the PDPO are not particularly helpful here because the damage will already have been done in these circumstances. An aggrieved individual seeking speedy redress would have to try his luck in the courts.

14.25   The exemptions relating to safeguarding Hong Kong's security interests, the prevention of crime and financial regulation also exclude the protection of principle 6 and the right to copies of the personal data in question, as well as the notification duty. However, they do not restrict the Commissioner's freedom to investigate a complaint about other abuses (such as unlawful collection) although the Chief Executive or the Chief Secretary do have power to warn the Commissioner off from carrying out an investigation or inspection where Hong Kong's security interests are at stake.

14.26   There are also important exemptions from data protection principle 3 which are relevant here. These exemptions may apply in respect of data held for the purposes of safeguarding Hong Kong's security interests or, data used for preventing crime or for financial regulation if restriction is imposed by principle 3 against *the use of the data for other non-approved purposes would be likely to prejudice such matters*. Thus, for example, data collected from an investigation into one crime may be transferred to another government department for investigating another unrelated crime without the consent of the data subject. However, it seems unlikely that this exemption would apply if the police wanted to disclose data obtained from investigation into a crime to the employer of the person being investigated because inability to so disclose should not prejudice the prevention or detection of crime etc. In this regard, note the pre-PDPO decisions of *Hall v Commissioner of the Independent Commission against Corruption* and *Ho Shau-Hong v Commissioner of Police* considered in the section on the common law below.

14.27   There is another exemption which permits a person to disclose personal data to a newspaper or other media company, if he has reasonable grounds to believe (and does believe) that the publishing or broadcasting of the data is in the public interest. This exemption attempts to reflect the common law on breach of confidence (as to which see below).

4   Post Office Ordinance

14.28   This Ordinance contains a number of provisions allowing Post Office officers to open mail (such as where the incorrect postage has been paid, the letter has been wrongly addressed or if a letter is otherwise sent in contravention of the Ordinance). However, the widest powers are perhaps contained in section 13 of the Ordinance. This gives power to the Chief Secretary of the Hong Kong Government to grant a warrant to the Postmaster General or officers of the Post Office to open and delay specified postal packets. The Postmaster General also has power to delay sending packets until the Chief Secretary has had time to issue a warrant. This provision, therefore, gives an unlimited discretion to the Chief Secretary to authorise interception of mail.

In spite of these powers, sections 27 and 29 of the Ordinance prohibit opening mail addressed to other persons without lawful excuse. Breach of these provisions is a criminal offence.

5 *Telecommunication Ordinance*

14.29   Section 33 of this Ordinance (which dates back to 1963) gives the Chief Executive of Hong Kong or any public officer authorised by the Chief Executive, either generally or for a particular occasion, power to order that any message or class of message transmitted or received via telecommunication be intercepted, detained or disclosed to the Government or the relevant public officer.

14.30   Notwithstanding the wide powers afforded to the authorities, it is an offence under sections 27 and 27A of this Ordinance for any person to interfere with telecommunication installations with intent to intercept or discover the contents of a message or to use telecommunication techniques to hack into computers.

6 *Interception of Communications Ordinance (not yet law)*

14.31   Immediately prior to the handover of sovereignty to China on 1 July 1997, the then partially democratically elected Legislative Council of Hong Kong passed the Interception of Communications Ordinance following the 1996 Consultation Paper upon Regulating Surveillance and the Interception of Communications issued by the Privacy Sub-Committee of the Law Reform Commission of Hong Kong. The purpose of this ordinance was to make telephone tapping without a warrant a criminal offence (although it should be noted that the Privacy Sub-Committee had also recommended creating a regulatory framework to control physical surveillance of private premises, amongst other things). Up to now, the Government of Hong Kong has declined to specify a starting date for the law, arguing that it is still reviewing the legislation and also that the law might interfere with certain longer investigations.
Judging from the Government's responses to questions in the new Legislative Councils it is unlikely that this law will be fully enacted, at least not in the foreseeable future. However, it is worth mentioning briefly its main provisions.

14.32   Section 3 would prohibit interception of communications by post or a 'telecommunications system' without a court order; unless the person making the communication consented; or the interception was made pursuant to the Post Office Ordinance or the Telecommunication Ordinance (so it will be seen that the wide powers under these last two ordinances would not be curtailed). Section 4 would empower High Court judges to authorise by court order *senior* public officers (including officers from the Hong Kong Police, the Customs and Excise Service, the Independent Commission against Corruption and the Immigration Department) to intercept specified communications by post or by telecommunications systems. Orders would only be granted for the purposes of detecting or preventing serious crime, or in the interests of Hong Kong's security. 'Serious crime' is defined as an offence punishable by imprisonment of seven years or more, but the security of Hong Kong is left undefined (the definition used in the PDPO might have been useful here). In addition, fairly strict conditions would have to be met before a judge could make the order:

(1) reasonable grounds to believe that an offence had been, was being, or was about to be, committed;

(2) reasonable grounds to believe that information about the offence would be obtained by the proposed interception;

(3) all other methods of investigation had been tried but had failed or were not likely to succeed; and

(4) good reason to believe that the interception would result in a conviction.

Orders could be made for a maximum period of 90 days, renewable once *only* by order of a judge. The requirements of the Ordinance could be relaxed if there was a serious threat of death or harm to a person. Any intercepted material not obtained under a court order would be inadmissible, unless the prosecution proved otherwise.

C   Reports by Law Reform Commission of Hong Kong, Sub-Committee on Privacy

14.33   Over the last few years, the Hong Kong Law Reform Commission has produced a number of other Consultation Papers on privacy issues (in addition to the one mentioned above which resulted in the Interception of Communications Ordinance). The various reports and papers are discussed below.

1   'Stalking'

14.34   In May 1998, the Commission's Privacy Sub-Committee issued its report on 'stalking'. Stalking (or conduct so persistent as to amount to harassment or molestation) has been identified as a major social problem, particularly for women and certain public figures, leading to emotional distress and sometimes personal injury to the victims. The issue is particularly topical now in view of the extraordinary behaviour of some sections of the media in Hong Kong recently including the harassment of a judge by a newspaper company after he had decided a court case against the company. Although there are a number of common law and statutory remedies available to protect people against this kind of harassment[7] the Commission concluded that the existing protection was 'fragmented, ad hoc and piecemeal' and simply not extensive enough to deal with the full intent and degree of many stalkers' behaviour. It proposed the creation of a new criminal offence of 'harassment' where a person pursues a course of conduct amounting to harassment of another which he knew or should have known amounted to harassment. 'Harassment' would include causing

---

7   Domestic Violence Ordinance and s 19 of the Legislative Council (Powers and Privileges) Ordinance which gives special protection to members of the Legislative Council – persons, inter alia, molesting, obstructing or interfering with LegCo members are guilty of an offence and liable to imprisonment for up to 12 months.

alarm or distress and a 'course of conduct' must have involved conduct on at least two occasions. The following further recommendations were made:

(1) maximum penalty – 2 years' imprisonment;

(2) defences – the conduct was pursued to prevent or detect crime, or otherwise under lawful authority, or the conduct was reasonable in the relevant circumstances;

(3) restraining orders to be added to any sentence, at the court's discretion;

(4) conduct constituting the offence of harassment also to give rise to civil liability and render the stalker liable to damages for emotional distress etc;

(5) the Government to consider reforming law on domestic violence, debt collection and landlord and tenant in the context of harassment.

At present these are still only proposals but it is possible that legislation will be introduced in Hong Kong to deal with this social evil. At the time of writing, no timetable had been set though.

2 *'Invasion of Privacy'*

14.35 In August 1999, the Privacy Sub-Committee issued its consultation paper on Invasion of Privacy. The Sub-Committee concluded that the PDPO could not always provide satisfactory protection against invasion of privacy, particularly where data is collected by journalists in connection with a newsworthy event or where the relevant data is not 'in a form in which access to or processing of the data is practicable' (see definition of 'personal data' above), the Court of Appeal's decision in the *Eastweek* case springs to mind here. The Sub-Committee decided it would not go so far as to recommend the creation of a general tort of invasion of privacy in view of the difficulty of devising a satisfactory definition. However, it did feel able to make the following recommendations:

(1) A person who intentionally or recklessly intrudes, physically or otherwise, upon the solitude or seclusion of another or into his private affairs or concerns, should be liable for a statutory tort of invasion of privacy provided the intrusion is seriously offensive and objectionable to a reasonable person of ordinary sensibilities;

    – a person should be liable for this tort if he gives publicity to a matter concerning another's private life, in the knowledge that this would be seriously offensive to and objectionable to a reasonable person of ordinary sensibilities;

    – the surreptitious use of a device to collect visual data relating to a person by another person who is lawfully on relevant premises where the relevant data is visible but not open to public view should be deemed to constitute an intrusion for the purposes of the new tort.

(2) Defences:

    – invasion was authorised by law or statute;

    – invasion was reasonably necessary for the protection of the person or property of the defendant or some other person;

    – public disclosure of private facts would have been privileged in a defamation case;

–'private' facts are already in the public domain through no fault of the defendant;

– the matter publicised was of legitimate public interest. Matters of public interest would be deemed to include:

(a) prevention, detection or investigation of crime;

(b) prevention of unlawful or seriously improper conduct, public dishonesty or serious malpractice;

(c) the ability of a person to discharge public or professional duties;

(d) the fitness of a person for a public office or profession;

(e) the protection of public health or safety;

(f) the protection of national security.

(3) Victims of sex offences should be afforded statutory anonymity.

(4) New statutory torts should be actionable without proof of damage.

(5) Court's powers:

– award damages (which may compensate mental distress, embarrassment or humiliation);

– grant injunctions;

– account of profits from invasion to be made;

– order destruction or delivery up of documents obtained from the invasion;

– publication of an apology.

(6) Limitation period – no action to be brought after 3 years from the time of the invasion.

(7) Actions under the torts – only available to individuals.

The Sub-Committee further recommended that the Privacy Commissioner should consider issuing codes of practice on surveillance in the workplace and on the use of personal data in advertising materials, and that the Broadcasting Authority should also include provisions governing the use of personal data in advertisements broadcast on TV and radio in its Codes of Practice on Advertising Standards.

3 'Regulation of Media Intrusion'

14.36 The Privacy Sub-Committee also issued a consultation paper on Regulation of Media Intrusion on 20 August, 1999. The stated purpose of the paper was to see whether legislative or other measures were needed to protect individuals' privacy against undue interference by news media. The Sub-Committee concluded that some sections of the press have been abusing press freedom and that there is a pressing social need to protect the public from unwarranted media intrusion. The Sub-Committee thought that prohibiting the use of intrusive means to collect personal data would not violate freedom of the press – investigative journalism could still be practiced without the need to employ intrusive means. Having reached these general conclusions, the Sub-Committee made a number of recommendations including the following:

(1) Privacy Commissioner to issue a code of practice on collection and

use of personal data for journalistic purposes (although it was recognized that such a code would likely have limited effect, principally because the PDPO did not really address invasion of privacy).

(2) Broadcasting Authority to adopt provisions relating to unwarranted invasion of privacy when obtaining material for broadcasting in its Codes of Practice on Programme Standards. Both the Privacy Commissioner and the Broadcasting Authority were directed to take into account codes of practice issued by British and German press councils when drawing up their own codes.

(3) Independent body, the Press Council for the Protection of Privacy ('Press Council'), to be established to deal with complaints from the public about breaches of a press code on privacy-related matters by newspapers and magazines;

> – newspaper proprietors, publishers and editors to be held responsible for breaches of the press code by the newspapers or their staff;

> – Press Council to be appointed by an 'Independent Appointments Commission'.

(4) Press Council to draw up and keep under review its press code of conduct on privacy-related matters.

(5) Press Council to receive complaints about breaches of the press code, to initiate its own investigations if it had reasonable grounds to believe there had been a breach, to attempt conciliation and to make rulings on alleged breaches.

(6) Press Council's powers in relation to a complaint:

> – declare there has been a breach of the press code;

> – reprimand the newspaper;

> – require publication of an apology, correction, details of the complaint, together with the Press Council's findings, decision and any observations about the complaint;

> – no power to award compensation to complainant;

> – power to impose a fine for serious breaches of the press code of up to HK$500,000 for a first offence and up to HK$1,000,000 for a second or further offence.

(7) Failure to comply with a Press Council ruling to give rise to liability for a fine recoverable as a civil debt.

(8) Right of appeal against a Press Council ruling to Court of Appeal.

As one might have expected, the recommendations have caused considerable controversy in Hong Kong particularly amongst the press. It remains to be seen whether the Government will take any steps to implement the recommendations.

D Common law

14.37 The Basic Law (at Article 8) confirms the continued applicability of the common law in Hong Kong (except to the extent the common law is inconsistent with the Basic Law or any law passed by the Hong Kong legislature). Thus any survey of Hong Kong law in relation to any particular issue must take into account the common law. In this regard, decisions of the courts of the United Kingdom (and other common law jurisdictions) still have a major influence.

14.38   Privacy, as such, is not protected by the law of torts. This can be seen in the English case of *Malone v Commissioner of Police*,[8] a case which involved telephone tapping of a suspect by the police. The suspect issued a writ claiming, inter alia, that the telephone tapping constituted a breach of his rights of privacy, property and confidentiality and was unlawful. The court held, however, that:

(1)   there was no general right of privacy under English law;

(2)   the police were entitled to tap telephones if to do so would not involve trespass or other breach of the law provided they had grounds to suspect that tapping would materially assist in detecting or preventing crime; and

(3)   telephone tapping, provided it did not involve anything unlawful, was permitted anyway on the general principle that everything was permitted except that which was expressly forbidden.

14.39   This last decision has been followed in two decisions (pre-handover) of the Hong Kong Court of Appeal,[9] both of which related to the disclosure by the police of evidence (gathered in connection with abortive investigations into possible corruption and illegal gambling) to the plaintiffs' employers, the Royal Hong Kong Jockey Club (as it then was), in connection with the Club's disciplinary proceedings. The Court of Appeal in both cases followed *Malone*, holding that in Hong Kong everything was permitted except what was expressly prohibited. The reasoning behind these cases and the *Malone* decision is that legal restraints must be lawfully created and the onus is on the complainant to prove illegality. It is interesting to note that both the Hong Kong cases might have been decided differently today following enactment of the Bill of Rights, the Basic Law and in view of data protection principle 3 and the PDPO (see above). However, the principle is clear enough: in the absence of any legal restraint on telephone tapping or invasion of privacy, both are permitted to the extent no other law is broken. However, protection of privacy may be afforded under various other heads of action. This survey will briefly consider breach of confidence and the torts of infliction of emotional distress, trespass and nuisance.

1   Breach of confidence

14.40   Breach of confidence is a complicated area. The law is perhaps best summarised in *Attorney-General v Guardian Newspapers*[10] (better known as the 'Spycatcher' case) where Lord Goff of Chieveley said that a 'duty of confidence arises when confidential information comes to the knowledge of a person (the confidant) in circumstances where he has notice, or is held to have agreed, that the information is confidential, with the effect that it

---

8   [1979] 2 All ER 620.
9   See *Hall v Commissioner of the Independent Commission against Corruption* [1987] HKLR 210; and *Ho Shau-Hong v Commissioner of Police* [1987] HKLR 945.
10   (No 2) [1990] 1 AC 109.

would be just in all the circumstances that he should be precluded from disclosing the information to others.'

14.41 These principles can be illustrated by looking at a number of cases, including two Hong Kong decisions. In *Lam v Koo and Chiu*,[11] an academic conducting cancer research was sued by two colleagues for using a questionnaire they had prepared for similar research. It was found that the questionnaire was obtained by the academic surreptitiously and that the academic must have known the questionnaire was confidential because of the amount of work which had gone into it and should have realised he was not entitled to use it. The Court of Appeal therefore found that the academic had committed a breach of confidence in respect of the questionnaire.

14.42 In *Li Yau-wai v Genesis Films Ltd*[12] an insurance salesman was photographed by a film company on the understanding that the photo be used to consider whether he should be cast in an upcoming film. Without his permission the photo was then used by the company in a 'ribald comedy' film. The context of the use of the photo exposed the insurance salesman to ridicule and caused him great embarrassment. It was held, among other things, that the film company owed a duty of confidence in respect of the photo – he allowed the photo to be taken on the basis that it would only be used to check whether the insurance salesman was suitable for a role in a film. The insurance salesman had agreed to be photographed in circumstances where he could expect confidentiality to be respected, so a duty of confidence on the part of the film company arose.

14.43 In *Francome v Mirror Group Newspapers Ltd*,[13] the English Court of Appeal had to decide on an appeal by a newspaper company in respect of its application to set aside an injunction restraining it from publishing articles based on tapes obtained by illegal tapping of telephone conversations. The newspaper company argued, inter alia, that the tapes of the conversations revealed iniquity by the plaintiffs, that there was no confidence in iniquity and that it was in the public interest that the plaintiffs' iniquity be disclosed.

The Court of Appeal declined to set aside the injunction. The court seems to have been heavily influenced, in so far as the 'confidence' issues were concerned, by the fact that the tapes *were* obtained illegally and that the action was only an interlocutory one: if the injunction were lifted, there would be little point in the plaintiffs continuing with their case even if they were ultimately to succeed. The public interest could be served by the newspaper applying to vary the injunction to permit disclosure to the authorities alone, but this was not the same as publishing the story in the newspaper. As far as the *Malone* case was concerned, the court distinguished it on the basis that *Malone* was only dealing with a case of tapping by the police and not by private individuals. The issues as to confidentiality and the public interest deserved to be heard at a full trial.

14.44 Other aspects of the principle of confidentiality may be summarised as follows:

(1) it only applies to information which is confidential – once information

---

11 [1993] 2 HKC 1.
12 [1987] 2 HKLR 711.
13 [1984] 1 WLR 892.

is in the public domain, the principle no longer applies;

(2) it does not apply to useless or trivial information;

(3) the public interest of preserving confidentiality can be outweighed by some other public interest (cf *Francome*).

It will be seen therefore that an action for breach of confidence may certainly lie where information is obtained surreptitiously or it is clear that there is a 'quality' of confidence attached to it.

2 *Intentional infliction of emotional distress*

14.45 *Wilkinson v Downton*[14] established a cause of action where an act (or acts) has (or have) been done wilfully, calculated to cause physical harm, and which have caused such harm. It would appear to be necessary to show that:

(1) the defendant, by doing relevant acts, intended, or was at least reckless as to, their consequences; and

(2) the 'emotional distress' inflicted became something physical (such as a recognisable psychiatric illness) and was more than transitory.

In *Khorasandjian v Bush*,[15] the English Court of Appeal felt able to grant injunctive relief to restrain the defendant from conduct constituting severe harassment (unsolicited phone calls, threats of violence etc) after his relationship with the plaintiff broke down, even though the plaintiff was not suffering a psychiatric illness as a result of the harassment. It was felt that there was an obvious risk of such an illness if the harassment were to continue.

Khorasandjian was overruled by the House of Lords to the extent it expanded the tort of nuisance [see below] in *Hunter v Canary Wharf Ltd*.[16] However, it seems unfair to deny a plaintiff relief where mental distress has been deliberately inflicted.[17]

3 *Trespass*

14.46 This tort can be summarised as any unauthorised intrusion by one person upon land in the possession of another or any unauthorised interference with another person's goods. Principal elements of trespass include the following:

(1) possession of land involves occupation or physical control and may depend on the interpretation of a lease eg a landlord may not be able to sue in trespass if not in possession;

(2) intrusion into air space over land may constitute trespass depending on the height of the intrusion. Flying over land at a reasonable and safe height does not constitute trespass.[18] However, intrusion by a low-flying aircraft might constitute a trespass;

14 [1897] 2 QB 57.
15 [1993] 3 WLR 476.
16 (1997) The Times, 25 April.
17 See Berthold and Wacks, *Data Privacy Law in Hong Kong*, at p 56.
18 See *Bernstein v Skyviews and General Ltd* [1978] QB 479.

(3) the intrusion/interference should be voluntary and there must be an element of intent (or recklessness or negligence). Involuntary, non-negligent intrusion may not constitute trespass;

(4) There is no need to prove loss or damage (unlike nuisance). Injunctive relief would seem to be available to prevent threatened trespass.

The *Malone* case[19] confirmed that, unless a wire or other bugging device was attached to a telephone on someone's premises, telephone tapping could not constitute trespass. Following from this, it is also difficult to see how computer hacking could constitute trespass.

4   Nuisance

14.47   This tort was defined by Lord Westbury in the English case of *St Helen's Smelting Co v Tipping*[20] as 'interference with one's enjoyment, one's quiet, one's personal freedom, anything that discomposes or injuriously affects the senses or the nerves.' An action for nuisance will usually only lie for someone who has a *proprietary* interest in land and wishes to protect that interest or enjoyment of it. The conduct complained of should constitute a 'state of affairs' meaning that it must have been continuing for a period of time for it to constitute a 'nuisance'. Blatant 'staking out' or 'paparazzi' style investigation by journalists outside someone's home could therefore constitute a nuisance.

5   Protection of a person's name and likeness

14.48   To the extent the laws summarised above do not apply, the following statements can be made about legal protection of a person's name and likeness in Hong Kong.

(1) The law of defamation is obviously highly relevant here. In Hong Kong defamation is: a published, false statement about a living individual which lowers that individual in the estimation of right-thinking members of the public. A statement will not be defamatory if it is true or, where the statement is an opinion, if it constitutes 'fair comment'. It is for the defendant to prove these defences and, in the case of 'fair comment', he must show the comment was fair or honest, made in good faith and on a matter of public interest. Note that members of the Legislative Council are granted immunity from prosecution in respect of statements they make in the Council or in reports to the Council.[1] Damages, injunctive relief or a simple apology are appropriate remedies for defamation.

Assuming there are no other factors involved, publishing or use of a person's name or biography would seem to be permissible provided the relevant publication or use is fair and accurate.

(2) A public figure's likeness cannot be used without authority for advertising or other gain. In *Tam Wing Lun Alan v Tam Kwok Hung*,[2]

19 At 664.
20 (1865) 11 HLC 642 650.
1   See the Legislative Council (Powers and Privileges) Ordinance, ss 3 and 4.
2   [1991] 2 HKC 384.

the Hong Kong court held the defendants liable for passing off when they sold audio cassettes recorded using the voices of unknown singers where the cassettes bore the name and image of the plaintiff, a famous Hong Kong singer. The court held that the plaintiff did not have to prove damage to reputation or goodwill as these would all be presumed – it accordingly awarded damages for injury to the plaintiff's goodwill and reputation.

In *Li Yau-wai v Genesis Films*,[3] the court also held that the film company had defamed the insurance salesman in that he was exposed to ridicule in the minds of right-thinking individuals (the use of the photo of the insurance salesman suggested that the person in the photo had, whilst he had been alive, been unable to fulfil his wife sexually). Damages of HK$25,000 (a little over US$3,000 at current exchange rates) were awarded.

(3) In so far as public authorities and public officers are concerned, they do not have any special privileges and can be criticised openly subject to the same laws as apply to private citizens. In addition, the likeness of public officers can be used in news reporting and marketing campaigns provided the reporting and marketing is limited to matters concerning the public office or matters of public interest. Thus, the health of a public officer is a matter of public interest as it may affect his/her work performance, but details of his/her private life such as an unusual hobby may not be relevant.

(4) A person's name or likeness can be protected by registration as a trade mark. Section 9 of the Trade Marks Ordinance allows registration of, inter alia, the name of an individual if represented in a special or particular manner. Consent of the person involved is required if it is not this person who is applying for registration. If the person has died, consent from his/her personal representatives is required unless he/she died more than 15 years before the application.

E   Some practical examples

1   Example 1

14.49   Police are conducting a covert investigation into a suspected drug dealer. The investigation involves telephone tapping, covert filming using powerful zoom lenses, a break-in to the suspect's flat and examination of the contents of unopened mail and desk drawers.

14.50   The Basic Law and the Bill of Rights Ordinance prohibit invasion of privacy, home and correspondence except pursuant to law. So in this example the police investigation would be unlawful unless the correct procedures and warrants are obtained under relevant legislation. The principle of common law laid down in *Malone* that everything is permitted except where expressly forbidden could not be relied on by the police – the law does forbid invasion of privacy except pursuant to the law.

---

3   See the section above on breach of confidence.

14.51 The telephone tapping would require specific authorisation from the Chief Executive of Hong Kong under section 33 of the Telecommunication Ordinance or, if the Interception of Communications Ordinance were in force, an authorisation from a High Court judge under section 4 of that Ordinance. As for opening mail, the Chief Secretary has power to grant a warrant authorising the Postmaster General or Post Office officers to do this under section 13 of the Post Office Ordinance and the Postmaster General can himself open mail if he has reason to believe that, inter alia, it contains anything with respect to which any offence has been or is being committed (see section 12).

14.52 As for the PDPO, data protection principle 1 applies, prima facie, to collection of the data. However, the police are exempt from the obligation under subsection (3) of principle 1 to give notice to the suspect of his rights and the purposes for which the data will be used. Subsections (1) and (2) of principle 1 would also not seem to prevent use of telephone tapping, covert filming or the break in:

(1) the data is being collected for a lawful purpose related to the functions of the police;

(2) the police should be able to argue easily enough that collection of the data is necessary for the police's purposes, and that the data being collected is not excessive for their purposes;

(3) subject to the obtaining necessary warrants and permissions, the collection is lawful; and

(4) in the context of a criminal investigation of a drug dealer and assuming the police have reasonable grounds for their investigation, the means being used are probably fair.

Any claims under common law would depend to some extent upon whether the police had obtained warrants and other necessary permissions. An action in trespass might lie in respect of the break-in and the opening of mail if these permissions had not been obtained.

14.53 As for breach of confidence, it was held in the *Malone* case that if there was a just cause or excuse for the telephone tapping and for the use made of material obtained by the tapping, then this would justify 'breach of confidence' (and, by implication, any nuisance or other tort). Thus, in our case, if the police had reasonable grounds to believe that the telephone tapping would materially assist in detecting or preventing crime, they would be justified in carrying it out.

2   *Example 2*

14.54 The police investigation of Example 1 is inconclusive and does not produce evidence sufficient to warrant a prosecution. However, it does reveal that the suspect is consorting with known triad members. The police disclose this information to the suspect's employers, a major bank in Hong Kong. The disclosure is a breach of data protection principle 3 of the PDPO and is unlawful. No exemption applies because the prohibition against disclosure would not seem to prejudice prevention or detection of crime etc.

14.55 The disclosure may constitute a breach of confidence under *Malone*. The court held in *Malone* that telephone tapping would be permitted if it would assist in detecting or preventing crime *provided* materials obtained were only used for these purposes and that information not relevant to such purposes was confined to the minimum number of persons reasonably required to carry out the tapping.

14.56   In the *Hall* case referred to above, the Court of Appeal allowed the ICAC to disclose information to the Royal Hong Kong Jockey Club which the latter then used in disciplinary proceedings against the jockey. The Court of Appeal held that there was an exception to the duty to act confidentially:

(1)   where the evidence did not constitute an offence within the ICAC's remit but was within the jurisdiction of some other body; or

(2)   the ICAC believed that the other body could better deal with the relevant conduct or practice. In our example, *Hall* probably would not apply because there was no evidence of any crime.

3   Example 3

14.57   A very famous film actor in Hong Kong begins an affair with a secretary at a law firm who had previously had no public exposure. Certain newspapers start a round-the-clock surveillance operation on the secretary. The operation involves:

(1)   filming and photographing her in her own flat from an adjacent flat using powerful zoom lenses;

(2)   use of an assumed identity to gain access to her flat and covertly videoing it;

(3)   a team of reporters following her and videoing/photographing her whenever she leaves her flat;

(4)   sifting her rubbish;

(5)   opening her mail and tapping her telephone; and

(6)   two operations vans conspicuously parked right outside her flat for the purpose of co-ordinating operations and monitoring her movements.

The operation has been going on for one month and the secretary, although patient at first, is near the end of her tether and is beginning to exhibit signs of nervous stress.

14.58   The press operation may be in breach of provisions in the Basic Law declaring the inviolability of Hong Kong residents' homes and prohibiting arbitrary or unlawful intrusion, and protecting freedom and privacy of communication. Except to the extent the Basic Law might extend the effect of the Bill of Rights Ordinance (as discussed briefly above), the Bill of Rights Ordinance does not apply here because the operation is not being carried out by public authorities.

14.59   All of the modes of collection of the data about the secretary would seem to involve breaches of subsections (1) and (2) of data protection principle 1 of the PDPO:

(1)   the data being collected is excessive for the purpose required;

(2)   some of the means of collection are unlawful (see below); and

(3) no reasonable person would argue that the methods used were fair in the circumstances.

Applying the principles laid down by both courts in the *Eastweek* case, (a) there was clearly 'collection' of data here for the purposes of the Court of Appeal's test as the newspapers knew the identity of the secretary and were compiling information about her for publication, (b) the operation probably does constitute 'news activity' which means that the standards of 'fairness' which should be applied are not so high, but (c) the use of covert and deceptive methods to collect data would probably be unfair enough to outweigh any 'news activity' defence; other issues raised by the *Eastweek* case such as whether the secretary consented to the use of her personal data and the relevant newspapers' policies on use of such data would not be so important in deciding this case because the whole point of the story was her identity.

Subsection (3) of principle 1 would probably not apply as to comply with its requirements would be likely to prejudice the purpose for which the data is being collected and the purpose is probably protected by the 'news activity' exemption under the PDPO. The secretary's remedies under the PDPO would include the right to complain to the Privacy Commissioner and thus instigate an investigation into the press's conduct, a civil claim against the newspaper companies under section 66 of the PDPO for injury to her feelings, and a claim for injunctive relief.

14.60 Opening the secretary's mail constitutes an offence under section 29 of the Post Office Ordinance (maximum sanctions: fine of HK$20,000 and two years' imprisonment). The telephone tapping does not seem to constitute an offence under the Telecommunication Ordinance but it is in contravention of Article 30 of the Basic Law (no sanctions are specified for breach). If it were law, the telephone tapping would be an offence under section 3 of the Interception of Communication Ordinance (maximum sanctions: HK$25,000 fine and two years' imprisonment). Publication of intercepted material would constitute an offence under section 9 of this Ordinance. The secretary would be able to apply to the court under section 10 for remedial relief. The court has a discretion as to what relief to grant but it could include:

(1) a declaration that the interception was unlawful;

(2) damages; and/or

(3) injunctive relief.

Publication of the data gathered from the operation would seem to constitute a breach of confidence. The public interest in reading about the secretary should not outweigh the public interest in protecting her privacy. Injunctive relief restraining publication and/or an action for damages would be available.

14.61 The newspaper companies' activities constitute severe harassment and, as they are beginning to affect the secretary's nervous state, might found an action for intentional infliction of emotional distress. Damages and injunctive relief would be available.

14.62 The use of an assumed identity to gain access to the flat, subsequent covert videoing and the rubbish sifting constitute trespass. In the unlikely event that the reporter succeeded in arguing that he entered the flat with the secretary's authority, his subsequent covert videoing would constitute an abuse of that authority and render him a trespasser *ab initio*. Remedies available here would be injunctive relief and general and exemplary damages.

14.63 The reporters' operation may found an action in private nuisance provided the secretary has some proprietary interest in her flat. The combination of the filming from the adjacent flat, the reporters waiting for her outside her flat in the vans and to follow her together with all the other activities almost certainly constitutes nuisance. The usual remedies of injunctive relief and damages to compensate for loss suffered would lie.

F   Conclusion

14.64   In conclusion, it will be seen that the authorities in Hong Kong are aware of the increasing threats to the privacy of individuals and have in recent years been fairly active in trying to extend individuals' rights to privacy, in particular, through the Bill of Rights Ordinance and the PDPO. This activity has, however, slowed down since the handover of sovereignty to China as has been seen by the failure to implement the Interception of Communications Ordinance and the possible low priority being given to the legislation on 'stalking', Invasion of Privacy and Regulation of Media Intrusion (recommended by the Law Reform Commission). Up to now the courts have only rarely been asked to interpret provisions in these laws protecting individual privacy (see, for example, the *Eastweek* case discussed above), so it is difficult to gauge how the courts will wield their new powers and to what extent the new statutory rights will replace or supplement existing common law rights. It is submitted, however, that concentration will now focus on the courts in respect of the development of a coherent body of law on individual privacy in Hong Kong.

15 ICELAND

S B Einarsdóttir

A Privacy

1 Constitutional protection of private life

15.01 The Icelandic Constitution,[1] contains a provison regarding the inviolability of private life, home and family. Article 71 of the Icelandic Constitution states that everyone shall enjoy inviolability of private life, home and family. This is the most basic provision to this effect and secures the human rights of individuals in society.

15.02 Iceland is also a signatory to the European Convention on Human Rights (ECHR).[2] The provisions contained in the ECHR, which will not be described here, regarding the protection of private life, family, home and correspondence are of course fully applicable in Iceland.

15.03 The provison of Article 71 of the Icelandic Constitution is meant to protect the privacy and personal matters of the public, whether at home or at work. It states that physical investigation or search may not be made without a court order or a special permission by law. The same applies to searching an individual's home or personal belongings, as well as documents and communications by post, telephone conversations and other telecommunications, as well as any comparable restriction of privacy. However, special permission by law may restrict in some other way the inviolability of private life, home and family, if there is an urgent necessity due to the rights of others.

2 Sanctions in relation to violations of privacy

15.04 The Penal Act,[3] also contains some specific provisons regarding violations of privacy. Pursuant to Article 228, snooping into the personal matters of others, such as their letters, documents or diaries, may be punishable by fines, custody or imprisonment. Pursuant to Article 229, making the private matters of others public without having sufficient reasons to do so is also punishable by fines or custody. This wording is rather unclear

---

1   Act of 17 June 1944, No 33/1944.
2   Cf Act No 62/1994 which came into force on 19 May 1994.
3   No 19/1940, which came into force in 1940.

and it is the duty of the court to evaluate and define what 'private matters' and 'sufficient reasons' are. However, this lack of clarity also means that the provision is capable of being applied to many different incidents.

15.05   The only exceptions to the above rules are to be found in the Act concerning the Handling of Official/Police Matters.[4] Staking out/use of assumed identity to obtain information may only be done within certain (strict) limits. It is not permitted by the public, and the police may do this only as far as it is absolutely necessary to solve crimes of a serious nature. However, it is clear that matters relating to the private lives of individuals may not be published, and such publication may be prevented by individuals. This is true of all activities such as covert filming, filming on private property, recording of conversations, both open and covert, sifting of rubbish, use of security camera footage for reporting events and use of telephoto lens. Personal and private matters are of course often made public in judgments and orders of the court. However, in sensitive cases such as rape and child care cases, the names of the persons involved are withheld and substituted by X, Y, etc.

3   Covert filming

15.06   Filming over private property is permitted, although it would probably be considered a violation of privacy if an especially strong lens was used to obtain photos of personal behaviour or belongings.

15.07   In 1997, employees at an airport shop found out that they were being videotaped at work without their knowledge or consent. These employees have now filed suit against the Icelandic State, claiming damages for illegal taping. The case has not yet been tried, but the outcome will certainly be of interest and help to form this field of the law in Iceland.

15.08   It should be stressed that the use of video cameras for the sake of security and protection of property, whose existence has been thoroughly advertised, is of course an entirely different matter. However, taping of conversations between two or more employees or an employee and a customer is considered a violation of their privacy, as is videotaping in staff quarters, either during coffee breaks or throughout the day, whether with or without consent, as this is not necessary for security reasons.

4   Data protection

15.09   Specifically, the Act concerning the Registration and Handling of Personal Data.[5] The Act applies to all forms of systematic registration and other handling of personal data, whether it is effected mechanically or by hand.

15.10   The Act applies to registration by employers, companies, societies and institutions and to registration carried out under the auspices of public bodies. These parties must of course be acting within Icelandic jurisdiction. This would probably be deemed to extend to anyone posting information contrary to the provisions of the law on the Internet.

---

4   No 19/1991.
5   No 121/1989, which came into force on 1 January 1990.

15.11 Systematic registration of data refers to the collection and registration of particular data as part of a systematic whole. Personal data refers to data concerning private affairs, financial affairs or other affairs of individuals, institutions, companies or other legal persons which it is reasonable and natural to keep secret.

15.12 Systematic registration of personal data as covered by the Act shall only be permitted if the registration constitutes a normal part of the activity of the relevant party and concerns only those who are connected with this work or sphere of operations, such as customers, employees or members.

15.13 Registration of the following data concerning the private affairs of individuals is not permitted:

(1) data concerning skin colour, race, political opinion and religion;

(2) data on whether a person has been suspected of, charged with or sentenced for a punishable deed;

(3) data on people's sexual behaviour, health matters and use of medicines, alcohol or drugs;

(4) data concerning substantial social problems; and

(5) data on private affairs of the same sort as referred to in (1) to (4).

15.14 However, registration of the above data is permitted if specially authorised according to other Acts, also if the individual himself has provided the data or if the data is collected with his consent. It is a condition for such collection that the data be collected in circumstances such that the person about whom the data is registered cannot be unaware of the intention to register the relevant data.

15.15 Recently, there has been extensive discussion in Iceland regarding a parliamentary bill concerning a database in the health care area. It is proposed that a genetics company will be given an exclusive right for 12 years to compile, utilise and exploit the database. One of the points stressed has been that the privacy of the individuals, whose health problems will be filed on the database and researched in order to cure diseases and develop new medicines, will be securely protected. This is proposed to be done by coding the personal information in a complex manner. The bill has yet to be discussed in parliament, and there are several other issues that must be resolved before it can be passed.

15.16 An individual whose privacy has been violated can seek an injunction to restrain the activity which has caused this violation, as well as damages from the responsible party.

B Publicity

1 Protection of one's likeness

15.17 The relevant law is the Trade Marks Act.[6]

---

6 No 45/1997, which came into force on 1 June 1997.

15.18   According to Item 4, paragraph 1, Article 14 of the Trade Marks Act,[7] a trade mark may not be registered if it contains anything which may give cause to conclude that it is the name of an active commercial operation or the *name or portrait of another person*, providing this does not involve individuals long dead or if the mark includes a distinctive name of real property or an illustration of it. Also, according to Item 5 of the same Article, a trade mark may not be registered if it contains anything which may cause it to be interpreted as the distinctive title of a protected literary or artistic work or if it infringes the copyright of another person to such work or other intellectual property right.

15.19   For instance, the Icelandic Patent Office was not willing to register the trade mark SALVADOR DALI, in the form of the signature of the deceased artist, without his consent. Such consent had in fact been given prior to his death, and the matter was resolved. This provision therefore offers protection to both national residents and citizens of foreign states.

15.20   The provision of Article 229 of the Penal Act[8] mentioned earlier makes it unlawful to make public the private matters of others without having sufficient reason to do so, a contravention of the provision is punishable by fines or custody. This provision can be used to restrict the use of a person's biography.

15.21   In a recent court case, the writer of a doctor's biography was fined for publishing private matters relating to a patient of the doctor, and for disclosing them in the biography. The patient had suffered mental problems, and had been romantically involved with the doctor at one time. The patient was deceased by the time of the publication of the biography, but the publication was considered a violation of her privacy, as well as the family's privacy.

C   Personality

1   Use of one's likeness

15.22   If a person is photographed or videotaped at a public event or gathering by eg a photographer for a newspaper or a TV station, it is probably very difficult for that person to prohibit the publishing of this photograph. In cases such as this one, a person's likeness can be used without their consent.

15.23   It is of course usual for the 'yellow press' to use a person's likeness without their consent to report their private life. If the person involved wanted to take action against the publishing of those photographs, it would probably be difficult, unless the pictures were of a very intimate and personal nature. Then Article 229 of the Penal Act would be applied.

15.24   A person's likeness may not be used for advertising for publicity purposes without the consent of the person involved. As mentioned before, a trade mark may not be registered if it contains anything which may give

---

7   No 45/1997.
8   No 19/1940.

cause to conclude that it is the name or portrait of another person, providing this does not involve individuals long dead. This is provided in Item 4, paragraph 1, Article 14 of the Trade Marks Act.[9]

9   No 45/1997.

16 INDIA

Pravin Anand
Gitanjli Duggal

A Privacy

1 Right of privacy defined

16.01   The right of privacy is defined as the right to be let alone, the right of a person to be free from unwarranted publicity and the right to live without unwarranted interference by the public in matters with which the public is not necessarily concerned. The term 'right of privacy' is a generic term encompassing various rights recognised to be inherent in the concept of ordered liberty and such a right prevents governmental interference in intimate personal relationships or activities, freedom of the individual to make fundamental choices involving himself, his family, and his relationships with others. Privacy laws prohibit an invasion of a person's right to be left alone (eg not to be photographed in public) and also restrict access to personal information (eg income tax returns, credit reports) and overhearing of private communications (eg electronic surveillance). The right of privacy, simply put, is merely the right to live as one chooses.

16.02   J Thomas McCarthy, in *The Rights of Publicity and Privacy*, defined the right to privacy as one's right to control the dissemination of information about oneself. According to him the right to privacy is the cluster of fundamental constitutional rights of citizens against various forms of government intrusion and the tort of invasion of privacy lies in the public disclosure of embarrassing private facts.

16.03   Breach of privacy lies in knowingly and without lawful authority:

(1) intercepting, without the consent of the sender or receiver, a message by telephone, telegraph, letter or other means of private communications;

(2) divulging, without the consent of the sender or receiver, the existence or contents of such message if such person knows that the message was illegally intercepted, or if he learned illegally of the message in the course of employment with an agency in transmitting it.

The right of privacy is said to exist only so far as its assertion is consistent with law or public policy, and in a proper case, equity will therefore interfere to prevent an injury threatened by the invasion of, or infringement upon, this right from motives of curiosity, gain or malice.

2   Invasion of privacy

16.04   Privacy is invaded by the unwarranted appropriation or exploitation of one's personality, publicising one's private affairs with which public has no legitimate concern, or wrongful intrusion into one's private activities, in such a manner as to cause mental suffering, shame or humiliation to person of ordinary sensibilities. In other words invasion of privacy is the violation of the right, which everyone has, to be left alone and unnoticed if he so chooses.

16.05   William Prosser[1] divided the tort of invasion of privacy into four separate and discrete categories:

(1)   intrusion into the private affairs/seclusion/solitude (trespass, nuisance, intentional infliction of mental distress);

(2)   disclosure – the public disclosures of embarrassing private facts even if true and so no action will lie for defamation;

(3)   false light privacy – present the plaintiff to the public in a false light or falsely attribute some opinion or statement. For example, a picture of an innocent person is used to illustrate a story on some controversial issue. Defamation is not necessary; it is enough to give the person publicity and to attribute to him characteristics, conduct or beliefs that are false; and

(4)   appropriation – unpermitted use, usually for commercial purposes of a person's identity, name, likeness, picture for advertising, and trade purposes.

16.05   India is a very close-knit society with strong ties of kinship, where the intensely private and personal affairs of an individual may, more often than not, become the 'public' affairs of all. There is in fact, a lack of awareness among the people in general about this most fundamental of rights concerning personal liberty and freedom. This is reflected in the absence of any comprehensive, all-encompassing legislation dealing with all aspects of the law in relation to a person's right to privacy.

16.06   However, the legislators in India have not been completely oblivious to the necessity of such a right. They have therefore, from time to time, included provisions relating to the right of privacy in various pieces of legislation, which govern or deal with special circumstances and/or special classes of people. In addition the lower courts in India, following the practice initiated, evolved and developed by the Supreme Court, have consistently derived the right to privacy from constitutional provisions guaranteeing to the people of India certain fundamental rights. India is also committed to upholding and protecting this right in conformity with the provisions of International Law. Let us examine each one of these sources of the right to privacy separately and in detail.

3   International conventions

16.07   India is a signatory to the International Covenant on Civil and Political Rights, 1966, Article 17 of which provides:

---

1   Privacy; 48 Calif L Rev 383.

(1) no-one shall be subject to arbitrary or unlawful interference with his privacy, family, human or correspondence, nor to unlawful attacks on his honour and reputation;

(2) everyone has the right to the protection of the law against such interference or attacks.

16.08   India is also a signatory to the Universal Declaration of Human Rights, 1948, Article 12 of which is in almost similar terms to Article 17 of the International Covenant on Civil and Political Rights, 1966.

16.09   It is an accepted proposition of law that rules of customary International Law which are not contrary to the municipal law shall be deemed to be incorporated in the domestic law. Since Article 17 of the International Covenant is not contrary to any part of Indian municipal law, Article 21 of the Constitution of India has, therefore, to be interpreted in conformity with the International Law. This view was also upheld by the Supreme Court in *People's Union for Civil Liberties v Union of India*.[2]

4   Legislation

16.10   Individual items of legislation which contain statutory prohibition against disclosure of information regarding special categories of individuals, giving protection to the individual's right to privacy, applicable to all persons including those specially directed to the press are set out below.

Code of Criminal Procedure, 1973

16.11   The code came into force with effect from 25 January 1974.

16.12   Section 327 (1) provides that the place in which any criminal court is held for the purpose of inquiring into or trying any offence shall be an open court but the second sub-clause provides that any inquiry into, trial and punishment for an offence of rape,[3] or an offence involving intercourse by a man with his wife during separation,[4] or an offence involving intercourse by a public servant with woman in his custody,[5] or an offence involving intercourse by a superintendent of jail, remand home, etc,[6] or an offence involving intercourse by any member of the management or staff of a hospital with any woman in that hospital[7] shall be conducted *in camera*, and only with the special permission of the presiding judge can any person be allowed to have access to, or be or remain in, the room or building used by the court. Further, in any proceedings under this subsection it shall not be lawful for any person to print or publish any matter in relation to any such proceedings except with the prior permission of the court.[8] Even in open trial, the Presiding Judge may order that the public generally or any named persons shall not have access to or be or remain in the room/building used by the court.

---

2 (1997) 1 SCC 301.
3   Sections 375 and 376 of the Indian Penal Code, 1860.
4   Section 376A of the Indian Penal Code, 1860.
5   Section 376B of the Indian Penal Code, 1860.
6   Section 376C of the Indian Penal Code, 1860.
7   Section 376D of the Indian Penal Code, 1860.
8   Section 327(3) of the Criminal Procedure Code, 1973.

16.13   This Act applies to every person, whether an Indian or a foreign citizen.

Hindu Marriage Act, 1955

16.14   The Hindu Marriage Act came into force on 18 May 1955.

16.15   Section 22 – Every proceeding under this Act, shall be conducted in camera and it shall not be lawful for any person to print or publish any matter in relation to any such proceeding except a judgement of the High Court or of the Supreme Court printed or published with the previous permission of the court. If any person prints or publishes any matter in contravention of the provisions this shall be punishable by a fine which may extend to 1,000 rupees.[9]

16.16   The provisions of this Act are applicable to marriages where both the parties are Hindus by religion.

16.17   Section 33 of the Special Marriages Act, 1954 though on the same terms as Section 22 of the Hindu Marriage Act, 1955 is less restrictive as it provides that a proceeding under that Act shall be conducted *in camera* if either party thereto, desires or if the District Court desires to do so.

The Children Act, 1960

16.18   This Act came into force on 26 December, 1960 and apples to a child who is defined as a boy under the age of 16 years and a girl under the age of 18 years.

16.19   Section 36 of the Act provides that no report in any newspaper, magazine or news-sheet of any inquiry regarding a child under this Act shall disclose the name, address or school or any other particular calculated to lead to the identification of the child, nor shall any picture of any such child be published. Any person contravening the provisions of this section shall be punishable by a fine, which may extend to 1,000 rupees.[10] Such disclosure may, however, be permitted by the authority for reasons to be recorded in writing if in its opinion such disclosure will be in the interest of the child.

The Juvenile Justice Act, 1986

16.20   This Act came into force on 1 December 1986 and apples to a juvenile who is defined as a boy under the age of 16 years and a girl under the age of 18 years.

16.21   Section 36 of the Act provides that no report in any newspaper, magazine or news-sheet of any inquiry regarding a juvenile under this Act shall disclose the name, address or school or any other particular calculated to lead to the identification of the juvenile, nor shall any picture of any such juvenile be published. Any person contravening the provisions of this section shall be punishable with fine, which may extend to 1,000 rupees.[11] Such disclosure may however be permitted by the authority for reasons to be recorded in writing if in its opinion such disclosure will be in the interest of the juvenile.

9   US $ 25 (approximately).
10   US $ 25 (approximately).
11   US $ 25 (approximately).

16.22 Both these Acts are enacted with the intention of safeguarding the image of a child and/or juvenile who is particularly vulnerable to acquiring any stigma or disrepute which would jeopardise their chances of leading a normal life.

The Emblems and Names (Prevention of Improper Use) Act, 1950

16.23 This Act came into force with effect from 1 March 1950.

16.24 Section 3 – No person shall except in conditions and cases as may be prescribed by the Central Government, use or continue to use for the purpose of any trade, business, calling or profession or in the title of any patent, or in any trade mark or design, any name or emblems specified in the schedule or any colourable imitation thereof without the previous permission of the Central Government or of any authorised officer of the Government. The bar extends to any competent authority registering any Company, firm, trade mark, design or granting a patent.

16.25 This Act is also applicable to citizens of India outside India.

16.26 Penalty for contravention of the provisions of this Act is fine which may extend to 500 rupees.[12]

16.27 The Schedule annexed to the Act lists the names of institutions and personalities, which come under the bar.

16.28 Entry 9 of the Schedule – the name or pictorial representation of the President (of India).

16.29 Entry 9A of the Schedule – the name or pictorial representation of Chhatrapati Shivaji Maharaj or Mahatama Gandhi, or Pandit Jawaharlal Nehru or Shrimati Indira Gandhi or the Prime Minister of India except on calendars not used for advertising goods.

The Indecent Representation of Women (Prohibition) Act, 1986

16.30 This Act came into force with effect from 23 December 1986.

16.31 Section 3 – No person shall publish, or cause to be published or arrange or take part in the publication or exhibition of, any advertisement which contains indecent representation of women in any form.

16.32 Section 4 – No person shall produce or cause to be produced, sell, let for hire, distribute, circulate, or send by post any book, pamphlet, paper, slide, film, writing, drawing, painting, photograph, representation or figure which contains indecent representation of women in any form, except if the said book etc is in the interest of science, literature, art or learning or other objects of general concern or for religious purposes.

16.33 Indecent representation of women is defined in section 2 (c) of the Act to mean, the depiction in any manner of the figure of a woman, her form or body or any part thereof in such a way as to have the effect of being indecent, or derogatory to, or denigrating, women, or is likely to deprave, corrupt, or injure the public morality or morals.

12 US $ 13 (approximately).

16.34   The penalty for the first conviction under the Act is imprisonment of either description for a term which may extend to two years and with fine which may extend to 2,000 rupees[13] and for second or subsequent conviction with imprisonment for a term of not less than six months but which may extend to five years and also with a fine of not less than 10,000 rupees[14] but which may extend to one lakh rupees.[15]

The Medical Termination of Pregnancy Act, 1971

16.35   This Act came into force with effect from 10 August 1971.

16.36   Under section 7(1) (c) of this Act, the State Governments are empowered to make regulations prohibiting the disclosure, except to such persons and for such purposes as may be specified in such regulations, of any information regarding the particulars of a woman having undergone termination of any pregnancy under the Act. Any person who willfully contravenes or willfully fails to comply with the any such regulations shall be liable to be punished with fine which may extend to 1,000 rupees.

16.37   It is evident that these special provisions were enacted to essentially safeguard the special interests of women and children in extraordinary circumstances.

5   Constitutional rights

16.38   The Constitution of India came into force on 26 January 1950.

16.39   The Supreme Court has derived the right to privacy from two sources in the Constitution namely, the Preamble and Articles 19(1)(a) and 21 of Part III of the Constitution which include, which guarantee to the people of India certain freedoms in the form of fundamental rights:

Preamble

> The Preamble to the Constitution seeks, inter alia, to '...assure the dignity of the individual...'. This has been interpreted by the Supreme Court in *Kharak Singh v State of Uttar Pradesh*[16] to safeguard those cherished human values as the means of ensuring his full development and evolution.

Article 21

> No person shall be deprived of his life or personal liberty except according to procedure established by law.
> Privacy primarily concerns the individual and therefore, relates to and overlaps with the concept of liberty. The expression 'life and personal liberty' has been construed very widely by the Supreme Court, and the process of expansion of the scope of the term is an ongoing one. It has now been conclusively laid down in numerous decisions that deprivation of life and personal liberty of an individual would occur if he is forced to live a life which may be incomplete in any manner or which takes away the pleasure of living with dignity, honour and self-respect to which every human is entitled.

---

13   US $ 50 (approximately).
14   US $ 250 (approximately).
15   US $ 2500 (approximately)
16   AIR 1963 SC 1295.

Article 19 (1)(a)

> Every citizen shall have the freedom of speech and expression subject
> to laws containing reasonable restrictions on the grounds, inter alia,
> decency or morality and defamation as laid down in Article 19 (2).
> Right to free speech does not entitle one to violate the right of others.
> It follows from this that the individual has the right to seek protection
> of the courts of law if he is faced with a situation of unwarranted
> intrusion by the press or media on his personal life. Since, the
> constitution exhaustively enumerates the permissible grounds of
> restriction on the freedom of expression in Article 19(2), it will not be
> possible for the courts to add 'privacy' to that list. But such exposure
> of private affairs as might be called 'obscene' or 'indecent' can be
> legitimately suppressed by the State on the ground of 'morality or
> decency'.

16.40   While the rights in Article 21 are available to all individuals whether
Indian or foreign, the fundamental rights enumerated in Article 19 are
available only to citizens of India. The right of privacy emanating from
Article 21 is a much stronger right as the same cannot be suspended even
on the proclamation of national emergency under Article 352 of the
Constitution while Article 19 can be suspended. It is perhaps, for this reason
that the Supreme Court has laid a greater emphasis in reading the right of
privacy in Article 21.

16.41   However, the violation of the right to personal liberty by a private
individual is not within the purview of Article 21. This protection is available
to individuals only against the acts of omission and commission by the State.
Therefore, a person whose right to personal liberty is infringed by a private
individual, must seek his remedy under the ordinary law and not under
Article 21. It is only against the might of the State that an individual needs
constitutional protection. State has been defined in Article 12 of the
Constitution to include Government and the Parliament of India,
Government and the Legislatures of each of the States, local authorities,
other Authorities within the territory of India or under the control of the
Government of India.

16.42   The form of remedy to seek redressal for the violation of one's
constitutional right to privacy would be by moving a Writ of Mandamus to
the Supreme Court under Article 32 or to the High Court of any of the
States under Article 226 of the Constitution.

6   Personal liberty

16.43   In *Kharak Singh v State of Uttar Pradesh*[17] the words 'Personal
Liberty' in Article 21 were given a very wide and liberal construction, ie to
be used in the Article as a compendious term to include within itself all the
varieties of rights which go to make up the personal liberties of man. Justice
Subba Rao, in his dissenting judgment stated that 'It is true our constitution
does not expressly declare a right to privacy as a fundamental right, but the
said right is an essential ingredient of personal liberty'. The bench
comprising seven judges read the right to privacy as part of the right to life

---

17   AIR 1963 SC 1295.

under Article 21 of the Constitution. Reliance was placed on the US decision of *Munn v Illinois*[18] wherein the term 'life' occurring in the 5th and 14th Amendment of the US Constitution (which corresponds to Article 21 of the Indian Constitution) was interpreted to mean not merely the right to the continuance of a person's animal existence. The Court noted that 'The right to personal liberty takes in not only a right to be free from restrictions placed on his movements, but also free from encroachments on his private life…Indeed, nothing is more deleterious to a man's physical happiness and health than a calculated interference with his privacy.' The court also relied on *Wolf v Colorado*[19] wherein it was held that the security of one's privacy against arbitrary intrusion by the police…is basic to a free society. It is therefore, implicit in the concept of ordered liberty. The court further held that the right of personal liberty in Article 21 can be defined as a right of an individual to be free from restrictions or encroachments on the person, whether those restrictions are directly imposed or indirectly brought about by calculated measures.

7 Right of privacy

16.44 The right of privacy as an independent and distinctive concept has two aspects which are but two faces of the same coin:

(1) the general law of privacy which affords a tort action for damages resulting from an unlawful invasion of privacy.

(2) the constitutional recognition given to the right to privacy which protects personal privacy against unlawful governmental invasion.

The Supreme Court summarised the broad principles regarding exercise of the said rights (Annex 'A').

16.45 The Supreme Court of India has therefore, given protection to the individual from unwarranted intrusion into his private life and has thereby, given common law recognition to the broadly understood meaning of the right of privacy.

16.46 So far in India, the civil law does not recognise any independent right of privacy. Hence, if anyone publishes anything which brings an individual into unwanted publicity or exposes to the public his family or other private affairs, he can bring legal proceedings against such person only if he can bring his case under any of the existing causes of action recognised by law, such as, defamation (which is both a civil wrong and a criminal offence under section 499 of the Indian Penal Code, 1860), breach of confidence and the like.

16.47 In *Gobind v State of Madhya Pradesh*[20] for the first time the Supreme Court granted recognition to the right to privacy in the sense that the fundamental right of the citizens embodied in Article 21 of the Constitution can be described as contributing to the right to privacy. One of the judges asserted that the rights and freedoms of citizens set forth in the constitution guaranteed that the individual, his personality and those things stamped

---

18 94 US 113.
19 338 US 25.
20 AIR 1975 SC 1378.

with his personality should be free from official interference. The judgment brought into focus the nexus between the right to privacy and the dignity and the happiness of the individual. It was considered necessary, at this stage, that the concept of the right to privacy goes through a process of case-by-case development. Here right to privacy was derived from the right to personal liberty (Article 21), the right to move freely throughout the territory of India [Article 19(1)(d)] and the right to speech and expression [art 19(1)(a)], which cumulatively create an independent right of privacy as an emanation of them, which one can characterise as a fundamental right. However, this right too cannot be absolute and would always be subject to reasonable restrictions on the basis of compelling public interest.

16.48   In *State of Maharashtra v Madukar Narayan Mandikar*[1] it was held that even a woman of easy virtue is entitled to privacy and no-one can invade her privacy as and when he likes. In *State of Maharashtra v Prabhakar Panndurang*[2] a detenu's right to write a book and to get it published was upheld by the Supreme Court.

8   Privacy right overrides copyright

16.49   In the celebrated case of *M/s Kaleidoscope (India) P Ltd v Phoolan Devi*[3] the trial judge had prohibited exhibition of a controversial film titled 'Bandit Queen' both in India and abroad. The court in its preliminary opinion held that the film infringed the right to privacy and publicity of Phoolan Devi, notwithstanding that she had assigned her copyright to her writings to the film producers. This was upheld in appeal by the Division Bench which granted an interim injunction restraining the exhibition of the film in India and abroad, even going to the extent of directing the appellants to recall the film from the Academy of Motion Pictures and Sciences before which the film had been submitted for nomination in the Oscar Awards.

9   Telephone tapping

16.50   In the recent case of *People's Union for Civil Liberties v Union of India*,[4] it was held that Telephone tapping is a serious invasion of an individual's privacy. A citizen's right to privacy has to be protected from being abused by the authority of the day. Though the right to privacy is not identified under the Constitution, the right to privacy would certainly include telephone conversations in the privacy of one's home or office without interference. Telephone tapping would, thus, infract Article 21 of the Constitution of India unless it is permitted under the procedure established by law. A valuable constitutional right can only be canalised by civilised processes.

---

1   AIR 1991 SC 207.
2   AIR 1966 SC 424.
3   AIR 1995 Del 316.
4   (1997) 1 SCC 301.

10 *Governmental interference with freedom of speech through privacy*

16.51 The Supreme Court in the case of *Smt Prabha Dutt v Union of India*,[5] wherein a petition had been filed by a journalist seeking permission allowing her to interview two convicts who were under the sentence of death. It was categorically laid down that the press could claim no such right unless in the first instance the person sought to be interviewed is so willing. The existence of a free press does not imply or spell out any legal obligation on the citizens to supply information to the press. In the present case since there was nothing on record to show that the convicts were unwilling to be interviewed, permission to interview them was granted.

16.52 In the case of *R Rajagopal v State of Tamil Nadu*,[6] the Supreme Court discussed the law relating to the convict's right to publish his autobiography was discussed in detail.

16.53 This petition raises a question concerning the freedom of press vis-à-vis the right to privacy of the citizens of this country. Some journalists wanted to publish the autobiography of the condemned prisoner, Auto Shankar, in their magazine, Nakkheeran. This was being interfered with by the prison authorities, who by exerting pressure on the convict had made him withdraw the permission earlier granted to the journalists. The convict had written his autobiography running into 300 pages, while in jail and given it to his wife to be handed over for publication in the said magazine. Auto Shankar was convicted and sentenced to death for having committed as many as six murders. In his autobiography he had set out the close nexus between himself and several high-ranking government officers who were his partners in several crimes.

11 *Intrusion by life insurance companies*

16.54 In *Neera Mathur v Life Insurance Corporation of India*,[7] the Supreme Court held that a declaration form requiring details of personal problems from lady applicants was indeed embarrassing, if not humiliating. Modesty and self-respect may perhaps preclude the disclosure of personal problems. The respondent was directed to delete such columns and the practice of including such questions in declaration forms was deprecated.

12 *Overt filming*

16.55 In the absence of any public issue, the press should not be allowed to make commercial use of materials obtained by invading the privacy of any individual.

16.56 The following are instances of matters in respect of which no individual including the Press has any special rights or privileges:

---

5   AIR 1982 SC 6.
6   AIR 1995 SC 264.
7   AIR 1992 SC 392.

(1) the right to enter private property, which is protected by the tort law of trespass, nuisance etc;

(2) even as regards public places, members of the public including newsmen may be excluded from a scene of crime or disaster.

The question that remains to be answered is whether the taking of a photograph of a person's premises or household without their permission should not be constituted a statutory wrong, if necessary, to add privacy as an additional limitation, in Article 19(2) of the constitution, in order to uphold such legislation.

13 Public order

16.57   The right of privacy as derived from constitutional provisions is not absolute. Its scope is subject to the concept of Public Order and the State can, in larger public interest, indulge in phone tapping and surveillance. An individual's right of privacy would always be secondary to and would consequently bow before the interests of the community. However, the said right cannot be curtailed except according to procedure established by law, which must not be arbitrary, unjust or wilful but must be fair and reasonable.

16.58   This has also been the view consistently held by the Supreme Court. In the case of *People's Union for Civil Liberties v Union of India*[8] concerning instances of telephone tapping, the Supreme Court, upheld section 5(2) of the Telegraph Act, 1885 as being substantively conforming with the requirements of a just and reasonable requirement, however was not backed by sound procedures.

16.59   Section 5(2) permits the interception of messages on the occurrence of any public emergency or in the interest of public safety. The court defined 'public emergency' to mean the occurrence of a sudden condition or state of affairs affecting the people at large calling for immediate action, and 'public safety' to mean the state or condition of freedom from danger or risk for the people at large. The existence of these two conditions is the *sine qua non* for the exercise of powers under this section by the Government. Once this stage is over, the competent authority is empowered to pass an order of interception after recording its satisfaction that it is necessary or expedient so to do in the interest of:

(1) sovereignty and integrity of India,

(2) the security of the state,

(3) friendly relations with foreign states,

(4) public order, or

(5) for preventing incitement to the commission of an offence.

14 Judicial decisions under Article 21 of the Constitution

16.60   The court has held that telephone tapping by the Government under section 5(2) amounts to infraction of the fundamental right under

---

8   (1997) 1 SCC 301.

Article 21 which included the right of privacy, hence it can be resorted to only in accordance with procedure established by law. Though substantive provisions of section 5(2) clearly laid down conditions/situations for interception of messages but in the absence of rules under section 7(2)(b) laying down what constitutes a just, fair and reasonable procedure rights granted under Articles 19(1)(a) and 21 cannot be safeguarded. The court then went on to lay down detailed guidelines for the exercise of these powers till the Central Government drafted rules under section 7(2)(b) of the Act.

16.61   The Supreme Court in *Kharak Singh's case*,[9] held that 'surveillance by domiciliary visits at night' under Chapter XX of the UP Police Regulations, was violative of Article 21 on the ground that there was no law under which the said regulation could be justified.

16.62   In *Gobind v State of Madhya Pradesh*,[10] the Supreme Court upheld the validity of the regulations under the Madhya Pradesh Police Regulations, which provided surveillance by way of several measures indicated in the said regulations, by holding that Article 21 was not violated because the impugned regulations were 'procedure established by law' in terms of the said Article.

16.63   It has been held that the publication of photos as preventive action by the police is not violative of the right to live with dignity and reputation. No right will be protected at the risk of public interest.[11]

16.64   If the court does find that a claimed right is entitled to protection as a fundamental privacy right, a law infringing it must satisfy not only the compelling State interest test but must also be according to 'procedure established by law', which has now been consistently interpreted on the same lines as the American doctrine of 'due process of law'.

B   Publicity

1   Right of publicity

16.65   Right of publicity is the right of a person to control the commercial use of his or her identity. It developed from a law of privacy into a right to control when, where and how any person desired his/her identity to be so used. Property right in the commercial value of every person's identity. It is a part of unfair competition law and as a part of intellectual property. In other words it is a mixture of personal rights, property rights and rights under unfair competition law.

16.66   Right to publicity protects persona, arising from the uniqueness of the human identity as a property right. The question whether it can be used to protect the identity of legal persons like corporations, partnerships, institutions and the like can be partially answered by taking a look at The Emblems and Names (Prevention of Improper Use) Act 1950, which

9   AIR 1963 SC 1295.
10   AIR 1975 SC 1378.
11   1987 CrLJ 1593.

prohibits the use of the name or logo or symbol of some institutions listed in its schedule, for the purpose of any trade, business, calling or profession or in the title of any patent, or in any trade mark or design, any name or emblems specified in the schedule or any colourable imitation thereof without the previous permission of the Central Government or of any authorised officer of the Government.

16.67 Similarly the commercial uses of identity of political figures whether living or deceased is also governed by the Emblems and Names (Prevention of Improper Use) Act 1950.

16.68 The circumstances under which the use of a person's biography can be restricted are discussed in detail by the Supreme Court in *R Rajagopal's Case*.[12]

2 *Trade and Merchandise Marks Act 1958*

16.69 Registerability of a personal name as a trade mark, is governed by the provisions of this Act, which applies to both foreign and Indian applicants of trademarks. The said Act came into force on 17 October 1958.

16.70 The law of trade marks is based on the principle that every trader is entitled to the right to adopt a mark in relation to his goods and to the continued use thereof to the exclusion of all others. The Act serves to benefit the interests of the consumers as much as those of the trade mark owners as it ensures that the product being bought has its origin in a particular manufacturer. However, to be able to claim exclusive use of a trade mark, the same must be distinctive or capable of acquiring distinctiveness.

16.71 Section 9(1)(d) provides that a trade mark shall not be registered in Part A of the register unless it contains or consists of at least one or more words '... not being, according to its ordinary signification a geographical name or a surname or a personal name or any common abbreviation thereof or the name of a sect, caste or tribe in India.'

3 *Registration of names and signatures as trade marks*

16.72 A mark must be distinctive ie adapted to or capable of distinguishing the goods of the applicant for registration from those of all others. Name of a person, surname, personal name etc are all considered *prima facie* not distinctive for the purpose as they are not adapted to distinguish the goods of one person from those of others bearing the same surname. However, such marks are registerable upon evidence of distinctiveness and for this it is important to bear in mind, the extent of distinctiveness inherent in the mark and whether it has acquired distinctiveness by virtue of use or of any other circumstances.

16.73 Personal name etc includes any abbreviation of a name. A misspelt name or surname or any phonetic equivalent thereof including a foreign surname should also be considered on the same footing.

16.74 Signature of an applicant is considered prima facie distinctive as they have a visual value when written in a distinctive style but may be refused

12 AIR 1995 SC 264.

registration as offending sections 11 or 12(1) ie on the ground of likelihood of confusion and deception being caused.

16.75 It is, however, possible to register a surname upon proof of its distinctiveness under section 9(2). A application for registration of a surname is closely scrutinised and acceptance granted only where its distinctive character is quite clearly established. The following are the relevant factors to be borne in mind while registering a personal name as a trade mark as laid down in *Burford & Co Ltd's Application:*[13]

(1) extent of actual user;

(2) probability of distinctiveness being maintained in the future;

(3) characteristics of the name;

(4) nature of trade or manufacture in which the name is employed – one restricted to small section of the community;

(5) the class of goods of the mark is distinctive and the way in which it is used in connection with them;

(6) are there any circumstances to induce the belief that the present distinctiveness is due to temporary or exceptional causes, and;

(7) the extent to which registration will control the freedom of individual having the same surname or personal name who may in future embark on the manufacture of the same goods.

The practice followed in India is on the same lines.

16.76 The courts in India have repeatedly laid down that the plaintiff would be entitled to the continued exclusive use of his personal name as a trade mark if the said trade mark has acquired distinctiveness as a result of which the members of trade and public associate the mark exclusively with the goods and business of the plaintiff. In *Kirloskar Diesel Recon Pvt Ltd v Kirloskar Proprietary Ltd,*[14] the court held that the respondent, who had commenced business in 1888 under their surname Kirloskar, could restrain the defendants from subsequently adopting an identical trade mark for their goods. The same was the proposition of law laid down in *Bajaj Electricals Ltd v Metal & Allied Products,*[15] *M/s KG Khosla Compressors Ltd v M/s Khosla Extraktions Ltd*[16] among many other decisions.

C Personality

1 *Personality rights*

16.77 Just as the freedom of the press is necessary for the dissemination of information about public affairs and other matters of public interest, it is equally in the public interest to see that not merely the reputation of an individual but his private affairs, which are unrelated to public affairs, should be protected from unwanted publicity in the press. The need for protection

13 36 RPC 139.
14 AIR 1996 Bom 149.
15 AIR 1988 Bom 167.
16 AIR 1986 Del 181.

of privacy of the personality achieves greater significance in the case of a private individual who has no public importance.

16.78 The Supreme Court has in *R Rajagopal's Case*,[17] stated that the right to privacy must be said to have been violated where, a person's likeness is used, without his consent, for advertising, or non advertising purposes. Therefore, even in the absence of any legislation on the subject the Supreme Court has granted recognition to the right of an individual to preserve his personality.

2   *The Monopolies and Restrictive Trade Practices Act 1969*

16.79   Section 36A defines Unfair Trade Practice to be a trade practice which for the purpose of promoting the sale, use or supply of any goods or for the provision of any services, adopts one or more of the following practices and thereby causes loss or injury to the consumers of such goods or services, whether by eliminating or restricting competition or otherwise, namely:

'(1) the practice of making any statement, whether orally or in writing or by visible representation which,– (...)

(iv) represents that the goods or services have sponsorship, approval, performance, characteristics, accessories, uses or benefits which such goods or services do not have;

(v) represents that the seller or the supplier has a sponsorship or approval or affiliation which such seller or supplier does not have.'

16.80   The remedy is provided under section 48 C – 'If any person contravenes any order made by the Commission under section 36D ie for Unfair Trade Practice, he shall be punishable with imprisonment for a term which may extend to three years or with a fine which may extend to 10,000 rupees'.

16.81   Though this provision is meant to be a protection to consumers against misleading advertisements and false representations and statements, the question which arises is whether this provision can be invoked on behalf of a famous personality in case of use of his or her name or image to portray an impression of endorsement. This is moreso, since it has been interpreted that the phrase 'or otherwise' is a very wide term and not to be read '*ejusdem generis*' – has to be construed to mean loss or injury to other interests of consumers whether they are economic interests or interests of health, welfare, safety etc. This provision generally applies to certification by institutions. It remains to be seen if it may also be extended to false statements portraying approval by a personality eg, sports equipment being endorsed by a famous sportsman or an educational institution by a known literary figure such as Gurudev Rabindranath Tagore etc.

16.82   The remedy includes injunction and damages and interim relief pending inquiry can also be granted. This provision can be invoked only by consumers, whether Indian or foreign.

17   AIR 1995 SC 264.

3   *Advertising codes*

16.83   The Advertising Council of India has also laid down certain code of ethics in this regard. They are as follows:

Code of Ethics for Advertising in India Issued by the Advertising Council Of India

16.84   The code aims to eliminate unfair advertising practice likely to alienate public confidence. This code is intended to be applied in the spirit as well as in the letter and should therefore be taken to set out the minimum standards to be observed by the parties concerned.

The Code for Commercial Advertising on All India Radio

16.85   'Standards of Practice for Radio Advertising:

> 4 – Any pretence in advertising copy must be avoided and such copy shall not be accepted by commercial stations. "The simulation" of voices of a personality in connection with advertisements for commercial products is also prohibited unless *bona fide* evidence is available that such personality has given permission for the simulation of his or her voice and it is clearly understood that stations broadcasting such announcements are indemnified by the advertiser or advertising agency against any possible legal action.'

Code for Commercial Advertising on Doordarshan[18]

16.86   '2– No advertisement shall be permitted which —

> (vi) exploits the national emblem, or any part of the Constitution or the person or personality of a national leader or State Dignitary.
>
> (...)
>
> 12– Imitation likely to mislead viewers shall be avoided.
>
> (...)
>
> 21– Any pretence in advertising copy must be avoided and such copy shall not be accepted by Doordarshan Kendras. The "simulation" of appearance or video of a personality in connection with advertisements for commercial products is also prohibited unless *bona fide* evidence is available that such personality has given permission for the simulation and it is clearly understood that stations telecasting such announcements are indemnified by the advertiser or advertising agency against any possible legal action.'

The Code of Advertising Practice of the Advertising Standards Council of India

16.87   To ensure the truthfulness and honesty of representations and claims made by Advertisements and to safeguard against misleading advertisements:

> '3. Advertisements should not contain any reference to any person, firm or institution without due permission; nor should a picture of any generally identifiable person be used in advertising without due permission.'

18 The state-controlled broadcasting corporation.

4 Annex 'A'

16.88 The Supreme Court of India[19] has summarised the law on privacy (see section 16.7) in the following manner:

'28. We may now summarise the broad principles flowing from the above discussion:

(1) the right to privacy is implicit in the right to life and liberty guaranteed to the citizens of this country by Article 21. It is a "right to be let alone." A citizen has a right to safeguard the privacy of his own, his family, marriage, procreation, motherhood, child bearing and education among other matters. None can publish anything concerning the above matters without his consent – whether truthful or otherwise and whether laudatory or critical. If he does so, he would be violating the right to privacy of the person concerned and would be liable in an action for damages. Position may, however, be different, if a person voluntarily thrusts himself into controversy or voluntarily invites or raises a controversy.

(2) The rule aforesaid is subject to the exception, that any publication concerning the aforesaid aspects becomes unobjectionable if such publication is based upon public records including Court records. This is for the reason that once a matter becomes a matter of public record, the right to privacy no longer subsists and it becomes a legitimate subject for comment by press and media among others. We are, however, of the opinion that in the interests of decency (Article 19(2)) an exception must be carved out to this rule, viz, a female who is the victim of a sexual assault, kidnap, abduction or a like offence should not further be subjected to the indignity of her name and the incident being published in press/media.

(3) There is yet another exception to the Rule in (1) above – indeed, this is not an exception but an independent rule. In the case of public officials, it is obvious, right to privacy, or for that matter, the remedy of action for damages is simply not available with respect to their acts and conduct relevant to the discharge of their official duties. This is so even where the publication is based upon facts and statements which are not true, unless the official establishes that the publication was made (by the defendant) with reckless disregard for truth. In such a case, it would be enough for the defendant (member of the press or media) to prove that he acted after a reasonable verification of the facts; it is not necessary for him to prove that what he has written is true. Of course, where the publication is proved to be false and actuated by malice or personal animosity, the defendant would have no defence and would be liable for damages. It is equally obvious that in matters not relevant to the discharge of his duties, the public official enjoys the same protection as any other citizen, as explained in (1) and (2) above. It needs no reiteration that judiciary, which is protected by the power to punish for contempt of Court and the Parliament and Legislatures protected as their privileges are by Articles 105 and 104 respectively of the Constitution of India, represent exceptions to this rule.

---

19 *R Rajgopal v State of Tamil Nadu*, AIR 1995 SC 264 at 276 and 277.

(4) So far as the Government, local authority and other organs and institutions exercising Governmental power are concerned, they cannot maintain a suit for damages for defaming them.

(5) Rules 3 and 4 do not, however, mean that Official Secrets Act, 1923, or any similar enactment or provision having the force of law does not bind the press or media.

(6) There is no law empowering the State or its officials to prohibit, or to impose a prior restraint upon the press/media.'

17   ITALY

Patrizio Menchetti

A   Privacy and publicity

1   *General framework*

17.01 The Italian legal system focuses on rights of personality (*diritti della personalità*), which also include the categories of privacy and publicity. Since the traditional classification is made on rights of personality in Italian law, the rights of publicity have been defined by legal scholars for violation of the rights of personality to image, and for some authors to the name as well,[1] under a recent judicial trend which recognises a different structure of claims in the case of undue commercial exploitation of a celebrity's likeness.

There is no general law in Italy establishing a detailed catalogue of rights of personality. They have been, therefore, specified by legal scholars.

Italian legal theory is divided on whether the protection is provided by the system with respect to a single, general right of personality extending to protection of privacy and publicity[2] or to several separate rights of personality.[3] The identification of single rights, or situations which are subject to specific protection, varies according to the different schools of thought. This has an impact on the evolution of judicial trends. Although Italy has a full civil law legal system, the courts have a wide latitude in interpreting the law in this area, as no detailed and homogeneous legal framework of ordinary law has been established with respect to rights of personality.

Among the rights or situations subject to specific protection as a right of personality (or under a general right of personality) the following have been identified:

(1)   the right to life, health and to a healthy environment (Article 32 of the Constitution and Articles 1 and 5 of the Civil Code);

---

1   See P Vercellone *Diritti della personalità e rights of publicity*, Rivista trimestrale di diritto e procedura civile, 1995, 1163-1174.
2   See V Zeno Zencovich *Personalità [diritti della]*, Digesto Civile.
3   A De Cupis, *I diritti della personalità*, in Trattato di diritto civile e commerciale diretto da Cicu e Messineo, Milano 1982, 43.

(2)   the right relating to detached parts of the body and the corpse (Article 5 of the Civil Code);

(3)   the right to honour and reputation, (Articles 585 to 595 of the Criminal Code and Article 97 of the Copyright Act, and, for some legal scholars, Article 3 of the Constitution);

(4)   the right to privacy (Article 2 of the Constitution);

(5)   the right to one's name and personal identity (Article 7 of the Civil Code);

(6)   the right to one's image (Article 10 of the Civil Code);

(7)   the author's moral right (Article 2575 of the Civil Code);

(8)   the inventor's moral right (Article 2589 of the Civil Code).

In the following text, reference will be made to those rights of personality which relate to the protection of privacy, including data protection, to the use of a person's name and to the use of an individual's likeness. When general reference is made to rights of personality, protection of privacy, of the use of a person's name and of the use of an individual's likeness are assumed to be covered.

2   Rights of legal persons and non-Italians

17.02 A school of thought and a judicial trend are developing which recognise that in the Italian legal system rights of personality can cover both natural and legal persons,[4] where applicable on a case-by-case approach.

Protection of rights of personality with respect to foreign persons and entities is subject to Article 16 of the Provisions on the Law in General of the Civil Code, which states that foreign legal and natural persons enjoy the protection of civil rights attributed to the citizen on condition of reciprocity and unless otherwise provided in specific laws. This provision was enacted before the current Constitution came into force, and the Constitutional Court in a series of rulings held that the condition of reciprocity cannot be applied to the fundamental human rights recognised by Article 2 of the Constitution.[5] This constitutional provision is construed by legal theory as incorporating by reference to all the other specific Articles of the Constitution protecting specific areas of the right to intimacy. It also refers to other constitutional provisions protecting specific areas, such as the rights to liberty under Article 13, to the inviolability of the domicile under Article 14 and to the secrecy of correspondence under Article 15. In the other cases, unless a specific treaty or convention provides otherwise, the condition of reciprocity must be proved by the foreign citizen or legal entity.[6] The right to start legal proceedings is recognised as a fundamental human right and therefore it is granted also to non-EU citizens and entities.[7] EU citizens and legal entities enjoy the same degree of protection as Italian ones, as the obligation of reciprocity is incompatible with Community law and therefore subject to the general rule established by the Constitutional

4   For a general analysis see D Messinetti *Personalità [diritti della]* Enciclopedia del diritto.
5   Corte Costituzionale, 67/120, 69/104, 69/1329, 79/54, 93/1681.
6   Corte di Cassazione, 95/12978.
7   Corte Costituzionale, 72/50, 93/1681, 93/1309, 66/1680.

Court which requires disapplication of incompatible internal provisions by the judiciary, or directly by the administration without the need of a prior judicial ruling.[8]

3 Privacy (including data protection)

17.03 Although no general statutory provision exists in Italy providing a definition of privacy, most Italian legal scholars refer to the approach taken by Warren and Brandeis,[9] in defining it as the right 'to enjoy life' and 'to be let alone'. Specifically, the right to privacy has been defined as 'the protection of the choices of life from public control and social reprobation'.[10]

The protection of privacy has traditionally been considered as being incorporated into the Italian legal system as a fundamental human right protected by constitutional provisions, international conventions and ordinary law.[11]

4 International conventions and EC Directives

17.04 Italy is party to several treaties and conventions which include an express reference to privacy protection. Since Italy has a dualistic legal system, the simple signing of a treaty is insufficient to establish it as a domestic source of law, and ratification by Parliament is required.

The 1966 International Covenant on Civil and Political Rights, which expressly refers to protection of privacy at Articles 17 and 19, was ratified by the Italian Parliament in 1977. The 1989 Convention on the Rights of the Child, Article 16 of which grants protection of the law with respect to arbitrary or illegal interference with private life, was ratified in 1991.

Italy is also a party to the European Convention for Protection of Human Rights and Fundamental Freedoms ('ECHR') and its additional protocols, and it has accepted the jurisdiction of the European Court of Human Rights. Article 8 of the ECHR, on the right to respect for private and family life, and Article 10 (2) on the protection of the reputation or rights of others, and prevention of the disclosure of information received in confidence with respect to the freedom of expression, are applicable by the Italian courts under Article 13 of the same Convention. Italy differs from several other European countries, in that ECHR has been construed by legal theorists as having a status which is no higher than ordinary law in the Italian legal system.[12] A recent judicial trend, however, construes ECHR provisions as general principles of law, and therefore more resilient than ordinary law.[13]

Italy is also party to Convention 108 of the Council of Europe for the protection of individuals with regard to automatic processing of personal

---

8   Corte Costituzionale, 89/389.
9   SD Warren, L Brandeis *The Right to Privacy*, Harvard Law Review, 4, 1890.
10 S Rodotà *Repertorio di fine secolo* Roma 1992, 190.
11 Corte di Cassazione, 75/2129.
12 M Chiavario *La convenzione europea dei diritti dell'uomo nel sistema delle fonti normative in materia penale* Milano, 1996, 29.
13 See G Raimondi *Un nuovo 'status' nell'ordinamento italiano per la convenzione europea dei diritti dell'uomo (nota a sent Cass, Sez I, 12 maggio 1993, Medrano)*, Cassazione penale 1994, 443.

data. Law 121/81 was believed to be preparatory to the adoption of Convention 108 and the Convention was signed in 1983, but in practice there was no implementation of its provisions in the domestic legal environment until 31 December 1996. The main incentive to adopting provisions implementing Convention 108 was provided when Italy became a party to the Schengen Agreement and its implementing Convention of 1990 on elimination of controls at common borders. The Schengen Convention established, inter alia, the Schengen Information System, providing transborder interchange of personal data for matters related to the Convention. As a measure of protection, Article 117 of the Schengen Convention provides that no contracting party thereto may operate the interchange of data, which is necessary for the practical implementation of the Convention, unless such contracting party adopts a level of personal data protection at least equivalent to the principles established by Convention 108 and Recommendation R15 [87] of 17 September 1987 of the Committee of Ministers of the Council of Europe. As Italy had no general law on data protection at the time it was impossible to implement the Schengen Convention, and, under strong pressure to solve the problem, the Italian Parliament enacted Law 675/96 on data protection on 31 December 1996, *de facto* also implementing Convention 108.[14]

By enacting Law 675/96 Italy complied with most of the basic requirements provided in Directive 95/46/EC on protection of personal data. However, the law has not been adopted under the specific framework existing in Italy for implementation of Community measures, and certain provisions of Law 675/96 do not appear to be exactly in line with the Directive. Legislative Decree (D Lgs) 171/98 implements Directive 97/66/EC on protection of privacy in the telecommunications sector.

5 Data protection

17.05 Law 675/96 establishes the first general system of data protection in Italy. The law covers treatment of personal data belonging to natural and legal persons, both in electronic and hard copy form.

The law also establishes the *Garante per la protezione dei dati personali* (hereinafter the Data Protection Authority), an independent regulatory body having *inter alia* the power to hear complaints, inspect premises and issue administrative penalties as well as cease and desist orders for violation of the law. Concurrent judicial protection is established by the law.

6 Personal data

17.06 Personal data is defined by Article 1 as 'any information relating to a natural or legal person, body or association, identified or identifiable directly or indirectly by reference to any other information, including a personal identification number'. The definition of data is also construed as covering images in so far as they relate to the identification of a person. The law provides that personal data subject to processing shall be:

---

14 See on the point G Buttarelli *Banche dati e tutela della riservatezza - la privacy nella società dell'informazione* Milano, 1997, 121.

(1) processed fairly and lawfully;

(2) collected and stored for specified, explicit and legitimate purposes, and not further processed in a way incompatible with those purposes;

(3) accurate and, when necessary, kept up-to-date;

(4) adequate, relevant and not excessive in relation to the purposes for which they are collected or further processed;

(5) kept in a manner which allows identification of data subjects for no longer than necessary for the purposes for which the data were collected or for which they are further processed.

The general exemptions from the reach of the law are very strict. The law exempts (a) the processing of personal data by a natural person in the course of a purely personal activity when this data is not intended to be systematically disclosed or to be disseminated, and (b) the operations of certain bodies of police, judiciary and national security services.

Under Law 675/96, as a general rule the data subject must freely consent to the processing. The data subject has the right to receive information on the processing of the data, and, in the case that the processing exceeds the purposes for which the data was given, such additional processing is to be expressly authorised by the data subject.

Unlawful processing of personal data is a criminal offence under Article 35, Law 675/96.

7 *Information to be provided when data collected*

17.07 The following information is to be provided to the data subject at the time the data is collected:

(1) the purposes and means of the processing;

(2) whether provision of the data is mandatory or voluntary;

(3) the possible consequences of failure to provide data;

(4) the recipients or categories of recipients to whom data may be disclosed, and the sphere of data dissemination;

(5) the name, denomination or trade name, and the address of the data holder and, when designated, of the data processor;

(6) failure to do so impairs the consent given to treatment of data, exposing the data processor to civil liability, administrative penalties, and criminal prosecution.

On collection of data, the data subject must also be informed that Article 13 of Law 675/96 provides him with the right to:

(1) access the registry of processes mandated by Law 675/96, free of charge, in order to determine the existence of data processing that could contain data relating to him;

(2) be given certain information specified in the notification filed with the Data Protection Authority;

(3) object, on legitimate grounds, to any or all operations involving the processing of personal data relating to him, even when related to the purposes of the data collection;

(4) object to any or all operations involving the processing of personal data relating to him with the intended purpose of providing business information or advertising or direct marketing, or for marketing research or interactive business communications and to be informed by the data holder of his right to object free of charge, not later than the time in which the data is communicated or disseminated;

obtain from the data holder or processor, without delay:

(1) confirmation of the existence of personal data relating to him, even if it is not yet recorded, and the communication to him in intelligible form of such data and of its origin, as well as of the logic involved in the processing and of its purposes. The request may be repeated after a period of not less than ninety days, or after a shorter period only on reasonable grounds;

(2) the erasure, transformation into anonymous data or blocking of data, the processing of which is in violation of the law, including data whose storage is not necessary for the purposes for which they have been collected and processed;

(3) the update or rectification of the data, or their integration if the data subject has a legitimate interest in it;

(4) a certification that the operations described in Numbers (2) and (3) above have been notified to third parties to whom the data has been disclosed or disseminated, unless this proves impossible or involves a clearly disproportionate effort with respect to the protected right. The certification must include the actual content of the operations performed on the data.

8 Transmission and dissemination of data

17.08 In addition, the use, transmission or dissemination of data for marketing purposes is always forbidden unless specific consent has been given, and the export of data (even in hard copy) outside the European Union or export of sensitive data (as identified below) even within the EU is forbidden unless the data subject has given his consent or the Data Protection Authority has so authorised. The entities processing data in Italy or exporting data outside the EU or exporting sensitive data, must also lodge a notification form with the Data Protection Authority. The omission of notification to the Data Protection Authority or notification not corresponding to the facts is a criminal offence under Article 34 of Law 675/96. Subsequent amendments to Law 675/96 have introduced a simplified notification or an exemption from notification with respect to certain categories of processing.

Data that may lead to the disclosure of racial or ethnic origin, religious, philosophical or other beliefs, political opinions, membership of political parties or trade unions, membership of organisations and associations with a religious, philosophical, political or trade-union orientation, and personal data concerning sexual life can only be processed, transmitted or disseminated with the prior written consent of the data subject and the prior authorisation of the Data Protection Authority. Data related to health is subject to the same provisions but can be disseminated only in connection with criminal law enforcement activities. Provisions on sensitive data apply to all activities, including those necessary to, or requested by, the data subject. The Data Protection Authority has, however, issued six general authorisations, on a principle similar to the block exemption regulations under EC competition law. The general authorisations have been renewed each year so far and cover the most common processing activities of sensitive data.

Article 15 Law 675/96 requires that state-of-the-art security measures are adopted to protect personal data. Failure to adopt such measures implies liability in tort. Unlike Directive 95/46/EC, Italian law does not provide a balance between costs and results to be provided, and therefore no defence is allowed in such respect.

Failure to adopt minimum data security measures established by Government, and to update every two years in order to take into account technology developments, is a criminal offence under Article 36 of Law 675/96. The regulation establishing a first set of minimum security measures became legally binding on 31 March 2000.

9   General provisions related to privacy

17.09 Constitutional provisions play a significant role in the area of protection of privacy and rights of personality generally, and are directly applied by courts in their judgments, thus often providing the legal basis for courts to rule on a claim for damages in the absence of other specific provisions.[15]

The constitutional protection of the right to privacy has been construed on the basis of Article 2 of the Italian Constitution, which guarantees respect for fundamental rights and human dignity.[16] The constitutional limit to the right to privacy is contained in Article 21 of the Constitution which provides the principles of freedom to express thoughts by oral and written means as well as other means of communication. This provision also sets out the basic rules guaranteeing press freedom, limiting the seizure of press to cases where obscene content is involved. Freedom of expression under Article 21 of the Constitution is also guaranteed as a human right, and therefore also applicable to foreign citizens.[17] Article 21 sets out as the only limit to the freedom of expression the obscene content of information. The right to privacy is however protected by a provision of equal ranking in Article 2 on the basis of the doctrine of 'implied limits', established by the Constitutional Court to protect all the other rights guaranteed by the Constitution on the same footing.[18] The Italian system of protection of privacy with respect to the activities of the press and of media programmes having an informational content is therefore based upon striking an adequate balance between the protection of the opposite rights granted under Articles 2 and 21 of the Constitution.

---

15 Corte di Cassazione, 98/5658.
16 Corte Costituzionale, 95/37 94/63, 73/38.
17 Corte di Cassazione, 93/1681.
18 Corte Costituzionale, 74/20.

10 Application of constitutional provisions by the courts

17.10   The civil courts have applied the constitutional provisions extensively in deciding cases where the balance between the right to inform and the right to privacy, the right to image or more generally the right to honour, is involved. In accordance with the judicial trend of the Court of Cassation[19] with respect to claims of damages in civil suits, the press, in order to exercise its right to inform, must demonstrate compliance with the following basic requirements:

(1)   the social utility of the information published;

(2)   the truth of facts published and an obligation not to alter the truth, by, for instance, omitting related facts which could alter the general perception of the public; and

(3)   civil and proportionate exposition of the facts and their evaluation.

Italian courts mainly focus, therefore, on the need for information to be published even if it is clear that such information has been collected by legitimate means. Where the above criteria are not met, publication or diffusion of images may be considered to be a violation of the right to image or to privacy or defamation. Assessment is made on a case-by-case basis. Media programmes having an informational content are assimilated to the press for these purposes.

Privacy of minors always takes the priority over the right to inform, and the self-regulation code prohibits the disclosure of names, or details allowing identification, of minors involved in facts that are reported. The only exception is made when a relevant public interest exists which justifies publication of the image of the minor; however, the balance of interest must always be in favour of the minor.

11 Internet services and filming events

17.11   The courts have issued conflicting rulings on Internet services such as publications on web pages, and it is not currently clear whether an Internet service can be assimilated to the press as regards to requirements of registration, liability or constitutional guarantees.[20] However, Internet services are subject to the application of Law 675/96 on data protection, and Internet access providers are also subject to the applicable provisions of D Lgs 171/98 on privacy in telecommunications.

17.12   Filming or taking pictures of public incidents or disorders by press or media information programmes has been generally assumed as legitimate, provided the above criteria are met.

Under Article 147 of the Provisions Implementing the Code of Criminal Procedure, filming or recording of criminal proceedings and subsequent

19   See, for instance, Corte di Cassazione, 84/5259.
20   Tribunale di Napoli, order of 13 March 1997 refusing registration of a Website as press; Tribunale di Roma, order of 6 November 1997 authorising registration of a web site as press; Tribunale di Teramo, civil injunction of 11 December 1997 ordering removal of information from a Website on a U.S. server not construing it as press; Procura della Repubblica di Vicenza, order of 23 July 1998 authorising penal seizure of a Website for diffusion of content which was not obscene; Tribunale di Roma, judgment of 4 July 1998 holding that a Website is not press for purposes of liability on informational content.

diffusion by the media is allowed on condition that the activities are exercised only for the purposes and the limits of the rights of the press and that such filming or recording does not interfere with the judicial proceedings. The filming or recording of criminal proceedings must be authorised by the presiding judge with the consent of all parties, or without such consent the judge considers that there is a particularly relevant public interest. In this case, parties, witnesses or other persons taking part in the proceedings who have not given their consent cannot be filmed or recorded.

17.13   Photos or filming of detained persons are allowed only with their consent, and images of handcuffed persons cannot be shown in newspapers or on television except when the image is necessary to identify abuse. Images of violence can be used only when there is a relevant and justified social interest.

17.14   Italy does not have a general law on the use of video surveillance systems. Article 4 of Law 300/70 forbids the use of video surveillance systems to check workers' activities. When relevant security reasons are involved, the consent of the trade unions is required. In the case of disagreement, the issue is decided by the Workers' Inspectorate, a public sector entity. The Data Protection Authority has ruled that use of video surveillance systems is also covered by Law 675/96, in particular with respect to the principle of proportionality of treatment and non-disclosure of information, and that entities adopting video surveillance systems, including public sector entities, must implement provisions regulating at least the storage of camera footings, access thereto and disclosure thereof to other entities.[1]

17.15   Under Article 615 *bis* (1) of the Penal Code the use of image- and sound-collecting devices to fraudulently collect information or images relating to private life in a third party's private premises is a criminal offence. Under Article 615 *bis* (2) of the Penal Code, the diffusion of such information and images to the public by any means of information is a separate offence. Use of a telephoto lens to collect images of events occurring in private premises in violation of Article 615 *bis* of the Penal Code has been held by a lower court as not being justified by the exercise of the right to inform under Article 21 of the Constitution, as this must be based on lawful collection of information.[2] Under a judicial trend related to civil suits, a claim for damages is also allowed when there is no socially appreciable interest exists to know published facts about an individual's personal or family life or events occurring outside private premises.[3]

12   Public figures

17.16   A well-established judicial trend has applied the constitutional principle of the right to privacy as prevailing over the media's right to inform of facts relating to public figures or celebrities. The courts have stated that

1   Garante per la protezione dei dati personali. Comune di Milano - 17 dicembre 1997; Ospedale Luigi Sacco Azienda ospedaliera-polo universitario di Milano - Modalità della videosorveglianza - 31 dicembre 1998; Impianti per la rilevazione degli accessi di veicoli ai centri storici - 24 febbraio 1999; Videosorveglianza sui mezzi di trasporto pubblico urbano - 23 marzo 1999; Realizzazione di un sistema di videosorveglianza - 21 ottobre 1999; Città di Portici - 17 febbraio 2000
2   Tribunale di Milano, 8 April 1991.
3   Corte di Cassazione, 75/2199.

public figures maintain their right to privacy with respect to such personal interests and activities as are not related to the circumstances of or reasons for their popularity.[4] The collection and assembling of information already known about public figures in such a manner as to enhance its general coverage, such as the publishing by the press of city map on which the telephone numbers, addresses and social habits of celebrities are reported was also held to be a violation of the right to privacy guaranteed by Article 2 of the Constitution.[5]

In accordance with the code of self-regulation, of journalists (see below at para **17.17**), a public figure's right to privacy must be respected in preventing the diffusion of information which has no relevance to his public life or role.

13 Position of journalists

17.17 Journalists are subject to specific rules of ethics. Infringement of the principles of professional conduct or of codes of self-regulation may lead to disciplinary sanctions up to and including expulsion from the journalists' roster.[6]

Law 675/96 as amended requires the self-regulation code of the journalists' professional body on privacy issues, as approved by the Data Protection Authority, to be published in the Official Journal.[7]

The self-regulation code affects professional journalists, trainees and others exercising the activity of journalists on an occasional basis.

The journalist is, inter alia, always required to disclose his identity and the purposes of the collection of information. Exceptions are made when the journalist's life is in danger and when the collection of the information may be compromised.

In an informal ruling the Data Protection Authority has confirmed that under Law 675/96 the journalist must always inform the interviewed person of the purposes for which the personal data collected will be treated.[8]

14 Interference with communications generally

17.18 The basic right to secrecy in communications is granted by Article 15 of the Constitution. This provides that the liberty and secrecy of correspondence and any other form of communications are inviolable, and that such liberty and secrecy can be limited only by an act of the judiciary under the guarantees established by law. The Italian Constitution provides

---

4   Tribunale di Milano, 17 November 1994.
5   Pretura di Roma, 15 July 1986.
6   Law 69/93 forbids the exercise of the professional activity of journalist, which has the status of a regulated profession, to those not enrolled in the journalists' roster. An access examination is provided by law for enrolment in the professional journalists' roster and the journalists' activities are overseen by a professional body.
7   Provvedimento Garante Protezione Dati 29 luglio 1998. Codice di deontologia relativo al trattamento dei dati personali nell'esercizio dell'attività giornalistica ai sensi dell'art 25 della L 31 dicembre 1996, n 675. Gazzetta ufficiale della Repubblica italiana, 3 August 1988.
8   Garante per la protezione dei dati personali, press release of 11 August 1998.

an extremely wide guarantee of the secrecy of correspondence and communications, not limiting it under decency provisions, and barring any intervention from public authorities other than the judiciary. The Constitutional Court has ruled that the provision is to be given a wide construction.[9] The holders of this right are both natural persons and legal entities not having the status of public authorities.[10] Article 15 of the Constitution has been expressly held to apply also to non-EU citizens.[11]

15 Interfering with post

17.19 Looking at, removing or opening post, telegrams, faxes, communications on IT systems, telematic communications, e-mail and any other form of distance communication directed to third parties is a criminal offence under Article 616 of the Penal Code. Courts have applied this provision to anything sent in a sealed envelope not necessarily including a message, such as cheques and photographs.[12] Disclosing such post, telegrams, faxes, communications on IT systems, telematic communications, e-mail and any other form of distance communication without just cause is also a criminal offence under the same provision. Disclosure of the fraudulently acquired content of correspondence intended to be secret is not contemplated by Article 616 is a criminal offence under Article 618 of the Penal Code.

17.20 Article 93 of the Copyright Law provides that letters, collection of letters exchanged, personal memories and other writings of the same nature cannot be published, reproduced or disclosed to the public in any manner without the prior consent of the author, and, in the case of letters or collection of letters, of the recipient, when they have a confidential nature or refer to the intimacy of private life. In the case of death, consent is to be obtained from the relatives of the deceased up to the fourth degree. Under Article 94 of Copyright Law, consent is not necessary when the content of the correspondence is necessary in a civil or criminal case or for the purpose of preservation of personal or familiar honour. As provided by Article 95 of Copyright Law, this protection also applies when the correspondence is a work protected under the general provisions of Copyright Law, and even if such work has come into the public domain. However, official correspondence of the administration or other correspondence which is of special interest to the State is not covered by these provisions.

16 Interception and interruption of telephone calls

17.21 Fraudulent interception or interruption of telephone calls is a criminal offence under Article 617 of the Penal Code. Under the same provision, disclosure of such conversations through any means of communication to the public is also a criminal offence. Installation of telephone interception devices is a criminal offence under Article 617 *bis* of the Penal Code. Interception of communications on an IT or a telematic

9   Corte Costituzionale, 93/81.
10 R Zaccaria *Diritto dell'informazione e della comunicazione*, Padova 1997, 181.
11 Corte di Cassazione, 93/1681.
12 Corte di Cassazione, 69/110215.

system is a criminal offence under Article 617 *quater* of the Penal Code. Under the same provision, disclosure of such communications through any means of communication to the public is also a criminal offence. Installation of devices aimed at intercepting or interrupting communications on an IT or a telematic system is a criminal offence under Article 617 *quinquies* of the Penal Code.

17 Privacy and data protection in telecommunications

17.22   D Lgs 171/98 implementing Directive 97/66/EC extends the provisions of Law 675/96 to the telecommunications sector. In addition, it also establishes a specific set of rules to protect privacy in telecommunications.

D Lgs 171/98 provides for the adoption of minimum standards of internal and network security measures for telecom operators in data processing and handling, in order to protect customers' privacy. The network security measures are to be adopted by telecom operators in co-operation with the incumbent telecom operator managing the public switched telephone service, and disagreements are to be arbitrated by the Communications Authority after consultation with the Data Protection Authority. In applying the principles of Law 675/96 to the telecom sector, D Lgs 171/98 makes non-adoption of minimum security measures a criminal offence, and requires, inter alia, that data on numbers called from every Italian telephone be cancelled after five years' storage. D Lgs 171/98 requires that telecom operators inform users of the service when a lack of security on the system or network exists. Lack of compliance with privacy provisions may, inter alia, result in the licence being suspended by the Ministry of Communications.

18 Junk faxes, calling line identification and use of 'hands-free'

17.23   D Lgs 171/98 also introduces, inter alia, the use of anonymous pre-paid cards for payment of all kinds of telecommunications services, the masking of the last three digits on each statement of numbers called through the telephone operator and the prohibition of automatically sent 'junk faxes' for commercial purposes. It also regulates the use of calling line identification ('CLI') with respect to protection from phone calls. The use of automated faxes and harassing phone calls for marketing purposes without the subscriber's prior consent are made a criminal offence.

D Lgs 171/98 requires that during a telephone conversation the other party be informed of the possibility that the conversation will be heard by third parties. Use of hands-free telephone sets with a loudspeaker without first informing the other party or parties in the conversation, is prohibited.

19 Remedies

17.24   Law 675/96 establishes the possibility of obtaining orders restoring the rights granted under Article 13 thereof (see para **17.07** above) as well as wide civil liability for unfair treatment, disclosure or dissemination of data or for failure to respect the obligations on information or consent.

Contrary to the traditional structure of Italian remedies for damages, Law 675/96 expressly provides for recovery of moral damages in civil suits for violation of the law. In addition, while actions for damages, even in this area, are generally governed by the ordinary rule of the duty of care, Law 675/96 mandates application of Article 2050 of the Civil Code, which establishes an aggrieved test for exemption from liability in the case of dangerous activities. In this case, the defendant is held liable unless he can prove that he adopted all the precautions provided by the state-of-the-art to prevent the event causing damage.[13] The burden of proof in practice shifts to the defendant when Article 2050 applies.

17.25   An injunction restoring the rights granted under Article 13 Law 675/96 can be requested, by the claimant, to courts or to the Data Protection Authority. The Data Protection Authority decides within thirty days from the lodging of the complaint, under a specific quasi-judicial procedure. An injunction of the Data Protection Authority can be opposed before civil courts. Failure to comply with the orders of the Data Protection Authority absent an opposition is a criminal offence under Article 37 Law 675/96. The Data Protection Authority held that its jurisdiction extends to articles published by press. However, a court quashed an order of the Data Protection Authority addressed to a newspaper, holding, inter alia, that a statute empowering a regulatory authority to issue such orders violates the constitutional provisions on freedom of press.[14] The issue remains an open one, as it has not been brought before the Constitutional Court.

17.26   Damages can be claimed before courts only. When a situation occurs which is covered by Law 675/96 or D Lgs 171/98 only, or by the provisions of the Civil Code or other provisions establishing civil liability jointly with Law 675/96 or D Lgs 171/98, an additional claim for moral damages can be made and the burden of proof as regards the duty of care will shift to the defendant. In cases which are covered by the general provisions of the Civil Code or other provisions establishing civil liability, the law does not provide that moral damages can be claimed and the burden of proof does not shift. In cases where a criminal offence is involved moral damages can always be claimed.

17.27   Interim measures can be demanded for the violation of rights of personality. The Constitutional Court has ruled on judicial interim remedies applicable to the press, stating that under Article 21 of the Constitution, press publishing pictures which violate the intimacy of a person can be seized, even under a court order, only when these pictures have an obscene content. Conversely, the Constitutional Court has ruled that a court order to seize photographic pictures held by the press, but not yet published, is constitutionally admissible.[15] The Data Protection Authority can issue interim orders for claims under Article 13 Law 675/96.

17.28   Disciplinary proceedings against professional journalists are conducted at the instance of the regional professional body where the journalist is enrolled, where complaints may be filed.

---

13 Corte di Cassazione, 91/4710.
14 Decisione del Garante per la protezione dei dati personali del 19 aprile 1999 – Giornalismo: richiesta di rettificazione dati personali. Tribunale di Milano, 29 November 1999.
15 Corte Costituzionale, 70/125. Corte Costituzionale, 73/38.

B   Personality

1   Right to one's name

17.29   The right to the name is protected under Article 6 of the Civil Code and Article 21 (2) and (3) of the Trade Mark Law.

Article 6 of the Civil Code provides that every person has the right to their name as attributed by law. Article 6 gives protection both to the right to the exclusive use of the name and to request third parties using the name to identify the bearer of the name. Article 9 of the Civil Code extends the protection to a pseudonym where it has acquired the force of a name.

17.30   The right to one's name is closely connected to the right to personal identity, and the use of a person's likeness in all cases where use of an image is not involved is construed under the legal basis of the right to the name. This set of provisions covers also the right of publicity, construed under Italian law as the right of economic exploitation of the name of the celebrity, while the general right to the proper treatment of the name as personal data is governed by Law 675/96. The protection of the right of publicity is identified by the greater patrimonial content in a claim for damages, but this does not imply the right to exclusively use the name as a trade name.[16] Articles 6 and 7 of the Civil Code have been construed as granting the right of protection of the name also to legal entities, including public sector legal entities.[17] In one case the right to the name was been taken into account in order to grant protection to a publisher with respect to the protection of an electronic identifier on the Internet, which was erroneously qualified as an Internet domain name.[18] The right to one's name is also the only legal basis in Italy for disputes on titles of rank in accordance with Transitory Provision XIV of the Republican Constitution.[19]

Italian trade mark law does not generally forbid the use of another person's name as a trade mark, but it seeks to prevent parasitic reliance on someone else's celebrity.[20]

17.31   Article 21 (2) of the Trade Mark Law provides that names of persons other than the name of the person filing for trade mark registration can be registered as trade marks provided that their use does not affect the fame, credit or honour of the persons having the right to bear these names. The provision also empowers the Patent and Trade Mark Office to require the consent of the person bearing the name or, in the case of his or her death, the consent of relatives up to the fourth degree, before accepting the

---

16   Corte di Cassazione, 93/2740.
17   Corte di Cassazione, 91/1185; Tribunale di Cagliari, 1 June 1988; Tribunale di Milano 9 November 1992, on the applicability to the banner and denomination of *contrade*, the seventeenth century boroughs in the city of Sienna which maintained their identity after the unification of Italy.
18   Tribunale di Modena, 23 October 1996. For a short discussion of the case see P Menchetti *Trademarks and Convergence* in Proceedings of the 1997 European Lawyers' Union International Forum on the Law of Telecommunications, Information Super-Highways and Multimedia (also available at http://www.giuristi.thebrain.net/zaleuco/menchetti.htm).
19   Corte Costituzionale, 67/101, Corte di Cassazione, 91/2426.
20   Corte di Cassazione, 79/1257.

registration. Registration of the trade mark does not, however, affect the use of the name by the holder. Article 21 (3) of the Trade Mark Law forbids, unless consent is given by the rightholder, the registration of a trade mark containing:

(1) a well-known name;

(2) a sign used in the field of art, literature, science, politics or sports;

(3) the denominations and acronyms of events and of non-profit making bodies, as well the emblems of the latter.

Article 21 (3) has been construed by courts as to extend to well-known pseudonyms or religious names.[1]

2   Remedies for unauthorised use of a name

17.32   Article 7 of the Civil Code grants the right to request a cease and desist court order and claim damages in all cases where the name is unlawfully used by third parties and such use may cause prejudice to the bearer of the name. The courts may order the judgment to be published on one or more newspapers. Under Article 9 of the Civil Code, the pseudonym that has acquired the force of a name is subject to protection under the same actions provided by Article 7 of the Civil Code. Under Article 8 of the Civil Code, an action provided by Article 7 may also be raised by a person who is not the bearer of the name, but has a relevant interest because of a family connection. Violation of the rights of publicity by the use of the name of a celebrity carries a cease and desist order and an award of damages. When the name of a celebrity has also been given to a company, as is common in the fashion sector, the action is to be taken by the physical person bearing the name and not by the legal entity.[2] Under Article 8 of the Civil Code, an action with respect to the right to the name can also be raised by members of the family not bearing that name when there is a relevant interest to do so. Before the enactment of Law 675/96 and the liberalisation of the telecommunications market, Articles 6 and 7 of the Civil Code had been construed as the only legal basis for a legal action with respect to the incorrect publication of the name in telephone directories,[3] but requests for judicial interim measures covering rectification of telephone directories have been refused.[4] When a violation of the right to the name occurs which is also covered by the provisions of Law 675/96, moral damages can be awarded. An action for declaration of nullity of a trade mark can be brought for violation of Article 21 of the Trade Mark Law.

3   Right to one's image

17.33   The right to image is protected both under Article 10 of the Civil Code, Articles 96 and 97 of the Copyright Law and Article 21 (1) of the Trade Mark Law. Article 10 of the Civil Code provides for a general protection of the right to one's image and it is customarily read and applied

---

1   Tribunale di Torino, 20 September 1996.
2   Corte di Cassazione, 91/4795.
3   Pretura di Milano, 26 October 1990, Pretura di Udine 21 November 1990.
4   Pretura di Milano, 26 November 1990.

in connection with Article 96 of the Copyright Law, which provides that the portrait of a person cannot be reproduced, exposed or put on the market without the person's consent. These Articles substantially forbid the reproduction and the use of the portrait or the image of an individual without his or her express consent. The right to image is also strictly linked both to the right to personal identity and to the right to privacy. In practice, the same legal basis can cover situations which may be related to protection of privacy, personality and publicity when the right to image is involved. The analysis is made by courts on a case-by-case basis.

17.34 Article 97 of the Copyright Law provides for some fair use exemptions to the prohibitions set forth in Article 96, and these exemptions also apply with respect to Article 10 of the Civil Code. Under Article 96 of the Copyright Law the reproduction of the image of an individual is allowed without his consent where such individual is a celebrity, or when it is associated with a public event. However, this exemption is construed very strictly, and it is allowed by the courts only in the case of fair use of the image for information purposes. The criteria defining information purposes are the general criteria defined under Article 21 of the Constitution, as already examined at para **17.09** above. Therefore, misuse of images collected under reporting activities by the media or press can give rise to action for civil damages on the basis of the right to one's image or personal identity. Courts have, for instance, constantly ruled that publication of images of children associated with criminal events, illness or moral degradation violates the right to one's image as it disproportionately affects the child's likeness.[5]

17.35 A uniform judicial trend tends to exclude from the exemption under Article 97 all cases in which no substantial information is given and the image is commercially exploited, as in advertising.[6] In such cases, the consent of the portrayed person is always necessary. Every use of the image of a celebrity in advertising for which consent has not been given is held by the courts to restrict not only moral rights but also the right of economic exploitation of the image, construed by legal theory as right of publicity, and therefore not covered by the exemption under Article 97 of the Copyright Law.[7] This can also extend to the reproduction of images already legitimately collected in other contexts, such as film clips used in a commercial,[8] the image of a fashion designer used in a commercial in association with a press release issued by him[9] or the image of a physician taken by a medical centre for other purposes and displayed on its advertising leaflet.[10] Use of a double of the celebrity has also been held to be a violation of the right to image and to personal identity.[11]

Borderline situations between informational content and commercial exploitation of the image are decided by courts on a case-by-case approach. For instance, the sale of collection cards with images of football players

---

5   See for instance Pretura di Torino, 3 January 1990, Pretura di Chieri, 3 January 1990, Tribunale dei Minorenni di Catania, 21 June 1990.
6   Corte di Cassazione, 93/1503.
7   Pretura di Perugia, 10 October 1992.
8   Tribunale di Roma, 22 December 1994.
9   Corte di Cassazione, 91/4785.
10   Tribunale di Milano, 7 April 1997.
11   Tribunale di Roma, 28 November 1992.

was held as not to be covered by the exemption of Article 97, since commercial exploitation prevailed over the informational content.[12]

Article 21 (1) of the Trade Mark Law provides that the portrait of a person cannot be registered as a trade mark without his consent, and, after his death, without the consent of the relatives up to the fourth degree. This provision was amended in its present form by the implementation of Directive 89/104/EEC, but was modified only in order to give a more detailed wording, and it substantially maintains the principles contained in the prior text.

4 Remedies for unauthorised use of an image

17.36 Actions for damages can be brought under the law. The courts may order the judgment to be published in one or more newspapers. When a violation of the right to the image occurs which is also covered by the provisions of Law 675/96, the strict liability test of Article 2050 of the Civil Code can be applied and moral damages can be awarded in judicial proceedings. Violation of the rights of publicity involves a higher award of damages for the use of the image of a celebrity. Interim measures of seizure and destruction of images can be awarded. Interim measures for seizure cannot be awarded when the images are published and the publication is assimilated to press because of its informational content, but they can be awarded when the publication does not have an informational content and is therefore assimilated to advertising or other commercial exploitation.[13]

An action for a declaration of nullity of a trade mark can be brought for violation of Article 21 (1) Trade Mark Law.

C   Conclusion

17.37 Before the enactment of Law 675/96 an imbalance existed in the Italian legal system between the very high level of protection granted by the criminal sanctions on illegal interception of communications and the weak protection in tort which existed in the area of privacy not covered by criminal sanctions. As Law 675/96 is probably the toughest piece of legislation on data protection which is currently in force in a EU Member State, its provisions grant an extensive protection to privacy, also in respect of judicial claims for damages and requests for injunctions. Law 675/96 has been amended by nine subsequent statutes in order to smoothen it; however, its formalistic approach, associated with the large number of criminal sanctions punishing violation of specific provisions and with remaining inconsistencies with Directive 95/46/EC, may still cause some difficulties in its practical implementation by the data controllers. Reasonable legal protection exists in Italy in respect of the use of celebrities' name and images for commercial communication, whilst in the area of press and media journalism courts strike the balance between the right to privacy and right to inform on a case-by-case basis.

---

12 Tribunale of di Modena, 18 June 1996.
13 Pretura di Milano, 23 January 1992.

18   JAPAN

Yoshimi Ohara

A   Overview

18.01   In Japan, the right to privacy is typically considered not to include the right to protection of one's likeness and the right to protection of one's name. Each is regarded as a separate constitutional moral right, rather than the latter rights forming a part of a single right to privacy. The right to publicity, on the other hand, although it has an effect similar to the right to protection of one's likeness and the right to protection of one's name, is regarded as a separate economic right, rather than a moral right.

This chapter explains and discusses each of these separate rights:

(1) the right to privacy;

(2) the right to protection of one's likeness;

(3) the right to protection of one's name; and

(4) the right to publicity.

It should be noted that the concepts underlying these rights and the protection afforded by them have only relatively recently been recognised by the courts. The necessary elements to establish the existence of a particular right, the defences and the remedies available are not yet always settled. Where there is no settled precedent, reference is made to lower court decisions and academic views.[1]

---

1   The treatises and books which are referred to in this chapter are as follows; Atsushi Naitoh and Sadayuki Tashiro 'Outline of the Right to Publicity' (1999), Minoru Takeda 'Invasion of privacy and Civil Liability' (1998), Masao Horibe 'Comparative Law on Information Disclosure and privacy' (1997), Takeshi Kawai 'Infringement of the Right to protection of Name' in *Lecture of Modern Compensation Law II* (1972), Kensuke Kobori 'Moral Rights of Well Known Figures' in *Lecture of Modern Compensation Law II* (1972), Tsuneo Matsumoto 'Customer List in Direct Marketing and privacy' in *Hanrei-Times*, vol 840 (1994), and Zen Tatsumura 'Current Status and problems of protection of Right to publicity' in *Copyright* No 415, vol 35 Number 7 (1995). These treatises and books are all written in Japanese.

B The right to privacy

1 Outline of the right to privacy

18.02 Although the constitution does not explicitly provide for the 'right to privacy' and although the Supreme Court has never used the term the 'right to privacy', many lower court decisions and academics have recognised a constitutional moral right to privacy for individuals as one of the 'rights to pursue happiness' as set forth in Article 13. There is no specific statute of general application such as a 'privacy act' which aims to protect privacy and therefore, the right is protected by means of the general legal doctrine of tort pursuant to the Civil Code.

To date, the extent and the scope of this right has not yet been determined. The conventional opinion is that a right to privacy is the right to be left alone, ie, the right to protection against undue invasion into, including disclosure of, one's private life. Recently, significantly more academics believe that the right to privacy also includes an active element, that being the right to certain controls in respect of one's own personal data, more precisely:

(1) the right to control the way that personal data is acquired, and used;

(2) the right to request disclosure of personal data; and

(3) the right to request that corrections be made to inaccurate, untimely or incomplete personal data.

This view is primarily the result of a massive increase in data collection by both the government and private entities, particularly through the utilisation of computer technology. The issue of data privacy is discussed separately in paras **18.25** and **18.26** below.

2 What constitutes an invasion of privacy?

18.03 In Japan a substantial amount of the litigation with respect to invasion of privacy relates to tabloid articles or so-called 'model novels'[2] which have disclosed a person's private matters to the public. Therefore, this section initially focuses on situations where a person's private matters have been exposed to the public and then refers to the other types of privacy invasions.

The disclosure of certain aspects of a person's private life constitutes a tort. The elements necessary to constitute this tort were set out in the *Utageno Ato* case[3] and have been subsequently supported by numerous judicial decisions. Essentially, the elements necessary to constitute this tort, include:

(1) disclosure has been made of certain facts, or matters that may be viewed as facts, about a person's private life;

---

2 The so-called 'model novel' is different from a biography. It is a novel using an actual person (not necessarily a famous figure) as the model of a character in the novel, but at the same time it usually contains some fictitious aspects.

3 Tokyo District Court, 28 September 1964, *Hanrei-Jiho* vol 385, p 12 (*Utageno Ato* case). This case involved a model novel written by Yukio Mishima which used as a model a former foreign minister who was also a former candidate for the governor of Tokyo Metropolitan City: *Namonaki Michiwo* case.

(2) the information disclosed must be of the type that the ordinary person would not wish to have disclosed about themselves (based on the ordinary person's level of sensitivity), in other words information, disclosure of which would cause mental suffering to the ordinary person; and

(3) the information must not yet have been disclosed to the public.

The issue of whether or not certain matters that have been disclosed to the public may be viewed as facts about a person's private life typically arises in model novel cases because a model novel mingles facts and fiction about a person's private life. In one case where a model novel referred to a person's private affairs and readers were able to recognise who the model was, the court held that the right to privacy is not breached if the character and activities of the model were modified to the extent that readers consider it to be a fictional novel in its entirety, more particularly readers do not view the descriptions about the person's private affairs in the novel as actual facts about the model's private life.[4] Further, another court precedent held that the right to privacy is breached if fact and fiction in a model novel are co-mingled to the extent that these two aspects become indistinguishable and they provide any information which ordinary people would not wish to have disclosed.[5]

The question of which aspects of a person's private life, if disclosed, would constitute an invasion of privacy is difficult to answer. Although the answer varies depending upon the manner and context of the disclosure, the courts have found that disclosure of the following matters constitutes an invasion of privacy: age, home address, home telephone number, profession, office address, office telephone number, educational background, professional background, criminal record, medical record (HIV positive), financial record (value of savings), romantic affairs, family problems and lists of books to which one subscribes.

Please note that 'disclosure' in the context of privacy invasion is not limited to disclosure to the public, but also includes disclosure to any number of people depending on the context of disclosure. Thus disclosure of certain of a person's private matters to merely one person could satisfy the requirement of 'disclosure'.[6] Basically the information, disclosure of which violates the right to privacy, must not yet have been disclosed to the public. However, even if certain private information has been disclosed to the public for a certain purpose, the same information could still be protected under the right to privacy for other purposes. In a case involving an eye doctor whose private information (such as his name, occupation, telephone number and address of his clinic) was disclosed on a net bulletin board causing harassment to the eye doctor, although the eye doctor published an advertisement containing the same information in a directory of a telephone company, the court still found an invasion of privacy, reasoning that the name, occupation, address and telephone number of the clinic in the advertisement is, in a sense, disclosed to only those who wish to see an eye doctor and not yet disclosed to the general public.[7]

---

4 Tokyo District Court, 19 May 1995, *Hanrei-Jiho*, vol 1550, p 49(*Namonaki Michiwo* case).
5 Osaka District Court, 19 December 1995, *Hanrei-Jiho*, vol 1583, p 98, supported in Osaka High Court, 8 August 1997, *Hanrei-Jiho*, vol 1631, p 80 (*Sousa Ikkachou* case).
6 Tokyo District Court, 29 August 1990, *Hanrei-Jiho*, vol 1382, p 92.
7 Kobe District Court, 23 June 1999, *Hanrei-Jiho*, vol 1700, p 99.

3 Other types of privacy invasion

18.04 Set out below is an alphabetical list of other conceivable situations involving an invasion of privacy. Other than the building construction case explained in para **18.05**, both published court cases or academic discussions of such types of privacy invasion are almost non-existent. Hence, the elements of these offences have not yet been determined. However, a court would recognise that privacy has been invaded in each of the following situations, provided that the ordinary person would feel unease or pressure in relation to such conduct, based on the ordinary person's level of sensitivity, considering the particular manner, nature and situation of the conduct.

Construction of a building close to an existing residence

18.05 In Japan the most typical type of privacy invasion dispute to be litigated, other than disclosure of a person's private matters, involves the situation where a new building is constructed close to an existing residence, which enables the residents of the new building to look into the next-door residence and observe the internal goings on. In fact, the Civil Code obligates a person who constructs a building at a distance of less than one metre from the boundary to erect screens over windows or verandas that overlook the adjoining property of another person (Article 235, para 1). This type of privacy invasion does not always constitute a tort. In order to determine whether or not such an invasion is 'tortious', the courts have designed a test that asks whether the particular interference with one's privacy exceeds the level of what a reasonable person should endure in society, or not. This threshold level is based upon the idea that in our society, where many people live in close proximity, it is impossible to entirely eliminate intervention into one's private life by third parties and secure complete privacy. Thus an award of damages and/or any equitable relief is available only to those who have suffered an invasion of privacy in excess of such level. The level varies depending on the type and necessity of the new building, the residential surroundings and various other factors. In cases where the courts have found that a tortious invasion of privacy existed, proprietors of the new building were requested to alter the building plans or to take other appropriate measures to prevent privacy invasion (eg placing screens on the windows of the new building which face the existing residence).

Filming on private property

18.06 Filming a person's private life on private property may constitute a tort depending on the manner of the conduct. In addition, as discussed in detail below in para **18.27** et seq, filming a person on his or her property such as at his or her personal residence would likely constitute a tortious infringement of the right to protection of one's likeness. Entering private property for the purpose of filming may itself constitute the tort of trespass, should it be against the will of the legitimate occupants of the property and if the manner of entrance intrudes on their privacy. Such trespass may also violate the Penal Code resulting in up to three years' imprisonment or up to a ¥100,000 fine (Article 130).

Filming over private property (from the air)

18.07 Like filming on private property, filming a person's private life over private property may constitute a tortious invasion of privacy depending upon the manner of the conduct. In addition, aerial filming of a person on his or her property such as at his or her residence, would be likely to constitute a tortious infringement of the right to protection of one's likeness.

Interception of mail

18.08   To intercept mail and to identify the content, sender or recipient of such mail may constitute a tortious invasion of privacy. Provided that the intercepted mail is being handled by the Ministry of Posts and Telecommunications, this type of conduct is in breach of the Mail Law (*Yubin Hô*) and results in up to one year imprisonment or up to a ¥200,000 fine (Articles 9 and 80).[8] In addition, the unauthorised opening of a sealed letter without any justifiable reasons breaches the Penal Code which can also result in up to one year imprisonment or up to a ¥200,000 fine (Article 133). If the letter in question is being handled by the Ministry, such action will also violate the Mail Law resulting in up to three years' imprisonment or up to a ¥500,000 fine (Article 77).

Interception of telephone conversations

18.09   Interception of telephone conversations constitutes a tortious invasion of privacy of the parties to such a telephone conversation. In addition, provided that the intercepted telephone conversation is being handled by telecommunications carrier, the interception is in breach of the Telecommunications Business Law (*Denki Tsushin Jigyô Hô*)(Article 4, para 1).[9] This can result in up to one year's imprisonment or up to a ¥300,000 fine (Article 104, para 1).

Peeping into another's residence

18.10   To peep into another person's residence may constitute a tortious invasion of privacy depending on the circumstances and the manner of the conduct. In addition, it may breach the Minor Offence Law (*Kei-Hanzai Hô*), which can result in less than 30-day imprisonment or a fine of less than ¥10,000 (Article 1, item 23).

Recording of conversations

18.11   The recording of a conversation by a party other than parties to the conversation without consent may constitute a tortious invasion of privacy, should the recording occur in a situation where the ordinary person may reasonably expect privacy in light of the content, place and context of

---

8   The Mail Law prohibits anyone from invading the 'secrecy of mail being handled by the Ministry of Posts and Telecommunications'. Therefore the interception of mail that has already been delivered to the mailbox of the recipient does not violate the law.
9   The Telecommunications Business Law prohibits anyone from invading the secrecy of telecommunications being handled by telecommunications carriers. 'Telecommunications being handled by telecommunications carriers' means those telecommunications being controlled by a telecommunications carrier, such as a telephone company. For example, recording a telephone conversation by way of installing a hidden microphone in a handset does not breach the law because a handset is not controlled by a telecommunications carrier. Also, the secrecy of a communication can only be invaded by a party other than parties to the communication. Therefore, the recording of a communication by a party to that communication does not constitute a violation of the law.

the conversation. The recording of a conversation by a party to the conversation without consent of the other party may also constitute a tort depending on the context of the conversations and the recording.[10] However, academic discussions are divided on whether such conduct breaches the right to privacy or other rights of the other party to the conversation. Some scholars argue that it does not breach the right to privacy because the other party to the conversation has disclosed his or her personal information or any other matters at his or her will during the conversations.

Sifting through rubbish

18.12 Sifting through a person's rubbish may constitute a tortious invasion of privacy depending on the manner and context of the conduct. For example, to sift through a person's rubbish to investigate his or her activities or private life is likely to constitute an invasion of privacy.

Staking out

18.13 Staking out may constitute a tortious invasion of privacy depending on the manner and context of the conduct. In one instance, the Supreme Court recognised that a tortious invasion of privacy had occurred when an employer staked out an employee who was a member of the communist party and monitored his activities.[11] Such conduct could also violate the Minor Offence Law which can result in less than 30 days' imprisonment or a fine of less than ¥10,000 (Article 1, para 1, item 28).

Use of an assumed identity to obtain information

18.14 To obtain information by the use of an assumed identity will constitute an invasion of privacy if:

(1) the person would not have provided the information if he or she knew the real identity; and

(2) the information provided relates to a person's private life and is protected by the right to privacy as described above in para **18.03**.

In one case where a newspaper reporter interviewed a detained suspect whilst disguised as a housewife who was interested in the impact of a certain law on detained suspects, a lower court recognised that there had been an invasion of privacy.[12] The court held that, in principle, newspaper reporters should disclose their identity when gathering data for reporting purposes if the right to privacy protects the information gathered.

Use of a security camera for reporting events

18.15 The use of a security camera for any purpose may constitute an invasion of privacy depending on the manner and the place where the camera is installed. Whether or not any defence is available to such use depends

---

10 In one case where a newspaper reporter secretly recorded an interview for the sake of ensuring accuracy, the Supreme Court held that such secret recording of the conversation without consent of the other party was not illegal. Supreme Court, 20 November 1981, *Hanrei-Jiho*, vol 1024, p 128.

11 Supreme Court, 5 September 1995, *Hanrei-Jiho*, vol 1546, p 115.

12 Tokyo District Court, 29 July 1991, *Hanrei-Jiho*, vol 1400, p 70.

upon the purpose and other factors. A defence is likely to be available for the use of a security camera for security purposes so long as the need for security protection and the manner of use of the security camera in light of such purpose can be considered as reasonable. The freedom of speech defence may be available to the use of the security camera for reporting purposes. The requirements of the freedom of speech defence are discussed in detail in para **18.17**.

Use of a telephoto lens

18.16   To observe a person's activities or private life by using a telephoto lens may constitute an invasion of privacy depending on the manner and context of such conduct. In addition, peeping into another's residence by the use of a telephoto lens may breach the Minor Offence Law and may result in less than 30 days' imprisonment or a fine of less than ¥10,000 (Article 1, item 23).

4   Defences

Freedom of speech

18.17   The most important defence to allegations of an invasion of privacy is the defence of freedom of speech. In addition to the right to privacy, freedom of speech is also regarded as one of the fundamental human rights which is pivotal to democracy. The issue, therefore, is how to balance these two rights. In order to achieve a balance, the courts have considered the following issues:

(1)   whether the disclosed personal information is of due social concern;

(2)   whether disclosure was for a public purpose; and

(3)   whether the manner of the disclosure was proper in light of the purpose of the disclosure.

For example, it has been held that facts related to crimes are, in principle, of due social concern. However, facts related to the family of the criminal suspect are not regarded in a similar light, unless such facts are essential to specify the crime(s) or are necessary to understand the motive behind such crime(s).[13] As a further example, a criminal record is, in principle, regarded as of no due social concern if a number of years have passed since the crime was committed and the criminal has already served a sentence, even if such crime was publicly reported at the time the crime was committed.[14] Private affairs of people who engage in certain social activities could be of due social concern. In one case, the court found that a sex scandal involving a medical professor working at a private university who was also a Rotarian

---

13   Tokyo District Court, 14 April 1995, *Hanrei-Jiho*, vol 1547, p 88.

14   Tokyo High Court, 5 September 1989, *Hanrei-Jiho*, vol 1323, p 37 (*Gyakuten* case). This case involved a non-fiction novel which covered a crime actually committed more than ten years prior and used the actual name of the criminal. The court held that a criminal has a legitimate interest in keeping his or her criminal record unrevealed for rehabilitation purposes, while societal concern over the crime gradually lessens when many years have passed since the crime was committed.

was of due social concern.[15] The reason for this decision being that the professor had the power to influence society in general through his educational and research activities therefore his social activities were of due social concern. Further, the fact that the chairman of a well-known consumer finance company was suffering from an unknown disease was also found to be of due social concern as the chairman influenced people's lives through his control over the company.[16]

Consent

18.18 Having the consent of those whose private matters have been disclosed is, of course, an effective defence. However, in order to constitute an effective defence, consent should be procured from all the relevant parties involved in the matter. In one court case, a famous actress consented to newspapers printing articles about her trouble with her husband while the newspaper did not procure consent from her husband.[17] The court found that there had been an invasion of her husband's privacy.

5   Remedies

Award of damages

18.19 The amount of damages awarded in tort cases is generally very small and there are no exceptions to this with regard to victims of privacy invasion. In general the courts have awarded victims damages amounting in tens of thousands to a few million yen, including compensation for legal fees incurred by the victim. Compensation for legal fees is also very limited, generally being somewhere between tens of thousands and hundreds of thousands, regardless of the amount of the legal fees actually incurred. Nowadays, there is substantial criticism of the pitiful amount of damages typically awarded. The major reason behind such criticism is that in the majority of instances, large media companies invade privacy and such amounts mean nothing to them. In fact, as only a small amount of damages are ever awarded, the media can value the risk of invading privacy as being at most a few million yen, and this simply encourages them. Despite significant criticism, court practices have not yet changed.

Injunction

18.20 In principle, a person whose moral right is about to be, or is being infringed is entitled to injunctive relief and thus prevailing academics hold the view that injunctive relief should be also available as a remedy to avoid imminent infringements, or to eliminate on-going infringements, of the right to privacy, one of the moral rights. In fact injunction can be a very crucial remedy for those whose right to privacy is about to be, or is being infringed. On the other hand, injunction, particularly one enjoining publication in advance, is also regarded as a critical threat to freedom of speech, because such injunction could completely deprive people of the

---

15 Tokyo District Court, 28 February 1987, *Hanrei-Jiho*, vol 1242, p 76.
16 Tokyo District Court, 22 May 1990, *Hanrei-Jiho*, vol 1357, p 93.
17 Tokyo District Court, 22 September 1993, *Hanrei-Times*, vol 843, p 234.

opportunity to express their ideas. Thus, the issue arises as to when advance injunction should be available. In a defamation case, the Supreme Court held that, in light of the prohibition of censorship in the Constitution, advance injunction may be granted only when:

(1) defamatory description is false or the description is apparently not for any due public purpose; and

(2) the victim would sustain serious and irremediable damage as a result of the publication.[18]

In reference to the above Supreme Court decision, the lower court held that injunction prohibiting the release of publication invading privacy is only available if:

(1) the content is apparently false or that the description is apparently not for any due public purpose; and

(2) a victim would sustain serious and irremediable damage as a result of the publication.[19]

In this case a private high school and its principal as co-applicants applied for an injunction prohibiting the release of a book that criticised them, the court applied the above criteria to the case and granted only deletion of certain descriptions, rather than an injunction of the entire publication.

Further remedy

18.21 In Japan, compensation by way of damages is the typical remedy available to victims of torts and only those who suffer, or are about to suffer, an infringement of certain rights (such as moral rights, including the right to privacy), are entitled to apply for injunctive relief. Interestingly however, in cases of defamation, the Civil Code provides a special remedy in addition to these two types of remedies. The court may order the defaming party to take any measures necessary to reinstate the defamed party's fame or reputation. The most typical 'reinstatement measure' is the publication of a notice of apology notifying the public that the article/statement was inaccurate and defamatory, and apologising for such defamation. Although defamatory articles often contain descriptions that also invade the privacy of the defamed party, the Code does not offer this type of remedy in the event of an invasion of privacy. Thus, the issue arises as to whether such remedy can be utilised in circumstances such as where there is only an invasion of privacy.

Court precedents and prevailing academics hold the view that such a remedy is not available to victims of an invasion of privacy. This is due to the fact that once personal matters are disclosed to the public, publication of any notice of apology simply has the effect of repeating the disclosure of the private matters previously disclosed and will not have the effect of 'reinstating' the status which the party enjoyed prior to the information being disclosed. In fact, several victims have requested an apology from people who have invaded their privacy. However, the courts have rejected such requests, reasoning that this type of remedy is not intended to provide

---

18 Supreme Court, 11 June 1986, *Hanrei-Times* No 605, p 42 (*Hoppou Journal* case).
19 Tokyo District Court, 24 March 1989, *Hanrei-Times*, vol 713, p 94.

the right for a victim to request a subjective apology from the defaming party, but to provide a right for the defamed party to attempt to recover their status by publishing a notice that the defamatory description was inaccurate, which cannot be achieved in the case of an invasion of privacy, as described above.

6   Who enjoys the right to privacy?

Public figures

18.22   Public figures enjoy less protection of their privacy than ordinary people by virtue of the so-called 'public figure theory' and the freedom of speech defence. Pursuant to the public figure theory, those whose activities attract public attention and who become 'public figures' are deemed to have waived a certain amount of privacy protection. Although in dictum some lower courts seem to have accepted this theory as a general rule, we are not aware of any published court decisions that have rejected an alleged invasion of privacy based on this theory. Nor has there been any sufficient academic analysis of this theory and thus who constitutes a public figure and to what extent public figures are deemed to have waived protection of their privacy, has not yet been established.[20] In addition to the 'public figure theory', certain public figures, such as publicly-elected officials or election candidates, often encounter successful freedom of speech defences to their allegations of an invasion of privacy. This is because, in many cases, their private matters could be regarded as being of due social concern so long as the matters in question are necessary and effective for evaluating or criticising that person's public activities.

The deceased

18.23   The deceased do not enjoy protection against an invasion of their privacy if the invasion is committed after that person's death. The right to privacy is regarded as a moral right which is neither alienable nor assignable and can only be enjoyed by the person in question.[1] Therefore, theoretically speaking, the members of the deceased person's family cannot claim damages that could be sustained by the deceased if he or she were alive at the time of an invasion of their privacy, based on a claim of an invasion of the deceased's privacy. However, family members are entitled to compensation for their own suffering (ie mental anguish) caused by conduct that would constitute an invasion of the deceased's privacy if the deceased were still alive at the time of such conduct.

---

20   One lower court case discussed some examples of what type of privacy protection public figures do and do not enjoy. The case involved a successful injunction on the publication of books featuring various data of well-known actresses (including date of birth, blood type, hobbies as well as maps to their homes and pictures of their homes so that their fans could follow them). Although the court did not explicitly adopt the 'public figure theory', it held that disclosure of date of birth, blood type and hobbies did not constitute an invasion of privacy. On the other hand the court found that disclosure of home addresses and pictures of their homes interfered with their private lives and therefore it constituted an invasion of privacy and accordingly the court granted the injunction to prohibit publication of the books. Kobe District Court, Amagasaki branch, 12 February 1997, *Hanrei-Jiho*, vol 1604, p 127.

1   Osaka District Court, 27 December 1989, *Hanrei-Jiho*, vol 1341, p 53.

Citizens of foreign states

18.24   The Supreme Court has held that citizens of foreign states also enjoy the fundamental human rights provided for in the Constitution as long as that such rights are not by their nature only available to Japanese citizens.[2] The right to privacy as described above is not by its nature only available to Japanese citizens and thus citizens of foreign states may likely enjoy it.

7   *Data protection*

Legislative movement

18.25   Due to recent rapid increases in the collection of massive amounts of personal information by both the government and the private sector, especially through the utilisation of computer technology, the protection of personal information as a part of the right to privacy has come into focus more and more frequently. Protection of personal information includes not only a conventional right, ie the right to prevent disclosure of personal information, but also includes the right to control the way personal data is acquired and used, the right to request disclosure of personal data, and the right to request that corrections be made to inaccurate, untimely or incomplete personal data.

In spite of heated discussions on the current need for the above types of protection for personal data, legislation and judicial precedents have not yet been developed to bring about such comprehensive protection. In terms of legislation, for example, there is the so-called Personal Data Protection Law (*Kojin Jôhô Hogo Hô*) which was enacted in 1988. However, this law only applies to personal data held by national administrative organisations which is controlled through computer processing. In addition, although this law provides individuals with the right to request disclosure of data about themselves held by the government, certain sensitive data (including individual medical and criminal records) was not subject to such right. Moreover the law does not provide individuals with the right to request corrections to data about themselves.

Currently, there is no law regulating treatment of personal information collected and databased by the private sector in general.[3] Certain ministries have set out guidelines regarding the protection of private data and these have been directed to business entities within that ministry's jurisdiction. Unlike the Personal Data Privacy Protection Law, these guidelines provide for a more comprehensive protection of personal data. For example, some guidelines not only restrict the way that personal information is acquired, stored, used and disclosed, but they also require that data should be up-to-date and accurate. In addition, they also provide that upon the request of an individual, entities that have collected the individual's information should,

---

2   Supreme Court, 4 October 1978, *Minshu*, vol 32, No 7, p 1223.
3   Some special laws provide limited data-privacy protection in certain private sectors. For instance, Law on the Regulation of Credit and Loan Business (*Kashikin Kisei Gyô Hô*)(art 30) and Instalment Sales Law (*Kappu Hanbai Hô*)(art 42 *bis* 4) prohibit moneylenders, credit sales companies and credit information organisations from using customers' credit information other than for the purpose of investigating their solvency.

to the greatest extent possible, disclose that information to such an individual and facilitate the correction of any inaccurate information. However, these are mere guidelines and they fail to contain any sanctions or enforcement measures in the event that they are breached.

In response to the strong societal concerns about massive storage, distribution and usage of personal data via information telecommunication technology, on October 11 2000, the Japanese government issued the 'General Principles of Personal Data Protection Basic Law', which outlines a personal data protection policy to be implemented by legislation ('General Principles').[4] The personal data protection policy constitutes five basic rules applicable to both public and private institutions ('Basic Rules'), to:

(1) specify purposes for using personal data and handle personal data only to fufill the specified purposes;

(2) obtain personal data by lawful and proper means;

(3) keep personal data accurate and updated to the extent necessary for the specified purposes;

(4) take appropriate measures to protect collected personal data by security safeguards; and

(5) keep transparent the way personal data is handled.

The General Principles provide that the government should implement the Basic Rules as to personal data collected by the government by way of new legislation or amendment of existing laws. On the other hand they take a position that the private sector should protect personal data privacy primarily through their own self-regulation rather than through legislation. In this connection the General Principles list minimum obligations of the private sector regarding personal data privacy to be implemented in their self-regulation. The obligations of the private sector to handle personal data ('Parties') set forth in the General Principles are as follows:

(1) **Limitation on using personal data in light of purposes**:
   (i) Parties should specify purposes for using personal data and acquire, process, and otherwise handle personal data only to fulfill the specified purposes. Parties may not unreasonably amend the specified purposes.
   (ii) Parties should notify, announce or otherwise make available their specified purposes, unless such notification or announcement might impede the legitimate interests or proper undertakings of Parties. In case of the prior consent of the data subject or urgent need to protect lives, bodies, or assets, the above obligations are exempted;

(2) **Proper Acquisition**: Parties should acquire personal data by lawful and proper means;

(3) **Proper Management**: Parties should strive to keep personal data accurate and updated to the extent necessary for the specified purposes for utilising personal data. Parties should strive to take necessary measures to protect personal data privacy and should properly supervise their employees and third party contractors that are engaged in handling personal data on behalf of the parties;

4   http://www.kantei.go.jp/jp/it/privacy/houseika/taikouan/1011taikous.html.

(4) **Limitation on distribution of personal data**: Parties may not distribute personal data to third parties without the prior consent of the data subject or urgent necessity to protect lives, bodies or assets;[5]

(5) **Announcement**: Parties should announce the purposes for handling personal data, the identity of Parties in charge of handling personal data, the procedures for individuals to request disclosure of their personal data, and any other matters necessary to protect data privacy, unless such announcement might impede the legitimate interests or proper undertakings of Parties or Parties individually notify the data subject thereof. Parties should announce any changes to the above listed information unless the changes are minor or Parties individually notify the data subject thereof;

(6) **Disclosure**: At the request of individuals, Parties should disclose personal data about the requesting parties, unless such disclosure might endanger the lives, bodies or assets of the requesting parties or any other parties or impede the legitimate interests of proper undertakings of the Parties. In case Parties do not disclose all or any part of personal data in spite of the request, Parties should so notify the requesting parties and strive to explain the reasons therefore;

(7) **Correction**: In the event individuals request Parties to correct and/or update personal data about the requesting parties, and Parties find such requests legitimate, the Parties should correct, add, delete personal data or take other appropriate measures to the extent necessary for the specified purposes, unless such corrections might endanger the lives, bodies or assets of the requesting parties or any third parties or impede the legitimate interests or proper undertakings of Parties. In case Parties do not correct all or any part of personal data in spite of the request, Parties should so notify the requesting parties and strive to explain the reasons therefore;

(8) **Suspension of using personal data**: In the event that individuals request Parties to suspend using personal data about the requesting parties due to Parties' breach of the obligations set forth in items (1)(i), (2) or (4) and Parties find such requests legitimate, Parties should suspend the use of, delete personal data or take any other appropriate measures, unless such supension might endanger the lives, bodies or assets of the requesting parties orany third parties or impede the legitimate interests or proper undertakings of Parties. In case parties do not correct all or part of personal data in spite of the request, Parties should so notify the requesting parties and strive to explain the reasons therefore;

---

5   The obligations set forth in item (iv) are not applicable in cases of which; (a) Parties transferring personal data as one of the assets to be transferred in the course of a business transfer, splitting companies or the like; (b) third parties handling personal data, either together with Parties or under a subcontracting arrangement to implement the purposes of handling personal data specified by Parties; (c) Parties exchanging persoinal data with certain other parties if Parties properly notify, or announce to, individuals regarding purposes for exchanging data as well as parties to which data is exchanged; and (d) Parties collecting personal data for the purposes of distributing to third parties, ensuring that they cease distributing personal data or take any appropriate measures at the request of individuals and notify or announce to individuals, the way personal data is distributed and the fact that they may cease distribution of personal data to third parties or take any appropriate measures upon the individuals' request.

(9) **Complaint processing**: Parties should strive to establish any necessary system to handle compaints regarding personal data privacy and to process those complaints in a proper and expeditious manner;

(10) **Organisations handling complaints**: Parties may establish organisations (consisting of Parties) to handle complaints regarding personal data privacy; and

(11) **Ministers involvement**: Competent ministers may authorise the establishment of organisations to handle complaints regarding personal data privacy. The ministers may request Parties or authorised organisations to submit reports and may provide advice or instructions to improve implementation of the above obligations.

Please note that parties subject to the above obligations are limited to those that utilise a database of personal data in their undertakings and parties in the field of the press, religion, academia and politics are explicitly exempted from the above obligations. On the other hand, the General Principles set forth only minimum obligations of the above parties, and the government may impose heavier obligations on those who handle certain sensitive personal data. The legislation to implement the General Principles is expected to come in due course.

Court cases on data protection

18.26   In the absence of laws providing comprehensive protection of data privacy, several courts have indicated availability of general legal doctrines, such as contract and/or tort, to ensure data protection as described below, although with one exception every plaintiff lost in the following cases.

With respect to the right to control the way that personal information is used or disclosed, in one case, a trust bank allegedly disclosed its customer's credit and asset information to a housing corporation and then the two together organised a seminar on asset management and invited customers to attend. The court found banks have an obligation to keep certain customer data (such as credit information, savings data, asset information and other private information) confidential and disclosure of such information to any third party without justifiable reason, constitutes breach of contract and/or tort.[6] In another case, a department store disclosed the profession and work telephone number of one of its customers. In those circumstances, the court found that information about a person's occupation and office telephone numbers is personal information and disclosure of such to any third party, without justifiable reason, constitutes a tortious invasion of privacy.[7]

With respect to protection to ensure the accuracy of information, the courts have found that it constitutes a breach of contract to release inaccurate credit information. In one case a credit company released information regarding a customer's default on a loan to a credit information company. This occurred despite the fact that the customer was in default due to an error in the credit company's internal systems. Here, the court found that the credit company had a special obligation to ensure that customers' credit information was accurate, so as not to damage a customer's credibility.[8]

6   Tokyo District Court, 28 March 1991, *Hanrei-Jiho*, vol 1382, p 98.
7   Tokyo District Court, 29 August 1990, *Hanrei-Jiho*, vol 1382, p 92.
8   Osaka District Court, 23 July 1990, *Hanrei-Jiho*, vol 1362, p 97.

With respect to the right to request correction of one's own personal information, in one case, the court found that an individual may request correction of his or her own inaccurate personal information if inaccuracy would cause harm to that person in excess of the level of what the ordinary person should endure in society.[9] In addition, it held that in determining whether or not a correction request should be granted, the court should balance the potential impact of the inaccurate information on the individual and the potential impact of facilitating the correction on those being requested to correct the information.

Although the above court cases do not encompass all the issues surrounding personal data privacy, in the absence of adequate legislation to protect personal data, such cases certainly indicate the possibility of protecting data privacy through existing legal doctrines.

C   The right to protection of one's likeness

1   Outline of the right to protection of one's likeness

18.27   Although the Constitution does not explicitly provide for a right to protection of one's likeness, the Supreme Court has recognised the freedom to not have pictures of one's face or body unduly taken.[10] Lower court decisions and academics both recognise this as a constitutional moral right and that it includes the right to protection against undue disclosure of pictures once taken. Further the right to protection of one's likeness is not limited to restrictions about photos, but also includes restrictions on any method of utilising or disclosing someone's likeness, including creating a statue.

Like the right to privacy, there is no specific law that aims to protect the right to protection of one's likeness and therefore, the right is protected by means of the general legal doctrine of tort. However, the concept of the right to protection of one's likeness is reflected in other laws. For example, the Japanese trademark law does not allow registration of a trademark which includes the likeness of other persons without first obtaining their consent (Article 4, para 1, item 8). Even if the applicant is allowed to register another person's likeness as a trademark with such person's consent, the trademark owner may not prevent them from using their own likeness as a trademark (Article 26, para 1, item 1).

The test that determines whether the taking or disclosure of certain photographs is undue, is whether or not such conduct would cause suffering (such as feeling uncomfortable, shameful or humiliated) to the victim, based upon the ordinary person's level of sensitivity. It also takes into account the manner, place and other circumstances of the filming as well as the position of the victim when the photo was taken. For instance, in one case, the court found that there had been an infringement of the right to protect one's

---

9   Tokyo High Court, 24 March 1988, *Hanrei-Jiho*, vol 1268, p 15.
10   Supreme Court, 24 December 1969, *Hanrei-Jiho*, vol 577, p18.

likeness where a tabloid magazine photographer had stretched up over a wall and taken a picture of a woman cooking at home in her kitchen.[11] In another case where a tabloid magazine photographer had taken a picture of the chairman of a consumer finance company sitting in a wheelchair in the hospital where he was hospitalised, the court again found that there had been an infringement of the right to protect one's likeness.[12] The court reasoned that a hospital, being a place where people disclose confidential information to doctors in order to receive proper medical treatment, should be regarded in the same manner as a private residence. However, even when the pictures are taken in a public space, the court sometimes finds that an infringement of this right has occurred. The courts can take other factors, including the manner of the filming and the position of the victim into consideration. In one case where a woman who was mistaken as a member of a controversial religious group, was filmed walking along a street by means of a hidden camera, the court recognised an infringement of the right to protection of her likeness.[13] Also in a case where a criminal suspect being escorted by police officers in a public place was filmed, the court found that there had been an infringement of the right to protection of one's likeness and then further examined whether or not defences were available.[14]

2   Defences

18.28   As in the invasion of privacy cases, the most important defence is again freedom of speech. The defence of freedom of speech is available when:

(1)   the subject of the picture relates to an issue that is of due public interest;

(2)   the picture was taken or disclosed for a valid public purpose; and

(3)   the taking of the photograph or the disclosure of pictures was appropriate and necessary in order to achieve such valid public purpose.

For example, disclosing pictures of a criminal suspect was found to be of due social concern. However, in cases where tabloid magazines featured a picture of a male criminal suspect who was completely naked without any retouches and a female criminal suspect only wearing a swimsuit, the courts did not allow any defences.[15] A picture of a medical professor who was involved in an infamous sex scandal[16] and a picture of a person who was evading taxes[17] were found to be of due public interest. On the other hand, a picture of the fiancée of a famous novelist was found not to be of due public interest, on the basis that the subject had no connection with the

11   Tokyo District Court, 23 June 1989, *Hanrei-Jiho*, vol 1319, p 132.
12   Tokyo District Court, 22 May 1990, *Hanrei-Jiho*, vol 1357, p 93.
13   Tokyo District Court, 15 June 1987, *Hanrei-Jiho*, vol 1243, p 54.
14   Tokyo High Court, 24 November 1993, *Hanrei-Jiho*, vol 1491, p 99.
15   Tokyo District Court, 14 March 1990, *Hanrei-Jiho*, vol 1357, p 85, Tokyo District Court, 31 January 1994, *Hanrei-Times*, vol 827, p 186.
16   Tokyo District Court, 28 February 1987, *Hanrei-Jiho*, vol 1242, p 76.
17   Tokyo District Court, 29 February 1996, *Hanrei-Times*, vol 915, p 190.

novelist's social and literary activities or reviews of these.[18]

Pictures of a person's likeness are often published together with an article that relates to the person so that the article may send a clearer and livelier message to the public. In such cases the courts have often considered whether or not the pictures of the person are necessary and essential to the article to which they relate. In the case where a tabloid magazine ran a feature on the chairman of a consumer finance company who was hospitalised, together with a picture of him sitting in a wheelchair in the hospital corridor, the court allowed the defence of freedom of speech with respect to the article, but denied the defence in connection with the picture.[19] The court reasoned that the tabloid magazine could have reported the fact that the chairman of that consumer finance company was hospitalised and suffering from an unknown disease without including the picture of him in the hospital.

3   Remedies

Award of damages

18.29   Most cases involving an infringement of the right to protection of one's likeness also involve an invasion of privacy. Hence, it is difficult to determine the amount of damages awarded in respect of an infringement of the right to protection of one's likeness alone. In general the damages payable with respect to an infringement of both the right to privacy and the right to protection of one's likeness range between tens of thousands and a few million yen, including compensation for legal fees incurred by the victim. As with the invasion of privacy cases, there is substantial criticism of such insubstantial amounts. Despite such criticism, there have been no changes to the Japanese court practices.

Injunction

18.30   Since the right to protection of one's likeness is regarded as one of the moral rights, injunctive relief is available to an imminent or on-going infringement of the right to protection of one's likeness. However, the elements necessary to obtain such relief have not yet been established either by court precedents or by academics. No doubt the criteria adopted by the courts to determine whether injunction is available in the privacy invasion cases would assist in the analysis of the criteria required for injunctive relief in the case of an infringement of the right to protection of one's likeness.

4   Who enjoys the right to protection of one's likeness?

Public figures

18.31   People who intentionally involve themselves in the public arena enjoy a limited right to protection of their likeness.[20] That is, their rights can only be infringed when the use of their likeness has a detrimental effect on their reputation, fame or image as a star and much depends on the context

---

18   Tokyo District Court, 23 June 1989, *Hanrei-Jiho*, vol 1319, p 132.
19   Tokyo District Court, 22 May 1990, *Hanrei-Jiho*, vol 1357, p 93.
20   Tokyo District Court, 29 June 1976, *Hanrei-Jiho*, vol 817, p 23 (*Mark Lester* case).

and manner in which their likeness is used. This is because people in occupations such as actors, actresses and professional sports players, the essence of whose activities requires public exposure, are deemed to have comprehensively agreed to the exposure of their likeness to the public or to have waived a certain amount of protection of their likeness. In many cases, such people actually prefer to have their likeness frequently exposed to the public and, as a consequence, do not suffer any mental anguish from public exposure. In the event that the likeness of public figures is misappropriated in a manner that does *not* detrimentally affect on their reputation or fame, they may still prevent such misappropriation based on the right to publicity, rather than the moral right to protection of one's likeness. To date, the precise determination of who constitutes a public figure and to what extent public figures are deemed to have waived protection of their likeness has not yet been established. The freedom of speech defence is more likely to be available when pictures of certain well-known figures, such as publicly-elected officials or election candidates are involved. This is because the subject of the pictures could often be regarded as being of due public interest.

The deceased

18.32 Deceased persons do not enjoy the right to protect their likeness if the infringement is committed after their death. This is because the right to likeness is regarded as a moral right, which is neither alienable nor assignable and can only be enjoyed by the particular person.[1] However, conduct, which would constitute an infringement of the deceased's right to likeness if the deceased were still alive at the time of the conduct, may constitute an independent tortious act against the bereaved family to cause them mental anguish. Hence, the bereaved are entitled to compensation for their own suffering.

Citizens of foreign states

18.33 The Supreme Court has held that citizens of foreign states also enjoy the fundamental human rights provided for in the Constitution so long as those rights are not by nature only provided to Japanese citizens.[2] The right to protection of one's likeness, one of the fundamental human rights, is not by nature available only to Japanese citizens and thus citizens of foreign states may likely enjoy such a right.

D   The right to protection of one's name

1   Outline of the right to protection of one's name

18.34 The right to protection of one's name is regarded as a moral right and breach of this right constitutes a tort. However, unauthorised use of a person's name does not always constitute a tort.

---

1   Osaka District Court, 27 December 1989, *Hanrei-Jiho*, vol 1341, p 53.
2   Supreme Court, 4 October 1978, *Minshu*, vol 32-7, p 1223.

In one case, the court provided that:

(1) a name's function is to distinguish one's self from others;

(2) this function only works when a person is able to use his or her name in an exclusive manner; and

(3) if others misappropriate that person's name 'causing damage to that person's interests', such misappropriation should be ceased.[3]

In another case, involving a famous poet, a lower court rejected a claim for an infringement of a right to protection of one's name on the basis that the particular use of the name did not in any way have a detrimental effect on the fame or reputation of the person whose name was used.[4] To date, however, it has not yet been established what else is required, in addition to unauthorised use of one's name, to constitute a tort.

Further, the right to protection of one's name includes a right to prevent others from misappropriating one's name as well as any other names that are so similar to the original name as to mislead the public to believe that the person with the similar name is actually the person with the original name.[5]

There is no special law that purports to protect the right to protection of one's name, however such right is protected by the general legal doctrine of tort pursuant to the Civil Code. In addition, the concept of the right to protection of one's name is also reflected in the trademark law. If an applicant applies for the registration of a trademark that includes a name other than the applicant's name and if it incorporates the actual name or famous pen or stage name of another person or any famous abbreviations thereof, this law prohibits registration of that trademark unless the applicant can show evidence of that person's consent (Article 4, para 1, item 8). Needless to say, once a person registers his or her own name as a trademark, like other marks in connection with certain products or services, that person can then prevent others from using the registered mark or any similar marks in connection with such products or services and any products or services similar to them. The only exception being that a registered trademark owner may not prevent others from using their registered name or similar name that is their own name, pen name or stage name (Article 26, para 1, item 1).

2   *Defences*

18.35   There is a defence that is unique to a claim for a breach of the right to protection of one's name. This is where there is a certain relationship between the user of another's name and the name owner that justifies such use. For example, courts have allowed a divorced woman and extra-marital children to use her ex-husband's family name and their father's family name, respectively.

---

3   Tokyo District Court, 31 July 1930, *Shinbun*, vol 3218, p 4.
4   Yokohama District Court, 4 June 1992, *Hanrei-Jiho*, vol 1434, p 116: *Doi Bansui* case. In this case, a city named a street after a famous but then deceased poet and his family sued the city to seek for injunction and award of damages. The court, in rejecting the claim, reasoned that it is quite common practice to name a street after a deceased person of historical importance and such conduct does not in any way have a detrimental effect on the fame or reputation of that person.
5   Tokyo District Court, 21 October 1987, *Hanrei-Jiho*, vol 1252, p 108.

3   Remedies

Award of damages

18.36   Few courts have awarded damages caused by infringement of the right to protection of one's name and hence, it is difficult to establish any trends in amounts of damages awarded. However, in light of the small amounts typically awarded in tort cases in general and also the trends in the amounts of damages in privacy invasion cases, the amount of damages in the case of an infringement of the right to protection of one's name is likely to be somewhere between tens of thousands and a few million yen, including compensation for legal fees incurred by the victim. In fact, in one case where a company repeatedly misappropriated its customer's name and likeness in advertisements despite repeated complaints from that person and his attorney, the court awarded ¥1,500,000 as compensation for mental suffering and ¥300,000 as compensation for legal fees.[6]

Injunction

18.37   Since the right to protection of one's name is regarded as a moral right, injunctive relief is available with respect to imminent or on-going infringements of such right. Again the elements necessary to obtain such relief have not yet been established either by court precedents or by academics. However, criteria adopted by the courts in the privacy invasion cases would no doubt be used to assist in the analysis of criteria required for injunctive relief in the case of an infringement of the right to protection of one's name.

4   Who enjoys the right to protection of one's name?

Public figures

18.38   As with the right to protection of one's likeness, people who intentionally place themselves in the public arena enjoy a limited right to protection of their names and this right may only be infringed upon when their names are used in a manner that injures or detrimentally affects their reputation or fame.[7] It should be noted, however, that in the event that names of public figures are misappropriated in a manner that does *not* detrimentally affect their reputation or fame, they may still prevent such misappropriation based on the right to publicity, rather than the moral right to protection of one's name. Please refer to para **18.39**, which explains protection of the likenesses of public figures.

The deceased

18.39   Similar to the rights to protect one's privacy and likeness, the right to protection of one's name is regarded as a moral right. Hence, deceased persons do not enjoy the right to this kind of protection if an infringement is committed after the person's death. However, the bereaved family would

---

6   Tokyo District Court, 29 August 1989, *Hanrei-Jiho*, vol 1338, p 119.
7   Tokyo District Court, 29 June 1976, *Hanrei-Jiho*, vol 817, p 23 (*Mark Lester* case).

be entitled to compensation by way of damages for their own emotional suffering, if any were found to exist.

Citizens of foreign states

18.40 Citizens of foreign states may also enjoy the right to protection of their names. In one case where citizens of foreign states requested Japanese TV broadcasting companies to pronounce their names in the same manner as that in their home country, the Supreme Court, whilst rejecting the existence of tortious conduct in the actual case, in dictum held that a person, including a citizen of a foreign state, is entitled to have his or her name pronounced accurately as a corollary to the right to protection of one's name.[8] This indicates that the Supreme Court recognises that foreign citizens also enjoy the right to protection of their names.

E   The right to publicity

1   Outline of the right to publicity

18.41 The right to publicity is the exclusive right to exploit and control the economic value associated with one's ability to attract public attention. Names or likenesses of celebrities, such as famous singers, actors, actresses and professional sports players, once used on products or in advertising have a function to promote sales and/or business activities through their fame, celebrity and favorable impression. Those celebrities generally wish to make their names or likenesses publicly known and therefore, while unauthorised use of such a person's name or likeness would be less likely to cause them mental suffering, it could cause them economic loss.[9] As said economic value derives from celebrities' fame or reputation, they should be entitled to exploit such value, and therefore, the right to publicity is regarded as an economic right rather than a moral right.[10]

There is no special law that purports to protect the right to publicity, rather this right is protected by the general legal doctrine of tort pursuant to the Civil Code. This right has been recently recognised by court precedents and there are still a number of issues that remain unresolved as described below.

8   Supreme Court, 16 February 1988, *Hanrei-Jiho*, vol 1266, p 9.
9   Those who enjoy the right to publicity may suffer from moral right infringement in the event that their name or likeness is used in a way detrimental to their fame or reputation.
10 Tokyo High Court, 26 September 1991, *Hanrei-Jiho*, vol 1400, p 3 (*Onyannko Club* case). Various academic discussions have been conducted as to whether a right to publicity is a pure economic right or an economic right inseparable from a moral right. Different conclusions could be reached regarding issues such as the scope, assignability or length of the right depending on which view is taken as to the nature of a right to publicity.

2 Who enjoys the right to publicity?

Celebrities

18.42　The issue as to who is entitled to enjoy the right to publicity has not yet been settled. There is no question that famous singers, actors and actresses may enjoy this right, but what about other categories of famous people such as politicians or novelists? In one case, the court rejected a claim for an infringement of a famous poet's right to publicity.[11] The court reasoned that a poet's main activity is the creation of poems rather than to exploit the economic value of his or her name or likeness, as would be the case for a singer or actor, therefore he had no right to publicity. There is no prevailing opinion with respect to this issue and we have to wait for the accumulation and evaluation of judicial decisions before this issue settles.

The deceased

18.43　When those who enjoyed the right to publicity die, will their heirs inherit the right? As stated in paras **18.23**, **18.32** and **18.39**, the rights to privacy, and protection of one's name and likeness are all regarded as moral rights, which can only be enjoyed by that person and hence their heirs do not inherit those rights. Unlike those rights, the right to publicity is more like an economic right, therefore, in theory, the right to publicity is likely to be inheritable. However, there has been no court precedent[12] and academic views are currently divided.

Citizens of foreign states

18.44　The courts have recognised a foreign citizen's right to publicity without any particular discussions or reasoning. The leading case which recognised the right to publicity involved an actor who was a citizen of a foreign state.[13]

3 What is protected under the right to publicity?

18.45　There is no question that names and likenesses of certain famous people are protected under this right. However, to date there have been very few discussions about what else (such as soundalikes or lookalikes) may be protected. Recently a lower court recognised that record or CD jackets of a famous rock group could be protected under this right regardless of whether or not names or likenesses of the rock group appear on those jackets.[14] The court reasoned that:

(1)　the essence of the right to publicity is the power to attract public attention; and

---

11　Yokohama District Court, 4 June 1992, *Hanrei-Jiho*, vol 1434, p 116: *Doi Bansui* case.
12　In the *Racehorse Publicity* case involving the product publicity right, the district court held that those who hold a title at the time when the product ceases to exist may still enjoy the right to publicity associated with the product thereafter so long as the publicity value remains. Nagoya District Court, 19 january 2000, http//www.courts.go.jp/ (*Racehorse Publicity* case).
13　Tokyo District Court, 29 June 1976, *Hanrei-Jiho*, vol 817, p 23: *Mark Lester* case.
14　Tokyo District Court, 21 January 1998, *Hanrei-Jiho*, vol 1644, p 141: *King Crimson* case.

(2) therefore, not only names or likenesses but also any matter with economic value, arising out of that celebrities' fame or reputation due to the attraction of public attention, should be protected under the right to publicity.

There is another recent development in the court precedents as to the subject of the right to publicity. In the case of a game software company that created and sold horserace game software using names and features of actual racehorses with the advertisement of 'your dream will come true to become a jockey and participate in a horse-race with THAT HORSE', a district court recognised that certain famous racehorses may be protected under the right to publicity.[15] It stressed the similarity between racehorses and sports players and reasoned that certain famous products might acquire the power to attract public attention in a manner similar to famous people and hence would be the subject of the right to publicity. However, some scholars are sceptical about expanding the scope of the subjects to be protected under the right to publicity because the right originally derives from the right of privacy which is unique to humans.

4 Assignability

18.46 As stated in previous sections, the right to privacy, and protection of one's name and likeness are all regarded as moral rights that are not alienable or assignable and can only be enjoyed by that person. Unlike those rights, the right to publicity is the right to exploit economic value and therefore, is more like a purely economic right. Generally speaking, an economic right is both alienable and assignable. In theory, this aspect of the right to publicity tends to lead to the conclusion that the right to publicity is both alienable and assignable. There is no court precedent[16] on this point and this theory has been untested.

5 Duration

18.47 The rights to privacy and protection of one's name and likeness, being moral rights, last until a person who holds the rights dies. Unlike those rights, the right to publicity has an economic right aspect and therefore, in theory it tends to lead to the conclusion that the right to publicity survives the death of the celebrities. Then the issue remains as to how long the right lasts after their death. There has been no court precedent and currently academic opinions are divided. One scholar argues that based on the similarity between copyright neighbouring rights and rights to publicity and in light of the balance between the two, heirs may enjoy the right for 50 years after death,[17] while another argues that the right should last forever so long as the publicity value is still commercially utilised.[18]

---

15 *Race horse publicity* , Nagoya District Court, 19 January 2000, http//www.courts.go.jp/.
16 In the *Racehorse Publicity* case, the district court recognised assignability in conjunction with the assignment of property title while it was silent as to the assignability of the right separate from the title of the product. See para **18.45**.
17 Koji Abe, Civil Law Annotation XVIII, p 584 (1991).
18 Toshikazu Ushiki, 'Relationship between the Right to Publicity and the Trademark law' in *Patent* vol 47, no 5, p 7 (1994).

Another argues that, in the absence of a specific statute that limits the duration of the rights in a civil law country, the rights last indefinitely; however, heirs of the celebrities could be restricted from exercising their rights by the right of abuse doctrine (Article 1 of the Civil Code).

6 Remedies

Award of damages

18.48 The courts have awarded damages in an amount equivalent to the normal royalty fees. In the *Onyannko Club* case involving sales of calendars using pictures of popular television personalities, the court awarded an amount equivalent to what they could have received from the infringer under the existing agreements with other licensees.[19] In the *King Crimson* case, involving a book feauring a famous rock group which contained pictures of its members and record jackets, the court awarded an amount equivalent to the standard royalty fee on a book, ie, 10 per cent of the retail sales price.[20] The leader of the rock group requeste double the amount of the standard royalty fee on books (ie, 20 per cent) as a penalty, which was rejected by the court.

Injunction

18.49 In principle, injunctive relief is unquestionably available for the infringement of moral rights, while only the infringement of exclusive economic rights (such as jus ad rem) afford injunctive relief. In spite of the principle, most recent court cases, without any particular analysis, granted injunctive relief, including disposition of infringing products that had remained in the infringers' possession. In the *Racehorse Publicity* case, however, the district court distinguished the product publicity right from the personal publicity right and denied injunctive relief. It reasoned that injunctive relief causes tremendous damage to infringers and unlike personal publicity right, a product publicity right is nothing but a mere economic right and accordingly injunctive relief is not available in the absence of statute.[1]

7 Defences

18.50 The most important defence in infringement of the right to publicity is again freedom of speech. As stated above, injunction of a publication could have a chilling effect on freedom of speech and therefore, criteria for injunction should be strict and clear. Several courtss have granted injunctions of publications infringing the right to publicity, however, most of them failed to analyse in detail the balance between freedom of speech and the right to publicity. Recently in the *King Crimson* case, the high court introduced certain criteria for determining an infringement of the right to publicity by a publication featuring celebrities: that is whether or not the

---

19 Tokyo High Court, 26 September 1991, *Hanrei-Jiho*, vol 1400, p 3 (*Onyannko Club* case).
20 Tokyo District Court, 21 January 1998, *Hanrei-Jiho*, vol 1644, p 141 (*King Crimson* case).
1 The *Race horse publicity* case at para **18.45**.

use of one's name, likeness or so on is found to be mainly for the purpose of utilising their publicity value.[2] This case involved a book published by an FM broadcast station, as one of its book in a series entitled 'The Earth Music Library', which features famous contemporary music and artists. The book in the dispute comprehensively covers a rock group, named King Crimson and its members ('sort of dictionary of the group' stated the district court), including their biographies, music and comments thereon. The book has the same name as the name of the famous rock group itself and contains 11 pictures of its members as well as all the pictures of its record jackets. The district court, in granting an injunction, applied another criteria: that is, whether or not the publicity value of the celebrities constituted a major part of the publication. Or more specifically whether or not the publication, in essence, utilised the celebrities' power to attract public attention.[3] The high court, however, overruled the lower court, applying the above criteria and denied the infringement. It reasoned that any publication covering the celebrities inevitably reflects their power to attract public attention and the district court decision was inappropriate because it compared the celebrities' power to attract public attention and freedom of speech on the same level. The above high court decision was supported by the Supreme Court.[4]

2   Tokyo High Court, 24 February 1999, unpublished, cited in 'Outline of the Right to Publicity' written by Atsushi Naitoh and Sadayuki Tashiro, p 254 (1999).
3   The district court applied the above criteria to the case and held that the defendant intentionally appealed to fans by using many pictures of the record sleeves and thereby promoted sales of that book. Tokyo District Court, 21 January 1998, *Hanrei-Jiho*, vol 1644, p 141.
4   Supreme Court, 9 November 2000, unpublished.

19 LUXEMBOURG

Anne Baudoin
Stéphan Le Goueff

A Introduction

19.01 The protection of privacy in Luxembourg has been safeguarded for many years from legislative interference because of the Constitutional rules regarding home privacy and secrecy of correspondence.[1] Further to the ratification of the Convention for Protection of Human Rights and Fundamental Freedoms of 4 November 1950, the protection of privacy has also been based upon the general principle of Article 8 of this Convention pursuant to which 'everyone has the right to have his private and family life, his home and correspondence respected'.

19.02 Case law has also safeguarded individuals privacy and likeness on the basis of the general principles of liability.[2] However, due to the development of technology, Luxembourg has enacted new laws in recent decades in order to offer to individuals a better protection against any interference with their private life.

19.03 Luxembourg has faced fewer problems regarding the protection of privacy than other European countries such as France, Germany or the United Kingdom. This situation may be explained by the size of the country and of its population but also by the lack of local tabloids and by the fact that the most popular newspaper is controlled by the Church. Therefore, Luxembourg case law relating to this subject is rather limited.

19.04 This chapter examines successively the protection provided to individuals by Luxembourg law regarding the following issues:

(1) privacy;

(2) publicity; and

(3) personality.

---

1 Constitution of 17 October 1868, arts 15 and 28.
2 T A Luxembourg, 2 June 1976, in Pasicrisie 23, p 553; T A Luxembourg 14 February 1990, nE 100/90.

B Privacy

1 Privacy legislation

19.05 Currently, privacy is mainly safeguarded by the following legislation:

(1) Articles 15 and 28 of the Constitution of 17 October 1868;

(2) the general rules regarding liability of Articles 1382 and 1383 of the Civil Code;

(3) the provisions of the Criminal Code on home privacy, professional secrecy, secrecy of correspondence;

(4) the law on the protection of privacy of 11 August 1982;

(5) the law on the use of personal data in data processing of 31 March 1979; and

(6) Article 4(1) of the telecommunications law of 21 March 1997.

19.06 The courts have also resorted to Article 8(1) of the Convention for Protection of Human Rights and Fundamental Freedoms to which direct effects in Luxembourg legal system have been recognised.[3]

19.07 As specific and detailed rules apply to data protection, we will examine separately privacy protection and data protection.

2 Privacy protection

19.08 Before the enactment of the law of 11 August 1982 on the protection of privacy, privacy protection was safeguarded either by the Articles 15 and 28 of the Constitution or by the courts on the basis of the general rules regarding liability. Now, the law relating to the protection of privacy mainly applies.

19.09 The following analysis will focus upon:

(1) the general principle set up by the law;

(2) the scope of privacy;

(3) the unlawful acts;

(4) the limits to privacy; and

(5) the available remedies and penalties.

3 The general principle

19.10 Article 1 of the law relating to the protection of privacy provides, as a general rule, that:

> 'Everyone has a right to the respect of his privacy. Judges may, without prejudice to the reparation of the damage suffered, prescribe any measures, such as sequestration, seizure and others, suitable to prevent or interrupt an interference with privacy; these measures may, in case of emergency, be ordered by injunction.'

3   Cass 17 January 1985, *Engel v Engel*.

19.11   This legal provision is the same as the provision of Article 9 of the French Civil code. Therefore, as Luxembourg has a similar legal provision to France, the courts may refer to the French doctrine or case law to decide a case.

4   Scope of privacy

19.12   Currently, there is no legal definition of the term 'privacy' and no case law relating to this point. However, according to parliamentary documents leading to the adoption of the law, privacy may be defined as 'what is totally private and generally kept hidden from others'.[4] Such a right to privacy is granted to unknown and famous persons alike as far as their privacy is concerned.

19.13   Privacy may be opposed to public life, ie when a person is the subject of a public event, that person cannot ask for the protection regarding such activities. It also seems that it may be opposed to professional life. For example, legal provisions regarding privacy shall not apply to recordings exclusively made during the performance of professional activities.[5]

19.14   As the legal protection of privacy is a civil right, everybody, without regard to his or her citizenship, may refer to it. However, the principle of reciprocity of treatment will apply.[6]

19.15   The scope of privacy may include, among others:

(1)   love and friendship;

(2)   family life, including facts regarding members of the family of a person;

(3)   social, political or religious information regarding a person;

(4)   health of a person, even a public person;

(5)   leisure; and

(6)   all patrimonial aspects of a person.

19.16   However, no protection will be recognised for facts that have already been disclosed either by the person or with his or her consent. Protection will also be excluded if the facts are well known to the public.

5   Unlawful acts

19.17   According to Article 2 of the law relating to the protection of privacy, unless the consent of the persons concerned has been obtained, the following acts are prohibited:

(1)   to listen, to record or to transmit private words or to require someone to do the same;

(2)   to watch a person who is in a private place, to fix and to transmit the image of the person or to require someone to do the same (it should be noted that, according to the law, the consent of the persons concerned is implied when such acts occurred publicly during a meeting); and

4   Chambre des députés, Bill relating to privacy protection, nE 2177, p 2.
5   T A Luxembourg, 11 July 1989, nE999/89.
6   Civil code, art 11.

(3) to open a message sent in a closed envelope, to acquire knowledge of its content or to destroy it without the consent of the sender or the receiver.

19.18 The following acts are prohibited so long as they concern people's privacy and are done without their consent:

(1) covert filming (as it may be assumed that the persons who are filmed have not given their consent to such act);

(2) filming on private property or filming over private property (from the air); however, if no person is being filmed, it is arguable whether such filming is a interference with privacy;

(3) interception of post and telephone calls which is prohibited, not only by the law regarding the protection of privacy, but also by Article 149 et seq of the Criminal Code, Article 88-1 et seq of the Code of Criminal Instruction and Article 4(1) of the Telecommunications Law;

(4) opening or reading of letters, the right to correspondence secrecy even being even safeguarded by Article 28 of the Constitution; and

(5) recording conversations, whether openly or covertly.

19.19 The violation of the law occurs irrespective of the equipment used, ie use of telephoto lens, microphone, etc.

19.20 A provision of the law allows the Government to adopt regulations regarding the import or export, sale or purchase, manufacturing or use of equipment made in order to permit a violation of privacy. However, it would seem that no such regulation has been enacted yet.

19.21 The following acts are also prohibited:

(1) the use or the installation of equipment in order to commit one of the prohibited acts mentioned under Article 2 of the law;[7]

(2) the disclosure of any information regarding privacy obtained as above mentioned, except with the consent of the person concerned;[8]

(3) the publication of montage of images or wording of a person without his or her consent, unless it is mentioned or it is obvious that it is a montage;[9]

(4) telephone or written harassment.[10]

6 Limits to privacy protection

19.22 Freedom of the press is safeguarded by Article 24 of the Luxembourg Constitution and a right of information has been recognised to the public.[11] However, journalists may be held liable on the basis of Articles 1382 and 1383 of the Civil Code (the basic provision regarding civil liability) in case of breach to their duty of truthfulness and discretion. In some areas, especially areas relating to privacy, their duty of discretion

---

7 Law of 11 August 1982, art 3
8 Law of 11 August 1982, art 4.
9 Law of 11 August 1982, art 5.
10 Law of 11 August 1982, art 6.
11 Cour, 21 February 1914 and 28 March 1914, in Paiscrisie 9, p 32.

must prevail over their duty of truth. As a result, the press must not publish facts regarding privacy, except with the consent of the persons concerned by these facts.[12]

19.23   Facts which have been recorded in a judicial decision in open court may be published, but the name of the parties or any detail which permits to identify these parties shall not be published. However, an exception to this rule has been admitted by the courts for crimes, based on the seriousness of the facts, their consequence on the public order and the character of the parties.[13]

19.24   The law on the protection of privacy also prohibits the voluntary disclosure of any document or recording regarding the privacy of a person, to the public or to a third party, unless the consent of this person has been obtained.[14] Such consent must be proved by the person who wants to proceed with the publication. As privacy is an indefeasible right, such consent can always be revoked.[15]

7   *Remedies and penalties*

19.25   The person whose privacy is violated may commence legal proceedings in order to prevent the publication of such document or recording, on the basis of Article 1 of the law relating to the protection of privacy or on the basis of Articles 806 and 807(1) of the Code of civil procedure which relate to summary proceedings. In the first instance, a violation of privacy has to be established. In the second instance, it must be established that it is necessary either to prevent an imminent damage or an obvious illegality.

19.26   The judge may prevent the publication of documents, recording or articles concerning privacy, order the restitution of the documents or recording or their destruction.

19.27   A person who seeks remedies for a violation of their privacy may also claim damages on the basis of Articles 1382 and 1383 of the Civil code. In such case, they will have to prove default on the part of the defendant, ie a violation of their privacy, a damage which will often be only moral, and a causal relationship between this default and the damage suffered.

19.28   Some criminal sanctions may also be incurred by the person who has violated the private life of another person, ie an imprisonment sentence and/or a fine for any violation of:

(1)   the provisions of Articles 2 to 7 of the law of the 11 August 1982 on the protection of privacy;

(2)   a person's domicile by a public officer[16] or any other person;[17]

---

12   T A Luxembourg, 17 March 1993, nE rôle 244793; T A Luxembourg 14 February 1990, nE 100/90.
13   T A Luxembourg, 17March 1993, nE rôle 244793; T A Luxembourg 30 October 1989, nE rôle 532/89; T A Luxembourg 29 March 1995, n'rôle 15758.
14   Law of 11 August 1982 concerning the protection of privacy, art 4.
15   Référé Luxembourg, 20 November 1978 in Pasicrisie 25, p 358 and subs; T A Luxembourg, 26 March 1987 nE rôle 33260.
16   Criminal Code, art 148.
17   Criminal Code, arts 439 and 440.

(3) the secrecy of the telegraphic messages by a depository;[18]

(4) the secret of correspondence by a public officer;[19] and

(5) the professional secrecy.

8 Data protection

19.29 In order to protect personal data, a specific law has been enacted, the law of 31 March 1979 regulating the use of personal data in data processing, as amended.

19.30 This section will examine successively the scope of data protection, the general rules governing data bases, the obligations of the processor, the rights of the data subject and the available penalties.

9 Scope of data protection

19.31 Protection against incorrect use of personal data is granted to legal entities and natural persons. The data protected is personal data, ie information regarding a person identified or identifiable.

19.32 In order to ensure data protection, an advisory commission has been established, with consulting and informative duties. Further to the enactment of the European Directive on personal privacy rights and computerised information, the independence of this authority should be secured and its powers should be increased[20] and the law should be amended according to ministerial information. However, due to recent procedural events, the Data Protection Bill has been withdrawn from Parliament.

10 General rules governing databases

19.33 A preliminary authorisation from the Minister in charge of the national directory of databases is requested for the creation and processing of any database, except State databases for which a legal authorisation is requested.

19.34 The gathering and processing of some sensible data is prohibited. This data relates to racial or ethnic origin, political opinions, religious or philosophical beliefs, trade union membership or data concerning the intimacy of privacy (such as sexual life). Exception to this prohibition concerns associations which can have files of their members or trade union memberships (subject to the consent of the concerned persons).

11 Obligations of the processor

19.35 Data protection is also ensured by obligations imposed on the persons responsible for processing.

---

18 Criminal Code, art 150.
19 Criminal Code, art 149.
20 European Directive on personal privacy rights and computerised information.

19.36   The processor is subject to professional secrecy. He must keep accurate and, where necessary, up-to-date the personal data. Personal data must be processed fairly and lawfully. The data must be collected for specified and lawful purposes and be relevant in relation with the purpose for which it is collected.

19.37   The processor has the duty to inform the individuals where data is collected, the purpose of the data processing, the compulsory or optional nature of the answers, the consequence of a refusal of answer, etc.

19.38   Security measures must be taken in order to ensure data security and, especially, to avoid any alteration, damage or unauthorised access.

12 Rights of the data subject

19.39   Data subjects have been granted certain rights of protection against any interference with privacy or any infringement to the law. These rights include:

(1)   a right of information (see above);

(2)   a right to access, through which the data subject can ascertain the accuracy of the data relating to such person and the lawfulness of the processing; and

(3)   the data subject's consent prior to processing or obtaining some personal data.

13 Available penalties

19.40   Criminal penalties (a custodial sentence and/or a fine) are incurred by persons that:

(1)   create, process or use a database without the requested authorisation or without fulfilling the terms of this authorisation;[1]

(2)   obtain and process prohibited data or data obtained fraudulently;[2]

(3)   do not respect the right of access of data subjects;[3]

(4)   use a false name or quality in order to obtain access to personal data;[4]

(5)   do not comply with his obligations to keep the data accurate and up to date;[5] and

(6)   impede or prevent the performance of his or her duties by either the Ministry or the advisory commission.[6]

19.41   These persons may also be held liable for damages on the basis of the general principles of liability already mentioned. Therefore, civil liability action must be brought before the relevant court.

---

1   Law of 31 March 1979, art 32.
2   Law of 31 March 1979, art 33.
3   Law of 31 March 1979, art 34.
4   Law of 31 March 1979, art 35.
5   Law of 31 March 1979, art 36.
6   Law of 31 March 1979, art 37.

C   Publicity

1   Use of a person's name

19.42   Use of a person's name, either in public or in a biography, without his or her consent may be restricted, on the basis either of some specific legal provisions or of the general rules of liability. This protection will apply to any person, without regard to their citizenship. However, the principle of reciprocal treatment may be applied as mentioned above.

19.43   This section examines name protection, the protection against unauthorised biography and protection of trade marks.

2   Name protection

19.44   Protection of one's name has been recognised by the Criminal Code. Under these provisions, any person who uses a false name incurs criminal penalties (custodial sentence and/or fine) in case of:

(1)   use of a false name or first name or use of a false quality or domicile in an official document (passport, identity card, commercial authorisation or any other document from a national or foreign public authority) or use of such public documents;[7]

(2)   public use of a name by a person who has no right to use it;[8]

(3)   delivery of funds, goods, receipt, release owing to the use of a false name or quality for the purpose of appropriation of goods belonging to an other person.[9]

19.45   Protection may also be ensured by the application of Articles 1382 and 1383 of the Civil Code. In such case, as mentioned above, the plaintiff will have to prove a fault from the defendant, ie the use of his or her name without having any right therefore, either the moral or material damage suffered and the causal link between this fault and the damage.

3   Use of biography

19.46   It is generally admitted that a conflict may exist between, on the one hand, the freedom of the press[10] and the right to be informed and, on the other hand, privacy or the right to reputation.

19.47   If the biography relates to public or historical events in which the person has taken part, publication is permitted, even if the consent of the person concerned has not been obtained, so long as the facts are truthfully objectively and impartially described.

---

7   Criminal Code, art 199.
8   Criminal Code, art 231.
9   Criminal Code, art 496.
10   Luxembourg Constitution, art 24.

19.48   Facts relating to privacy may not be disclosed in a biography, except with the consent of the person concerned. Publication would otherwise constitute an infringement of the law relating to the protection of privacy, and the penalties will be the same as those mentioned in para **19.25** et seq.

19.49   Publication of public events may be punished as a violation of a person's reputation, in the following cases:

(1)   a specific fact has been maliciously and publicly attributed to a person, a fact that may cause an injury to the person's reputation (defamation if the proof of this precise fact is prohibited and libel if the proof is legally permitted and the fact is not proved);[11] the penalties (custodial sentence and fine) incurred will depend on the circumstances of the defamation, libel or slander;[12]

(2)   the person is insulted when the above mentioned facts are not specific;[13] the penalties (custodial sentence and fine) incurred will also depend on the circumstances of the insult.

19.50   Under the legislation regarding press[14] and media,[15] a right to reply has been granted to any person whose name or assumed name is publicly mentioned in a newspaper, a radio or broadcasting programme without their consent.

4   Name and trade mark protection

19.51   According to Article 2 of the Benelux Uniform Law on trade marks, as amended, trade mark protection may be granted to a person's name. This protection may be extended to first name and pseudonyms.

19.52   However, this protection will be limited as no monopoly may be granted to prohibit the use of homonyms.

D   Personality

1   Use of one's likeness

19.53   In Luxembourg, case law has established, as a general principle, that the use of an individual's likeness is subject to their consent. This protection applies to everybody, without regard to citizenship, but the principle of reciprocal treatment may apply.

19.54   More precisely, anyone may prohibit the reproduction and the use of their image or voice without their consent.

19.55   This right is considered an aspect of privacy when the image relates to private events. In such a case, either the taking of the image or using by

---

11   Criminal Code, art 443 and subs.
12   Criminal Code, art 444 and subs.
13   Criminal Code, art 448 and subs.
14   Law of 20 July 1867 on the press and the offences performed by the different means of publication, art 23.
15   Law of 27 July 1991 on electronic media, art 26.

any means may be punished under the provisions of the law of the 11 August 1982 concerning the protection of privacy. This right may also be regarded as a specific right called *'droit à l'image'* (the right to image or likeness), protected by the provisions of Articles 1382 and 1383 of the Civil Code above mentioned.

19.56   When images are taken of activities performed in public or public events, no sanction may be incurred by a person who has taken the images.

19.57   According to case law, the consent of a person who took part in a public event may not be required when the image is used to report this public event. The public interest may also justify the publication of an image taken in public[16] of a person who is taking part in a public event. However, persons responsible for publication may be liable in the event of malicious intent or unfaithful reporting.

19.58   According to relevant case law,[17] the right of a person in relation to their likeness is an exclusive right. As a result, the prior consent of the person is required for the publication of their image, unless public interest in a public event justifies publication. Consent must be proved by the person responsible for publication and may always be withdrawn in good faith.[18]

19.59   So far as concerns the use of a person's likeness for advertising, the consent of the person will always be required prior to any use as a consequence of their rights in respect of their image or likeness.

---

16   T A Luxembourg 17 March 1993, nE 244/93; T A Luxembourg 29 March 1995, nE rôle 15758.
17   T A Luxembourg 17 March 1993, nE 244/93; T A Luxembourg 29 March 1995, nE rôle 15758.
18   Référés Luxembourg, 20 November 1978, in Pasicrisie 25, p 358.

20 THE NETHERLANDS

J C S Pinckaers

A Privacy

1 General right to respect for one's private life

20.01   All privacy rules stem from the right of every individual to respect for his or her private life. This basic right was incorporated in Article 10 of the Constitution of the Kingdom of the Netherlands (Constitution) with the constitutional revision of 1983. Article 10 provides:

(1)   Everyone shall have the right to respect for their private life, without prejudice to restrictions laid down by or pursuant to Act of Parliament.

(2)   Rules to protect one's private life shall be laid down by Act of Parliament in connection with the recording and dissemination of personal data.

(3)   Rules concerning the rights of persons to be informed of data recorded concerning them and of the use that is made thereof, and to have such data corrected shall be laid down by Act of Parliament.

20.02   Pursuant to Article VI Additional Articles, Article 10(1) of the Dutch Constitution came into force on 17 February 1988.[1] However, even before this date, courts have recognised the right of every individual to respect for his or her private life under Article 8(1) of the European Convention for the Protection of Human Rights and Fundamental Freedoms ('ECHR').[2] Article 8(1) of the ECHR provides:

'Everyone has the right to respect for their private and family life, their home and their correspondence.'

Article 17(1) of the International Convention on Civil and Political Rights (ICCPR)[3] provides:

'No one shall be subjected to arbitrary or unlawful interference with

---

1   Acts of 11 February 1988, Stb 33 and 34, and 1 February 1990, Stb 60.
2   The EHRC (Treaty of Rome of 4 November 1950), Trb 1951, 154, has been ratified by Act of 28 July 1954, Stb 335, and came into effect on 31 August 1954.
3   The ICCPR of 19 December 1966, Trb 1969, 99, came into effect in the Netherlands on 11 March 1979, Trb 1978, 177.

his privacy, family, home or correspondence, nor to unlawful attacks on his honour and reputation.'

In 1987, the Netherlands Supreme Court ruled that:

'a right to respect for one's private life should be accepted, that fits with similar developments in other countries and that, as far as its content is concerned, is also defined by Article 8 ECHR, of which it should be presumed that it is also effective between citizens. A violation of this right will in principle result in a tort in the sense of Article [6:162] Civil Code'.[4]

20.03 Although Article 8 of the ECHR is directed at the various governments, the Supreme Court recognised that this Article directly affects the relationship between private citizens without any need to incorporate its norms in any specific statute. Citizens should also respect each other's privacy in their mutual relations. One citizen can infringe the right to respect for the private life of another citizen. The Court explicitly referred to the recognition of right to respect for one's private life in other countries.

2   Personal Data Protection Act

20.04   Article 10(2) and (3) of the Constitution provide that the rules concerning the recording and dissemination of personal data shall be laid down by Act of Parliament. In 1988 the Personal Data Registration Act ('PDRA') was enacted (Wet persoonsregistraties).[5] Under the PDRA, the owner of a personal data system ('registration') was held to comply with various requirements in respect of the compilation and use of personal data, the accuracy of the data and the security of the system. On 6 July 2000, the legislator passed the new Personal Data Protection Act ('PDPA') which replaced the PDRA. This Act implemented Directive 95/46/EC of the European Parliament and of the Council of 24 October 1995 on the protection of individuals with regard to the processing of personal data and on the free movement of such data.[6]

20.05   The PDPA focuses on the *processing* of personal data rather than on the registration thereof as under the old PDRA. 'Personal data' is defined 'as any information relating to an identified or identifiable natural person'. The term 'processing' is defined as 'any operation or any set of operations concerning personal data', which includes the collection, compilation, storage, use, dissemination by transmission, making available, and erasure or destruction.

Personal data must be processed in accordance with the PDPA and in a proper and careful manner. It must be collected for *specific, explicitly defined and legitimate purposes*. The PDPA provides that personal data may *only* be processed on the following *six grounds*:

(1)   the data subject has unambiguously given his consent for the processing;

(2)   the processing is necessary for the performance of a contract to which the data subject is party, or for actions to be carried out at the request

---

4   Supreme Court, 9 January 1987, NJ 1987, 928 (*Edam welfare mother*).
5   Law of 28 December 1988, Stb 1988, 655.
6   OJ 1995 L 281/31. Implementation of this Directive was due before 24 October 1998, but the Dutch Government did not manage to succeed in time.

of the data subject and which are necessary for the conclusion of a contract;

(3) the processing is necessary in order to comply with a legal obligation to which the responsible party is subject;

(4) the processing is necessary in order to protect a vital interest of the data subject;

(5) the processing is necessary for the proper performance of a public law duty by the administrative body concerned or by the administrative body to which the data is provided; or

(6) the processing is necessary for upholding the legitimate interests of the responsible party or of a third party to whom the data is supplied, except where the interests or fundamental rights and freedoms of the data subject, in particular the right to protection of individual privacy, prevail.

In practice, the last ground will be important, eg for companies that are involved in database marketing.[7]

20.06 Personal data may not be further processed in a way incompatible with the purposes for which they have been obtained. They may not be kept in an identifiable form for any longer than is necessary for achieving the purposes for which they were collected or subsequently processed.

20.07 The person involved may request the responsible party to give or send him a specification of the personal data concerning him which have been processed. In response to such information he or she may request that the data be corrected or supplemented, or removed because of lack of relevance, etc.

20.08 A set of very strict rules applies to so-called *'special personal data'*. It is prohibited to process personal data concerning a person's religion or philosophy of life, race, political persuasion, health and sexual life, or personal data concerning trade union membership, or a person's criminal behaviour, unless it comes under one of the specific exceptions stated in the PDPA. For example, processing personal data concerning a person's criminal behaviour may be carried out by bodies, charged by law with applying criminal law and by responsible parties who have obtained these data in accordance with the Police Registers Act or the Judicial Documentation Act.

20.09 The automated processing of personal data must be reported to the Personal Data Protection Board. In addition, the PDPA introduces the so-called 'privacy officer,' who supervises the observance of privacy requirements within the organisation of the processor or within the branch it is active in.

20.10 The PDPA applies to all processing of personal data in the course of activities conducted in a responsible party's place of business anywhere in the Netherlands. Personal data which is subject to processing or intended for processing after it has been transferred, shall only be transferred to a *country outside the European Union* in the case that, without prejudice to

---

7   See A Artz, C Ebbers, E Schreuders and S Nouwt, Marketing en de WBP-proef, *Privacy & Informatie*, 1998, 37.

compliance with the PDPA, that country guarantees an adequate level of protection.

20.11 The PDPA does not apply in certain particular cases stated in that Act, such as processing in the course of a purely personal or household activity or processing for purposes of implementing other Acts, such as the Police Act, Municipal Database Personal Records Act or Judicial Documentation Act. In respect of certain particular data processing the government may by Administrative Decree determine that it need not be reported.

3   Criminal acts

20.12 In 1971, Articles 139a–139g were added to the Criminal Act[8] in order to protect a person's right to respect for their private life against unwanted invasions by, for example, long-focus lenses, eavesdropping or recording. In addition, Article 441b of the Criminal Act penalises the secret taking of a photograph of persons in places where food, drinks or other goods are sold to the public.

In 1998, the Parliament proposed the Dutch Stalking Act,[9] which penalises 'stalking' (*belaging*) in a new Articles 285b or 301a of the Criminal Act. Stalking is considered to be the invasion of a person's privacy by systematically contacting this person, eg by following, phoning, writing, contacting family members etc.

4   Different aspects of privacy

20.13 The Netherlands Supreme Court has recognised each citizen's 'general right to respect for their private life'. Synonyms for this right are 'privacy right', 'right to privacy',[10] 'personality right' or 'general personality right'.[11]

20.14 Traditionally the term 'personality rights' refers to the non-assignable moral rights of the author of a work, protected by Article 25 of the Copyright Act 1912, such as the right to oppose the publication of this work without the author's name or under a different name, alterations in the work, or distortion or mutilation of their work that could be prejudicial to their honour or reputation or to their value as such. These rights protect the personality interests of the author, who is vulnerable in his person, since the work bears their personal mark. The author can exercise these rights even after the author has assigned his copyright. However, since the 1990s, the term 'personality right' has also been used outside the scope of copyright law as a synonym for the general privacy right.

20.15 The privacy right protects against the violation of the different personality interests of a person. An analysis of case law shows that the following distinctions can be made:

---

8   Act of 7 April 1971, Stb 180.
9   Proposal 25 768.
10 Supreme Court, 12 June 1992, NJ 1992, 589.
11 Supreme Court, 6 January 1995, NJ 1995, 422 (*Het Parool et al/Van Gasteren*), para 5.10: right to be let alone derives from the 'general personality right'.

(1) *physical* privacy: protection against violation of physical integrity;

(2) *spatial* privacy: protection of the private sphere;

(3) *informational* privacy: protection against abuse of information concerning one's person.

5 Physical integrity

20.16 Physical integrity is explicitly protected by Article 11 of the Constitution, which recognises the 'inviolability of the body'. This right is relevant for instance in cases concerning:

(1) protection against rape;

(2) sexual harassment;

(3) examination of or with the body;

(4) the obligation or freedom to undergo medical examination;[12]

(5) protection against unlawful deprivation of freedom;

(6) protection against harassment in the streets;[13] or

(7) noise pollution.[14]

These are discussed below.

6 Spatial privacy

20.17 Spatial privacy is inter alia protected by Article 12 of the Constitution, which states under what strict circumstances the entry into a home against the will of its inhabitant shall be authorised. The issue here is protection against unlawful entry of a person's spatial privacy by intrusion, as a result of, for example:

(1) trespassing;

(2) spying on;[15]

(3) peeping at, whether or not with technical aids such as long-focus lenses;

(4) eavesdropping[16] or photographing;[17]

(5) intruding through constantly phoning;[18]

(6) interference with the family life or the private communication; or

(7) reading or copying of private documents such as diaries.[19]

---

12 Supreme Court, 18 June 1993, NJ 1994, 347 (*Compulsory Aids test after rape*).
13 President District Court Amsterdam, 12 June 1986, KG 1986, 285 (*injunction to visit neighbourhood of victim*).
14 District Court Amsterdam, 12 February 1974, NJ 1974, 121 (*Noise pollution by Schiphol Airport*).
15 Supreme Court, 9 January 1987, NJ 1987, 928 (*Edam welfare mother*).
16 District Court Zutphen, 29 August 1980, NJ 1981, 43 (overhearing mobile phone conversation).
17 Supreme Court, 25 June 1974, NJ 1974, 455 (*Party W Oltmans*).
18 President District Court Haarlem, 12 January 1990, KG 1990, 91 (*Phone nuisance*).
19 President District Court Arnhem, 8 August 1990, KG 1991, 14 (*Reading another's diary*).

20.18   There is a distinction made between the different spheres that a person can be in: public life, social life, private life and the intimate life.[20] The more intimate this sphere is, the sooner intrusion will be unlawful.[1]

Even employees at work have some privacy protection. For example, the President of the Roermond District Court granted an injunction against an employer who used television-cameras within the company to keep an eye on its employees.[2]

20.19   As a rule of thumb, the publication of information is unlawful if this information has been obtained through unlawful invasion of another person's private sphere, for example under false pretences. The Dutch Supreme Court upheld a case of the Amsterdam Court of Appeal which considered the manner in which weekly magazine *Privé* gathered its news an unlawful invasion of the right to respect for the private life of Princess Irene's children. The defendant had posted a reporter in a car outside the new school of Princess Irene's eldest son for four days, in an attempt to gather news about him and/or to take photographs. The President of the Amsterdam District Court prohibited defendant from forcing itself on plaintiffs or to follow them for its (photo) press activities in a manner that was annoying to them. The Court of Appeal upheld the injunction. It took into consideration as relevant circumstances that, though the young members of the Royal Family were in fact public figures (although of minor importance), they had in no way whatsoever given cause for a greater interest of the media in their private lives, and that the news value of the news facts purportedly gathered (the start of a new education) was marginal.[3]

7   Informational privacy

20.20   Informational privacy is associated with the right of the individual to decide in principle for himself about the release and the use of personal data. In this respect, the right to respect for one's private life may be infringed:

(1)   by *interference* in the communication between the individual and third parties, for instance by breaching the confidentiality of the mail, or telephone and telegraph,

(2)   by *recording* personal data on a medium, multiplying this medium, or storing personal data on a database and by abusing this data, or

(3)   by the *publication* of information concerning a person.

The interference in the communication between the individual and third parties or the *recording* of personal data is in principle unlawful in the event that it comes under the Criminal Act (see para **20.03**) or constitutes an invasion of the spatial privacy (see para **20.06**). In addition, the recording can be unlawful if there exists a threat that the data will be made public,

---

20   Cf Hubmann, *Das Persönlichkeitsrecht*, 1967, at 262–270.
1   Cf President District Court Alkmaar, 2 June 1967, NJ 1967, 284 (*'Ongewijde aarde'*): motion picture producer invaded private life of family by filming during funeral. Injunction to prevent the showing of the motion picture in part of the Netherlands.
2   President District Court Roermond, 12 September 1985, KG 1985, 299.
3   Supreme Court, 4 March 1988, NJ 1989, 361 (*Children Princess Irene*).

and the publication in itself will constitute an unlawful invasion of the privacy right.

The question under what circumstances *publications* concerning a person may be unlawful is dealt with separately below in paras **20.08** et seq and paras **20.13** et seq.

B Personality

1 *Right to one's personal name*

20.21 Article 1:8 of the Civil Code states that whoever uses another person's name without this person's permission, commits a tort against this person if his action creates the impression that he is this person, or belongs to his lineage or family. Loeb writes about the right to one's personal name:

> 'Should a person wish to oppose the use of his name by another person, he needs to have a certain exclusive right to the personal name. [...] Nowadays it is generally accepted that the right to one's personal name is not a property right or something similar, but a so-called personality right. Infringement of such a personality right – a 'subjective right' – may constitute a tort toward the owner of this right'.[4]

The owner of the right to one's name can only oppose the unauthorised use of his or her name in so far as this creates confusion amongst third parties. If a lookalike gives a performance, for payment, under the name of a well-known artist, this artist can state a claim for infringement of the right to his or her personal name, if the audience does not realise that the performance is given by a lookalike. This confusion will be more easily created if a first name or surname or a relatively rare or unique combination of both is involved.

20.22 The advertising standards authority (*Reclameraad*) found that an advertisement for the Post Office Giro (*postgiro*) in which an actress contrary to the truth and without permission presented herself as 'Mrs Dudok van Heel,' violated Article 1:8 of the Civil Code, because in this particular case an uncommon family name was involved and the actress created the impression of belonging to the lineage of the bearer of that surname.[5]

20.23 However, the content of the right to one's personal name is very limited. It only protects against the use of another person's name, as if it is one's own name. The legislator thought of the situation in which B starts calling himself A in everyday life. However, A will not be able to appeal to the right to his personal name, if B uses A's name as an eye-catcher in commercials for B's products. The right to one's personal name also only protects the official first name and/or surname, not, for instance, a pseudonym or a stage name.

---

4 Loeb, *Naam en recht, Praktische beschrijving van het naamrecht in Nederland*, 1990, at 122.
5 Advertising Standards Council (Reclame Raad), 17 January 1983, no 333, PRAR IVN no 8 (*Dudok van Heel*).

2 *Protection of name against unwanted press publications*

20.24   Until 1992 the Civil Code provided special rules for the actions against the torts of slander,[6] defamatory writing,[7] libel[8] or mere insult.[9] Since 1 January 1993 these rules have been left out and an action against a tort can be instituted as a result of any disclosure, press publication or public insult under the general tort clause of Article 6:162 of the Civil Code.

20.25   Article 6:162(1) provides that whoever commits a tort against another person, which can be imputed to him, is liable for damages caused by this tort. Under Article 6:162(2) of the Civil Code, the following acts are deemed to be unlawful: the infringement of a right (eg the right to one's name of Article 1:8 of the Civil Code, copyright, trade mark right or privacy right), an act or omission violating a statutory obligation (eg provisions of the Criminal Act) or an act contrary to what is regarded proper social conduct according to unwritten law. In principle, the publication of an unauthorised biography of a person is not unlawful.

20.26   In most press publication cases, courts have to balance the privacy interest of the plaintiff against the public interest in freedom of speech. In the above-mentioned decision about Princess Irene's children, the Dutch Supreme Court held that:

> 'In the answer, to be found by balancing, to the question whether a press publication that invades another person's right to respect for his private life, is justified by the freedom of speech – the assertion of which constitutional right is inter alia restricted by the rights of others – all particular circumstances of the case in question should be considered'.[10]

In this case, the Amsterdam Court of Appeal had ruled that not only was the manner of news gathering unlawful, but also the report itself. According to the Court of Appeal, the reflections on and suggestions about the children's private affairs constituted an unlawful invasion of their private lives. In appeal, the Dutch Supreme Court held that, in its balancing as meant above, a court may take into account both the nature of the facts that the press publication is based on, and the interests that the newspaper in question endeavours to serve in general, or with the involved publication in particular. Thus the Court of Appeal was allowed to take into consideration that, according to its judgment, the news value of the facts concerned was marginal.

20.27   In the '*Municipal Councillor*' decision (*Gemeenteraadslid X*),[11] the Dutch Supreme Court mentioned circumstances that can be relevant for the question whether the privacy right or the freedom of speech right prevails.

---

6   Article 261(1) Criminal Act defines slander as 'intentional assault of a person's honour or good reputation by charging a specific offence, with the obvious purpose to give it publicity' ('smaad').
7   Article 261(2) Criminal Act defines defamatory writing as 'slander by publication of writings or pictures' ('smaadschrift').
8   Article 262 Criminal Act: slander or libel, while knowing that the charge is false ('laster').
9   Article 266(1) Criminal Act: intentional defamation which is not slander nor libel ('eenvoudige belediging').
10 Supreme Court, 4 March 1988, NJ 1989, 361 (*Children Princess Irene*), para 3.5.
11 Supreme Court, 24 June 1983, NJ 1984, 801 (*Municipal Councillor*).

20.28 The court must balance the interests of individual citizens in not being exposed to rash imputations by publications in the press against the interest that abuses which concern society may survive, due to a lack of information among the general public. Which of these interests should be the prevailing in a given case depends, inter alia, on:

(1) the nature of the imputations made public and the seriousness of the consequences that may be expected with respect to the person they concern;

(2) the seriousness – in the light of public interest – of the abuse that the publication endeavours to denounce;

(3) the extent to which the imputations were, at the time of publication, supported by the factual material available at that time;

(4) the presentation of the imputations viewed in relation to the factors mentioned under (1), (2) and (3);

(5) the extent to which it is likely that, even without the litigated press publication, the goal which is pursued in the public interest could have been achieved with a reasonable chance of a rapid success through other means, less harmful to the opposing party;

(6) a possible limitation of the damage caused by the press publication to the person who is affected by it, considering the likelihood that the question would have become public even without the litigated publication being at the disposal of the press;

(7) the authority of the medium;[12]

(8) the public position of the plaintiff;[13]

(9) a possible financial interest in accusing the plaintiff;

(10) the extent to which the plaintiff had an opportunity to answer the imputations.[14]

20.29 In the '*Haarlem building fraud*' case (*Haarlemse Bouwfraude*), the Dutch Supreme Court upheld the decision of the Amsterdam Court of Appeal, in which it stated that daily newspaper *De Telegraaf* acted unlawfully against A, since it accused him of having been the brain behind the so-called 'Haarlemse Bouwfraude' (Haarlem building fraud). Here the Court of Appeal took into consideration that, at the time of publication, the published accusations of A were little supported by the then available factual material, which made it fairly likely that the accusations were unfounded. It also took into consideration the nature of the published accusations, the seriousness of the consequences that could be expected by A and the fact that the goal pursued by publication could be considered of minor

---

12 The authority that third parties may assign to whoever made an actual statement public can be relevant: Supreme Court, 27 January 1984, NJ 1984, 803 (*Vara and Bom/Leading Succes People*).

13 Supreme Court, 27 January 1984, NJ 1984, 802 (*De Telegraaf and the Haarlem building fraud*).

14 President District Court Amsterdam, 2 February 1995, KG 1995, 146 (*Van Sprundel/ TROS*): tv-broadcasting by TROS in consumer television programme 'Radar' which showed reporter's unannounced confrontation of plaintiff with complaints of a consumer without giving plaintiff opportunity to reply is contrary to principle of hearing. However, the President did not enjoin the television program because plaintiff was unable to provide a valid reason for the problems raised.

importance, since the accusations were already known to the police and the Public Prosecutor.[15]

20.30 Most press publications that are challenged in court are those in which the plaintiff is accused of some wrongful act. In such cases, the most important question seems to be the extent to which the imputation was, at the time of publication, supported by the then available factual material. However, this factor is not relevant in publications in which the truth of the alleged facts is not an issue. For example, the Arnhem Court of Appeal ruled that a (true) press publication of the Police of Arnhem about a criminal action against the plaintiff, owner of a garage, was unlawful, because there was no specific need for the police to publish it.[16]

20.31 Article 10(2) of the ECHR states that freedom of speech may only be limited if necessary in a democratic society, and for the protection of the rights of others. Since the mid-1990s, in press publication cases, the Supreme Court has explicitly applied the analysis of Article 10(2) of the ECHR by investigating whether the outcome of the balancing of the specific circumstances by the Court of Appeal is necessary in a democratic society and for the protection of the rights of others.[17]

20.32 In addition to an injunction against the publication, and compensation for material and immaterial damages, the injured party may also claim rectification of the defendant's unlawful press publication under Article 6:167 of the Civil Code (see para **20.02**).

3 Protection of name against unwanted fictitious stories

20.33 Persons recognising themselves in fictitious stories or movies may under certain circumstances oppose publication, if the public is led to believe that the described negative context in which this person is placed is not fiction but reality. For example, the President of the Amsterdam District Court prohibited KRO's television screening of Pinto's story *The Woman's Angle* under the title *Louise*, since the plaintiff recognised herself in the main character, who was portrayed in the movie as an indecent woman whose political trustworthiness was questioned. The judge was of the opinion that there was sufficient similarity between the life story of the plaintiff and that of the main character, whose middle name was Louise. This was not altered by the fact that the plaintiff had not opposed (the translation of) the English book by Pinto, on which the television story had been based.[18] The Amsterdam Court of Appeal prohibited the publication of the book *Seizoenarbeid* (Seasonal Work) by Lodewijk H Wiener, in so far as it contained the 27-page short story 'Jansen'. The court found that the plaintiff could recognise himself in the character 'Jansen,' a Zandvoort restaurant owner, who was caught in a compromising situation with a waitress in the story. The court held that it would be difficult for those readers who were familiar with Zandvoort to distinguish between reality

---

15 Supreme Court, 27 January 1984, NJ 1984, 802 (*De Telegraaf and the Haarlem building fraud*).
16 Court of Appeal Arnhem, 25, July 1989, KG 1989, 323 (*State/J*).
17 Supreme Court, 21 October 1994, NJ 1996, 346 (*Blijf van m'n lijf/Multi Magazines*), and Supreme Court, 6 January 1995, NJ 1995, 422 (*Het Parool et al/Van Gasteren*).
18 President District Court Amsterdam, 4 December 1962, NJ 1963, 64 (*Louise*).

and fiction, and the reading public would therefore be generally inclined to accept the situations described as the truth.[19]

20.34   However, the sister of Margaretha Geertruida Zelle (better known as Mata Hari) could not oppose the showing of a movie about Mata Hari, in which there is a scene where Mata Hari kills general Shubin. The President of the Rotterdam District Court found that the movie about the exotic dancer and spy for the German government, who stole the heart of Russian lieutenant-airman Alexis Rosanoff, and was eventually executed after the French court-martial, does not represent a historically accurate picture of the life story of Mata Hari. Neither would the public interpret the movie as such. This was not altered by the announcement of the movie as *Mata Hari's Life Story*, according to the President.[20]

4   Protection of name against unwanted commercial use

20.35   The District Court of the Hague held that the unauthorised mention of the names of the eleven football players of the Dutch National Football Team in an advertisement for milk in the national newspapers, immediately before an international match, was not unlawful towards the players. Profiting from a current event on a once-only basis in a commercial, in which the name of a popular person is mentioned, was not held to be unlawful as long as the advertised product is not linked to the person involved in such a way that it leads the public to think that person endorses the defendant's product. The advertiser did not act unlawfully since he did not create the false suggestion that the players endorsed his product.[1]

20.36   However, the Rotterdam District Court ordered car manufacturer Honda to pay damages of NLG 50,000 to concert pianist *Pogorelich* because Honda had used his name without his permission as an eye-catcher in an advertising campaign in national and regional newspapers and magazines for the promotion of the Honda Accord car.[2] The Court rejected Honda's defence that Pogorelich could not appeal to the protection of the commercial value of his name, since he was not very well-known to the general public. The Court also rejected Honda's defence that 'they might just as well have used the name of another concert pianist' stating that the incorrectness of this defence is evident from the fact that Honda did use his name for its advertisement. Finally, the Court rejected the defence that Pogorelich did not suffer damages, since Honda had increased his popularity with its advertising campaign. The Court held that Honda had acted unlawfully by taking away Pogorelich's freedom to decide for himself whether or not and under what circumstances he would like to see his name and qualities connected with another's sales activities. Unlike the Hague Court, the Rotterdam Court did not require any false endorsement.

19 Court of Appeal Amsterdam, 12, October 1967, NJ 1968, 21 (*Wiener' novel, Jansen*).
20 President District Court Rotterdam, 24 Octoer 1932, NJ 1932, at 1602 (*Zelle/Tuschinsky*).
1   District Court the Hague, 16 May 1986, IER 1986, no 56, at p 120 (*Dutch Football team*).
2   District Court Rotterdam, 4 February 1994, NJ 1995, 39; IER 1996, no 20, at 113 (*Pogorelich/Honda*). In its interlocutory judgment, the District Court found that a damage award of NLG 10,000 was a reasonable, and in the relevant sector common compensation. In so far as Pogorelich claims more damages, he had to prove it. In its final judgment, the District Court granted an award of NLG 50,000, see District Court Rotterdam, 22 June 1995, IER 1996, no 20, at 116 (*Pogorelich/Honda*).

5 Names and trade mark law

20.37 Personal names can be registered as a trade mark so long as that serves to distinguish the goods or services of an enterprise. Problems may arise if someone does not register his own but *another's* name. In a 1957 case the Dutch Supreme Court determined that Dutch law does not prohibit the unauthorised use of another person's name as a trade name or a trade mark in general. In the *'Elkington'* decision the Dutch Supreme Court considered that the use of another person's name as a trade mark does not constitute a tort on the mere basis that it causes damages to the bearer of that name, but that additional circumstances are required.[3]

20.38 The Benelux Countries did not implement in the Benelux Trade Mark Act ('BTMA') the optional provision of Article 4(4)(c)(i) of the European trade mark Harmonisation Directive, which provides that an EU Member State may rule that no right to a trade mark shall be acquired if it conflicts with a 'right to a name'. However, one may argue that the registration of another person's name as a trade mark may be unlawful towards the bearer of that name, if at the time of registration of the trade mark the public already associates that name with its bearer as a result of his fame, and if the depositor attempts to profit from this fame. In addition, one may also argue that under Article 4(6) of the BTMA no right to a mark can be acquired by a filing effected in bad faith.

C Publicity

1 Likeness right

20.39 In the Netherlands, the likeness right is recognised in the Copyright Act 1912 ('CA'). Article 21 of the CA provides:

> 'If a portrait has been produced without any particular instructions given to the author by or on behalf of the portrayed, or to his benefit, the publication of that portrait by the person who owns the copyright, is prohibited, as far as *a reasonable interest* of the portrayed or, after his death, of one of his next of kin, opposes publication.'

Literally, Article 21 of the CA only regulates the legal relation between the person portrayed and the copyright owner of the likeness. However, it is generally recognised that the likeness protection can also be invoked against any third party who publishes the likeness. One may summarise the likeness right of Article 21 of the CA as a right to oppose the publication of one's likeness on the basis of a *'reasonable interest'*. The portrayed can exercise his likeness right during his lifetime. After his demise, under Article 25a of the CA, only the 'parents, spouse, and children,' as next of kin, can oppose the publication of the likeness of the deceased on the grounds of their own reasonable personality interest.

20.40 The 'reasonable interest' criterion is therefore the pivot of Dutch likeness law. The publication or exploitation of the non-ordered likeness

---

3 Supreme Court, 29 November 1957, NJ 1958, 31 (*Technisch Bureau/Dover*).

by the author or any third party is not allowed in so far as a reasonable interest of the portrayed opposes this. In 1912, the legislator presumed that a reasonable interest was purely a *personality/privacy interest* (see para **20.14**). However, since 1959, courts have also acknowledged as reasonable the *financial interest* of a popular person to oppose the unauthorised commercial exploitation of his likeness (see para **20.20**).

2 *Personality interests*

20.41 In so far as Article 21 of the CA protects personality or privacy interests, it can be considered as a particular form of the general privacy right as recognised by Article 10 of the Constitution and Article 8 of the ECHR. The Netherlands Supreme Court perceives the right of privacy as the legal basis for the protection of the portrayed.[4]

20.42 Before 1994, some courts had held that the presence of a reasonable interest of the portrayed makes a publication per se unlawful. If the portrayed has a reasonable interest in the likeness not being published, one should not balance this interest against other (free speech) interests. However, in the *Ferdi E* case, the Supreme Court ruled that any reasonable interest of the portrayed must be balanced with other (important) interests. The Court considered that Article 21 of the CA on the one hand affords the portrayed protection against invasion of the right to respect for his or her private life, but that this right does not carry an absolute weight, which is, in principle, more important than that of the right of freedom of speech. According to the Dutch Supreme Court it:

> 'concerns two kinds of freedom, that are essential to both the development of the individual and the democratic society as such, and there are no grounds on which one should accept a hierarchy between these two kinds of freedom, as where the plea [of Ferdi E] starts from'.[5]

As a result, the answer to the question whether the publication of a likeness, which invades the right to respect for one's private life, is unlawful, can only be found by a balancing of interests, considering all the particular circumstances of the given case, in order to discover which of the two fundamental rights, privacy or freedom of speech, is more important.

20.43 It is possible to distinguish several categories in case law with respect to the personality interest. As a rule of thumb, one may say that a publication of a likeness will be considered an unlawful invasion of a person's private life if it:

(1) shows intimate parts of the body of the portrayed;

(2) is publicised in connection with an unwanted commercial product;

(3) falsely suggests a connection between the portrayed and the publication;

(4) causes physical danger to the portrayed or destroys the portrayed's new life.

---

4   Supreme Court, 1 July 1988, NJ 1988, 1000 (*Vondelpark I*).
5   Supreme Court, 21 January 1994, NJ 1994, 473 (*Ferdi E/Uitgeverij Spaarnestad*).

3 Intimate parts of the body

20.44   The mere fact that a person has been portrayed naked, in principle, constitutes a reasonable interest which opposes publication. Only under particular circumstances can this be otherwise. This was decided by the Dutch Supreme Court in the *'Naturist'* case. It concerned a photograph of an eighteen-year-old girl, taken during the holidays, when she was staying, naked, in a naturist camp in France. The photograph, that was taken with the permission of the girl, was published eleven years later on the back cover of the international naturist travelling guide of 1984–1985, which was generally available in bookstores. She successfully opposed this publication. The Dutch Supreme Court considered that 'the decision of the Court of Appeal that the mere fact that X has been portrayed in the nude constitutes a reasonable interest which opposes publication, apart from specific circumstances,' is correct. The circumstances that the portrayed is a naturist herself, and that the guide was solely intended for naturists, did not influence the decision, since the guide was also available to non-naturists.[6]

20.45   However, actress Van Drumpt could not oppose the publication of stills, consisting of nude photographs taken of her from the movie *De gulle minaar* (The Generous Lover), in the monthly magazine *Playboy* with an additional text about the movie and about Van Drumpt. The Haarlem District Court considered that the interest of the defendant in publication of the photographs prevailed since the monthly magazine came out just before the release of the movie, which should be considered a news fact. Playboy has a legitimate interest in publishing items about the course of the plaintiff's career.[7]

4 Invasion of privacy by commercial use of a likeness

20.46   The Netherlands Supreme Court held that a person portrayed, in principle, *will always* have a reasonable interest to oppose the use of his likeness as support *in a commercial advertisement.*[8] According to the Court, use of a likeness in an advertisement for goods or a service will cause the public to associate the portrayed with those goods or that service, and the public will, in general, assume that such use is not without permission and a testimony of public support of that good or service by the portrayed. The Supreme Court confirmed that persons have a privacy interest not to be used for commercial products and advertisements by a third party. The Court did not require the plaintiff to prove mental damages. Thus (non-famous and famous) persons can oppose the unauthorised use of their portraits in advertisements on the ground that the public will wrongly assume that a permission was granted.

However, some authors have argued that the words 'in principle' make clear that persons cannot oppose the unauthorised commercial use of their portraits if the public *will not* get this wrong assumption. For example, one

---

6   Supreme Court, 30 October 1987, NJ 1988, 277 (*Naturist*).
7   District Court Haarlem, 8 February 1994, Mf 1994, B35 (*Van Drumpt/Uitgeverij Spaarnestad*).
8   Supreme Court, 2 May 1997, NJ 1997, 661 (*Disco dancer in advertisement for gay party*).

author argued that the use of portraits of four politicians (ministers) in an advertisement for services of a leasing company should not be held unlawful, since the public will not assume that they granted permission.

20.46　In 1988, cafe 'Bukowski' was opened in Haarlem. Two glass doors with the likeness of the writer Charles Bukowski embellished the entrance of the cafe. Posters with the likeness of the writer were distributed around the town. The President of the Haarlem District Court considered this use of the writer's likeness for commercial purposes as an infringement of his reasonable personality interest. Bukowski had a strong aversion to publicity because he did not want to see his personality connected with any form of commerce.[9]

5　False suggestion of connection between portrayed and context of publication

20.47　Courts have generally recognised the reasonable interest in opposing the creation of a false impression that the portrayed has anything to do with the subject matter of a publication, which is undesirable in his opinion. The unlawfulness is a result of the *false* suggestion that was given to the public. The false suggestion can be created by

(1)　manipulating a photograph;

(2)　placing a likeness in an undesirable context, or with an undesirable text;

(3)　falsely suggesting a contribution to the publication; or

(4)　the false suggestion that the portrayed has received a payment for the publication.

20.48　Examples of subject matters of publications which a portrayed does not want to be identified with, are sex/pornography, criminality, drugs, gambling, prostitution, unpopular political ideas, or social problem cases.

For example, the President of the Amsterdam District Court granted an injunction against an integral broadcasting by television station NCRV in the programme *Surveillance*, which showed the plaintiff, a mother, and her children in the context of a police investigation into her life. The President found that the NCRV has the right to inform the public about the police's method of working including the investigation into the mother's life. However, in this case, the interests of the plaintiff prevailed because the criminal case against the plaintiff had been dismissed, and the program contained disapproving remarks of the police about the plaintiff, which caused the impression that the plaintiff acted ina blameworthy fashion towards her children. The President ordered the NCRV to make the plaintiff and her children unrecognisable.[10]

9　President District Court Haarlem, 8 August 1989, BIE 1990, no 71, at 227 (*photograph of Bukowski*).

10　President District Court Amsterdam, 20 January 1995, KG 1995, 83 (*PHB/NCRV*).

6 Exposing the portrayed to physical danger or danger to a newly-built life

20.49 Publication of a likeness is unlawful if physical danger can arise for the portrayed because of this publication. For example, the publication of the likeness of the only witness of a robbery, of which, at the time of publication, the offenders are still at large, is unlawful. The Netherlands Supreme Court considered that there can be a reasonable interest 'if there is [an] actual possibility that the portrayed [...], also as a result of that publication, will suffer damages'.[11]

20.50 In the '*Zwerven in het Paradijs*' case, the President of the Amsterdam District Court granted an injunction against television station NCRV to broadcast a recognisable likeness of the plaintiff in a film about homeless young persons. The plaintiff had co-operated in a recording of her private life when she was a 17-year old. However, 18 months later the plaintiff opposed the broadcast of her likeness because the film showed intimate data about her life, such as her motherhood, problems keeping her former boyfriend, a possible new pregnancy, and her venereal disease, for which she did not want to have medical treatment. After the recording, the plaintiff had built a new life, with new friends, schoolmates, and in-laws, who did not know about her past. The President ruled that under these circumstances, the plaintiff's privacy interest outbalanced NCRV's interests to broadcast her recognisable likeness.[12]

20.51 In the *Ferdi E* case, on 17 February 1989, the defendant had published an article in its weekly magazine *Panorama* about 'The Six Most Notorious Postwar Killers'. In this article the author gave an account of his investigation into the backgrounds and motives of these convicts. The article was illustrated with six photographs, one of which was a photograph of the plaintiff Ferdi E, the murderer of industrialist G J Heijn. One month later, defendant published the photograph again in an article which gave information about the awarding of the Silver Camera to the best press photograph of 1988. Next to this article were fourteen prize-winning photographs, one of which was a likeness of Ferdi E, the photograph that won the first prize in the category 'News'. Toward the end of 1988, Ferdi E was sentenced irreversibly to 20 years' imprisonment for the murder on G J Heijn. This offence had attracted a lot of public attention. Ferdi E stated that both publications of his likeness after his conviction were unlawful. The Haarlem Court decided that Ferdi E had a reasonable interest in opposing the publication, and declared that the publications were unlawful.[13]

In appeal, the Amsterdam Court of Appeal decided that the publications were not unlawful, since the interests of *Panorama* in the publications under the given circumstances, ranked higher than the interests of Ferdi E. The Court of Appeal considered that the defendant did not obtain the photographs in an unlawful way, that the photographs in themselves were of a neutral nature, and that in both cases the publication of the photograph was functional for the provision of news and information to the readers.

11 Supreme Court, 21 October 1969, NJ 1971, 124 (*Witness robbery*).
12 President District Court Amsterdam, 2 February 1995, KG 1995, 137 (*X/NCRV*).
13 District Court Haarlem, 15 March 1991, Mf 1991, B53 (*Ferdi E/Uitgeverij Spaarnestad*).

The photograph of Ferdi E in the article of the 'Six Most Notorious Postwar Killers' added to the expressiveness of the article. The Court of Appeal acknowledged that the publication of the photographs could interfere with the rehabilitation of Ferdi E, since it is likely that he will be recognisable to the public in future, but this interest was considered less important. The Court of Appeal considered relevant that, at the time of publication by the defendant, more than one photograph of Ferdi E was already in circulation. The Dutch Supreme Court rejected Ferdi E's cassation plea.[14]

7   Balance of interests

20.52   Judging all the circumstances of the actual case, it must be decided whether a publication of a likeness infringes the personality right of the portrayed. In principle it can be stated that outside the four categories mentioned in para **20.18**, the freedom of expression prevails. However, in exceptional cases, courts have recognised that a publisher is obliged to take reasonable care that the privacy interests of the portrayed will not be endangered. This is the case if publication entails *special risks* with respect to the privacy of the portrayed, which could and should have been foreseen by the publisher. Whether that risk exists, depends again on all the circumstances of the case. It becomes apparent from case law that the following non-exhaustive list of circumstances can be relevant:

(a)   Questions with respect to the likeness:

    (1)   Under what circumstances was the likeness produced? On private property/in public? How was it produced? Unexpectedly or openly? What equipment was used: long-focus lens?

    (2)   What is the nature of the likeness? How old is this likeness? What is the size of the likeness? Was the likeness generally obtainable before?

    (3)   In what way is the plaintiff portrayed? Does it involve intimacy? Has the likeness been manipulated?

    (4)   What is the degree of identification?

(b)   Questions with respect to the medium:

    (5)   In what particular medium was the likeness made public? What is the nature of the public that the medium is focusing on? What is the size of the public? Does the medium have a direct financial interest in harming the portrayed?

    (6)   In what context is the likeness placed? What is the nature of the additional text? How will the public read the context?

    (7)   What is the function and purpose of the publication? Could the purpose of the medium be pursued in any other way but publication? Was is it, in light of this purpose, possible to verify whether the portrayed had any objections?

    (8)   What is the informational or entertainment value of the publication?

---

14   Supreme Court, 21 January 1994, NJ 1994, 473 (*Ferdi E/Uitgeverij Spaarnestad*).

(c) Questions with respect to the portrayed:

>   (9) What kind of person is the portrayed? Did the portrayed 'provoke' the publication? Is the portrayed a private or a public figure? Did the portrayed act as a public or private person?

>   (10) What are the actual objections of or disadvantages to the portrayed? What is the seriousness of the consequences that may be expected with respect the publication?

20.53   In the '*Vondelpark*' case, after a referral by the Supreme Court,[15] the Amsterdam Court of Appeal[16] came to the conclusion, with the help of a checklist of questions suggested by the Dutch Supreme Court, that the portrayed did have a reasonable interest in opposing the publication of her likeness in a weekly magazine. It concerned a photograph that was published in the weekly magazine *Nieuwe Revu*, in an article about the Vondelpark in Amsterdam. On that particular photograph the face and the body, down to the knees of the plaintiff L, are portrayed, while she is taking a walk with her fiancé of that time. They are holding each other very close. In the background one can see trees, a pond and a tea house. The Court of Appeal investigated whether L's right to respect for her private life had been infringed by this publication of the photograph, so that a reasonable interest of L could oppose the publication of her likeness. The Court of Appeal considered that the photograph, because of the fixation of L on her boyfriend (3), was of an obvious intimate nature (2), that L was clearly recognisable (4) on the photograph, which was quite large: it covered 2/3 of two adjoining pages (2). Regarding the circumstances under which the photograph was taken (1), the Court of Appeal considered that the photograph was taken deliberately at a moment that was totally unexpected to the person portrayed in it, in a park, a public place, albeit with a certain reputation for attracting lovers.

20.54   With respect to the medium (5), the Court of Appeal considered that the photograph was published in a weekly magazine with a circulation of 200,000 copies. Because of this fact the possibility was greater that acquaintances from the plaintiff's neighbourhood would recognise her. The photograph was published in an article entitled 'Vondelpark, vrijplaats voor geluk' (Vondelpark, Refuge for Happiness), in which a suggestion of eroticism, freedom of opinions and behaviour in the Vondelpark, came into prominence (6). Subsequently the Court of Appeal came to the conclusion that '*Nieuwe Revu,*' by publishing this by no means offensive or degrading photograph, still took the risk that publication without her permission could be perceived by L as very disturbing. Since it did indeed appear later that L felt aggrieved by the publication, L's right to respect for her private life had been invaded. The relationship with her new boyfriend ended when he saw the photograph of L with her former boyfriend (9). The publication led to uncomfortable feelings, shame and grief (10).

The defence of *Nieuwe Revu*, that the photograph was taken on the public road and that it could not have foreseen the exceptional reaction of L, was rejected. The Dutch Supreme Court stated explicitly that the question whether L had a reasonable interest, should be judged in the light of her

15 Supreme Court, 1 July 1988, NJ 1988, 1000 (*Vondelpark I*).
16 Court of Appeal Amsterdam, 27 April 1989, NJ 1990, 370 (*Vondelpark II*).

actual circumstances and her background, and that it was not relevant whether similar objections would exist for other persons.

According to the Court of Appeal, the publication without permission of the photograph in question (questions 1–4) in the chosen context (questions 5–6), entailed special risks to the publisher with respect to the person and the privacy of the portrayed, which the defendant could and should have foreseen. According to standards of fairness, the Court of Appeal assessed the immaterial damages at NLG 1,000.

20.55   The term *'reality television'* is a term that refers to the growing phenomenon of television programs which show local real life, such as reports about the daily life of policemen, firemen, ambulancemen. Often the persons who feel that they are filmed in a disqualifying context, submit legal claims against the stations that broadcast such programs. Recently, some authors have suggested that the interests of the persons portrayed in reality television programs are insufficiently protected, and proposed to give them a few days time for reflection in order to decide whether they wished to oppose the broadcast. However, courts have not recognised specific rules for reality television cases, and solved such cases according to the general principles as outlined above. In principle, the broadcast of reality television programs is not unlawful, unless the person portrayed can show specific circumstances leading to the conclusion that the right to respect his or her private life must prevail. The Arnhem District Court ruled that the detailed broadcast of the likeness of a car driver after an accident constituted an infringement of the likeness right, that was not justified by the public interest in news about the accident. The court found it relevant that the victim had protested against the filming and that it was possible to broadcast the news without showing the victim's identity by making the likeness unrecognisable.[17]

8   Commercial interests

20.56   With the changing of public opinion and the rise of new media, it frequently occurred that well-known persons, who had no fundamental objections, gave permission to use their likeness for commercial purposes. The consequence of this was that portrayed persons also started to appeal to *commercial interests* in legal proceedings. A court recognised a commercial interest in opposing an unauthorised publication of plaintiff's likeness for the first time in 1959.[18]

20.57   Twenty years later, in 1979, the Netherlands Supreme Court has also acknowledged a commercial interest as a reasonable interest within the meaning of Article 21 of the CA. In this case it concerned the publishing of a photo book entitled *'t Schaep met de vijf Pooten* (the sheep with the five legs), in which colour photographs of several scenes from the television series of the same name were printed. The actors from these scenes had only given permission for publication of their photographs in newspapers and magazines in order to inform the reading and viewing public. They opposed the publication of their photographs in a photo book since they

17   22 January 1998, AMI 1998, 120 (*Van Hesteren/Ordelman*).
18   President District Court Rotterdam, 14 April 1959, NJ 1959, 648 (*Teddy Scholten*).

did not receive any financial compensation for this. They were of the opinion that the publisher unlawfully took advantage of their popularity, which enabled them to gain a financial benefit. They stated that they had a reasonable commercial interest within the meaning of Article 21 of the CA, and claimed damages of NLG 10,000.

20.58 The Amsterdam District Court awarded the sum of NLG 6,000. The Court considered a reasonable commercial interest present, since the private commercial interest of the publisher was very prominent when the photo book was put on the market. The photo book contained a reproduction of the text of the television series with the photographs as an additional illustration. The plaintiffs could ask for financial compensation for their permission because they were popular. The Amsterdam Court of Appeal upheld the decision in appeal and the Dutch Supreme Court rejected the appeal. In appeal to the Supreme Court, the publisher stated that Article 21 of the CA only protects immaterial interests, but this was rejected by the Dutch Supreme Court:

> 'Although, at the time of enactment of the Copyright Act, by using the words 'reasonable interest' in Article 21, the legislator must mainly have thought of non-financial interests, there can – also in view of the development of public opinion in this regard – also be a reasonable interest, when the popularity of the portrayed persons, obtained in their profession, is of such a nature that a commercial exploitation of that popularity, by any form of publication of their portraits becomes possible. The interests of the portrayed to be able to share the advantages of such exploitation by not agreeing to publication of their portraits for commercial purposes without receiving financial compensation, is a reasonable interest within the meaning of Article 21.'[19]

20.59 The Supreme Court only recognised the reasonable *commercial* interest with respect to persons:

(1) who have a certain popularity;
(2) which is obtained in their profession; and
(3) which can be commercially exploited.

20.60 The Court has not yet rendered a decision with respect to *commercial* interests of other (non-famous) persons. However, such persons are not without any right, since they can also invoke their privacy interests under the rule of the Court's 1997 decision discussed in para **20.16**.

20.61 The persons who meet the three requirements, can oppose the unauthorised 'commercial exploitation' of their likeness. In case law, three types of commercial exploitation are recognised:

(1) use of a likeness in order to promote the sale of commercial products;
(2) use of a likeness in advertisements for these products; and
(3) use of a likeness in connection with information media if the portrayed could have stipulated a financial compensation.

---

19 Supreme Court, 19 January 1979, NJ 1979, 383 (*'t Schaep met de vijf Pooten*).

20.62 The categories (1) and (2) are not problematic. For example, the Hague District Court held that the distribution of free photographs of members of the Beatles to buyers of chewing gum is unlawful since Beatles did not give permission.[20] The Cantonal Court Harderwijk ruled that the unauthorised use of a photograph of professional iceskater Yep Kramer in an advertisement for heaters in two magazines, constituted an infringement of Article 21 of the CA. The court awarded NLG 5,000 for damages.[1]

20.63 The third category is more problematic since in that case forms of likeness use in an information medium are labelled as '*commercial exploitation*'. Here courts have to balance the commercial interest of the plaintiff versus the public interest in freedom of speech.[2] For example, the Haarlem District Court held that unauthorised publication of a likeness of amateur boxer Arnold Vanderlijde in magazine *Panorama* was contrary to his commercial likeness right. The defence that it concerned an illustration to an article was rejected, since the way in which the likeness was published clearly went beyond the illustrative use and pointed to an intention of commercial exploitation. It was relevant that the likeness was printed on a double page, exactly in the centre of the magazine, and was advertised as a 'poster'. Besides, the 'poster' was announced on the cover of the magazine, and the name of the magazine was printed in a misleading way on the boxing gloves and the boxing outfit of Vanderlijde.[3] In appeal, the case was upheld. The Amsterdam Court of Appeal rejected Spaarnestad's free speech defence to publish an illustration next to an article because the way of publication made clear that in this case it was 'a publication for *primarily* commercial purposes'.[4]

9   *Civil remedies*

20.64 A person whose privacy is invaded or whose name or likeness is illegally made public, can institute the following actions:

(1) a claim for an injunction;
(2) a claim for damages;
(3) other actions, such as a claim for the statement in court regarding the unlawfulness of the publication; a claim for publication of the decision;
(4) a claim for rectification; a claim for taking back the objects on which the publication has been made public.

Article 6:162(1) of the Civil Code provides that whoever commits a tort against another which can be imputed to him, must compensate the damages which the other person suffers as a consequence thereof. Since the mid-1980s, an *advance* of approximately NLG 5,000–10,000 has increasingly been awarded in summary proceedings, in cases of unlawful competition. Article 6:96(1) of the Civil Code provides that both loss suffered and profit of which the plaintiff has been deprived may be considered commercial damages.

---

20   President District Court the Hague, 15 April 1964, NJ 1964, 483 (*Beatles*).
1   Cantonal Court Harderwijk, 4 June 1991, PRG 1991, 3507 (*Yep Kramer/Burnham Europa*).
2   See for an extensive discussion of this problem: JCS Pinckaers, From *Privacy Toward a New Intellectual Property Right in Persona*, Chs 9 and 10 Kluwer Law International, 1996.
3   District Court Haarlem, 6 November 1990, AMI 1991, at 198.
4   Court of Appeal Amsterdam, 27 May 1993, NJ 1994, 658 (*Vanderlijde/Panorama*).

20.65   The following forms of material damages are generally distinguished in the event of infringement of intellectual property rights:

(1)   loss of a licence compensation;
(2)   limited sales potential for one's own or authorised products, because potential clients have purchased defendant's product;
(3)   depreciation of the right itself, as a result of damage to the reputation or exclusivity of the protected object; and
(4)   other types of damages mentioned by Article 6:96(2) of the Civil Code, such as costs for the prevention of damage and costs for the assessment of damage.

Under Article 6:104 of the Civil Code, the judge can also assess the damage according to the amount of the profit or a part thereof that defendant has gained as a result of his tort. A plaintiff may claim his lost profit or defendant's profit, but the judge will be able to award only one of these two claims, which in his opinion agrees most with the nature of the damage.

20.66   If a person's privacy is invaded, or if the portrayed has a reasonable privacy interest to oppose the publication of his likeness, he is entitled to compensation for *immaterial damages*, fixed in accordance with what is considered fair, if, as a result of the publication his honour or good reputation has been harmed, or if he has otherwise been *injured in his person.*[5] Immaterial damage does not consist of commercial damages or reduction of property, but involves mental grief, mental discontent or a reduction in one's sense of pleasure or joy in life. The judge must assess the amount, in accordance with what is considered fair, since feelings, such as irritation, offence, or grief, cannot be expressed exactly in terms of money. The amount of immaterial damages that the judge awards in the event of infringement of the likeness right, depends on the seriousness of the infringement of the private life and usually lies somewhere between NLG 500 and NLG 10,000.

---

5   See art 6:106(1) Civil Code using the words 'harm other than commercial damage'.

21 NEW ZEALAND

Ken Moon
Bona Lee

A Privacy

Privacy generally

21.01 It appears that the tort of privacy is now established in New Zealand.[1] The courts had previously followed English common law[2] in refusing to recognise such a tort. In addition, statutory protection for the privacy of personal information exists in the form of the Privacy Act 1993 and the Broadcasting Act 1989 regulates the activities of radio and television broadcasters in relation to the privacy of individuals. Privacy claims may have to be made by way of proceedings for defamation, breach of confidence and/or breach of copyright where circumstances admit.

21.02 At least in the first instance, complaints under the more specific statutory provisions must be taken to tribunals outside the general court hierarchy in New Zealand. Thus complaints under the Privacy Act are heard by the Complaints Review Tribunal while complaints under the Broadcasting Act are heard by the Broadcasting Standards Authority. Until recently, privacy complaints would only be heard by judges if appeals were taken from the lower special-purpose tribunals.

21.03 The New Zealand Bill of Rights Act 1990 contains in section 14 a right of freedom of expression. The right of freedom of expression and in particular freedom of the media to publish matters in the public interest will be a defence to privacy claims in appropriate cases.[3] The media are essentially excluded from the ambit of the Privacy Act provided they are engaged in news-gathering activities.

Common Law Privacy Protection

21.04 The 'new' tort of privacy in New Zealand encompasses public disclosure of private facts. According to the High Court in *P v D & Independent News Auckland Ltd*, breach of the tort is determined by considering four factors:

---

1 *P v D & Independent News Auckland Ltd* [2000] 2 NZLR 591;*Tucker v News Media Ownership Ltd* [1986] 2 NZLR 716; *Bradley v Wingnut Films Ltd* [1993] 1 NZLR 415; *Hobson v Harding* (1995) 1 HRNZ 342.
2 Eg *Kaye v Robertson* [1991] FSR 62, CA.
3 *TV3 Network Services Ltd v Fahey* (Unreported, CA, 1 December 1998, CA 276/98).

(1) that the disclosure of the private facts must be a public disclosure and not a private one;

(2) facts disclosed to the public must be private facts and not public ones;

(3) the matter made public must be one which would be highly offensive to a reasonable person of ordinary sensibilities; and

(4) the nature and extent of legitimate public interest in having the information disclosed.

The right of freedom of expression under the New Zealand Bill of Rights Act 1990, section 14, was said by the court to be 'subject to limitations of privacy as well as other limitations such as indecency and defamation'.

The development of this tort is still in its infancy in New Zealand, but since the High Court in both the *Independent News Auckland Ltd* case and the *Bradley* case[4] relied on US texts, it is likely much of the US jurisprudence on privacy will now be applicable in New Zealand.

Privacy Act 1993

21.05 The object of the Privacy Act is to promote and protect individual privacy in accordance with the 1980 Organisation for Economic Co-operation and Development ('OECD') Guidelines Concerning the Protection of Privacy and Transborder Flows of Personal Data. It is thus primarily, although not exclusively, a data protection law. It is the essential purpose of the Act to establish privacy principles in respect of the collection, use and disclosure by public and private sector agencies of information relating to individuals and also principles establishing access by individuals to information relating to them.

21.06 Complaints are made in the first instance to the Privacy Commissioner. The Commissioner makes an investigation (which can be made on his own initiative in the absence of the complaint) and forms an opinion about whether there has been an interference with the privacy of an individual. There must be a breach of one of the 12 information privacy principles set out in the Act. The Commissioner may act as a conciliator or he may refer the matter to the Proceedings Commissioner of the Human Rights Commission. Only the Proceedings Commissioner has the power to take a case to the Complaints Review Tribunal which has powers to grant enforcement orders and award compensation. Decisions of the Complaints Review Tribunal may be appealed through the general court system with the first level of appeal to the High Court. The Complaints Review Tribunal may make one or more of the following orders:

(1) a declaration that a privacy principle has been breached;

(2) an order restraining the agency in breach;

(3) an award of damages to the complainant;

(4) a remedial order; or

(5) other relief it considers appropriate to the circumstances.

21.07 A recent media-related case taken to the Complaints Review Tribunal is *Talley Family v National Business Review*.[5] The Talley family were named in a 'Rich List' as published by the weekly business newspaper

---

4   See para **21.01**, n1 above.
5   (1997) 4 HRNZ 72.

National Business Review. The Talley family complained that their naming was a breach of their privacy. The Tribunal held that the publication of the Rich List was a 'news activity' since it involved the gathering or dissemination of news and observations on news or current affairs. The Privacy Act applied to 'agencies' and agencies did not include the news media when involved in news activities. National Business Review did not therefore infringe the Privacy Act.

21.08 All individuals are entitled to protection under the Privacy Act whether nationals or citizens of foreign countries.

Broadcasting Act 1989

21.09 The Broadcasting Standards Authority exercises jurisdiction under this Act and is in practice the major regulator of media-related privacy in New Zealand.

21.10 Under section 4(1)(c) a radio or television broadcaster is responsible for maintaining in its programmes and their presentation standards which 'are consistent with the privacy of an individual'. In its first decision in 1990[6] the Broadcasting Standards Authority formulated a set of privacy principles which it would apply to complaints under section 4(1)(c). It decided that it could not simply apply general lay notions of privacy and in the absence of a developed tort of privacy in New Zealand decided to adopt concepts from US privacy jurisprudence. There would be a breach of privacy where there was:

(1) public disclosure of highly offensive private facts, the disclosure of which would be objectionable to a reasonable person of ordinary sensibilities;

(2) public disclosure of highly offensive public facts including public facts which have become private again through, for example, the effluxion of time; and

(3) situations involving the intentional intrusion of a person's solitude or seclusion. The intrusion must be offensive to a reasonable person of ordinary sensibilities. It is not an intrusion under this principle to be pursued or photographed while in a public place.

21.11 The Authority's reliance on elements of US case law was upheld by the High Court in an appeal brought in 1995.[7]

21.12 The penalties which the Authority may impose under section 13(1) include compensatory damages and an award of costs. The maximum damages that can be awarded is modest being only $5,000. Where it is known in advance that a damaging television programme is to be screened an injunction application may only be made to the High Court. No practical mechanism is available via the Broadcasting Standards Authority for such pre-emptive action. Since the Broadcasting Act provisions can only be invoked in a complaint taken to the Authority, the causes of action which must be relied upon to support an application to the High Court must be such as defamation, trespass and/or the new tort of breach of privacy.

---

6 *Re Macallister* [1990] NZAR 324.
7 *TV3 Network Services Ltd v Broadcasting Standards Authority* [1995] 2 NZLR 720.

21.13 It is, however, rare that injunctions are granted in cases such as this. One of the usual considerations for granting an interim injunction (arguable case) does not apply where defamation is a cause of action. 'Any prior restraint of free expression requires passing a much higher threshold than the arguable case standard'.[8] Indeed freedom of expression, public interest and consent (which may be implied) are three of the more significant defences to complaints of invasion of privacy.

21.14 At least in relation to broadcasters, case law in New Zealand has established that the filming of a person on private property irrespective of where the camera may be located may breach a persons privacy where there is no consent.[9] The situation is different where the person being filmed is aware of the situation and chooses to continue an interview, especially if that person is a public figure.[10] The use of a telephoto lens per se will only breach privacy if used for the purpose of permitting the filming camera to be concealed. The use of an assumed identity to obtain information and the sifting through a person's rubbish to ascertain information would be unlikely to breach any laws in New Zealand and it is considered that the use of security camera footage for reporting events would not infringe existing law although in some circumstances may breach any future tort of privacy which may be developed. On the other hand covert filming and the covert recording of a conversation may be permissible provided the purpose is the exposure of possible serious misconduct which is in the public interest.[11]

B Publicity

Passing off, trade marks and fair trading

21.15 There is no general right of publicity recognised under New Zealand law. That is, there is no specific tort or statute which provides persons with the right to control the commercial exploitation of their identity. Protection, if available at all, must be sought in the laws of defamation, registered trade marks, passing off or breach of the Fair Trading Act 1986. For the moment it is still an unresolved issue as to whether the courts will adopt an expansive formulation of the law of passing off to provide protection for personas as has happened in Australia.[12]

21.16 It is possible for a person to register their name as a trade mark in relation to particular goods or services although there must be a bona fide intention to use the mark. It would then be an infringement to use that name as a trade mark or in a trade mark sense in relation to the registered goods or services. As a defensive measure to secure control over the use of a person's name trade mark registration has limitations. First the registration could be removed from the register if not used in the course of trade for a

8   *TV3 Network Services Ltd v Fahey* (CA, 1 December 1998, CA 276/98).
9   *TV3 Network Services Ltd v Broadcasting Standards Authority* [1995] 2 NZLR 720.
10 *Laws v TV3* (BSA 1997, 24, 6 March 1998).
11 *TV3 Network Services Ltd v Fahey* (CA, 1 December 1998, CA 276/98).
12 *Henderson v Radio Corporation Pty Ltd* [1960] NZWR 279; *Hogan v Koala Dundee Pty Ltd* (1988) 12 IPR 508; *Hogan v Pacifica Dunlop Ltd* (1988) 12 IPR 225; *Pacific Dunlop v Hogan* (1989) 14 IPR 398.

five-year period and, secondly, could not be used to stop unauthorised non-commercial use such as in news reporting, documentations and gossip columns. That said, trade mark registration must be considered an essential part of any authorised merchandising programme.

21.17   The law of passing off in New Zealand (at least in its core form) is essentially the same as it is in the United Kingdom.[13] It provides a remedy where the reputation or goodwill of a trader is appropriated by another trader. A plaintiff must show:

(1)   a reputation or goodwill in his goods or business;

(2)   a misrepresentation made to consumers by the defendant in the course of trade so as to cause confusion in the minds of consumers as to whether the defendant's activities are those of the plaintiff; and

(3)   damage or likelihood of damage as a result of the defendant's actions.

21.18   The classic requirement for a misrepresentation considerably limits this cause of action as a remedy for persons whose names have been associated with the goods or services of another without their consent. The New Zealand courts have not considered cases where the name or persona of a real person has been appropriated but there has been an indication that they may[14] adopt the more liberal requirements for passing off as have been formulated by the Australian courts.[15]

21.19   The New Zealand courts have in the main not required that the defendant be engaged in a common field of activity with the plaintiff[16] and deal with this issue as a factor in determining confusion.[17] This indicates a preparedness to move beyond the restrictive line of English case law and removes at least one of the barriers to the use of the law of passing off to protect unauthorised use of persons' names.

21.20   The Fair Trading Act 1986 provides remedies for deceptive conduct in the course of trade. Some misrepresentation is inevitably required for there to be deception and mere confusion without deception, as arises in many unauthorised uses of a person's name, cannot be remedied under this law. Unlike passing off, there is no requirement for a plaintiff to show damage and on this count the Fair Trading Act may offer an avenue of redress in appropriate cases involving trade.

---

13   The principles enunciated by Lord Diplock in *Erven Warnink BV v J Townsend and Sons* [1979] 2 All ER 927 are followed by the New Zealand courts.

14   Per Fisher J in *Tot Toys Ltd v Mitchell* [1993] 1 NZLR 325.

15   *Henderson v Radio Corporation Pty Ltd* [1960] NZWR 279; *Hogan v Koala Dundee Pty Ltd* (1988) 12 IPR 508; *Hogan v Pacifica Dunlop Ltd* (1988) 12 IPR 225; *Pacific Dunlop v Hogan* (1989) 14 IPR 398.

16   *Weight Watchers International Inc v Quality Bakers of New Zealand Ltd* (1980) 1 NZIPR 293.

17   *Taylor Bros Ltd v Taylors Group Ltd* [1988] 2 NZLR 1, 20.

C Personality

Protection of likeness

21.21 As with the right to control publicity, New Zealand does not recognise any general law protecting a person's likeness or image ('persona'). Unlike many of the states in the US the law in New Zealand has not evolved to keep pace with the multiplicity of ways and the ease with which personality can be exploited at the end of the twentieth century. Protection of the misuse of a person's likeness has traditionally only been available when the use has been defamatory[18] or where a breach of photographic copyright[19] has been involved.

21.22 As mentioned in relation to publicity there are some indications that the courts may adopt a more liberal view of the law of passing off, to protect at least the personas of real people if not those of fictitious characters. In *Tot Toys Ltd v Mitchell*, a case dealing with a famous New Zealand toy, 'Buzzy Bee', Fisher J commented:

> 'I think that a distinction should immediately be drawn between the promotional use of the names, reputations and images of real persons and artificial character merchandising. Few would dispute that real persons should generally have the right to prevent the unauthorised promotional use of their persona. There may be a case for going beyond existing causes of action to ... North American causes of action for appropriation of personality and/or breach of rights of privacy and publicity. That, however could have no bearing upon rights with respect to artificial images .... [for which] .... there is already considerable protection from trade marks, registered designs, patents, the Fair Trading Act and copyright....'

21.23 Much of what has been stated under publicity above equally applies in relation to the protection of likenesses. New Zealand law is really only starting to move away from a regime where well-known figures had little control over their personas apart from defamation law. Although the practice is not uncommon there is probably no need for film and television producers to obtain 'releases' from persons interviewed in their place of business or home - provided of course there is no issue of trespass.

---

18 In accordance with the 1930s English case *Tolley v Fry* [1931] AC 333.
19 In the case of actors, any such copyright will usually be owned by a production company.

22   NORWAY*

Lee A Bygrave
Ann Helen Aarø

A   Privacy

1   Provisions providing for protection of privacy

22.01   Privacy is protected in Norway not only by specific constitutional and statutory legislation but also by non-statutory means derived from decisions in specific reported cases.**

2   Constitutional protection

22.02   There is no provision in the Norwegian Constitution (*'Grunnlov'*) of 1814 dealing specifically with the protection of privacy. The closest to such a provision is section 102, which prohibits searches of private homes except in cases of criminal investigation. More generally, section 110c of the Constitution places state authorities under an express duty to 'respect and secure human rights'. However, the Constitution itself lacks a comprehensive catalogue of basic human rights and freedoms. This shortcoming, though, has been mitigated to some extent by the recent incorporation into Norwegian law of, inter alia, the European Convention on Human Rights and Fundamental Freedoms ('ECHR') of 1950 and the International Covenant on Civil and Political Rights ('ICCPR') of 1966 – both of which contain such a catalogue, including express rights to privacy.[1] Formally, neither the ECHR nor ICCPR enjoy constitutional status in Norway, but they do enjoy a relatively strong, semi-constitutional status in light of section 110c of the Constitution (see above) together with the fact

---

*Unless otherwise specified, all legislative references are to statutes in their amended state as of 1.8.2000.
***Abbreviations*
EC   European Community
RG   Rettens Gang (Norwegian Court Reporter)
Rt   Norsk Retstidende (Norwegian Law Reports)

1   See the Human Rights Act 1999 (*lov om styrking av menneskerettighetenes stilling i norsk rett av 21 mai 1999 nr 30*).

that the provisions of the ECHR and ICCPR shall prevail over conflicting provisions in other Norwegian statutes.[2]

Note should also be made of the 'principle of legality' (*'legalitetsprinsippet'*) in Norwegian law. This is an unwritten norm rooted in customary law and enjoys constitutional status. In a nutshell, it requires that actions by public authorities which infringe significantly on the rights and freedoms of private citizens (eg police surveillance), be authorised by statute.[3]

3 Statutory protection

Public disclosure of information

22.03 Currently, the most direct statutory protection for privacy is provided by section 390 of the Criminal Code 1902 (*almindelig borgerlig straffelov 22 mai 1902 nr 10*). Section 390 punishes violation of 'privacy' (*'privatlivets fred'*) caused by 'public disclosure of information relating to personal or domestic affairs'. Although this provision has long featured in the Criminal Code, it has rarely been applied or commented upon by the courts. Moreover, the relevant *travaux préparatoires* say little about the provision. Thus, the exact ambit of the provision remains relatively uncertain. One unresolved issue, for instance, is whether or not section 390 may protect the privacy interests of legal/juristic persons. Nevertheless, the provision has a potentially wide-ranging area of application given that it does not require that information be disclosed via a specified type of medium nor that the disclosed information be gathered by a specified means. Section 390 could apply, for example, to situations in which information gleaned from the sifting of a person's household rubbish, is made public. It could equally apply to situations involving public disclosure of information gleaned from the filming (aerial or at ground-level) of a person's home. However, section 390 will not prohibit the actual act of sifting garbage or filming. Such acts, though, could arguably be prohibited by section 390a of the Criminal Code which punishes violation of a person's 'peace of mind' (*'fred'*) brought about by 'frightening or irritating behaviour' or other 'inconsiderate actions' (*'hensynsløs atferd'*).

Privacy of communications

22.04 Several other provisions in the Criminal Code also serve to protect privacy. One such provision is section 145 which punishes unauthorised opening of sealed correspondence together with the cracking of security mechanisms in order to gain unauthorised access to, inter alia, data stored or transmitted electronically. Complementing section 145 is section 145a, which punishes the covert monitoring and/or recording of telephone conversations and other conversations in closed settings.

Video surveillance

22.05 The Criminal Code contained provisions punishing covert television surveillance of public areas or workplaces (section 390b). These

---

2   See s 3 of the Human Rights Act.
3   As such, the principle of legality complements the requirements of, inter alia, art 8(2) of the ECHR.

provisions – along with others on video surveillance – have now been incorporated (with some amendments) into Norway's new data protection legislation, and are dealt with further below under the rubric of 'data protection'.

Breach of confidence

22.06 Section 121 of the Criminal Code punishes breaches of statutory duties of confidence. Such duties are created by a large number of statutes: central examples are section 13 of the Administrative Procedures Act 1967 (*lov om behandlingsmåten i forvaltningssaker 10 februar 1967*), section 31 of the Medical Doctors Act 1980 (*lov om leger 13 juni 1980 nr 42*) and section 9-3 of the Telecommunications Act 1995 (*lov om telekommunikasjon 23 juni 1995 nr 39*).

Defamation

22.07 Also pertinent in the Criminal Code are sections 246 ff, which punish defamation. It is noteworthy that proof of truth is not an absolute defence to a defamation action: under section 249(2), a truthful defamatory statement is still punishable if it is issued without any 'worthy ground' (*'aktverdig grunn'*) or is otherwise 'improper' (*'utilbørlig'*) on account of the form or manner in which it is issued.

Sanctions for breach

22.08 In all of the above cases, punishment for the illegal action may take the form of either fine or imprisonment.

Protection of foreigners

22.09 All of the above provisions may serve to protect the privacy interests of not only Norwegian nationals but also foreign citizens on Norwegian territory (cf section 12 of the Criminal Code).

Wire tapping

22.10 Derogation from some of the above provisions is permitted in furtherance of police investigation of crime. Thus, chapter 16a of the Criminal Procedure Act 1981 (*lov om rettergangsmåten i straffesaker 22 mai 1981 nr 25*) permits police wire tapping for the purposes of investigating narcotics crime, while section 1 of the Control of Postal and Telephonic Communications Act 1915 (*lov om kontroll med post- og telegrafforsendelser og med telefonsamtaler 24 juni 1915 nr 5*) provides statutory authority for police wire tapping in cases involving risks to national security. Wire tapping in both cases must be approved by a magistrates' court before it may be initiated. In essence, court approval in cases concerning narcotics crime may only be given when there is 'reasonable ground' (*'skjellig grunn'*) for suspecting criminal conduct and the wire tapping is of 'essential significance' for the police investigations: see further sections 216b ff of the Criminal Procedure Act. As for cases concerning national security, court approval may only be given when there is a 'grounded suspicion' (*'Når noen med grunn mistenkes ...'*) of criminal conduct and the wire tapping is viewed as 'necessary' (*'påkrevd'*) with respect to national security: see further section 1 of the Regulations on Postal and Telephonic Control (*forskrifter om post-*

og telefonkontroll 19 august 1960 nr 2). It should be noted that police do not have any legal authority to bug rooms.

4 Data protection

Legislation

22.11   Norway's principal piece of data protection legislation over the last two decades has been the Personal Data Registers Act 1978 (*lov om personregistre mm av 9 juni 1978 nr 48*). The Act is in the process of being replaced and repealed by the Personal Data Act 1999 (*lov om behandling av personopplysninger av 14 april 1999 nr 31*), in force as of 1.1.2001. This legislative renewal has come about partly in order to meet new technological developments and partly in order to bring Norwegian law into conformity with the requirements of the 1995 EC Directive on data protection.[4] Thus, the provisions of the Personal Data Act 1999 (PDA) follow closely those of the Directive.

As with the 1978 Act, the PDA has been drafted as framework legislation that is to be supplemented by more detailed rules – primarily in the form of regulations.[5] Nevertheless, the PDA contains more numerous and detailed substantive rules than the 1978 legislation. For example, it delineates more clearly core data protection principles, such as that of purpose specification (ie that personal data should be collected and processed for specified, legitimate purposes and not further processed in a way that is incompatible with those purposes: see section 11(1)(c)). To take another example, the PDA includes an objects clause (section 1) – unlike the 1978 Act. Further, the regulatory focus of the PDA differs somewhat to its predecessor. The 1978 legislation focuses to a considerable extent on the creation and use of *registers* of personal data. The new Act – in line with the EC Directive – shifts regulatory focus to the 'processing' of data largely irrespective of the way the data is organised and largely irrespective of the technology used.

Institutional arrangements

22.12   The PDA partly preserves and partly changes the institutional arrangements established under the 1978 Act. The Data Inspectorate ('*Datatilsynet*') – a special, independent agency established to oversee implementation of the 1978 legislation – has been retained to monitor and enforce implementation of the PDA (section 42). The Inspectorate also retains many of the broad discretionary powers it has enjoyed under the 1978 Act, even though the PDA cuts back significantly on the licensing requirements of the old legislation (see further below). A major change is

---

4   Directive 95/46/EC of the European Parliament and of the Council of 24 October 1995 on the protection of individuals with regard to the processing of personal data and on the free movement of such data (OJ L 281, 23.11.1995, p 31). Although Norway is not an EU member state, it is party to the 1992 Agreement on the European Economic Area (EEA). As such, Norway is legally bound to comply with the Directive once the latter has been formally incorporated into the EEA Agreement. Incorporation took place on 25.6.1999.

5   At the time of writing this chapter, no such regulations had been issued. Hence, the following presentation of data protection rules is confined to the provisions of the PDA.

the establishment under the PDA of a new quasi-judicial body – the Data Protection Tribunal (*'Personvernnemda'*) – to handle appeals from decisions of the Inspectorate (section 43). Under the old legislation, such appeals have been handled directly by an ordinary government department (usually the Ministry of Justice) – an arrangement that risks undermining the independence of the Inspectorate.

Decisions of the Data Protection Tribunal may be appealed to the courts on questions of law. There is reason to doubt that numerous such appeals will eventuate. During the life of the 1978 Act, extremely few decisions of the Inspectorate have been appealed relative to the number of cases handled by it. Moreover, the courts have played a marginal role in interpreting and applying the legislation.

Legal/juristic persons

22.13 Whereas the 1978 legislation expressly protected data on private corporations and other legal/juristic persons to much the same extent as data on individual natural/physical persons, the PDA dispenses completely with express protection for legal person data. However, the PDA does permit protection for legal person data to be introduced in the future with respect to credit-reporting activities (section 3(4)). At the same time, it should not be forgotten that legal person data capable of being linked back to a specific individual will be regarded as 'personal data' pursuant to the new Act. Data on small companies will often be of this character.

Basic rules for processing

22.14 As a point of departure, the processing of personal data for non-private purposes[6] is prohibited unless it satisfies one or more conditions (section 8). These conditions basically follow Article 7 of the EC Directive and are, in summary, as follows:

(a) the data subject (ie the person to whom the data relates) consents to the processing;

(b) the processing is authorised by statute;

(c) the processing is necessary for concluding a contract with the data subject;

(d) the data controller is legally required to carry out the processing;

(e) the processing is necessary for protecting the 'vital interests' of the data subject;

(f) the processing is necessary for performing a task executed in the public interest or in exercise of official authority; or

(g) the processing is carried out in pursuance of a 'legitimate interest' that overrides the conflicting interests of the data subject.

Following Articles 8 and 20 of the EC Directive, the PDA lays down somewhat sharpened conditions for the processing of certain kinds of especially sensitive data. This data concerns a person's racial or ethnic origin, political, religious or philosophical beliefs, criminal record, trade-union membership, health or sex life (section 2(8)). In addition to having to satisfy

---

6   The PDA – like the EC Directive – does not cover data processing for purely personal or other private purposes (s 3(2)).

one of the conditions set out in section 8, the processing of such data must also meet one of a set of conditions laid down in section 9. These conditions basically follow Article 8 of the EC Directive. More significantly, the processing of such data is also made conditional upon formal approval (in the form of a licence) being obtained from the Data Inspectorate (section 33). There are, however, several exceptions to this licensing requirement (see para **22.18** below).

22.15 The processing of personal data must otherwise conform to a large number of ground rules the most important of which are set out in section 11 and which essentially replicate the provisions of Article 6 of the Directive. Thus, personal data must only be processed for specifically given purposes that are 'objectively justifiable' (*'saklig begrunnet'*) with respect to the activities of the data controller (ie the person/organisation responsible for the data processing)(section 11(1)(b)). The data must not be subsequently used for purposes that are incompatible with the original purposes, unless the data subject consents to such use (section 11(1)(c)). Further, the data must be adequate and relevant for the purpose(s) for which it is processed (section 11(1)(d)), correct and up-to-date, and not stored for longer than necessary (section 11(1)(e)). Certain exceptions to these rules are permitted for the processing of personal data for historical, statistical or scientific purposes (section 11(2)).

22.16 Moreover, data controllers are placed under a duty to implement 'planned and systematic measures' for ensuring information security and for otherwise ensuring that the requirements of the PDA are met (sections 13–14). Data controllers must additionally document these measures.

22.17 With regard to regulating transfers of personal data to countries outside the EU/EEA (ie so-called 'third countries'), the PDA basically repeats what is contained in Articles 25 and 26 of the EC Directive.

Notification and licensing

22.18 The 1978 legislation has required, with some exceptions, that all personal data registers which are computerised or contain certain sensitive data must be licensed by the Data Inspectorate prior to their establishment. A licensing requirement has also been stipulated for certain kinds of businesses, such as credit-reporting agencies. In line with the EC Directive, the PDA cuts back extensively on such requirements. As noted above, licensing is now necessary only for the processing of sensitive data as defined in section 2(8), unless the data subject has voluntarily supplied the data or the processing is carried out by a government agency pursuant to statutory authorisation (section 33(1)) or the processing consists of television surveillance (defined below) for the purposes of crime control (section 37(2)). At the same time, though, the Data Inspectorate is empowered to determine, on a case-by-case basis, that other data-processing operations require licensing when they 'obviously infringe weighty data protection interests' (*'åpenbart vil krenke tungtveiende personverninteresser'*) (section 33(2)). One indication of what such interests may involve is provided in section 1(2), which elaborates the need for 'personal integrity' (*'personlig integritet'*), 'privacy' (*'privatlivets fred'*) and 'adequate information quality' (*'tilstrekkelig kvalitet på personopplysninger'*) as figuring amongst 'fundamental data protection concerns' (*'grunnleggende personvernhensyn'*).

22.19 The bulk of data-processing operations are subject only to a requirement that they be notified to the Data Inspectorate (sections 31–32). Exemption from this requirement is provided for non-automated data registers, unless they contain sensitive data as defined in section 2(8) (section 31(1)(b)).

Data subjects' rights

22.20 Data subjects enjoy a large number of rights under the PDA. Arguably, the most important of these rights is data subjects' right of access to data on them held by others (section 18). This right of access supplements, and is co-ordinated with, access rights provided under other legislation, notably the Administrative Procedures Act 1967 – which provides parties to an administrative case access to the case documents (see especially section 18) – and the Freedom of Information Act 1970 (*lov om offentlighet i forvaltningen av 19 juni 1970 nr 69*) – which provides citizens a general right of access to government-held information.

Other examples of data subjects' rights are a right not to be subject to direct marketing (section 26) and a right not to be subject to fully automated decision making based on use of a personal profile (section 25).

Duty to inform

22.21 Under the influence of Articles 10 and 11 of the EC Directive, data controllers are placed under a duty to inform, of their own accord, the data subject of basic details about their data-processing practices (sections 19–20). At the same time, the Norwegian legislation goes further than the Directive by including a duty of information when, on the basis of a personal profile, either the data subject is approached/contacted or a decision, directed at the data subject, is made. In such a case, the data subject must be automatically informed of the data controller's identity, the data constituting the profile and the source of these data (section 21).

Television surveillance

22.22 The PDA – like the 1978 Act – includes rules dealing specifically with television surveillance (defined as 'continuous or regularly repeated personal surveillance with the aid of a remotely controlled or automatically operational television camera, photographic apparatus or similar equipment': section 36). The concept of television surveillance is sufficiently broad to cover operations in which personal data is not actually registered or stored (eg on film). Surveillance involving the registration/storage of personal data must conform with all of the general rules of the PDA. Surveillance which is directed at a location 'regularly trafficked by a limited number of persons' (eg a workplace) is permitted only if there is 'special necessity' ('*særskilt behov*') (section 38). Adequate warning (eg through use of signs) must be given about such surveillance and of surveillance in public places (section 40; cf former section 390b of the Criminal Code). The Data Inspectorate is also given competence to step in and prohibit surveillance that does not meet with the above rules (section 46).

Sanctions for breach

22.23 A variety of sanctions and remedies are stipulated for breach of the rules in the PDA. Provision is made for a combination of penalties (fines and/or imprisonment), compensatory damages and, where applicable, revocation of licences (sections 46 ff). New in relation to the 1978 Act is that the Data Inspectorate is empowered to impose ongoing enforcement damages during the time in which a data controller fails to comply with the Inspectorate's orders (section 47). Also new is that compensation may be awarded for purely non-economic injury (section 49(3)). Strict/objective liability for damages is stipulated in relation to harm caused by credit-reporting agencies (section 49(2)). No express allowance is made for class actions to be brought.

5 Case law

Privacy and personality

22.24 In addition to statutory protection for privacy, there exists in Norwegian law a general protection of personality which exists independently of statute law but which helps constitute the normative underpinnings of the latter, and which can be developed and applied by the courts on a case-by-case basis. There are only a handful of judicial decisions in which this non-statutory protection of personality has been applied. Nevertheless, it is clear from these decisions that a major dimension of such protection is the safeguarding of a person's interest in privacy.

This privacy dimension was first drawn out in a famous decision of the Norwegian Supreme Court in 1952.[7] The case concerned plans to publicly screen a film that, though primarily fictional in character, was based upon a set of brutal crimes committed some twenty years earlier by two men. One of the latter – who had since served a prison sentence for the crimes, changed his name and begun a new life – objected to the planned screening of the film for fear that it would reveal his background and thereby damage his attempt to embark on a new existence. The Court found in his favour, holding that the screening of the film would breach non-statutory protection of the plaintiff's personality.[8]

Surreptitious surveillance

22.25 More recently, doctrine on non-statutory protection of personality has been applied to cases involving surreptitious surveillance. The leading case here concerned the lawfulness of video recordings surreptitiously made by a snack-bar owner of the activities of a woman working in the snack-bar.[9] The Supreme Court ruled that the video recordings violated non-statutory protection of the employee's privacy as the woman had not

---

7 Rt 1952, p 1217.
8 If this case were to come up for judicial consideration today or in the near future, it is – at the very least – questionable whether the Court would go so far as to issue such an injunction, given that the right to freedom of expression appears to be gaining greater prominence and weight in the Norwegian legal system. This development is due in no small part to the case law of the European Court of Human Rights pursuant to art 10 of the ECHR. Indeed, the above decision of the Norwegian Supreme Court would quite likely fail to satisfy the requirements established in the art 10 case law, particularly the requirement (pursuant to art 10(2)) that interference with the right to freedom of expression be anchored in a legal norm that is precise enough to enable citizens reasonably to foresee its consequences.
9 Rt 1991, p 616.

been informed beforehand that the recordings would be made. Accordingly, the court refused to allow the recordings to be admitted as evidence in prosecution of the woman for the crime of embezzlement. The same line was subsequently taken by the Agder Court of Appeal in a case involving a broadly similar set of facts, though in relation to prosecution for a civil offence.[10]

Electronic data

22.26   Also noteworthy is a decision by the Asker and Bærum Court of First Instance concerning covert surveillance of electronic data files.[11] In this case, the court ruled that a company director's surreptitious monitoring of the contents of private data files kept on the company computer system by an employee was in breach of non-statutory rules on privacy protection.

Remedies

22.27   It should be emphasised that violation of non-statutory rules for protection of personality and privacy is strictly a civil law offence; criminal law sanctions cannot apply. Remedies may take the form of injunction, payment of compensatory damages and/or exclusion of evidence attained as a result of the violation.

B   Publicity

1   Use of a person's name and/or biography

Specific issues

22.28   Use of a person's name and/or biography is restricted to some degree by both civil and criminal law. The rationale for such restrictions is viewed in Norway as partly concerned with safeguarding individuals' rights to protection of personality and privacy as described in Part A above. The rationale is also partly economic, rooted in protecting individuals' ability to commercially exploit their names and/or biographies. The restrictions are instituted pursuant to a variety of legal rules, each of which relate to quite specific and different situations. In the following, we deal mainly with three sets of issues:

(1)   the extent to which persons who are parties to a civil law suit, or persons who are suspected of, or indicted or convicted for, a criminal offence, may be identified by the mass media;

(2)   the extent to which a person's name may be used for marketing purposes; and

(3)   the extent to which persons can obtain trade mark protection of their names.

---

10   Decision of 5.10.1992, reported in (1992) *Lov & Data* no 34, p 8.
11   RG 1993, p 77.

Right to identify

22.29 Regarding the first set of issues, the general rule is that court proceedings – both criminal and civil – are public. This rule follows from sections 124 and 131 of the Courts Act 1915 (*lov om domstolene 13 august 1915 nr 5*). Under the rule, representatives for the mass media (hereinafter termed 'journalists' for short) may be present at, and report on, official court proceedings. However, should journalists reveal the identity of parties and/or indicted persons *prior* to the initiation of court proceedings, they may be held liable pursuant to two sorts of actions. First, if the person identified is subsequently found innocent or if charges against him or her are dropped, he or she may bring an action for defamation pursuant to chapter 23 of the Criminal Code and demand damages if the information concerned is shown to be false or misleading.[12] Secondly, even if the person is actually convicted, his or her identification prior to the court proceedings may be in breach of section 390 of the Criminal Code and/or of the non-statutory rules on protection of personality, as described in Part A above.

22.30 A general principle of Norwegian law is that journalists' reports of court proceedings have a privileged status *vis-à-vis* actions for defamation. This means that a person identified in such a report usually cannot bring an action for defamation against the journalist concerned (or the organisation for whom the latter works) even if the report contains information that is defamatory under the Criminal Code, as long as the report accurately repeats or describes what has been said in the court proceedings.[13] This rule does not cover, however, the journalist's *own* evaluation of the case or the persons involved. As for defamatory material contained in an indictment, a journalist will also be able to escape an action for defamation based on his or her report of the indictment, if the report simply provides an accurate record of what the indictment contains.[14] Further, journalists have a privileged right to report other events (eg house searches) that result in a person's indictment.[15] However, journalists' reports of the fact that a person has been reported to the police are usually not privileged, although the Supreme Court has held that there might be an exception here for serious cases of public interest.[16] It should also be noted that in all of the above cases, the privileged status of journalists' reports can be lost if the object of the reporting cannot be said to serve any objectively proper or decent purpose; eg if the report is written up and published simply in order to harm the person concerned, or if the journalist only wants to create 'a good story' in a sensationalist sense.[17]

22.31 As indicated above, identifying a person by name may constitute an interference with the person's right to privacy under section 390 of the

---

12 Further on this possibility, see Part C below, under the rubric of 'photographs of court proceedings and suspected criminals'.

13 See eg the Supreme Court decision in Rt 1976, p 1055. The privilege also covers journalists' summaries of court proceedings as long as these give a balanced, correct and objective picture of events.

14 Note that journalists have a right to copies of indictments pursuant to s 22-7 of the Prosecution Instruction 1985 (*forskrift om ordningen av påtalemyndigheten 28 juni 1985 nr 1679*).

15 See eg the Supreme Court decision in Rt 1979 p 807.

16 Rt 1994, p 50.

17 See eg the Supreme Court decisions in Rt 1986, p 1307, Rt 1979, p 1590 and Rt 1987, p 1082.

Criminal Code. However, a person's ability to bring an action pursuant to section 390 is considerably narrowed in relation to journalists' reports of court proceedings, in line with the privileged status of these reports *vis-à-vis* defamation actions.[18] Whether the public disclosure of the identity of a party to a civil-law suit or the identity of a person who is suspected of, or indicted or convicted for, a criminal offence, breaches section 390 will depend on various factors. Reporting at an early stage of the process leading to conviction will interfere more easily with section 390 than will reporting directly after conviction is secured. Disclosure of relatively sensitive personal information (eg information about sexual behaviour) will violate section 390 more easily than disclosure of relatively non-sensitive information. There might often be an interference if the persons' family or other innocent parties is/are identified.

Use of name for marketing purposes

22.32   Regarding issue (2), no statutory rules explicitly protect individuals against use of their personal names. However, both section 1(1) of the Marketing Act 1972 (*lov om kontroll med markedsføring og avtalevilkår 16 juni 1972 nr 47*) and the non-statutory rules on protection of personality (described in Part A above) are applicable. Section 1(1) of the Marketing Act provides, inter alia, that business activities must be conducted in conformity with 'good business practice' (*'god forretningsskikk'*) and 'good marketing practice' (*'god markedsføringsskikk'*).

22.33   There has only been one civil law suit in Norway regarding a company's exploitation of an individual's personal name for marketing purposes.[19] In this case, a well-known Norwegian country-music artist pressed charges against a company for use of his name for marketing purposes without his consent. The Oslo City Court found that the use of his name was not in conformity with 'good business practice' pursuant to section 1(1) of the Marketing Act.[20] Neither was it in conformity with the non-statutory rules for protection of the artist's personality, as described in Part A above. The plaintiff was awarded compensatory damages, independent of financial loss, to the sum of NOK 20,000. It is important to note that the application of the particular part of section 1(1) of the Marketing Act utilised in the case was preconditioned by the fact that the plaintiff was a business entrepeneur who used his name for business purposes, though it seems from the court's judgment that this precondition may be met fairly easily. In any case, it appears from the wording of section 1(1) that such a criterion need not be met if one sues on the ground that the use of one's name is in violation of 'good marketing practice'. Such a criterion also need not be met if one sues on the ground that the use of one's name is in breach of non-statutory rules for protection of one's personality.

---

18   See eg the Supreme Court decision in Rt 1952, p 1259.
19   See the decision of the Oslo City Court in RG 1995, p 151.
20   Note that in construing the content of s 1(1) of the Marketing Act, the court made reference to standards found in the International Code of Advertising Practice issued by the International Chamber of Commerce in 1997, especially arts 9 (on 'portrayal or imitation of personal property') and 10 (on 'exploitation of goodwill').

Trade mark protection of names

22.34 Moving to issue (3), it is generally not possible to obtain, pursuant to the Trade Marks Act 1961 (*lov om fellesmerker 3 mars 1961 nr 4*) a trade mark protection of a personal name *solely* to avoid other private persons using one's name. Only special family names may enjoy such protection, pursuant to section 7(2) of the Personal Names Act 1964 (*lov om personnamn 29 mai 1964 nr 1*). If one is involved in some kind of business, one may use one's name as a trade mark for the business, or a combination of one's name and a figure/logo, as long as the use does not conflict with use of other registered trade marks: see generally section 3 of the Trade Marks Act. The user of the name is then protected against others taking the same or similar name to market the same categories of goods or services. Persons can, and are to some degree obliged to, register their business enterprises pursuant to sections 2-1 and 2-2 of the Enterprises Registration Act 1985 (*lov om registrering av foretak 21 juni 1985 nr 78*). The title of a one-person enterprise ('*enkeltmannsforetak*') must contain the surname of the person responsible: see section 2-2 of the Firms Act 1985 (*lov om enerett til firma og andre forretningskjennetegn 21 juni 1985 nr 79*). Registration of the name of a one-person enterprise will prevent others using the same name within the same branch of activity, and in some cases also in other branches: see sections 3-2 to 3-3 of the Firms Act.

C Personality

1 *Personality rights*

Reproduction of photographs

22.35 Section 45c of the Intellectual Property Act 1961 (*lov om opphavsrett til åndsverk mv 12 mai 1961 nr 2*) states that a photograph of a person cannot be copied or shown *in public* without the individual's consent. It follows from the criterion of publicity that the provision is not applicable if the photograph is only shown amongst a small group of persons. Section 45c applies not just to photographs but also video films. It also applies to every medium for publishing photographs of persons – eg newspapers, billboard advertisements, television and the Internet. However, section 45c does not restrict the act of photography itself.

22.36 The prohibition in section 45c does not apply if the photograph is of current and general interest (section 45c(a)). According to the *travaux préparatoires*, this exception means that public figures – eg the royal family, politicians, athletes, artists – and to some degree their families, must accept that photographs of them are published without their consent, especially when the photographs are published as part of news of general interest. Persons involved in a special event of current public interest must also accept non-consensual publication of photographs of them, even though they are not otherwise public figures. At the same time, however, some restrictions on such publication will follow from section 390 of the Criminal Code, described in Part A above.

Another exception from the prohibition in section 45c is if the person on the photograph is less important than the photograph itself – eg if a person is photographed while passing by a political demonstration, unless the photograph focuses on the person directly (section 45c(b)).[1] A further exception is for photographs of groups of people in public places or situations of general interest (section 45c(c)).

Use of photographs for advertising

22.37   As for non-consensual use of a person's likeness for advertising or publicity purposes, this is not explicitly regulated by section 45c. It is, nevertheless, fairly obvious that such use falls within the scope of the provision's general prohibition. Such use may also breach section 390 of the Criminal Code. At the same time, though, such use is not strictly forbidden, on account of consideration for freedom of expression. For example, a writer may be able to publish a biography of a person which contains photographs of the latter, without the latter's consent. But if there is no such close relation between the person and the product in which the person's likeness is depicted, the use of the person's likeness may be illegal. There has only been one case on this issue in Norway, and that case concerned a company which stamped the picture of an artist on a button they produced, without the artist's consent.[2] The company argued that its use of the artist's likeness was covered by section 45c(a) of the Intellectual Property Act. The Horten City Court rejected this argument, stating that even though the artist was well known, the company used her photograph solely for marketing purposes; consequently, the exception in section 45c(a) did not apply. The plaintiff sued for compensatory damages for both economic and non-economic loss. The court awarded her a small sum (NOK 6,000)[3] in damages for economic loss, but held that 'Norwegian tort law does not authorise compensation for personal discomfort in a case of this kind'.

Photographs of court proceedings and suspected criminals

22.38   Section 131(a) of the Courts Act prohibits the taking of any photographs of persons during court proceedings in criminal cases, or taking pictures of the indicted or convicted on his/her way to and from such proceedings. Breach of this prohibition will be punished (only by fines) pursuant to section 198(3) of the Courts Act. Section 6(8) of the Freedom of Information Act provides that pictures of persons stored in the personal data registers of government agencies are not publicly available documents, but journalists will in any case often have pictures of the involved parties, and the question therefore arises if and when such pictures may be used in journalists' case reporting. This question is closely related to the issue of whether journalists are allowed to publish the names of persons involved in a civil or criminal law suit. If the case concerned is serious, and a person has been indicted or convicted, a picture of the person may be published. However, even in such cases, there can be limitations on this ability to publish. The most recent court decision of relevance here concerned a case in which an assistant nurse was indicted for the murder of ten patients at a

---

1   See also eg Rt 1983, p 637.
2   See RG 1983, p 822.
3   The sum was equivalent to the net profit that the defendant was estimated to have made through using the plaintiff's likeness.

nursing home for the aged. Shortly afterwards, a television station identified the nurse with both name and picture. Charges against the nurse were later dropped. The Bergen City Court held that the television station had acted in violation of section 249(2) of the Criminal Code (as set out in Part A above). The court referred especially to the fact that the way in which the television station identified the nurse insinuated that she was guilty. The court's decision, however, was reversed on appeal, first by the Gulating Court of Appeal then by the Supreme Court. In a unanimous decision, the Supreme Court ruled that publication of the name and picture of the nurse did not violate section 249(2) as the matter of the deaths was of serious and extraordinary dimensions and had been justifiably of public concern.[4] The court also ruled that a relevant factor in assessing whether section 249(2) has been breached is the moment at which publication of identity occurs in relation to how far the investigation/prosecution of the matter has come. In the case at hand, the court found that it was not improper to publish the name and picture of the assistant nurse before the magistrates' court had reached a decision regarding her custody.

If the case is less serious – eg concerning a speeding offence or drug abuse – publication of the person's picture will often violate section 390 and/or section 249(2) of the Criminal Code. However, this will not necessarily be the case where the person is a public figure,[5] unless especially intimate matters are involved or respect for the person's family requires non-disclosure.

---

4   Rt 1999, p 1742.
5   For instance, the newspaper publication of a picture of a Norwegian government minister upon losing her driving license as a result of a speeding offence, has been accepted as unproblematic.

23 PORTUGAL

César Bessa Monteiro
Rita Paínho

A Privacy

1 Relevant laws

23.01 Listed below are the laws relevant to the issue of privacy in Portugal.[1]

2 Portuguese constitution

23.02 The Portuguese Republic Constitution ('PRC') expressly guarantees the right to intimacy relating to a person's private life and family in Article 26° in its Rights, Freedom and Guarantees section. In this section it is also possible to find articles relating to correspondence and other private communication systems and data protection. Private life and family intimacy are, therefore, protected by constitutional law, which also requires that guarantees, legal procedures and means of compensation must be established by law, in accordance with constitutional principles. Furthermore, the PRC, in Article 15°, establishes a principle of equal treatment between national citizens and citizens of foreign states, which means that in all respects (other than political rights) the citizens of foreign states who are resident in Portugal are subject to the same constitutional rights and duties as national residents.

3 Criminal Code

23.03 The Criminal Code, in section VII on 'Crimes Against Private Life Intimacy', enumerates conduct which may give rise to criminal proceedings:

(1) intercepting, recording, utilising or transmitting conversations,

---

1 Portuguese Republic Constitution, to rule from 1976 (last reviewed in 1997)
Criminal Code, Decree-law n° 48/95, from 15 March 1995, to rule from 1 October 1995. (Last reviewed in 1998)
Civil Code, Decree-law n° 47344, from 25 November 1966, to rule from 1 June 1967. (Several reviews).
Press Law, Decree-law n° 85-C/75, from 26 February 1975, to rule from 13 March 1975. (Last reviewed in 1996).
Data Protection, Law n° 67/98, from 26 October 1998, to rule from 27 October 1998.
Data Protection Regarding Telephone Transmissions, Law n° 69/98, from 28 October 1998, to rule from 24 October 1998.
Private Security Activities, Decree-law n° 231/98, from 22 July 1998, to rule from 20 October 1998.

including telephone conversations;

(2) recording, filming, taking of photos, recording or disclosing a person's image, objects or private spaces;

(3) watching or listening to persons who are in a private place from a concealed position;

(4) disclosing information regarding a person's private life or their serious illness.

In each of these cases the conduct could lead to criminal proceedings. However, criminal law also requires that two other conditions be satisfied: there must be no prior consent of the victim and there must be a deliberate act aimed at disclosing the victim's private life to the public. Similar provisions relating to correspondence and other private communication systems are also contained in the Portuguese Criminal Code. It is also important to note that the penalties will be greater if violation of private life occurs through the media (Articles 192° to 198°).

Article 199°, section VIII, which deals with 'Crimes Against Another Person's Assets', prohibits recording or disclosure to the public of words, as well as taking photos or filming, without the individual's consent.

Article 290° relates to highway safety and expressly forbids any conduct intended to obstruct any terrestrial communication way, where such conduct may endanger the life or physical well-being of any individual.

The Criminal Code provisions are applicable to all acts performed in Portuguese territory and those whose direct results occur in Portuguese territory, in accordance with Article 7°.

4   Civil Code

23.04   The Civil Code also contains provisions relating to privacy, but the most significant provisions relate to civil liability – Article 483°. Under Portuguese Law, for liability to exist it is necessary for the victim to know of the individual who committed the tort, and it is also necessary to establish default on the part of that person. Civil liability is limited to direct damages, indirect and punitive damages being excluded.

5   Press laws

23.05   The Press Law and Television Law besides containing some provisions relating to the protection of private lives, also provides the possibility of exercising a right of reply. This means that if a person sees a newspaper article or a television programme which makes reference to some aspect of their private life and contains errors, the person may, according to the Press Law, use their right of reply, and under certain conditions require a reply to be published or broadcast on television in which the true and correct facts are presented.

6   Security archives

23.06 The Private Security Activities Law contains provisions regarding filming, the use of security cameras and the storage of recordings. According to Article 12° the use of security cameras is only allowed for the protection and safety of individuals and property and the video recordings must be destroyed within 30 days. Furthermore, the video recordings may only be used as evidence under the terms of the criminal law. It is also necessary that all public places under the surveillance of security cameras give written information to the public (eg 'This place is under video/audio surveillance for your security').

7 Data protection

23.07 So far as data information is concerned, a new law has been published (Law 67/98) as a result of the European Data Protection Directive 95/46/EC. Its scope is defined in Article 4 and it essentially refers to the processing of personal data, whether wholly or partly by automatic means, and includes obtaining, recording, holding, using, disclosing or erasing data.

The main principles regarding data protection are that the data:

(1) should be fairly and lawfully processed;

(2) should only be obtained for certain specified lawful purposes;

(3) should not be further processed in a manner which might be incompatible with those purposes; and

(4) should only be processed once the individual's consent has been obtained.

There are specific rules relating to sensitive personal data, being those concerned with political, philosophical, religious or trade union matters as well as private life information, racial, health and sexual data. In these cases processing is only allowed with the express consent of the individual and upon authorisation of the National Data Protection Commission.

Any individual whose data has been processed in contravention of the provisions of Law 67/98 may complain to the National Data Protection Commission and take administrative or legal action against the offender.

8 Telephone communications

23.08 There are also some specific provisions about data protection regarding telephone transmissions, as a result of the European Telephone Communications Directive 97/66/EEC, which are complementary to the Data Protection Law. For present purposes the most relevant provision is contained in Article 5°, regarding the confidentiality of phone conversations (being applicable also to mobile phone companies). The surveillance or tapping of phones or communications is only permitted with the knowledge and express consent of the individual. Violation of this provision is punishable under Article 33°, n°2 of the Decree-law n° 381-A/97, from 30 December 1997, accordingly with Article 15° of the Data Protection Regarding Telephone Communications Law.

9 Other provisions relating to privacy

23.09 There are a large number of other provisions at law covering aspects of privacy and private life or family intimacy. In fact, there are diverse positions in a large number of state laws relating to recording conversations, taking photos or filming as well as relating to disclosure of matters from the private lives of individuals. Some of these actions may result in criminal, disciplinary or administrative liability and also give rise to claims for compensation. Portuguese law also forbids the film from security cameras being used for reporting events. This kind of filming is permitted for the purpose of the protection and safety of individuals and valuables in public places or places which are open to the public.

Filming on private property without the consent of the owner may be considered trespassing which means that it is always necessary to have the prior consent of the owner. If the filming is carried out with the intent of revealing aspects of the private life of an individual without their consent, this will infringe criminal provisions relating to the individual's privacy. However, in such cases, in order to commence criminal proceedings, it is not only necessary to demonstrate the absence of prior consent, but also the performance of a deliberate act aimed at disclosing the victim's private life to the public.

10 Remedies

23.10   So far as concerns *prevention*, few measures can be taken. In fact, according to Portuguese criminal law, attempt may only be punished in specific cases, data protection legislation being the only relevant legislation for these purposes. It may be possible to obtain an injunction from a civil court in order to prevent the publication or broadcast of private matters. This kind of preventive measure will be difficult to obtain and its results may not be satisfactory. Even if the court retains all the offending material, the reporter already knows the story and may print or broadcast it anyway. Additionally the victim may experience difficulties in producing evidence that the private matters were going to be published or broadcast.

On the other hand, if the violation has occurred, several measures may be taken by the victim, including a complaint in order to obtain disciplinary procedure, criminal procedure and a claim for compensation. The victim may commence criminal proceedings and at the same time bring an action for compensation. The conditions for these legal procedures have already been mentioned.

B   Publicity

1   Relevant laws

23.11   Listed below are the laws relevant to the issue of publicity in Portugal.[2]

---

2   Portuguese Republic Constitution, to rule from 1976 (last reviewed in 1997).
   Criminal Code, Decree-law n° 48/95, from 15 March 1995, to rule from 1 October 1995. (last reviewed in 1998).
   Civil Code, Decree-law n° 47344, from 25 November 1966, to rule from 1 June 1967. (Several reviews).
   Industrial Property Code, Decree-law n°16/95, from 24 January 1995, to rule from 1 June 1995.

2 *Publicity rights generally*

23.12 The Portuguese Republic Constitution, besides protecting individuals' private lives, also considers their right to their good name and reputation and again provides that the guarantees, legal procedures and means of compensation must be established by law.

So far as concerns citizens of foreign states, the same principles and rules that are established regarding 'Privacy' are applicable to the following provisions referred to 'Publicity'.

There are no specific provisions regarding biography in Portuguese law. However, it is necessary to bear in mind that most of the time, the use of a person's biography, necessarily includes several aspects of the individual's private life. Therefore, whenever those aspects are disclosed without the person's consent the provisions mentioned above are applicable.

Article 72° of the Civil Code, states that any individual has the right to use their name and also to oppose its use by someone else for the purpose of identification or for any other purposes. Article 72° permits the commencement of legal proceedings whenever a person's name is used without their consent.

3 *Trade mark protection*

23.13 So far as concerns trade mark protection two aspects should be considered, namely the conditions required to obtain trade mark protection and the possibility of obtaining trade mark protection in respect of a person's name.

In Portuguese law, a mark is a distinctive sign used to identify products or services to be rendered to the consumer. Trade mark signs may have a distinctive character or may be generic. The name 'Pierre', per se, has no distinctiveness (there are numerous individuals named Pierre around the world) but the name 'Pierre Cardin' has distinctiveness, and may be protected as a trade mark.

Article 165° of the Industrial Property Code foresees the possibility of obtaining trade mark protection of a person's name in order to distinguish products or services of a company from the ones offered by other companies. Anyone who has a legitimate interest may apply for the registration of a trade mark, the legitimate interest being defined in Article 168°. However in order to obtain trade mark protection of a name, the distinctive sign must be considered a strong one. Several examples are found in Portugal: Pierre Cardin, Hugo Boss, Calvin Klein, Chanel, among others.

C Personality

1 Relevant laws and codes

23.14 Listed below are the laws relevant to the issue of publicity in Portugal.[3]

2 Personality rights generally

23.15 So far as concerns the Portuguese Republic Constitution and the Criminal Code, the same provisions mentioned at the 'Privacy' and 'Publicity' topics are applicable. In fact, the use of a person's likeness to publish or broadcast public events or private life matters, without the person's consent, may also violate the rights to intimacy, to good name and reputation as well as the right to their image.

The Civil Code contains a provision regarding the right to image in Article 79°, but it essentially refers to portraits of a person and does not mention an individual's likenesses.

So far as concerns advertising for publicity purposes, the Publicity Code, makes reference to the use of a person's image or words, without previous consent, in Article 7°. However, the provision relates to a specific person or someone with a physical resemblance to them.

The most significant provisions are found in various *Codes* related to the advertising business. In fact the Loyal Publicity Practices Code contains some rules regarding private person's protection. Article 8° states that in advertising, the image or representation of a person or words spoken by them should not be used without their prior consent.

Article 14° of the Code also provides that the advertiser, the advertising agency and the editor must ensure that all advertising material created by them complies with all rules. Similar provisions are contained in the International Loyal Publicity Practices Code.

The Conduct Code of the Civil Autodiscipline Publicity Institute defines the competent authorities for the adjudication of any violations of the rules and sets out the procedures and sanctions to be adopted in case of breach. However, the sanctions to be applied are merely internal, not judicial.

---

3 Portuguese Republic Constitution, to rule from 1976 (last reviewed in 1997)
   Criminal Code, Decree-law n° 48/95, from 15 March 1995, to rule from 1 October 1995. (Last reviewed in 1998).
   Civil Code, Decree-law n° 47344, from 25 November 1966, to rule from 1 June 1967. (Several reviews).
   Publicity Code, Decree-law n° 330/90, from 30 October 1990, to rule from 31 October 1990. (Last reviewed in 1998).
   Codes
   Loyal Publicity Practices Code.
   International Loyal Publicity Practices Code.
   Conduct Code of the Civil Autodiscipline Publicity Institute.

3   *Recent case law*

23.16   The Portuguese legal system is a continental law system, meaning that the precedent rule does not have the same extension or importance that it has in a common law system. Previous court decisions in Portugal may be taken into account or referred to in order to decide similar cases, but the Portuguese courts are not bound by those previous decisions or even bound to take them in consideration.

The most common legal actions relate to the press, on which several decisions can be found. The Lisbon Court of Appeal, in a decision dated 21 May 1987,[3] states that civil liability concerning the right to one's good name and reputation, arises not only in relation to untrue facts, but also true facts which describe a person in a false light. The same Court of Appeal, in a decision dated 29 November 1994,[4] considered that the right to inform can only be exercised if it clearly respects a person's right to their good name and reputation.

The Supreme Court of Justice, in a decision dated 29 October 1996,[5] refers to the rights of freedom of expression, media expression and the right to one's good name and reputation. As all these rights are constitutionally granted, it is necessary to define boundaries, whenever a collision between them occurs. The right of freedom of expression and right of media expression must not infringe a person's right to their good name.

D   Conclusion

23.17   Concerning to Privacy, Publicity and Personality rights it is possible to find several dispositions in the Portuguese Legislation. Most of the Laws and Decree-laws, like Data Protection law, Data Protection Regarding Telephone Transmissions or the Press Law are quite recent and supposed to be more effective. However, only with time and the continuous application of same laws it will be possible to make a balance concerning its efficiency.

---

3   Lisbon Court of Appeal, in a decision dated 21 May 1987, case entitled '*Civil Responsibility - Press*': 'Article 484° of the Civil Code is valid not only for the non real facts but also to the real facts interpreted in unfaithful way (...)'. (Free translation).
4   Lisbon Court of Appeal, in a decision dated 29 November 1994, case entitled '*Press Crimes*': 'The rigth to inform must be exercised protecting the right to good name; sensationalism can not go against personal rights.' (Free translation).
5   Supreme Court of Justice, decision dated 29 October 1996, case entitled '*Press Freedom*': 'The Constitution imposes as immediate limits to the press freedom the moral integrity, the right to image, good name, reputation, private life and family intimacy (...). (...) 'People who perform a role in public life also have the rigth to the protection of their private lives, unless that private behaviour causes direct influence in their public life. A person who has public responsibilities is also entitled to private life intimacy.' (Free translation).

24 SINGAPORE

Michael Hwang*
Andrew Chan**

A Introduction

24.01 Singapore's laws comprise common law, equity and statutory law. This chapter seeks to provide an overview of the laws in Singapore:

(1) on protection against the intrusion of privacy of individuals, including the unauthorised use, mining or procurement of information concerning individuals and their private matters;

(2) restricting publicity of an individual's name or biography; and

(3) on protection against the use of an individual's name, likeness or personality.

24.02 There are no general laws in Singapore on privacy, publicity and personality. The laws relevant to these areas are mostly piecemeal and are to be derived mainly from various branches of the law. However, it is possible that specific torts may be developing in the areas of privacy and personality which, when fully developed, could well provide general remedies.

B Privacy

1 Privacy generally

24.03 Privacy connotes the state or condition of being alone or undisturbed as a matter of choice or right, or freedom from interference or intrusion.[1] This Part of the chapter is concerned with the interference and intrusion into the privacy of individuals, including the unauthorised use or procurement of information relating to individuals. The Singapore courts have on occasion

---

* BCL, MA (Oxon), Senior Partner and Head, Litigation Department, Messrs Allen & Gledhill, Singapore. Formerly Judicial Commissioner (acting High Court judge) of the Supreme Court of the Republic of Singapore.
** LLB (Hons) (NUS), Partner, Litigation Department, Messrs Allen & Gledhill, Singapore.
1 The *Oxford English Dictionary* Vol XII, 2nd edn, p 515.

given regard to the right of privacy of parties. This is demonstrated, for instance, in cases where *Anton Piller* orders[2] are sought. In deciding whether an *Anton Piller* is justified, the courts will balance the plaintiff's right to recover his property or to preserve evidence against violation of the privacy of a defendant who has had no opportunity to put his side of the case.[3]

24.04   However, no Singapore case has recognised a legally enforceable right to privacy. The prevailing view at common law is that there is no general remedy available against an intrusion of privacy.[4] Even the great innovator, Lord Denning, could only say in *Re X*[5] that there was 'as yet no general remedy for infringement of privacy'. It is likely that the Singapore courts, when faced with the question of whether to recognise a general tort of intrusion of privacy will adopt the prevailing view at common law.

24.05   That having been said, it is not possible to rule out altogether the development of a general tort against intrusion of privacy. It must be said here that there are no Singapore cases which necessarily preclude the recognition in Singapore of a general tort of intrusion of privacy.[6] The developing tort of intentional harassment discussed in paras **24.59** ff below provides the greatest promise for the development of a general remedy against invasion of privacy.

At any rate, what is clear is that intrusion of privacy may amount to a violation or infringement of some other legal right[7] and, where this takes place, the privacy of individuals may also indirectly be protected.

2   Confidentiality

24.06   The law of confidentiality is a useful branch of law which may be utilised to protect confidential information concerning a person or his activities. In *AG v Guardian Newspaper Ltd*,[8] Lord Keith indicated that the right to privacy is one which the law of confidence should (where possible) protect. Further, parties may enter into contractual arrangements to protect confidential information. Such arrangements may be particularly useful, for instance, in cases where personal information is to a provider or seller of goods or services. Apart from contractual arrangements, there is also the equitable duty of confidence.

---

2   An *Anton Piller* order is essentially a court order, ordinarily obtained ex parte, to allow a party to enter into premises of another to seize and obtain documents and other objects of evidence. Further, in *Microsoft Corpn v Summit Holdings Ltd* [2000] 1 SLR 343, the court noted that one purpose of the rule prohibiting (in general) the use of documents discovered pursuant through the court discovery process was to protect the privacy and confidentiality of the documents.
3   See eg *Computerland Corpn v Yew Seng Computers Pte Ltd* [1991] SLR 247.
4   *Clerk & Lindsell On Torts*, 17th edn, para 1-23, *Canadian Tort Law*, Linden, 5th edn, at 52, *The Law Of Torts In New Zealand*, Todd, et al, at 757, and *Privacy, The Individual And Data Mining* (1995) Singapore Law Gazette, August, p 39, Gilbert Leong.
5   [1975] 1 All ER 697 at 704e–f.
6   There is, however, a suggestion in *Teo Siew Har v Lee Kuan Yew* [1999] 4 SLR 560 (at 578 E to F) that an invasion of privacy is not a recognised head of claim on a contractual basis. On the other hand, the Chief Justice remarked in passing in *Soh Yang Tick v PP* [1998] 2 SLR 42 at 62H, a criminal case relating to the use of force to outrage modesty, 'for those who wish to protect their privacy, the law should do its bit to see that this is respected'.
7   *Clerk & Lindsell On Torts*, 17th edn, para 1-23.
8   [1990] 1 AC 109.

In *X Pte Ltd v CDE*,[9] an attempt was made (during an application for an interlocutory injunction, inter alia, to prevent the use or disclosure of certain potentially confidential information) to challenge the existence of the equitable duty of confidence in Singapore on the basis that the doctrine was unconstitutional as being contrary to Article 14 of the Constitution of Singapore (which deals with the right to freedom of speech and expression). The argument proceeded on the basis that the equitable doctrine of confidentiality compromised the right of a person to freely speak and express his opinion. At the interlocutory stage, it was not necessary for the judge hearing the matter to decide on the correctness of the constitutional challenge. All that was required at that juncture was for the plaintiffs to show that they had a good arguable case. The judge, while making clear that she was not prejudging the issue, noted, however, that there were considerable difficulties in the way of the constitutional challenge being successfully mounted.

24.07   It has been assumed in several Singapore cases[10] decided before and after *X Pte Ltd v CDE*,[11] that the equitable duty of confidence is part of Singapore law. Further, it is unlikely that the constitutional challenge would succeed given that the right to freedom of speech and expression is, as the court in *X Pte Ltd v CDE*[12] recognised, not absolute. In the premises, it is very likely (although the Singapore courts have not squarely decided the question of constitutionality of the equitable duty of confidence) that the equitable duty of confidence forms part of Singapore law.

24.08   In general, the equitable duty of confidence arises where:

(1)   the information to be protected had the necessary quality of confidence about it;

(2)   the information had been imparted in circumstances importing an obligation of confidence; and

(3)   there was an unauthorised use of the information by the defendant to the detriment of the party who originally communicated it.[13]

24.09   In *X Pte Ltd v CDE*,[14] the judge accepted that information relating to a person's sexual conduct had the necessary quality of confidence. The judge was further prepared to accept[15] that it was at least seriously arguable (for the purpose of a grant of an interlocutory injunction) that the obligation of confidentiality was attracted where confidential information was improperly or surreptitiously obtained.

24.10   The English cases cited for this proposition were *Lord Ashburton v Pape*[16] and *Francome v Mirror Group Newspapers Ltd*.[17] In the latter, the English

---

9   [1992] 2 SLR 996 at 1003G–1006B.
10 See eg *Federal Computer Services Sdn Bhd v Ang Jee Hai Eric* [1991] 3 MLJ 341, *Chiarapurk Jack v Haw Par Brothers International Ltd* [1993] 3 SLR 285 and *Tang Siew Choy v Certact Pte Ltd* [1993] 3 SLR 44, all of which are decisions of the Singapore Court of Appeal.
11 [1992] 2 SLR 996 at 1003G–1006B.
12 [1992] 2 SLR 996 at 1003G–1006B.
13 *X Pte Ltd v CDE* [1992] 2 SLR 996 at 1007B–D, citing and accepting *Coco v AN Clarke (Engineers) Ltd* [1969] RPC 41.
14 *Stephens v Avery* [1988] 1 Ch 449, cited with approval in *X Pte Ltd v CDE* [1992] 2 SLR 996 at 1007H–I.
15 [1992] 2 SLR 996 at 1008E–1009C.
16 [1913] 2 Ch 469 at 475.
17 [1984] 2 All ER 408.

Court of Appeal granted an interlocutory injunction against the use by a newspaper of tape recordings of a number of telephone conversations between two plaintiffs. It was alleged on the facts of that case that the tapes revealed breaches of criminal law, and that the tapes were the result of unauthorised taping of the plaintiffs' telephones.

24.11   If, which is likely, the English cases are to be followed in Singapore, the surreptitious or improper obtaining of confidential information would attract the duty of confidentiality. The duty may then prevent the party having such information from disclosing the information. The circumstances in which information may be held to have been surreptitiously or improperly obtained are varied.

In this connection, the discussion in paras **24.20** to **24.31**, and **24.46** to **24.53** below relating to various offences under Singapore criminal law (in particular, those in relation to computer misuse and unauthorised access to telecommunication facilities) would be relevant to a finding that information had been improperly obtained. In other words, confidential information obtained in the course of commission of offences under the various criminal statutes may give rise to a finding that the information was surreptitiously or improperly obtained, thereby subjecting the party obtaining the information to a private duty of confidentiality. It should be mentioned that the mere use of surveillance equipment or devices (such as telephoto cameras and binoculars) do not automatically give rise to a finding that the use was surreptitious, or import a duty of confidentiality.[18]

24.12   Further, the following passage from the decision of Justice Laws in *Hellewell v Chief Constable of Derbyshire*[19] (a case in which the plaintiff unsuccessfully sued for a breach of confidence for the use by the police of a mug shot photograph of the plaintiff) is worth noting:

> 'I entertain no doubt that disclosure of a photograph may, in some circumstances, be actionable as a breach of confidence. If a photographer is hired to take a photograph to be used only for certain purposes but uses it for an unauthorised purpose of his own, a claim may lie against him…If someone with a telephoto lens were to take from a distance and with no authority a picture of another engaged in some private act, his subsequent disclosure of the photograph would, in my judgment, as surely amount to a breach of confidence as if he had found or stolen a letter or diary in which the act was recounted and proceeded to publish it. In such a case, the law would protect what might reasonably be called a right of privacy, although the names accorded to the action would be breach of confidence.'[20]

The courts in Singapore have yet to show whether these words will be judicially approved in Singapore.

---

18 *Confidentiality*, Toulson and Phipps, at paras 9-01 and 9-02. Neither, it would seem is there any general remedy for the invasion of privacy by the use of surveillance devices. It would then be necessary to fit a claim against the use of such devices under the individual headings of claims wrongs.
19 [1995] 1 WLR 804 at 807G–H.
20 *R v The Chief Constable For The North Wales Police Area; The Secretary Of State For The Home Department; The National Association For The Care And Resettlement Of Offenders, ex p Ab* (1998) EWCA 1315.

24.13   Finally, in situations where information is protected by an obligation of confidentiality, it is possible to obtain an injunction restraining the improper use or disclosure of confidential information,[1] and to obtain damages, alternatively an account of profits, for breaches of the duty of confidentiality.[2]

3   Copyright

24.14   Copyright in Singapore is governed by the Copyright Act,[3] which Act is largely based on the Australian Copyright Act of 1968. The Copyright Act protects for a period of time, inter alia, copyright in original literary works and artistic works.[4] Artistic works include a painting or photograph, whether the work is of artistic quality or not.[5]

24.15   An unauthorised publication of literary or artistic works (eg an unauthorised publication of a photograph) is a breach of copyright.[6] The party owning the copyright may sue for infringement of the copyright.

24.16   Copyright may, in appropriate circumstances, be relied upon by the owner of the copyright to protect privacy (eg where a photograph containing personal matters is sought to be published without authorisation).

24.17   Broadly speaking, the owner of the copyright is the author of the works in which copyright subsists.[7] An exception is that, where a person enters into a contract with another for the taking of a photograph, the painting or drawing of a portrait, or the making of an engraving, by the latter, the former is entitled to the copyright in the works made pursuant to the contract.[8] If the person depicted in the works owns the copyright in the works, or if the owner of the copyright is (in aid of the person depicted) prepared to take action in respect of any infringement of copyright, copyright may be relied upon to protect the privacy of individuals depicted.

The remedies for infringement of copyright are:

(1)   an injunction preventing infringement of copyright;

(2)   damages, or alternatively an account of profits; and

(3)   delivery up of infringing copies.[9]

---

1   See eg *X Pte Ltd v CDE* [1992] 2 SLR 996 and *Tang Siew Choy v Certact Pte Ltd* [1993] 3 SLR 44.
2   *Clerk & Lindsell On Torts*, 17th edn, para 26-22.
3   Copyright Act, s 4 provides that subject to the provisions of the Act, no copyright shall subsist otherwise than by virtue of the Act. The present Copyright Act (which repealed and replaced the previous Copyright Act 1911) came into force on 10 April 1987.
4   Sections 26, 27 and 28 of the Copyright Act.
5   See the definition of 'artistic work' in the Copyright Act, s 7(1).
6   See s 26 read with s 31 of the Copyright Act.
7   Copyright Act, s 30(2). In general, the owner of the copyright may by contract assign, transfer or sell, the copyright to another.
8   Copyright Act, s 30(5).
9   *The Law Of Copyright In Singapore*, George Wei, pp 201–213.

4   Banking secrecy

24.18   In addition to the civil law aspects of copyright law discussed above, there are several offences relating to copyright which may be relied upon to protect privacy.

24.19   Section 136(1) of the Copyright Act provides that a person who at a time when copyright subsists in a work:

(1)   makes for sale or hire;

(2)   sells or lets for hire, or by way of trade offers or exposes for sale or hire; or

(3)   by way of trade exhibits in a public,

any article which he knows, or ought reasonably to know, to be an infringing copy of the work shall be guilty of an offence and shall be liable on conviction to a fine not exceeding S$10,000 for the article or for each article in respect of which the offence was committed or S$100,000, whichever is the lower, or to imprisonment for a term not exceeding five years or to both.

24.20   Section 136(2) of the Copyright Act provides that a person who at a time when copyright subsists in a work has in his possession or imports into Singapore any article which he knows, or ought reasonably to know, to be an infringing copy of the work for the purpose of:

(1)   selling, letting for hire, or by way of trade offering or exposing for sale or hire, the article;

(2)   distributing the article for the purpose of trade, or for any other purpose to an extent that will affect prejudicially the owner of the copyright in the work; or

(3)   trade exhibiting the article in public;

shall be guilty of an offence and shall be liable on conviction to a fine not exceeding S$10,000 for the article or for each article in respect of which the offence was committed or S$100,000, whichever is the lower, or to imprisonment for a term not exceeding five years or to both.

24.21   Section 136(3) of the Copyright Act provides that any person who, at a time when copyright subsists in a work, distributes either:

(1)   for purposes of trade; or

(2)   for other purposes, but to such an extent as to affect prejudicially the owner of the copyright,

articles which he knows, or ought reasonably to know, to be infringing copies of the work, shall be guilty of an offence and shall be liable on conviction to a fine not exceeding S$50,000 or to imprisonment for a term not exceeding three years or to both.

24.22   Section 136(6) of the Copyright Act provides that any person who for his private profit causes, inter alia, a literary or dramatic work to be performed in public, or causes a cinematograph film to be seen or heard or seen and heard in public, other than by the reception of a television broadcast or cable programme, where he knows, or ought reasonably to know, that copyright subsists in the work or cinematography film and that the performance constitutes an infringement of the copyright, shall be guilty of an offence and shall be liable on conviction to a fine not exceeding S$20,000 or to imprisonment for a term not exceeding two years or to both.

24.23   Section 47(3) of the Banking Act provides that, subject to various exceptions contained in section 47(4) of the Banking Act, no official of any bank and no person who by reason of his capacity or office has by any means access to the records of the bank, registers or any correspondence or material with regard to the account of any customer of that bank shall, while his employment in or professional relationship with the bank, as the case may be, continues or after the termination thereof, give, divulge or reveal any information whatsoever regarding the money or other relevant particulars of the account of that customer.

24.24   Section 47(12) of the Banking Act provides as punishment for any contravention of section 47 of the Banking Act, a fine not exceeding S$50,000 or imprisonment for a term not exceeding three years or both.

5   Computer misuse

24.25   The main Act in Singapore dealing with the criminal offences relating to the use of computers is the Computer Misuse Act ('CMA').[10] The provisions of the CMA are useful in preventing unauthorised procurement or mining of data stored on computers or related peripherals.

In *Public Prosecutor v Muhammad Nuzaihan bin Kamalluddin*,[11] the Chief Justice accepted that the commission of crimes under the CMA must be viewed seriously. As such, the court decided on the facts in favour of a deterrent jail sentence and that probation was not suitable.

24.26   There are three basic offences under the CMA which may be relied upon to protect the privacy of individuals, namely the offences of

(1)   unauthorised access to computer material (section 3 of the CMA);

(2)   unauthorised modification of 'computer material' (section 5 of the CMA); and

(3)   unauthorised use or interception of 'computer service', etc (section 6 of the CMA).

Each of these offences is elaborated upon below.

Unauthorised access

24.27   First, section 3(1) of the CMA[12] makes it an offence for any person knowingly to cause a computer to perform any function for the purpose of securing access without authority to programs or data held in any computer.

24.28   Where no damage is caused, a conviction of an offence under section 3(1) of the CMA attracts the punishment of a fine not exceeding S$5,000 or imprisonment for a term not exceeding two years, or both. In the case of a second or subsequent conviction, the punishment is a fine not exceeding S$10,000 or imprisonment for a term not exceeding three years, or both. Where damage is caused as a result of the commission of an offence under

---

10   The Act came into force in Singapore on 30 August 1993. There is an extensive discussion of the Act in an article entitled '*Offences Created By The Computer Misuse Act 1993*' [1994] SJLS 263, by Christopher Lee.

11   [2000] 1 SLR 34.

12   The section is based on the UK Computer Misuse Act 1990. See '*Offences Created By The Computer Misuse Act 1993*' [1994] SJLS 263, Christopher Lee, at 272.

section 3(1) of the CMA, the punishment is a fine not exceeding S$50,000 or imprisonment for a term not exceeding seven years, or both.

Unauthorised modification

24.29 Secondly, it is an offence under section 5(1) of the CMA[13] for any person to do an act which he knows will cause an unauthorised modification of the contents of any computer.

24.30 Where no damage is caused as a result of the commission of the offence under section 5(1) of the CMA, the punishment is a fine not exceeding S$10,000 or imprisonment for a term not exceeding three years, or both. In the case of a second or subsequent conviction, the punishment is a fine not exceeding S$20,000 or imprisonment for a term not exceeding five years, or both. Where damage is caused as a result of the commission of an offence under section 5(1) of the CMA, the punishment is a fine not exceeding S$50,000 or imprisonment for a term not exceeding seven years, or both.

Unauthorised use

24.31 Third, section 6(1) of the CMA[14] makes it an offence for any person knowingly to:

(1) secure access without authority to any computer for the purpose of obtaining, directly or indirectly, a 'computer service';

(2) intercept or cause to be intercepted without authority, directly or indirectly, any function of a computer by means of an electromagnetic, acoustic, mechanical or other device; or

(3) use or cause to be used, directly or indirectly, the computer or any other device for the purpose of committing an offence under paragraph (1) or (2) above.

Section 2 of the CMA defines 'computer service' to include computer time, data processing and the storage or retrieval of data.

24.32 A person convicted of an offence under section 6(1) of the CMA may be punished, where no damage is caused as a result of the offence, by (a) a fine not exceeding S$10,000 or imprisonment for a term not exceeding three years, or both, in the case of a first conviction, and (b) a fine not exceeding S$20,000 or imprisonment for a term not exceeding five years, or both, in the case of a second or subsequent conviction.

24.33 Where damage is caused as a result of the commission of an offence under section 6(2) of the CMA, the punishment is a fine not exceeding S$50,000 or imprisonment for a term not exceeding seven years, or both.

24.34 Finally, where access to any protected computer is obtained in the course of a commission of an offence under, inter alia, sections 3, 5 or 6 of the CMA, section 9(1) of the CMA provides, in lieu of the punishment prescribed in those sections, for punishment on conviction to a fine not exceeding

13 This section is based (although not entirely) on the UK Computer Misuse Act 1990. See '*Offences Created By The Computer Misuse Act 1993*' [1994] SJLS 263, Christopher Lee, at 295.

14 This section is based on the Canadian Criminal Code (as amended by s 45 of the Canadian Law Amendment Act 1985). See '*Offences Created By The Computer Misuse Act 1993*' [1994] SJLS 263, Christopher Lee, at 303.

S$100,000 or to imprisonment for a term not exceeding 20 years, or to both. For the purpose of the enhanced sentencing provision under section 9(1) of the CMA, section 9(2) of the CMA provides that a computer is to be treated a 'protected computer' if the person committing the offence knew or ought reasonably to have known, that the computer or data or program is used directly with or necessary for, inter alia:

(1)   the existence or identity of a confidential source of information relating to the enforcement of a criminal law; or

(2)   the provision of services directly related, inter alia, to communications infrastructure, banking and financial services, public utilities, public transportation or public key infrastructure.

24.35   Information on offenders and their criminal records, and the personal particulars of customers of banks are some matters which individuals may wish to keep private, and unauthorised interception or access to such information from protected computers may attract the enhanced penalties under section 9(1) of the CMA.

6   Outrage of modesty

24.36   Section 509 of the Penal Code provides, 'Whoever, intending to insult the modesty of any woman…intrudes upon the privacy of such woman, shall be punished with imprisonment for a term which may extend to one year, or with fine, or with both.' In *Tan Pin Seng v PP*,[15] an accused, who had been peeping through a hole in the bathroom door while a woman was having a shower, was recently convicted under the section and sentenced to one month's imprisonment.

7   Public order and harassment

24.37   Public order and harassment offences may, in appropriate cases, also be relied upon to protect against the intrusion of privacy.

24.38   Section 13A of the Miscellaneous Offences (Public Order And Nuisance) Act ('MOA') makes it an offence for any person in a private place to use threatening, abusive or insulting words or behaviour to cause harassment, alarm or distress to another person. A person guilty of an offence under the section may be fined up to S$5,000.

24.39   Section 13B of the MOA makes it an offence for any person in a private place to use threatening, abusive or insulting words or behaviour within the hearing or sight of any person such as to be likely to cause harassment, alarm or distress. The difference between the offences constituted by sections 13A and 13B, is that, in the case of the former, the acts must actually cause harassment, alarm or distress, whereas in the case of the latter, the acts need only be likely to cause harassment, alarm or distress. A person guilty of an offence under section 13B of the MOA may be fined up to S$2,000.

24.40   Sections 13A and 13B of the MOA may be relied upon to protect privacy in cases where the acts of intrusion of privacy amount to threatening,

15 [1998] 1 SLR 418.

abusive or insulting behaviour such as to cause or be likely to cause harassment, alarm or distress. Although untested, the provisions are potentially wide enough to cover at least serious cases of stalking.

24.41 In the case of intrusion of privacy by reason of harassment of debtors and their families by moneylenders or persons on their behalf, the Moneylenders Act may be relied upon.

24.42 Section 33(1) of the Moneylenders Act provides that any moneylender who harasses or intimidates his debtor, any member of the debtor's family or any other person in connection with the loan to the debtor at, or watches or besets, the residence or place of business or employment of the debtor, the member of the debtor's family or that other person, shall be guilty of an offence. The punishment is a fine of not less than S$2,000 and not more than S$20,000 or imprisonment for a term not exceeding twelve months or both. Where the offender is a company, the punishment is a fine of not less than S$4,000 and not more than S$40,000.

24.43 Section 33(2) of the Moneylenders Act provides that any person who, acting on behalf of a moneylender, commits or attempts to commit any of the acts specified in section 33(1) of the Moneylenders Act, shall be guilty of an offence and shall be liable on conviction to a fine of not less than S$2,000 and not more than S$20,000, or to imprisonment for a term not exceeding twelve months, or to both.

24.44 Section 33(3) of the Moneylenders Act provides that a person who, whilst committing an offence under sections 33(1) or 33(2) of the Moneylenders Act, causes hurt to another person shall on conviction be liable to be punished with caning with not more than six strokes.

24.45 The court may, where 'family violence' has been or is likely to be committed against a family member, issue a protection order under Part VII of the Women's Charter. The family order restraints the person from committing family violence against a family member. Also, where appropriate the court may further grant exclusive possession of shared premises of part thereof to the protected person. These provisions are useful in protecting against harassment, as 'family violence' is widely defined to include, in addition instances where physical violence is threatened or caused, a situation of continued harassment with the intent to cause or knowing that it is likely to cause anguish to a family member.

8   Telecommunications

24.46 Privacy may also be invaded by a person unlawfully intercepting or acquainting oneself with messages intended for another person.

24.47 The Telecommunications Authority of Singapore Act ('TAS Act'), which, inter alia, regulates the telecommunications and postal industry, creates certain offences which may be relied upon to the protect privacy of individuals.

24.48 Section 77 of the TAS Act provides that any person who, intending to:

(1) prevent or obstruct the transmission or delivery of any message or postal article;

(2) intercept or to acquaint himself with the contents of any message or letter; or

(3) commit mischief, damages, removes, tampers with or touches any installation or plant or any part thereof used for telecommunications or for posts belonging to a public telecommunication licensee or a public postal licensee, as the case may be, or interferes with the radio-communication service or system of a public telecommunication licensee, shall be guilty of an offence and shall be liable on conviction to a fine not exceeding S$10,000 or to imprisonment for a term not exceeding three years or to both.

24.49   Section 81 of the TAS Act provides, inter alia, that any person who fraudulently retains or wilfully secretes, makes away with or detains a message or record of a message which ought to have been delivered to some other person shall be guilty of an offence, and shall be liable on conviction to a fine not exceeding S$10,000 or to imprisonment for a term not exceeding three years or to both.

24.50   Section 431A of the Penal Code provides that whoever commits mischief by cutting or injuring any electric telegraph cable, wire, line, post, instrument or apparatus for signalling, shall be punished with imprisonment for a term which may extend to two years, or with fine, or with both. Section 425 of the Penal Code defines 'mischief' as follows:

> 'Whoever, with intent to cause, or knowing that he is likely to cause, wrongful loss or damage to the public or any person, causes the destruction of any property, or any such change in any property, or in the situation thereof, as destroys or diminishes its value or utility, or affects it injuriously, commits "mischief".'

9   Theft

24.51   Section 378 of the Penal Code defines theft as:

> 'Whoever, intending to take dishonestly any movable property out of the possession of any person without that person's consent, moves that property in order to such taking, is said to commit theft.'

A case of simple theft is punishable under section 379 of the Penal Code with imprisonment for a term which may extend to three years, or with fine, or with both.

24.52   Two points concerning the offence of theft under the Penal Code are worth noting. First, unlike England,[16] the temporary deprivation of possession of property would suffice for the purpose of the offence of theft under the Penal Code.[17] In the result, if, for example, there is a dishonest unauthorised temporary removal, of documents or other materials containing personal information with the intention of extracting or copying relevant information, an offence of theft may be made out under the Penal Code.

---

16 In *R v Lloyd* [1985] 1 QB 829, the English Court of Appeal held that an offence of theft was not made out under the English Theft Act 1968 where there was a mere borrowing without authority of films with the intention of making pirated copies of the films and returning them after the pirated copies were made. In this respect, it is worth noting that s 1(1) of the English Act provides as a requirement of the offence of theft, a 'dishonest appropriation of property belonging to another with the intention of *permanently* depriving the other of it'. (emphasis added).

17 *Ward v PP* (1953) 19 MLJ 153 and *Criminal Law in Singapore and Malaysia*, Koh, Clarkson and Morgan, at pp 537–538.

24.53 Secondly, the definition (in particular the illustration thereto) of 'movable property' (which phrase appears in section 378 of the Penal Code) in section 22 of the Penal Code is worth noting. Section 22 provides:

> 'The words "movable property" are intended to include corporeal property of every description, except land and things attached to the earth, or permanently fastened to anything which is attached to the earth.
> Illustration
> *Writings, relating to real or personal property or rights, are movable property.*'
> (emphasis added).

10 Criminal Trespass

24.54 Section 441 of the Penal Code provides,

> 'Whoever enters into or upon property in the possession of another with the intent to...intimidate, insult or annoy any person in possession of such property, or having lawfully entered into or upon such property, or having lawfully entered into or upon such property, unlawfully remains there with intent thereby to intimidate, insult or annoy any such person, or with intent to commit an offence, is said to commit "criminal trespass".'

A simple case of criminal trespass is punishable under section 447 of the Penal Code with imprisonment of up to three months, or with a fine not exceeding S$500, or with both.

24.55 Section 442 of the Criminal Code provides,

> 'Whoever commits criminal trespass by entering into, or remaining in, any building, tent or vessel used as a human dwelling, or any building used as a place for worship or as a place for the custody of property, is said to commit "house-trespass".'

A simple case of house-trespass is punishable under section 448 of the Penal Code with imprisonment of up to one year, or with a fine not exceeding S$1,000, or with both. There are heavier penalties where house-trespass takes place with an intention to commit, or with the commission of, certain crimes.[18] These provisions are useful in ensuring privacy of persons in possession of premises.

11 Vandalism

24.56 Section 3 of the Vandalism Act provides that any person who commits, attempts to commit or cause any act of vandalism may be punished upon conviction with a fine not exceeding S$2,000, imprisonment for a term not exceeding three years, and caning with not less than three strokes and not more than eight strokes.

24.57 However, caning may not, in the case of a first conviction, be imposed for certain forms of vandalism.[19] Further, offenders who are women, men sentenced to death, and men above the age of fifty years, may not be caned.[20]

---

18 Sections 449–452 of the Penal Code.
19 See the proviso to s 3 of the Vandalism Act.
20 Section 3 of the Vandalism Act and s 231 of the Criminal Procedure Code.

24.58 The definition of what constitutes 'vandalism' in section 2 of the Vandalism Act is broad, and hence may in some circumstances be relied upon to protect privacy (ie where the form of intrusion of privacy includes an act of vandalism). An act of vandalism is defined in section 2 of the Vandalism Act to include:

(1) writing, drawing, painting, marking or inscribing on any private property any word, slogan, caricature, drawing, mark, symbol or other thing;

(2) affixing, posting up or displaying on any private property any poster, placard, advertisement, bill, notice, paper or other document; or

(3) hanging suspending, hoisting, affixing or displaying on or from any private property any flag, bunting, standard, banner or the like with any word, slogan, caricature, drawing, mark, symbol or other thing,

without the written consent of the owner or occupier of private property.

12 Harassment (tort)

24.59 *Wilkinson v Downton*[1] and *Janvier v Sweeney*[2] are English authorities which establish that false words or verbal threats calculated to cause, and uttered with the knowledge that they are likely to cause, and actually cause physical injury to persons to whom they have been uttered are actionable.[3] In *Wilkinson v Downton*,[4] 'nervous shock' (manifested by a recognised medical condition) was suffered and the plaintiff had a remedy.

24.60 Dillon LJ, who delivered the leading judgment of the majority in *Khorasandjian v Bush*,[5] appears to have understood *Wilkinson v Downton*[6] and *Janvier v Sweeney*[7] as requiring physical injury before false words or verbal threats made intentionally were actionable. Further, his Lordship drew a distinction between 'nervous shock' on one hand and 'mere emotional distress' on the other.

24.61 In *Hunter v Canary Wharf Ltd*[8] (a case where the House of Lords disagreed with the view of the majority in *Khorasandjian v Bush*[9] which held that ownership or exclusive possession in land is not necessary for a person to sue in private nuisance)[10] Lord Hoffman stated:[11]

'The perceived gap in *Khorasandjian v Bush* was the absence of a tort of intentional harassment causing distress without actual bodily or psychiatric illness. This limitation is thought to arise out of cases like *Wilkinson v Downton* [1897] 2 QB 57 and *Janvier v Sweeney* [1919] 2 KB 316. The law of harassment has now been put on a statutory basis (see the Protection from Harassment Act 1997) and it is unnecessary to consider

1   [1897] 2 QB 57.
2   [1919] 2 KB 316.
3   *Khorasandjian v Bush* [1993] 3 All ER 676e to 677a.
4   [1897] 2 QB 57.
5   [1993] 3 All ER 669 at 676h to 677a.
6   [1897] 2 QB 57.
7   [1919] 2 KB 316.
8   [1997] 2 WLR 684.
9   [1993] 3 All ER 669.
10 See further the discussion of the tort of private nuisance in paras **24.62–24.67** below.
11 [1997] 2 WLR 684 at 709G–H.

how the common law might have developed. But as at present advised, *I see no reason why a tort of intention should be subject to the rule which excludes compensation for mere distress, inconvenience or discomfort in actions based on negligence*: see *Hicks v Chief Constable of the South Yorkshire Police* [1992] 2 All ER 65. *The policy considerations are quite different.* I do not therefore say that *Khorasandjian v Bush* was wrongly decided. But it must be seen as a case on intentional harassment, not nuisance.' (emphasis added)

This passage from the decision of Lord Hoffman provides material for the development in Singapore of a common law tort of intentional harassment. Positive statements in this direction can also be found in Lord Hope's judgment in *Hunter v Canary*,[12] *Robert Fine v Eileen May McLardy*,[13] and *Janice Ward v Scotrail Railways Ltd.*[14]

If, and when this takes place, there would be much scope for the protection of privacy, since the tort may, if fully developed, protect against 'distress, inconvenience and discomfort'. The main difficulty against the adoption of the tort of harassment in Singapore is a passage from the decision of Selvam J in *Arul Chandran v Gartshore*[15] which suggests that mental distress is not actionable. It is submitted that Selvam J's statement that mental distress is not actionable should not preclude the development and acceptance of a tort of intentional harassment in Singapore for several reasons. First, the statement of Selvam J was only an *obiter dicta* in respect of recovery for mental distress in tort, since the case before Selvam J involved a claim for breach of contract. Secondly, Selvam J relied on old judgments that mental distress was not recoverable. Selvam J's attention was not drawn to the modern cases including these cited in this part of the chapter that support the view that there can be a cause of action based on intentionally causing mental distress. Thirdly, Selvam J's suggestion that such damages should not be recoverable on the basis that they are difficult to quantify is not a good reason to deny a remedy. The courts are adept in quantifying damages. Thus, in *Perharic v Henessey*,[16] the English Court of Appeal observed as follows; 'The recorder, taking a broad-brush approach and not directing himself by reference to moderate psychiatric damage or anything of that character but simply asking himself what amount should properly reflect the distress to which the plaintiff had been wickedly subjected by the conduct of which complained, might well have come to the conclusion that £5000 was an apt amount.'

13 Private nuisance

24.62 The common law tort of private nuisance is part of Singapore law.[17] The essence of the tort of private nuisance is a condition or activity which unduly interferes with the use or enjoyment of land.[18] Broadly, nuisance takes place where:

---

12 [1997] WLR 684 at 726D.
13 (1998) EWCA 2991.
14 (1998) Scot CS 95.
15 [2000] 2 SLR 446.
16 (1997) CLY 4895 and available on Lexis.
17 See eg *Hygeian Medical Supplies Pte Ltd v Tri-Star Rotary Screen Engraving Works Pte Ltd (Seng Wing Engineering Works Pte Ltd, third party)* [1993] 3 SLR 309 and *X Pte Ltd v CDE* [1992] 2 SLR 996.
18 *Clerk & Lindsell On Torts*, 17th edn, para 18-01.

(1) there is an encroachment into land (where nuisance closely resembles trespass to land),[19]

(2) physical damage is caused to land, or building or works or vegetation on it, or

(3) undue interference with the enjoyment of land.[20]

Traditionally, a private nuisance is primarily a wrong to the person having possession of land affected.[1]

24.63   In the Canadian case of *Motherwell v Motherwell*,[2] the Alberta Supreme Court held that the harassment by a defendant of a plaintiff by unwanted telephone and mail gave rise to a cause of action in private nuisance. On the facts, a wife staying in her matrimonial home was held to be entitled to sue for private nuisance. In the court's view, it was sufficient if the occupancy was of a substantial nature. The occupancy need not be founded on a legally demonstrable right.

24.64   Later, in *Khorasandjian v Bush*,[3] the English Court of Appeal held that the court had the jurisdiction to grant an interlocutory injunction restraining the defendant from harassing the plaintiff by unwanted telephone calls, notwithstanding the plaintiff had no interest in land. On the facts, the plaintiff was a mere licensee on the land and the action against the defendant was bought in private nuisance.

24.65   Subsequently, the English House of Lords in *Hunter v Canary Wharf Ltd*[4] overruled the decision of the Court of Appeal in *Khorasandjian v Bush*[5] to the extent that the Court of Appeal suggested that there was a right to sue notwithstanding that the plaintiff had no right of exclusive possession of land. The decision of the House of Lords, however, does not detract from the view that unwanted telephone calls may constitute acts of private nuisance. The House of Lords was concerned primarily with title to sue.

24.66   It is possible that the traditional position (requiring an interest in land) will be followed in Singapore, given that conceptually the tort of private nuisance is essentially intended to protect the use or enjoyment of land. If so, the tort of private nuisance would only be available to protect privacy in cases where the use or enjoyment of land by a person having an interest in land is affected by acts which constitute private nuisance, such as unwanted telephone calls.

24.67   The remedies for the tort of private nuisance are damages resulting from the acts of nuisance and to obtain an injunction to prevent the nuisance from continuing.[6]

---

19 The tort of trespass to land is discussed in paras **24.68–24.70** below.
20 *Clerk & Lindsell On Torts*, 17th edn, paras 18-05 to 18-24.
1   *Clerk & Lindsell On Torts*, 17th edn, paras 18–19.
2   (1976) 73 DLR 62.
3   [1993] 3 All ER 669.
4   [1997] 2 WLR 684.
5   [1993] 3 All ER 669.
6   *Clerk & Lindsell On Torts*, 17th edn, paras 18-22 and 18-26–18-27.

14 Trespass

24.68   The common law tort of trespass to land is part of Singapore law.[7] In *King's Tanglin Shopping Pte Ltd v Chee Kim Neo*[8] Chan Sek Keong J stated that the tort of trespass to land consists in the acts of:

(1)   entering upon land in the possession of the plaintiff, or

(2)   remaining on such land, or

(3)   placing or projecting any object upon it, in each case without lawful justification.

In this connection, it has been said that the slightest crossing of the boundary is sufficient to found an action for trespass to land.[9] Trespass to land is not merely limited to the physical land but also the air space above the land necessary for the enjoyment of the land.[10]

In *King's Tanglin Shopping Pte Ltd v Chee Kim Neo*,[11] Chan Sek Keong J also accepted that trespass is actionable per se without proof of damage.

24.69   The person who may sue for trespass to land is the person having possession of the land, that is generally to say occupation or physical control of land.[12] The person in possession need not necessarily be the owner of the land.[13]

24.70   Where a case for trespass is made out, the party having possession of the land may, as it is appropriate to the circumstances of the case,

(1)   obtain an injunction to put a stop to the act of trespass or to prevent the act of trespass from continuing,

(2)   obtain an order for recovery of possession of the land, and

(3)   seek damages.[14]

The tort of trespass and the remedies which may be obtained in connection therewith provides a useful weapon in the armoury of the person having possession of land from acts of intrusion upon the land (which acts may sometimes also amount to an invasion of privacy, albeit the remedy is to be found in the tort of trespass rather than the invasion of privacy). In closing, it is worth noting that in *Sheen v Clegg*,[15] damages were awarded for trespass in a case where a bugging device in the form of a microphone was installed on the plaintiff's marital bed.

---

7   See eg *Tay Tuan Kiat & Anor v Pritam Singh Brar* [1987] 1 MLJ 276 and *King's Tanglin Shopping Pte Ltd v Chee Kim Neo* [1991] 3 CLJ 1933.

8   [1991] 3 CLJ 1933 at 1395 lhc G.

9   *Clerk & Lindsell On Torts*, 17th edn, para 17-01.

10   *Kim Beng Lee Pte Ltd v Kosion Enterprise (S) Pte Ltd* [1994] 1 SLR 700 at 702H–703A and *Clerk & Lindsell On Torts*, 17th edn, para 17-03.

11   [1991] 3 CLJ 1933 at 1935 rhc D.

12   *Clerk & Lindsell On Torts*, 17th edn, paras 17-09 and 17-10.

13   *Clerk & Lindsell On Torts*, 17th edn, para 17-09 and *Koh Ah Kow v PP* [1995] 2 SLR 342 at 346I.

14   *King's Tanglin Shopping Pte Ltd v Chee Kim Neo* [1991] 3 CLJ 1933 at 1935 rhc D–E and *Clerk & Lindsell On Torts*, 17th edn, paras 17-59–17-70.

15   *Daily Telegraph* 22 June 1961, as cited in *State Security, Privacy & Information*, Baxter, p 147.

15 Singapore Code of Advertising Practice

24.71 The Singapore Code of Advertising Practice ('Advertising Code') is a fundamental part of a system by which players in the local advertising community regulate their own activities. The Advertising Code has the support of, inter alia, the Consumer Association of Singapore ('CASE'), the Singapore Advertisers Association, the Association of Accredited Advertising Agents, Singapore, the Advertising Media Owners' Association of Singapore, various professional and trade bodies, and government ministries.[16] The Advertising Code is administered by the Advertising Standards Authority of the Singapore Advisory Council of CASE ('ASAS').[17]

24.72 While the Advertising Code itself does not have the force of law, the scheme of the Advertising Code is such that ASAS may ask an advertiser or advertising agency to withdraw or amend an advertisement which in the opinion of ASAS is contrary to the Advertising Code. ASAS may also ask media owners to support their decisions.[18]

24.73 Article 10.1 of Part II of the Advertising Code provides that, subject to certain exceptions,[19] advertisements should not portray or refer to (by whatever means), any living persons, unless their prior permission has been obtained. The Article further makes it clear that the requirement applies to all persons, including public figures and foreign nationals. Article 10.3 of Part II of the Advertising Code further provides that the depiction in advertisements of the President of Singapore and members of his family is prohibited.

B Publicity

1 Publicity generally

24.74 There are no established general laws in Singapore restricting publicity of individuals, that is to say restricting the use by a person of his name, picture or biography. There are, however, laws which govern specific situations. These laws are discussed below.

In addition, regard should also be had to the Advertising Code[20] which is a non-binding code to which the local advertising community adheres to as a means of self-regulation.

---

16 See pages (ii) and (iv) of the Advertising Code.
17 See pages (ii) and (iv) of the Advertising Code.
18 See page (iv) of the Advertising Code.
19 The exceptions are provided for in art 10.2 of the Advertising Code. Exceptions include
    (1) the use of crowd or background shots in which individuals are recognisable, provided that neither the portrayal, nor the context in which it appears, is defamatory, offensive or humiliating,
    (2) advertisements in which there appear portrayals of, or references to, individuals who form part of the subject matter of the advertisements, and
    (3) the rare occasion when in the opinion of the ASAS council, the reference or portrayal is not inconsistent with the subject's right to a reasonable degree of privacy and does not constitute an unjustifiable commercial exploitation of his fame or reputation.
20 See the general discussion of the Advertising Code at paras **24.71–24.73** above.

2 Criminal law

24.75 The criminal offences having an impact on the publicity of individuals include the following.

Indecent advertisements

24.76 Section 5 of the Indecent Advertisements Act essentially makes it an offence to exhibit in the public view any picture or printed or written matter which is of an indecent or obscene nature. A person convicted under the section may be punished with a fine up to S$100 or imprisonment for a term not exceeding one month or both.

Obscene material

24.77 Section 292 of the Penal Code, inter alia, makes it an offence to sell, distribute, publicly exhibit or put into circulation obscene objects, including books, drawings, paintings, representations or figures. A person convicted of an offence under the section may be punished with imprisonment for a term which may extend to three months, or with a fine, or with both.

Religious feelings

24.78 Section 298 of the Penal Code provides that whoever, with deliberate intention of wounding the religious feelings of any person, places any object in the sight of that person, shall be punished with imprisonment for a term which may extend to one year, or with fine or with both.

3 Professions and service providers

24.79 There are numerous laws which prohibit a person from advertising or holding himself out to belong to certain professions or to provide certain services, unless various requirements under the relevant laws are satisfied.

24.80 The laws include those restricting on the advertising or holding out by persons as:

(1) an accountant or a tax consultant, unless registered under the Accountants Act as a public accountant (the contravention of which is punishable by a fine not exceeding S$5,000 or imprisonment for a term not exceeding one year or to both, and in the case of a second or subsequent conviction, a fine not exceeding S$10,000 or imprisonment for a term not exceeding two years or to both);[1]

(2) a contact lens practitioner, unless registered or licensed under the Contact Lens Practitioners Act (the contravention of which is punishable by a fine not exceeding S$10,000 or imprisonment for a term not exceeding six months or both, and in the case of a second or subsequent conviction, a fine not exceeding S$20,000 or imprisonment for a term not exceeding one year or both);[2]

(3) a person ready to undertake for payment or other remuneration the functions of a private investigator, unless he is a holder of a private

---

1   Accountants Act, ss 48(1)(b) and 51.
2   Contact Lens Practitioners Act, s 16.

investigator's licence under the Private Investigation And Security Agencies Act (the contravention of which is punishable by a fine not exceeding S$10,000 or imprisonment for a term not exceeding two years or to both);[3]

(4) a licensed electrical worker, or as a person competent or qualified or legally permitted personally to carry out electrical work, unless licensed as an electrical worker in accordance with the Electrical Workers And Contractors Licensing Act (the contravention of which is punishable by a fine not exceeding S$5,000 or imprisonment for a term not exceeding one year or both);[4]

(5) a person who is authorised to supply professional engineering services in Singapore, unless registered as a professional engineer who has in force a practising certificate under the Professional Engineers Act (the contravention of which is punishable by a fine not exceeding S$5,000 and in the case of a second or subsequent conviction, a fine not exceeding S$10,000 or to imprisonment for a term not exceeding six months or both);[5]

(6) a person authorised to supply land survey services, unless registered and holding a practising certificate which is in force in accordance with the Land Surveyors Act (the contravention of which is punishable by a fine not exceeding S$4,000);[6]

(7) a person carrying out the business of a futures broker, unless licensed, and the relevant trading takes place in accordance with the rules and practices of a futures exchange, in accordance with the Futures Trading Act (the contravention of which is punishable by a fine not exceeding S$30,000 or to imprisonment for a term not exceeding three years or to both);[7]

(8) a futures trading adviser or a futures pool operator, unless he holds a licence under the Futures Trading Act (the contravention of which is punishable by a fine not exceeding S$30,000 or imprisonment for a term not exceeding three years or both);[8]

(9) a futures broker's representative, a future trading adviser's representative or a futures pool operator's representative unless he holds a licence under the Futures Trading Act (the contravention of which is punishable by a fine not exceeding S$10,000 or imprisonment for a term not exceeding one year or to both);[9]

(10) a martial arts instructor, unless licensed under the Martial Arts Instruction Act (the contravention of which is punishable by a fine not exceeding S$2,000 or imprisonment for a term not exceeding six months or both);[10]

(11) a dentist, unless registered under the Dentists Act, sections 22 and 28, (the contravention of which is punishable by a fine not exceeding S$25,000

---

3   Private Investigation And Security Agencies Act s 5.
4   Electrical Workers And Contractors Licensing Act, s 6.
5   Professional Engineers Act, s 10.
6   Land Surveyors Act, s 10.
7   Futures Trading Act, s 11.
8   Futures Trading Act, s 12.
9   Futures Trading Act, s 12.
10 Martial Arts Instruction Act, s 21.

and in the case of a second or subsequent conviction, to a fine not exceeding S$50,000 or to imprisonment for a term not exceeding six months or both);

(12) a person qualified to practice medicine or surgery, unless registered or exempted under the Medical Registration Act (the contravention of which may be punished with a fine not exceeding S$500 for each offence and to a further fine of S$50 for every day during which the offence continues),[11]

(13) an advocate or solicitor, unless authorised under the Legal Profession Act (the contravention of which is punishable by a fine not exceeding S$1,000 or imprisonment for a term not exceeding six months or both).[12]

In addition, some professions have rules governing publicity by their individual members.

4   Singapore Code of Advertising Practice

24.81   The Advertising Code (discussed generally in paras **24.71** to **24.73** above) contains several guidelines which may impinge on the publicity of individuals. The preamble to the Code (which may be found in Part I of the Advertising Code) provides, inter alia, that:

(1)   all advertisements should be legal, decent, honest and truthful;

(2)   all advertisements should be prepared with a sense of responsibility to the consumer;

(3)   all advertisements should conform to the principles of fair competition as generally accepted in business;

(4)   no advertisement should bring advertising into disrepute or reduce confidence in advertising as a service to industry and to the public.

24.82   Some of the specific provisions of the Advertising Code which may have an impact on publicity of individuals include the following:

(1)   advertisement should not contain statements or visual presentations offensive to the standards of decency prevailing among those who are likely to be exposed to them;[13]

(2)   advertisements should not be so framed as to abuse the trust of the consumer or exploit his lack of experience or knowledge;[14]

(3)   all descriptions, claims and comparisons which relate to matters of objectively ascertainable fact should be capable of substantiation;[15]

(4)   advertisements should not contain any statement or visual presentation which, directly or by implication, omission, ambiguity, or exaggerated claim, is likely to mislead the consumer about the product advertised, the advertiser, or about any other product or advertiser;[16]

(5)   advertisements should not contain or refer to any testimonial or

---

11 Medical Registration Act, s 26.
12 Legal Profession Act, s 33(1).
13 Article 1.1 of Part II of the Advertising Code.
14 Article 2.1 of Part II of the Advertising Code.
15 Article 4.1 of Part II of the Advertising Code.
16 Article 4.2.1 of Part II of the Advertising Code.

endorsement unless it is genuine and related to the personal experience over a reasonable period of the person giving it. Testimonials or endorsements which are obsolete or otherwise no longer applicable should not be used.[17]

C Personality/likeness

1 *Personality generally*

24.83 There are no general laws in Singapore protecting or restricting the use by a person of another individual's likeness. In the earlier part of the century, Lord Lindley sitting in the English House of Lords in *Cowley v Cowley*[18] stated 'Speaking generally, the law...allows any person to assume and use any name, provided its use is not calculated to deceive or to inflict pecuniary loss.' There is also a tort of appropriation of personality which is developing in Canada and which may well find favour with the Singapore courts.

24.84 At any rate, there are specific laws which may, depending on the circumstances of the case, be relied upon to protect individual likeness. Further, the Advertising Code (discussed more fully in paras **24.71** ff above) may also have effect in protecting the use of the likeness of an individual by another.

2 *Appropriation of personality*

24.84 While there are no cases in Singapore which have recognised a general remedy against the wrongful appropriation of personality or likeness of a person, there appears also to be no Singapore cases which stand in the way of the recognition of such a general remedy.

In the result, it is open to a Singapore court applying common law to look to the developments in Canada for guidance. In *Remedies In Tort*[19] the author states:[20]

'The common law of appropriation of personality is developing in Canada and is primarily based on two cases: obiter dicta from the Ontario Court of Appeal in *Krouse v Chrysler Can Ltd*[1] and a decision of the High Court of Ontario in *Athans v Can Adventure Camps Ltd*.[2] The tort is actionable where "the defendant has appropriated for his own purposes some attribute of the plaintiff's name or identity" and protects two distinct interests: the right of a person desiring privacy not to be the object of publicity for another's ends without consent; and secondly, what has been called "the right of publicity", "an exclusive right in the celebrity to the publicity

---

17 Article 9.3 of Part II of the Advertising Code.
18 [1901] AC 450 at 460.
19 Published by Carswell, Thomson Professional Publishing.
20 Chapter 24, Cullingham, para 8, and see further *Canadian Tort Law*, Linden, 5th edn, pp 53–54.
1 (1973), 1 OR (2d) 225, 40 DLR (3d) 15, 13 CPR (2d) 28.
2 (1977), 17 OR (2d) 425, 4 CCLT 20, 80 DLR (3d) 583, 34 CPR (2d) 126.

value of his persona". Although the latter is a proprietary rather than a privacy interest, the trend in Canada has been to apply the doctrine equally to both situations.'

24.86 It has been said that the law supporting the tort of appropriation of personality is derived primarily from areas of defamation and passing off[3] Both defamation[4] and passing off[5] are torts recognised in Singapore. The question which is yet to be raised or answered in Singapore is whether it is possible to develop, utilising the law of defamation and passing off as a foundation, the new tort of appropriation of personality.[6]

3 Confidentiality

24.87 The law of confidentiality (discussed more fully in para **24.03** above) may also apply to protect against the unauthorised use of an individual's likeness in cases where the means or methods of obtaining the medium of an individual's likeness attracts the duty of confidentiality.

4 Copyright

24.88 An individual's likeness may be captured in a photograph or a painting, or some other medium which copyright may attach to. In situations where there is copyright in the particular medium which the individual likeness is captured, there is the right of the copyright owner to sue to restrain the breach of copyright, and to claim damages, or alternatively, an account of profits, for breaches of the copyright.[7]

5 Criminal law

Cheating

24.89 Section 415 of the Penal Code provides that a person is said to 'cheat' within the Penal Code when the person, by deceiving any person, fraudulently or dishonestly induces the person so deceived to deliver any property to any person, or to consent that any person shall retain any property, or intentionally induces the person so deceived to do or omit to do anything which he would not do or omit if he were not so deceived, and which act or omission causes or is likely to cause damage or harm to that person in body, mind, reputation or property.

24.90 Section 416 of the Penal Code further provides that a person is said to 'cheat by personation' where he cheats by pretending to be some other person,

---

3   *Remedies In Tort*, Carswell, Thomson Professional Publishing, Chapter 24, para 11.
4   See paras **24.95–24.100** below.
5   For cases recognising the action in passing off as part of Singapore law, see eg *Chiarapurk Jack v Haw Par Brothers International Ltd* [1993] 3 SLR 285, *Tong Guan Food Products Pte Ltd v Hoe Huat Hng Foodstuff Pte Ltd* [1991] SLR 133 and *Pontiac Marina Pte Ltd v CDL Hotels International Ltd* [1997] 3 SLR 726.
6   Some of the issues involved in utilising the traditional torts of defamation and passing off as foundations of a new tort of appropriation of personality are discussed in *Remedies In Tort*, Carswell, Chapter 24, Cullingham, paras 12–14.
7   Please see the general discussion on the law of copyright in Singapore in paras **24.18** ff above, in particular the discussion on who owns the copyright.

or by knowingly substituting one person for another, or representing that he or any person is a person other than he or such other person really is. The punishment for cheating by personation is imprisonment for a term which may extend to three years, or a fine, or both.

Defamation

24.91   In cases where the use of the individual likeness gives rise to an offence for defamation under the Penal Code, the Penal Code may be relied upon to protect an individual's likeness through the sanction of criminal punishment.

24.92   Section 499 of the Penal Code provides, subject to exceptions, that criminal defamation takes place when whoever, by words either spoken or intended to be read, or by signs, or by visible representations, makes or publishes any imputation concerning any person, intending to harm, or knowing or having reason to believe that such imputation will harm, the reputation of such person. Where a case is made out for criminal defamation, the punishment is imprisonment for a term which may extend to two years, or a fine, or both.[8]

24.93   Further, section 501 of the Penal Code provides that whoever prints or engraves any matter, knowing or having good reason to believe that such matter is defamatory of any person, shall be punished with imprisonment for a term which may extend to two years, or with fine, or with both.

24.94   Finally, section 502 of the Penal Code provides that whoever sells or offers for sale any printed or engraved substance, containing defamatory matter, knowing that it contains such matter, shall be punished with imprisonment for a term which may extend to two years, with fine, or with both.

6   Defamation (tort)

24.95   The law of defamation is part of Singapore law.[9] The elements of the tort of defamation are that the matter complained of:

(1)   is defamatory,

(2)   refers to the plaintiff, and

(3)   has been published to a third person.[10]

24.96   There are two forms of defamation, namely:

(1)   libel (that is to say broadly where the defamatory matter is published in a permanent form or in a form which is deemed to be permanent), and

(2)   slander (that is to say broadly defamation published by spoken word or in some other transitory form).[11]

24.97   Libel is actionable per se, that is to say, actionable without the plaintiff having to show actual damage, and substantial rather than merely nominal

---

8   Section 500 of the Penal Code.
9   See eg *Gabriel Peter & Partners (suing as a firm) v Wee Cheong Jin* [1998] 1 SLR 374, *Tang Liang Hong v Lee Kuan Yew* [1998] 1 SLR 97 and *Shunmugam Jayakumar v Jeyaretnam JB* [1997] 2 SLR 172.
10   *Carter-Ruck On Libel And Slander*, Carter-Ruck and Starte, 5th edn, p 35.
11   *Gatley On Libel And Slander*, 9th edn, para 3.6.

damages may be awarded even in the absence of proof of such substantial damage.[12] In contrast, slander is not actionable unless some actual damage is shown. The four exceptional cases are:

(1)   where the words impute a crime for which the plaintiff can be made to suffer physically by way of punishment;

(2)   where the word impute to the plaintiff a contagious or infectious disease;

(3)   where the words are calculated to disparage the plaintiff in any office, profession, calling, trade or business held or carried on by him at the time of publication; and

(4)   where the words impute adultery or unchastity to a woman or girl.[13]

24.98   The law of defamation may be relied upon to protect against the use of the likeness or personality of an individual by another where the use thereof is defamatory towards the individual. In particular, it is worth noting that statutes, pictures or other physical representations of a person which convey a defamatory imputation are actionable.[14]

24.99   In *Chiam See Tong v Xin Zhang Jiang Restaurant Pte Ltd*,[15] the plaintiff, who was a member of parliament and a lawyer, sued successfully for defamation in respect of a photograph in an advertisement (in a English newspaper) of the defendant's restaurant showing the plaintiff holding a microphone. The plaintiff previously had a birthday celebration at the restaurant and had agreed to take part in karaoke singing to raise funds. The Chinese words in a newspaper made clear that the plaintiff's single rendition of a song raised S$1,000. The court, however, held that the use of the photograph in the advertisement would convey to an ordinary English reader who did not read Chinese that the plaintiff had consented to the use of his photograph for publicity, either for gain or to sponsor a private restaurant. The photograph further suggested that the plaintiff was taking advantage of his position as a member of parliament and had also used the opportunity to promote himself as an advocate and solicitor. On the facts of the case, which included acts of aggravation on the part of the managing director of the defendant, the court awarded the plaintiff S$50,000. More recently, a well-known Singapore model was awarded S$30,000 when a picture of the model was used in an advertisement of a social escort agency in a telephone directory.[16]

24.100   In addition to a claim for damages, it is possible to obtain the remedy of an injunction to restrain the continued publication of the defamatory material.

---

12 *Gatley On Libel And Slander*, 9th edn, para 3.6.
13 *Gatley On Libel And Slander*, 9th edn, para 3.6.
14 *Gatley On Libel And Slander*, 9th edn, para 3.4.
15 [1995] 3 SLR 196.
16 *Straits Times* (1998) 10 August, p 27. See further *Tolley v JS Fry & Sons Ltd* [1931] AC 333 and *Datuk Syed Kechik Bin Syed Mohamed v Datuk Yeh Pao Tzu Lor* [1977] 1 MLJ 56.

7 Passing off

24.101 It is well established that the tort of passing off is part of Singapore law.[17] The elements of the tort of are:

(1) goodwill or reputation attached to goods or services supplied by the plaintiff;

(2) misrepresentation by defendant (that the goods or services supplied by the defendant are in fact those of the plaintiff) to the public leading to the deception of the public; and

(3) damage due to the plaintiff by such misrepresentation.[18]

In principle, if the plaintiff's business is associated with the name or likeness of an individual, misrepresentation by the defendant by utilising the name or likeness of the individual may give rise to an action in passing off.[19]

8 Trade mark

24.102 It is in appropriate cases possible to register a name of an individual as a trade mark. An unauthorised use of the name protected by a trade mark may amount to an infringement of the trade mark.[20] In general, the remedies for infringement of trade mark are for:

(1) an injunction restraining further infringement;

(2) the delivery for destruction, or erasure of the marks, of goods marked with the spurious mark, as well as of deceptive labels, advertising material, etc; and

(3) an inquiry as to damages in respect of past infringement, or alternatively, an account of profits.[1]

9 Singapore Code of Advertising Practice

24.103 The discussion of the Advertising Code above would also be relevant to the question of protection against the unauthorised use of an individual's likeness.

---

17 See eg *Chiarapurk Jack v Haw Par Brothers International Ltd* [1993] 3 SLR 285, *Tong Guan Food Products Pte Ltd v Hoe Huat Hng Foodstuff Pte Ltd* [1991] SLR 133 and *Pontiac Marina Pte Ltd v CDL Hotels International Ltd* [1997] 3 SLR 726.

18 *CDL Hotels International Ltd v Pontiac Marina Pte Ltd* [1998] 2 SLR 550 (at 583G to 584C) citing with approval a passage from the decision of Lord Oliver in *Reckitt & Colman Products Ltd v Borden Inc* [1990] RPC 341 at 406.

19 If the other elements of passing off are also present. See further *Tavener Rutledge Ltd v Trexapalm Ltd* [1977] RPC 275

20 See the definitions of 'trade mark' and 'mark' in s 2(1) the Trademarks Act 1998. For the requirements of registration, please see generally Part II of the Trademarks Act 1998.

1 Kerly DM *Law of Trade Marks & Trade Names* (12th edn) para 15-58.

D Conclusion

24.104   There may in the future be a need for Singapore to develop or have general laws dealing with privacy, publicity and personality. At the moment, there does not appear to be any moves to legislate or enact general laws in these areas. In the result, the laws in these areas would continue at least for sometime to be piecemeal. Further, in the absence of legislation, any development of the general law would probably have to be found by the common law developing torts protecting privacy and personality, which torts, as seen above, may well at present be in their embryonic stages.

25 SOUTH AFRICA

Owen Dean

A Introduction

1 *Relevant laws*

25.01   The privacy of individuals, publicity regarding details of their lives, and the protection and exploitation of aspects of their personality are matters that are primarily governed by the common law relating to privacy and publicity but are also governed by specific statutory enactments, and by the Constitution of the Republic of South Africa[1] ('the Constitution'). The Constitution is the supreme law of the country.

25.02   The Constitution contains several basic provisions relating directly to privacy, publicity and personality, namely section 10 (human dignity),[2] section 14 (privacy)[3] and section 16 (freedom of expression).[4] Section 14(d) more particularly provides that the right to privacy includes everyone's right not to have the privacy of their communications infringed. Against this right must be balanced the right of freedom of expression (section 16), which includes the freedom of the press and other media.

2 *Basis of common law of personality rights*

25.03   The common law of South Africa is Roman Dutch Law. The common law recognises and protects an individual's personality. Personality rights are divided into several categories such as protection against defamation, impairment of dignity and invasion of privacy. The law relating to personality rights seeks to prevent violation of the relevant aspect of the individual's personality and to provide the individual with monetary compensation for the violation of his personality. Protection of personality rights is derived basically from the Roman common law remedy, the *actio injuriarum*. To this remedy is

---

1   Act No 108 of 1996.
2   Section 10: 'Every person has inherent dignity and the right to have their dignity respected and protected.'
3   Section 14: 'Everyone has the right to privacy, which includes the right not to have—
    (a)   their person or home searched;
    (b)   their property searched;
    (c)   their possessions seized; or
    (d)   the privacy of their communications infringed.'
4   Section 16: 'Everyone has the right to freedom of expression, which includes—
    (a)   freedom of the press and other media; ...'.

allied the Roman law remedy, the *actio legis aquiliae*, the remedy by means of which the individual can claim in respect of economic damage caused to him by unlawful acts.

25.04   It can be stated as a general rule that the laws of South Africa apply to all persons in the country, including foreign citizens. Accordingly, non-South African nationals or residents can, in principle, obtain the protection set out in this work.

25.05   The remedies available to a person consequent to infringement of his personality rights are substantially the same no matter whether one is dealing with the right of privacy, the right of publicity, passing off or trade mark infringement. These remedies will be discussed below as they are equally applicable to all the various rights discussed.

B   Privacy

1   *Defining the protectable interest: private facts*

25.06   Privacy consists of the sum total of information of facts which pertain to an individual in the state of solitude and are thus excluded from disclosure to outsiders; it embraces all personal facts. The criterion for determining what are personal facts is the choice of the individual himself and thus the ambit of his privacy is what he chooses to keep private.[5] An actionable invasion of privacy occurs when another party commits an act which has the effect of violating an individual's privacy, and that act is unlawful and intentional. An act which amounts to an invasion of privacy is unlawful when it is contrary to the subjective desire on the part of the aggrieved person that the facts should remain private and is objectively unreasonable. The *boni mores*, or norms prevailing in the community, is the standard by which the objective unreasonableness of an act is determined.

25.07   Information about another person can be obtained, broadly speaking, by means of communication by such person himself or by another person, by means of observation of such person's conduct, and by accessing information which relates to such person. The Appellate Division of the Supreme Court of South Africa (now referred to as the Supreme Court of Appeal) has stated that:

> 'there is a public interest in preserving confidentiality in regard to private affairs and in discouraging the leaking of private and confidential information, unlawfully obtained, to the media (and others)'[6] (per Corbett CJ).

Not all information about a person will, necessarily, be private.

25.08   Even when information is disclosed by a person himself or herself, there may nevertheless be restrictions on the further communication of such information. The Appellate Division indicated in *National Media Ltd v Jooste*[7]

---

5   *Neethling's Law of Personality*, p 36.
6   *Financial Mail (Pty) Ltd v Sage Holdings* 1993 (2) SA 451 AD 464G–H. See also *Janit v Motor Industry Fund Administrators (Pty) Ltd & Anor* 1995 (4) SA 292 AD.
7   1996 (3) SA 262 271G.

that a right to privacy encompasses the competence to determine the destiny of private facts (the individual concerned can communicate such information or authorise its communication). The individual concerned may dictate the ambit of disclosure (for example to a circle of friends, a professional adviser or the public), and may also prescribe the purpose and method of the disclosure or the conditions under which private facts may be made public. A medical practitioner is under a duty to respect the confidentiality of his patient and not to disclose private medical facts.[8]

25.09   The case of *National Media Ltd*[9] involved the publication of certain private facts which concerned 'important and highly intimate details' of the respondent which she had disclosed to a journalist, subject to certain restrictions concerning the publication of the information. The article complained of consisted of a word-for-word narrative between quotation marks of the relationship between the complainant and a well-known sports figure. In the court's view the narrative of this relationship was private and worthy of protection. The information had been published without the respondent's consent. The court referred to 'private facts' as facts worthy of protection that had not become public before their publication, the facts in question being 'important and highly intimate detail'. The private facts which the court deems worthy of protection include facts the disclosure of which will cause 'mental distress and injury to anyone possessed of ordinary feelings and intelligence, situated in like circumstances as the complainant' (citing *American Jurisprudence* 2d 'Privacy' para 40). This protection does not extend to hypersensitivity beyond ordinary and reasonable sensibilities.

25.10   The court in *National Media Ltd* also accepted, as a general proposition, that a fact that the interested party has no wish to keep private will not be protected. It is to be noted that some of the facts in question disclosed related to a child, and the court observed that the mother and/or guardian of the child is entitled to prescribe, within some limits, the child's exposure to the public eye. The court held that the child's private facts are in a sense also the mother's private facts.

25.11   In *Financial Mail (Pty) Ltd v Sage Holdings Ltd*,[10] the Appellate Division endorsed the view that an invasion of the right to privacy may take the following forms, namely:

(1)   an unlawful intrusion upon the personal privacy of another; and

(2)   the unlawful publication of private facts about a person.

2   *Intrusion upon the personal privacy of another*

25.12   When demarcating the dividing line between lawful and unlawful intrusions upon personal privacy or unlawful publication of private facts about a person, the court will have regard to the contemporary *boni mores* (good morals) and sense of justice of the community as perceived by the court. An act relevant to a person's privacy will be unlawful if it is *contra bonos mores*.

---

8   *Jansen Van Vuuren & Anor NNO v Kruger* 1993 (4) SA AD 842.
9   *National Media Ltd & Anor v Jooste* 1996 (3) SA 262.
10 1993 (2) SA 451 AD 462E.

25.13   In *Financial Mail (Pty) Ltd v Sage Holdings Ltd*,[11] the court observed that a decision on the issue of unlawfulness will involve a consideration and a weighing of competing interests. The Appellate Division cited with apparent approval the approach by the Appellate Division of the former Rhodesia in *S v I & Anor*,[12] where that court had regarded as justified an invasion of privacy when an estranged wife, accompanied by a private detective, peeped at night into the husband's bedroom 'solely with the *bona fide* motive of obtaining evidence of the husband's adultery', the wife's interest in obtaining evidence of her husband's infidelity being seen by the court as outweighing the husband's right to privacy.

25.14   In terms of section 4(1) of the Divorce Act,[13] a court may grant a decree of divorce on the ground of the irretrievable breakdown of a marriage if it is satisfied that the relationship between the parties to the marriage has reached such a state of disintegration that there is no reasonable prospect of the restoration of a normal marriage relationship between them. The court may accept evidence of the defendant's adultery as indicative of the irretrievable breakdown of a marriage. The permissibility of evidence relating to the defendant's adultery arguably does not translate into a sanctioning of methods of invasion of privacy which may be in conflict with the protection accorded by section 14 of the Constitution.

25.15   The Appellate Division in *Financial Mail (Pty) Ltd v Sage Holdings Ltd* did not refer to *S v A*,[14] a case where private detectives had installed a listening device in a person's hotel room with a view to obtaining possible evidence of adultery. Botha AJ held that the 'encroachment on a person's privacy by a private individual, albeit a private detective, by means of planting a listening-device in his apartment and listening in to his private conversations' amounted to a serious impairment of the complainant's *dignitas*.[15] McQuoid-Mason has pointed out that *S v A* can be distinguished from *S v I* on the basis that in *S v A* the accused had indulged in *continuous* surveillance.[16]

25.16   The fact that in *S v A* nothing had been said in any of the eavesdropped conversations that the complainant would have been ashamed of was held to be entirely irrelevant:

'The offence of *crimen injuria* on the facts of this case does not depend on whether the complainant was overheard to say something shameful, something of which he could or would have been ashamed. The offence consists simply in the fact that there was a wrongful and intentional breach of the complainant's right to privacy'.[17]

25.17   The lawfulness of conduct amounting to an intrusion upon the personal privacy of another, and which may have been resorted to in order to discover or obtain publishable information or images, may in itself be important for various reasons. The intrusive conduct may constitute the commission of an offence, for instance trespassing, giving rise to criminal prosecution and/or a

---

11 1993 (2) SA 451 AD 462H–I.
12 1976 (1) SA 781 (RA).
13 Act No 70 of 1979.
14 1971 (2) SA 293 (TPD).
15 At 299C.
16 McQuoid-Mason *The Law of Privacy in South Africa* (1978), p 150.
17 1971 (2) SA 293 (TPD), 299C–D.
18 *Neethling's Law of Personality* (1995), p 296.

civil action. The conduct in question may have the effect of tainting the information which has been obtained by means of objectionable methods, thus ultimately affecting the lawfulness of the publication of such information.

Specific manners of acquiring private facts will be discussed in the ensuing paragraphs.

Covert filming in public

25.18 If camera equipment is used in such a way as to penetrate the private sphere of an individual, the user of the equipment may exceed the limits of permissible behaviour. It is submitted that covert filming must be justified by a legitimate purpose, for example, to obtain evidence regarding the commission of a crime, to protect public safety, etc. If the purpose is to obtain information regarding 'private facts', use of the equipment could, arguably, amount to an unlawful intrusion upon personal privacy.

Data protection

25.19 The view has been expressed that there is an urgent need for the creation of effective legislative measures to protect the individual's privacy against unlawful intrusion by means of collection of personal particulars for compiling a database.[18] Any misuse of personal information in a database can amount to an unlawful invasion of privacy.

Filming on private property

25.20 Filming on private property such as a residence or abode can be regarded as an intrusion into the privacy of a person. Klopper[19] also states that the publication of photographs of a person where he relaxes in a private garden will, in principle, be unlawful without that person's permission.

Filming over private property (from the air)

25.21 It is submitted that the technique or technology employed is irrelevant in determining whether particular conduct amounts to an invasion of privacy. The critical issue is the effect which the conduct has on the privacy of the individual. There may, however, be specific rules prescribed by the public authorities to govern particular kinds of activity. Aerial photography is, for example, subject to safety regulation by the Department of Civil Aviation.[20]

Recording of conversations (open and covert)

25.22 The court in *Financial Mail (Pty) Ltd v Sage Holdings Ltd*[1] unequivocally condemned as an unlawful invasion of the privacy of the complainant (an incorporated company) and of its corporate executives the telephone tapping which had occurred. From this situation must be distinguished the so-called fixation of facts on tape without the speaker's knowledge or consent. Despite judicial opinion to the contrary,[2] Neethling submits that such clandestine

---

19 Klopper, op cit 308.
20 Aviation Act 74 of 1962.
1   1993 (2) SA 451 AD 463C.
2   *Human v East London Daily Despatch (Pty) Ltd* 1975 2 PH J24(E), discussed by Neethling *Law of Personality*, p 261.

embodiment of facts should, in principle, be seen as unlawful.[3] This issue has not yet been authoritatively settled. The provisions of the Interception and Monitoring Prohibition Act[4] as discussed below, are, however relevant.

25.23 This Act defines a monitoring device as meaning any instrument, device or equipment which is used or can be used, whether by itself or in combination with any other instrument, device or equipment, to listen to or record any conversation.[5] In terms of section 2(1)(b) of the Act, no person is allowed, without a direction by a judge, to monitor intentionally a conversation by means of a monitoring device so as to gather confidential information concerning any person, body or organisation. A contravention of the provisions of s 2(1) constitutes an offence and renders the person convicted of such contravention liable to a fine or imprisonment.

Sifting of rubbish

25.24 South Africa does not have specific laws dealing with the sifting of rubbish. It is submitted that the general principles relating to privacy will be applicable. Depending on the circumstances, it could amount to an infringement of the individual's right of privacy.

Staking out/following, use of assumed identity

25.25 There is no general offence regarding impersonation or the use of an assumed identity to obtain information.[6] Various laws, however, prohibit the impersonation of officials such as police officers[7] and postal officers.[8]

25.26 According to the writers Neethling, Potgieter and Visser,[9] the observation of people in public may very well amount to an infringement of privacy. Neethling et al submit,[10] with regard to the collection of personal information, that the total picture presented by the record of such facts is usually of such a nature that the person in question would like to restrict others from having knowledge thereof, despite the fact that some of the data, viewed in isolation, is not 'private'. It may be argued by analogy that the shadowing or stalking of a person may similarly amount to infringement of privacy.

Telephone and computer communication

25.27 The Interception and Monitoring Prohibition Act applies to telephone tapping and computer hacking. The Act imposes a prohibition on the interception of any communication which is transmitted by telephone or in any other manner over a telecommunications line. A telecommunications line includes any apparatus, instrument, pole, mast, wire, pipe, pneumatic or other tube, thing or means which is or may be used for or in connection with the sending, conveying, transmitting or receiving of signs, signals, sounds, communications or other information.

3 J Neethling, Potgieter JM and Visser PJ *Law of Personality* (1996), p 261.
4 Act No 127 of 1992.
5 Section 1, Interception and Monitoring Prohibition Act (No 127 of 1992).
6 See *The Law of South Africa* (ed WA Joubert), First Reissue Vol 6 *Criminal Law*.
7 Section 66, South African Police Service Act (Act No 68 of 1995).
8 Section 102, Post Office Act (No 44 of 1958).
9 *Neethling's Law of Personality* (1995), p 247.
10 *Neethling's law of Personailty* (1995), p 297.

25.28　The prohibition applies if the interception is executed intentionally and without the knowledge or permission of the dispatcher of the communication. The prohibition extends to communications which have already been made as well as to communications intended to be transmitted.

Trespassing

25.29　Unlawful entry of private premises may also constitute the offence of 'trespass'. In terms of the Trespass Act,[11] any person who enters or is upon land or in a building without the permission of the lawful occupier of the land or building shall be guilty of an offence unless he has a lawful reason to enter or be there.

Use of security camera footage for reporting events

25.30　There is no specific legislation regarding the use of camera footage for reporting events. Provided that the use of the camera footage is reasonable it should, in principle, be permissible.

Use of telephoto lens

25.31　There is no specific legislation regarding the use of telephoto lenses, although any use which amounts to an intrusion on privacy may infringe the individual's right of privacy.

3　*The unlawful publication of private facts about a person*

25.32　As regards press (and therefore also television) publication of private facts about a person, the court will weigh the person's interest in preventing the public disclosure of such facts against the interest of the public, if any, to be informed about such facts.[12] The court in *Financial Mail (Pty) Ltd v Sage Holdings Ltd* noted that although the media have a private interest of their own in publishing what appeals to the public, this does not constitute an overriding consideration of public interest justifying publication.[13]

25.33　It may constitute a defence that private facts have been communicated during a privileged occasion. The Appellate Division considered this defence in *Jansen van Vuuren NNO v Kruger*,[14] holding that the duty or right to communicate and the reciprocal duty or right to receive the communication may be legal, social or moral. The court applied the following test stated by Burchell *Principles of Delict*[15] in the context of defamation:

> 'It is lawful to publish ... a statement in the discharge of a duty or the exercise of a right to a person who has a corresponding right or duty to receive the information. Even if a right or duty to publish material and a corresponding duty or right to receive it does not exist, it is sufficient if the publisher had a legitimate interest in publishing the material and the publishee had a legitimate interest in receiving the material.'

11　Act No 6 of 1959.
12　*Financial Mail (Pty) Ltd v Sage Holdings* (supra) 462I–463A.
13　*Financial Mail (Pty) Ltd v Sage Holdings* (supra) 465I–J.
14　1993 (4) SA 842 (A) 851.
15　1993, p 180.

25.34   In *National Media Ltd, Sibiya, Khulu, Allied Publishers Ltd, and Perskor Ltd v Bogoshi, Nthedi Morole*,[16] the Supreme Court of Appeal also referred to the 'circumstantial test' used by the Court of Appeal in *Reynolds v Times Newspapers Ltd*,[17] enquiring as to whether the nature, status and source of the material, and the circumstances of the publication, were such that the publication should in the public interest be protected in the absence of proof of express malice.

4   Permissible and non-permissible methods for obtaining information regarding private facts

25.35   The fact that a specific method for obtaining information is either unlawful or illegal will not necessarily be sufficient to determine the legality of the public disclosure of such facts, but is likely to be an important factor regarding whether or not publication will be allowed or may give rise to an infringement of a person's right of privacy.

25.36   *Financial Mail (Pty) Ltd v Sage Holdings* was concerned with the publication of confidential financial information of a company, which reflected negatively on the company's credit-worthiness. The information had been obtained from a confidential internal memorandum as well as from telephonic eavesdropping. The court held that use of the information gleaned from confidential sources was unlawful. While the court agreed that, as a general proposition, the publication of private facts about another would infringe that person's right to privacy, the court would not go so far as to hold that this rule could not be subject to any exceptions:

> '...if in the case of information obtained by means of an unlawful intrusion the nature of the information were such that there were overriding grounds in favour of the public being informed thereof, the court would conclude that publication of the information should be permitted, despite its source or the manner in which it was obtained.'

25.37   The crisp point for decision by the court was, however, not the lawfulness of the tapping itself, but 'whether appellants, having come into possession of the tapes that were produced in the tapping process, were entitled to use information derived therefrom in an article to be published in the *Financial Mail*.' The court deemed the fact that the information in question had been obtained by means of an unlawful intrusion to be a factor of major significance and concluded that there was no overriding consideration of public interest justifying publication.

25.38   The court referred with approval to the English case of *Lion Laboratories Ltd v Evans*[18] where former employees of the plaintiff had leaked to the press information, 'in flagrant breach of confidence' regarding the reliability and accuracy of an intoximeter used to determine alcohol intoxication levels, and where it was held that the interest of the public in the accuracy and reliability of an instrument, on which depended the liability of a person to be convicted

---

16 Unreported judgment, Supreme Court of Appeal, 29 September 1998.
17 Unreported judgment of the English Court of Appeal, 8 July 1998.
18 [1984] 2 All ER 417 (CA).

and punished for a drink-driving offence, prevailed over the confidentiality of the plaintiff's documents. The South African court emphasised that, although the general rule might permit of exceptions, the overriding considerations of public interest, which would permit publication of such information, would need to be very cogent and would be present only in extremely rare circumstances (a *rara avis*); a good reason would have to be advanced to justify publication of private facts in these circumstances.[19]

25.39   Certain forms of conduct, whether or not they are aimed at gathering information of a private nature, are proscribed or regulated. While certain statutes may make provision for the use of camera and or sound-recording equipment in specific circumstances (for example, in relation to public safety and prisons), the use of such equipment in public is not generally prohibited. Klopper[20] asserts that no-one can force another to be photographed and that there is no basic right to take photographs. According to Klopper, the 'right' to film and take photographs arises when the photograph and its publication thereof is justified in the public interest. This would be the case, for example, when an accused is photographed leaving court or when the purpose of the filming is to record a newsworthy event involving a public figure. It is nevertheless clear that no authority is required to operate camera equipment in public. As long as the equipment is used for a legitimate purpose in a way which can be justified in the public interest, for example to cover a newsworthy event or the public activities of a public figure, the use of such equipment will be permissible.

C   Publicity

1   *Laws and restrictions relating to the use of a person's name and/or biography*

25.40   The right of the individual to restrain the unauthorised use of his name or the writing of unauthorised biographies is not clear-cut or unqualified. The provisions of the law giving a measure of protection are discussed below.

25.41   South African law does not grant a law of publicity to an individual and in practice, a publicity right only exists on a somewhat indirect basis.

Copyright

25.42   To the extent that a person's biography has been recorded in writing and qualifies for copyright protection, any unauthorised reproduction thereof will constitute copyright infringement. Copyright is regulated by the Copyright Act.[1]

25.43   The unauthorised publication of private letters or documents will amount to an invasion of privacy[2] and could also constitute copyright infringement.

---

19 *Financial Mail (Pty) Ltd v Sage Holdings* (supra) 465C–D.
20 Klopper HB Strauss, *Strydom & Van der Walt Mediareg* (1986), pp 306–307.
1   No 98 of 1978.
2   McQuoid-Mason *The Law of Privacy in South Africa* (1978), p 170.

Passing off

25.44   The remedy of passing-off is derived from the common law. Passing-off is considered to be a species of unlawful competition and in essence is a species of delict derived from the Roman law *lex aquila*.

25.45   In a situation where, by virtue of the renown or reputation which an individual has attained the use of that individual's name or some aspect of his personality is likely to cause such manner of use to be associated with the individual, when no such association exists, that individual can have recourse to the legal process to restrain the doing of the act which is incorrectly associated with that individual. The essence of a passing off claim is that the individual is able to protect the goodwill which he has built up in his own name from being misused by others.[3]

Pre-publication negotiations and agreements

25.46   The case of *National Media Ltd v Jooste*[4] revolved around discussions which the respondent had had with certain news magazines. The respondent had disclosed information relating to a personal relationship which she had with a national sport celebrity, one Naas Botha. The respondent had concluded an agreement to the effect that she would receive payment upon publication of the details of an exclusive personal interview. Publication was, however, only to occur after the respondent had approved both the contents of the article and any photographs to be used. After reviewing a draft of the article the respondent issued a provisional approval but requested certain amendments. She also requested to see the final and translated versions. A further draft was submitted to the respondent who still had certain reservations and proposed more amendments. She had a vague objection regarding the tone of the article, requiring a more positive tone, whatever that might mean. She subsequently informed the publishers that she was withdrawing her consent for publication of the article. The article was eventually published without the respondent's consent and in breach of the original agreement regarding publication.

25.47   Once the interested party has entered into an agreement of this nature, the general sense of justice of the community requires due compliance with the terms of such an agreement. If publication had taken place according to the terms of the agreement, publication of the erstwhile private facts would not have been unlawful. The mere fact that the respondent had (after publication) accepted payment of the amount agreed on did not serve as evidence that the agreement had been cancelled.

Defamation

25.48   Defamation is defined as the intentional infringement of another's right to his good name, status or reputation.[5] Publication of the act in question is a necessary element of the delict: If a person's name is used without his authority, or if an unauthorised biography is written and statements which are slanderous of that person are made, such person may have a claim of defamation against the author of the statement or the biography.

---

3   Webster and Page *South African Law of Trade Marks* (4th edn) para 15.15 et seq.
4   1996 (3) SA 262.
5   See *Neethling's Law of Personality* (1995), p 140.

Obtaining of trade mark protection for person's name

25.49 It is possible to obtain trade mark rights in a person's image and name. The Trade Marks Act[6] makes provision for the registration as a trade mark, of a mark that is capable of being represented graphically and this includes the name or representation of a person. The person whose name or representation is sought to be registered as a trade mark or, if he or she is deceased, his or her legal representative must consent to the inclusion of the name or representation in a trade mark.

25.50 Registration of a person's name as a trade mark constitutes the most effective means of regulating the use of that name.

D Personality

1 Protection of the use of a person's likeness

25.51 Under South African law, the term 'personality rights' is used to denote a *genus* of laws which deal with the inherent rights of an individual. The most common *species* of this *genus* are defamation, impairment of dignity and invasion of privacy. Invasion of privacy and defamation have already been dealt with above. Impairment of dignity takes place when an individual's self-esteem is impaired by the intentional conduct of another without the objectionable conduct necessarily coming to the public's attention or the attention of anyone else besides the aggrieved individual. It is, in essence, a remedy to compensate for 'hurt feelings'.

25.52 For the major part in this section various forms of conduct will be tested against whether such conduct can constitute defamation, impairment of the individual's dignity, or an invasion of his or her privacy.

Restrictions on use of person's likeness for reporting public event*s*

25.53 The use of a person's likeness in relation to the reporting of public events will, in principle, be lawful provided such person has some connection with the event in question and the report is not defamatory.

Restrictions on use of person's likeness in reporting the private life

25.54 The use of a person's likeness in reporting his or her private life can, depending on the circumstances, amount to an invasion of the person's privacy or to defamation. In this regard see the discussions of these subjects above. If the use does not constitute one of these delicts, it will generally be unobjectionable.

Restrictions on use of person's likeness in advertising for publicity purposes

25.55 In the absence of a right of publicity, an individual's right to restrain the use of his likeness in advertising for publicity purposes will depend upon whether the use of his or her image constitutes defamation, impairment of

---

6 Act No 194 of 1993.

dignity, invasion of privacy or passing off. There are circumstances where this manner of use of the likeness of an individual can very well infringe an individual's rights under one or more of these headings.

25.56 In *O'Keefe v Argus Printing & Publishing Co Ltd*[7] the plaintiff's image, as depicted in a photograph, was used in an advertisement for firearms without her permission. The plaintiff, who was a radio announcer, had previously been critical of the use of firearms. The court held that this manner of unauthorised use of the plaintiff's image had been degrading and humiliating, and infringed her right of dignity.

25.57 In the event that a photograph of an individual is used without the authority of the owner of the copyright in that photograph, copyright infringement will occur in addition to any invasion of the personality right of the individual depicted in the photograph.

25.58 The Advertising Standards Authority ('ASA') is a self-regulatory body organised by the advertising community and it has laid down a Code of Conduct. In terms of the Code of the ASA, the unauthorised use of a person's name or representation so as to endorse goods or services is prohibited.

25.59 The use of a person's likeness in advertising for publicity purposes could well give rise to the inference or deduction that the individual has endorsed the product or service which is the subject of the advertisement or is otherwise connected in the course of trade with such goods or services. If the use of the image of the individual is unauthorised and the suggestion of a trade connection is incorrect passing-off will occur, as discussed above, in connection with the use of the individual's name.

25.60 The question of whether the commercial exploitation of a person's likeness will amount to an impairment of his dignity will depend on the circumstances of each case, the nature of the use of the likeness, the personality of the plaintiff, his status in life and previous habits with regard to publicity and the like.[8]

Obtaining trade mark protection for person's likeness

25.61 The Trade Marks Act[9] makes provision for the registration of trade marks which may include the name or representation of a person. The Registrar may require the consent of that person or, where such person is deceased, of his legal representative before registration will be granted.

25.62 See the discussion on obtaining trade mark protection for a person's name or image in para **25.49** above.

Passing Off

25.63 Unauthorised use of a person's likeness in advertising for publicity purposes can constitute passing off in certain circumstances. In this regard see the discussion of passing off in para **25.44** above.

---

7 1964 (3) SA (C).
8 See discussion of *Mhlongo v Bailey* 1958 1 SA 370 (W) by Burns Y *Media Law* (1990).
9 Act No 194 of 1993.

2 Remedies

25.64 Infringements of personality rights or copyright and instances of passing off are actionable at the suit of the holder of the right which is impaired and such person can claim an interdict restraining the performance of the infringing act, damages and costs of suit. Infringements of personality rights and of copyright can also give rise to a criminal offence by the perpetrator of the act. These various remedies will be briefly discussed below.

3 Interdict

25.65 An interdict restraining the defendant from performing or continuing to perform a particular act is often the principal remedy sought by the aggrieved party. The criteria for the granting of an interdict are the following:

(1) the invasion or threatened invasion of a right;

(2) a reasonable apprehension that the offending conduct will be perpetrated or continue to be perpetrated unless the court intervenes; and

(3) the unavailability of a more satisfactory form of relief.

25.66 It is only in very unusual circumstances that the court would not be willing to grant an interdict in the case of invasions of personality rights, copyright infringement or passing off provided that elements (1) and (2) above are present.

25.67 An interdict is usually a negative remedy in that it restrains the performing of a specific act by a defendant. An interdict can, however, also be positive in the sense that it places an obligation on the defendant to do something, for instance, publish an apology in the media.

25.68 In *Mandela v Falati*[10] an application was made for an order restraining the respondent from holding a threatened press conference at which it was anticipated that defamatory remarks about the applicant would be made. The applicant was a well-known politician. It was held that while the dispute was private, it nevertheless related to a matter of grave social and political importance. In general, no politician could be permitted to silence his or her critics. The court declined to authorise what, in fact, amounted to a prior silencing order, holding that the private interest had to yield to the larger public one.

4 Damages

25.69 In the case of the infringement of personality rights, there are two types of damages available to the plaintiff. In the first place, the plaintiff is entitled to reparation for subjective prejudice (eg stress and anxiety) which he has suffered as a result of the defendant's conduct; such damages are largely discretionary and bear little or no relation to economic harm. In the second place, where a plaintiff can show that he has suffered patrimonial loss, he can claim compensation for the economic damage which he has suffered. Depending on the circumstances, the two forms of damages can be recovered

---

10 1995 (1) SA 251 WLD.

cumulatively. The case of *Jansen Van Vuuren & Anor NNO v Kruger*[11] involved a disclosure by a medical practitioner to other medical practitioners of the HIV positive status of one of his patients. The court held that there were no circumstances which justified the disclosure of this information in the public interest and awarded compensation of R5,000 by way of sentimental damages. In assessing the amount of compensation, the court noted that the right of privacy was a valuable right and that the award should reflect this fact.[12] The fact that a professional relationship had been abused was considered by the court to be an aggravating factor.

5   Costs

25.70   The general rule which applies to civil litigation in South Africa is that costs follow the cause. In other words, in normal circumstances the successful party is entitled to recover his or her so-called 'party and party costs' from the unsuccessful party. Party and party costs are those costs incurred by the plaintiff which are considered to be directly related to the litigation calculated in terms of an officially prescribed tariff. In practice, party and party costs usually amount to approximately 60 per cent of the parties' total costs.

25.71   Where the conduct of a defendant has been particularly reprehensible, courts have awarded so-called 'attorney and client costs', which are virtually all the plaintiff's costs attributable to the litigation but subject to specific items being at a level which the court considers to be reasonable.

6   Criminal offences

25.72   Defamation can constitute a common law criminal offence while impairment of a person's dignity or an invasion of privacy can constitute the common law offence of *crimen injuria*. Furthermore, certain forms of copyright infringement can constitute a criminal offence, while passing off could also bring about a criminal liability under the Merchandise Marks Act[13] where the misrepresentation giving rise to passing off can be considered to be a false trade description.

7   Code of the Advertising Standards Authority

25.73   Mention has been made above of the use of an individual's likeness offending against the ASA Code. The sanction for such a contravention of the Code is that an embargo is placed by the ASA on all forms of advertising by the offender until such time as the use of the offending advertisement has ceased.

---

11 1993 (4) SA AD 842.
12 1993 (4) SA AD 842 857J.
13 Act No 17 of 1941.

26   SPAIN

Professor Dr Isabel Hernando

A   Privacy

1   Privacy generally

26.01   Under Spanish legislation, the rights of privacy, publicity and personality are fundamental rights of the person. Their regulation is based upon Article 18 of the Spanish Constitution ('SC') and their observance constitutes a limit to the exercise of freedom of expression and of information, which the SC itself recognises and protects as being of the same fundamental nature.

The right to privacy in Article 18 (1) SC [1] is strictly linked to the dignity of the person recognised in Article 10 SC. According to the Constitutional Court this right implies 'the existence of a private and personal domain in relation to the actions and knowledge of others, necessary, according to the standards of our culture, for the maintaining of a minimum quality of human life'.[2] The private circumstances of a person's life are also included and although they may not be secret, they deserve the respect of all and protection from their improper disclosure.[3]

26.02   Privacy is basically governed by the *Ley Orgánica de protección del derecho al honor, a la intimidad personal y familiar y a la propia imagen*, of 5 May 1982 ('LOHII')[4] and by the *Ley Orgánica Protección de datos de caracter personal* of 13 December 1999 ('LORTAD').[5] Both laws are of territorial application and list the range of acts which constitute an invasion of privacy.

---

1   Article 18 (1) CE: 'the right to honour, to personal and family intimacy and to one's own image is guaranteed'.
2   *STC 231/1988, 2-XII-1988* (BOE 23-XII-1988).
3   *STS 26-VII-1995* (RJ1995/6596).
4   *LO 1/1982, 5-V-1982* (BOE no 115, 14-V-1982) modified its art 2 (2) with *LO 29-V-1985* (BOE no 129, 30-V-1985) and arts 1(2) and 7(7) by the *Disposición Final Cuarta of the Penal Codel LO 10/1995, 23-XI-1995* (BOE no 281, 24-XI-1995 and the correction of errors in BOE, no 54, 2-III-1996).
5   *O 15/1999, 13-X-1999*, (BOE no 298, *14-XII-1999*) implementing the Directive 95/46/EC of the European Parliament and of the Council of 24 October 1995, (DOCE L, 281/31, 23-XI-1995).

The unlawful acts, which are regulated in the LOHII[6] and in the LORTAD, have been considered criminal acts since the introduction of the new Penal Code of 1995.[7]

2   Unlawful acts

26.03   Those actions which constitute unlawful invasion of privacy are listed non-exhaustively in the above laws and include the following:

Covert filming, filming on private property and filming over private property (from the air)

26.04   The actions of covert filming, filming on private property and filming over private property (from the air) are included within the range of activities that are considered to be unlawful under Article 7 (2). The rule deems unlawful the recording or reproduction of people's private lives or of statements or private letters not intended for those who make improper use of such items.[8]

The same consideration under the law is given to the placement, wherever that might be, of filming devices used for the recording or reproduction of people's private lives (Article 7 (1) LOHII).[9]

Interception of post and telephone calls

26.05   The interception of communications constitutes an infringement of the constitutional principle that guarantees the secrecy of communications established under Article 18 (3) SC.[10]

The LOHII deals with this constitutional mandate and declares as illegal the use of listening devices for obtaining information about people's private lives, statements not destined for those who make use of such items as well as the recording and reproduction of this information.[11]

Likewise the placement, wherever that might be, of listening devices for the recording or reproduction of people's private lives is understood to be an unlawful invasion of privacy.[12]

---

6   Article 1 (2) LOHII.
7   Penal Code, arts 197–201. In the penal context, acts against privacy include, equally, the inviolability of the domicile in its two variations of illegal entry and search (arts 202–204) and the generic manipulation of the person (arts 152–161).
8   The *STC 231/1988, 2-XII-1988* (108/89), *Paquirri* case recognises the infringement of the right to privacy by the filming inside a nursing home of events concerning the health and life of a bullfighter as a result of injuries received during the celebration of a bullfight. The *STS 28-X-1986* (RJ1041/1986), which decided in the opposite sense, is annulled.
9   The clandestine visual surveillance of the person is punishable under the Penal Code in its basic form in art 197(1) with a penalty of one to four years in prison and a fine of twelve to twenty-four months. The penalty is increased if there is diffusion, disclosure or transfer to third parties of the captured images (art 197 (3) CP).
10 Article 18(3) CE: 'The secrecy of communications and especially, of postal, telegraphic and telephonic communications is guaranteed except where there is judicial resolution.'
11 Article 7 (2) LOHII.
12 Article 7 (1) LOHII.

In the penal context, the interception of communications to disclose secrets or to invade privacy is punishable by penalties of one to four years' imprisonment and fines[13] of twelve to twenty-four months.[14]

Public order aspects

26.06 The recording of the sound and images of a person, from the perspective of public order, is regulated by specific laws: the 1983 law concerning the right of assembly,[15] the 1992 law for the maintenance of public safety[16] and the 1990 law governing motor vehicles and road safety.[17]

According to the latter, the installation and use of video cameras and of any other means for the recording and reproduction of images for the control, regulation and organisation of traffic, will be unlawful if the provisions of the LOHII and of the LORTAD are not observed.

Finally, the utilisation by the Security Forces of video cameras, fixed or mobile, to record images and sounds in public places, through application of the *Ley Orgánica* 4-VI-1997,[18] will be unlawful if realised in the following circumstances:

(1) use in the interior of private residences, and in their entrances, except with the express consent of the property owner or with judicial authorisation;

(2) use in public areas, whether open or closed, when this impinges in a direct and serious way on people's privacy; and

(3) use for the recording of conversations of a strictly private nature.

However, if the images and sounds should be obtained in a fortuitous way in the situations previously described, the law calls for their immediate destruction by the person responsible for their safekeeping.

Publication of personal documents

26.07 The revelation or publication of the content of letters, memoirs or any other private documents are considered to be unlawful invasions of privacy by the LOHII.[19]

Moreover, the diffusion, disclosure or transfer to third parties of data or facts discovered through the access to papers, records, e-mails or any other documents or personal effects, is punishable under the penal code with a prison sentence of two to five years.[20]

---

13 Please note, 'fines' is used here and throughout this chapter in the context of a spanish legal text.
14 Basic category art 197 (1) CP. The disclosure, diffusion and transfer to third parties is an aggravated case with the penalty of two to five years in prison (art 197 (3) CP).
15 *LO 9/1983, 15-VII-1983* (RCL 1983/1534).
16 *LO 1/1992, 21-II-1992*, (RCL1992/421).
17 Real Decreto Legislativo 339/1990, 2-III-1990 (RCL1990/578 and 1653).
18 *LO 4/1997, 4-VIII-1997*, regulates the utilisation of video cameras by the Security Forces in public places (BOE no 186, 5-VIII-1997, art 6 (5).
19 Article 7 (3) LOHII. In *STS 11-X-1991* (RJ 1991/6911) it is considered to be an infringement when there is the publication in a book of the content of private letters.
20 Article 197 (3) CP.

Publication of personal data

26.08   Under the LOHII [Article 7 (4)] it is considered to be an invasion of privacy to reveal private data about a person, or his/her family, which became known through the professional or official actions of the person who reveals them.[1]

The duty of discretion is required from officials who, by reason of their responsibilities, may have access to personal information and also from persons who are in professional-client relationships.

There are also a number of professions where conduct is specifically subject to the obligation of confidentiality (eg attorneys and solicitors, bankers, journalists, doctors, private detectives).

Breach of this obligation can lead to the imposition of penal sanctions.[2]

Publishing of personal data

26.09   The publication[3] of data related to the private life of a person or family which affects their reputation or good name is declared to be an invasion of privacy under the LOHII.[4]

Recording of conversations, whether openly or covertly

26.10   The recording of conversations, without prejudice to what is specified in the *Ley Orgánica* 1997 on the use of video cameras, is regulated under the LOHII. According to this law, the positioning in any place[5] or the use of listening devices for the purpose of obtaining information about the private life of individuals, and the recording or reproduction of such information, is considered to be an unlawful invasion of the private lives of such individuals.[6]

The use of devices for the purpose of recording or reproducing sounds or discovering secrets or to invade privacy is punishable, under the penal code with prison sentences of one to four years and a fine of twelve to twenty-four months.[7]

---

1   In the *STS 13-III-1989* (RJ 1989/2040) the following were considered to be considered breaches of privacy: the revelation by an official of the Sports Federation to a press agency of the exclusion of an athlete for motives known by reason of the official's position, *STS 19-VI-1989* (RJ 1989/4699) the revelation to a newspaper by an administrative superior of a sanction imposed on a subordinate before notice had been given to the individual in question, *STS 14-XI-1992* (RJ 1993/3738) the questions of a personnel selection test for a job that involved access to matters related to National Security.
2   Article 199 (1) (2) CP, art 197 (4) CP.
3   *STS 23-III-1993*, (RJ 1993/3303).
4   Article 7 (3) LOHII. It was considered to be infringement of privacy, *STS 18-VII-1988* (RJ 1988/5726) when there appeared the journalistic publication on an architect with AIDS, *STS 19-VI-1990* (RJ 1990/4857) the journalistic revelation of data and personal motivations given confidentially by a public figure during a course of treatment, *STS 18-III-1992* (RJ 1992/2204), *STC 17-X-1991* (RTC 1991/197), *STS 7-XII-1995* (RJ 1995/9268) the revelation in a newspaper of data concerning the relationship of a minor adopted by persons in the public eye. The application of the notion of neutral reportage is reserved only for the right to honour *STS 24-I-1997* (RJ 1997/20).
5   Article 7 (1) LOHII.
6   Article 7 (2) LOHII.
7   Article 197 (1) CP in its basic form.

Use of security camera footage for reporting events and the use of telephoto lenses

26.11 As in the previous instances, the installation and utilisation of telephoto lenses or any other optical devices or means capable of gathering information about people's private lives or about statements which were not intended for those who seek to make use of such items, as well as the recording or reproduction of such information, are deemed to be unlawful by the LOHII.[8]

Use of automated personal data

26.12 The wrongful use of automated personal data constitutes an invasion of privacy, as established in Article 18 (4) SC [9] and of the principles regulated in the LORTAD.[10]

The following actions are unlawful:[11]

(1) collecting or storing personal data which is unnecessary, irrelevant and excessive;

(2) establishing unspecified and illegal purposes;

(3) using and transferring personal data for different purposes from those for which its collection was intended;

(4) maintaining personal data which isincomplete or out of date;

(5) storing data for a period of time in excess of what is necessary;

(6) unfair and unlawful obtaining and processing of data;

(7) failing to observe security measures; and

(8) infringing the rights of those affected (eg access, information, correction, cancellation).

The majority of these actions are reflected in the penal code (Article 197(2)) for which a more serious sanction is applied when sensitive personal data is involved: data revealing ideology, religion, beliefs, health, racial origin or sexual life, or when the affected party is a minor or disabled person.[12]

3   Lawful actions

26.13 The LOHII specifies the circumstances in which activities, which otherwise constitute an invasion of privacy, will be judged lawful. These

---

8   Article 7 (2) LOHII. In the *STS 29-III-1988* (RJ 1988/2480) it is considered to be an infringement of the privacy to obtain, by means of a telephoto lens, photographs of an artist without his consent. Equally, the CP includes this conduct in its art 197 (1).

9   Article 18 (4) CE 'Law will restrain the use of computers in order to guarantee the honour, the personal and family privacy of citizens and the full exercise of their rights'

10   The principles are similar to those of Council of Europe Convention for the Protection of Individuals with regard to Automated processing of Personal Data of 1981, ratified by Spain 27-I-1984 (BOE no 274, 15-XI-1985).

11   See, for the principles of the Lortad, Hernando I, *Data Transmission and Privacy*, edited by D Campbell and J Fisher, Martinus Nijhoff, 1994, pp 453-473. *STS 5-III-1994* (RJ 1994/2107) the consulting of the records of births and deaths by news reporting companies is a breach of privacy.

12   Article 197 (5), (6) CP.

circumstances, which will be interpreted in accordance with social criteria,[13] are the following.

Consent of the interested party

26.14   The consent of the interested party is the first circumstance, necessary for invasion of privacy to be lawful.[14] However, in order to be valid, this consent must comply with a number of conditions:

(1)   consent is of a limited nature.[15] Only a temporary and specific invasion of an individual's privacy is permitted since the right to a private life is irrevocable, inalienable, and imprescribable. Any relinquishment of this right is considered to be invalid;

(2)   consent must be specific and unequivocal;[16]

(3)   consent may be given before or after the invasion of privacy takes place;

(4)   consent may be withdrawn at any time. If revocation is likely to cause damage to the beneficiary of the consent, this party has the right to be compensated for the damage and financial loss caused, including consequential losses. However, the effectiveness of the revocation is not conditional on the payment of compensation; and

(5)   the subject of the consent must not be contrary to law, morality or considerations of public order.[17]

According to the law, minors and incapacitated persons may give consent in certain circumstances; otherwise consent must be obtained from their legal representatives, in writing, with the assent of the public prosecutor (*Ministerio Fiscal*).[18] So far as concerns minors, even if authorisation has been given on the part of their representatives, the use of their images or names in the media will be considered an unlawful invasion of privacy if it is contrary to their interests or to their reputation.[19]

Authorisation by law

26.15   Invasion of privacy is lawful if it is specifically authorised by Law.[20] The Law, however, must have the same status as that of the LOHII.[1]

Public interest

26.16   The third circumstance in which invasion of privacy may be lawful relates to the relative public interest of the facts disclosed. In this case, invasion of privacy is justified by the significance of the matter in question

---

13   Article 2 (1) LOHII, the social criteria are fixed in accordance with the private sphere which, by their own acts, each person reserves for himself or his family (art 3 (1) civil Code) *STS 18-III-1992* (RJ 1992/2204).
14   Article 1 (3) LOHII.
15   *STS 7-III-1990* (RJ 1990/1677), consent for a single television transmission.
16   *STS 11-VII-1991* (RJ 1991/5343), express consent contained in a leasing contract. *STS 7-IV-1992* (RJ 1992/3094), express consent by unequivocal conduct.
17   Article 1255 Civil Code.
18   Article 3 LOHII.
19   Article 4(3) LO 1/1996 (B.O.E. 17-I-1996) of *Protection of minors*.
20   Article 2 (2) LOHII.
1   Thus, the art 2 of the *LO 4-VIII-1997* on the utilisation of video cameras by the Security Forces, op cit, p 3.

or, by the legitimate interest of the public to be informed.[2] The actions which are considered valid invasions of privacy under the LOHII are the following:[3]

(1) existence of authorisation from the competent authority, in accordance with a law;[4] and

(2) existence of a relevant historical, scientific or cultural interest which prevails over considerations of privacy.[5]

4 *Judicial protection of privacy*

26.17 Privacy can be protected by penal, civil and administrative means.

Penal protection of privacy

26.18 The penal code protects privacy against illegal activities in Articles 197 to 201, 535 and 536. However, the criminal character of the intrusion does not preclude having recourse to the judicial procedures established in the LOHII. The criteria of this law are applicable, in every situation, in order to determine the extent of the civil liability arising from the criminal act.[6]

Civil protection of privacy

26.19 From the civil perspective, the judicial protection established in the LOHII can be effected through ordinary legal procedures or those established by the *Ley 62/1978 de protección jurisdiccional de los derechos fundamentales de la persona.*[7] The aim of these proceedings involves the adoption of the following measures of protection:

(1) Stopping the invasion of privacy. As a supplementary form of protection, preventive injunctions may be called for to bring about the immediate cessation of the invasion of privacy (eg seizure, impounding and halting the distribution of the offending material).

(2) Preventing or impeding subsequent invasions of privacy.

(3) Full and satisfactory reinstatement of the infringed right. In this respect the following actions are envisaged:

---

2 In this sense the *STS 11-XII-1989*, (RJ 1989/8817), *STC 17-X-1991* (RTC 1991/197, 11-IV-1992), *STC. 14-II-1992* (RTC 1992/20), *STS 2-II-1993* (RJ 1993/794), *STS 2-XII-1993* (RJ 1993/9483).

3 Article 8 (1) LOHII.

4 On the duty to collect taxes which in itself does not create an infringement of art 7 (4) LOHIII, the *STS 15-II-1994*, (RJ 1994/3447), *STS 8- II - 1994*, (RJ 1994/2856), *STS 11-III-1994* (RJ 1993/7221), *STS 29-III-1993*, (RJ 1993/2100), *STS 9-II-1993*, (RJ 1993/2100), *STS 9-V-1991*, (RJ 1991/6601), *STS 2-VII-1991* (RJ 1991/4229). Similarly, a biological paternity test in a filiation proceeding, *STS 1-III-1994*, (RJ 1994/1634), *STS 25-I-1992*, (RJ 1992/263), *STS 21-V-1988*, (RJ 1988/6543). Likewise, public access to the civil register on unknown paternity *STS 29-I-1990*, (RJ 1990/72).

5 *STS 30-XII-1989*, (RJ 1989/8880) the television broadcast of a criminal trial of 1959.

6 Article 1(2) LOHII.

7 *Law 62/1978, 26-XII-1978*, (BOE, no 3, 3-I-1979).

(a) *Acknowledgment of the right to reply.* Any person entitled to do so may exercise the right to rectify unlawful information spread by any means of social communication in accordance with the *Ley Orgánica 2/1984.*[8]

(b) *Acknowledgment of the right to publicise the sentence.* The publication should be by the same means of communication in which the unlawful invasion of privacy occurred in accordance with the conditions stipulated in the sentence.

(c) *Compensation for the damages caused.* In accordance with the LOHII, damage is presumed as long as unlawful action is proven. If several participants are involved in the invasion of privacy, they are jointly liable.[9]

Compensation relates both to material damage and moral damage. Moral damage is appraised in relation to the following criteria:[10]

(a) The circumstances of the case

(b) The gravity of the injury actually produced. To appraise gravity, the diffusion or medium through which the injury has been caused will be taken into account.

(c) The benefit or profit obtained by the infringer.

(4) Finally, the authorised party may present the *recurso de amparo* before the Constitutional Court against judicial sentences that do not recognise the right to privacy or its invasion.

These measures of protection of the LOHII may only be exercised within a four-year period commencing when the right first became exercisable.

In addition, the LORTAD grants a right to compensation to the affected parties. Article 9 (1) establishes a system of objective liability. However, the LORTAD distinguishes between two types of proceedings. Thus, if the breach occurs in the public sector, liability is determined in accordance with regulatory legislation governing Public Administrations.[11] In contrast, claims for compensation within the private sector should be brought before the civil jurisdiction bodies.

Administrative protection of privacy

26.20 Administrative protection of privacy is regulated in the LORTAD for breaches committed by those responsible for personal data files.

Responsible parties, both in the public and in the private sectors, are subject to disciplinary administrative proceedings before the Data Protection Agency and the administrative courts (*Agencia de Protección de Datos y los Tribunales contencioso-administrativos*).

---

8 *LO 2/1984, 24-III-1984 reguladora del Derecho de Rectificación* (BOE no 74, 27-III-1984 , rectifications BOE, no 90, 14 -IV - 1984).

9 The *Law 14/1996, 18-III-1966* (RCL 1996/519, NDL 24475) for the legislation of the press and printing industry applies, art 65, if the infringement of privacy has been committed through a means of public communication, *STC 12-XI-1990*, (RTC 1990/171 and RTC 1990/172)

10 In application of the assessment criteria, *STS 2-III-1997*, (RJ 1997/2188), *STS 25-IV-1997*, (RJ 1997/3401), *STS 7-XII-1995* (RJ 1995/9268).

11 *Law 30/1992, 26-XI-1992*, (BOE, no 285, 27-XI-1992).

B Publicity

1 Elements of publicity right

26.21 The commercial use of a person's image is placed within the context of the rights of personality, regulated by the LOHII of 1982. Publicity is defined, quite strictly, in Article 7 (6) as 'the use of the name, the voice or the image of a person for commercial, publicity or similar purposes'.

According to the LOHII, there is an infringement of publicity right when the following circumstances are found:

Identification of a person

26.22 First, it is necessary for a person to be identified. It is sufficient that there should exist the possibility that third parties might make an identification. Proof of identification is not necessary for the commencement of proceedings for infringement of this right.

The use of the identity of another person is prohibited in a number of ways:

(1) the appropriation of a person's *voice* for publicity purposes is an appropriation of their personality; and

(2) the use of a person's name includes the use of surnames, combination of first names and surnames, first name, nickname, professional name, pseudonym and also biographical facts.

The High Court has decided on various occasions in relation to the use of a name as a factor identifying the person, and prohibited its use by third parties. In the case *Cesar Manrique*,[12] the High Court considered the creation of a limited company with the name Cesar Manrique to be an unlawful action, since the name belonged to a well-known individual in the artistic and business world. In this case there was a confusion of identities and the Court held that the existence of the company's entry in the Official Mercantile Register (*Registro Mercantil*) did not constitute an authorisation to usurp the name of another person. This prohibition derived, in practice, from Article 7 (6) of the LOHII and Article 53 of the 1957 Civil Register Law (*Ley de Registro Civil*).[13]

In the case of *Marquis of Bradomín*,[14] the High Court found against the use of a noble title for the commercialisation of a wine. In this case, the name 'Marquis of Bradomin' was entered as a trade mark in the former Industrial Property Register (*Registro de la Propiedad Industrial*) to designate a product. However, despite this registration, under trade mark law[15] the registration of names or images which belong to a person other than the applicant is prohibited. Likewise, the name, surname, pseudonym or any other form by which the general public might identify a person other than the applicant, cannot be used without the person's prior authorisation. Finally, in relation

---

12 *STS 5-X-1989*, (RJ 1989/6886).
13 *LRC, 8-VI-1957*, (BOE, no 151, 10-VI-1957). The name (formed by the first name and the surnames, paternal and maternal) is protected '*erga omnes*'.
14 *STS 26-I-1990*, (RJ 1990/26).
15 *Law 32/1988, 10-XI-1988*, (BOE no 272, 12-XI-1988), arts 13, 81 (for trade names) and 85.

to the various forms of presenting the life of a person, (biographical, docudrama, fiction, fictionalisation)[16] the question of whether there has been an infringement of the right of publicity may depend on whether the pursuit of financial gain prevails over one of the exceptions stipulated for its authorised use.[17]

(3) Finally, the *image*, defined by the High Court as the graphical representation of the human figure through the use of mechanical or technical means of reproduction,[18] includes the imitation and appropriation of an individual's form of behaviour, the use of doubles and lookalikes.

The profit motive

26.23 The right of publicity is, under the Spanish Law, the recognition of the right which each person has to control the commercial use of one's image, to be remunerated for the economic value of one's own identity, without any detriment to one's reputation or good name.[19]

The uses that suppose an infringement of this right are stated in the LOHII:

(1) *Advertising purposes* – The following activities are identified as being within this category:

> (a) the use and appropriation of a person's image or name in commercial advertising and publicity features;[20]
>
> (b) the appropriation of the form of behaviour or character of a public person in commercial advertising;
>
> (c) the use of doubles and lookalikes of a person in commercial advertising; and
>
> (d) the use of the identity of a person in collateral advertising.

(2) *Commercial purposes* – The following activities are classified as being commercial purposes:

> (a) the use of the name, image or biographical data in games;[1]
>
> (b) the sale of products associated with an event or with a celebrity (merchandising); and

16 After Lisa A Lawrence, in 'Television , Docudramas and the Right of Publicity: Too bad Liz, That's Show Biz', 8 Comment LJ, 275.

17 The High Court has had occasion to pronounce in the case *La huella de la crimen (STS 30-XII-1989*, op cit , para **26.16**, n 5 on privacy protection) in which the story of a public criminal trial was made known by television and the facts that led to the death penalty for a woman in 1959, which were circulated by the media of the period. According to the Court, the social and historical significance of the event justified the verdict of non infringement of publicity rights argued by the heirs of the deceased.

18 *STS 11-IV-1987, STS 29-III-1988, STS 9-V-1988, STS 9-II-1989, 19-X-1992*, they cited in *STS 3-X-1996*, AC,3/13, 19-I-1997.

19 See, below, para **26.06**.

20 These proceedings are contained in the judgment of the Supreme Court of 3 October 1996 (*STS 3-X-1996*, op cit, n 18 above) in which it was accepted that there was an infringement of publicity rights of some Spanish Olympic athletes. It concerned the production, by a company dedicated to the manufacture and sale of beer, of calendars for the Christmas campaign of 1984 adorned with the photographs of the Olympic athletes who had obtained a medal in the Los Angeles Olympics of 1984.

1 *STS 9-V-1988*, (RJ 1988/4049) Unlawful infringement occurred in the case of 'professional footballers ' who gave their photographs to be used in collections of stickers during a soccer season. After the end of this period the company continued to publish the stickers despite the opposition of the footballers.

the utilisation of other people's names and identities as brand names.[2]

(3) *Analogous purposes* – Unless this is exempted by law, under analogous purposes we may include the use of images in electoral processes[3] and in the illustration of news.[4]

The non-existence of exemptions

26.24   For the infringement of the publicity right to be deemed unlawful, it is required that none of the exceptions established in the LOHII should be applicable.

General exemptions

26.25   These exemptions are common to the rights of personality regulated under the LOHII:

(1)   the right to honour, to privacy and to one's own image;[5]

(2)   existence of the consent of the person;[6]

(3)   existence of a law authorising the interference;[7]

(4)   existence of authorisation from the competent Authority according to the law; and

(5)   existence of a historical, scientific or cultural interest that prevails over the publicity right.

This last exception is especially relevant in relation to biographies.[8] However, where real or invented facts about the life of a person are used (docudrama, fiction, fictionalisation) the appraisal is stricter and such uses can be deemed to be an unlawful invasion of publicity if there is no overriding informative purpose or exercise of the right of freedom of expression.

---

2   Case *Cesar Manrique*, op cit, p 10 and case *Marquis of Bradomín* op cit, p 10.

3   In the case *Esquerra Republicana de Catalunya, STS 11-IV-1987*, (RJ 1987/2703), it was considered unlawful infringement by a political party to use for a propaganda poster a photograph of several workers leaving a factory, to which had been added as photo montage a Catalan flag.

4   In the *STS 25-IV-1989*, (RJ 1989/3260) with the *Paquirri* case(see para **26.04**, n 8), it is considered to be infringement of the publicity right for the diffusion by television to have been made of the video of the bullfighter taken in his death bed and, in the *STS 29-III-1988* (RJ 1988/2480) op cit, it is considered unlawful for the magazine Interviú to publish several photographs of a well-known actress, topless on a beach, taken by means of a telephoto lens. Similarly, *STS 22-IV-1992* (RJ 1992/3317) in which it was deemed unlawful for a newspaper to publish a photograph of two persons standing in front of a bus stop, attributing to them conduct which was prejudicial to their honour and, *STS 29-III-1996* (RJ 1996/2371) which found to be unlawful the publication of a photograph of a professional model taken without his consent.

5   Article 8 (1) LOHII.

6   *STS 16-VI-1990* (RJ 1990/4762) withdrawal of consent given by an actress for the publication of some photographs in Playboy was not admitted on account of the itme that had elapsed. For the requirements of the consent, see paras **26.07** ff.

7   See paras **26.07** ff.

8   See, case *La huella de la crimen*, see para **26.27**, n 17.

Specific exemptions

26.26   There are specific exemptions which apply to the publicity right. These exceptions are established in the LOHII, in Article 8 (2).

Public figures. It is not considered to be an unlawful invasion of publicity if the image recorded, reproduced or published relates to a person who holds public office, or follows a prominent or public profession and the image has been taken during a public activity or in places open to the public.

This exemption on the occasions that it has been cited in connection with Article 7 (6), has been dismissed by the High Court

(1)   Public figures are those who carry out public duties or follow a public profession;

(2)   public places and acts at which recording of the image is made are interpreted restrictively. This present exemption is not allowed if the public figure, by his actions, has made a clear attempt to protect his privacy, even when this is in a public place;[9] and

(3)   the exemption serves the interests of public information. This interest is excluded if the recording, reproduction and diffusion of the image infringe the rights to honour or privacy or if financial gain is the intention.[10]

2   *Judicial protection of the right of publicity*

26.27   Judicial protection is provided in civil proceeedings by the same procedural means and actions as those established in the LOHII (Article 9) to protect the right to privacy:[11]

(1)   measures for terminating the infringement of publicity;

(2)   measures for preventing or hindering further infringement of publicity;

(3)   measures for restoring the full enjoyment of the infringed right; and

(4)   the lodging of the *recurso de amparo* before the Constitutional Court.

C   Personality

26.28   The right to one's own image, outside of considerations of publicity, and the right to honour are, in Spanish law, the remaining rights of personality recognised in the LOHII of 1982, in Articles 7 (5) and, 7 (7) in the draft of 1985, respectively. However, the latter right is also regulated in the Penal Code, in Section XI on 'offences against honour', Articles 205 and 216, which deal with the crimes of calumny and insult, and in Article 620 (2) with regard to offences against the honour of a person.

---

9   *STS 29-III-1988*, (RJ 1988/2480).
10   *STS 9-V-1988* (RJ 1988/4049), *STS 3-X-1996* (RJ 1996/2371), *STS 3-X-1996*, (AC 3/13 19-I- 1997), *STS 17-VII-1993* (RJ 1993/6458).
11   See, paras **26.19** ff.

1   Unlawful activities

26.29   The following activities will be considered unlawful personality invasions in the absence of consent from the person concerned or their legal representative,[12] or authorisation from a competent authority or a specific legal exemption (*Ley Orgánica*).[13]

Advertising for publicity purposes

26.30   The use of an image for a relevant and overriding historical, cultural or scientific purpose[14] or use in an incidental manner is legal.

However, using a restrictive interpretation of the exceptions, the High Court, in the cases of publicity campaigns undertaken by the a Public Administration for cultural or scientific ends has declared such use to be unlawful.

Thus, in an informative campaign about 'respect for the elderly' in which the photograph of five adults and two children in a public park was taken and published, the Court, in its decision of 7 October 1996, established that the citizen does not lose the right to his own image by the simple fact of having entered a public place. In order to benefit from the exemption relevance must be established as well as the indispensable nature of the use in relation to the intended purpose.[15]

A further case where the Court held that the exemption did not apply was a production about infant health, which formed part of an educational campaign, which used the photograph of a minor at the moment of receiving treatment by dialysis.[16]

Reporting private life

26.31   Under Spanish law, it is unlawful to record, reproduce or publish images through photographs, films or any other means, at places and times either in or outside of the private life.

The use of the image of a person in literary works is not permitted if the ideas expressed do not require a controversial image and this is not essential to the freedom of expression of Article 20 SC. These requirements are strictly interpreted by the Court.[17]

In contrast, it is not considered to be unlawful to record the image of people holding public office or pursuing a public profession or activity, in places open to the public, nor to use their caricature in accordance with social

---

12 In the case of the image, consent must be explicit for each of the activities of recording, reproduction or publication, *STS 3-XI-1988*, (RJ 1988/8408). On the withdrawal of consent with regard to infringement of the right to honour, *STS 7-III-1990*, (RJ 1990/1677), *STS 30-XI-1992*, (RJ 1992/9458), the latter, in a television campaign against alcoholism.

13 *LO 4/1997, 4-VIII-1997*, on the utilisation of video cameras by the Security Forces, see para **26.06**, n 18.

14 Commercials are within the publicity (art 7 (6) LOHII), in paras **26.14** ff.

15 *STS 7-X-1996*, see para **26.26**, n 10.

16 *STS 19-X-1992*, (RJ 1992/8079).

17 *STS 11-XII-1995*, (RJ 1995/9477) a newspaper was fined for the publication of the photo taken in the forties at the wedding of the claimant to illustrate changes in the mores between bridal couples. Compensation remains that established in the Court at 3,000,000 pesetas.

usages. Nevertheless, in both cases, the use must not be prejudicial to their privacy or honour.

In relation to this last right, the LOHII, in its draft of 1985, deems unlawful the attribution of facts or value judgments through actions or expressions which may in any way injure the dignity of another person, damaging their reputation or act against their self esteem.

The disclosure of data which refers to private matters of private or public persons is not considered to be of sufficient general interest for the right to the freedom of expression to prevail over that to honour.[18]

Reporting public events

26.32   In relation to public events or occasions, the recording, reproduction or publication by any means of a person's image is unlawful unless the following circumstances are found to apply:

(1)   the images belong to a person in public office or in public professions and are taken during a public event;

(2)   the image of a given person appears as a merely incidental occurrence. This incidental character is determined by the High Court with reference to the whole photograph and to the photograph itself within the global context of the information; and

(3)   there is an overriding and relevant historical, cultural or scientific interest in the graphical information.[19]

This last exception is one which both the High Court and the Constitutional Court have consistently applied so that it may not be considered an offence against honour when the information divulged contains data or commentaries about people or their professional good name.[20]

In practice, the conditions that the High Court demands to this end are the following:[1]

(1)   *the information must be truthful*. This requirement (Article 20 (1) (d) SC) means that the informant has a special duty to verify the information, employing a sufficient level of diligence expected of a professional.[2] All the information must be reliable, though inaccuracies in some points, or circumstantial errors may be allowed if they do not affect the essential substance of the information[3] or, if it is given in the context of neutral reporting.[4]

(2)   *the information be relevant*. Relevance in the sense that it refers to public matters that will be of general interest for the issues they deal with

---

18   In application of art 8 (1) LOHII and art 20 CE, *STC 138/96, 16-IX-1996, R3241/93*, (BOE 21-X-1996). Except for social uses or if the persons by their own actions express the contrary, *STS 14-III-1997* (RJ 1997/2105) calling press conferences and making public appearances.

19   The scientific interest is not accepted in *STS 29-IX-1992*, (RJ 1992/7424).

20   *STC 223/1992, 24-XII-1992*, (RTC 1992/223).

1   *STS 20-III-1997*, (RJ 1997/1985), *STS 13-II-1997*, (RJ 1997/943), *STS 25-III-1995*, (RJ 1995/2138), *STS 28-III-1994*, (RJ 1994/2527), *STS 30 -1993*, (RJ 1993/7671), *STS 11-IV-1992*, (RJ 1992/86 3094), *STS 17-V-1991*, (RJ 1991/3711).

2   *STC 6/1988*, (RTC 1988/6), *STS 1-IV-1997* (RJ 1997/2723).

3   *STS 24-IV-1997*, (RJ 1997/3252), *STS 10-IV-1997*, (RJ 1997/2911), *STS 25-III-1991* (RJ 1991/2441).

4   *STS 20-II-1997* (RJ 1997/1009), *STS 24-I-1997*, (RJ 1997/20).

and for the persons who are involved. Use of freedom of expression as a defence is weakened if the revelations do not refer to public figures.

2   *Judicial protection of the personality*

26.33   Protection of the personality may be effected through penal and civil procedures.

Penal protection of honour

26.34   At the request of the injured party, honour is protected in the Penal Code, (Articles 205 to 216 and 620 (2). However, as in the case of privacy, in application of Article 1 (2) of the LOHII, the criminal nature of the infringement does not preclude recourse to the judicial procedures established in this law. Furthermore, the criteria of this law will be applicable for determining any civil liability deriving from the offence.

Civil protection of the personality

26.35   With regard to the right to the image and the right to honour, the judicial protection recognised in the LOHII is applied and put into effect through ordinary procedural channels or by the procedures regulated in the *Ley* 62/1978.[5]
The measures for protection, which are applied in the same way as for the privacy and publicity, are the following:[6]

(1)   action to end infringement, including preventive injunctions;

(2)   action to prevent or hinder further infringement;

(3)   action to restore the full enjoyment of rights; and

(4)   exercise of *recurso de amparo* before the *Constitutional Court*.

D   Conclusion

26.36   By way of conclusion it is important to note that, in relation to the rights previously analysed (privacy, publicity, personality) protection is accorded to the person who has suffered the unlawful infringement, or their legal representatives.[7]

In the event of death, whether the infringement occurred before or after the death, the rights of action survive and the following persons are authorised to act:[8]

(1)   the legal or physical person that the deceased may have nominated for such purpose in his will;

(2)   in his absence or, if the appointee has died, the responsibility passes to the spouse, descendants, and parents, who were alive at the time of his death; and

---

5   See para **26.19**, n7.
6   See paras **26.13** and **26.24** ff.
7   Article 6 (1) LOHII.
8   Article 4 LOHII.

(3) finally, in the absence of family members, the responsibility passes to the public prosecutor, as long as no more than eighty years have elapsed since the death of the affected party.

These persons are equally authorised to continue with any action already commenced by the affected when he or she died.[9]

---

9   Article 6 (2) LOHII.

27 SWEDEN

Thomas Lindqvist
Claes Langenius

A Introduction

27.01 In order to be able to describe Swedish law in relation to the aspects of privacy, publicity and personality it is necessary to understand the structure of Swedish law with regard to these aspects.

27.02 Protection of an individual's integrity and personality has by tradition been given a rather limited attention in Swedish law. The constitution states that the public shall protect the individual's privacy, but this principle has only partly resulted in binding legislation. In Sweden, it is therefore not possible to say that the rights of privacy and personality are clearly defined as a distinctive jurisprudence. This matter has been discussed from time to time and various legislative proposals have been presented. However, the matter is politically sensitive as the contradiction between the right of privacy and the constitutional rights of publicity and freedom of speech is delicate. The legislative proposals have therefore not resulted in any legislation so far.

27.03 The right of personality may to some extent be found within the laws of copyright. Swedish copyright laws do contain some aspects of personality protection. As an example, the author's moral rights (*'droit moral'*) and the author's right to be mentioned by name when the work is used should be mentioned. The author is also protected against any insulting change or presentation of the work. The right of 'moral' damages in the context of copyright can also be seen as an aspect of protection of personality.

27.04 The Swedish Names Act[1] protects distinctive surnames against use of the protected name, or a name which is confusingly similar to the name, without consent. An infringement of those provisions may result in 'moral' damages.

1   1982:670.

B   Privacy

1   Privacy generally

27.05   Some rules relating to privacy can be found within the criminal law. In order to describe whether Swedish law permits publication of matters relating to the private lives of individuals and the applicable limits, it is necessary to outline some parts of Swedish criminal law.

27.06   An individual's right to privacy may be protected through regulations under criminal law such as eg breach of domiciliary peace, molestation, eavesdropping and defamation. These provisions can be found in the Swedish Penal Code from 1962, which since then has been amended several times. The Penal Code[2] is applicable to both national residents and citizens of foreign states.

27.07   Before evaluating whether specific acts would be permitted under Swedish law it is, in our opinion, necessary, by way of summary, to state some of the most relevant aspects of the different prohibitions in the Penal Code with regard to the privacy of individuals.

2   Breach of domiciliary peace (trespassing)

27.08   A person who unlawfully intrudes or remains where another has his living quarters, whether it is a room, a house, a yard or a vessel, is liable for *breach of domiciliary peace*.

Further, if a person, without authorisation, intrudes or remains in an office, factory, other building or vessel or at a storage area or other similar place, he is liable for *unlawful intrusion*.

Normally such crimes are punishable by fine but if the crime is grave, a prison sentence of up to two years can be imposed.

3   Molestation

27.09   A person who manually molests or harasses another, by discharge of a firearm, throwing of stones, making loud noise or other heedless conduct is liable for *molestation* and can be sentenced to pay a fine or to imprisonment for a maximum of one year.

4   Breach of postal or telecommunication secrecy

27.10   If a person unlawfully obtains access to a communication which is being transmitted, in the form of mail or as a telephone conversation, telegram or other telecommunication by a public agency of communication, he can be sentenced for *breach of postal or telecommunication secrecy* to pay a fine or to imprisonment for a maximum of two years.

---

2   1962:700.

5   Intrusion in a safe depository

27.11   A person who, in circumstances not covered by the above mentioned provision, unlawfully opens a letter or a telegram or otherwise obtains access to something kept safely under seal or lock or otherwise enclosed, shall be sentenced for *intrusion in a safe depository* to pay a fine or to imprisonment for a maximum of two years.

6   Eavesdropping

27.12   A person who, in circumstances other than those stated above, unlawfully and secretly listens to or privately records a conversation between others or discussions at a conference or other meeting to which the public is not admitted and in which he himself does not participate, or to which he has improperly obtained access, shall be sentenced for *eavesdropping* to pay a fine or to imprisonment for a maximum two years.

7   Defamation

27.13   A person who identifies someone as being a criminal or as reproachable for his mode of life, or otherwise gives information likely to expose him to the disrespect of others, may be sentenced for *defamation* to pay a fine. If he was required to disclose the information or if, considering the circumstances, the disclosure of the information was defensible, and if he proves that the information was true or that he had reasonable grounds to believe it, no punishment shall be imposed.

27.14   If the above mentioned crime is regarded as serious, a fine or imprisonment for a maximum of two years may be imposed for *grave defamation*. In judging the gravity of the crime, special attention shall be given to whether the information, because of its content or the scope of its dissemination or otherwise, was likely to result in serious damage.

27.15   A person who has been the subject of a crime may always claim damages for eg physical and mental damages for injuries and any insult. However, the amount of such damages is rather low according to Swedish law and court practice.

8   Covert filming

27.16   Under Swedish law there exists no general prohibition against filming a person without their consent, or showing the film to others, even if doing so offends the person's integrity.

The Swedish Supreme Court has, in a 1992[3] case, stated several interesting principles with regard to this problem. In short, the case concerned a man who was prosecuted for defamation for having filmed a woman in an intimate situation with him without her knowledge. The man had shown the film extensively to other people. The Supreme Court found that the action fell within the provisions of defamation in the Penal Code. However, as this requires the victim to have been exposed to others' disrespect, the

---

3   'Filming sexual act'. NJA 1992, s 594.

court had to assess whether this was the fact. The court found that a person watching the tape might get the impression that the woman knew that she was filmed and that she did not mind the tape being shown to others. On the basis of this assumption the court stated that the film was disparaging for the woman. The court also found that the crime was grave due to the grade of insult and the circulation of the film. The defendant was sentenced to pay fines of SEK 8,000. It should be noted that the victim did not claim any damages in the case, but she had obtained damages of SEK 10,000 before the proceedings.

27.17   This case is quite illustrative of Swedish law in this aspect. Covert filming is accordingly not prohibited per se, but may constitute a crime if it results in an insult to a person's honour. This has to some extent been criticised as an action can be insulting even if it is not an insult to a person's honour.

27.18   Besides the above mentioned rules there is a specific Act[4] regarding the use of surveillance cameras in shops etc. According to this Act a licence is required for such use. The holder of a licence is obliged to state that their premises are under surveillance and agree that any information received from such a camera is confidential. The observance of the Act is monitored by the Swedish County Administrative Board. A person infringing this Act may be subject to fines or imprisonment for a maximum of one year.

9   Filming on private property

27.19   Besides the aspects mentioned above, the following points should be noted.

A person's right to privacy on his property is protected by some of the provisions in the Penal Code mentioned above. Where filming results in a person's unlawfully intruding or remaining in another person's home the intruder may be sentenced for breach of domiciliary peace. This also applies if a person without authorisation intrudes or remains in an office, factory or other similar place. The crime is then called unlawful intrusion.

A person who infringes these provisions can be subject to fines, or, if the crime is grave, imprisonment for a maximum of two years.

27.20   The courts have ruled on these issues several times. In one case[5] where three persons had entered an unoccupied house to look around and take some pictures, the Court of Appeal did not find that this was an unlawful intrusion, as the house was unoccupied and the persons had only looked around and taken a small number of pictures.

---

4   1990: 484.
5   *S v JT* rf s 34. The Court of Appeal also stated that normally it would be considered an unlawful intrusion when entering a building without prior authorisation. However, all circumstances must be taken into consideration. In this case, the building was not only unoccupied and kept in bad repair, but an entrance was also left open.

In another case[6] a reporter had followed several persons who had occupied a consulate, and refused to leave the building despite a warning from the tenant. The reporter was sentenced for intrusion. However, in another case[7] the Court of Appeal found that an editor who had entered an occupied building to take pictures etc had not acted unlawfully.

27.21   The state of the house or building in question, the way in which the intruder has entered the building and if he has left the building voluntarily when asked to, are all facts which will be taken into account by the courts. The Supreme Court has also stated that in principle only actions which can be seen as reprehensible should be punished.

In principle, covert filming is not prohibited, but the actions leading up to the pictures being taken etc may be considered as eg trespassing and the publication of a film or a picture may result in a crime such as defamation.

10   Filming over private property (from the air)

27.22   Apart from what has been mentioned above it should be noted that filming over private property requires permission from the Ministry of Defence if the filming is to take place over certain military sensitive areas. If filming takes place outside these areas, and the pictures are to be published, the pictures must be examined by the Ministry of Defence and approval is not given as a general permission to eg a magazine.

11   Public order aspects

27.23   Besides the above-mentioned restriction filming is not allowed during court procedures. According to special arrangements filming may only take place in prisons under certain conditions. Filming inside a hospital is, however, regulated through the general provisions in the Penal Code concerning breach of domiciliary peace etc mentioned above.

12   Recording of conversations, whether open or covert

27.24   The Swedish Penal Code states that a person who unlawfully and secretly listens to or privately records, by technical means for sound reproduction, a conversation between others or discussions at a conference or other meeting to which the public is not admitted and in which he himself does not participate, or to which he has improperly obtained access, may be sentenced for eavesdropping.[8]

---

6   RH 1986:16. The reporter stayed in the building despite the fact that the tenant showed him the tenancy agreement and despite the fact that security officers asked him to leave. The Court of Appeal did however take into account that the reporter was serving a public interest of information when imposing the penalty.

7   RH 1988:62. In this case, special emphasis was put on the fact that the reporter had entered the building after the start of the occupation, that he had not especially been requested to leave the building and that when he, at the arrival of the police authority, wanted to leave the building, was unable to do so due to the barricades built by the occupants.

8   Penal Code, Chapter 4, s 9a.

This provision is only applicable to covert eavesdropping and if the person who records the conversation himself takes part in the conversation he cannot be sentenced under this provision.

A person infringing this prohibition is subject to fines or imprisonment for a maximum of two years.

13 Sifting of rubbish

27.25 Going through someone's private things on someone's private property would most likely be deemed to be a breach of domiciliary peace or unlawful intrusion. A person infringing these provisions may be subject to fines or, if the crime is grave, imprisonment for a maximum of two years.

14 Assumed identity

27.26 Under Swedish criminal law assuming an identity may be prohibited, but only if the assumed identity leads a person to undertake any actions, which result in an *economic* damage.

15 Use of security camera footage and telephoto lens for reporting events

27.27 The use of a security camera footage or telephoto lens per se does not constitute any crime. However, if such a camera has been used in a context which falls under the prohibition for eavesdropping, the camera may be seen as a means to the crime, and may therefore, in theory, be forfeited. This is, however, only possible if it can be assumed that the forfeiture of the camera or lens may lead to prevention of crime.

16 Data protection

27.28 The Swedish Data Protection Act has recently been replaced by a new Personal Data Protection Act[9] which entered into force on 24 October 1998. This Act protects the use of personal data in different contexts. According to the Act it is no longer necessary to obtain a licence in order to be allowed to hold a record of personal data. The new Act prescribes instead an obligation to notify the Data Inspection Board before carrying out any automatic processing operation.

The provisions of the Act are applicable to everything that can be done with such data, eg the retrieval, collection, storage and dissemination of personal data. Processing of personal data which is partly or wholly automatic, ie largely computerised, falls under the Act. Manual processing of such data (on paper) is only included if the data forms part of a proper record. Purely private use of personal data falls outside the Act.

27.29 The Act defines certain basic requirements for the processing of personal data. The person responsible for processing of personal data must

---

9   1998:204.

ensure that the data is only collected for certain expressly stated and justifiable purposes. The data may not be used for any purpose incompatible with the ones for which the data was originally collected. Superfluous data may not be processed – all data must be adequate and relevant. The data may be stored only as long as is necessary with respect to the purposes of processing.

27.30 The Act prohibits processing of personal data which reveals eg a person's race, political opinion, religion or membership in a trade union. However, personal data may always be processed if the individual in question has given his consent. In other cases processing must be necessary for the attaining of certain stated purposes. However, in some situations processing may be undertaken without consent, such as in order to fulfil an obligation under a contract with the individual in question, or in order to protect vital interests of the data subject or in order for the company responsible for the processing of personal data to fulfil a legal obligation.

27.31 As the Act came into force its implementation into Swedish law was criticised. One of the most important criticisms was that the existence of the Internet was not considered. As of 1 January 2000, section 33 of the Act has been amended in order to be better adapted to its purpose, in considering the Internet. The old section 33 prohibited the transfer of personal data that was undergoing processing to a third country (countries outside the EU). As from 1 January it is permissible to transfer personal data from Sweden to any country that provides adequate protection of personal integrity. When evaluating if adequate protection exists, all circumstances shall be taken into consideration. Special importance shall be attached to the nature of the data, the purpose of the processing, how long the processing will last, the land of origin, the final country of destination and the rules regulating the processing of personal data in the third country.

C   Publicity

1   Names and pictures in advertising

27.32 As mentioned above under part B Swedish law does not contain any distinct law of personality.

However, a law does exist concerning the use of a person's name and picture in advertising; the Swedish Act on Names and Pictures in Advertising, from 1979.[10] This Act regulates only the use of names and pictures in the context of *commercial marketing*. This law prohibits companies from using a person's names or picture without their consent in the marketing of goods and services. The main purpose of the law is to protect a person's integrity by allowing them to decide whether they want to be used in a commercial context.

27.33 The Act is applicable to all kinds of persons, also including citizens of foreign states and famous people. The Act protects common names as well as a person's stage-name and also applies if a person is identified by the

---

10 1978:800.

use of a denomination, which may be comparable to a name, for example the denomination 'prime minister'.

If a person's picture forms part of a larger subject, consent is required if the purpose of the advertising is to call attention to the specific person. This is often assumed if the subject contains the picture of a *public* person, but not if an unknown individual can be seen in the background of a picture.

According to the introduction to the Act, the law is not intended to protect deceased persons' names or pictures.

27.34   A person infringing this Act may be subject to fines and damages. A person can obtain not only economical but also 'moral' damages according to the Act. In addition to this, a court may also decide that a person being found to have breached the provisions of the Act should pay for the costs of printing the judgment in one or several newspapers.

27.35   In order to illustrate the practical application of this Act some relevant and recent cases are mentioned.

The Court of Appeal stated in 1993[11] that the use of the name of the then Minister of Finance in the advertisements of a firm of accountants and a bank was contrary to the law.

The Court of Appeal found that although the advertisements in question did not try to express that the Minister of Finance had recommended the services in question, ie the bank or the firm of accountants, it was obvious that the use of the picture of this very famous person was designated to draw attention to the advertisement and that the defendants accordingly had used the picture unlawfully. The defendants were sentenced to fines of SEK 2,000.

27.36   Another interesting case in this context is a judgment rendered by the Supreme Court in 1994.[12] A Swedish pornographic magazine had used the pictures of faces of famous Swedish people such as the Prime Minister, other politicians, and artists, which had by way of photomontage been put together with other persons' bodies. These persons instituted proceedings against the pornographic magazine and its editor.

The Supreme Court found that the publication of the pictures in combination with headlines and text constituted grave defamation. The editor was sentenced to pay fines of SEK 15,000. The court also decided on the aspect of damages, a decision which was given quite a lot attention, as the damages were considered to be rather high from a Swedish point of view. The court stated that the defendant should pay SEK 100,000 to each of the plaintiffs. The court especially noted that the photomontages with texts had been spread widely and had resulted in considerable discomfort for the plaintiffs, which was maybe even more serious as they were famous people who received great attention from the public. The court then referred to the character of the crimes and the economic consideration that was assumed being the reason for the publicity, and found that the damages should be set at such a high level that they would be preventive.

This case has, as mentioned above, received some attention owing to the fact that some lawyers are of the opinion that the judgment shows that Swedish legislation is insufficient and that the court had to use existing

11   RH 1993:20.
12   'The Swedish hustler versus several Swedish celebrities'. NJA 1994, s 637.

remedies in a strained way. The court's statements about the insult and the aspect of prevention in relation to the damages has also been interpreted as the court's using damages as a punishment.

27.37 In a recent decision from the Swedish Supreme Court,[13] another pornographic magazine was imposed to pay penalties to a Swedish actor/comedian. The case concerned an advertisement showing the famous Swede reading the magazine, along with text stating that he preferred that kind of magazine to a specific TV magazine for children, of which he used to be the host. The person in question had not in any way given his consent to the publishing of the picture in this magazine; the picture was taken in a totally different context. The defendant tried to plead the protection of the Freedom of the Press Act. The Supreme Court, however, pointed at the commercial nature of the picture and the text, which also stated the prize and how often the magazine was published and found the Swedish Act on Names and Pictures in Advertising applicable.

The District Court and the Court of Appeal have found that the advertisement was commercial and accordingly should be judged under the provisions of the Act of Names and Pictures in Advertising and that the advertisement constituted an infringement of this Act. The editor was sentenced to pay fines of SEK 8,800. The plaintiff obtained damages to an amount of SEK 125,000. The Court of Appeal affirmed the judgment of the District Court and added, in accordance with the principles laid down by the Supreme Court in the above mentioned case that the amount of 'moral' damages should be seen against the facts that the advertisements had been spread widely and had resulted in considerable discomfort for the plaintiff. The Court of Appeal also referred to the Supreme Court's statement that the damages should be set at such a high level that they would be preventive.

27.38 In this context it should also be noted that an advertisement may be found to be inappropriate if it wrongly gives the impression that the person in question has used or approved the goods or services in question. Such an advertisement can be judged in accordance with another Swedish act, the Swedish Marketing Act. An infringement of this Act may lead to a prohibition to continue with the marketing in question and fines.

27.39 In Swedish law, there is little difficulty obtaining trade mark protection of a person's name, provided the name is sufficiently distinctive. A family name, artist's name or the picture of a person may, however, be cited against the registration of a trade mark which is similar to such names or pictures, unless the person in question gives his consent or the name or the picture relates to a person who has been deceased for several years.

As mentioned above, a family name is protected according to the Names Act.[14] This protection means that a person may not take another similar family name. An infringement of this Act may result in damages.

13 'Aktuell rapport versus Robert G'. NJA 1999, s 749.
14 1982:670.

D Personality

1 Personality generally

27.40 In accordance with what has been mentioned above, the use of a person's personality may be contrary to the provisions of the Act on Names and Pictures in Advertising.[15] In this context it should be noted that the provisions of the Act may be applicable if an advertisement contains a picture of a famous person, but the person in the picture is a 'double' of that famous person. However, we do not know of any cases where the courts would have applied such a principle.

In addition to this it should be mentioned that the use of a person's personality or likeness could be deemed to constitute an infringement of the above mentioned criminal provision defamation. This could be the case where a person's likeness has been used in a way which would denigrate them. However, we do not know of any cases where the courts have applied such a principle.

15 1978:800.

28 SWITZERLAND

François Dessemontet

A Privacy

1 Relevant laws of privacy

28.01 Article 28 of the Swiss Civil Code of 10 December 1907 (hereafter CC) is a general provision protecting privacy, publicity and personality as well as all other personal interests.

28.02 The Federal Law on Data Protection of 19 June 1992 protects personal data under 39 Articles. It is also the basis of various new provisions throughout federal statutes, adopted on the same day:

(1) Code of Obligations of 30 March 1911 (hereafter CO), as amended from time to time, Article 328b restricting the right of the employer to deal with personal data of his employees (which is a mandatory provision according to Article 362 CO).

(2) Law on International Private Law of 18 December 1987 (hereafter LDIP), Articles 129, 130 and 139 of which deal with jurisdiction of the Swiss courts and applicable law in transborder data protection cases.

(3) Swiss Penal Code of 21 December 1937 as amended (hereafter CP); Article 179 *novies* deals with the theft or embezzlement of personal data; Article 321 *bis* regulates professional duties to secrecy and exceptions thereto where research is done in the interest of public health and medicine, anonymity being safeguarded; Article 351 *bis – septies* and Article 363 *bis* deal with transborder exchange of data between police authorities.

28.03 The Federal Ordinance on Data Protection of 14 June 1993 provides detailed guidance on the application of the Federal Law of 19 June 1992.

28.04 The Federal Ordinance on the Treatment of Personal Data Regarding Preventive Measures for State Security of 14 June 1993 regulates political police, fighting against terrorism, revolution, political intelligence and violent extremism, as well as against weapon smuggling and illegal transfer of technology, and fighting against the organised criminality. A new Law on the same topics has been accepted by the people of Switzerland on 7 June 1998 and is scheduled to enter in force shortly.

28.05 The Federal Ordinance on the Authorisation to Lift Professional Duties of Secrecy for Medical Research of 14 June 1993.

28.06 The Federal Law on Penal Procedure of 15 June 1934 as amended, Articles 27, 29 *bis*, 73 *bis*, 73 *ter*, 73 *quater*, 101 *bis*, 102 *bis*, 102 *ter*, 102 *quater*, 105 *bis*, 107 *bis* of which deal with data protection within criminal proceedings.

28.07 Finally, all Cantons have a law regulating, inter alia, the protection of data with cantonal administrations.

2   *Application of the law*

28.08 As regards national residents, they all benefit from the protection of Swiss Laws, Ordinances and Cantonal Statutes.

(1) As regards citizens of foreign states, they may benefit from the protection under Swiss Laws if there is Swiss jurisdiction according to Articles 129–130 LDIP.

  (a) jurisdiction: the domicile, residence or main place of business of the defendant, if within Switzerland, is the main connecting factor giving rise to jurisdiction;

  (b) if none of these factors are present, the jurisdiction may be given either:

   if the wrongful act against data protection is committed within Switzerland, or

   if the result is to be felt within Switzerland.

Contrary to the cases of *Marinari*[1] and *Fiona Shevill*,[2] Swiss jurisdiction is not limited to that part of the damage which is caused within Switzerland.[3]

(2) As to the applicable law, the injured party may according to Article 139 LDIP elect to have the case adjudicated under either of the three following laws:

  (a) the law of the State of his habitual residence, provided however that the defendant had to expect the damage would occur in that State;

  (b) the law of the State in which the defendant has his main place of business or his habitual residence;

  (c) the law of the State in which the damage is caused, provided however that the defendant had to expect that the result would occur in that State.

---

1 *Antonio Marinari v Lloyds Bank plc et Zubaidi Trading Company*, 19 September 1995, aff C-364/93, Rec 1995, pp I-2719 ss.
2 *Fiona Shevill e a c Presse Alliance SA*, 7 March 1995, aff C-68/93, Rec 1995, pp I-415 ss; see especially L Idot, *L'application de la Convention de Bruxelles en matière de diffamation*. See also the important informations about the interpretation of art 53, Europe, June 1995, chron, pp 1-2; H Ehmann/K Thorn, *Erfolgsort bei grenzüberschreitenden Persönlichketisverletzungen*, AfP (*Zeitschrift für Medien- und Kommunikationsrecht*) 1996, pp 24-25, n 60, citing the critical comment of G Hohloch, to the *Fiona Shevill* case, JuS (*Juristische Schulung*) 1995, pp 928-929.
3 See F Dessemontet, *Internet, les droit de la personnalité et le droit international privé*, in Medialex 2/1997, pp 77 *et seq*, especially at 80.

In fact, according to the prevailing doctrine, letters a and c of Article 139 LDIP envision the same State, so that the choice would be two-fold rather than three-fold.[4]

3   General provisions relating to privacy

28.09   It should be recalled that Article 18 CC inaugurated in 1907 the legislative approach of a general provision protecting personal interests against all and any encroachments on them in whatever manner. Due to that encompassing approach, it is first necessary to define the personal interests that are deemed worthy of protection (hereafter (a)) before setting out the methodology of balancing the need for protection of those interests and the need to maintain a free flow of information in an open society (hereafter (b)).

Personal interests

28.10   Article 28 CC protects the person and every personal interest of an individual. Legal entities also enjoy that protection, to the extent that the interests at stake are not related only to the characteristics of a human being as such (Article 53 CC).[5] Among the personal interests are their life and physical well-being, their psychological and moral wholeness, their privacy, name, honour and dignity as well as social reputation, likeness and voice, relation to one's father, anonymity,[6] relations to friends and relatives, the fate of the body after death, etc. There is no exhaustive list of the personal interests which are protectable by the Swiss courts. This would run contrary to the very spirit of an open, general provision.

Methodology

28.11   The law and cases distinguish between public, private and intimate life. The protection of privacy is given in all situations, but the limits of protection are not the same, under civil law, in all three cases. Appearances of a person in public life receive less protection than events within his or her private life, while a person's intimate life is most strongly protected. Further, persons pertaining to public life (prominent politicians, socialites, members of royal families, actors, sports champions, etc) have to accept more intrusion in their life through reporting, photographing, commenting on their public appearances.

28.12   The methodology is to balance a person's right to be left alone with the interest of the press to inform and of the public to be informed.[7] Switzerland does not know of a 'people's press' as do some other countries, maybe because Swiss Cantons were always organised as Republics in which it was poor taste to be prominent. Therefore, reporting on people is not as such seen as falling within the confine of the constitutional freedom of the

---

4   See F Dasser, in Honsell/ N P Vogt/A K Schnyder, *Kommentar zum Schweizerischen Privatrecht, Internationales Privatrecht,* nE 8 *ad* art 139 LDIP.

5   See F Dessemontet, *La presse et les sociétés commerciales,* in *Die Verantwortlichkeit im Recht,* Zurich 1981, vol 1, pp 183 ss with citations.

6   For example for a strip-tease dancer: Swiss Review of Jurisprudence (hereafter RSJ) 1985 NE 29 pp 161-164 (Cant Trib St-Gallen, 23 June 1983).

7   See F Dessemontet, *Le journalisme économique,* in Medialex 1998/2, p 89.

press, with the exception of public facts pertaining to public personalities. For example, when he was recently questioned by high-school students through the Internet (May 1998), the President of the Swiss Confederation Flavio Cotti could answer that he did not know his salary (answer: 'please ask my wife', who was not to be reached on the Internet).

28.13   In a few cases, however, the balance of interests is such that private facts may be disclosed by the press. For instance, as the General Manager of the Swiss Mail was recently under attack for his management techniques, it was disclosed that a severance payment had been paid on his recommendation to a marketing manager, the amount of which was finally published after much pressure by the media, without any legal action ensuing to restrain publication.

28.14   The main tests to be satisfied to determine whether private data may be published are:

(1)   Is there a superior interest of the public to know of the facts and data?

(2)   Does the report state truly and exactly the facts and data?

(3)   Is there any injury due to the innuendoes, or style and expression of the reporting?

28.15   All conflicts between the protection of personal interests and other interests worthy of consideration are solved taking into account the test of proportionality. The encroachment upon someone else's personal interests may be tolerated if it is not excessive in relation to the goal which is furthered by the report (better management of the Swiss Mail, for example). The intensity of the competing interests must be balanced against each other, as well as the need to publish the information (is there any other means to reach the same result?). Finally, the hierarchy of the interests (money making *versus* personal honour) may help to attain a balanced judgment.

4   Covert filming

28.16   Under Article 179 *quater* par 1 CP as amended on 20 December 1968, it is unlawful without the consent of the subject to record on a videotape or any similar device anything relating to that person's intimate life or anything relating to their privacy. Nevertheless, 'public appearance' is not defined as any and all appearances on public streets. Some commentators opine that Article 179 *quater* CP does apply when the shooting takes place in a public area or on the street, if the subject cannot escape the video camera or if the images are 'surreptitiously' taken.[8] Any covert filming should be deemed to be 'surreptitious' within that opinion.

28.17   Without going as far as that opinion, the Swiss Supreme Court (Federal Tribunal) has decided that a photograph taken in front of a private house when the owner is opening the door to two policemen constituted an intrusion into the private life of the house's owner, so that it fell under Article 179 *quater* CP.[9]

---

8   See quotations in *Arrêts du Tribunal Fédéral* 118 IV 41, at 46.
9   *Arrêts du Tribunal Fédéral* 118 IV 50-51.

5 Filming on private property

28.18 Most early commentators thought that Article 179 *quater* CP should not apply when the subject was in a public place.[10] Thus, the proper scope of the criminal provision would be filming on private property (of course, if there is trespass upon private property by the cameraman intruding into a garden or a building, a separate count will be held against him under Article 186 CP). (If filming takes place in a bar or other 'public' rooms, it is however 'private property').[11]

28.19 Confirmation of that opinion is not found in the only case on the point, which is a Legal Opinion of the Federal Department of Justice.[12] The case concerned the videotaping of unlawful immigrants over two small footpaths crossing over Swiss boundaries. The cameras were concealed, but there was 'no further ado' to focus on the passers-by, no impediment to be surmounted in order to get a clear picture of the subjects. Since this test is mentioned, the Department of Justice seems to have deemed Article 179 *quater* CP applicable per se; nevertheless, it should be noted that Article 27 of the Customs Act of 1 October 1925 authorising the control of the borders, there was an explicit defence against indictment under any criminal provision or the covert filming of the immigrants.

6 Filming from the air

28.20 Filming from the air over a private property cannot be done 'without further ado'. Someone needs to hire a plane or a helicopter, or to climb on a tree, or to have access to a tall building, all of which is the proof that shooting of the events was not possible without some obstacle to be surmounted. Therefore, it is always unlawful under Article 179 *quater* CP.

28.21 In a first phase, Swiss commentary was to the effect that privacy was invaded only if the 'private property' in which the recorded events took place was a building or a garden behind closed doors.[13] Of late, it has been however decided that videotaping of a person in a garden is contrary to Article 179 *quater* CP, even if the cameraman is outside and even if there is no physical barrier between him and the subject.[14]

7 Filming from the air over public ground

28.22 Filming from the air over public ground, or using a telephoto lens to focus on the face or the body of a person while in a soccer match, another sports event or on another occasion calls for a different treatment.

---

10 See quotations in *Arrêts du Tribunal Fédéral* 118 IV 46 litt b.
11 See H Schultz, *Der strafrechtliche Schutz der Geheimsphäre*, RSJ 1971 p 304.
12 *Jurisprudence des Autorités Administratives de la Confédération* (hereafter JAAC) 58 (1994) NE 75.
13 See Th Legler, *Vie privée, image volée*, thesis, Geneva, Berne 1997, pp 140-141.
14 Plädoyer 6/96, pp 63–65 (District Ct Meilen, 8 March 1996; unlawful video survey of the insured victim of a car accident through a private detective hired by the insurance company). On 18 December 1997, The Federal Tribunal decided to the contrary in an almost identical case. See Medialex 1998/2, 109-110 (the lawfulness of the videosurvey being admitted in view of the justified interest of the insurance company in view of the claim [SFr. 2'600'000.-]).

28.23 If the recorded facts are of an intimate nature, Article 179 *quater* CP protects the individual no matter where the events take place. For example, weeping at funerals cannot be recorded through telephoto lens or otherwise, whatever the legal status of the graveyard (ie private property or public ground).[15] The same is true for joyful behaviour, like kissing, and mild or wild sexual endearments. By their very nature, those are intimate acts.[16] The same should be said of someone buying or reading pornography.[17] Finally, the recording of someone who is wounded, having a broken nose or another visible injury is intrusion into his or her intimate sphere,[18] as well as recording someone who is making an indiscreet gesture.[19] If the recorded facts are not intimate, the test would appear to be whether the filming can be done 'without further ado'.

28.24 The Swiss commentary is restrictive of the use of telephoto lenses, seeing in it a technical means publicly to record something which is not intended for the public, with intention to do so.[20] Nonetheless, the Parliament seems to have entertained the notion that filming, for example, a spectator during a soccer game, even with a telephoto lens, would not fall under Article 179 *quater* CP.[1]

8   Use of security camera footage

28.25 Basically, the operating of security cameras in banks, department stores, and workshops, is not unlawful per se.   To this writer's knowledge, trade unions who protested against the use of security cameras in workshops never obtained a clear-cut condemnation of the practice, which is arguably contrary to the protection of the personality of employees under Article 328 CO.[2]

28.26 The use of the security camera footage for reporting (for example a hold-up or a fight between customers) is unobjectionable, according to Article 179 *quater* CP, to the extent that the events take place in a public area, at least according to one authority.[3] There are no behaviour nor acts pertaining to the intimacy of the people that are involved. If the security camera overlooks a private garden or private facilities such as workshops, then the reasoning which is referred to in para **28.10** above should hold true. Of course, the right to use the tape must be secured both in relation to its owner and the copyright owner if there is copyright in such tape. Swiss law would never accept the idea that the public's need to know justifies

---

15 Th Legler, p 141 n 570.
16 For the case of lovers in a public park, see the Legal Opinion of the Department of Justice JAAC 58 [1994] p 565 at 567 *et seq.*
17 Th Legler, p 134 *in fine* citing MP Bolla, Official Bulletin of Council of States 1968, p 187.
18 German case of 1996 cited with approval by Legler, p 139 n 559.
19 D Barrelet, *Droit suisse des mass media*, 2d ed nE 560.
20 See Legler, p 133, citing F Riklin, *Der Strafrechtliche Schutz des Rechts am eigenen Bild, in Festschrift für Leo Schürmann*, Fribourg 1987, p 547.
1   See Official Bulletin National Council 1968, p 340 (MP Bieri), and p 344, 631, 669 (MP Cevey).
2   See Arrêts du Tribunal Fédéral 114 II 345.
3   Riklin, pp 550-551.

broadcasting of a videotape (for example on the death through ecstasy pills in a disco) without the consent of the copyright owner.[4]

9   Interception of post and telephone calls

Post

28.27   Article 179 CP prohibits the opening of a letter or of a parcel as well as the disclosing of knowledge so gained or benefiting from this.

Telephone calls

28.28   Article 179 *bis* CP prohibits eavesdropping or the recording of a private conversation between other persons without their consent, as well as disclosing to a third party or personally benefiting from a fact known through such acts, or keeping or disclosing such a recording.

Article 179 *ter* CP prohibits the recording of a conversation in which one participates without the consent of the other participants, or keeping such a recording, benefiting from it, or disclosing it to a third party.

Those provisions cover not only the recording of telephone calls but also all private conversations, and the recording is unlawful even if the conversation takes place in public rooms such as a bar, a restaurant, the lobby of a hotel or of a hospital, etc.[5]

According to Article 179 *quinquies* CP, there is no penalty if the overhearing or recording of a conversation is made on a phone exchange or other ancillary installation. This exception is due to the technical necessity of overhearing some conversations when operating a business phone exchange, and to the lawfulness of recording devices incorporated into or connected with many phones. Nevertheless, it is only the hearing and recording that are authorised. Any further act undertaken in order to derive a benefit from a fact so discovered, or any disclosure to a third party will be punishable.[6]

10   Public order

28.29   Official measures of control of mail and phone conversations can be ordered by a competent authority according to Article 179 *sexies* CP. For the fight against terrorism, espionage, organised crime and drug trafficking, eavesdropping and recording will now even be ordered when there is no concrete act against which criminal proceedings could be taken.

28.30   Riots, public demonstrations, etc can be filmed both by TV reporters and police. Some cantons have enacted law prohibiting the wearing of masks during demonstrations (eg Canton of Berne, law of 1998).

28.31   Swiss commentary is to the effect that even in a demonstration, the focusing by a TV crew on one particular by-stander or participant who is not a leader would be unlawful without his or her consent, unless the said

---

4   See for an English decision peculiar in that respect *Beggars' Banquet Records Ltd v Carlton Television Ltd* [1993] EMLR 349 at 372.
5   Schultz, p 304.
6   Schultz, p 307.

individual has only an ancillary role in the whole picture (in which case the cameraman does not actually focus on him or her).[7] To sum up, the consent of all persons (other than politicians and leaders of the mob) who are clearly recognisable and stay for more than a very short period of time in the focus of the camera, should be obtained, for example, through the signature of a release before broadcasting the footage. Otherwise, their features should be electronically masked and their voice modified beforehand. The Guidelines of the Swiss Television and Broadcasting Society of 1 May 1979 are to this effect.[8]

28.32 The waiver or release is not required to be in any particular form. It has been opined by the Department of Justice that, under the Law on Protection of Personal Data of 19 June 1992, the waiver may be withdrawn at any time.[9] The same should not hold true for a release under the Swiss Penal Code or Article 28 CC. Of course, the release shall be valid only for the broadcasting which is mentioned and no second use, especially of a commercial nature, could be deemed to be covered by it. For example, if there is a release by two nice-looking joggers for the use of the tape in one political campaign, this release does not extend to the use of their image or posters for commercial advertising or by another political party in a later election.

11 Sifting of rubbish

28.33 Such a tasteless practice is nowhere mentioned in Swiss law. As concerns rubbish of socialites or politicians, there appears to be a violation of Article 28 CC, the general provision on the protection of personality. City authorities have from time to time made regulations allowing trash to be examined in order to establish who is violating city ordinances on the disposal of rubbish, that provide for a stated amount to be paid on each rubbish bag.

12 Assumed identity to obtain information

28.34 No specific rule deals with the impersonation of someone in order to obtain information. Of course, it may be a felony if it is at the same time a 'threat which frightens or scares a person' according to Article 180 CP.

13 Remedies

28.35 Criminal remedies vary with the crime, but the main articles above referenced provide for the felony to be punished with imprisonment for a period between three days and three years (Article 36 CP).

Civil remedies under Article 28 CC include a cease-and-desist order, an opportunity to have the court state the unlawfulness of the acts, a publication of the judgment and damages for pain and suffering under Article 49 CO.

---

7   D Barrelet, NE 559.
8   Th Legler, p 193.
9   JAAC 57 [1993] p 335.

Damages are subject to the requirement that a serious attack has been launched against the plaintiff. They can be paid to a charity if the claimant so agrees.

B Publicity

1 *Laws of publicity*

28.36 Article 29 CC is the main basis of protection for the name of physical persons and of those legal entities that are not commercial corporations, ie associations, foundations, churches, etc.

Article 956 CO is the main basis for protection of the trade names of corporations that are commercial entities, such as the company limited by shares, the company with limited responsibility, and the co-operative, as well as the individual enterprise.

Article 48 of the Ordinance on the Register of Commerce of 7 June 1937, as amended from time to time, but not in that respect (hereafter ORC), protects the shop-signs and by extension all uses of a trade name on letterheads, advertisements, delivery trucks, etc.

Article 28 CC provides the basis for protecting a person against a wrong use of his or her biography (see supra, para **28.01** for more details on Article 28 CC).

If applicable, the law against Unfair Competition of 19 December 1986 (hereafter LCD), especially Article 3(b) and (d) against misappropriation of trade names, may give effective relief.

2 *Application to citizen of foreign states*

28.37 As to the formation of the name, Swiss law applies to all persons who are registered in the Swiss birth and family registry offices.

The choice of the first name is not entirely free (Article 301 par 4 CC),[10] but there is of late some allowance for the customs of other countries (such as the family name of an ancestor given as middle name in the US, which can be registered as first name in Switzerland).[11]

There is no choice for the family name, which is inherited from the father (or from the mother for children born out of wedlock) (Article 270 CC).

28.38 Legal entities that are registered at the Register of Commerce have to follow Swiss rules.

28.39 Foreign citizens and companies are under the same duty to use their name as Swiss citizens are.

(1) The official first name and family name are to be born and used as they are. This is considered to be a duty necessary for the insertion of the individual into the community.[12] It is to be recalled that the duty

---

10 Arrêts du Tribunal Fédéral 118 II 243, 119 II 401.
11 See Arrêts du Tribunal Fédéral 116 II 504.
12 Arrêts du Tribunal Fédéral 108 II 161 at 162.

to bear this 'official' name appeared in Germany during the seventeenth and eighteenth centuries for military, taxation and administration purposes.[13] Therefore the interests of the Administration are still considered to be predominant.[14] For artistic purposes, pseudonyms may be chosen freely.[15]

(2) Legal entities have to use their trade name as registered in the Register of Commerce.

28.40 As to the protection of names, citizens of foreign countries and foreign companies that are not registered in Switzerland can invoke Articles 29 and 28 CC, as well as Article 3(b) and (d) LCD. Foreign companies that are not registered in Switzerland cannot invoke Article 956 CO.

3   Use of biography

28.41   As has been explained under the heading of privacy (see para **28.09**) protection of a person's intimacy is absolute; protection of his or her privacy is generally afforded unless some overwhelming interest directs otherwise; there is little protection of the public life. The application of this test requires a line to be drawn between public figures, who are deemed to be 'persons interesting for contemporary history', such as politicians, socialites, royals, heads of state, actors, famous sportsmen, etc, and private parties. An intermediate category is proposed by recent German literature, that of a 'person interesting for contemporary history only to a point'.[16]

Those persons are for example the victims of spectacular accidents, the relatives of public figures or their friends, and all other persons on whom a report may be made in the media but only because of a particular event, and thus only in connection with this event.

28.42   To the extent that they are not recognisable, private persons cannot oppose the use of their biography, for example in a fiction.[17] Otherwise, they are entitled to absolute secrecy if they do not wish to lift the veil surrounding their privacy and intimacy. For their public life, on the other hand, there is no protection save the protection of their honour.[18]

28.43   According to an unfortunate *obiter dictum* of the Federal Tribunal, there would be no 'right to be forgotten' (*droit à l'oubli/ Recht auf Vergessen*), at least for former opinions and political activities belonging to public life[19] – ie political life, even dating back to the thirties or forties.

---

13 See D Lack, *Privatrechtlicher Namensschutz*, thesis Berne 1992, p 7.

14 Arrêts du Tribunal Fédéral 99 Ia 561 at 564.

15 See for their protection Arrêts du Tribunal Fédéral 112 II 59 at 63 and cit. Arrêts du Tribunal Fédéral 108 II 163 even mentions pseudonyms in 'scientific activities'! On the other hand, it is doubtful that businessmen could select any pseudonym for their business dealings, at least if any swindle is hereby favored. See J-M Grossen, *in Schweizerisches Privatrecht II*, Basle 1967, p 340.

16 See A Meili, in *Schweizerisches Zivilgesetzbuch I*, Basle 1996, N 52 ad art 28 CC ('*relative Personen der Zeitgeschichte*').

17 See P Lalive, *Le romancier et la protection des intérêts personnels*, Geneva 1956. See the same author, *Sur la responsabilité civile de l'écrivain*, *Revue de la Société des Juristes bernois 104 (1968)*, pp 201 et seq.

18 See J-M Grossen, pp 369-370.

19 Arrêts du Tribunal Fédéral 111 II 209 at 214.

E contrario, a 'right to be forgotten', should indisputably exist for private and business affairs[20] and even public statements of otherwise private persons, for example businessmen, artists, etc.

28.44 Even if Swiss law should be construed as not encompassing a right to be forgotten, the protection of honour means that former publicly-held opinions shall not be presented in a biased manner, injuring the honour of politicians, bankers, etc. In that regard a publication shall be deemed wrongful if the use of the biography does not conform to the truth or implies mistaken connotations such as treason, or sympathy for fascist or Nazi opinions.[1]

4 Trade mark protection

28.45 In order to enjoy protection as a trade mark, the name has to be registered at the Swiss Institute of Intellectual Property or to benefit from an international registration. Basically, the Institute does not inquire on the title to a name, if it is a well-known name.[2] This is a strong departure from the practice until April 1993 (when the new Law on the Protection of Trade marks of 28 August 1992; hereafter 'LPM' came into force), where some important links between the applicant and the bearer of the name had to be shown.

Now, it is up to the courts to determine if the registration of the name as trade mark is null and void because it implies a business relationship that does not exist in fact.[3]

28.46 Two persons may have the same family name and be active in the same field. They both have the right to deposit their name as a trade mark, but the one coming later on must add a first name or some other distinctive sign or be active in another field; if this does not suffice to avoid passing-off, no trade mark with the same name shall be registered.[4] This protection is not necessarily open to foreigners who are inactive in Switzerland.[5]

5 Remedies

28.47 For remedies generally, see paras **28.41** and **28.42**. Recent cases allow for no generalisation as to the amount of damages for violation of Articles 28–29 CC and Article 3(d) LCD.[6]

---

20 See Arrêts du Tribunal Fédéral 122 III 449 et seq prohibiting the mention of an old (ie dating from 10 years ago) conviction for economic crimes in a report on a business 'trouble-shooter'. See also Arrêts du Tribunal Fédéral 109 II 353, at 360–361.

1   See Arrêts du Tribunal Fédéral 111 II 209 at 214 et seq.

2   For example, Mr Hovic Simonian has obtained the registration of a trade mark HAYEK (CH NE 408 455) for watches, although Mr Hayek, a well-known businessman who owns the SWATCH group, did not give his consent. See E Marbach, in *Schweizeriches Immaterialgüter- und Wettbewerbsrecht*, vol III, Kennzeichenrecht, Basle 1996, p 84 fn 310.

3   See Arrêts du Tribunal Fédéral 98 Ib 188, at 192 ('Sheila Diffusion' null and void if no connection with the French pop star Sheila).

4   Arrêts du Tribunal Fédéral 116 II 194, at 616 (*Guccio Gucci SpA v Paolo Gucci);* Comm Ct Zurich, RSPI 1988 p 155 (Bulgari).

5   Arrêts du Tribunal Fédéral 113 II 73 at 74 ' RSPI 1988 p 175 (Fortunoff).

6   See eg Just Ct Geneva, RSPI 1992, p 371 (2'000.- SFr. for unfair competition). In a settlement out-of-court, a TV station agreed to pay 10'000 SFr as damage for misuse of a photography in advertising (NZZ 17/18 September 1994, p 55).

C Personality

1 Relevant laws of personality

28.48   Article 28 CC and Article 179 *quater* CP are the basis for protection of the personality (understood as the 'right of publicity' in American parlance, ie the right to an individual's likeness).

2 Public events

28.49   For the individual being on the street or in a stadium, the protection of his or her intimacy is normally not at stake. There may be a violation of his or her privacy if the pictures taken focus on indiscreet gestures.[7] Therefore, there must be a precise relationship with the topic of the reporting.[8] Further, the new Law on Assistance to Victims of Crime of 4 October 1991 (hereafter 'LAVI') prohibits the giving away of the identity of the victim of a crime (art 5 par 2 LAVI), which could conceivably take place through publication of a picture of the victim. Consent of the victim is required by law.

28.50   On the other hand, reporting on a Parliament session, a soccer match or other public events cannot be done without focusing for some moments on individuals. Further, social or artistic events of a public nature can be reported freely.[9]

3 Private life

28.51   Photographs or video recordings cannot invade the private life of even well-known personalities.[10] Even if the public could conceivably have a justified interest to know about some private dealings of a public figure, no justification would exist for invading the private sphere through the use of cameras or recording devices, that are strictly prohibited under Article 179 *quater* CPS.[11]

4 Advertising for publicity purposes

28.52   The very first year after entry into force of the Civil Code, a Swiss court recognised the protection of personality against the misappropriation of a locomotive engineer's head as a trade mark for cigars.[12] The court ruled that under Article 28 CC the right of personality is an 'absolute right'. It did not matter that the defendant had believed that the picture was that of a deceased person. That case states rules that are still valid today. In no

---

7   For more details see hereabove I C 2.
8   See M Baddeley, *Le sportif, sujet ou objet*, Revue de droit suisse 1996, II 135, at 199.
9   See A Bucher, *Personnes physiques et protection de la personnalité*, 3rd ed, Basle 1995, Nos 481, 482 and 484.
10   See for more details see para **28.04**.
11   According to M Baddeley, p 223, well-known sportsmen and women would even enjoy a stronger protection than politicians, since sportsmen are not in charge of public interests.
12   Sup Ct Aargau, 27 September 1912, RSJ 1912/1913, p 241 NE 209.

case is the protection limited to public figures, actors, royalty, and socialites who are immediately recognised by the public. As an 'absolute' right, it can be asserted against anyone, even against someone who has had access to the picture through a photograph or an agency if they had no authority to consent to the use of the photography.

In given cases, the courts have accepted that a third party, be it a husband[13] or a widow,[14] may file the action because he or she has been hurt in his feelings by the use of the photograph.

28.53 As long as it is deemed to derive from Article 28 CC, the right of personality ends with the death of the person whose picture has been misappropriated.[15] This unsatisfactory situation leads to a new reasoning: the right of personality on one's likeness should be deemed to belong to the category of intellectual property, such as copyright, that last for 70 years after the death of the authors.[16]

28.54 Copyright protection is also afforded to fictitious characters.[17] The common goal of most intellectual property legislation is to secure a reward to the skilful, inventive, hard-working artists, authors, inventors and designers. The personality who is able to derive some benefit from his or her appeal to the public is basically in the same situation as are the other creators. He deserves the same protection, the monetary value of which will of course vary from time to time according to his appeal in the merchandising or sponsoring of products. This new intellectual property right might be inherited,[18] and taken into account in a divorce settlement as any other asset.

28.55 Most importantly, to envisage the right of personality as a property right is to give a valid and safe basis to licensing agreements that are extremely frequent in practice. For the time being, this theory is accepted by at least another author,[19] but is not yet the majority view.

For remedies, see paras **28.41** and **28.42**.

---

13 Sup Ct Zurich, 25 January 1944, RSJ 1944 p 331, NE 203.
14 Arrêts du Tribunal Fédéral 70 II 127.
15 Arrêts du Tribunal Fédéral 101 II 191.
16 See F Dessemontet, *Le droit à sa propre image* in Mélanges Grossen, Basle 1992, p 41, at 50 *et seq.*; *Les droits des acteurs face à la digitalisation*, 1996/3, *Droit de l'informatique et des télécoms* (Paris), pp 7 ss, with cit.
17 Sup Ct Zurich, 18 March 1949, RSJ 1949, p 204 NE 84 ('Professor Cekadete').
18 In order to determine how the heirs are to decide on a request to authorise the use of the deceased person's likeness, s 990 of the Civil Code of California could serve as model: no unanimous consent, but a majority vote should suffice.
19 See M Magda Streuli-Youssef, *Besonderkeiten des Urheberrechtes in Rechtsverkehr*, AJP 1996, p 358 at 962.

29 UNITED KINGDOM

Robyn Durie

A Privacy

1 Law relating to privacy in the UK

29.01 There is no general right to privacy under English common law.[1] This has been recognised as a gap in English law, but this is unlikely to change significantly in the near future[2] as UK governments have been reluctant to introduce such a right. The Government and the UK judiciary does, however, believe that the Human Rights Act 1998 will allow a common law right of privacy to develop.[3] To do so the courts will need to review existing cases such as *Kaye v Robertson* where a tabloid journalist ignored notices prohibiting entry to a room where a well-known actor was recovering from extensive head injuries, and interviewed and photographed him. Mr Justice Glidewell said obiter in that case that there had been a gross invasion of privacy which highlighted a failure in English law. Other judges have agreed with this conclusion and suggested that a general right of privacy should be recognised.[4] However, no cases currently establish such a right although its development has been envisaged.[5]

29.02 Issues of privacy dealt with by English law include privacy of private property, the right to be left alone, the right to communicate privately and the right to respect for private life. As a matter of public policy, any law relating to privacy must strike a proper balance between preserving privacy and confidentiality and preserving freedom of speech and access to public

---

1 *Bernstein v Skyviews and General Ltd* [1978] QB 579; *Malone v Metropolitan Police Comr* [1979] Ch 334.
2 *Kaye v Robertson* [1991] FSR 62. Such a right was also considered by the Younger Committee in 1972, 'The Report of the Committee on Privacy and Related Matters' chaired by David Calcutt in 1990, the 'Review of Press Self-Regulation' (1993) and 'The Report of the National Heritage Committee on Privacy'.
3 Lord Irvine, Hansard House of Lords, 24 November 1997, Col 784.
4 SI 1999/2093. For example, Lord Scarman in *Morris V Beardmore* [1981] AC 446 and Lord Keith in *A-G v Guardian Newspapers (No 2)* [1990] AC 10 at 281–282.
5 *Hellewell v CC Derbyshire* [1995] 1 WLR 804.

information which are central to a modern democracy. Indeed the Human Rights Act also contains the right of freedom of expression.[6] Some degree of protection of privacy is found in English law, this is examined in the paragraphs that follow.

Data Protection

29.03   Data Protection law ensures protection of living individuals with respect to the disclosure of personal data relating to them which is stored on computer. The current law, the Data Protection Act 1998, controls the compiling, and use of data relating to living individuals processed in the UK or elsewhere under the control of a UK established person or company, called a data controller The Act limits the extent of data which may be stored, the processing of data and how it can be disclosed. Data must be fairly and lawfully processed, relevant and kept up-to-date. Limits are put on the transfer of data outside the European Economic Area. Those who are the subject of processed data have rights including being informed of the purpose of the processing, access to the data, the right to prevent direct marketing, rights to correct or block the processing of data and to prevent the taking of decisions relating to them automatically.

The Act, which came into force on 1 March 2000, implements the EU Data Protection Directive (95/46/EC). It provides greater protection of individuals with regard to the processing of personal data than its predecessor, the Data Protection Act 1984, including by 2007 certain manual data, and the free movement of such data. The Act in certain cases requires the consent of individuals, or data subjects as they are known, to the obtaining of data, the giving of notice if data is processed, and limits such processing to the extent that it is 'fair and lawful'.[7] There are exceptions, most notably if data is processed pursuant to a contract. Stricter requirements apply, including the obtaining of specific consent, to what is defined as 'sensitive personal data'. This includes data in relation to health, race, religion and sexual preferences.

29.04   New provisions relate to the gathering of data for the purposes of investigatory journalism and literary and artistic purposes. They limit the access to data otherwise given to data subjects.

The Telecommunications (Data Protection and Privacy) Regulations 1999, as amended by the Telecommunications (Data Protection and Privacy) Regulations 2000,[8] implement the EU Telecommunications Data Protection Directive (97/66/EC).[9] The provisions of the Regulations supplement the Data Protection Act by providing for the processing of personal data in connection with the provision of publicly available telecommunications services and public telecommunications networks.

29.05   The Regulations include limiting the use of traffic and billing data by those operating in the telecommunications sector and in particular ban the sending of unsolicited direct marketing faxes to corporate subscribers and require consent of individuals to receive direct marketing phone calls.

---

6   Schedule 1, art 10.
7   Schedule 1 Part II of the Data Protection Act 1998.
8   SI 1999/2093 as amended by SI 2000/157.
9   Further proposals to amend and extend this Directive were published by the European Commission on 12 July 2000; COM (2000) 385.

Subscribers to telecommunication services will be able to protect their privacy, free of charge, in respect of Calling Line Identification, whereby incoming calls can be identified by either a Caller Display Service which requires equipment capable of displaying the calling number on a screen or by a Call Return Service whereby the previous caller's number can be identified. Conversely, receiving parties, such as charity helplines will be able to block access to incoming callers' numbers. Subscribers will also be able to determine the scope of their telephone directory entries and go ex-directory free of charge.

The Telecommunications (Data Protection and Privacy) Regulations were implemented concurrently with the new Data Protection Act. Article 5 of the Directive, which deals with confidentiality of communications, will have the greatest impact on privacy issues. It has been implemented by the Regulation of Investigatory Powers Act 2000, ('the RIP Act') which came into force on 24 October 2000.

The RIP Act prohibits listening, storage or other kinds of interception or surveillance of communications by means of a public telecommunications network or a publicly available telecommunications service without the user's consent, except when legally authorised. There is a limited exception which enables the Secretary of State, by regulations, to authorise the recording of communications in the course of lawful business practice for the purpose of providing evidence of a commercial transaction or any other business communication. Regulations, relating to lawful business practice in relation to the interception of communications, are currently being drafted.

2   The Human Rights Act 1998

29.06   The UK ratified the European Convention for the Protection of Human Rights and Fundamental Freedoms (Cmd 8969 (1953), European Convention) in 1951 but took until 2 October 2000 to implement the Convention into UK law. Prior to that time the Convention was merely a persuasive authority which could be used to clarify statute or common law where there are ambiguities.

29.07   The Human Rights Act 1998 refers to the relationship between public authorities and the individual, rather than between citizens. Schedule 1 to the Act sets out the Convention. Article 8 of the Convention provides for 'respect for private and family life, home and correspondence'. Article 8 was relied on unsuccessfully to challenge the legality of telephone tapping.[10] The introduction may encourage the development of privacy case law especially with respect to the media, although the limitations on the application of the Act make it unlikely that a general right to privacy will be established. Article 8 is counterbalanced by Article 10: freedom of expression, ideas and information.

29.08   The Human Rights Act makes it unlawful for public authorities to act in a way which is incompatible with the Convention. Courts will not be able to ignore previous law, but common law and legislation in so far as they relate to public authorities must be developed and interpreted taking

---

10 *Malone v Commissioner of Police of the Metropolis* [1979] Ch 344.

the Convention, as interpreted by the European Human Rights Commission and Court of Human Rights, into account. Section 12 of the Human Rights Act provides as follows:

'This section applies if a court is considering whether to grant any relief which, if granted, might affect the exercise of the Convention right to freedom of expression.

If a person against whom the application for relief is made ("the respondent") is neither present nor represented, no such relief is to be granted unless the court is satisfied:

    (a)   that the applicant has taken all practicable steps to notify the respondent; or

    (b)   that there are compelling reasons why the respondent should not be notified.

No such relief is to be granted as to restrain publication before trial unless the court is satisfied that the applicant is likely to establish that publication should not be allowed.

The court must have particular regard to the importance of the Convention right to freedom of expression and, where the proceedings relate to material which the respondent claims, or which appears to the court, to be journalistic, literary or artistic material (or to conduct connected with such material), to:

    (a)   the extent to which—

        (i)   the material has, or is about to, become available to the public; or

        (ii) it is, or would be, in the public interest for the material to be published;

    (b)   any relevant privacy code.

In this section:

    "court" includes a tribunal; and

    "relief" includes any remedy or order (other than in criminal proceedings).'

Section 12(2) codifies existing law. Section 12(3) arguably increases the threshold for an application for in a breach of confidence case. The current test requires a serious arguable case and that the balance of convenience favours the plaintiff. Section 12(3) equates breach of confidence with libel where as a general rule no interim relief is available.[11] Section 12(4) raises issues as to what is the public domain and its effect. It also refers to privacy codes such as the Press Complaints Commission Code of Practice. Unfortunately section 12(3) may block the development of a law of privacy based on the Human Rights Act, contrary to clear judicial wishes.

Intercepted Communications

29.09 Interception of post and the unauthorised telephone tapping of the public switched network for whatever purpose is currently a criminal offence, as is disclosure of any information acquired from it under section

---

11 *Bonnard v Perryman* [1891] 2 cn 269.

5(b) of the Wireless Telegraphy Act 1949, and sections 10 and 11 of the Interception of Communications Act 1985.[12] The penalty is a fine or imprisonment not exceeding two years.

The 1985 Act was prompted by litigation which established that telephone tapping was not a tort at common law[13] although it was a violation of the European Convention on Human Rights. That Act is to be replaced by the RIP Act.

The RIP Act also extends the networks to which it applies and applies to networks like the Internet, when used as a public network. The RIP Act makes it an offence to intercept communications on a private telecommunications system; unless a person has the right to control the system or the express or implied consent of the person whose calls are intercepted.[14] The RIP Act provides limited exceptions to the offence of interception and the new tort which the RIP Act establishes, covering the activities of the police and security services, and also for limited business purposes. Regulations are currently being drafted under the RIP Act setting out when such exceptions will apply, but also extending it to private networks, such as internal office networks. Currently there is a suggestion that both parties to a call will have to consent to this, unless it is a type of call for which there is a reasonable expectation that it will be taped to provide proof of business transactions, such as trading of securities.

The RIP Act has been the subject of controversy as it will permit the police and security forces to require access to de-encrypted versions of encrypted communications and, in limited circumstances, the cryptographic keys to enable such communications to be de-encrypted.

Trespass

29.10   The concept of trespass is one of the oldest principles in UK law: 'The house of everyone is to him as is his castle and fortress, as well as his defence against injury and violence, as for his repose'.[15] Trespass, even to a private dwelling house, is not a crime at common law. A criminal offence is only committed where the defendant possesses certain types of intent, which is the intent required by section 9 of the Theft Act 1968 to commit the offence of burglary, that is entry with intent to steal or commit rape or under the Public Order Act 1986 detailed below.

29.11   Trespass to land is a tort in English law. Mistakes, such as the defendant mistakenly believing that the land belongs to him, is no defence. There is no liability if the act is involuntary[16] and if the act is unintentional an action may only lie in negligence.[17] The right to bring an action in trespass belongs to the person in possession of the land at the time of the trespass.

If a trespasser peaceably enters the land the person in possession of the land may request him to leave and if he refuses to do so may remove him from the land by his own acts or by instructing another to do so, using no

---

12   *Paul v Ministry of Posts and Telecommunications* [1979] RTD 245 (DC); *DPP v Waite* (1966) 160 JP 726 DC.
13   *Malone v Metropolitan Police Commissioner* [1979] Ch 344.
14   Regulation of Investigatory Powers Act 2000, s 1 (2).
15   *Seymayne's Case* (1603) 5 Co Rep 91, 916.
16   *Smith v Stone* (1647) Sty 65.
17   *Letang v Cooper* [1965] 1 QB 232.

more force than is reasonably necessary. If the trespasser enters forcibly the person in possession does not need to request him to leave before removing him from the land.

The court can grant an injunction to prevent continued or threatened repetition of a trespass. Where the trespass is of a trifling nature or where damages are sufficient remedy an injunction may be refused.

29.12   The police have powers under the Public Order Act 1986 to move on trespassers who are attempting to live on privately-owned property where they have been threatening or abusive to the occupiers or where they have brought 12 or more vehicles onto the land. The trespassers commit an offence if they fail to leave the land or if they re-enter the land within three months of the notice to leave.

29.13   Placing a listening device in a room of a hotel will not amount to an action in trespass because the occupiers do not have 'possession' of the room. Trespass also does not prevent journalists from camping outside the gates of private property, from spying into gardens and houses, using telephoto lenses, from entering airspace over a property[18] or from taking aerial photographs.

Nuisance

29.14   Where there is no intrusion on another person's property tortious liability may arise in nuisance. For an action in nuisance to succeed the act must have interfered with a person's use or enjoyment of his land or some right connected with the land and the claimant must have suffered damage. Persistent harassment by telephone could amount to an actionable nuisance[19] but use of a telephoto lens to look into a private bedroom would not.

Harassment

29.15   Section 1 of the Protection from Harassment Act 1997 protects an individual from behaviour of another which amounts to harassment, unless that conduct was reasonable in the circumstances. The action must be hostile but an intention to injure is not a requirement. The remedies for a civil action are an injunction or damages for, among other things, any anxiety caused by and any financial loss resulting from the harassment. The defendant commits a criminal offence where an injunction has been granted and without reasonable excuse the defendant does something which is prohibited under the terms of the injunction. The courts have construed this legislation narrowly.

Permitted acts

29.16   Investigative journalists and private investigators are also operating within the law when recording conversations whether open or covert, other than those made by use of the public telephone network; sifting through rubbish, staking out a property and using an assumed identity for the purposes of obtaining information. Covert filming is allowed and the

18   *Baron Bernstein of Leigh v Skyviews and General Ltd* [1978] QB 479.
19   *Motherwell v Motherwick* [1976] 73 DLR 93d0 62 (Atla App Div).

resultant film can be used for any purpose; for example, security camera footage can legitimately be used for journalism.[20]

In *R v Khan*[1] the appellant failed in his appeal to exclude evidence of a recorded conversation which was admitted at his trial for importing Class A drugs into the UK. It was held that the appellant did not enjoy a right to privacy in respect of the recorded conversation and even if there was that right, the right to exclude evidence was at the judge's discretion at common law or under section 78 of the Police and Criminal Evidence Act 1984. In a case involving the same appellant the European Court of Human Rights found a violation of Article 8 of the European Convention on Human Rights as UK law did not provide protection against interference with an individual's right to private and family life. In *R v Broadcasting Standards Commission, ex p British Broadcasting Corpn*[2] secret filming appears to have been held to be an unwarranted invasion of privacy even if the events filmed were not conducted in secrecy. That case related to filming within a retail electronics store for the BBC's 'Watchdog' programme.

29.17   Under the Public Order Act 1986 and Criminal Justice and Public Order Act 1994 crowds are granted a right to assembly and a limited right to obstruct the highway. Individuals seeking privacy from large numbers of journalists, fans or even an abusive crowd have little power to disband a crowd.

Law of confidence

29.18   The law of confidence, or the equitable protection of confidential information as it is more properly called, seeks to ensure that confidential information disclosed under an obligation of confidence is not disclosed or used other than as contemplated by the person making the disclosure. The law of confidence protects the privacy or confidentiality of the information and not the person suffering the intrusion.

29.19   A duty of confidence may be imposed by statute or by codes of practice imposed by regulatory bodies. For example, civil servants must not disclose unauthorised information under the Official Secrets Acts, doctors must maintain the privacy of patient's medical records as part of their fiduciary duties, but also under the Data Protection Act. The Access to Medical Reports Act 1988 states that individuals who are the subject of any medical report which is to be used for employment or insurance purposes must give their consent before such a report can be disclosed by the medical practitioner. The legislation also gives the subject of the report other rights in relation to the relevant medical report, including those of access and correction. Those persons who obtain and use confidential financial information are restricted by the Financial Services Act 1986. Conversely, statutes can force the disclosure of information such as duties of disclosure under the Companies Act 1985, and disclosure required in civil procedure by way of discovery and under *Anton Piller* orders.

Contract, professional codes of conduct and fiduciary duties impose a duty of confidence between professional and client, employee and customer,

---

20   *R v Khan* [1996] 3 All ER 289.
1   [1996] 3 All ER 289.
2   *R v Broadcasting Standards Commission, ex p British Broadcasting Corpn* [2000] EMLR 587.

doctor and patient and so on. More generally, an equitable duty of confidence can arise between parties where confidential information was passed to another who knew or ought to have known that the information was not to be disclosed, provided it has the requisite quality of confidence.

29.20   To establish an action for breach of confidence in either contract or equity, the information communicated must be secret and not trivial and be given in circumstances where the recipient knew or ought to have known that it was to be kept confidential and used for a limited purpose.[3]

For any breach of confidence to be established the information must be confidential.[4] Recently, George Blake, a former MI5 employee and spy, faced an action for breach of confidence following the publication of his autobiography. The Court of Appeal held that there was no breach as the information given in his book was no longer secret. However, as Blake had committed an offence under the Official Secrets Act 1989 and as a matter of policy should not profit from his wrongdoings an injunction was granted to prevent Blake receiving royalties on sales of this book.

29.21   Information cannot be protected from disclosure if it is in the public domain. In the *Spycatcher* case[5] the Guardian and Observer newspapers published the main allegations in Peter Wright's book 'Spycatcher' at a time when the book was subject to breach of confidence proceedings in Australia. The book was to be published in the US and the Sunday Times began to serialise it in the UK. All were injuncted and the injunction was upheld by the House of Lords. The courts accepted that Peter Wright, a former intelligence agent, was under a lifelong duty to keep confidential any information he learnt in the course of his work. The book was subsequently published in the US and the courts refused to grant a permanent injunction because the Attorney General could not show that public interest would be harmed by the publication in the newspapers because of the widespread dissemination of the book's contents. The Sunday Times published its extract prior to the US publication and so had to account for the profits made by the increase in circulation.[6] An arguable breach of contract and arguable breach of confidence was also found in the *Princess Diana Gym Photographs* case.[7]

Anthony Cavendish, a former member of MI6, had copies of his memoirs distributed as Christmas cards and when the MI6 material was subsequently published by the Scotsman no injunction was granted, because there was no threat to national security and because the earlier publication by means of the Christmas cards meant the information was no longer secret.[8]

29.22   The courts have developed a general principle of balancing the public interest in disclosure against the public interests in preserving confidence.[9] Although the author of the book about Scientology had

3   *Coco v A N Clarke (Engineers) Ltd* [1969] RPC 41.
4   *Lennon v Newsgroup Newspapers and Twist* [1978] FSR 573.
5   *A-G v Guardian Newspapers Ltd (No 2)* [1988] 3 All ER 545.
6   *A-G v Times Newspapers Ltd* [1987] 1 WLR 1248.
7   Drake J, 1995 unreported.
8   *Lord Advocate v Scotsmen Publications Ltd* [1989] 2 All ER 852.
9   *Initial Services Ltd v Putterill* [1968] 1QB 396, followed in *Hubbard v Vosper* [1972] 1 All ER 1023.

described courses offered by the organisation based upon information obtained in breach of confidence an injunction was not granted because there was ground for thinking the courses contained such dangerous material that disclosure was in the public interest.[10]

The public interest defence is not limited to situations where there has been a serious wrongdoing by the claimant.[11] The Daily Express published internal documents from the manufacturer of an intoximeter which revealed doubts about the ethicacy of that machine to obtain convictions for drink driving. The court held that the possibility of wrongful convictions raised a matter of vital public interest.[12]

29.23   There is a distinction between matters in the public interest and those which are merely interesting to the public. In the *Francome* case use of telephone tapping which breached Jockey Club Regulations was found to have justified disclosure to the Jockey Club or the police but not to the world at large.[13]

29.24   Confidence can also be applied to non-contractual and domestic relationships.[14] In *Argyll v Argyll* a newspaper was not able to publish the Duke of Argyll's account of his marriage as this would have disclosed communications between husband and wife which would have betrayed the normal confidence and trust that is judicially assumed to exist in marriage. This has been extended to lesbian relationships and homosexual relations.[15] More recently, the pop group Oasis were granted an injunction to prevent publication of a photograph taken at a private photo-shoot for the cover of their new album.[16] In an obiter remark in *Hellewell v Chief Constable of Derbyshire*[17] Law J said:

> 'If someone with a telephoto lens were to take from a distance and with no authority a picture of another engaged in some private act, the subsequent disclosure of the photograph would, in my judgment, as surely amount to a breach of confidence as if he had found or stolen a letter or diary in which the act was recounted and proceeded to publish it. In such a case, the law should protect what might reasonably be called a right of privacy, although the name accorded to the cause of action would be a breach of confidence'.

Limitations on some breach of confidence actions may be introduced by the Human Rights Act, see para **29.06** above.

29.25   Actions for breach of confidence can only be brought by the person or organisation to whom the confidence is owed.[18] Furthermore, equity will not protect a person seeking to use confidence to cover up a wrongdoing on public interest grounds[19] and a duty of confidence will be balanced against public interest. Ernest Saunders, the former Chairman and Chief Executive

---

10 *Hubbard v Vosper* [1972] 1 All ER 1023.
11 *Lion Laboratories v Evans and the Express Newspapers* [1985] QB 526.
12 This was upheld in the House of Lords in *A-G v Guardian Newspapers Ltd (No 2)* [1990] 1 AC 109, HL ('*Spycatcher (No2)*' case).
13 *Francome v Mirror Group Newspapers Ltd* [1984] 1 WLR 892.
14 *Argyll v Argyll* [1967] CA 302.
15 *Stevens v Avery* [1988] 1 Ch 449 and *Barrymore v News Group Newspapers* [1997] FSR 600.
16 *Creation Records v News Group Newspapers Ltd*, Times Law Reports, 29 April 1997.
17 [1995] 1 WLR 804.
18 *Fraser v Evans* [1969] 1 All ER 8.
19 *Initial Service v Puttrell* [1968] 1 QB 396.

of Guinness plc, was denied an order under section 10 of the Contempt of Court Act 1981 requiring Punch to disclose the source of its article referring to discussions between Saunders and his former solicitors.[20] Mr Justice Lindsay dismissed the application having weighed up the public interest in legal professional confidence against the public interest in free speech.

29.26 The remedies for breach of confidence include the granting of an injunction, an account of profits and damages. Injunctions are commonly granted. However, if publication has already occurred, and the claimant has lost his or her right to privacy, only damages are available.

Confidence between employer and employee

29.27 Where information is given in confidence to an employee, the courts will imply an undertaking that the information will not be used to the employer's detriment.[1] The extent to which this undertaking operates will depend on the contract of employment. Under the Prevention of Corruption Act 1906 it is an offence to offer an incentive or reward to any employee to do any act in relation to his principals' business. For breach of that statute any payment must have been made corruptly.

The Official Secrets Act 1989

29.28 The Official Secrets Act 1989 makes it a criminal offence for civil servants and others subject to the Act to disclose unauthorised information. Unauthorised information is any information which relates to security and intelligence, defence or international relations or any information which is likely to result in an offence or other related consequential information resulting from unauthorised disclosures, and any information entrusted in confidence to other states or international organisations.[2]

Rehabilitation of Offenders

29.29 Offenders can be 'rehabilitated' whereby they no longer have to disclose their previous convictions. Under the Rehabilitation of Offenders Act 1974 certain prior convictions are to be removed from an individual's criminal record. The relevant convictions include those which have resulted in a sentence of no more than 30 months' imprisonment and where a period of five years has elapsed for a sentence of less than six months or where seven years have elapsed for a sentence of six months or more.

If a newspaper maliciously publishes information about a person's rehabilitated criminal past an action in defamation may lie.

Human Rights Convention

29.30 The European Human Rights Commission has developed privacy protection out of a breach of confidence action. Although in *Earl Countess Spencer v UK*[3] the complaint was not heard by the ECHR the Commission found a right of privacy enforceable by an action for breach of confidence.

---

20 *Saunders v Punch Ltd* (9 October, unreported).
1 *Faccenda Chicken v Fowler* [1987] Ch 117.
2 Official Secrets Act 1989, ss 1–6.
3 Application 28851/95 (1998) 25 EHRR CD 105.

In that case information about the former Countess Spencer being in a clinic being treated for an eating disorder and alcoholism, accompanied in one case by a photo taken with a telephoto lens of her in the clinic had been published.

Ancillary Regulations

29.31   Whereas statutory and fiduciary duties are part of English law professional codes are generally regulated by the professional body, the exception being the Broadcasting Standards Commission Code which is administered by the Commission set up under the Broadcasting Act 1996.

The Press Complaints Commission Code of Practice

29.32   The Press Complaints Commission is a private body funded by newspaper proprietors with half its members drawn from the public.

The voluntary Code of Practice includes guidance on privacy in the media, such as telephoto lens photography, hotel room surveillance and electronic bugging. It prohibits the photography of individuals in 'private places' without their consent, and sets out further general rules regarding the circumstances under which journalists and photographers may obtain information. The Code specifically prohibits the interviewing or photographing of a child under the age of 16 in the absence of or without the consent of a parent or other responsible adult.

Complaints about newspapers and journals may be made to the Commission and although it has no legal powers adjudications are usually published by the paper complained against and often by rival papers.

The Advertising Standards Authority

29.33   The Advertising Standards Authority, a private company funded by the advertising industry, hears complaints about legality and honesty in advertisements. The Authority, generally, requires the advertiser to obtain the consent of the individual featured in an advertisement and may refer offending advertisements to the Director General of Fair Trading who can seek an injunction from the court to prevent the advertisements further appearance. The Authority does not, however, have the power to order compensation.

The current Advertising Code allows the portrayal of entertainers and politicians and other persons with a high public profile as long as they are not portrayed in an offensive or adverse way. Prior permission may, however, not be needed if the advertisement contains nothing that is inconsistent with the position or views of the person featured (although this does not allow advertisers to claim endorsement by third parties without their consent).

29.34   References to the deceased and the Royal family are subject to additional controls.

The Broadcasting Standards Commission and its powers

29.35   The Broadcasting Standards Commission's Code of Fairness and Privacy came into effect on 1 January 1998. The Code, which unlike the Press Complaints Commission Code has statutory effect under section 107 of the Broadcasting Act 1996, seeks to limit the invasion of privacy and prevents interviewees being misled by programme makers. Under the Code, an invasion of privacy must be justified by an overriding public interest. This would include revealing or detecting crime or disreputable behaviour, protecting public health or safety, exposing misleading claims made by individuals or organisations, or disclosing significant incompetence in public office. The means of obtaining the information must be proportionate to the matter under investigation. Even where the material is not used in a broadcast, or where the matter under investigation is in the past, privacy could still be infringed. Those in the public domain and their friends and family are protected under the Code.

29.36   Secret recording is only permitted under the Broadcasting Standards Commission's Code where it is necessary and in the public interest. An individual's consent must be granted to broadcast secret recordings made for entertainment purposes. Investigative film documentaries can use secret filming where there is an overriding public interest and where the questions are fair. The Commission also considers privacy as a function of taste and decency.

The Broadcasting Act 1996

29.37   Section 110 of the Broadcasting Act 1996 places a duty on the Broadcasting Standards Commission to consider and adjudicate complaints which relate to an unwarranted infringement of privacy in, or in connection with the obtaining of material to be included in particular programmes.

In *R v Broadcasting Standards Commission, ex p British Broadcasting Corpn*[4] secret filming appears to have been held to be an unwarranted invasion of privacy even if the events filmed were not conducted in secrecy.

The BBC Royal Charter and Agreement

29.38   The BBC issues guidelines to its producers which include privacy. The Charter came into effect on 1 May 1996.

Government Guidelines

29.39   The Home Office produces non-statutory guidelines on the use of domestic surveillance by the police. Intrusion into domestic privacy is generally acceptable where it is in the public interest. Guidelines are also produced to govern disclosure by the National Health Service and regarding the disclosure of patients' and victims' identities.

Future of privacy law in the UK

29.40   The application of the Human Rights Act 1998 and the introduction of law relating to freedom of information is likely to promote the case for the development of a more sophisticated area of law concerning privacy and the flow of information which extends beyond the public sector. Any new law addressing privacy in the UK must not limit legitimate access to individuals. Where any such law could affect the media, clear guidance is required as to news investigations and reporting to balance the rights of privacy with freedom of information and disclosure in the public interest.

---

4   *R v Broadcasting Standards Commission, ex p British Broadcasting Corpn* [2000] EMLR 587.

Freedom of Information

29.41 The Freedom of Information Bill was introduced to the House of Commons on 18 November 1999. The Bill creates new rights of access to information and there is a presumption in favour of openness in the public sector with a right for any person or company to have access to information held by public authorities. The provisions in the Bill will be regulated by a Commissioner to whom the public will have direct access. The legislation will affect government departments, privatised utilities and functions of the public sector which are contracted out to private bodies. The proposed Act will increase the amount of public information and reduce the amount of privacy in government. For example, it would free-up the disclosure of information in relation to pharmaceutical and food safety. However, it also creates exemptions from the duty to disclose information and establishes rights of appeal.

29.42 Disclosure would be ordered if 'harm' could be shown in the case of policy advice and decision-making in government, or 'substantial harm' in relation to security services, defence and international relations, law enforcement, personal privacy, commercial confidentiality, public security and information supplied in confidence. Security and intelligence services, court records, staff records and records not relating directly to public functions would be exempt unless there was an overriding public interest in its disclosure. Only the administrative function of the police will be affected, for example there would be no duty to disclose information relating to deaths in custody. The proposed Act would apply to unrecorded information as well as all records in paper or electronic form.

The Bill also makes amendments to certain parts of the Data Protection Act 1998, which relate to subject access and data accuracy to all personal information held by public authorities. Schedule 6 makes specific provision to extend the 1998 Act to include relevant personal information processed by or on behalf of both Houses of Parliament and makes other minor amendments to the Act.

B   Publicity

29.43 The right of publicity is the right of all individuals, but principally celebrities, against the misappropriation by another of the commercial value of their own identity or performance. The right does not give a personality privacy but rather a financial interest in controlling the use of their identity.

1   UK law

29.44 In the UK there is no right to publicity; the unauthorised use of a celebrity's personality for commercial purposes is permitted provided the general public does not believe that the product or service is authorised or sponsored by the celebrity. Celebrities can make a large percentage of their income from the use of their name, characteristics and fame through advertising and commercial promotions but they have little power to prevent others from similarly benefiting from unauthorised use of their image. Sales of counterfeit goods may dent sales of authentic merchandise and celebrities may object to being linked with low-quality goods or those produced in bad taste. Strands of UK law give limited publicity rights to individuals as discussed below.

Malicious falsehood

29.45   An action for the tort of malicious falsehood may be brought where the celebrity has suffered economic loss caused by a maliciously-made falsehood or misrepresentation. In *Tolley v Fry*,[5] an amateur golfer successfully sued a sweet manufacturer which had featured the golfer in an unauthorised advertisement, for insinuating that the plaintiff had compromised his amateur status by being paid in his capacity as a golfer.

The well-known actor Gordon Kaye successfully sued for malicious falsehood when a tabloid newspaper, The Sunday Sport entered his private hospital room despite security provisions and managed to interview and photograph him.[6] It was held that Mr Kaye did not give his consent, given the attempts he had made to maintain his privacy and his poor state of health and because he might otherwise have sold his story and so he was able to obtain damages.

Defamation

29.46   Where false statements are made about an individual he or she may bring an action for defamation. However, as well as taking on the stress and cost of litigation and the risk of losing the case, a libel action keeps the issue in the public eye for longer than it might otherwise have been and can lead to further media intrusion into the claimant's family and private life.

Two actors, from the Australian soap opera 'Neighbours', failed in a libel action against a newspaper which had altered and used their images without their consent.[7] The newspaper had published a photograph of the claimants' faces superimposed onto the near-naked bodies of models in pornographic poses. The accompanying text made it clear that the photographs had been produced without the consent of the claimants. The House of Lords held that a claim for libel could not be founded on a headline or photograph in isolation from the related text. On the facts of the case the ordinary and reasonable reader would not have formed the opinion that the claimants were involved in making pornographic films.

There can be no libel where the statements made are true.

Advertising Codes

29.47   The Advertising Standards Authority Regulations for non-broadcast media and relevant advertising trade bodies for broadcasting media require that an advertiser has gained the consent of the relevant personality where his or her name or likeness is used in advertising. Where a complaint is upheld the Authority may refer the matter to the Director General of Fair Trading who may seek an injunction from the court to prevent the advertisement being shown but there is no power to order the offender to pay compensation.

---

5   *Tolley v JS Fry & Sons Ltd* [1931] All ER 131.
6   *Kay v Robertson* [1991] FSR 62.
7   *Charleston v News Group Newspapers Ltd* [1995] 2 AC 65.

Creating a publicity law in the UK

29.48   The right to a publicity law in the UK can be justified on the simple ground that what is worth copying is worth protecting. A publicity law in the UK would create a unified right which is drafted to cater for the requirements of a commercialised 21st century. It would also increase the harmonisation of international law to give celebrities who often have international fame equivalent protection from one county to another.

A publicity law could be an absolute right in determining the use of any facet of ones identity with respect to advertising and commercial use. Unlike the law of passing off there would be no requirement to show confusion or that the product is or isn't authorised and no need to prove damage. Use in the media, such as in television programmes, magazines and newspapers, would not be affected by the right so long as the use was not for commercial purposes such as an advertisement. However, the distinction between commercial and communicative products is not always clear, for example, pictures and names on sports sticker collections or cigarette cards could be categorised as either.

29.49   The term of the right following death would have to be clearly defined, such as the 50-year term of the right in California which must be registered on death. This right would not infringe on the right to free speech in the media. The right would have to clarify issues of assignability, inheritability and revocation of assignments.

C   Personality

29.50   A right to personality is the exclusive intellectual property right of each person to use his or her own name, image, voice, signature, and any other distinguishing characteristics which would identify a specific person. Unlike a publicity right, a personality right is not a financial right but rather a personal intellectual property right which, strictly speaking, is not inheritable or assignable.

The need to protect performance rights is likely to increase as technology remasters, recreates or impersonates the actor. There is little protection from film studios creating 'virtual actors' using computer technology to create convincing humans based on images of celebrities. This technology, seen in films from 'Roger Rabbit' to 'Jurassic Park', has already been used to complete the film, 'The Crow', starring an actor who died during production.

1   UK law

29.51   There is no right of personality or equivalent moral right under English law. Intellectual property rights may give limited protection to personality by way of registered trade marks or copyright and the law of passing off. Moral rights are currently limited to the rights of paternity and integrity and against false attribution of authorship.

Copyright Designs and Patents Act 1988

29.52 In the UK there is no copyright in name or in a person's name, face, features, voice, body or image apart from the copyright in a specific photograph or drawing. This was recently confirmed by Mr Justice Laddie in the *Elvis Presley Enterprises* case.[8]

The Copyright Designs and Patents Act 1988 ('CDPA') protects original literary, dramatic, musical or artistic works and sound recordings, films, broadcasts or cable programmes, specific photographs or paintings.[9]

29.53 Performers do have rights over their work but this is a statutory and not a copyright in that their consent is required for the exploitation of their performances.[10] The performer's rights are passed on to their estates on their death. However, the protection is limited in that it only applies to images that are obtained by unauthorised recordings of qualifying performances, that is, performances given by a citizen or, subject of, or resident in the UK, EEC or any other country enjoying reciprocal protection by an Order in Council made under section 208 of the CDPA, or takes place in such a country.

29.54 Copyright will subsist in the work, such as the photograph or performance, rather than with the individual. A limited exception is where a celebrity creates a caricature of himself. In most cases the person who owns the copyright will be the person who created the work or where the work is created in the course of his or her employment, his or her employer. This means that the subject matter of the work will only rarely have control over the copyrighted work. The exception is where a photograph has been commissioned for private and domestic purposes. Under section 85 of the CDPA the person commissioning the photograph has the right to prevent it from being issued to the public, displayed in public, broadcast or included in a cable programme without his or her permission, regardless of ownership of copyright.

The CDPA is part of international protection of copyright so that the protection given to UK nationals under that Act is extended under sections 153–162 to nationals of other countries which are parties to the Berne Convention or the Universal Copyright Convention.

29.55 Fair dealing defences are available for portrayal of a person's likeness which is protected by copyright where the image is used for reporting current events or for research or study, or for criticism or review, or for reporting current events (sections 29 and 30 of the CDPA). There is no general statutory definition of 'fair dealing'; what is fair is a matter of fact and degree in the individual case. Where work is copied for criticism or review or for reporting current events there must be 'sufficient acknowledgement' of the copyright work.

Copyright law gives automatic, albeit limited and indirect, protection to individuals. The extent of the protection granted is limited by the type of work which is capable of being protected, the extent of the ownership of the rights and by the defences available which permit use of the work which would otherwise be unlawful.

---

8 *Elvis Presley Trade Marks* [1997] RPC 543.
9 CDPA 1988, s 1.
10 CDPA 1988, s 180(1).

29.56   Moral rights are protected by the CDPA, as well as by the common law of contract, passing off and defamation. Section 77 contains the right of paternity whereby the author of a literary, dramatic, musical or artistic work in which copyright subsists, and the director of a copyright film, has the right to be identified as such each time the work is published, performed, broadcast, issued or displayed to the public. This right is only operational and capable of being infringed if it has first been asserted. Assertion can be by including a statement in the assignment of copyright or by a separate notice in writing. Section 80 contains the right of integrity, that is, an author's right not to be subject to derogatory treatment.

An author also has the right not to have work falsely attributed to him (CDPA, section 84). The right subsists until 20 years after the person's death so that it can be asserted by the author's personal representatives.

29.57   In the event of an author's breach of any moral rights he may be entitled to damages and, in addition, the court may grant an injunction. In the *Dorothy Squires* case,[11] Lord Denning awarded damages for false attribution of authorship but commented that, if a claimant obtains damages in libel or passing off, then there can be no duplication of damages in respect of the same complaint.

Trade marks

29.58   For a name, logo, mark or image to be registered as a trade mark it must be capable of being represented graphically and must be capable of distinguishing the goods or services of one undertaking from that of another (Trade Marks Act 1994, section 1(1)). The Trade Marks Act 1994 ('TMA') implements the EU Trademark Directive.[12] The registered proprietor of a trade mark has exclusive rights in the mark. Those rights can be infringed in four ways by any person who, in the course of trade, without the owner's consent uses the mark (TMA, section 10). First, by the use of an identical mark for good or services which are identical to those for which it was registered; secondly, for use of an identical mark for goods or services which are similar to those for which it was registered so that there is a likelihood of confusion on the part of the public; thirdly, for uses a similar mark to the registered mark for goods or services which are identical to those for which it was registered, so that there is a likelihood of confusion on the part of the public; and fourthly, where a mark identical to the registered mark which has an established reputation in the UK is used for dissimilar goods or services but in such a way as to take unfair advantage of or to be detrimental to the distinctive character or reputation of the mark. Injunctions, damages and accounts of profits may all be awarded in an action for trade mark infringement (TMA, section 4).

29.59   A trade mark is not infringed where a person is acting in accordance with the honest practices in industrial or commercial matters uses his own name or address provided the trader honestly thought that no confusion would arise and that he had no intention of diverting business to himself by using the name.[13]

11 *Moore v News of the World* [1972] 1 All ER.
12 OJ 1989 L40/T.
13 *Parker-Knoll v Knoll International* [1962] RPC 265.

29.60 Section 8 of the TMA has extended the previous law to include the use by a company of its registered name and assignment of the name.

In the recent *Elvis Presley Enterprises* case[14] Mr Justice Laddie rejected a series of trade mark applications for Elvis's name on the basis that people bought 'Elvis Presley' goods because fans wanted a souvenir of the singer, rather than because they thought the name identified a particular supplier of the goods. He went on to say that the general public did not care one way or the other who had produced or licensed it. Although, the judgment related to the Trade Marks Act 1938, the court is likely to have interpreted the TMA in the same manner.

29.61 The strict application of UK trade mark law as a badge of origin, rather than as a form of protection against unauthorised merchandising, was confirmed by Mr Justice Lightman in the recent *Spice Girls* case.[15] The Spice Girls were denied an ex parte injunction to prevent the sale of a 'Fab Five' sticker collection featuring their images, which did not state or imply that the collection had not been authorised by the pop group.

After the earlier case of *Mirage Studio v Counter-feat Clothing*[16] it had been suggested that character merchandising by third parties could and did constitute a misrepresentation that the characters had been licensed by the owner. In that case Teenage Mutant Ninja Turtles merchandise was successfully protected from counterfeiters. However, Laddie J in the *Elvis* case distinguished the *Teenage Mutant Ninja Turtles* case on its facts, and said that in general the public did not assume that the public believed or even cared who made, sold or licensed the product.

29.62 An individual can protect his or her name, signature or likeness where it is capable of distinguishing his or her own brand goods and services from those of others. For example, the likeness of 'Colonel Sanders' of Kentucky Fried Chicken has been protected for a long period of time. A number of personalities and bodies have successfully registered a trade mark relating to a name, signature or face. The 'Diana, Princess of Wales Memorial Fund' registered its name and logo as well as the name 'Diana, Princess of Wales', the signature 'Diana' and a number of photographs of Diana. The English footballers Alan Shearer, Paul Gascoigne and David Beckham have also registered trade marks.

In the light of recent the recent *Elvis* and *Spice Girls* cases these trade marks could be open to challenge in the courts. Trade marks can only offer protection to personalities where commercial activity is involved and the marks have been registered pro-actively at some cost.

Passing off

29.63 The tort of passing off protects individuals against the appropriation of another person's identity. English courts have also recognised character merchandise as protectable under the law of passing off.[17] For an individual to succeed in an action for passing off both parties must be in a trade or

---

14 *Elvis Presley Trade Marks* [1997] RPC 543.
15 *Halliwell v Panini* [1997] 6 June 1997.
16 *Mirage Studio v Counter-feat Clothing* [1991] FSR 145.
17 *Mirage Studios v Counter-Feat Clothing* [1991] FSR 145.

business and there must be a misrepresentation to the public leading them to believe that the goods are those of a particular individual and that as a result the individual has suffered damage. Damage could be loss of royalties from official goods or damage to reputation by the supply of inferior goods. In the *Advocaat* case[18] five characteristics must be present in order to create a valid cause of action for passing off:

(1)   a misrepresentation;

(2)   made by a trader in the course of trade;

(3)   to prospective customers of his or ultimate consumers of goods or services supplied by him;

(4)   which is calculated to injure the business or goodwill of another trader (in the sense that this is a reasonably foreseeable consequence); and

(5)   which causes actual damage to a business or goodwill of the trader by whom the action is brought or (in a quia timet action) will probably do so.

29.64   Confusion could be caused by the supply or offer of goods in such a way as to make it appear that the offer or supply is sanctioned by or connected with the celebrity or character. The law can never protect individuals who do not commercially exploit their name or image as there would clearly be no confusion in the eyes of the public and generally, they will not be operating in the course of a business. For example, images of Prince William would not be protected as he does not produce official merchandise.

Whether or not there is consumer confusion is a question of fact; however, recent case law has shown that the assumptions the court makes relating to consumers has changed. The court assumed in the *Mirage Studios* case that people will believe a product to be authorised unless there was a statement that it was not. That assumption has been doubted by Lightman J in the *Spice Girls* case and by the judgment in the *Elvis* case although these were trade mark decisions.

29.65   In some circumstances there is a defence to an action for passing off where the defendant was making normal use of his own name. The defence will operate where there is mere confusion because two people or companies have the same or similar names and there is no misrepresentation or attempt to pass off the goods as those of another.

29.66   It is a question of fact whether a particular name has acquired a secondary meaning so that if goods were produced by another under that name it would cause confusion in the minds of the public. If it is proven that that name has acquired such a secondary meaning then the court must decide whether a defendant, regardless of intention, is describing his goods in such a manner that it is likely that a substantial section of the purchasing public will be misled to believing that his goods are the goods of the claimant.

The proximity of the place where the defendant sets up business to that of the established trading area of a well known firm may be evidence that the defendant is seeking to take fraudulent advantage of the similarity of his own name to that of the claimant's, for example, where someone with a

18   *Ewen Warnink BV v J Townend & Sons (Hull) Ltd* [1972] 2 All ER 927.

surname 'Bass' set up a brewery at Burton-On-Trent called Bass & Co.[19] There is however no special right to trade under one's nickname.[20]

29.67   Remedies include an award of damages and or an injunction, an order for delivery up and destruction of the offending articles.

Impact of the Human Rights Act 1998

29.68   The incorporation of the European Convention of Human Rights into UK law may increase the protection of personality rights granted to living people.

Demand for a personality right in the UK

29.69   A personality law would prevent others from taking economic advantage of or morally abusing the personal rights of the individual. Recently, there has been public support for the attempts of the Diana, Princess of Wales Memorial Fund to protect the name and image of the late Princess of Wales and debate concerning the somewhat dubious commercial uses of the Memorial Fund's trade marks on cartons of margarine and lottery tickets.

29.70   A personality right would provide automatic equal protection to all individuals in contrast to the protection granted to the limited number of public figures who have protected their personality by registering trade marks at some expense. However, such a law could potentially limit freedom of speech and produce complex law. Exceptions would probably be required, including, for the use for providing factual information regarding a product or a service, parodies in certain circumstances and for use of a person in a crowd of persons.

29.71   Any personality law would have to define the duration of the right, such as whether or not the right would terminate on death or on a specific period after death. The need for protection of personality may decline after death because fame inevitably fades with time. Furthermore, if a personality right lasts for a substantial period of time there would be limits to the production of posthumous biographical accounts and films, thus infringing freedom of speech and literary and dramatic production.

Any rights in personality should be assignable and be capable of being licensed.

---

19   *Massam v Thorley* [1880] 14 Ch D 748.
20   *BIBA Group v BIBA Boutique* [1980] RPC 413.

30 UNITED STATES OF AMERICA

Bruce P Keller*
Jeremy Feigelson*
Craig Bloom*
Lisa Green**

A   Privacy and publicity

1   Introduction

30.01   This chapter sets forth a brief overview of United States law on privacy and publicity. To fully understand the substantive law of privacy and publicity in the United States, it is useful to review the basic structure of the US legal system.

The federal system: what law applies?

30.02   The US has a federal system. The national government has a body of laws, a legislature, and a judiciary that governs the conduct of all of the country's citizens. Each of the 50 States also has its own body of law, legislature, and judiciary that govern within its borders. Analysis of a particular legal problem often begins with the question of whether the problem is governed by State law, federal law, or a combination of the two. To the extent that an issue is governed by State law, often there is also a question as to which State's law applies.

In this chapter we focus on general principles that apply, for the most part, across State lines and across the State-federal boundary. We also note some of the major variations in the law that apply in prominent commercial States such as New York and California. There are, however, too many distinctions between State and federal law, and between the laws of different States, to be covered in detail in a general survey such as this one. Readers in need of a specific statement of the law of a particular jurisdiction are referred to the excellent and comprehensive *50-State Survey: Media Privacy and Related Law*.[1]

*   Of Debevoise & Plimpton.
**   Of the National Broadcasting Co. The authors would like to thank Marianna Vaidman Stone, Jonathan Perry and Eric Creizman for their assistance with this chapter.
1   Published annually by the Libel Defense Resource Center in New York City (www.ldrc.com).

455

Sources of law

30.03 In addition to determining what jurisdiction's law applies, one must consider the threshold question of what source of law is controlling: common law, statutory law, or constitutional law.

Federal law

30.04 The written US Constitution is the supreme source of law. The First Amendment to the US Constitution protects freedom of speech and the press.[2] The protections of the First Amendment limit many efforts to impose liability on the media, including liability for invasion of privacy and defamation.

Subsidiary to the Constitution are the statutes enacted by Congress and the regulations issued by relevant agencies such as the Federal Communications Commission. Court decisions construing the Constitution, statutes and regulations are also significant. There is no general federal common law.

State law

30.05 State law in the US generally takes the form of common law, that is, judge-made doctrines that are set forth in published court decisions. Authoritative scholarly works, such as the Restatement of Torts, summarise common law principles and are often treated as significant (if not controlling) authority.

Some States' legislatures have codified all or part of the common law of privacy. To the extent that a legislature has spoken, its statutes generally trump the common law. As a general rule, though, statutes are construed to harmonise with the common law where possible.

Each State also has a constitution that sets forth basic principles of organisation for the State's government. Some State constitutions, notably those of New York and California, also include specific provisions that protect civil liberties such as the right to privacy or the freedom of the press. Such constitutional protections trump any contrary common or statutory law at the State level, but do not trump federal law.

Procedural issues

30.06 There is often no crisp dividing line between the jurisdiction of state courts and federal courts. In many cases, a dispute could be heard in either type of forum. As a general rule, State and federal cases tend to follow similar procedural paths: a case begins with the submission of written pleadings by both sides, proceeds through a discovery process in which each side makes all relevant witnesses and documents available to the other, and concludes either with a dispositive motion or a trial. There are also opportunities to obtain preliminary injunctive relief, and opportunities to get a case dismissed at the outset if it lacks any legal basis. In certain situations, it is possible to move a case from State to federal court, from federal to State court, or from one court to another within either the state or federal system.

There are also significant differences between State and federal courts and

---

2 The First Amendment provides that the government 'shall make no law . . . abridging the freedom of speech or of the press.'

among particular judges. Analysis of the legal trends and procedural options available in a particular jurisdiction is often crucial to analysing a particular legal problem.

Liability for newsgathering

30.07   The most rapidly developing area of law governing journalists in the US concerns not what they print, but how they behave. As discussed elsewhere in this chapter, the First Amendment usually immunises the press from liability for the *content* of published information that the subject, or society, deems offensive.

The First Amendment, however, provides far less protection to the *conduct* by which the press obtains information. The First Amendment normally does not exempt the media from compliance with generally applicable laws. As the Supreme Court has observed, '[t]he press may not with impunity break and enter an office or dwelling to gather news.'[3] Nor is a journalist generally free to break the law while working 'undercover' to report about crime.[4]

Both tort law and statutes threaten the media with substantial liability for conduct that exceeds permissible boundaries. For example, most States recognise a form of the invasion of privacy tort called 'intrusion,' which is defined as follows:

'One who intentionally intrudes, physically or otherwise, upon the solitude or seclusion of another or his private affairs or concerns, is subject to liability to the other for invasion of privacy, if the intrusion would be highly offensive to a reasonable person.'[5]

In contrast to the form of the privacy tort called 'disclosure of private facts,' the newsworthiness of the information sought is not a defence to an intrusion claim.[6]

30.08   Other rules with which the media must contend include general laws proscribing offences such as trespass and fraud, and State and federal laws that regulate the taping of conversations and the use of hidden cameras and microphones. Moreover, as a consequence of Princess Diana's death (which some persons have blamed on aggressive photographers), California enacted a law intended to curb aggressive photojournalism, and other jurisdictions are considering similar legislation.

As a legal matter, the media cannot avoid liability for newsgathering offences by choosing not to publish the resulting information. Although, as a practical matter, publication might make a suit more likely (by upsetting the subject, or bringing the investigative techniques to light for the first time),

---

3   *Cohen v Cowles Media Co*, 501 US 663, 669 (1991) (media's breach of promise of confidentiality held to be actionable under general laws governing enforcement of promises).

4   In one recent case, a federal appellate court rejected a journalist's argument that he could not be prosecuted for sending and receiving child pornography because he allegedly did so only as a means of researching a story on the topic. The journalist was sentenced to 18 months in prison. *United States v Matthews*, 209 F3d 338 (4th Cir, 2000). In a different case, however, another federal court ruled that possession of child pornography by a researcher might be protected by the First Amendment. *United States v Lamb*, 945 F Supp 441, 450 (NDNY 1996).

5   Restatement (Second) of Torts, s 652B.

6   *Shulman v Group W Productions, Inc*, 18 Cal 4th 200, 240-41, 955 P2d 469 (Cal Sup Ct 1998).

publication is not normally an element of a newsgathering offence.[7] Courts have split on the question of whether harm caused by subsequent publication may increase the damages that are available because of the improper conduct.[8]

2 Taping conversations

30.09 Journalists face the risk of both criminal and civil liability if they violate federal or State laws that bar the taping of telephone conversations and other private conversations under certain circumstances.

Federal wire tap statute

30.10 Federal law prohibits the interception of oral or wire communications unless one party to the conversation consents to the taping. In practical terms, this statute does not substantially restrict the press because the one person consenting can be a journalist surreptitiously taping an interview.

The law also prohibits the use of illegally intercepted communications if the user knows, or has reason to know, the source.[9] Courts have split on the question of whether the First Amendment nevertheless enables a party who receives an illegally intercepted communication – but was not involved in the interception – to disclose the information.[10]

30.11 If a journalist violates section 2511, the law authorises punishment of up to five years in jail and a fine. Available civil penalties include actual damages, fines, and punitive damages for repeat offenders. Remedies probably would not include a prohibition against the publication of the intercepted information, see *In re King World Productions, Inc.*[11]

---

7 See, eg, *KOVR-TV, Inc v Superior Ct*, 31 Cal App 4th 1023, 37 Cal Rptr 2d 431 (Cal Ct App 1995) (although the videotape was never broadcast, the court finds triable the issue regarding whether the media intentionally inflicted emotional distress on children who were told by journalists of child killings and suicide next door).
8 Compare *Dietemann v Time, Inc*, 449 F2d 245, 250 (9th Cir 1971) (permitting damages for additional emotional distress when wrongfully obtained information is published), with *Food Lion, Inc v Capital Cities/ABC, Inc*, 194 F3d 505, 522–24 (4th Cir 1999) (plaintiff could recover token damages resulting from trespass by undercover journalists, but could not recover compensatory damages for subsequent broadcast of report, because First Amendment bars recovery for damage to reputation absent proof of falsity, and that the journalists either knew of the falsity or recklessly disregarded the truth).
9 18 USC s 2511.
10 Compare *Bartnicki v Vopper*, 200 F3d 109, 118–29 (3d Cir 1999) (First Amendment overcomes provisions of federal and state wire tapping laws that 'penalize the use or disclosure of illegally intercepted information where there is no allegation that the defendants participated in or encouraged that interception'), and *Peavy v New Times, Inc*, 976 F Supp 532 (ND Tex 1997) (First Amendment bars prosecution for publication), with *Boehner v McDermott*, 191 F3d 463 (DC Cir 1999) (First Amendment does not bar lawsuit alleging violation of wire tap statute against Congressman who received tape of illegally intercepted call, and passed tape along to news media), and *Natoli v Sullivan*, 159 Misc 2d 681, 606 NYS2d 504, 21 Media L Rep 2097 (NY Sup Ct 1993), aff'd, 206 AD2d 841, 616 NYS2d 318 (NY App Div 1994) (media may be held liable for initial disclosure of conversations intercepted by others; once information enters public domain, however, law does not prevent subsequent publication). This issue is expected to be resolved by the US Supreme Court, which will hear the *Bartnicki* case in the court's 2000/2001 term.
11 898 F2d 56, 59-60 (6th Cir 1990).

State statutes

30.12   Even if federal law permits the taping of a particular conversation under the 'one-party consent' approach, state law might ban it. Ten States – California, Connecticut, Florida, Illinois, Maryland, Massachusetts, Montana, New Hampshire, Pennsylvania and Washington – bar the taping of private conversations unless *all* parties to the conversation consent. Most other states have adopted statutes based on the federal law, and thus permit taping if one party consents.

One potential defence for a journalist who secretly tapes a conversation in an all-party consent State is to argue that the conversation was not 'confidential' in the first place, and thus not covered by the taping law. In one case a federal appeals court, interpreting California's taping law, held that an ABC reporter who secretly taped a conversation did not violate the law because he identified himself as a reporter; he was not asked to keep the conversation private; and he did not promise to keep it private. The court held that the other party thus could not reasonably expect that her disclosures would not be revealed.[12]

FCC telephone rule

30.13   Federal Communications Commission regulations require that before a broadcaster may record a telephone call, or broadcast a call live, the broadcaster must inform all parties of his or her intention to broadcast the call.[13] Although fines of up to $25,000 are authorised for a first offence, and fines of up to $250,000 are authorised for repeat offenders, the FCC tends to give only a warning for a first offence.

Interstate telephone calls

30.14   Choice-of-law issues arise when telephone calls cross state lines, and the laws of the respective states differ on the issue of all-party vs one-party consent. Either State's rule might be applied. The court's choice would turn on the specific facts, and the rules of the forum State for resolving such conflicts.

3   Hidden cameras

30.15   Hidden cameras are a potent and popular newsgathering tool, but their use by US television journalists has been constrained by State law and judicial decisions that weigh newsgathering rights against privacy interests.

Laws restricting use of hidden cameras

30.16   Twelve States have statutes that prohibit the use of hidden cameras under certain circumstances: Alabama, California, Delaware, Georgia, Hawaii, Kansas, Maine, Michigan, Minnesota, New Hampshire, South Dakota, and Utah. In general, these laws do not completely outlaw the technique, but instead bar hidden camera use only if the individuals captured on tape had a reasonable expectation of privacy.

---

12   *Deteresa v ABC Inc*, 121 F3d 460, 463-65 (9th Cir 1997).
13   47 CFR, s 73.1206.

A comparison of two cases in California illustrates the factors that can determine whether a plaintiff complaining about surreptitious videotaping is found to have a reasonable expectation of privacy. In one case, two journalists, who were co-operating with law enforcement officials, used false pretenses to enter the home of a man claiming to be a physician, and then secretly recorded and photographed that man. The Ninth Circuit Court of Appeals held that this surreptitious behavior was an intrusion, finding that the First Amendment does not grant 'a license to trespass, to steal, or to intrude by electronic means into the precincts of another's home or office.'[14] By contrast, in the *Deteresa* case described above, the use of a hidden camera was not punished because the source knew she was speaking with a journalist, and she was in public view when she was filmed. Significantly, in *Deteresa* the reporter did not gain access inside the source's home under false pretenses.[15]

Depending on the State, journalists sometimes can legally obtain hidden camera footage if their equipment is not recording sound. If a State statute bars only surreptitious recording of a conversation or communication, silent recording may fall outside the statute.

Advisability of obtaining consent

30.17 Journalists normally can protect themselves from suit if they obtain the subjects' consent before videotaping in places where people could reasonably expect privacy. These consents may be written, or obtained on-camera. Consents are particularly useful in settings where the camera is likely to capture people with particularly compelling privacy interests, such as children or medical patients, and in settings in which people are not free to leave, such as hospitals or prisons.

Effect of new technologies

30.18 The scope of hidden camera laws and court decisions is bound to change along with technology, as courts consider the privacy and newsgathering implications of equipment that captures high-quality footage and sound from great distances, and the increased popularity of aerial footage. Recent decisions suggest judicial discomfort with these techniques. In *Wolfson v Lewis*,[16] a federal judge granted a preliminary injunction – an extraordinary form of relief in a media case – to prevent journalists from employing sensitive cameras and microphones to capture, from afar, images and conversations of a family of high-paid executives of an insurance company that had been criticised for failing to pay adequate sums for members' health care. The judge described the issue raised by the case as 'the extent to which the First Amendment protects news gathering by TV journalists using modern technologies.'[17] The court did not need to rely on anti-eavesdropping statutes to restrain the journalists, but justified its action by finding that the executives likely would prevail on a common-law 'intrusion' claim. The case eventually settled.

---

14 *Dietemann v Time Inc*, 449 2d 245, 249 (9th Cir 1971).
15 paragrapgh **30.21** below explores in greater detail the media's potential liability for reporting from private homes, with or without hidden cameras.
16 924 F Supp 1413 (ED Pa 1996).
17 Ibid at 1417.

Responding to the death of Princess Diana, and Hollywood's frequent disdain for paparazzi, California has attempted to rein in photojournalists by statute. A law enacted in 1998 authorises triple damages, punitive damages, and the disgorgement of profits for trespassing (or for using image or sound enhancing technology as an alternative to trespassing) to record or observe 'personal or familial activity' of a person who has a reasonable expectation of privacy.[18]

Other implications of hidden camera use

30.19   Sometimes, a lawsuit prompted by a hidden camera investigation may not be decided on eavesdropping grounds, but the use of hidden cameras may nonetheless disturb the jury and influence the result. For a hidden camera investigation of a supermarket chain, journalists secured jobs at the chain by creating employment histories that did not reveal their profession. Wearing hidden cameras, the journalists recorded evidence of poor food-handling practices. The supermarket chain sued after the broadcast of a report that included some of this footage. A wire tapping claim against the journalists was dismissed, but they were found liable for, among other claims, trespass and fraud arising from their obtaining the jobs under false pretenses. Although the jury found only $1,402 in actual damages, it awarded more than $5.5 million in punitive damages. The trial court reduced that amount to $315,000.[19] Although an appellate court threw out all but $2 of the award,[20] the case has made journalists more reluctant to use hidden cameras in similar investigations.

4   Intrusion into private/sensitive places

30.20   Whether journalistic conduct constitutes actionable 'intrusion' often depends on where the conduct takes place. Although the media generally cannot be liable for observing or filming what is in public view, intrusions into private homes and other sensitive areas may expose the media to liability for intrusion, trespass, and related offences.

The home

30.21   US law exalts the home above other locations. The Fourth Amendment to the US Constitution, for example, protects people from unreasonable searches of their houses. The home also provides a limited sanctuary from obscenity laws. As a result of this approach, a home is one of the riskiest places for a journalist to gather news.

The media generally cannot enter a home without the consent of the owner or occupant. Exceptions to this general rule have been made in the event of natural disasters. In one case, a photographer who accompanied a fire marshal into a home destroyed by fire was not liable for intrusion, because the court found implied consent based on common custom and practice.[1]

Authorised police activity at a home, however, normally does not authorise media presence as well. Recent years have seen a proliferation of reality-

---

18 Cal Civ Code, s 1708.8.
19 *Food Lion, Inc v Capital Cities/ABC, Inc,* 984 F Supp 923 (MDNC 1997).
20 *Food Lion, Inc v Capital Cities/ABC, Inc,* 194 F3d 505 (4th Cir 1999).
1   *Florida Publishing Co v Fletcher,* 340 So 2d 914 (Fla Sup Ct 1976).

based television shows in which journalists follow police, emergency medical teams, and similar government agents to document high drama for the audience. To the extent these officials carry on their business in public, journalists generally are free to record what transpires.

That freedom, however, essentially stops at private homes, even when law enforcement officials have a valid search warrant and invite the media to join them inside. In *Wilson v Layne*,[2] the Supreme Court held that 'it is a violation of the Fourth Amendment for police to bring members of the media or other third parties into a home during the execution of a warrant when the presence of the third parties in the home was not in aid of the execution of the warrant.'

The *Wilson* decision followed a series of similar lower court rulings that denounced such arrangements between government officials and the media. As one court wrote: 'A private home is not a soundstage for law enforcement theatricals.' See *Ayeni v Mottola*,[3] finding that the Fourth Amendment would bar a federal agent from permitting journalists to join him while he executed a search warrant. Under these rulings, in addition to potential liability for trespass, intrusion, and intentional infliction of emotional distress, a journalist could even be found to violate a homeowner's constitutional rights. See *Berger v Hanlon*,[4] CNN personnel who contracted with US agents to join execution of search warrant were deemed to have acted jointly with federal agents, and thus 'under color of law', vacated on other grounds.[5]

Sensitive places outside the home

30.22 Although the media have more liberty outside the home, intrusion claims still can be brought under certain circumstances. In an important California case, a video camera operator employed by a television producer accompanied a medical rescue team as it flew by helicopter to a car accident scene, cared for the victims at the scene, and flew away with two victims to a hospital. The court held that the victims could not sue for intrusion based upon the cameraman's presence at and filming of the accident scene. That holding conforms with the general rule that intrusion claims cannot be brought when a journalist merely films what can be seen from a place open to the public. The court held, however, that a jury would be permitted to decide if either the cameraman's recording of a victim's conversations with rescue workers at the scene (via a wireless microphone worn by the flight nurse), or the cameraman's subsequent presence inside the helicopter when it returned to the hospital, satisfied the elements of the intrusion tort, see *Shulman v Group W Productions, Inc.*[6]

The workplace

30.23 Courts have held that people generally have less of an expectation of privacy when they are at work, and courts accordingly sometimes reject trespass and intrusion claims based on filming at a subject's workplace. See eg, *Desnick v ABC, Inc*,[7] no cause of action for undercover investigation of a

2   526 US 603 (1999).
3   35 F3d 680, 686 (2d Cir 1994).
4   129 F3d 505, 514–16 (9th Cir 1997).
5   526 US 808 (1999).
6   18 Cal 4th 200, 231–42, 955 P2d 469 (Cal Sup Ct 1998).
7   44 F3d 1345, 1351–53 (7th Cir 1995).

medical clinic; *PETA v Bobby Berosini Ltd*,[8] secret videotaping of an animal trainer at their workplace, where privacy expectation was reduced and where others could watch, did not intrude on seclusion; but see *Sanders v American Broadcasting Cos*,[9] a television reporter working undercover at a telepsychic hotline secretly videotaped her conversation with a worker; court permitted the worker's claim for invasion of privacy by intrusion, even though the worker lacked reasonable expectation of complete privacy in conversation, which could be seen and overheard by co-workers; *Food Lion, Inc v Capital Cities/ABC, Inc*,[10] upholding trespass verdict against ABC arising from undercover investigation of a supermarket.

5   Other offensive conduct

30.24   This section reviews the media's potential liability for other reporting conduct that subjects may claim is offensive.

Harassment

30.25   Even if a journalist operates only in public space, the journalist may be held liable for aggressive conduct that violates laws against harassment or 'stalking.' In one well-known case, a freelance photographer who aggressively pursued Jacqueline Onassis and her children was ordered to keep at least 25 feet away from Ms Onassis, and at least 30 feet away from her children, and not to take any action likely to frighten them, see *Galella v Onassis*.[11]

Deception

30.26   Journalists who obtain information under false pretenses have mixed success when they defend their conduct in court. Some judges have rejected fraud claims because they tend to chill First Amendment activity: *Sussman v ABC, Inc*.[12] Other judges reject them because of specific deficiencies, such as a failure to allege pecuniary loss as a result of the misrepresentation, see *Homsy v King World Entertainment, Inc*,[13] holding that damage to reputation based on the eventual broadcast did not count. In other cases, such as the *Food Lion* dispute discussed above in para **30.19**, courts have held undercover journalists liable for torts such as trespass and breach of the duty of loyalty, see *Food Lion, Inc v Capital Cities/ABC, Inc*.[14] Journalists also may be at risk under laws that bar a specific misrepresentation. For example, in one case a reporter was convicted of impersonating a public official after the reporter allegedly told the mother of a homicide victim that the reporter was from the county morgue.[15]

---

8   895 P2d 1269 (Nev 1995).
9   20 Cal 4th 907 (Cal 1999).
10   194 F3d 505 (4th Cir 1999).
11   487 F2d 986 (2d Cir 1973).
12   971 F Supp 432, 435 & n 3 (CD Cal 1997).
13   No 01-96-00708-CV, 1997 WL 52154 (Tex App Feb 6, 1997).
14   194 F3d 505 (4th Cir 1999).
15   *New Jersey v Cantor*, 221 NJ Super 219, 534 A2d 83 (NJ App Div 1987).

Conversion/theft of information

30.27 Although the media generally cannot be held liable for publishing information it receives from persons who were required to keep it confidential, the media is not free to steal information itself. In 1998, the Cincinnati Enquirer newspaper agreed to pay Chiquita Brands International Inc more than $10 million to avoid being sued over a series of articles that criticised the company. The newspaper did not admit that its stories were false; rather, the newspaper apparently paid to settle the matter because of allegations that its reporter had broken into Chiquita's voice mail system and stolen information. The reporter later pleaded guilty in Ohio State court to charges of unlawful interception of wire communications and unlawful access to computer systems, and was sentenced to five years of probation.

Nor is the media necessarily entitled to keep original documents that were stolen by others, especially if the theft victim does not have any copies. *FMC Corp v Capital Cities/ABC Inc*,[16] journalists had to return originals, but could retain copies and publish contents. In such cases, retention of the documents might constitute the tort of conversion, defined as an 'intentional exercise of dominion or control over a chattel which so seriously interferes with the right of another to control it that the actor may justly be required to pay the other the full value.'[17] A conversion claim is not stated when the media merely records images and voices, which are not chattel.[18]

A conversion claim, and related intrusion claims, likely would also fail if brought against a journalist who sifted through garbage that was set out for collection. The producer of the garbage likely would be viewed as having abandoned control. Similarly, most courts have ruled that police searches of garbage do not require a search warrant because the producers of the garbage have no reasonable expectation of privacy with respect to their garbage. See *Colorado v Hillman*,[19] finding that nationwide, most jurisdictions have not found a privacy right in garbage; noting New Jersey, Washington, and Hawaii as exceptions.

B   Disclosure of private facts

1   Introduction

30.28 The branch of the invasion of privacy tort known as 'disclosure of private facts' imposes liability for the dissemination of embarrassing and true private facts regarding an individual's life. In order to prevail, a claimant must prove that there was public disclosure of private facts, that the

---

16 915 F2d 300 (7th Cir 1990).
17 Restatement (Second) of Torts, s 222A.
18 *Berger v Hanlon*, 129 F3d 505, 517 (9th Cir 1997), vacated on other grounds, 526 US 808 (1999).
19 834 P2d 1271, 1273-76 (Col Sup Ct 1992).

disclosure would be highly offensive to a reasonable person, and that the facts are of no legitimate concern to the public.[20]

Because this tort permits liability for the publication of true facts, it conflicts with the First Amendment principle that truth is a defence to publication torts. Virtually all States, however, recognise a defence of newsworthiness to this tort, which somewhat alleviates the tension. Because the courts have broadly defined 'newsworthiness,' the action of public disclosure of private facts has limited application. Most States have recognised the tort. Nebraska, New York, North Carolina, and Oregon are among those that have not.[1] Some State statutes also prohibit the publication of certain sensitive information, such as the names of rape victims. As discussed below, the First Amendment generally renders these statutes unconstitutional.

2 Elements

30.29 To give rise to a claim of disclosure of private facts, a communication must satisfy four main criteria: (1) the disclosure must be public; (2) the publication must identify the plaintiff; (3) the facts disclosed must have been private; and (4) the disclosure of the facts must be highly offensive to a reasonable person – that is, offensive in an objective sense.[2] In addition, the facts must be true; inaccuracies or mischaracterisations concerning the details of the plaintiff's private life do not give rise to a cause of action in private facts.[3] Although 'lack of newsworthiness' may be considered an element of the tort, the newsworthiness requirement is discussed below in paras **30.34–30.38**, which address defences.

Public disclosure

30.30 The majority rule is that the disclosure must be communicated to the public at large, or to so many persons that the matter must be regarded as substantially certain to become one of public knowledge. In general, a communication to a single person, or even to a small group of persons, is not enough; this distinguishes disclosures actionable under this tort from 'publication' in the context of defamation, where disclosure to any third

---

20 The Restatement (Second) of Torts, s 652D provides that:

> 'One who gives publicity to a matter concerning the private life of another is subject to liability to the other for invasion of privacy, if the matter publicized is of a kind that
> (a) would be highly offensive to a reasonable person, and
> (b) is not of legitimate concern to the public.'

1 Neb Rev Stat, ss 20–201 to 211; *Howell v New York Post Co*, 596 NYS2d 350 (NY Ct App 1993); *Hall v Post*, 372 SE2d 711 (NC Sup Ct 1988); *Anderson v Fisher Broadcasting Cos*, 712 P2d 803 (Or Sup Ct 1986).

2 The disclosure does not have to be express; it may be symbolic speech that implies the underlying facts. In *Santiesteban v Goodyear Tire & Rubber Co*, 306 F2d 9 (5th Cir 1962), the defendants removed tyres and tubes from the plaintiff's car and left the car in full view of the plaintiff's business. The court held that this action constituted publicity because it was a 'demonstrative' communication that the defendants believed the plaintiff owed them money.

3 See *Langworthy v Pulitzer Publishing Co*, 368 SW2d 385 (Mo Sup Ct 1963) (allegedly false report about plaintiff's complaint to the police about delinquent children did not give rise to invasion of privacy claim; among other reasons, the court noted that '[n]o action for damages lies against a newspaper for merely inaccurate reporting when the publication does not constitute libel').

party normally suffices,[4] see *Henry v Conner*,[5] disclosure of plaintiff's bad credit history in a loud voice in hospital waiting room was not sufficient publicity for disclosure of private facts claim.

Several States, however, permit liability for disclosures of private facts to individuals or small groups, if the disclosure is made to a 'particular public' with a special relationship to the plaintiff. See *Beaumont v Brown*,[6] employer's communication to an army official that said employee was an inadequate worker, and mentioned unnecessary details, constituted publicity because employer knew that the communication would reach other army officials; in fact, plaintiff was investigated because of the communication; *McSurely v McClellan*,[7] disclosure of a person's sexual history to that person's spouse held actionable; see generally *Doe v Methodist Hospital*,[8] reviewing split in authority, and holding that disclosure of plaintiff's HIV condition to a co-worker was not 'publicity' even under the looser standard because the co-worker did not have a special relationship with the plaintiff.

In most media cases, the 'publicity' requirement will be met, because a media outlet is open to the public, even if few observe its messages.[9]

Identification of plaintiff

30.31 The disclosure must identify the plaintiff to the reasonable person. Plaintiff's name need not be mentioned for the plaintiff to be identified. The facts, however, must reveal unique characteristics of the plaintiff so that the plaintiff is identifiable.

Rawls v Condé Nast Publications, Inc,[10] plaintiff is not identifiable where defendants published photographs of the inside of a home without revealing any unique characteristics.

Private information

30.32 The third element of a private facts claim is that the facts disclosed must have been kept private. In general, neither matters of public record nor activities open to public view can be deemed 'private' for the purposes of this cause of action.

Heath v Playboy Enterprises, Inc,[11] pictures taken of plaintiffs at a courthouse were not private because they were taken in a public place where the plaintiffs were in full view.

Jaubert v Crowley Post-Signal, In,[12] photo of plaintiff's home taken without plaintiff's consent; court holds no privacy interest in home visible to the public.

Neff v Time, Inc,[13] photograph of plaintiff's unzipped trousers was taken at

---

4   Restatement (Second) of Torts, s 652D cmt a.
5   226 NW2d 921 (Minn Sup Ct 1975).
6   257 NW2d 522 (Mich Sup Ct 1977).
7   753 F2d 88, 112-13 (DC Cir 1985).
8   690 NE2d 681, 692-93 (Ind Sup Ct 1997).
9   See, eg, Restatement (Second) of Torts, s 652D cmt a ('[A]ny publication in a newspaper or a magazine, even of small circulation, or any broadcast over the radio ... is sufficient to give publicity.').
10 446 F2d 313 (5th Cir 1971).
11 732 F Supp 1145 (SD Fla 1990).
12 375 So 2d 1386 (La Sup Ct 1979).
13 406 F Supp 858 (WD Pa 1976).

a football game; no claim because plaintiff was in a public place, and encouraged the photographer to take his picture; but see *Daily Times Democrat v Graham*,[14] plaintiff had cause of action for photograph of her taken when a fan blew her dress above her waist and exposed her underwear.

Gill v Hearst,[15] publication in magazine of married plaintiffs, in an affectionate but not obscene pose, taken without consent at an ice cream concession; no claim.

Once a matter is part of the public record, publishing truthful details of the matter generally is not actionable because no 'private' fact is being disclosed, and because the First Amendment prevents liability.

Cox Broadcasting Corpn v Cohn,[16] under First Amendment, broadcaster could not be held liable for revealing name of rape victim whose identity was obtained through open court records: 'Once true information is disclosed in public court documents open to public inspection, the press cannot be sanctioned for publishing it'.

Some courts have fashioned an exception to this general rule, and have permitted liability for reporting on the past crimes of rehabilitated criminals. *Briscoe v Reader's Digest Assocn*,[17] former hijacker, who had obeyed the law for the 11 years since his crime, had a cause of action for invasion of privacy over article that described his conviction. Subsequent US Supreme Court cases, however, such as *Cox Broadcasting Corpn v Cohn*, suggest that cases like *Briscoe* no longer are good law.[18]

Offensiveness

30.33 The fourth element of the private facts tort is that the facts disclosed must be offensive and embarrassing to a person of reasonable sensibilities. Courts have approached the 'offensiveness' issue on a case-by-case basis. In the following illustrative cases, courts have found the 'offensiveness' standard satisfied:

Horne v Patton,[19] unauthorised disclosure of plaintiff's medical records.

Daily Times Democrat v Graham,[20] plaintiff photographed with her dress blown in the air by a funhouse wind machine, exposing her undergarments.

The facts in the following cases were found insufficient to meet the requisite level of 'offensiveness':

Virgil v Sports Illustrated,[1] magazine published that plaintiff engaged in outrageous activities such as 'putting out cigarettes in his mouth and diving off stairs to impress women, hurting himself in order to collect unemployment so as to have time for bodysurfing . . . , fighting in gang fights as a youngster, and eating insects'.

---

14 276 Ala 380 (Ala Sup Ct 1964).
15 253 P2d 441 (Cal Sup Ct 1953).
16 420 US 469 (1975).
17 4 Cal 3d 529 (Cal Sup Ct 1971).
18 For a fuller discussion of the First Amendment defence to disclosure of private facts claims, see paras **30.14–30.38** below.
19 287 So 2d 824 (Ala Sup Ct 1973).
20 162 So 2d 474 (Ala Sup Ct 1964).
1   424 F Supp 1286 (SD Cal 1976).

Bitsie v Walston,[2] picture of child used in fundraising effort for cerebral palsy.

3 Defences

30.34 In addition to defending a private facts claim on the basis that the elements have not been satisfied, or on privileges available in defamation claims, a defendant may cite its First Amendment right to publish truthful matters of public significance, and the similar common law provision that a private facts claim must fail if the published facts are newsworthy.

Supreme Court decisions

30.35 The tension between the private facts action and the First Amendment arises because publication of true facts is generally thought to be protected. Both the common law and the First Amendment, for example, bar liability for defamation when the offending statement is true. When addressing claims for disclosure of private facts, however, the Supreme Court has not unequivocally held that truthful publication is protected by the First Amendment. Rather, the court has held that 'where a newspaper publishes truthful information which it has lawfully obtained, punishment may lawfully be imposed, if at all, only when narrowly tailored to a State interest of the highest order.' *Florida Star v BJF*.[3] In the several private facts cases that the court has reviewed, it consistently has barred liability:

Cox Broadcasting Corpn v Cohn,[4] broadcaster could not be held liable for revealing name of rape victim whose identity was obtained through open court records: 'Once true information is disclosed in public court documents open to public inspection, the press cannot be sanctioned for publishing it'.

Oklahoma Publishing Co v District Court,[5] First Amendment barred judge from prohibiting the media from printing the name of a juvenile murder suspect who had been identified at a court hearing open to the media.

Landmark Communications, Inc v Virginia,[6] First Amendment bars the criminal punishment of the news media for publishing truthful information regarding confidential proceedings of a commission that investigates judicial misconduct.

Smith v Daily Mail Publishing Co,[7] newspaper could not be held liable for publishing the name of a juvenile charged with murder, in violation of a State statute requiring the permission of the juvenile court prior to publication.

Florida Star v BJF,[8] newspaper could not be held liable for negligence where it published name of a rape victim whose identity was obtained from a police report.

---

2   515 P2d 659 (NM Ct App 1973).
3   491 US 524 (1989).
4   420 US 469 (1975).
5   430 US 308 (1977) (per curiam).
6   435 US 829 (1978).
7   443 US 97 (1979).
8   491 US 524 (1989).

Lower court decisions

30.36   Relying on both the First Amendment and common law limitations on the disclosure tort, courts refuse to hold the media liable for revealing private facts that are 'newsworthy,' or have some logical connection to matters of legitimate public interest.[9] To avoid unconstitutional interference with the right of the press to report truthfully on matters of legitimate public concern, the courts usually grant considerable deference to the decisions made by reporters and editors.[10] Moreover, the definition of 'newsworthiness' includes more than just hard news: 'It extends also to the use of names, likenesses or facts in giving information to the public for purposes of education, amusement or enlightenment, when the public may reasonably be expected to have a legitimate interest in what is published.'[11] Sensitive facts about a person can become a matter of public interest when that person, voluntarily or otherwise, becomes involved in events that are important to the public: 'People who do not desire the limelight and do not deliberately choose a way of life or course of conduct calculated to thrust them into it nevertheless have no legal right to extinguish it if the experiences that have befallen them are newsworthy, even if they would prefer that those experiences be kept private, *Haynes v Alfred A Knopf, Inc*.[12] In light of these principles, the courts have held that a broad range of information is newsworthy.

In *Haynes*, a book chronicled the migration of black Americans from the rural South to cities in the North. The plaintiff, a man who appeared in the book, sued because he objected to the revelation of unpleasant facts regarding his personal life. The court, however, found that the work was protected because the plaintiff's private life provided a concrete example of the black American experience.

Shulman v Group W Productions, Inc involved the broadcast of a medical team's attempt to rescue the victims of a car accident. The court held that the broadcast of the appearance and words of one of the victims was not actionable because the scene was of legitimate public interest.[13]

Dresbach v Doubleday & Co,[14] book revealed private facts about a man whose brother was a convicted murderer, including his alleged abandonment of his brother, and his refusal to share inheritance; publication was held to be newsworthy because a nexus was shown between the newsworthy item and the facts revealed.

---

9   See generally *Shulman v Group W Productions, Inc*, 14 Cal 4th 200, 223-25 (Cal Sup Ct 1998).

10   See case in n 9 above. In non-media cases, courts will more readily reject a newsworthiness defence. An example is *Norris v King*, 355 So 2d 21 (La Ct App 1978). The defendant, a store owner, posted on the store's wall pictures of plaintiff committing a theft (as caught by the store's hidden cameras). Accompanying the picture were captions disclosing plaintiff's guilty plea and suspended sentence. The court held that the publication was not privileged, despite the Supreme Court's holding in *Cox Broadcasting Corpn v Cohn*. The court reasoned, questionably, that because the defendant was not a newspaper the First Amendment concerns were not as crucial. The court stated that defendant was a self-interested property owner, concerned only with deterring others from committing crimes. The court held that the state's interest in rehabilitation outweighed the interest of the store owner in deterring crime.

11   Restatement (Second) of Torts, s 652D cmt j.

12   8 F3d 1222, 1232 (7th Cir 1993).

13   As discussed above in para **30.22**, however, the court also found that the victim could sue over certain objectionable conduct by the media in obtaining the footage.

14   518 F Supp 1285 (DDC 1981).

Virgil v Sports Illustrated,[15] article, describing plaintiff's wild exploits such as eating insects and fighting as a teen in gang battles, was not actionable because plaintiff was a talented body surfer who surfed at dangerous locales – a matter of legitimate public interest – and the facts helped create a better understanding of the plaintiff's style.

30.37   In the following cases the courts have declined to hold publications newsworthy as a matter of law.

Capra v Thoroughbred Racing Association of North America, Inc,[16] defendant issued a press release identifying the plaintiffs as members of the federal witness protection program.

Times-Mirror Co v Superior Court,[17] State interest in the protection of witnesses may override press right to print the name of the witness who found the murder victim's body and confronted the murder suspect, who had not been caught when the story was published.

McCabe v Village Voice, Inc,[18] picture of the plaintiff in a bathtub.

Harms v Miami Daily News, Inc,[19] plaintiff stated a claim based upon an article instructing readers to call her at her office and ask for 'Louise' in order to hear a 'sexy telephone voice'.

Barber v Time, Inc,[20] picture of a woman with a physical ailment while she was being treated in the hospital.

30.38   Reports are more likely to be considered newsworthy if they concern public figures. Because the lives of such persons generally are of public interest, permitting tort recovery would hamper the First Amendment objective of disseminating information of public importance. As the Restatement explains: 'Revelations that may properly be made concerning a murderer or the President of the US would not be privileged if they were made concerning one who is merely injured in an automobile accident.'[1] Thus a disclosure that the President was having an extra-marital affair probably would not be actionable, while a disclosure that a non-famous accident victim was having an extra-marital affair probably would be actionable.

Klein v McGraw-Hill, Inc,[2] plaintiff was a child inventor who once had achieved fame for his contributions to science; publishing his photograph along with a description of his contributions in a science book years later did not give rise to a cause of action because the plaintiff 'had become a public figure' and was therefore 'not entitled to privacy to the same extent as an ordinary member of the public'.

Macon Telegraph Publishing Co v Tatum,[3] plaintiff became a public figure when she shot and killed an intruder in her home; newspaper had the right to publish facts about the incident, including her name.

---

15   424 F Supp 1286 (SD Cal 1976).
16   787 F2d 463 (9th Cir 1986).
17   244 Cal Rptr 556 (Cal Ct App 1988).
18   550 F Supp 525 (ED Pa 1982).
19   127 So 2d 715 (Fla Dist Ct App 1961).
20   159 SW2d 291 (Mo Sup Ct 1942).
1   Restatement (Second) of Torts, s 652D cmt h.
2   263 F Supp 919 (DDC 1966).
3   263 Ga 678 (Ga Sup Ct 1993).

4   *Who may sue?*

30.39   The majority rule is that a private facts claim may be brought only by the individual who is the subject of the disclosure, and that a cause of action does not survive the death of the plaintiff. See eg, *Fitch v Voit*,[4] (because the right of privacy is a personal right, family members had no privacy claim against a newspaper that published a photograph of their deceased relative, taken when she was dying of cancer); *Justice v Belo Broadcasting Corpn*,[5] adopting majority view that 'deceased's relatives may not maintain an action for invasion of privacy, either based upon their own privacy interests or as a representative for the deceased, where the alleged invasion was directed primarily at the deceased';[6] but see *Reid v Pierce County*,[7] defendants' conduct in passing around autopsy photographs was sufficiently egregious that the families of the deceased could maintain their own actions for invasion of privacy.

Only human beings, and not corporations, partnerships, or unincorporated associations, may bring a cause of action for disclosure of private facts.[8]

C   False light

1   *Introduction*

30.40   The tort of 'false light' involves the publication either of a false statement, or of a literally true statement presented in such a manner as to convey to the public a false or misleading factual impression, that a reasonable person would find highly offensive.[9] Although false light is classified as a form of invasion of privacy, it is closely related to the tort of defamation (which generally is defined as the publication of false facts causing reputational injury). Often, a plaintiff who asserts a false light claim also asserts a defamation cause of action. The key distinction is that false light plaintiffs seek compensation for, and must prove, emotional distress rather than injury to reputation.

The false light cause of action is recognised at common law by about thirty States, the most notable of which is California.[10] The state of Rhode Island provides for false light claims by statute. About ten States, however, including New York,[11] Ohio, Texas, Virginia, and most recently Minnesota,[12] have

---

4   624 So 2d 542 (Ala Sup Ct 1993).
5   472 F Supp 145 (ND Tex 1979).
6   Restatement (Second) of Torts, s 652I & cmts a, b.
7   961 P2d 333 (Wash Sup Ct 1998).
8   Restatement (Second) of Torts, s 652I cmt c.
9   The Restatement (Second) of Torts, s 652E provides: One who gives publicity to a matter concerning another that places the other before the public in a false light is subject to liability to the other for invasion of his privacy, if (a) the false light in which the other was placed would be highly offensive to a reasonable person, and (b) the actor had knowledge of or acted in reckless disregard as to the falsity of the publicised matter and the false light in which the other would be placed.
10   See *Gill v Curtis Publishing Co*, 38 Cal 2d 273, 239 P2d 630 (Cal Sup Ct 1952).
11   Although New York courts once recognised false light claims, the New York Court of Appeals has made it clear that New York 'has no common law of privacy' and that the New York's privacy statute (Civil Rights Law, ss 50–51) does not provide for false light actions. *Howell v New York Post Co*, 596 NYS2d 350 (NY Ct App 1993).
12   *Lake v Wal-Mart Stores, Inc*, 582 NW2d 231 (Minn Sup Ct 1998).

rejected the tort of false light. The courts of the remaining States have yet to clearly indicate a position on whether the false light action is cognisable.

Elements of false light

30.41   There are five elements that a plaintiff must prove if asserting a false light claim: (i) public disclosure; (ii) falsity; (iii) identification of the plaintiff; (iv) offensiveness; and (v) fault.

(i)   Public disclosure: the publicised material must be communicated to the public, not merely to a private group of people. Thirty mailings to twenty people has been held to be sufficient public disclosure, *Kinsey v Macur*.[13] Distribution of a report to a small group of individuals with a professional interest in the matter was not public disclosure, *Cabanas v Gloodt Associates*.[14]

(ii)   Falsity: the published depiction must be false, not merely unflattering. Generally, the falsity must be substantial and material. Statement that a lawsuit was instituted against plaintiff, when in fact a lawsuit was only considered but never commenced, contained inaccuracies 'too minor to be actionable,' *Rinsley v Brandt*.[15]
The falsity, however, need not be defamatory.

(iii)   Identification of the plaintiff: as with defamation claims, the publication must be about, or 'of and concerning,' the particular plaintiff. The publication need not specifically name the plaintiff; it must, however, 'be reasonably capable of being understood as singling out, or pointing to, the plaintiff,' *Aroonsakul v Shannon*.[16]
Groups or organisations cannot bring a false light claim. When a group is placed in a false light, an individual member cannot bring a false light claim either, unless that group is so small that any publicity reasonably can be understood as referring to that individual, or circumstances surrounding the publicity give rise to the reasonable conclusion that there is particular reference to that individual.
Individual hunters were not placed in a false light because television broadcast referred to Michigan hunters as a group, *Michigan United Conservation Clubs v CBS News*.[17]

Similarly, a corporation cannot bring a false light action because such an entity, as a matter of law, cannot experience emotional distress.

(iv)   Offensiveness: the false light in which the plaintiff was placed must be 'highly offensive to a reasonable person'; 'hypersensitive' persons cannot recover for their subjective responses.
Statements made by a radio host that the plaintiff must have married his wife, who suffered from the Elephant Man's disease, in a shotgun wedding and that his wife and son had abnormally large heads, were sufficiently offensive to support a false light action, *Kolegas v Heftel Broadcasting Corpn*.[18]
Newspaper publication of false obituary, retracted the following day, was not offensive to a reasonable person, *Thomason v Times-Journal, Inc*.[19]

13   165 Cal Rptr 608 (Cal Ct App 1980).
14   942 F Supp 1295, 1310 (ED Cal 1996).
15   700 F2d 1304 (10th Cir 1983).
16   664 NE2d 1094 (Ill App Ct 1996).
17   485 F Supp 893 (WD Mich 1980).
18   607 NE2d 201 (Ill Sup Ct 1992).
19   379 SE2d 551 (Ga Ct App 1989).

(v)   Fault: actual malice v negligence: States are divided on the level of fault required to subject a publisher to liability for false light invasion of privacy. Most States follow the Restatement of Torts, which requires that the defendant publish the falsity with 'actual malice'; that is, the 'actor had knowledge of or acted in reckless disregard as to the falsity of the publicised matter and the false light in which the other would be placed.'[20]

The 'actual malice' standard is stringent and difficult for a plaintiff to meet. Photograph of plaintiff mistakenly identifying him as a convicted murderer did not give rise to false light action because the newspaper did not act with actual malice, despite the failure to correct or retract the story after the plaintiff notified the newspaper of the error, *Colbert v World Pub Co.*[1]

The courts are divided as to whether the First Amendment requires States to apply the actual malice standard of fault. In *Time, Inc v Hill,*[2] the US Supreme Court held that material concerning 'matters of public interest' allegedly placing the plaintiff in a false light cannot give rise to liability unless it was published with 'actual malice.' This holding effectively extended to false light the same constitutional standards that the court applied to defamation in *New York Times Co v Sullivan.*[3] In the defamation case *Gertz v Robert Welch, Inc,*[4] however, the court held that although an 'actual malice' standard must be applied to claims by public figures, States are free to adopt a lower negligence standard of fault if the plaintiff is a private figure. The court has not since clarified whether the two-pronged *Gertz* standards apply in the context of false light. State courts have split as to which rule to follow.

False light categories

30.42   There are four generally recognised categories of false light claims:

(1)   Falsity/distortion: a story or photo conveys a false or misleading impression of the plaintiff because of the context in which it is placed, such as by a caption or story accompanying a photograph. Elderly newspaper carrier placed in a false light where her photograph accompanied a false story about a different elderly woman who allegedly quit her paper route because she became pregnant, *People's Bank and Trust v Globe Int'l Publishing, Inc.*[5]

(2)   Omission/Implication: an inaccurate overall impression is conveyed through the inclusion of selected true information and the omission of other information. Although a model had consented to publication of nude photographs in a relatively respectable sexually explicit magazine, Playboy, the photographs instead were published in a degrading magazine, Hustler. The model had a false light cause of action because her appearance in Hustler suggested that she was the type of person who willingly would appear in such a publication, *Douglass v Hustler Magazine, Inc.*[6]

---

20   Restatement (Second) of Torts, s 652E.
1   747 P2d 286 (Okla Sup Ct 1987).
2   385 US 374 (1967).
3   376 US 254 (1964).
4   418 US 323 (1974).
5   978 F2d 1065 (8th Cir 1992).
6   769 F2d 1128 (7th Cir 1985).

The omission of facts will not lead to liability, however, so long as the facts included, and the reasonable inferences from those facts, are substantially true, *Machleder v Diaz*.[7]

(3) Embellishment: False information is added to an otherwise true news story. Newspaper feature story, which contained several false statements about the impact upon the plaintiff's family of the death of the father, gave rise to a successful false light action, *Cantrell v Forest City Publishing Co*.[8]

(4) Fictionalisation: A story or dramatisation falsely depicts a character reasonably identifiable as the plaintiff. This category of false light claims is difficult to prove because courts generally afford defendants literary licence. In particular, fictional accounts of 'public figures' or 'matters of public concern' usually are protected, on the theory that 'dramatic interpretation of events and dialogue filled with rhetorical flourishes' rarely satisfy an 'actual malice' standard of fault – that is, a standard requiring that defendants publish with conscious awareness of falsity, or with reckless disregard as to falsity.[9] Further, the material will be protected if a reasonable viewer would understand the account as purely fictional and not as a presentation of fact.

False light v defamation

30.43 As discussed earlier, false light and defamation are similar torts, but are designed to remedy different wrongs: emotional harm and reputational injury. Many States, including California, allow a plaintiff to recover either for false light or defamation, but not both, in connection with the same publication. Additionally, the similarity of the two causes of action has led courts to apply to false light claims many of the same procedural requirements (such as statutes of limitation) and substantive defences that apply to defamation claims.

Procedural aspects

30.44 (1) Burden of proof: courts have disagreed about whether the plaintiff must prove the elements of false light by 'preponderance of the evidence' or by 'clear and convincing evidence.' Most States have not resolved this issue.

(2) Statutes of limitation: statutes of limitation for false light actions range from one year to four years, with most States adopting a one- or two-year limit.

(3) Retraction statutes: a few States, including California, require a plaintiff to provide notice to or demand retraction by the defendant of the false or misleading statement. A few States provide for mitigation of damages if the publicised matter is retracted, either after a demand or voluntarily.

---

7   801 F2d 46, 55 (2d Cir 1986).
8   419 US 245 (1974).
9   *Partington v Bugliosi*, 56 F3d 1147 (9th Cir 1995).

2   Defences

30.45   In general, courts will allow defendants in a false light action to use any defences that would be available in a defamation action.

Truth: substantial truth constitutes an absolute defence to false light claims. Photograph of automobile accident and accompanying article explaining that the driver had been charged with drunk driving three weeks earlier did not constitute false light because they were accurate, despite possible inference that drunk driving caused this accident, *Prescott v Bay St Louis Newspapers*.[10]

Lack of actual malice: as already noted, a defendant can argue in certain courts that he did not publish with the requisite actual malice.

Newsworthiness: a small number of jurisdictions go beyond the constitutional requirements and provide a complete defence for publications involving matters of legitimate public interest;[11] therefore, a false light claim would not be actionable even if there was 'actual malice.'

Appearance in public: some courts have dismissed false light suits when they involve photographs taken in a public place or any other place in which the plaintiff does not have a reasonable expectation of privacy. Generally, these cases involve situations in which the false context is not provided by the defendant, but is inherent in the plaintiff's appearance in the public place. A newspaper did not invade the plaintiff's privacy, where the plaintiff was included in a photograph of people in line to collect unemployment benefits, even though he was there only to act as a translator, *Cefalu v Globe Newspaper Co*.[12]

Not presented as fact: in order for a plaintiff to state a false light claim, the hypothetical 'reasonable reader' must be able to construe the publicised material as conveying a statement of fact. Therefore, publishers can defend against a false light claim by showing that the publication instead was presented as opinion, critique, parody or pure fiction. A pornographic magazine that published a critical column about an anti-pornography activist was not liable for false light invasion because the column constituted the magazine's opinion: *Leidholdt v LFP, Inc*.[13] False light action dismissed because a picture and caption in a school yearbook 'Funny Pages' implying that the plaintiff had made sexual propositions to another teacher was clearly understood as humour and parody: *Salek v Passaic Collegiate School*.[14] This defence was rejected, however, in the case of the allegedly pregnant elderly newspaper carrier discussed above: *People's Bank and Trust v Globe Intern Pub*.[15] Although the court acknowledged that the notion of a hundred-year-old woman becoming pregnant was improbable, it found that the article's implication of sexual impropriety was subject to reasonable belief.

Overlap with defamation claim: some States, including California, provide

---

10   497 So 2d 77 (Miss Sup Ct 1986).
11   See, eg, *Hagler v Democrat-News, Inc*, 699 SW2d 96 (Mo Ct App 1985) (publication describing police activity cannot give rise to a false light claim because it concerns a matter of public interest).
12   391 NE2d 935 (Mass App Ct 1979).
13   860 F2d 890 (9th Cir 1988).
14   605 A2d 276 (NJ Super Ct App Div 1992).
15   978 F2d 1065 (8th Cir 1992).

for dismissal of a false light claim if the plaintiff also has alleged a defamation action on the same facts.

Miscellaneous common law and statutory defences: Several common law and statutory defences, generally applicable to most publication torts, often apply to false light claims. For example, California's absolute statutory privilege for statements made in official proceedings will apply to false light claims. Although the courts of many States have not addressed the issue of such privileges in the false light context, it is likely that a court would apply the same defences available in defamation claims.

Consent: permission to use the photograph or written statement, in the manner in which it is presented, constitutes a complete defence.

Remedies

30.46　The basic remedy is monetary damages to compensate the victim for emotional distress resulting from the publication. In general, States permit the awarding of punitive damages, in addition to compensatory damages, to punish the defendant for acting with actual malice. Damage awards for successful false light actions vary considerably.

An elderly newspaper carrier falsely accused of being pregnant was awarded $1 million in compensatory and punitive damages: *Mitchell v Globe Int'l Publishing, Inc.*[16]

$1 million compensatory damages awarded to a woman placed in a false light by the publication of nude photos, along with a caption implying she was a lesbian, deemed excessive, but court suggested that $100,000 punitive damage award fixed by lower court was insufficient to deter conduct, *Douglass v Hustler Magazine, Inc.*[17]

$100 nominal damage award sufficient because plaintiff did not show any specific injury or emotional distress: *Bowling v Missionary Servants of Most Holy Trinity.*[18]

D　Personality and publicity

1　Introduction

30.47　The right of publicity is a subset of the right of privacy that limits unauthorised uses of the name, likeness, and other aspects of the identity of individuals. Most journalistic uses of identity are exempt from regulation. Thus, although a cereal company cannot feature a person's picture (be it a celebrity or a non-celebrity) on a box of corn flakes without consent, a newspaper could publish that same picture to illustrate an article about the person without violating their right of publicity.

Right of publicity laws serve two distinct purposes. First, they protect persons from the anguish and loss of dignity that may arise from the unauthorised use of their identity. Secondly, they protect the property interest that persons, especially celebrities, possess in his or her identities.

16　817 F Supp 72 (WD Ark 1993).
17　769 F2d 1128, 1143-45 (7th Cir 1985).
18　20 Med L Rptr 1496 (6th Cir 1992).

2 Sources of right of publicity: State and federal laws

State laws

30.48 Most States protect the right of publicity through the common law, a statute, or both. States that are major media centers, such as California and New York, tend to have the most highly developed right of publicity laws. Although several less prominent States have no specific laws that address the right of publicity, courts in these states almost certainly would recognise a common law right if they were presented with an appropriate case.

The scope of the right of publicity varies from State to State. In the case of a national publication, any State might have jurisdiction over a dispute. Savvy plaintiffs may attempt to file suit in the forum with the broadest applicable right of publicity. That forum often is California, which protects the right of publicity both through a statute and the common law.

The California statute provides in relevant part that: 'Any person who knowingly uses another's name, voice, signature, photograph, or likeness, in any manner, . . . for purposes of advertising or selling, . . . without such person's prior consent . . . shall be liable for any damages sustained by the person or persons injured as a result thereof.'[19] Punitive damages may also be awarded, and attorneys' fees are available to the prevailing party. (This differs from the basic rule in US litigation, under which each side, win or lose, must pay its own attorneys' fees.)

To prevail on the common law claim in California (and other jurisdictions that have adopted a similar formulation), the plaintiff must prove: (1) the defendant's use of the plaintiff's identity; (2) appropriation of the plaintiff's identity to the defendant's advantage, commercial or otherwise; (3) lack of consent; and (4) resulting injury.[20] A key difference between California's common law and statutory formulations is that the 'identity' protected by common law covers more than the specific elements of identity protected by statute.

Federal law

30.49 The federal Lanham Act – which prohibits the use in commerce of, inter alia, symbols or devices likely to deceive consumers as to the sponsorship of goods or services by another person[1]– has been applied to those right of publicity claims styled as false endorsement claims. Simply stated, 'false endorsement' means that the person portrayed did not consent to endorse the product concerned. The Lanham Act, therefore, prevents 'the unauthorised use of a celebrity's identity . . . [through] the misuse of a trademark, ie, a symbol or device such as a visual likeness, vocal imitation, or other uniquely distinguishing characteristic, which is likely to confuse consumers as to the plaintiff's sponsorship or approval of the product,' *Waits v Frito-Lay, Inc.*[2] Because the Lanham Act is a federal statute, it applies in all States.

---

19 Cal Civ Code, s 3344.
20 *Eastwood v Superior Court*, 149 Cal App 3d 409, 417, 198 Cal Rptr 342 (Cal Ct App 1983).
1   15 USC s 1125(a).
2   978 F2d 1093, 1106-10 (9th Cir 1992).

3 Protected features of identity

30.50 Controversy sometimes arises over whether particular elements of a person's identity are protected. An advertiser may not actually use a person's name or photograph, but still may evoke that person's identity through other means. The trend among courts, especially when interpreting the common law, is to permit celebrities to bring suit whenever an advertisement evokes thoughts of the celebrity. In all of the following cases, the court found that a celebrity could bring suit under at least one State or federal right of publicity law:

Robots: an advertisement for an electronics company parodied a television game show hostess, Vanna White, by depicting a robot wearing a dress like she typically wore on a set that resembled the set of her show, 'Wheel of Fortune.'[3] The hostess won about $400,000 in damages. In a similar case, a heavy actor and a thinner actor, who had appeared in the television comedy 'Cheers,' objected to the use of a heavy robot and a thinner robot in airport bars modeled upon the television show's set.[4]

Lookalikes: the designer Christian Dior used a Jacqueline Onassis lookalike, who wore a pillbox hat, pearls, and otherwise imitated Onassis's appearance, in an advertisement for Dior products.[5]

Soundalikes: Frito-Lay hired a singer whose voice closely resembled singer Tom Waits' unusual, gravelly tones to sing its jingle in Waits' style. Waits won $2.5 million in compensatory damages, punitive damages, and attorneys fees.[6] After the singer Bette Midler declined to sing for a car commercial a song that she had popularised, the advertising agency hired one of Midler's back-up singers to perform the song, and told her to sound as much like Midler as possible.[7] A jury awarded Midler $400,000 in damages.[8]

Distinctive car: a cigarette company depicted an automobile racer's car – altered, but still recognisable as the racer's – in a television commercial. The racer appeared in the photograph, but his features were not visible.[9]

Retired athlete's stance, skin colour, number: a beer company advertisement included an illustration that copied a decades-old photograph of a retired baseball pitcher. The court permitted the pitcher to have a jury determine whether he was recognisable, given the distinctiveness of the pitcher's stance, and the additional facts that the illustration (1) matched his skin tone, and (2) included a uniform number similar to the pitcher's.[10]

Catch phrases/nicknames/puns: Here's Johnny Portable Toilets evoked talkshow host Johnny Carson by using the phrase, 'Here's Johnny,' that Carson's sidekick used to introduce him.[11] Pornography magazine evoked

---

3 *White v Samsung Electronics America, Inc* 971 F2d 1395 (9th Cir 1992).
4 *Wendt v Host Int'l, Inc*, 125 F3d 806 (9th Cir 1997).
5 *Onassis v Christian Dior-New York, Inc*, 472 NYS2d 254 (NY Sup Ct 1984), aff'd, 488 NS2d 943 (NY App Div 1985).
6 *Waits v Frito-Lay*, 978 F2d 1093 (9th Cir 1992).
7 *Midler v Ford Motor Co*, 849 F2d 460 (9th Cir 1988).
8 *Midler v Young & Rubicam, Inc* 1991 US App LEXIS 22641 (9th Cir 1991).
9 *Motschenbacher v RJ Reynolds Tobacco Co*, 498 F2d 821 (9th Cir 1974).
10 *Newcombe v Adolph Coors Co*, 157 F3d 686 (9th Cir 1998).
11 *Carson v Here's Johnny Portable Toilets, Inc*, 698 F2d 831 (6th Cir 1983).

boxer Muhammad Ali by using Ali's nickname, 'The Greatest,' to refer to a drawing of a nude black boxer.[12] Department store evoked musician Don Henley through advertisement featuring a man wearing a henley shirt; text included 'This is Don,' 'This is Don's henley' and 'Don loves his henley'.[13]

Abandoned former name: before a car commercial asked a trivia question about the car, it asked a trivia question about basketball, and printed the answer 'Lew Alcindor', the former name of the basketball star Kareem Abdul-Jabbar. At the time of the suit, Mr Abdul-Jabbar had not used the name 'Lew Alcindor' commercially for more than 10 years.[14]

As the above cases demonstrate, advertisements and other works that evoke virtually any aspect of a celebrity's persona may result in liability. Several of the cases have been highly controversial. The Vanna White and 'Cheers' robot cases, for example, yielded stinging dissents from a judge concerned about their impact on free expression.[15] Thus far, however, neither the Supreme Court nor State legislatures have acted to scale back the law.

4   Persons who may claim right of publicity

30.51   Persons who may challenge a violation of the right of publicity include the person whose identity was infringed and, if the applicable law permits, an assignee, an exclusive licensee, or the heir of the right of publicity. Most States that protect the right of publicity provide that after a person dies, the right may be enforced by heirs. Of these States, most limit the term of the right's survivability. In California, for example, the term is 70 years. In a minority of States, including New York, the right of publicity ends at death.

5   Remedies

30.52   Successful plaintiffs in right of publicity suits generally may obtain both injunctive relief to bar future use of their identity, and damages for past harm.

Injunctions

30.53   As in other actions regarding rights to intellectual property, injunctions are a common form of relief, and courts usually do not apply the general First Amendment bar on prior restraints. The division of the US into many different jurisdictions, however, may frustrate plaintiffs who seek a nationwide injunction. Some courts may enjoin distribution only in their own State.[16] Even if a court does order a nationwide injunction, it may permit a defendant to exclude certain States if the defendant can show that the activity is legal in those States.[17]

---

12 *Ali v Playgirl, Inc*, 447 F Supp 723 (SDNY 1978).
13 *Henley v Dillard Department Stores*, 46 F Supp 2d 587 (ND Tex 1999).
14 *Abdul-Jabbar v General Motors Corpn*, 85 F3d 407 (9th Cir 1996).
15 See *White*, 989 F2d 1512 (9th Cir 1993) (denial of motion for rehearing) (Kozinski, J, dissenting); *Wendt*, 197 F3d 1284 (9th Cir 1999) (denial of motion for rehearing) (Kozinski, J, dissenting).
16 Eg, *Shamsky v Garan, Inc*, 632 NYS2d 930 (NY Sup Ct 1995).
17 Eg, *Carson v Here's Johnny Portable Toilets, Inc* 810 F2d 104 (6th Cir 1987).

Damages

30.54 Damages for a right of publicity claim are determined by the finder of fact. To the extent that plaintiffs vindicate their dignitary rights in controlling the use of their identity, there is no commonly accepted means of calculating damages (much like the situation with pain and suffering damages in personal injury cases). If the use is particularly offensive, the jury might award enormous damages. Judges, however, frequently reduce such awards substantially. In one case a jury awarded a writer $7 million in compensatory damages after a magazine misidentified her as a participant in an orgy. An appellate court, which dismissed the case on other grounds, stated that such an award was grossly excessive, and noted that in similar cases awards of less than $50,000 were found appropriate.[18]

To the extent that plaintiffs vindicate their property interest in their identity, damages are calculated based on the commercial value of the persona. In an age of multi-million dollar endorsement deals for top celebrities, the damages for the unauthorised use of their identities can be substantial.[19]

A successful plaintiff also may be entitled to punitive damages if the defendant's conduct was willful or malicious. Several States, including California, also permit recovery of reasonable attorneys' fees, which could total hundreds of thousands of dollars. All told, liability could amount to millions of dollars. See *Waits v Frito-Lay*,[20] permitting an award of $2.5 million for use of a soundalike in a commercial; *Hoffman v Capital Cities/ABC, Inc*,[1] judge awarded actor Dustin Hoffman $3 million in compensatory and punitive damages, plus $270,000 in attorney's fees, from a magazine that altered an old photograph of Hoffman from the film 'Tootsie' to make it appear he was wearing contemporary designer clothing.

6 Defences

Newsworthiness

30.55 If the law permitted persons to control *all* uses of their identities, the First Amendment would be gutted and journalism would be crippled. A newsworthiness privilege prevents that result. Thus a newspaper can, for example, illustrate an article about a celebrity's wedding with a photograph of the celebrity. Some courts, however, have taken a narrow view of what is newsworthy. In the Dustin Hoffman case, for example, the trial court judge refused to extend this privilege to a magazine article that featured old photographs of celebrities altered to make it appear they were wearing contemporary fashions. The judge held that the use of Dustin Hoffman's 'famous face bears no reasonable (or other) relationship to the fashions themselves, but only serves to attract attention to the magazine.'[2] As of this writing the magazine's lawyers were appealing that decision to the US Court

---

18 *Lerman v Flynt Distributing Co*, 745 F2d 123, 141–42 (2d Cir 1984).
19 Some amount of damages is presumed to exist even for an obscure plaintiff. To accommodate the difficulty of showing the value of a non-celebrity persona, California has adopted statutory minimum damages of $750, Cal Civ Code s 3344(a).
20 978 F2d 1093 (9th Cir 1992) .
1 33 F Supp 2d 867 (CD Cal 1999).
2 *Hoffman*, 33 F Supp 2d at 875.

of Appeals, Ninth Circuit. See also *Titan Sports, Inc v Comics World Corpn*,[3] fact finder should determine whether oversized photographs of professional wrestlers stapled into magazine primarily were protected speech, or used the likenesses for purposes of trade; uses not privileged as a matter of law. Once a newsworthy use has been made of a celebrity's image, the publication can feature the image in advertising for the publication. The defence may even apply where the advertisement is carried on an item that may be considered a product independent of the newspaper. In a case brought by the American football quarterback Joe Montana, a newspaper published a photograph of Montana, taken during the 1990 Super Bowl, to accompany a story about the game. The newspaper then sold posters of the photograph that bore the newspaper's logo. The court found that the use of the photograph for the poster was incidental to its original newsworthy use, and thus Montana's right of publicity was not infringed.[4] A media outlet would likely lose this defence, however, if its advertisement affirmatively and falsely suggested that the celebrity endorsed the outlet.

Political figures are especially vulnerable to the newsworthiness defence. The First Amendment is particularly solicitous of speech on political matters, and thus the use of a political figure's persona may be protected even in a commercial context, especially if the publication contains some political message.

The newsworthiness privilege, although strong, is not absolute. In one case, the Supreme Court ruled that a television company violated the publicity rights of a man who performed a 'human cannonball' act because it aired his entire 15-second act and thus sapped its commercial value.[5] Courts also have ruled that the media are not immune from right of publicity laws if their purported news publications are in fact calculated falsehoods.[6] *Hoffman*,[7] fabricated image of actor's head superimposed on another's body not entitled to First Amendment protection; but see *Messenger v Gruner + Jahr Printing & Publishing*,[8] under New York law, newsworthiness privilege generally applies to pictures used to illustrate articles of public concern, even if juxtaposition creates false impression about the person in the picture. Moreover, an advertiser generally may not override the right of publicity by surrounding its advertising with information on matters of public interest. *Beverley v Choices Women's Medical Center, Inc*,[9] a medical facility's promotional calendar included text and photos that celebrated the women's movement; facility held liable for $75,000 for including plaintiff's photograph without her consent.

Art

30.56 Like the newsworthiness privilege, the First Amendment protection for novels and movies generally outweighs the publicity rights of persons whose identities are incorporated within. Eg, *Rogers v Grimaldi*,[10] title of Fellini film 'Ginger and Fred,' about dancers who imitated Ginger Rogers

---

3   870 F2d 85, 87 (2d Cir 1989).
4   *Montana v San Jose Mercury News, Inc*, 40 Cal Rptr 2d 639 (Cal Ct App 1995).
5   *Zacchini v Scripps-Howard Broadcasting Co*, 433 US 562 (1977).
6   *Eastwood v Superior Court*, 149 Cal App 3d 409, 425, 198 Cal Rptr 342 (1983).
7   33 F Supp 2d at 875.
8   208 F3d 122 (2d Cir 2000).
9   78 NY2d 745 (NY Ct App 1991).
10 875 F2d 994 (2d Cir 1989) .

and Fred Astaire, did not violate Rogers' publicity rights under State or federal law; *DeClemente v Columbia Pictures Indus*,[11] no violation where plaintiff claimed that film 'The Karate Kid' resembled his life.

Parody

30.57   When the commercial use of a person's identity occurs in a parody, the First Amendment may bar liability for what otherwise would be a violation of the right of publicity. Support for this principle comes from a copyright case, *Campbell v Acuff-Rose Music, Inc*, in which the Supreme Court ruled that a rap parody of a song (Roy Orbison's 'Oh Pretty Woman') might be entitled to the Copyright Act's fair use defence.[12] The *Campbell* case and its progeny suggest that First Amendment protection is more likely when: (1) the parody makes fun of the celebrity, rather than uses the celebrity's image to make fun of another target; and (2) the parody itself is sold, rather than used to promote sales of other goods or services. These distinctions help explain why Samsung could not use a Vanna White robot to sell videocassette recorders, but a company could sell baseball cards that lampooned the players.[13]

Incidental use

30.58   If a person's identity appears in a work briefly and insignificantly, that person probably will not have a cause of action for violation of his or her right of publicity. This doctrine recognises the practical difficulties involved in obtaining consents from every person whose image might appear in a commercial use, and that the fundamental purpose of these laws is to protect blatant abuses of a person's right to control the use of his or her identity. See *Preston v Martin Bregman Productions, Inc*,[14] a prostitute who was depicted for just several seconds during opening credits of a feature film could not claim a violation of her right of publicity.

First sale doctrine

30.59   The first sale doctrine may also provide a defence to certain claimed violations of the right of publicity. The doctrine provides that once the holder of a right sells an item bearing the holder's intellectual property (ie, a patented, trademarked or copyrighted work), that item may be resold without regard to the original rightholder's wishes. Thus, once a publisher sells a book to a consumer, it has no further say about the resale of that book by a second hand bookstore, despite the copyright it retains in the text. In the right of publicity context, the first sale doctrine was applied to protect a defendant who purchased sports trading cards that featured pictures of plaintiffs, mounted them with plaques and clocks produced by the defendant, and sold the resulting product to consumers.[15]

---

11   860 F Supp 30 (EDNY 1994).
12   510 US 569 (1994).
13   *Cardtoons, LC v Major League Baseball Players Assoc*, 95 F3d 959 (10th Cir 1996).
14   765 F Supp 116 (SDNY 1991).
15   *Allison v Vintage Sports Plaques*, 136 F3d 1443 (11th Cir 1998).

APPENDIX

Convention for the Protection of Human Rights and Fundamental Freedoms

Rome, 4.XI.1950

The governments signatory hereto, being members of the Council of Europe;

Considering the Universal Declaration of Human Rights proclaimed by the General Assembly of the United Nations on 10th December 1948;

Considering that this Declaration aims at securing the universal and effective recognition and observance of the Rights therein declared;

Considering that the aim of the Council of Europe is the achievement of greater unity between its members and that one of the methods by which that aim is to be pursued is the maintenance and further realisation of human rights and fundamental freedoms; Reaffirming their profound belief in those fundamental freedoms which are the foundation of justice and peace in the world and are best maintained on the one hand by an effective political democracy and on the other by a common understanding and observance of the human rights upon which they depend;

Being resolved, as the governments of European countries which are like-minded and have a common heritage of political traditions, ideals, freedom and the rule of law, to take the first steps for the collective enforcement of certain of the rights stated in the Universal Declaration,

Have agreed as follows:

Notes
1   Headings added according to the provisions of Protocol No 11 (ETS No 155).

Article 1[1] – Obligation to respect human rights

The High Contracting Parties shall secure to everyone within their jurisdiction the rights and freedoms defined in Section 1 of this Convention.

SECTION 1[1] — RIGHTS AND FREEDOMS

Article 2[1] – Right to life

1   Everyone's right to life shall be protected by law. No one shall be deprived of his life intentionally save in the execution of a sentence of a court following his conviction of a crime for which this penalty is provided by law.

2   Deprivation of life shall not be regarded as inflicted in contravention of this article when it results from the use of force which is no more than absolutely necessary:

   a in defence of any person from unlawful violence;
   b in order to effect a lawful arrest or to prevent the escape of a person lawfully detained;
   c in action lawfully taken for the purpose of quelling a riot or insurrection.

Article 3[1] – **Prohibition of torture**

No one shall be subjected to torture or to inhuman or degrading treatment or punishment.

Article 4[1] – **Prohibition of slavery and forced labour**

1   No one shall be held in slavery or servitude.

2   No one shall be required to perform forced or compulsory labour.

3   For the purpose of this article the term 'forced or compulsory labour' shall not include:

    a   any work required to be done in the ordinary course of detention imposed according to the provisions of Article 5 of this Convention or during conditional release from such detention;

    b   any service of a military character or, in case of conscientious objectors in countries where they are recognised, service exacted instead of compulsory military service;

    c   any service exacted in case of an emergency or calamity threatening the life or well-being of the community;

    d   any work or service which forms part of normal civic obligations.

Article 5[1] – **Right to liberty and security**

1   Everyone has the right to liberty and security of person. No one shall be deprived of his liberty save in the following cases and in accordance with a procedure prescribed by law:

    a   the lawful detention of a person after conviction by a competent court;

    b   the lawful arrest or detention of a person for noncompliance with the lawful order of a court or in order to secure the fulfilment of any obligation prescribed by law;

    c   the lawful arrest or detention of a person effected for the purpose of bringing him before the competent legal authority on reasonable suspicion of having committed an offence or when it is reasonably considered necessary to prevent his committing an offence or fleeing after having done so;

    d   the detention of a minor by lawful order for the purpose of educational supervision or his lawful detention for the purpose of bringing him before the competent legal authority;

    e   the lawful detention of persons for the prevention of the spreading of infectious diseases, of persons of unsound mind, alcoholics or drug addicts or vagrants;

    f   the lawful arrest or detention of a person to prevent his effecting an unauthorised entry into the country or of a person against whom action is being taken with a view to deportation or extradition.

2   Everyone who is arrested shall be informed promptly, in a language which he understands, of the reasons for his arrest and of any charge against him.

3   Everyone arrested or detained in accordance with the provisions of paragraph 1.c of this article shall be brought promptly before a judge

or other officer authorised by law to exercise judicial power and shall be entitled to trial within a reasonable time or to release pending trial. Release may be conditioned by guarantees to appear for trial.

4   Everyone who is deprived of his liberty by arrest or detention shall be entitled to take proceedings by which the lawfulness of his detention shall be decided speedily by a court and his release ordered if the detention is not lawful.

5   Everyone who has been the victim of arrest or detention in contravention of the provisions of this article shall have an enforceable right to compensation.

Article 6[1] – Right to a fair trial

1   In the determination of his civil rights and obligations or of any criminal charge against him, everyone is entitled to a fair and public hearing within a reasonable time by an independent and impartial tribunal established by law. Judgment shall be pronounced publicly but the press and public may be excluded from all or part of the trial in the interests of morals, public order or national security in a democratic society, where the interests of juveniles or the protection of the private life of the parties so require, or to the extent strictly necessary in the opinion of the court in special circumstances where publicity would prejudice the interests of justice.

2   Everyone charged with a criminal offence shall be presumed innocent until proved guilty according to law.

3   Everyone charged with a criminal offence has the following minimum rights:

a   to be informed promptly, in a language which he understands and in detail, of the nature and cause of the accusation against him;

b   to have adequate time and facilities for the preparation of his defence;

c   to defend himself in person or through legal assistance of his own choosing or, if he has not sufficient means to pay for legal assistance, to be given it free when the interests of justice so require;

d   to examine or have examined witnesses against him and to obtain the attendance and examination of witnesses on his behalf under the same conditions as witnesses against him;

e   to have the free assistance of an interpreter if he cannot understand or speak the language used in court.

Article 7[1] – No punishment without law

1   No one shall be held guilty of any criminal offence on account of any act or omission which did not constitute a criminal offence under national or international law at the time when it was committed. Nor shall a heavier penalty be imposed than the one that was applicable at the time the criminal offence was committed.

2   This article shall not prejudice the trial and punishment of any person for any act or omission which, at the time when it was committed, was criminal according to the general principles of law recognised by civilised nations.

Article 8[1] – Right to respect for private and family life

1   Everyone has the right to respect for his private and family life, his home and his correspondence.

2   There shall be no interference by a public authority with the exercise of this right except such as is in accordance with the law and is necessary in a democratic society in the interests of national security, public safety or the economic well-being of the country, for the prevention of disorder or crime, for the protection of health or morals, or for the protection of the rights and freedoms of others.

Article 9[1] – Freedom of thought, conscience and religion

1   Everyone has the right to freedom of thought, conscience and religion; this right includes freedom to change his religion or belief and freedom, either alone or in community with others and in public or private, to manifest his religion or belief, in worship, teaching, practice and observance.

2   Freedom to manifest one's religion or beliefs shall be subject only to such limitations as are prescribed by law and are necessary in a democratic society in the interests of public safety, for the protection of public order, health or morals, or for the protection of the rights and freedoms of others.

Article 10[1] – Freedom of expression

1   Everyone has the right to freedom of expression. This right shall include freedom to hold opinions and to receive and impart information and ideas without interference by public authority and regardless of frontiers. This article shall not prevent States from requiring the licensing of broadcasting, television or cinema enterprises.

2   The exercise of these freedoms, since it carries with it duties and responsibilities, may be subject to such formalities, conditions, restrictions or penalties as are prescribed by law and are necessary in a democratic society, in the interests of national security, territorial integrity or public safety, for the prevention of disorder or crime, for the protection of health or morals, for the protection of the reputation or rights of others, for preventing the disclosure of information received in confidence, or for maintaining the authority and impartiality of the judiciary.

Article 11[1] – Freedom of assembly and association

1   Everyone has the right to freedom of peaceful assembly and to freedom of association with others, including the right to form and to join trade unions for the protection of his interests.

2   No restrictions shall be placed on the exercise of these rights other than such as are prescribed by law and are necessary in a democratic society in the interests of national security or public safety, for the prevention of disorder or crime, for the protection of health or morals or for the protection of the rights and freedoms of others. This article shall not prevent the imposition of lawful restrictions on the exercise of these rights by members of the armed forces, of the police or of the administration of the State.

Article 12¹ – Right to marry

Men and women of marriageable age have the right to marry and to found a family, according to the national laws governing the exercise of this right.

Article 13¹ – Right to an effective remedy

Everyone whose rights and freedoms as set forth in this Convention are violated shall have an effective remedy before a national authority notwithstanding that the violation has been committed by persons acting in an official capacity.

Article 14¹ – Prohibition of discrimination

The enjoyment of the rights and freedoms set forth in this Convention shall be secured without discrimination on any ground such as sex, race, colour, language, religion, political or other opinion, national or social origin, association with a national minority, property, birth or other status.

Article 15¹ – Derogation in time of emergency

1   In time of war or other public emergency threatening the life of the nation any High Contracting Party may take measures derogating from its obligations under this Convention to the extent strictly required by the exigencies of the situation, provided that such measures are not inconsistent with its other obligations under international law.

2   No derogation from Article 2, except in respect of deaths resulting from lawful acts of war, or from Articles 3, 4 (paragraph 1) and 7 shall be made under this provision.

3   Any High Contracting Party availing itself of this right of derogation shall keep the Secretary General of the Council of Europe fully informed of the measures which it has taken and the reasons therefor. It shall also inform the Secretary General of the Council of Europe when such measures have ceased to operate and the provisions of the Convention are again being fully executed.

Article 16¹ – Restrictions on political activity of aliens

Nothing in Articles 10, 11 and 14 shall be regarded as preventing the High Contracting Parties from imposing restrictions on the political activity of aliens.

Article 17¹ – Prohibition of abuse of rights

Nothing in this Convention may be interpreted as implying for any State, group or person any right to engage in any activity or perform any act aimed at the destruction of any of the rights and freedoms set forth herein or at their limitation to a greater extent than is provided for in the Convention.

Article 18¹ – Limitation on use of restrictions on rights

The restrictions permitted under this Convention to the said rights and freedoms shall not be applied for any purpose other than those for which they have been prescribed.

SECTION II[1] — EUROPEAN COURT
OF HUMAN RIGHTS

Article 19 – Establishment of the Court

To ensure the observance of the engagements undertaken by the High Contracting Parties in the Convention and the Protocols thereto, there shall be set up a European Court of Human Rights, hereinafter referred to as 'the Court'. It shall function on a permanent basis.

Article 20 – Number of judges

The Court shall consist of a number of judges equal to that of the High Contracting Parties.

Article 21 – Criteria for office

1   The judges shall be of high moral character and must either possess the qualifications required for appointment to high judicial office or be jurisconsults of recognised competence.

2   The judges shall sit on the Court in their individual capacity.

3   During their term of office the judges shall not engage in any activity which is incompatible with their independence, impartiality or with the demands of a full-time office; all questions arising from the application of this paragraph shall be decided by the Court.

Article 22 – Election of judges

1   The judges shall be elected by the Parliamentary Assembly with respect to each High Contracting Party by a majority of votes cast from a list of three candidates nominated by the High Contracting Party.

2   The same procedure shall be followed to complete the Court in the event of the accession of new High Contracting Parties and in filling casual vacancies.

Article 23 – Terms of office

1   The judges shall be elected for a period of six years. They may be re-elected. However, the terms of office of one-half of the judges elected at the first election shall expire at the end of three years.

2   The judges whose terms of office are to expire at the end of the initial period of three years shall be chosen by lot by the Secretary General of the Council of Europe immediately after their election.

3   In order to ensure that, as far as possible, the terms of office of one-half of the judges are renewed every three years, the Parliamentary Assembly may decide, before proceeding to any subsequent election, that the term or terms of office of one or more judges to be elected shall be for a period other than six years but not more than nine and not less than three years.

4   In cases where more than one term of office is involved and where the Parliamentary Assembly applies the preceding paragraph, the allocation of the terms of office shall be effected by a drawing of lots by the Secretary General of the Council of Europe immediately after the election.

5   A judge elected to replace a judge whose term of office has not expired shall hold office for the remainder of his predecessor's term.

6   The terms of office of judges shall expire when they reach the age of 70.

7   The judges shall hold office until replaced. They shall, however, continue to deal with such cases as they already have under consideration.

Article 24 – Dismissal

No judge may be dismissed from his office unless the other judges decide unanimously that he has ceased to fulfil the required conditions.

Article 25 – Registry and legal secretaries

The Court shall have a registry, the functions and organisation of which shall be laid down in the rules of the Court. The Court shall be assisted by legal secretaries.

Article 26 – Plenary Court

The plenary Court shall

   a   elect its President and one or two Vice-Presidents for a period of three years; they may be re-elected;

   b   set up Chambers, constituted for a fixed period of time;

   c   elect the Presidents of the Chambers of the Court; they may be re-elected;

   d   adopt the rules of the Court, and

   e   elect the Registrar and one or more Deputy Registrars.

Article 27 – Committees, Chambers and Grand Chamber

1   To consider cases brought before it, the Court shall sit in committees of three judges, in Chambers of seven judges and in a Grand Chamber of seventeen judges. The Court's Chambers shall set up committees for a fixed period of time.

2   There shall sit as an *ex officio* member of the Chamber and the Grand Chamber the judge elected in respect of the State Party concerned or, if there is none or if he is unable to sit, a person of its choice who shall sit in the capacity of judge.

3   The Grand Chamber shall also include the President of the Court, the Vice-Presidents, the Presidents of the Chambers and other judges chosen in accordance with the rules of the Court. When a case is referred to the Grand Chamber under Article 43, no judge from the Chamber which rendered the judgment shall sit in the Grand Chamber, with the exception of the President of the Chamber and the judge who sat in respect of the State Party concerned.

Article 28 – Declarations of inadmissibility by committees

A committee may, by a unanimous vote, declare inadmissible or strike out of' its list of cases an application submitted under Article 34 where such a decision can be taken without further examination. The decision shall be final.

Article 29 – Decisions by Chambers on admissibility and merits

1   If no decision is taken under Article 28, a Chamber shall decide on the admissibility and merits of individual applications submitted under Article 34.

2   A Chamber shall decide on the admissibility and merits of inter-State applications submitted under Article 33.

3   The decision on admissibility shall be taken separately unless the Court, in exceptional cases, decides otherwise.

Article 30 – Relinquishment of jurisdiction to the Grand Chamber

Where a case pending before a Chamber raises a serious question affecting the interpretation of the Convention or the protocols thereto, or where the resolution of a question before the Chamber might have a result inconsistent with a judgment previously delivered by the Court, the Chamber may, at any time before it has rendered its judgment, relinquish jurisdiction in favour of the Grand Chamber, unless one of the parties to the case objects.

Article 31 – Powers of the Grand Chamber

The Grand Chamber shall

a   determine applications submitted either under Article 33 or Article 34 when a Chamber has relinquished jurisdiction under Article 30 or when the case has been referred to it under Article 43; and

b   consider requests for advisory opinions submitted under Article 47.

Article 32 – Jurisdiction of the Court

1 The jurisdiction of the Court shall extend to all matters concerning the interpretation and application of the Convention and the protocols thereto which are referred to it as provided in Articles 33, 34 and 47.

2 In the event of dispute as to whether the Court has jurisdiction, the Court shall decide.

Article 33 – Inter-State cases

Any High Contracting Party may refer to the Court any alleged breach of the provisions of the Convention and the protocols thereto by another High Contracting Party.

Article 34 – Individual applications

The Court may receive applications from any person, non-governmental organisation or group of individuals claiming to be the victim of a violation by one of the High Contracting Parties ofthe rights set forth in the Convention or the protocols thereto. The High Contracting Parties undertake not to hinder in any way the effective exercise of this right.

Article 35 – Admissibility criteria

1   The Court may only deal with the matter after all domestic remedies have been exhausted, according to the generally recognised rules of international law, and within a period of six months from the date on which the final decision was taken.

2   The Court shall not deal with any application submitted under Article 34 that

a   is anonymous; or

b   is substantially the same as a matter that has already been examined by the Court or has already been submitted to another procedure of international investigation or settlement and contains no relevant new information.

3   The Court shall declare inadmissible any individual application submitted under Article 34 which it considers incompatible with the provisions of the Convention or the protocols thereto, manifestly ill-founded, or an abuse of the right of application.

4   The Court shall reject any application which it considers inadmissible under this Article. It may do so at any stage of the proceedings.

Article 36 – Third party intervention

1   In all cases before a Chamber of the Grand Chamber, a High Contracting Party one of whose nationals is an applicant shall have the right to submit written comments and to take part in hearings.

2   The President of the Court may, in the interest of the proper administration of justice, invite any High Contracting Party which is not a party to the proceedings or any person concerned who is not the applicant to submit written comments or take part in hearings.

Article 37 – Striking out applications

1   The Court may at any stage of the proceedings decide to strike an application out of its list of cases where the circumstances lead to the conclusion that

a   the applicant does not intend to pursue his application; or

b   the matter has been resolved; or

c   for any other reason established by the Court, it is no longer justified to continue the examination of the application.

However, the Court shall continue the examination of the application if respect for human rights as defined in the Convention and the protocols thereto so requires.

2   The Court may decide to restore an application to its list of cases if it considers that the circumstances justify such a course.

Article 38 – Examination of the case and friendly settlement proceedings

1   If the Court declares the application admissible, it shall

a   pursue the examination of the case, together with the representatives of the parties, and if need be, undertake an investigation, for the effective conduct of which the States concerned shall furnish all necessary facilities;

b place itself at the disposal of the parties concerned with a view to securing a friendly settlement of the matter on the basis of respect for human rights as defined in the Convention and the protocols thereto.

2 Proceedings conducted under paragraph 1.b shall be confidential.

Article 39 – Finding of a friendly settlement

If a friendly settlement is effected, the Court shall strike the case out of its list by means of a decision which shall be confined to a brief statement of the facts and of the solution reached.

Article 40 – Public hearings and access to documents

1 Hearings shall be in public unless the Court in exceptional circumstances decides otherwise.

2 Documents deposited with the Registrar shall be accessible to the public unless the President of the Court decides otherwise.

Article 41 – *Just satisfaction*

If the Court finds that there has been a violation of the Convention or the protocols thereto, and if the internal law of the High Contracting Party concerned allows only partial reparation to be made, the Court shall, if necessary, afford just satisfaction to the injured party.

Article 42 – Judgments of Chambers

Judgments of Chambers shall become final in accordance with the provisions of Article 44, paragraph 2.

Article 43 – Referral to the Grand Chamber

1 Within a period of three months from the date of the judgment of the Chamber, any party to the case may, in exceptional cases, request that the case be referred to the Grand Chamber.

2 A panel of five judges of the Grand Chamber shall accept the request if the case raises a serious question affecting the interpretation or application of the Convention or the protocols thereto, or a serious issue of general importance.

3 If the panel accepts the request, the Grand Chamber shall decide the case by means of a judgment.

Article 44 – Final judgments

1 The judgment of the Grand Chamber shall be final.

2 The judgment of a Chamber shall become final

a when the parties declare that they will not request that the case be referred to the Grand Chamber; or

b three months after the date of the judgment, if reference of the case to the Grand Chamber has not been requested; or

c when the panel of the Grand Chamber rejects the request to refer under Article 43.

3   The final judgment shall be published.

Article 45 – Reasons for judgments and decisions

1   Reasons shall be given for judgments as well as for decisions declaring applications admissible or inadmissible.

2   If a judgment does not represent, in whole or in part, the unanimous opinion of the judges, any judge shall be entitled to deliver a separate opinion.

Article 46 – Binding force and execution of judgments

1   The High Contracting Parties undertake to abide by the final judgment of the Court in any case to which they are parties.

2   The final judgment of the Court shall be transmitted to the Committee of Ministers, which shall supervise its execution.

Article 47 – Advisory opinions

1   The Court may, at the request of the Committee of Ministers, give advisory opinions on legal questions concerning the interpretation of the Convention and the protocols thereto.

2   Such opinions shall not deal with any question relating to the content or scope of the rights or freedoms defined in Section 1 of the Convention and the protocols thereto, or with any other question which the Court or the Committee of Ministers might have to consider in consequence of any such proceedings as could be instituted in accordance with the Convention.

3   Decisions of the Committee of Ministers to request an advisory opinion of the Court shall require a majority vote of the representatives entitled to sit on the Committee.

Article 48 – Advisory jurisdiction of the Court

The Court shall decide whether a request for an advisory opinion submitted by the Committee of Ministers is within its competence as defined in Article 47.

Article 49 – Reasons for advisory opinions

1   Reasons shall be given for advisory opinions of the Court.

2   If the advisory opinion does not represent, in whole or in part, the unanimous opinion of the judges, any judge shall be entitled to deliver a separate opinion.

3   Advisory opinions of the Court shall be communicated to the Committee of Ministers.

Article 50 – Expenditure on the Court

The expenditure on the Court shall be borne by the Council of Europe.

Article 51 – Privileges and immunities of judges

The judges shall be entitled, during the exercise of their functions, to the privileges and immunities provided for in Article 40 of the Statute of the Council of Europe and in the agreements made thereunder.

SECTION III[1,2] — MISCELLANEOUS PROVISIONS

Notes

1   Headings in this section added according to the provisions of Protocol No 11 (ETS No 155).
2   The articles of this section are renumbered according to the provisions of Protocol No 11 (ETS No 155).

Article 52[1] – Inquiries by the Secretary General

On receipt of a request from the Secretary General of the Council of Europe any High Contracting Party shall furnish an explanation of the manner in which its internal law ensures the effective implementation of any of the provisions of the Convention.

Article 53[1] – Safeguard for existing human rights

Nothing in this Convention shall be construed as limiting or derogating from any of the human rights and fundamental freedoms which may be ensured under the laws of any High Contracting Party or under any other agreement to which it is a Party.

Article 54[1] – Powers of the Committee of Ministers

Nothing in this Convention shall prejudice the powers conferred on the Committee of Ministers by the Statute of the Council of Europe.

Article 55[1] – Exclusion of other means of dispute settlement

The High Contracting Parties agree that, except by special agreement, they will not avail themselves of treaties, conventions or declarations. in force between them for the purpose of submitting, by way of petition, a dispute arising out of the interpretation or application of this Convention to a means of settlement other than those provided for in this Convention.

Article 56[1] – Territorial application

1[2]   Any State may at the time of its ratification or at any time thereafter declare by notification addressed to the Secretary General of the Council of Europe that the present Convention shall, subject to paragraph 4 of this Article, extend to all or any of the territories for whose international relations it is responsible.

2   The Convention shall extend to the territory or territories named in the notification as from the thirtieth day after the receipt of this notification by the Secretary General of the Council of Europe.

3   The provisions of this Convention shall be applied in such territories with due regard, however, to local requirements.

4[2]   Any State which has made a declaration in accordance with paragraph 1 of this article may at any time thereafter declare on behalf of one or more of the territories to which the declaration relates that it accepts the competence of the Court to receive applications from individuals, non-governmental organisations or groups of individuals as provided by Article 34 of the Convention.

Notes
1   Heading added according to the provisions of Protocol No 11 (ETS No 155).
2   Text amended according to the provisions of Protocol No 11 (ETS No 155).

Article 57[1] – Reservations

1   Any State may, when signing this Convention or when depositing its instrument of ratification, make a reservation in respect of any particular provision of the Convention to the extent that any law then in force in its territory is not in conformity with the provision. Reservations of a general character shall not be permitted under this article.

2   Any reservation made under this article shall contain a brief statement of the law concerned.

Article 58[1] – Denunciation

1   A High Contracting Party may denounce the present Convention only after the expiry of five years from the date on which it became a party to it and after six months' notice contained in a notification addressed to the Secretary General of the Council of Europe, who shall inform the other High Contracting Parties.

2   Such a denunciation shall not have the effect of releasing the High Contracting Party concerned from its obligations under this Convention in respect of any act which, being capable of constituting a violation of such obligations, may have been performed by it before the date at which the denunciation became effective.

3   Any High Contracting Party which shall cease to be a member of the Council of Europe shall cease to be a Party to this Convention under the same conditions.

4[2]   The Convention may be denounced in accordance with the provisions of the preceding paragraphs in respect of any territory to which it has been declared to extend under the terms of Article 56.

Notes
1   Heading added according to the provisions of Protocol No 11 (ETS No 155).
2   Text amended according to the provisions of Protocol No 11 (ETS No 155).

Article 59[1] – Signature and ratification

1   This Convention shall be open to the signature of the members of the Council of Europe. It shall be ratified. Ratifications shall be deposited with the Secretary General of the Council of Europe.

2   The present Convention shall come into force after the deposit of ten instruments of ratification.

3   As regards any signatory ratifying subsequently, the Convention shall come into force at the date of the deposit of its instrument of ratification.

4   The Secretary General of the Council of Europe shall notify all the members of the Council of Europe of the entry into force of the Convention, the names of the High Contracting Parties who have ratified it, and the deposit of all instruments of ratification which may be effected subsequently.

Done at Rome this 4th day of November 1950, in English and French, both texts being equally authentic, in a single copy which shall remain deposited in the archives of the Council of Europe. The Secretary General shall transmit certified copies to each of the signatories.

Protocol [No 1]
to the Convention for the Protection
of Human Rights and Fundamental Freedoms[1]

Paris, 20.III.1952

The governments signatory hereto, being members of the Council of Europe,

Being resolved to take steps to ensure the collective enforcement of certain rights and freedoms other than those already included in Section 1 of the Convention for the Protection of Human Rights and Fundamental Freedoms signed at Rome on 4 November 1950 (hereinafter referred to as 'the Convention'),

Have agreed as follows:

Article 1 – Protection of property

Every natural or legal person is entitled to the peaceful enjoyment of his possessions. No one shall be deprived of his possessions except in the public interest and subject to the conditions provided for by law and by the general principles of international law.

The preceding provisions shall not, however, in any way impair the right of a State to enforce such laws as it deems necessary to control the use of property in accordance with the general interest or to secure the payment of taxes or other contributions or penalties.

Notes
1   Headings of articles added and text amended according to the provisions of Protocol No 11 (ETS No 155) as from its entry into force.

Article 2 – Right to education

No person shall be denied the right to education. In the exercise of any functions which it assumes in relation to education and to teaching, the State shall respect the right of parents to ensure such education and teaching in conformity with their own religious and philosophical convictions.

Article 3 – Right to free elections

The High Contracting Parties undertake to hold free elections at reasonable intervals by secret ballot, under conditions which will ensure the free expression of the opinion of the people in the choice of the legislature.

Article 4[1] – Territorial application

Any High Contracting Party may at the time of signature or ratification or at any time thereafter communicate to the Secretary General of the Council of Europe a declaration stating the extent to which it undertakes that the provisions of the present Protocol shall apply to such of the territories for the international relations of which it is responsible as are named therein.

Any High Contracting Party which has communicated a declaration in virtue of the preceding paragraph may from time to time communicate a further declaration modifying the terms of any former declaration or terminating the application of the provisions of this Protocol in respect of any territory.

A declaration made in accordance with this article shall be deemed to have been made in accordance with paragraph 1 of Article 56 of the Convention.

Notes
1 Text amended according to the provisions of Protocol No 11 (ETS No 155).

Article 5 – Relationship to the Convention

As between the High Contracting Parties the provisions of Articles 1, 2, 3 and 4 of this Protocol shall be regarded as additional articles to the Convention and all the provisions of the Convention shall apply accordingly.

Article 6 – Signature and ratification

This Protocol shall be open for signature by the members of the Council of Europe, who are the signatories of the Convention; it shall be ratified at the same time as or after the ratification of the Convention. It shall enter into force after the deposit of ten instruments of ratification. As regards any signatory ratifying subsequently, the Protocol shall enter into force at the date of the deposit of its instrument of ratification.

The instruments of ratification shall be deposited with the Secretary General of the Council of Europe, who will notify all members of the names of those who have ratified.

Done at Paris on the 20th day of March 1952, in English and French, both texts being equally authentic, in a single copy which shall remain deposited in the archives of the Council of Europe. The Secretary General shall transmit certified copies to each of the signatory governments.

Protocol No 4 to the Convention for the Protection of Human Rights and Fundamental Freedoms securing certain rights and freedoms other than those already included in the Convention and in the First Protocol thereto[1]

Strasbourg, 16.IX.1963

Notes
1 Headings of articles added and text amended according to the provisions of Protocol No 11 (ETS No 155) as from its entry into force.

The governments signatory hereto, being members of the Council of Europe,

Being resolved to take steps to ensure the collective enforcement of certain rights and freedoms other than those already included in Section 1 of the Convention for the Protection of Human Rights and Fundamental Freedoms signed at Rome on 4th November 1950 (hereinafter referred to as the 'Convention') and in Articles 1 to 3 of the First Protocol to the Convention, signed at Paris on 20th March 1952,

Have agreed as follows:

Article 1 – Prohibition of imprisonment for debt

No one shall be deprived of his liberty merely on the ground of inability to fulfil a contractual obligation.

Article 2 – *Freedom of movement*

1   Everyone lawfully within the territory of a State shall, within that territory, have the right to liberty of movement and freedom to choose his residence.

2   Everyone shall be free to leave any country, including his own.

3   No restrictions shall be placed on the exercise of these rights other than such as are in accordance with law and are necessary in a democratic society in the interests of national security or public safety, for the maintenance of ordre public, for the prevention of crime, for the protection of health or morals, or for the protection of the rights and freedoms of others.

4   The rights set forth in paragraph 1 may also be subject, in particular areas, to restrictions imposed in accordance with law and justified by the public interest in a democratic society.

Article 3 – *Prohibition of expulsion of nationals*

1   No one shall be expelled, by means either of an individual or of a collective measure, from the territory of the State of which he is a national.

2   No one shall be deprived of the right to enter the territory of the state of which he is a national.

Article 4 – Prohibition of collective expulsion of aliens

Collective expulsion of aliens is prohibited.

Article 5 – *Territorial application*

1   Any High Contracting Party may, at the time of signature or ratification of this Protocol, or at any time thereafter, communicate to the Secretary General of the Council of Europe a declaration stating the extent to which it undertakes that the provisions of this Protocol shall apply to such of the territories for the international relations of which it is responsible as are named therein.

2   Any High Contracting Party which has communicated a declaration in virtue of the preceding paragraph may, from time to time, communicate a further declaration modifying the terms of any former declaration or terminating the application of the provisions of this Protocol in respect of any territory.

3[1]   A declaration made in accordance with this article shall be deemed to have been made in accordance with paragraph 1 of Article 56 of the Convention.

4   The territory of any State to which this Protocol applies by virtue of ratification or acceptance by that State, and each territory to which this Protocol is applied by virtue of a declaration by that State under this article, shall be treated as separate territories for the purpose of the references in Articles 2 and 3 to the territory of a State.

5[2]   Any State which has made a declaration in accordance with paragraph 1 or 2 of this Article may at any time thereafter declare on behalf of one or more of the territories to which the declaration relates that it accepts the competence of the Court to receive applications from individuals, non-governmental organisations or groups of individuals as provided in Article 34 of the Convention in respect of all or any of Articles 1 to 4 of this Protocol.

Notes
1   Text amended according to the provisions of Protocol No 11 (ETS No 155).
2   Text added according to the provisions of Protocol No 11 (ETS No 155).

Article 6[1] – *Relationship to the Convention*

As between the High Contracting Parties the provisions of Articles 1 to 5 of this Protocol shall be regarded as additional Articles to the Convention, and all the provisions of the Convention shall apply accordingly.

Notes
1   Text amended according to the provisions of Protocol No 11 (ETS No 155).

Article 7 – Signature and ratification

1   This Protocol shall be open for signature by the members of the Council of Europe who are the signatories of the Convention; it shall be ratified at the same time as or after the ratification of the Convention. It shall enter into force after the deposit of five instruments of ratification. As regards any signatory ratifying subsequently, the Protocol shall enter into force at the date of the deposit of its instrument of ratification.

2   The instruments of ratification shall be deposited with the Secretary General of the Council of Europe, who will notify all members of the names of those who have ratified.

In witness whereof the undersigned, being duly authorised thereto, have signed this Protocol.

Done at Strasbourg, this 16th day of September 1963, in English and in French, both texts being equally authoritative, in a single copy which shall remain deposited in the archives of the Council of Europe. The Secretary General shall transmit certified copies to each of the signatory states.

Protocol No 6 to the Convention for the Protection of Human Rights and Fundamental Freedoms concerning the Abolition of the Death Penalty[1]

Strasbourg, 28.IV.1983

The member States of the Council of Europe, signatory to this Protocol to the Convention for the Protection of Human Rights and Fundamental

Freedoms, signed at Rome on 4 November 1950 (hereinafter referred to as 'the Convention'),

Considering that the evolution that has occurred in several member States of the Council of Europe expresses a general tendency in favour of abolition of the death penalty;

Have agreed as follows:

Notes

1   Headings of articles added and text amended according to the provisions of Protocol No 11 (ETS No 155) as from its entry into force.

Article 1 – Abolition of the death penalty

The death penalty shall be abolished. No-one shall be condemned to such penalty or executed.

Article 2 – Death penalty in time of war

A State may make provision in its law for the death penalty in respect of acts committed in time of war or of imminent threat of war; such penalty shall be applied only in the instances laid down in the law and in accordance with its provisions. The State shall communicate to the Secretary General of the Council of Europe the relevant provisions of that law.

Article 3 – Prohibition of derogations

No derogation from the provisions of this Protocol shall be made under Article 15 of the Convention.

Article 4[1]

Prohibition of reservations

No reservation may be made under Article 57 of the Convention in respect of the provisions of this Protocol.

Notes

1   Text amended according to the provisions of Protocol No 11 (ETS No 155).

Article 5 – Territorial application

1   Any State may at the time of signature or when depositing its instrument of ratification, acceptance or approval, specify the territory or territories to which this Protocol shall apply.

2   Any State may at any later date, by a declaration addressed to the Secretary General of the Council of Europe, extend the application of this Protocol to any other territory specified in the declaration. In respect of such territory the Protocol shall enter into force on the first day of the month following the date of receipt of such declaration by the Secretary General.

3   Any declaration made under the two preceding paragraphs may, in respect of any territory specified in such declaration, be withdrawn by a notification addressed to the Secretary General. The withdrawal shall become effective on the first day of the month following the date of receipt of such notification by the Secretary General.

Article 6 – Relationship to the Convention

As between the States Parties the provisions of Articles 1 and 5 of this Protocol shall be regarded as additional articles to the Convention and all the provisions of the Convention shall apply accordingly.

Article 7 – Signature and ratification

The Protocol shall be open for signature by the member States of the Council of Europe, signatories to the Convention. It shall be subject to ratification, acceptance or approval. A member State of the Council of Europe may not ratify, accept or approve this Protocol unless it has, simultaneously or previously, ratified the Convention. Instruments of ratification, acceptance or approval shall be deposited with the Secretary General of the Council of Europe.

Article 8 – Entry into force

1   This Protocol shall enter into force on the first day of the month following the date on which five member States of the Council of Europe have expressed their consent to be bound by the Protocol in accordance with the provisions of Article 7.

2   In respect of any member State which subsequently expresses its consent to be bound by it, the Protocol shall enter into force on the first day of the month following the date of the deposit of the instrument of ratification, acceptance or approval.

Article 9 – Depositary functions

The Secretary General of the Council of Europe shall notify the member States of the Council of:

a any signature;

b the deposit of any instrument of ratification, acceptance or approval;

c any date of entry into force of this Protocol in accordance with Articles 5 and 8;

d any other act, notification or communication relating to this Protocol.

In witness whereof the undersigned, being duly authorised thereto, have signed this Protocol.

Done at Strasbourg, this 28th day of April 1983, in English and in French, both texts being equally authentic, in a single copy which shall be deposited in the archives of the Council of Europe. The Secretary General of the Council of Europe shall transmit certified copies to each member State of the Council of Europe.

Protocol No. 7
to the Convention for the Protection
of Human Rights and Fundamental Freedoms[1]

Strasbourg, 22.XI.1984

Notes

1   Headings of articles added and text amended according to the provisions of Protocol No 11 (ETS No 155) as from its entry into force.

The member States of the Council of Europe signatory hereto,

Being resolved to take further steps to ensure the collective enforcement of certain rights and freedoms by means of the Convention for the Protection of Human Rights and Fundamental Freedoms signed at Rome on 4 November 1950 (hereinafter referred to as 'the Convention'),

Have agreed as follows:

Article 1 – Procedural safeguards relating to expulsion of aliens

1   An alien lawfully resident in the territory of a State shall not be expelled therefrom except in pursuance of a decision reached in accordance with law and shall be allowed:

a   to submit reasons against his expulsion,

b   to have his case reviewed, and

c   to be represented for these purposes before the competent authority or a person or persons designated by that authority.

2   An alien may be expelled before the exercise of his rights under paragraph 1.a, b and c of this Article, when such expulsion is necessary in the interests of public order or is grounded on reasons of national security.

Article 2 – Right of appeal in criminal matters

1   Everyone convicted of a criminal offence by a tribunal shall have the right to have his conviction or sentence reviewed by a higher tribunal. The exercise of this right, including the grounds on which it may be exercised, shall be governed by law.

2   This right may be subject to exceptions in regard to offences of a minor character, as prescribed by law, or in cases in which the person concerned was tried in the first instance by the highest tribunal or was convicted following an appeal against acquittal.

Article 3 – Compensation for wrongful conviction

When a person has by a final decision been convicted of a criminal offence and when subsequently his conviction has been reversed, or he has been pardoned, on the ground that a new or newly discovered fact shows conclusively that there has been a miscarriage of justice, the person who has suffered punishment as a result of such conviction shall be compensated according to the law or the practice of the state concerned, unless it is proved that the nondisclosure of the unknown fact in time is wholly or partly attributable to him.

Article 4 – Right not to be tried or punished twice

1   No one shall be liable to be tried or punished again in criminal proceedings under the jurisdiction of the same state for an offence for which he has already been finally acquitted or convicted in accordance with the law and penal procedure of that state.

2 The provisions of the preceding paragraph shall not prevent the reopening of the case in accordance with the law and penal procedure of the State concerned, if there is evidence of new or newly discovered facts, or if there has been a fundamental defect in the previous proceedings, which could affect the outcome of the case.

3   No derogation from this Article shall be made under Article 15 of the Convention.

Article 5 – Equality between spouses

Spouses shall enjoy equality of rights and responsibilities of a private law character between them, and in their relations with their children, as to marriage, during marriage and in the event of its dissolution. This Article shall not prevent States from taking such measures as are necessary in the interests of the children.

Article 6 – Territorial applications

1   Any State may at the time of signature or when depositing its instrument of ratification, acceptance or approval, specify the territory or territories to which this Protocol shall apply and state the extent to which it undertakes that the provisions of this Protocol shall apply to this or these territories.

2   Any state may at any later date, by a declaration addressed to the Secretary-General of the Council of Europe, extend the application of this Protocol to any other territory specified in the declaration. In respect of such territory the protocol shall enter into force on the first day of the month following the expiration of a period of two months after the date of receipt by the Secretary-General of such declaration.

3   Any declaration made under the two preceding paragraphs may, in respect of any territory specified in such declaration, be withdrawn or modified by a notification addressed to the Secretary-General. The withdrawal or modification shall become effective on the first day of the month following the expiration of a period of two months after the date of receipt of such notification by the Secretary-General.

4[1]   A declaration made in accordance with this Article shall be deemed to have been made in accordance with paragraph 1 of Article 56 of the Convention.

5   The territory of any State to which this Protocol applies by virtue of ratification, acceptance or approval by that State, and each territory to which this Protocol is applied by virtue of a declaration by that State under this Article, may be treated as separate territories for the purpose of the reference in Article 1 to the territory of a State.

6[2]   Any State which has made a declaration in accordance with paragraph 1 or 2 of this Article may at any time thereafter declare on behalf of one or more of the territories to which the declaration relates that it accepts the competence of the Court to receive applications from

505

individuals, non-governmental organisations or groups of individuals as provided in Article 34 of the Convention in respect of Articles 1 to 5 of this Protocol.

Notes
1   Text amended according to the provisions of Protocol No 11 (ETS No 155).
2   Text added according to the provisions of Protocol No 11 (ETS No 155).

Article 7[1] – Relationship to the Convention

As between the States Parties, the provisions of Article 1 to 6 of this Protocol shall be regarded as additional Articles to the Convention, and all the provisions of the Convention shall apply accordingly.

Notes
1   Text amended according to the provisions of Protocol No 11 (ETS No 155).

Article 8 – Signature and ratification

This Protocol shall be open for signature by member States of the Council of Europe which have signed the Convention. It is subject to ratification, acceptance or approval. A member State of the Council of Europe may not ratify, accept or approve this Protocol without previously or simultaneously ratifying the Convention. Instruments of ratification, acceptance or approval shall be deposited with the Secretary General of the Council of Europe.

Article 9 – Entry into force

1   This Protocol shall enter into force on the first day of the month following the expiration of a period of two months after the date on which seven member States of the Council of Europe have expressed their consent to be bound by the Protocol in accordance with the provisions of Article 8.

2   In respect of any member State which subsequently expresses its consent to be bound by it, the Protocol shall enter into force on the first day of the month following the expiration of a period of two months after the date of the deposit of the instrument of ratification, acceptance or approval.

Article 10 – Depositary functions

The Secretary General of the Council of Europe shall notify all the member States of the Council of Europe of:

a   any signature;

b   the deposit of any instrument of ratification, acceptance or approval;

c   any date of entry into force of this Protocol in accordance with Articles 6 and 9;

d   any other act, notification or declaration relating to this Protocol.

In witness whereof the undersigned, being duly authorised thereto, have signed this Protocol.

Done at Strasbourg this 22nd day of November 1984, in English and French, both texts being equally authentic, in a single copy which shall be deposited in the archives of the Council of Europe. The Secretary General of the Council of Europe shall transmit certified copies to each member State of the Council of Europe.